Selected Writings on Media, Propaganda, and Political Communication

....
NEW DIRECTIONS IN CRITICAL THEORY

NEW DIRECTIONS IN CRITICAL THEORY

Amy Allen, General Editor

New Directions in Critical Theory presents outstanding classic and contemporary texts in the tradition of critical social theory, broadly construed. The series aims to renew and advance the program of critical social theory, with a particular focus on theorizing contemporary struggles around gender, race, sexuality, class, and globalization and their complex interconnections.

For a complete list of titles, see page 453

Selected Writings on Media, Propaganda, and Political Communication

Siegfried Kracauer

Edited by Jaeho Kang, Graeme Gilloch, and John Abromeit

Columbia University Press

New York

Columbia University Press
Publishers Since 1893
New York   Chichester, West Sussex
cup.columbia.edu

Copyright © 2022 Columbia University Press
All rights reserved

Library of Congress Cataloging-in-Publication Data
Names: Kracauer, Siegfried, 1889–1966, author. | Kang, Jaeho, 1969– editor. | Gilloch, Graeme, editor. | Abromeit, John, 1970– editor.
Title: Selected writings on media, propaganda, and political communication / Siegfried Kracauer ; edited by Jaeho Kang, Graeme Gilloch, and John Abromeit.
Description: New York : Columbia University Press, [2022] | Series: New directions in critical theory | Includes bibliographical references and index.
Identifiers: LCCN 2021036436 (print) | LCCN 2021036437 (ebook) | ISBN 9780231158961 (hardback) | ISBN 9780231158978 (trade paperback) | ISBN 9780231555661 (ebook)
Subjects: LCSH: Mass media—Political aspects. | Mass media and propaganda. | Communication in politics.
Classification: LCC P95.8 .K73 2022 (print) | LCC P95.8 (ebook) | DDC 320.01/4—dc23/eng/20211102
LC record available at https://lccn.loc.gov/2021036436
LC ebook record available at https://lccn.loc.gov/2021036437

Cover design: Noah Arlow
Cover image: Henrik Hjort, *Siegfried Kracauer*

For Ulrich Oevermann

Contents

Preface xi

Acknowledgments xv

General Introduction 1

PART I
Studies of Totalitarianism, Propaganda, and the Masses (1936–1940) 37

1. Exposé. Mass and Propaganda. An Inquiry Into Fascist Propaganda 49

2. Totalitarian Propaganda 56

3. Abridged Restricted Schema 107

4. Schemata 109

5. Disposition 113

PART 2
The Caligari Complex (1943–1947)   127

6. The Conquest of Europe on the Screen:
   The Nazi Newsreel, 1939–40   135

7. The Hitler Image   152

8. Below the Surface: Project of a Test Film   155

PART 3
Postwar Publics (1948–1950)   211

9. Re-education Program for the Reich   217

10. How and Why the Public Responds
    to the Propagandist   220

11. Popular Advertisements   223

12. A Duck Crosses Main Street   233

13. National Types as Hollywood Presents Them   238

14. Deluge of Pictures   263

PART 4
Cold War Tensions (1952–1958)   267

15. Appeals to the Near and Middle East:
    Implications of the Communications Studies
    Along the Soviet Periphery   275

16. Attitudes Toward Various Communist Types in Hungary, Poland, and Czechoslovakia   309

17. Proposal for a Research Project Designed to Promote the Use of Qualitative Analysis in the Social Sciences   316

18. The Challenge of Qualitative Content Analysis   322

19. On the Relation of Analysis to the Situational Factors in Case Studies   333

20. The Social Research Center on the Campus: Its Significance for the Social Sciences and Its Relations to the University and Society at Large   350

....

Appendix 1: T. W. Adorno, "Report on the Work 'Totalitarian Propaganda in Germany and Italy' by Siegfried Kracauer, pp. 1–106"   *391*

Appendix 2: John Abromeit, "Siegfried Kracauer and the Early Frankfurt School's Analysis of Fascism as Right-Wing Populism"   *395*

Bibliography   *423*

Sources   *431*

Index   *435*

Preface

This anthology is intended as a contribution to the wider dissemination of the work of the German social, cultural and film theorist Siegfried Kracauer (1889–1966), a highly original and critical thinker, whose manifold and varied writings are gaining an ever wider and increasingly appreciative readership across the humanities and social sciences. In presenting a selection of his numerous works examining propaganda, political communication, and media research, we address themes, concepts, and motifs that, while clearly corresponding to many of Kracauer's other works, have nevertheless not hitherto been prominent in its anglophone reception. Many of his concerns in these writings are all too relevant for us today. The "prophets of deceit"—as Leo Lowenthal and Norbert Gutermann so memorably described them back in 1949—are not only still among us, but they prosper now in new guises and have at their disposal unprecedented technological means of mass propagation and circulation, modes of ideological transmission and forms of interaction unimaginable in Kracauer's own lifetime—satellite channels, digital platforms, the internet and social media. The mediascape of the mid-twentieth century was very different from that of today—there are probably very few still living who can recall watching newsreels at the cinema. So if the medium is indeed the message, then the message now would bear little relation to that even of the recent past. But reading Kracauer's explorations of, for example, fascist propaganda, one is struck repeatedly by the pertinence and perspicacity of his work, and by its relevance. Time and again, his pioneering insights into the promulgation of deceptions and duplicities by "charismatic" leaders—charlatans invoking the "people" while stereotyping and stigmatizing "others"; promoting prejudice and pandering to racism, xenophobia, and anti-Semitism; mythologizing the "nation" and its "history"—reveal the authoritarian fulminations of our post-truth world as the nothing-new of rancid rhetoric, the poisonous regurgitations of lies and hand-me-down hate. We are certainly not the first generations to encounter political leaders and pretenders asserting "alternative facts," decrying the "fake news" of critical alternative voices, and peddling conspiracy theories to listeners all too willing to conspire. It seems some messages—shrill, verbose, toxic—have changed less than the media which configure and carry them. Reading Kracauer the question arises: how different are digital demagogues from analogue ones?

The texts in this anthology explore themes beyond the hucksters of authoritarian propaganda, be they twentieth or twenty-first century specimens. In the 1950s, Cold War politics also looked to strategies of ideological persuasion targeting national populations, what now goes under the rubric of "soft power." Kracauer was commissioned to report on the efficacy of media operating transnationally and interculturally in the propagation of pro-Western, pro-liberal-democratic, pro-capitalist values, sentiments, and sensibilities. He was also to attend to and assess the "satellite mentalities" of Soviet-controlled Eastern Europe and the influence and reach of American radio broadcasts on popular perceptions in the "peripheral" countries around the Mediterranean. In short, he was tasked by American government agencies and others with investigating and evaluating the potentialities of, and challenges to, American ideological and cultural global hegemony, the universalization of the American "way of life" as an ideal, the dream of the "American dream." At the same time, Kracauer's critical eye was also turned to matters closer at hand, to what this American "lifestyle" comprised, how it was configured and, in particular, how it was insistently promoted. Indeed, the formation and inculcation of a particular habitus, of everyday ways of living and seeing, the adoption of certain attitudes and validation of tastes claimed as one's own, were the mundane, routine work of the American advertising and marketing industries. Envisioning and celebrating youthfulness, vitality and "clean-living," advertising does much more than promote this or that individual product. Rather, it works normatively, enforcing and policing the normativity of the "normal," disciplining, domesticating, and fashioning our all-too-docile bodies. Even the most banal advertising plays its part in the creation of predictability, homogeneity, and conformity—the production of the mass for the profits of mass production and, concomitantly, for the contemporary prophets of deceit too. For it is precisely this, the dissolution of the individual, the subject, the distinctive, the idiosyncratic, the other, the heretical, into the compliant complacent mass that is central to Kracauer's critique of capitalist modernity and the work of contemporary media. The mass media produce the mass. And the mass is the very stuff of fascism. This is the "message" of these media. And so, this might beg the question today: what kind of "social" is produced by social media is the question we confront today.

We were rather naïve. When we first embarked upon this anthology we had little sense of how long and how complex the process of its completion and publication would prove to be. To begin with: how do you solve a problem like NYANA? Following Kracauer's death in 1966, the rights for his works passed to the New York Association for New Americans (NYANA), a charitable organization set up in 1949 to help immigrants establish themselves in the United States in the wake of the Second World War. The association was, however, dissolved in 2008, leaving the issues of copyright and permissions completely opaque. Thanks to the kind support, good-will and industry of the Deutsche Literatur Archiv (DLA) in Marbach am Neckar, the holders of Kracauer's archive, of Suhrkamp Verlag, the University of California Press and our own publishers at Columbia University Press, the copyright issue was fortunately resolved. Then there was the selection of materials. The inclusion of some materials was straightforward; but what to do with the 150-page *Totalitäre Propaganda* work which, painstakingly transcribed from manuscripts held in the DLA, was simply too extensive to include in its entirety in an anthology of this kind? If we were to translate and include a selection of this study, what should we choose and on what basis? And, moreover, what should be done with Theodor W. Adorno's substantially abridged, revised and edited version of this text, a rewrite repudiated by Kracauer himself and one which is, after all, technically a piece by Adorno? We have chosen here to honour Kracauer's own preferences in translating and including sections E (on the masses) and G (his conclusion) and excluding Adorno's version altogether. And this is just Part I! Moving on ... there are three extant versions of the 'Below the Surface' script: which one should we include?

We have had plenty of causes and pauses for thought during this project. And this is as it should be: for interruptions and impediments, obstacles and quandaries, are very much in accord with the spirit of Kracauer's writings, work which, eschewing shortcuts, leads into the snagging "thicket of things." And indeed, as the scope and intricacies of the anthology increased, as this thicket became thicker, so too has both our own appreciation of the texts we have selected here and our confidence in their intellectual value and contemporary relevance. We hope that we have made justifiable decisions, wise choices.

We hope, above all, that this anthology will invite new readers of his work, stimulate new interest, provoke new engagement, encourage new scholarship, prompt new practices. For of this we are certain: we have much to learn from Kracauer and his Critical Theory colleagues for the struggles of the present.

This anthology is for all those who refuse, refute, repudiate, and resist the prophets of deceit then and now.

Acknowledgments

Central to Kracauer's understanding of film is the recognition that movies are never the product of any one single individual – the fallacy of the director-as-auteur – but rather collaborative product of numerous different specialists: script and screenplay writers, set and costume designers and makers, casting directors, camera and lighting crews, make-up specialists, sound and soundtrack engineers, musical directors and composers, production assistants and technicians of all kinds, editors and many many others. The seemingly endless credits that roll after each and every film today attests to this collective effort. The same is true of the book, of this book. Without the author of these texts, Kracauer, there would be no anthology. But he is only one of many contributors to the publication and production of this volume. And so we, the editors, without shirking any responsibility for this book, would like to thank all those who have collaborated on this project.

This anthology would not have been possible without the kind and continuous support of the staff of the DLA. Our sincere thanks to you all for your help. And special thanks are due to Janet Dilger for her kind assistance in locating and reproducing manuscripts that would not have been included here otherwise. The archivist Herr Jochen Stollberg at the Literaturhaus in Frankfurt was extremely helpful with the manuscript for "Below the Surface." We thank you and wish you a long and happy retirement. Preparatory archive work was undertaken with the generous support of the Alexander von Humboldt Stiftung and the DAAD (Deutscher Akademischer Austauschdienst).

We are deeply grateful too to Suhrkamp Verlag and in particular Dr. Petra Hardt and Nora Mercurio for their wholehearted support of this anthology. We would like to thank and express our deep appreciation for the editorial team who worked on the Suhrkamp publications of Kracauer's "Totalitäre Propaganda" in both the paperback edition (2013) and the *Werke* 2.2 (2012): Christian Fleck, Bernd Stiegler, Joachim Heck, and Maren Neumann. We are particularly indebted to them not only for the text itself but also for the accompanying "Notes" (*Anmerkungen*) which provide remarkable detail on so many of the figures and events mentioned in Kracauer's texts, materials that we précis here in our own endnotes for part 1. We would also like to extend our thanks to the editors of the Kracauer *Werke*, Inka Mülder-Bach and Ingrid Belke, for their work, support, and encouragement. We are grateful to Clare Wellnitz of the University of California Press for her help in clarifying the issue of copyright.

Our thanks also go to the Éditions de la Maison des sciences de l'homme in Paris for giving us permission to republish John Abromeit's essay, "Siegfried Kracauer and the Early Frankfurt School's Analysis of Fascism as Right-Wing Populism." The essay first appeared in 2020 in their volume *Theorie Critique de la Propagande*, edited by Pierre-François Noppen and Gérard Raulet. Henrik Hjört kindly allowed us to use his striking painting of Kracauer for our book cover. Thank you, Henrik! We love your artwork!

We would like to thank Nicholas Baer for kindly allowing us to include his translation of the *Exposé*; Bernadette Boyle for her meticulous and attentive work as translator of several texts in part 1; and Doh-Yeon Kim for her scrupulous archival and bibliographical research and careful transcription work.

We are also very grateful to Amy Allen, Stefano Brenna, Vinayak Chaturvedi, Gerd Gemünden, Noah Isenberg, Hans Lind, Johannes von Moltke, and Marcos Nobre. Your kind interest in and support for our project throughout has been most welcome. Thank you!

We are indebted to a number of scholars who were inspirational for us in this project: Nancy Fraser, the late David Frisby, Jeffrey Goldfarb, the late Miriam Hansen, Axel Honneth, Andreas Huyssen, Anton Kaes, Elihu Katz, Ruth Katz, Martin Jay, Thomas Levin, and John B. Thompson.

Finally, we would to thank the editorial, production, and marketing teams at Columbia University Press for all their amazing work and enduring support: Emily Shelton, Lowell Frye, Susan Pensak, Zachary Friedman, and Noah Arlow.

Above all, we would like to thank our editor from the start, Wendy K. Lochner, whose unwavering support and endless patience have been amazing. Wendy, you have been wonderful!

The editors of this anthology first met in Frankfurt many years ago while each was working on a different project. Ulrich Oevermann acted as host and "supervisor" (*Gastgeber und Betreuer*) for Graeme's Humboldt Research Fellowship in the Fachbereich Soziologie at the Goethe Universität. Without his kind and generous support, we three may never have met, and this book would not exist. Professor Oevermann (28.02.1940–11.10.2021) was a unique and inspirational scholar; he was also a dear friend who will be greatly missed. This book is dedicated to him.

Selected Writings on Media, Propaganda, and Political Communication

General Introduction

SCOPE AND PURPOSE

This anthology brings together for the first time a specific selection of the writings by the German Jewish social and critical theorist Siegfried Kracauer (1889–1966), a figure who is now widely regarded as one of the most original and insightful cultural theorists of the twentieth century and, in particular, a genuine pioneer in the critical analysis of modern popular culture and film. Its publication just as the third decade of the twenty-first century begins is especially timely—for the best of reasons, and for the worst.

For the best: our anthology appears in the context of an increasing recognition of Kracauer's writings by a new generation of contemporary scholars working in a variety of interdisciplinary fields across the social sciences, arts, and humanities—a renewal of interest attested to by a wealth of recent publications, including new volumes of his *Werke* by Suhrkamp Verlag.[1] The last few years have seen the appearance of new Anglophone collections[2] and other translations of his key texts[3] and correspondence.[4] These new and newly available primary sources have been accompanied by the welcome proliferation of scholarly books and journal articles exploring his studies, themes, and concepts,[5] including a major biography.[6] Moving beyond earlier misreadings and misunderstandings of Kracauer as primarily a "realist" film theorist, there is now a significant and ever-increasing appreciation of, for example, his carefully differentiated and highly nuanced accounts of mass cultural forms during the Weimar years, studies that, while taking due account of the popular appeal and the pleasures of distraction afforded by these everyday entertainments, nevertheless remain resolutely critical of their ideological role. To be sure, popular movies were indeed part and parcel of the profit-driven capitalist "culture industry," but, for Kracauer, the medium of film was at the same time something much more. It could be a symptomatic expression of prevailing unconscious predispositions among audiences and hence a diagnostic or interpretive tool for cultural analysis; it could serve as an innovative and privileged research instrument for the social-psychological study of prejudices and anti-Semitism; and it could constitute an aesthetic medium that promised through its envisioning of the world around us a revitalized, rejuvenated sensitivity to physical reality, an enrichment of human experiences, and a new sense of our everyday urban environment as "home."

This continuing renewal of interest is certainly pleasing to see and bodes well, but it is also long overdue, and there is much still to be done. Kracauer's diverse and provocative writings generally have attracted considerably less scholarly attention and critical acclaim than the works of his friends and colleagues associated with the Frankfurt Institute for Social Research (Institut für Sozialforschung), the so-called Frankfurt School, such as, most notably, Walter Benjamin and Theodor W. Adorno. The relative neglect of Kracauer's work is a condition of neglect nonetheless.

In bringing together here a selection of Kracauer's diverse materials on propaganda and political communication—texts hitherto unavailable in English or strewn among different (sometimes now obsolete or obscure) journals, periodicals, and magazines—we hope that his numerous and varied analyses of the manifold and complex relationships between power, mass culture, spectacle, and different media (film, newsreels, radio) in modern society will stimulate further academic interest and provoke fresh scholarly debate. Our anthology is therefore intended as a contribution to the development and diversity of the Anglophone reception, perception, and appreciation of the intellectual scope and critical insights of Kracauer's work.

Our collection is also timely for the worst of reasons: the prevailing social, economic, and political circumstances in so many countries today mean that the critical interrogation of authoritarian and totalitarian propaganda and the refutation of forms of prejudice and intolerance are more urgent tasks than at any time in the last half-century. We see today populist support for chauvinist, misogynist "strongmen" as leaders, even within long-standing liberal democratic societies; established legal frameworks and systems of safeguards increasingly challenged or circumvented by regimes invoking "states of exception" and the need to "get things done"; the incitement of prejudice and xenophobia in numerous pernicious guises (misogyny, racism, homophobia, anti-Semitism, Islamophobia) and the vicious stigmatization of vulnerable minorities as political expediency and petty nationalist rhetoric; the proliferation of a new generation of "prophets of deceit" peddling pernicious lies, mythologizing the past ("Make America Great Again"), spewing forth vacuous and tautological slogans ("Brexit means Brexit"), vilifying their opponents ("traitors," "enemies of the people"); the posturing of media-savvy, digitally adept demagogues who accuse their accusers of "fake news" and "project fear" as they decry expert analysis, scorn scientific research, disdain reasoned argument, and either contemptuously consign universities and intellectuals to the role of paid lackeys, or scorn them as parts of "liberal metropolitan elites," or both. These and many more aspects of twenty-first-century global neoliberalism are evidence that the "dialectic of Enlightenment" thesis formulated back in the 1940s by Theodor W. Adorno and Max Horkheimer (and heavily indebted to Kracauer) was not so very wide of the mark as to the catastrophic trajectory of the West when "instrumental reason" in the service of capital and hegemonic elites reigns triumphant. When we first published our work on Kracauer's long-forgotten "test film" project back in 2007, we noted how a particular set of themes once central to Critical Theory—namely, authoritarianism, totalitarianism, anti-Semitism, prejudice, fascist agitators and personality structures—had become sidelined in the reception of the Frankfurt School, albeit unintentionally. Perhaps these numerous studies, primarily written in the 1940s and 1950s, were viewed with some discomfort and as writings very much of their time—as exercises, expedients, and experiments now only of interest to a few intellectual historians. This is no longer the case, if indeed it ever was. These writings—a small selection of which appear in this anthology—are all too relevant, actual, pertinent, and prescient. They speak to us today in a way that is clear, critical, and compelling. *They illuminate our world here and now; not just their world there and then.* That they do so is no cause for celebration.

INTELLECTUAL BACKGROUND: KRACAUER'S MAJOR WRITINGS

Overview

Siegfried Kracauer was part of a generation of European intellectuals that lived through one of the most catastrophic periods of human history: from the mechanized carnage of World War I; through the chaos of revolution, civil war, and the descent into brutal totalitarianism and Stalinist terror; through the catastrophic rise and fall of Fascism and Nazism and the horrors of total war, genocide, and the Holocaust; and through the paranoid machinations of the Cold War, the perverse logic of mutually assured destruction, and the atrocities of saturation bombing, napalm, and Agent Orange. Accordingly, it should be no surprise that, as one of the most original and astute critics of Western modernity, Kracauer should write extensively and repeatedly on the themes of propaganda, ideology, and political communication. It is rather puzzling that this central aspect of his work has been so neglected by scholars and commentators. These particular writings can be understood not simply as attempts to understand and learn from some of these calamitous moments in recent Western civilization, but also as elements of an intense interrogation and a thoroughgoing critique of modernity itself. As such, they may be interpreted within the constellation formed by—or, indeed, at the very convergence point of—three principal themes which might be seen as leitmotifs of his entire oeuvre.

Firstly, at the very heart of Kracauer's work is an enduring preoccupation, indebted to the works of his erstwhile tutor Georg Simmel, with the fate of the modern individual as s/he seeks to give meaning and expression to the inclinations and yearnings of their "inner life" amid the constraints and impositions of the wider society, outer or "objective culture." Kracauer largely shared Simmel's pessimistic vision, encapsulated in his famous 1903 essay "The Metropolis and Mental Life," of the modern large-scale urban environment as the preeminent site of abstraction—of value (money) and of time (the clock)—wherein the individual is compelled to be ever on guard against, and feigning indifference toward, the multiplicity of fleeting sensations and stimuli that otherwise threaten to overwhelm her/him. Even the adoption or cultivation of a characteristically metropolitan, blasé personality may prove insufficient, however, to stave off the neurasthenia and other pathological psychological conditions induced by the intense and relentless demands of living at such an accelerated tempo and among so many equally indifferent strangers. Atomized and alienated, the once autonomous individual is increasingly subject to the rationalizing and homogenizing tendencies of the modern city, such that s/he is eventually engulfed by the multitude itself, absorbed into the anonymous masses. Simultaneously, and paradoxically, just as the individual is threatened with such eradication, the very notion of "individuality" itself, of being a distinctive and unique individual subject, is lauded as the defining principle and ultimate good of such a society. The individual is thus celebrated in theory in the very same moment as it is abolished in practice. *Individualism* thereby serves as the very ideology of a *deindividualized mass existence.*

Secondly, and much to his credit, Kracauer was *the* Critical Theorist who took mundane popular culture and the mass media seriously as objects of scrutiny and interrogation. Popular culture was not merely to be dismissed as the domain of ideology and the pacification of the masses, as all those banal and commodified products spawned by the "culture industry" (*Kulturindustrie*), identified by Horkheimer and Adorno in their 1947 *Dialectic of Enlightenment*, that served to stultify and stifle the critical imagination. For Kracauer, as journalist and sociologist, even the seemingly most trivial aspects of mass culture could provide invaluable insight into those conditions of modern metropolitan existence already described. In his 1930 essay "The Biography as an Art Form of the New Bourgeoisie," for example, he astutely interprets the growing popular interest in life histories as forms of compensation and consolation.[7] The tedium and routine of ordinary lives stimulate an escapist demand for narratives of extraordinary ones. In a world in which the individual has actually been reduced to a minimum of significance, the biographical form serves to propagate the mythological potency of the exceptional individual. Politicians, sovereigns, generals, artists, scholars—these appear as inspired and inspiring figures who fashion history, who change the course of world events. In their celebration of supposed genius, heroism, and charisma, such hagiographies of national figures, along with self-serving autobiographies, all played their part in encouraging authoritarian dispositions and inducing the cultic adoration of demagogues as extraordinary personalities, as we will see in due course.

Importantly, Kracauer's work demonstrates a lasting preoccupation with the proliferation and prevalence of new forms and technologies of cultural production—in particular, of course, the rise of the mass media themselves as corollaries of this emergent mass society. His interest is a complex and multifaceted one. Visual media in general, and the significance and promise of the camera in particular, prove of enduring fascination for him. The technological capacity of camera—both photographic or cinematic—to capture and record everything that stands before the lens at a given moment leads him in contrasting directions: writing in 1927, he laments photography as the banal inventorying of the world of appearances, a superficial stock-taking that, unlike the images borne in human memory, have no particular significance or meaning. Photography makes for banal indifferent pictures for banal indifferent times. By 1960, in *Theory of Film*, it is precisely this same ability to record what was present but perhaps went unnoticed at the time that promises a revitalization of an otherwise ever-more-impoverished human perception, counteracting and perhaps even overcoming Simmelian indifference. Kracauer, then, is not only at pains to identify the inherent logics, tendencies, and possibilities of these new media for representing and reshaping this modern world, but also, as we will see, comes to consider how film itself may provide a distinctive research instrument for the disclosure of collective social-psychological states and predispositions.

Thirdly, one finds in Kracauer's work an ongoing concern with dialectical analysis and forms of critique which, while antithetical to the instrumental, scientized, quantifying technocratic systems of our contemporary world, nevertheless resolutely reject any reactionary relapse into irrationalism, prejudice, religious mysticism, or political fanaticism. As Kracauer points out as early as 1927 in his key "The Mass Ornament" essay, it is not that capitalist modernity has rationalized society too much, but that it has done so too little. Indeed, this essay is in many ways the fundamental point of intersection of Kracauer's three overarching concerns set out here: the masses, popular culture, and the practice of dialectical critique. It opens with an insistence upon a depth hermeneutic, one in which what might be dismissed as merely superficial phenomena of an epoch are not simply privileged as the best mode of reading a prevailing social formation, but are deemed the only truly dialectical way of doing so. Kracauer writes:

> The position that an epoch occupies in the historical process can be determined more strikingly from an analysis of its inconspicuous surface-level expressions than from that epoch's judgements about itself. Since these judgements are expressions of the tendencies of a particular era, they do not offer conclusive testimony about its overall constitution. The surface-level expressions, however, by virtue of their unconscious nature, provide unmediated access to the fundamental substance of the state of things. Conversely, knowledge of this state of things depends on the interpretation of these surface-level expressions. The fundamental substance of an epoch and its unheeded impulses illuminate each other reciprocally.[8]

The specific "surface-level expression" Kracauer identifies and explores in his essay is the Tiller Girls, the internationally popular English "kick and tap" dance troupe famous for their tightly choreographed routines in which up to thirty-two dancers combined to form complex geometrical figures and patterns with precisely synchronized movements. Of similar build and appearance and dressed identically to the others, the individual performer became one functioning part of a total mechanistic assemblage—not a distinctive dancer, but a subset of "indissoluble girl clusters" (1995, 76) composed of heads, arms, and legs set in perpetual motion. As for these endlessly evolving and dissolving patterns and configurations themselves, they were devoid of any actual meaning as such, existing instead simply as ends in and of themselves. *This is ornament for its own sake*, as pure spectacle by the masses, for the masses, a spectacle of the rationally ordered and organized, of obedient and compliant de-eroticized, de-individualized, dismembered bodies. This is the aestheticization of abstractness. The Tiller Girls thus serve as a perfect expression of both the disappearance of the autonomous subject and the triumph of the technocratic reason of the machine age (or the *Ratio*, as Kracauer terms it).

The critical exploration of the struggles of various individual selves within and against the disenchanted life-world of the metropolis and of modernity; the consequences attending the advent of the masses and the mass media as defining phenomena of social, cultural and political life in the twentieth century; and the search for modes of dialectical critique—these, then, are the central and recurrent motifs of Kracauer's work. Spanning more than forty years of intellectual endeavor, these fundamental concerns inform and find expression in the many and varied textual forms taken by his writings, including feuilleton fragments and reviews, a couple of novels, some government reports, and several film treatments and potential scripts. Above all, these abiding concerns run through the four main books published by Kracauer in his lifetime: a pioneering urban ethnography of contemporary Berlin: *The Salaried Masses* (*Die Angestellten*, 1930); *Jacques Offenbach and the Paris of Time* (1937), an equally original so-called "societal biography" (*Gesellschaftsbiographie*) examining Paris in the Second Empire; *From Caligari to Hitler* (1947), a social-psychological history of film and cinematic audiences; and *Theory of Film* (1960), a critical exposition of the very ontology of the film medium itself. It is in relation to these themes—the mass, the mass media, dialectical critique—and against the backdrop of these four major studies that Kracauer's writings on propaganda and political communication took shape.

Berlin Calling

On February 28, 1933, the day following the infamous Reichstag Fire, Kracauer, then feuilleton editor for the Berlin edition of the relatively liberal daily *Frankfurter Zeitung* (*FZ*), together with his wife, Elizabeth (Lili), former librarian at the Institute for Social Research, hastily packed their belongings and quit the city—indeed, left the country altogether. At the behest of the newspaper's proprietors, they fled (via Frankfurt) to Paris, a city then becoming home to an increasing number of exiles and refugees fleeing Nazi Germany, among them, of course, Walter Benjamin, Kracauer's acquaintance and colleague in Critical Theory.

Kracauer was at least able to find some consolation in the prospect of becoming the paper's designated correspondent in the French capital, though this was to prove perhaps the most bitter disappointment of all: only a few weeks later, his journalistic and editorial services were dispensed with altogether when the newspaper finally deemed it too damaging to continue employing Jewish left-wing intellectuals even as foreign correspondents abroad. Thus, Kracauer's hitherto productive and prolific journalistic career, in which he penned some two thousand pieces for publication in the course of a dozen years, came to an abrupt and acrimonious end.

Kracauer had first started as a freelance local reporter with the *FZ* back in January 1921 when, increasingly drawn to sociological, philosophical, and cultural ideas and issues, he abandoned his chosen career as an architect, for which he had trained in Darmstadt, Berlin, and Munich and been engaged professionally since before the Great War. The Berlin lectures of the sociologist and philosopher Georg Simmel, and his weekly Frankfurt discussions of Kant with the precocious Theodor W. Adorno, some fourteen years his junior, were rather more inspiring than drawing up plans for housing estates in Osnabruck. And so it was that while architecture remained one of Kracauer's journalistic specialisms—reviewing contemporary exhibitions and designs and reporting on the construction and opening of new buildings in Frankfurt and elsewhere—his writings took both a broader and deeper perspective, his subject matter the whole sweep of everyday cultural life in the modern city. These texts met with no little success: in November 1924, he became a full-time, permanent member of the newspaper staff. In 1930, when he was invited to assume an editorship position with the Berlin issue, he and his wife relocated to the capital of the Weimar Republic.

Although Kracauer's writings were many and varied during the 1920s (a full-length philosophical treatise on the detective story, an epistemological and theoretical consideration of sociology as science, a semiautobiographical novel entitled *Ginster*), the pages of the *FZ* were without doubt the principal site for the articulation and presentation of his preoccupations and predilections. The exigencies of newspaper publishing were to be the tough schooling for the precise and concise expression of his ideas and insights. His fundamental concerns were the contemporary cultural conditions he witnessed and came to describe as "the newest Germany" during the fraught years and amid the fragile institutions of the Republic. In particular, his attention was drawn to the expanding cosmopolitan center that was Berlin in the jazz age with its radically transforming class patterns, its rapidly emerging consumer culture, its pioneering and proliferating entertainment industries, and its modern technologies, traffic, crowds, edifices, and structures: opulent department stores, extravagant cinemas conceived as picture palaces, radio masts piercing the urban skyline, seedy nightclubs, burlesque cabarets and theatrical revues, popular bestsellers, fashion magazines, and, of course, the newspapers themselves.

Just prior to his final move to Berlin, in the guise of an intrepid metropolitan ethnographer, Kracauer collected an eclectic array of material (interviews, anecdotes, newspaper and commercial reports, various statistics, conversations, and other reflections) for a series of articles in which he hoped to document, or provide a panoramic vision of, the everyday lifestyle of what he regarded as the distinctive and increasingly dominant socioeconomic class of the city, that broad stratum of petit bourgeois employees whose very ordinariness and obviousness had made them seemingly invisible to social commentators and critics: the white-collar workers, mundane office and clerical staff—in short, the salaried masses. First published in twelve installments commencing in 1929 and then collected in book form the following year, *The Salaried Masses* sought to map the "terra incognita" of these employees, not only with respect to their experiences of the occupational structure, but also in terms of their fundamental roles as customers, consumers, and clientele; as shoppers and browsers; as spectators, audiences, and readers.

It should come as no surprise that, in bearing witness to the incipient phases of those structures and identities constituting bureaucratic, Fordist modernity, *The Salaried Masses* is permeated with Kracauer's bleak Simmelian vision of a disenchanted, functionalized, mechanized life-world. Above all it brings the two central paradoxes, the double double-binds, of the white-collar world of this time into sharp focus. Firstly, since the bureaucratized apparatus itself is premised, as Max Weber famously recognized, upon impersonality, anonymity, and objective criteria of formal, technical expertise, the whole principle undergirding such rationalized systems is the dispensability and seamless substitution of individual office holders. Posts are filled and refilled with more or less competent functionaries. At the same time, however, significance is attached in ever greater measure to the distinctive personal attributes, morals, and virtues of the individual employee. Secondly, aspiring vainly to haute bourgeois notions of education (*Bildung*) and culture (*Kultur*), all the while disdaining the working classes, these office employees find themselves situated in a comfortless intermediary socioeconomic position, one that leaves them bereft of any sense of social solidarity. These salaried masses are, as Kracauer memorably puts it, "spiritually shelterless [*geistig obdachlos*]."[9] They are indebted for their very existence to this rationalized, bureaucratized, impersonal, modern system and at the same time the main bearers of its miseries and misfortunes: frustration, resentment, repression, boredom, fatalism.

As we will see, this is of the utmost importance for Kracauer's writings on propaganda and communication in the mid-to-late 1930s because these socio-economic strata—obliging, and obsequious to those above them, haughty and high-handed to those below—were the very ones most susceptible and predisposed to the promises and prejudices promulgated by National Socialist propaganda.

Parisian Exile

Kracauer himself, like Benjamin, was to lead a precarious financial existence in Paris as a freelance writer devoting his time and energy to three main projects: a second novel, *Georg*, which was to remain unpublished at the time; his 1937 study of the French composer and impresario Jacques Offenbach, a book that he styled as a "societal biography," critically exploring the "dreamworld" of the Second Empire through the satirical lens of one of its outstanding cultural figures, and a work Kracauer hoped would become, if not exactly a bestseller, then at least popular enough to provide some much-needed income; and, most significantly for us here, at the instigation in late 1936 of Max Horkheimer, then-director of the Institute for Social Research while in exile in New York, an extensive study of contemporary totalitarian propaganda in Fascist Italy and National Socialist Germany, a work that, like the Offenbach book, was to become the subject of a bitter and acrimonious exchange with Adorno.[10]

Kracauer's "Totalitarian Propaganda" writings will be introduced in part 1. Here, some words on his Offenbach book are needed by way of context, especially because this work—written in parallel with Benjamin's ongoing study of the same historical moment as manifested in the Parisian arcades and the poetry of Charles Baudelaire—was intended as something other than a conventional biography, the kind he himself had critically discussed just a few years earlier. Exploring the Paris of his time as much as the life of the composer, it was an attempt (perhaps a little too often implicit) to redeem what Kracauer identified as the satirical energies and utopian intimations of Offenbach's music for contemporary political interventions. The composer was no arbitrary choice: his comic operettas and other musical theater enjoyed remarkable and sustained success in a dreamworld that was itself, Kracauer claims, "operetta-like" in its illusions and pretensions. Paris under Napoleon III was home to the spectacular proliferation of commodities, fashions, and luxuries imported from around the empire framed amid new urban consumption sites and spaces (arcades, boulevards, world exhibitions); to cycles of financial speculation and economic crisis as new industries, grand public works, and colonial trade flourished and failed; and to the accelerating tempo of modern metropolitan society and its burgeoning distractions and entertainments. Kracauer thus posits a correspondence, or an elective affinity, between the fanciful world of the operetta and the ostentatious and outlandish world of the Second Empire. For a while, the realities of dictatorship and class struggle were forgotten, sidelined, or ameliorated by short-term prosperity. Theatricality, artifice, and pretense took center stage. The operetta both expressed and was an essential part of the phantasmagoria of this farcical (as Marx observed) regime. It was to be short lived: the Franco-Prussian War saw the catastrophic defeat of the Second Empire in 1870–1871. It was the end, too, for Offenbach's operettas. Turning to gloomier themes, the composer died in 1880 just prior to the first performance of his melancholic *Tales of Hoffmann*.

Kracauer's Offenbach book is of particular interest for us in this anthology for both thematic and methodological reasons. Significantly, Kracauer sees Offenbach's music as providing the signature tune to the hegemony of a dictatorial regime combining brutality and repression with spectacular and superficial "joy and glamour"; mobilizing mass populations for civic projects, urban and infrastructural renewal, and military adventures; embarking on ruthless colonial exploits to appease a people familiar with *la gloire* and avaricious for pomp and pageantry; and destined to war and defeat at the hands of one of its neighbors. All these features of the recent past would have been only too familiar to those forced to flee Nazi Germany in the 1930s.

Additionally, in taking the life of Offenbach as a kind of monadological entity from which to unpack critically the wider society of which he was such an integral part—that is to say, to see in, read through, and unfold from the life of a single individual the fundamental features of her/his times—Kracauer reconfigures the depth hermeneutic with which he opened his "Mass Ornament" essay written ten years earlier. Jacques Offenbach's popular operettas are not so much surface-level expressions as the very *musical embodiment* of the Second Empire. Indeed, Kracauer claims his study of the composer as nothing less than a model of and for historical materialist cultural analysis: "By disclosing the connections between the operetta and society, the book demonstrates through an exemplary case the dependence of every genre of art on specific social conditions."[11] In this sense, Kracauer offers up his Offenbach study as a *case study*—or, more precisely, *as a kind of test case* of the historical materialist analysis of popular cultural phenomena and cultural production. The "societal biography" here becomes for Kracauer an essential Marxist method for reading the relationship between artist, artwork, and society.

Weimar in Retrospect

First published while in American exile in 1947, Kracauer's *From Caligari to Hitler: A Psychological History of the German Film* (arguably still the book for which he is best known in the Anglophone academy) is Janus-faced. In many ways it represents the culmination of his writings on Weimar culture and society, the attempt to make some sense of a time, place, and people now seen in retrospect through the horrors that were foreshadowed by them. At the same time, the book constitutes his first major study of the cinematic medium that had long fascinated him as a reviewer and feuilleton editor for the *FZ*. In the Caligari book it is not just the "little shop girls" who "go to the movies" in search of romance, solace, and escapism, but rather *all* those "spiritually shelterless" white-collar workers whose workaday lives and commonplace tastes had earlier been revealed by the intrepid ethnographer and author of *Die Angestellten*.[12] It was above all to the ever-changing but always conservative tastes and preferences of these numerous "middle strata" (*Mittelschichten*) that the German film industry pandered in its production of popular and predictable cinematic treats. For Kracauer, popular films—not those technical and aesthetic experiments in the medium created by the avant-garde—are the focus of his critical attention precisely because they provide a point of access into the deep-seated inclinations and predispositions of their ordinary, everyday audiences.

The book is significant for us here for at least three reasons. Firstly, and most important, is the fact that the *Caligari* book—or, more specifically, the archival work and other research undertaken to write it—played a fundamental role in saving the Kracauers' lives. While Kracauer hoped that his commission from Horkheimer and the Institute for the "Totalitarian Propaganda" study and its subsequent publication in the *Zeitschrift für Sozialforschung* might be the first of a series of collaborations eventually facilitating an American visa and passage from Europe to the safe haven of New York, the debacle that ensued, leaving his text unpublished and creating considerable rancor on both sides, put a sorry end to any such aspirations. It was instead to be the offer from the Film Library at the New York Museum of Modern Art for Kracauer to become a special research assistant and undertake a project on the historical and sociological significance of German cinema that proved decisive in securing Siegfried and Lili the necessary financial guarantees and requisite transit documentation for their escape from occupied France in February 1941. Others, Benjamin among them, were not so fortunate.

Secondly, it is a key work thematically and methodologically. In the "Mass Ornament" essay, Kracauer first expounded upon and then elaborated the crucial critical insight that forms of modern metropolitan mass culture had a diagnostic or symptomatic significance as surface-level expressions of much deeper processes and tendencies. The Offenbach book had reworked this notion into a historical undertaking, the societal biography, in which the life of a particular and carefully chosen individual could provide for a monadological reading of an entire epoch and society: Paris in the "era of high capitalism," as Benjamin termed it. Such practices of unfolding and interpreting were decisive for the Kracauer's psychological history of German cinema that was to constitute the *Caligari* book. The popular films of a particular time together formed a rich collection or constellation of surface-level expressions for discerning and interrogating what he saw as a historically specific though ever-changing collective, national unconscious. Films are, he argued, especially important as expressions of underlying psychological patterns and proclivities. This is because of *how they come into being*; they are themselves collective cultural products, necessarily involving the collaboration of numerous specialists and hence never, *pace* theories of the director as auteur, the work of a single individual. And *for whom they come into being*: commercial pressures and the need to fill cinemas ensure that most films look to appease widely shared tastes and to "satisfy existing mass desires."[13] Films of a particular time and place—in this case, the Germany of the recent past—will display certain recurrent themes and motifs, "visible hieroglyphs" (2019, 7), whose critical decipherment would reveal the shared sensibilities and secret longings of mass audiences. The analysis of film was to proceed in an analogous manner to the interpretation of dreams—not so much individual dreams as *collective* ones.

Dividing the history of the German film industry into four main periods based on fluctuating socioeconomic and political conditions instead of, for example, technological innovations such as the advent of sound and new techniques in cinematography, Kracauer discloses the "secret history" (2019, 11) of the German unconscious prior to 1933 as manifested on the screens of Weimar movie houses.[14] It is a story of increasing irrationalism and psychological retrogression in which the German psyche, marked by an absence of critical reasoning and an immature fear of genuine freedom, came to embrace, even to crave, authoritarianism and totalitarianism.

Taking the eponymous *Das Cabinet des Dr. Caligari* (Robert Wiene, 1919) as his point of departure, Kracauer observes how by means of a framing device, "a revolutionary film was turned into a conformist one" (2019, 67). In their "outspoken revolutionary story" (64), the pacifists Hans Janowitz and Carl Mayer, horrified by the carnage of the Great War, penned a critical vision of tyranny and obedience as the fiendish Dr. Caligari uses his hypnotic powers to send the strange figure of the somnambulist Cesare—an innocent instrument of evildoing—on errands of murder and abduction.[15] Bracketing this narrative such that it is no more than the delusions of an asylum inmate, the film version transforms Dr. Caligari from a showground charlatan and murderous manipulator into a benign hospital director.

This was a first taste of things to come. Craven submissiveness to authority, spurious reconciliations between classes (as in the final scenes of Fritz Lang's "pompous" *Metropolis* of 1927), and the all-too "timid heresies" of the street film genre—with their youthful bourgeois rebels who dally with life on the edge before finding comfort again back with their well-heeled and forgiving families—were all to feature largely in the films that followed, indications for Kracauer of the fundamental paralysis of critical faculties. True, he observes, the economic crises of 1929 did lead to some politically progressive films,[16] but these were no match for the spate of "national epics" and war films in which visions of heroism, duty and sacrifice, of national liberation and inspirational charismatic leadership on the battlefield are played out in costumes borrowed from the eighteenth and nineteenth centuries.[17] German films were forms of both gratification and preparation for their audiences. Unquestioning loyalty and devotion to the national leader-as-genius, patriotism and self-sacrifice, blind obedience unto death: such sentiments repeatedly pervaded and provided the finale of Weimar film.

Kracauer's original psychological-sociological-historical thesis is certainly not without its flaws, as numerous subsequent commentators have pointed out—not just inconsistencies and questionable readings of particular films, but the whole retrospective teleological thrust of the argument itself. But it is still important for this anthology in a number of ways: it reiterates Kracauer's critique of mass metropolitan culture and, in particular, focuses attention on the salaried masses; it reorients this critique toward *film*, for Kracauer the mass medium par excellence; it makes the fundamental connection between film audiences and prevailing psychological conditions and circumstances; it designates the deciphering of films as the method of tracing these psychological traits; and it recognizes film as an instrument or gauge for exploring underlying states of mind.

Finally, it is important to recognize that *Caligari* occupies a key moment in the trajectory of Kracauer's work. In a sense, it bookends the "Totalitarian Propaganda" study of 1936–1938 in that it takes as its historical focus the preceding period (the Weimar years) but itself appears a full decade later. The thematic complexes of the masses, psychological regression, the role of popular media, and forms of political power and domination are common to both. What were to emerge as the book's central principles concerning the psychology of audiences were earlier being deployed and refined by Kracauer as part of, for example, his social-psychological "test film" project ("The Accident"/"Below the Surface"), whose script and other accompanying documents we include in this anthology. Designed specifically to reveal latent anti-Semitism among American students, as indicative of wider populations and prejudices, Kracauer proposed to use audience reactions to a film to explore their deep-seated values, attitudes, and preconceptions; this is a kind of *Caligari in reverse*. Also, research for *Caligari* developed in parallel with various other studies of propaganda and prejudice undertaken by the Institute during the 1940s, many on behalf of the American Jewish Committee. These, like *Caligari*, were conceived as a significant contribution to understanding the problem of authoritarianism in modern industrial societies, and—more urgently—to the Allied psychological warfare research effort and the defeat of Nazi Germany. Several former affiliates of the Institute worked directly for the U.S. government during and after the war, conducting intelligence work on Nazi Germany.[18] It was to this end that Kracauer was employed as a special research assistant: his work had a pertinent, practical, and political purpose.

In the light of this, the *Caligari* study may be understood as the very centerpiece of Kracauer's various writings on authoritarianism and propaganda. Paradoxically, we do not present any material from the book itself here. Nevertheless, for us it is the sun around which the works in this anthology orbit, albeit at different distances and, in some cases, eccentrically.

Film in Our Time

Kracauer's *Caligari* study is a significant text in that, as will become clear, it anticipates many concepts, techniques, and examples explored in Kracauer's

Theory of Film: The Redemption of Physical Reality (1960), the fourth and last of his books to be discussed here. For example, one reads in *Caligari* of the camera's ability "to scan the whole visible world" (2019, 6) and, importantly, of its penchant for capturing the contingencies and happenstances of everyday urban existence—the "flow of life," as he terms it, as witnessed on the busy streets. There are due references, too, to various techniques and practices of cinematic montage and editing and to the increasing importance of sound and music as forms of emotional intensification and the creation and accentuation of mood. Such insights would later be extended and reconfigured in Kracauer's ambitious attempt to articulate the redemptive possibilities and restorative promise inherent in the medium of film. And, like *Caligari*, film is here to be considered in the context of a double catastrophe: the alienation and "spiritual shelterlessness" of the subject in a disenchanted modern world are placed in a new light by the unspeakable, perhaps unrepresentable, horrors of the Holocaust.[19]

Although Kracauer's *Theory of Film* appeared after his Cold War studies from the 1950s—studies that, much to his frustration, repeatedly delayed progress on the book manuscript—it is still highly relevant as the backdrop to the propaganda writings collected in this anthology. This is the case not least because, as Miriam Hansen points out in her lucid introduction to *Theory of Film* as well as elsewhere, the book was originally conceived *before* the *Caligari* study as an analysis of film aesthetics sketched in a series of notebooks in Marseilles in 1940 while the Kracauers were still trapped in Occupied France.[20] In fact, the origins of the project go much further back. The search for the genuine subject matter of the new film medium was one of the principal concerns of Kracauer's very earliest writings on cinema and imbue his numerous film reviews for the *FZ* in the 1920s.

In seeking to identify and establish both the essential qualities of the film medium and its inherent possibilities, Kracauer's *Theory of Film* takes as its point of departure the not unreasonable view that the so-called "moving" images of film and the "still" images of photography fundamentally share the same logic and capacity for revealing and recording the visible world—what he variously terms "physical," "material," or "camera" reality. Film finds itself in accord with this inherent "realistic tendency" when it attends to and captures the serendipitous and spontaneous movements and patterns of life that ceaselessly unfurl and unfold before the lens of the camera.[21] The hurry-scurry of pedestrians; the stop-start of traffic; the happenstances of chance encounters; things in transit; life in passing and passing away; the ephemeral, marginal, and improvised—all are among the true subject of the film medium which is dedicated to perceiving and preserving this 'real' world as it is manifested in the moment. This realistic tendency—or "cinematic approach" (1997, 35), as Kracauer terms it—contrasts with the "formative tendency," with the work of the filmmaker to give structure, shape, and sequence to these images, cutting, splicing, and editing them, fashioning them through montage and relay into a narrative, rendering them as works of art. These two opposing tendencies are not, of course, mutually exclusive; on the contrary, all films involve a compromise between realistic and formative tendencies for their content and form, for their very existence.

Foregrounding and privileging the realistic tendency of the film medium, *Theory of Film* continues with the exploration of cinematic techniques and the use of, for example, diegetic and nondiegetic sound and music. In so doing, Kracauer offers readings of numerous movies that accord with and exemplify his principles and others that contravene or conflict with them. His argument, then, is neither a dogmatic insistence upon realism in film nor a naïve advocacy of, for example, Italian neorealist cinema. It is one that leads him nonetheless to some idiosyncratic and, to his credit, highly unpretentious evaluations of particular films and film genres. While he celebrates the unpredictable world and ad hoc methods of improvisation displayed in popular slapstick comedies, as well as the interruption of narrative progression for the sake of singing and dancing in Hollywood musicals, Kracauer is also not afraid to decry the lamentably *uncinematic* qualities of much avant-garde, experimental "film art"—that is, films more concerned with displaying the technical inventiveness and skills of the filmmakers themselves than with depicting the life-world in which we are immersed. Walter Ruttmann's 1927 *Berlin: Symphony of a Great City* is a particular case in point. Kracauer's attitude toward films like Ruttmann's—not just mild distaste for but outright rejection of—is highly instructive as to the principles and precepts of *Theory of Film* and the significance of these for the propaganda studies in our anthology.

In many ways, one might expect Kracauer to be appreciative of Ruttmann's "city symphony," which was based on an original idea by Carl Mayer (none other than the coauthor of *Caligari*) and shot by his close associate Karl Freund. The film was supposed to depict the mundane sights and scenes of an ordinary day in Berlin, with images set to an original musical score by the Austrian composer Edmund Meisel. The visual and the acoustic were to combine in various ways to capture the hither and thither, the hustle and bustle of quotidian metropolitan existence: busy streets; criss-crossing pedestrians; traffic at speed; crowded streetcars; the comings and goings of local trains laden with commuters; office workers at their desks tap tapping away on typewriters; factories filled with wheels spinning, machinery pumping, engines turning; thriving shops, cafés, and bars; cinemas and theaters packed with appreciative audiences; even the

Tiller Girls themselves (or a dance troupe like them) make a brief appearance. Walter Ruttmann was brought in as editor to give a very particular shape and distinctive direction to Freund's images while collaborating closely with Meisel. All this activity and energy captured on film was edited according to the demands of rhythmic montage to ensure the correct dynamic tempo and proper sense of kaleidoscopic fragmentation. Mayer was appalled. And Kracauer loathed the film. Why?

For one thing, Kracauer detested what he saw as the overly self-conscious editing and stylization of the film: the emphasis time and again on the formative tendency, which celebrated the contrivances and cleverness of the filmmaker at the expense of the material depicted. Experimental aesthetics here equated to cinematic self-indulgence and narcissism, style over substance. And it produced what Kracauer detested most: *abstractness*. Here, the logic and speed of machines and engines are not simply privileged over human life, but become the very measure and pace for the responses of the body; here, the citizens of Berlin appeared either as aggregations, as masses, as otherwise meaningless constituent elements of larger patterns, or as banal types, as representatives of roles and responsibilities; Berliners never feature as distinctive individuals. Automation, atomization, anonymity: these are the main features of the featureless world conjured up by the Berlin symphony. For Kracauer, such things betray the radical promise of the film medium. In his epilogue, "Film in Our Time," he returns to his earlier critical vision of the disenchanted Simmelian life-world, one beset by the onward march of rationalization, calculation, and quantification. These processes, he reiterates, have led to a diminution of the human senses and an indifference to the unique qualities of things around us. It is precisely these tendencies, this work of reification, that the film medium promises to counteract. In its very ability to penetrate, record, and (re)present reality—revealing what was previously invisible, revitalizing perception by the use of unconventional camera angles, defamiliarizing and questioning the everyday and taken-for-granted—the film camera enhances our faculties, heightens our sensitivity and receptivity, and restores our aesthetic appreciation of the world around us.[22] Kracauer thus sees film as promising a twofold redemption: of the physical reality it (re)discovers, and of those who bear witness to this renewed world, an emancipated humanity.

Images of choreographed anonymous masses moving in and out of step to the relentless tempo of the machine and the rhythms of the Ratio were scrupulously edited into a kind of posthuman city-as-cyborg *Gesamtkunstwerk*. Ruttmann's film, then, is a kind of cinematic "mass ornament" and, as such, constitutes the very antithesis of Kracauer's precepts in *Theory of Film*. Little wonder, then, that

Ruttmann later worked with Leni Riefenstahl on *Triumph of the Will* (1934). He was to die of injuries sustained on the Russian front while shooting footage as a cameraman making Nazi propaganda films extolling "total war." Ultimately, for Kracauer, *film is not a neutral medium* that can simply be put into the service of any number of political persuasions and purposes. Rather, film is only true to its own ontological imperatives when it serves the radical redemption of human faculties and senses. *Propaganda films are always and everywhere a betrayal of the very medium of film itself, for they seek to blind us to very reality they should, as films, reveal and redeem.*

The leitmotifs of Kracauer's main works are hopefully evident: modern metropolitan mass society and the forms and possibilities of individual and collective experience this environment engenders and endangers; the significance of cultural phenomena, and film in particular, as manifestations of the prevailing social, cultural, political, and spiritual conditions of the masses; the complex and subtle strategies and textual techniques by means of which the Critical Theorist can undertake modern cultural analysis, reading the dialectical play between surface and depth, individual and society, conscious and unconscious states; and the possibilities of film, not only as a phenomenon through which the contemporary collective psyche may be discerned and deciphered, but also as the most important modern medium whose essence, for Kracauer, is to restore human perception and appreciation of the physical world so as to reveal it anew and thereby redeem it from a state of oblivion. The aesthetics of film were antithetical to the anaesthetics, the amnesia and alienation, of existence under the exigencies of modern capitalism.

CONTEXTUALIZATION OF MATERIALS

In bringing together this selection of Kracauer's writings on media, propaganda, and political communication for the first time in English, we hope that this anthology will lead to a new appreciation of the scope of his interests and expertise. Kracauer was a witness to the traumatic occurrences of the first half of the twentieth century, events that imbue his writings even as they seek to explicate and illuminate them. Not surprisingly, in Kracauer's case, this chronological time frame also corresponds to significant thematic reconfigurations and reconceptualizations as the Marxist critique of (German) mass culture as ideology develops into an increasingly sophisticated and detailed analysis of film as a medium (including its techniques, practices, and potentialities) and of its reception and interpretation by cinema audiences. Written over some twenty-five years, the various chosen texts collected here are invaluable for any proper understanding of the developments and trajectories of Kracauer's thought.

The truly alarming political developments of recent years have prompted a much-needed reassessment and long-overdue recognition of the Frankfurt School's many insightful writings on authority and authoritarianism, on Fascist agitators and propaganda techniques, and on anti-Semitism and prejudice.[23] For too long there was perhaps a widespread perception of much of the Institute's empirical research agenda in American exile as mere exercises in financial expediency (*Brotarbeit*) and institutional politicking both to win favor with influential organizations and, as Marxist German émigrés, to minimize unwelcome scrutiny from the authorities. Such studies were perhaps overlooked because they were seen at first to be characterized and compromised by precisely the kind of naïve methodology, empirical simplifications, and pseudoscientific experimental style characteristic of mainstream American social sciences—the very forms of knowledge against which Critical Theory configured and indeed defined itself. Overshadowed (or, perhaps more accurately, outshone) by the sophisticated critical analyses of the triumph of instrumental reason and the many essays in ideology-critique dissecting the culture industry, these texts are being subject to renewed interest and investigation. Not only is their continuity with and contribution to the more celebrated writings of Critical Theory increasingly evident, but also the prescience of their insights, the relevance of their conceptual armature, is newly and appreciable. They speak clearly, cogently, and urgently to the politics of our twenty-first-century world today.

Kracauer's writings on propaganda and political communication are exemplary in this regard. True, these analyses may seem to lack some of the philosophical sophistication and richness that make his other writings so demanding and provocative. However, we would argue that this does not diminish their value and significance, both as historical documents and as sources of theoretical and critical insight. Indeed, for Kracauer, the propaganda studies constituted essential and urgent intellectual contributions to the Allied war effort and the desperate struggle of liberal democratic regimes against Fascism and National Socialism.[24] Spanning a quarter of a century, these writings constitute a pioneering attempt to examine the social-psychological and cultural dimensions of the mobilization of the masses for "states of exception" that saw the accession to power and the legitimation of ruthless dictatorship, the acquiescence to if not actual willing participation in violence and terror, and the perpetration of total war and genocide. As such, these studies were developments of, rather than departures from, his long-standing intellectual trajectories. As we have already sought to suggest in this introduction, they demonstrate a clear correspondence with, and are primarily intelligible in terms of, those very cultural and aesthetic studies that have since eclipsed them.

While not wishing to create discontinuities in Kracauer's work, our anthology groups his texts into four main constellations under rubrics that are both chronological and thematic. In what follows, we provide a more specific and detailed contextualization of the selected works.

Studies of Totalitarianism, Propaganda, and the Masses (1936–1940)

This first section focuses on Kracauer's various writings—sketches, notes, schematic plans, and two substantial extracts—involved in his ill-fated "Totalitarian Propaganda" study, a project begun in 1936 at the behest of Max Horkheimer, which was to remain unpublished in his lifetime. Kracauer's initial outline or exposé of the work, entitled "Mass and Propaganda" (chapter 1), identifies three main questions: "How did the propaganda emerge? What is its underlying reality? And what function does it fulfill?" To address and answer these questions, he proposes a categorical framework for the project in four dimensions: 1) The Crisis After the War and Its Consequences; 2) The Decisive Phase of the Crisis; 3) The Approach of the Fascist Sham Solution; and 4) The Role of Propaganda in Fascism. The exposé highlights the potency and reach of emerging forms of mass communication, mediation, and spectacle, and the concomitant demise of individual identity and subjectivity as the distinctive individual personality is atomized and incorporated into the undifferentiated mass. Importantly, the exposé demonstrates that his propaganda project was conceived as a continuing investigation of the transformation of the urban masses as pioneered in *Die Angestellten* and adopting its pivotal conception of "spiritual shelterlessness." Thus, Fascist propaganda deceitfully promises to deliver the masses from the fundamental existential crises and ideological vacuum of modernity. The exposé also reveals how, in its critical disenchantment of the joy and glamour of the Second Empire and the hollow spectacle of imperial dictatorship, Kracuaer's 1937 study *Jacques Offenbach and the Paris of His Time* takes on an acutely critical significance in the era of totalitarianism.

In the exposé, Kracauer emphatically links the unprecedented penetration of the new media of the time into mundane lives and quotidian settings. For instance, he argues that radio has transformed the home into a public space, resulting in a "totalization of the inwardness of the individual" and a "politicization of the everyday lives of the masses." Fascist propaganda plays a distinctive and destructive role in the transformation of both private and public spheres and, importantly, of the borders and thresholds that have traditionally separated them. Furthermore, Kracauer considers his propaganda project to be a rigorous sociological investigation of the complex relationship between the urban masses and totalitarian regimes in high capitalism, a relationship that is inextricably interwoven with ideology and propaganda. Unlike communist propaganda, fascist propaganda's goal is not concerned with the disappearance or transcendence of the masses since fascism itself cannot exist without their constant mobilization. For Kracauer, this is an intrinsic dilemma that fascist regimes face. Herein lie noteworthy affinities and subtle differences between Benjamin's famous yet still enigmatic characterization of fascism as the "aestheticization of politics" and Kracauer's critical vision of mass spectacle and ornament. Benjamin's thesis constitutes an attempt to reflect upon the total crisis and alienation of the human sensorium in conjunction with the high capitalist entertainment industry. In Kracauer's conception, however, the masses always present themselves in the "aesthetically seductive form of an ornament or of an effective image." This insight is less akin to the formation of false consciousness than to the psychological reception of a mass mediated iconography of power, one exploring Fascist strategies in terms of the very visibility of the masses themselves (or "ornamentalization" of the masses, to use Kracauer's own terminology).

Developed from this exposé, Kracauer's 150-page typescript was completed two year later. It was duly sent to the Institute in New York, where it received scathing criticisms from Adorno in his "evaluative report" (*Gutachten*) provided to Horkheimer (see appendix 1). Dissatisfied with what he saw as a lack of theoretical insight and methodological rigor, Adorno took it upon himself to edit and abridge the manuscript (or, in Kracauer's view, "distort" it) under the title "On the Theory of Authoritarian Propaganda" (*Zur Theorie der autoritären Propaganda*).

After some heated correspondence and debates, Kracauer rejected Adorno's bowdlerized version and, when his own proposal of a compromise—the publication of two sections of the text—was declined, furiously withdrew his text altogether.[25] In accordance with Kracauer's wishes, we include here in original English translation the two key sections (E, exploring the formation of masses, and G, the concluding section) that he himself argued should be published (chapter 2). The original typescript for this was subsequently lost, and only a handwritten manuscript has survived in the Kracauer Nachlass in Marbach-am-Neckar. Painstakingly deciphered and transcribed, this was first published by

Suhrkamp Verlag in the second part of volume 2 of Kracauer's *Werke* in 2012. Moreover, again respecting Kracauer's own view, we have decided, after careful deliberation, *not* to include a translation of Adorno's rewritten version in this anthology. Whatever its own shortcomings and merits, this was and remains Adorno's text, not Kracauer's.

The Caligari Complex (1943–1947)

Written both during and in the immediate aftermath of World War II, the writings gathered in this section were inspired by two main factors: firstly, in examining propaganda techniques and audience psychologies, they were genuinely seen as a contribution to the American war effort; and, secondly, in experimenting on and examining American audiences, they were intended to identify, understand, and counteract fascist mentalities and anti-Semitism in the United States itself—the enemy within, so to speak. Here we group these writings under the sign of his major historical-psychological study of German cinema, *From Caligari to Hitler*, because it is in this book that so many of Kracauer's key ideas—especially the attempt to analyze the resonance of particular images and motifs for the inner psychological states of audiences—come to full fruition.

As we have already noted, Kracauer's propaganda projects were conceived against the background of his ongoing research on the *Caligari* book. Some of these first materialized in America with the help of the faculty of the New School for Social Research as well as the Museum of Modern Art Film Library. Kracauer's review article "Hollywood, the Movie Colony—*The Movie Makers* by Leo C. Rosten" was published in *Social Research* in 1942, a journal edited and published by the Graduate Faculty of the New School for Social Research, including Alvin Johnson and Hans Speier. The first tangible outcome was a pamphlet, *Propaganda and the Nazi War Film*, issued in 1942 by the Museum of Modern Art Film Library and later incorporated as a supplement to the *Caligari* book. As Kracauer explicitly acknowledged, Speier and Ernst Kris, another faculty member of the New School for Social Research, were deeply engaged in the development of his study of Nazi war film. The second piece, "The Conquest of Europe on the Screen: The Nazi Newsreel, 1939–1940" (chapter 6), was originally produced for the Experimental Division for the Study of War Time Communication in 1943. An abbreviated version was published in a 1943 issue of *Social Research*, one that included a major article by Hans Herm,

"Goebbels' Conception of Propaganda," and Speier's "Nazi Propaganda and Its Decline."

In the field of cultural sociology and communication studies in America in the 1940s, qualitative analysis of German cultural phenomena was not unfamiliar. Kris and Speier, among other émigré scholars, were undertaking extensive qualitative analyses of the German media and political communications. Kris's work "German Radio Propaganda" (1944) was highly influential in the early stages of media and propaganda research. It is little wonder to find close theoretical affinities between Kracauer's and Speier's views on the impact of Fascist propaganda on the transformation of white-collar workers. Since the mid-1930s, Speier had comprehensively researched the structural changes of salaried employees in modern society and, specifically, the role of German white-collar workers in the rise of Hitler. From the 1940s onward, Speier investigated how the radio communication of war news in Germany played a key role in the transformation of the masses.

As should be clear, for Kracauer film was not merely an ideological tool of the powerful, but also a new and innovative research instrument for the study of unconscious prejudices and a medium that promised a renewed sensitivity to physical reality and an enrichment of human experience. In his analyses of Nazi newsreels, Kracauer provides differentiated and nuanced accounts of Fascist propaganda as a form of mass culture, recognizing its popular appeal and the pleasure of distraction while retaining a resolute critical accent. In the essay "The Conquest of Europe on the Screen," he proceeds to analyze Nazi newsreels by characterizing their main aspects as "the unification of the news as a whole" and "the predominance of the visual element over commentary." He also offers a detailed examination of the role of the camera, of pictorial editing techniques, and the calculated combination of images, commentary and music. In these propaganda studies, we see Kracauer's search for an adequate and appropriate critical method for the concrete application of Critical Theory, for an approach that might combine European ideas and American methods into a sophisticated, powerful, and empirically grounded historical critique of the mass media and politics.

In exploring further the relatively sophisticated cinematography of Nazi newsreels—how camera angles and lighting can be used to create particular effects for example—Kracauer's "The Hitler Image" (chapter 7) from 1944 foregrounds the two key motifs from his earlier "Totalitarian Propaganda" study. An exemplary analysis of the aestheticization of politics, this essay considers not just the idolatry of the Führer—Hitler portrayed as genius and savior—but also the construction of his relationship with the masses, those adoring crowds from whom he retained a distinctive and necessary distance. Newsreels played their part in the fabrication of what one might term, following Benjamin, the "aura" of the Führer: a vision of both singularity and of remoteness.

Postwar Publics (1948–1950)

That the Kracauers decided to remain in America after the war and not to return to live in Germany—perhaps to engage in some way with its socioeconomic, cultural, and political reconstruction—or even elsewhere in Europe, should not be passed over without comment. While some, Adorno in particular, were seemingly only too keen to quit America and restore the Institute to its rightful home, Frankfurt-am-Main, Kracauer was to become one of those "permanent exiles"[26] like Leo Löwenthal and Herbert Marcuse, who chose to remain on the other side of the Atlantic.[27] As one-time editor of the *Zeitschrift* and hence part of the inner circle of the Institute, Löwenthal perhaps had more reason than most to return to his native city, but he, like Marcuse, was able to establish an academic career on the West Coast, first at Stanford and then at Berkeley. Much to his delight, and partly as a result of his own prompting, he was to be joined in California by Marcuse, who, after a spell at Brandeis University in Waltham, Massachusetts, took up a post at the University of California, San Diego. Kracauer, however, remained in New York. Despite close ties with Columbia University, he never held a proper full-time academic position. Their decision to stay in America and become naturalized U.S. citizens (in September 1946) is perhaps indicative of three things.

Firstly, it is undoubtedly indicative of Kracauer's own underlying attitude to Germany and the horrors of the Holocaust. Extraordinarily, the latter receives scant explicit mention in his published postwar works, with a late and oblique reference in *Theory of Film* to the role of cinema as a medium permitting audience to look upon and thereby overcome such atrocities, just as the hero of Greek myth Perseus uses his shield to reflect the petrifying image of, and then decapitate, the monstrous Medusa. Despite Kracauer's best long-distance efforts, first from Paris and then from New York, to enable his aging mother and aunt to leave Germany, they were expelled sometime in November 1941 from the modest Frankfurt apartment they shared and then deported to Theresienstadt in the middle of August 1942. All contact with them was then lost. They were just two of the many thousands who perished there. Reading Kracauer's review in the

New York Times of January 4, 1948 (chapter 9), of Marshall Knappen's *And Call It Peace*, one is left in no doubt as to his own skepticism regarding the ease with which Allied postwar reconstruction efforts would bring about denazification and welcome Germany into the happy family of postwar liberal democratic states. Knappen's focus on economic factors in accounting for Hitler's rise to power, Kracauer notes, leads him to the optimistic but naïve conclusion that the Marshall Plan—involving massive U.S. investment to stimulate and sustain economic growth and jobs—would radically and rapidly transform German sensibilities and attitudes, bringing a swift metamorphosis from authoritarian militarized masses to public-minded civilians. Kracauer's conclusion is telling: "For a historian, Mr. Knappen seems rather oblivious of Germany's past. We can only hope that a future Germany will not give lie to his rosy basic assumption." His skepticism was grounded, of course, in his own psychological-historical research, the work that was to culminate in the *Caligari* book. Here, the triumph of totalitarianism in Germany was not merely the result of particular economic crises during the 1920s and 1930s, but also because of the fertile ground it found in the prevailing national collective psyche, one whose predispositions to the rule of tyrants had repeatedly found symbolic expression on the cinema screens of the Weimar Republic since its very inception in 1919. For Kracauer, it would take considerably more than a job at steady wages to bring about the genuine denazification of German society.

Secondly, the decision to stay in New York is suggestive of Kracauer's confidence in his facility and fluency in the English language. For a writer who of necessity lives by means of the typewriter, especially a wordsmith praised even by Adorno for his gift for ironic expression and seemingly effortless literary style, this is no small matter.[28] For Kracauer, the economics of this were simple: insufficient English would mean no publications in America, which in turn would mean no money. The Kracauers had little if any English as they first stepped off the transatlantic steamship *Nyassa* in New York back in the spring of 1941. Nevertheless, at the age of fifty-two, Kracauer began writing in this alien tongue almost from the start, with his first English-language publication appearing just six months after their arrival.[29] Kracauer's resourcefulness and skills as a journalist and editor honed with the *FZ* in the Weimar years were to serve him well once again, this time in the very different context of postwar New York, where as a freelancer and frequent contributor Kracauer managed to establish a small network of outlets for his writings including such journals as the *New Republic*, *Public Opinion Quarterly*, and *Commentary*, as well as the book review section of the *New York Times*.

While Kracauer was never a full-time paid-up insider as such, he was nevertheless successful enough in integrating himself through the good offices of various friends and colleagues into the institutional fabric of the American academy,[30] of the various private research funding foundations, and even of several governmental agencies.[31] These did not make for a life of luxury, but they did suffice for a living. In any case, the prospect of getting by by means of these short-term fellowships, ad hoc journal pieces, and report-writing contracts was clearly preferable to the alternative: returning to Germany.

Finally, the decision to stay in America is significant in that it tells us something about his continuing relationship with Adorno, Horkheimer, and the Institute. Prior to his commission for the "Totalitarian Propaganda" essay in 1936, Kracauer had expressed his resolve not to have anything more to do with the Institute, a stance that the ensuing debacle around the study could only reaffirm. It might be pushing things too far to suggest that Kracauer stayed in New York *precisely because* Adorno and Horkheimer returned to Germany, but the fact remains that they left for Frankfurt, and he did not. Perhaps one could formulate it like this: *their* choice had, at best, little consequence for *his* decision. Not that he was invited to join the Institute, of course; not that he would have accepted such an invitation if it had been forthcoming. Neither the departures of Adorno and Horkheimer for Frankfurt, nor those of Löwenthal and Marcuse for the sunnier climes of California, were to persuade Kracauer to forsake his new home in Manhattan.

The seemingly diverse texts included in this section attest to Kracauer's enduring concern with the contrasting character of the techniques, forms, and contents of totalitarian propaganda, and those of other types of persuasive communication prevalent in capitalist liberal democracies—namely, advertising. This had originally been a part of this plan for the "Totalitarian Propaganda" study itself but had been dropped so as to sharpen the focus of the work. In his unpublished "Popular Advertisements" (chapter 11), dated January 15, 1949, Kracauer explores the recurrent motifs of American advertising, ones that—in promoting images of youthfulness, of health and vitality, of contentment and fitting in to the status quo—emphasize how correct fashion, brand, and lifestyle choices ensure social esteem, personal popularity, and all the other blessings of conformity. Two points are of particular interest here: that selling the "American dream" is here not so very different perhaps from promoting those "friendly face[s]" and "morally pink complexion[s]" (1998, 38) Kracauer scathingly identified as the secrets to success in the white-collar world of Berlin twenty years earlier; and that this incipient dreamworld of affluent consumerism was precisely that to which the "satellite mentalities" of those escaping the postwar Soviet bloc were drawn.

Not surprisingly, America's cinema screens are also the focus of Kracauer's attention in this period. In his satirically titled article "A Duck Crosses Main Street" (chapter 12), published in the *New Republic* in December 1948, Kracauer critically examines the American newsreel as it vies for the attention of audiences and struggles to fill screen time both in terms of economy and entertainment. The loosely linked pieces, air of eclecticism, and excessive chatty commentary of these newsreels are in stark contrast to those tightly crafted, intensely focused, and highly coherent image-led Nazi propaganda newsreels that Kracauer had critically explored earlier as part of the *Caligari* project, a study included in the previous section. American newsreels may exhibit "sloppiness, distortion and bias," but these are, he suggests, "unintentional" consequences of their being "indolent rather than totalitarian minded."

Such newsreels might be seen as part of the "Deluge of Pictures" identified by Kracauer in his January 1950 review of Lancelot Hogben's *From Cave Painting to Comic Strip* (chapter 14). Kracauer's critical comments here on the modern superfluity and superficiality of images recall themes articulated many years earlier in his 1927 essay "Photography": "The blizzard of photographs," he noted back then, "betrays an indifference toward what the things mean" (1995, 58), but now the proliferation of images and the concomitant diminution of meaning is given a new and rather different inflection. Now it is not so much the surfeit of images per se that is the problem, but the ever-more-intrusive and directive role of text and voice in steering interpretation and anchoring understanding. Captions, headlines, labels, slogans, and commentary increasingly tell viewers what to think of the picture, as opposed to allowing them to look for and find meaning in the pictures themselves. We are everywhere overwhelmed by the superabundance of pictures but simultaneously prevented from properly perceiving and questioning them. We are *told* the story; we are not permitted to see and make sense of it for ourselves. The "deluge," then, is not just of images, but of words—words that reduce pictures to mere illustrations.

Kracauer's study of "National Types" as depicted in Hollywood films (chapter 13) appeared in a number of different guises and was part of a 1949 UNESCO project exploring, and seeking to alleviate, "International Tensions."[32] In making linkages between recurrent cinematic motifs and unconscious attitudes of national audiences, his approach here echoes that of the (contemporaneous) *Caligari* study. Indeed, the essay partially fulfills Kracauer's interest in redirecting the critical interpretive approach developed in relation to Weimar cinema toward popular Hollywood films. Such parallels are clear when, for example, he notes, "The audiences also determine the way these films picture foreigners. The subjective factor in any such image is more or less identical with the notions American public opinion entertains of the people portrayed." Kracauer then proceeds to contrast the relatively wide and diverse representations of British characters—"American films offer a more complete cross-section of the English than they do of any other people"—emphasizing "British imperturbability, doggedness and, sportsmanship" with the much narrower portrayal of Russians, which, after a hiatus during the war years when negative depictions of allies would have been impolitic, revert to eccentric stereotypes of the "mad Russian" as postwar temperatures drop and the Cold War takes hold. Film here is not only a way of decoding popular sentiments and sensibilities, of deciphering latent public opinion and political attitudes, but also of assessing and evaluating the state and prevailing spirit of transcultural perceptions and international relations.

Marked Restricted: Cold War Tensions (1952–1958)

In this final section of our anthology we bring together a number of writings stemming from Kracauer's work with various American government agencies and other organizations in the postwar period, most notably Columbia University's Bureau of Applied Social Research (BASR), where he served as a research adviser on a part-time basis from 1951. Our selection of texts here, writings that provided repeated and unwelcome distraction from progress on the *Theory of Film* manuscript, focus on two main issues.

Firstly, this work was concerned with exploring the reach, efficacy, and proliferation of both American democratic and Soviet propaganda, especially along the newly established (indeed, still establishing) borders between Western and Eastern territories and spheres of influence. This particular topic was explored in two key ways. On the one hand, in relation to the success or otherwise of radio broadcasts (by the Voice of America and Radio Free Europe stations) in promulgating anti-Soviet messages in different countries and among diverse communities, classes, and other constituencies within those nation-states. In June 1952, for example, he completed a report entitled "The Voice and the BBC: A Comparison," based on broadcasts to Greece, of September 1951. In this anthology we include the more wide-ranging "Appeals to the Near and Middle East: Implications of the Communications Studies Along the Soviet Periphery," a summative report prepared in May 1952 for the International Information Administration (chapter 15).

On the other hand, Kracauer undertook research on the formation and articulation of attitudes among populations *within* the Soviet bloc itself, and in particular in Eastern Europe. Using interview data collected from some three hundred refugees from Hungary, Poland Czechoslovakia detained on the border and held temporarily in screening centers in Austria and elsewhere in central Europe (1951–1952), Kracauer and Paul L. Berkman's 1956 "Satellite Mentality" was a substantial report identifying not only the various grievances and sources of hostility towards Soviet systems, conditions, and apparatchiks in these different countries, but also the aspirations and expectations of those who had fled them for a new life in the capitalist West. Published in *Social Problems* in 1955, the essay included here, "Attitudes Toward Various Communist Types in Hungary, Poland, and Czechoslovakia" (chapter 16), is a summation of this larger report and investigates the attitudes of non-Communists to their country's Communist regime. It argues that the initial success of Communist propaganda in drawing people to the party quickly dissipated as the various promises made failed to materialize and the quality of daily life deteriorated. It also explores how the broadcasts of Radio Free Europe helped shape the perspectives of non-Communists toward their compatriots, toward the Soviet Union, and toward Western Europe and the United States.

Secondly, while it might be tempting to see Kracauer's Cold War reports as responses to financial necessity, this would be to do them, and him, an injustice. These writings were at the same time part of a much wider methodological exploration under the auspices of the Bureau of Applied Research: the search to devise appropriate methods for the empirical investigation and *qualitative* analysis of mass media texts, images, and other such data. Such epistemological and methodological issues were concerns dating back to Kracauer's early writings on sociology as a science, his ethnography of Berlin's white-collar workers, his societal biography of the Second Empire, and his interpretive schemas for film analysis underpinning *Caligari*. The three essays included in this section are particularly relevant here, for they demonstrate Kracauer's repeated attempt throughout the 1950s to elaborate a systematic qualitative communication research method, one that insists upon the need to move beyond the coding and counting techniques of conventional content analysis and recognize instead the critical role of situation and context in the hermeneutical interpretation of meaning. We include "Proposal for a Research Project Designed to Promote the Use of Qualitative Methods in the Social Sciences" (unpublished manuscript, 1950; chapter 17); "The Challenge of Qualitative Content Analysis" (*Public Opinion Quarterly*, 1953; chapter 18); and "On the Relation of Analysis to the Situational Factors in Case Studies" (unpublished manuscript, ca. 1958; chapter 19). Defending the virtues of qualitative techniques such as participant observation and in-depth interviews, these writings together constitute a critical response to the Columbia bureau's tendency to focus on quantitative methods. It may indeed be significant how often particular words and phrases occur in a text or transcript, but for Kracauer any one-sided reliance or overemphasis on quantitative content analysis leads to a neglect of how language is used and how meaning itself is produced, reproduced, expressed, conveyed, understood, and subverted. For us today this is perhaps a salutary and timely reminder of the role of intense and critical reading and interpretation in an era fascinated by the potential of "big data" and the ubiquity of computer-generated infographics.

The final text of our anthology, "The Social Research Center on the Campus: Its Significance for the Social Sciences and Its Relations to the University and Society at Large" (ca. 1954; chapter 20), draws heavily on his experiences working as a research adviser at the Bureau of Applied Social Research at Columbia University during the 1950s. This unpublished article was, as Kracauer writes, "intended as an inclusive and systematic contribution to the running controversy about the significance of organized social research in the university." Although the pursuit of such research at established, continuously functioning university institutions was still a relatively recent phenomenon in the United States, some reflection upon the problems and internal debates that had been most persistent so far was warranted. But rather than carrying out an ambitious comparative study of these institutions, Kracauer focuses on the history of BASRA itself, which was a pioneer in the field of media and communications research and became a model for similar institutions at other universities. He looks, in particular, at three main areas of controversy: autonomous research, commissioned research, and the training of aspiring social scientists at these institutions. Although Kracauer clearly made an effort to adopt the scientific-objective style of writing common among the positivist-dominated social sciences in the United States, his own voice and his criticisms of such hegemonic views are also apparent throughout the text.

We are also including as appendices two texts that were not written by Kracauer, which will contribute to a better understanding of his substantial manuscript on "Totalitarian Propaganda." The first is the *Gutachten*—that is, the brief assessment of Kracauer's essay, which was written by Adorno in March 1938. As mentioned earlier, Kracauer had hoped to publish his essay in the Institute's house journal, the *Zeitschrift für Sozialforschung*. The chief editor of the journal and director of the Institute, Max Horkheimer, had asked Adorno to pen an evaluation of Kracauer's essay. Adorno's harsh critique of it in his *Gutachten* undoubtedly delivered the final blow to any possibility of publication in the

Zeitschrift. The second text we are including is an article by John Abromeit that examines both Kracauer's "Totalitarian Propaganda" study and Adorno's evaluation of it. Abromeit's article has several aims. It provides a section-by-section overview of Kracauer's manuscript that will make its main contours and arguments familiar to a non-German-reading public; although we have translated and included in this volume two of the seven sections of the manuscript, the remaining five sections remain inaccessible to English speakers. Additionally, Abromeit argues that not all of Adorno's criticisms of Kracauer's essay were justified. In contrast to Adorno, who asserted a fundamental theoretical incompatibility between the Institute's and Kracauer's own analyses of fascism, Abromeit seeks to demonstrate how Kracauer's essay complements and supplements the Critical Theorists' writings on fascism, especially the work of Horkheimer and Erich Fromm from the 1930s, which Kracauer repeatedly cites in his essay. Finally, Abromeit makes a case for the ongoing relevance of both Kracauer's and the early Frankfurt School's sophisticated studies of fascism. Drawing on these studies and more recently theoretical and historical scholarship, he tries to show in particular why fascism should be seen as an extreme form of authoritarian, right-wing populism, and thus also how a careful study of historical fascism can still yield important insights into the less extreme—yet still deeply menacing—versions of authoritarian populism that have proliferated in Europe, the United States, and many other parts of the world in the past few decades.

In this anthology we bring together a diverse range of Kracauer's texts spanning more than twenty years. We hope that these writings will shed light on how manifold forms, techniques, and roles of political propaganda and persuasive communication may be subject to critical scrutiny and intense interrogation. We hope that the insightfulness and importance of Kracauer's writings on such themes will become evident and his contribution to Critical Theory as a vital and continuing critique of authoritarianism, totalitarianism, and irrationality will be increasingly recognized. Above all, we hope that this anthology will be an encouragement to all to read and engage with Kracauer's work in a critical and appreciative spirit, recognizing its enduring importance in the struggles of the present.

NOTES

1. Of particular significance for our work here is that the nine volumes of the German-language *Werke* issued by Suhrkamp Verlag now include vols. 9.1 and 9.2, "Early

Writings from the Archive" (2004); and vol. 2.2, "Studies in Mass Media and Propaganda" (2012).

2. Most notably, *Siegfried Kracauer's American Writings*, ed. Johannes von Moltke and Kristy Rawson (Berkeley: University of California Press, 2012).

3. See, for example, the publication by Suhrkamp in English of Kracauer's second novel, *Georg* (2016).

4. Including, most important, the publication of Kracauer's correspondence with Theodor W. Adorno, first by Suhrkamp in German (2008) and now by Polity in English translation (2020).

5. See, for example, Gerd Gemünden and Johannes von Moltke, eds., *Culture in the Anteroom: The Legacies of Siegfried Kracauer* (Ann Arbor: University of Michigan Press, 2012); Johannes von Moltke, *The Curious Humanist: Siegfried Kracauer in America* (Berkeley: University of California Press, 2016), very much a companion study for his edited collection with Kirsty Rawson, *Siegfried Kracauer's American Writings* (Berkeley: University of California Press, 2012); and Harry Carver, *Reluctant Skeptic: Siegfried Kracauer and the Crises of Weimar Culture* (New York: Berghahn, 2017). See also Miriam Hansen, *Cinema and Experience: Siegfried Kracauer, Walter Benjamin, and Theodor W. Adorno* (Berkeley: University of California Press, 2017). Kracauer's work is the focus of many of the essays in *The Detective of Modernity*, ed. Georgia Giannakopoulou and Graeme Gilloch (London: Routledge, 2020), a collection dedicated to the sociologist David Frisby, a pioneering figure in the Anglophone reception of Kracauer's Weimar studies. Gilloch's *Siegfried Kracauer: Our Companion in Misfortune* (Cambridge: Polity, 2012) provides an overview of his principal writings.

6. Jörg Später's magisterial *Siegfried Kracauer: Eine Biographie* was published by Suhrkamp in 2016 and is now available in an English translation by Daniel Steuer under the title *Kracauer: A Biography* (Cambridge: Polity, 2020).

7. As we will see, Kracauer's friend and colleague Leo Löwenthal was also to write on this theme in a 1944 essay proposing an interesting shift in focus away from so-called "idols of production" to "idols of consumption": Leo Löwenthal, "Biographies in Popular Magazines," in *Radio Research: 1942–1943*, ed. Paul Lazarsfeld and Frank Stanton (New York: Duell, Sloane & Pearce, 1944). See also Leo Löwenthal, "German Popular Biographies: Culture's Bargain Counter," in *The Critical Spirit: Essays in Honor of Herbert Marcuse*, ed. Kurt H. Wolff and Barrington Moore Jr. (Boston: Beacon, 1967), 267–83.

8. Siegfried Kracauer, *The Mass Ornament*, trans. T. Y. Levin (Cambridge, MA: Harvard University Press, 1995), 75. Hereafter cited parenthetically.

9. Siegfried Kracauer, *The Salaried Masses: Duty and Distraction in Weimar Germany*, trans. Q. Hoare (New York: Verso, [1930] 1998), 88. Hereafter cited parenthetically.

10. Regarding the Offenbach book, see their exchange of letters during May 1937 in *Theodor W. Adorno and Siegfried Kracauer: Correspondence, 1923–1966*, ed. Wolfgang Schopf, trans. Susan Reynolds and Michael Winkler (Cambridge: Polity, 2020), 240–50.

11. Siegfried Kracauer, *Jacques Offenbach and the Paris of His Time*, trans. G. David and E. Mosbacher (New York: Zone, [1937] 2002), 24.

12. "The Little Shopgirls Go to the Movies" was a series of eight pieces published in the *FZ* in March 1927. See Kracauer, *The Mass Ornament: Weimar Essays* (Cambridge, MA: Harvard University Press, 1995), 291–304.
13. Siegfried Kracauer, *From Caligari to Hitler: A Psychological History of the German Film* (Princeton, NJ: Princeton University Press, [1947] 2019), 5. Hereafter cited parenthetically.
14. These are: the "archaic" period (1895–1918); the immediate postwar era (1918–1924); the "stabilized period" (1924–1929); and the pre-Hitler years (1930–1933).
15. In his combination of showmanship, charlatanism, ruthlessness, and hypnotism, the figure of Dr. Caligari serves not only as the first in a series of onscreen tyrants, but also, as will see, embodies key characteristics of the totalitarian dictator examined in the "Totalitarian Propaganda" study.
16. For example, pacifist and antimilitarism films like G. W. Pabst's *Westfront 1918* (1930); films critiquing authority like Leontine Sagan's *Mädchen in Uniform* (1931); and even some more radical films such as Slatan Dudow's famous *Kuhle Wampe* (1930).
17. Kracauer notes the popularity of Luis Trenker's war films, the glut of Napoleonic costume dramas, and a series of "Fridericus" films (homilies to Frederick the Great).
18. On the work of Institute affiliates for the U.S. government during World War II, see Barry M. Kātz, *Foreign Intelligence: Research and Analysis in the Office of Strategic Services, 1942–1945* (Cambridge, MA: Harvard University Press, 1989); and Franz Neumann, Herbert Marcuse, and Otto Kirchheimer, *Secret Reports on Nazi Germany: The Frankfurt School Contribution to the War Effort*, ed. Raffaele Laudani (Princeton, NJ: Princeton University Press, 2013).
19. In *Theory of Film*, Kracauer suggests that Allied footage shot to document the extermination camps after their liberation may enable us to confront onscreen via the medium of film such horrors which we otherwise could not face.
20. See Hansen, *Cinema and Experience*.
21. Siegfried Kracauer, *Theory of Film: The Redemption of Physical Reality* (Princeton, NJ: Princeton University Press, [1960] 1997), 33. Hereafter cited parenthetically.
22. What Benjamin would famously term the "optical unconscious" in his 1936 "Work of Art in the Age of Mechanical Reproduction" essay.
23. These texts include, for example, Leo Löwenthal and Norbert Guterman, *Prophets of Deceit: A Study of the Techniques of the American Agitator* (Palo Alto, CA: Pacific, [1949] 1970); Adorno's own study of American Fascist agitators in the mid-1930s, *The Psychological Technique of Martin Luther Thomas' Radio Addresses* (Stanford, CA: Stanford University Press, [1975] 2000); and, subsequently, *The Authoritarian Personality* (London: Verso, [1950] 2019). For one recent assessment of the relevance of these writings to contemporary forms of authoritarianism, see *Critical Theory and Authoritarian Populism*, ed. Jeremiah Morelock (London: University of Westminster Press, 2018).
24. In the addendum to his 1936 exposé, "Masse und Propaganda," he particularly emphasized that propaganda studies should also examine "the corresponding conditions in the great democracies (especially in America)."

25. For Kracauer's rejection of Adorno's edited version of the text and counterproposal, see their exchange of letters (August 20 and September 12, 1938) in *Correspondence*, 269–74.
26. Martin Jay, *Permanent Exiles: Essays on the Intellectual Migration from Germany to America* (New York: Columbia University Press, 1986).
27. This was perhaps more the case with Adorno than Horkheimer. The former was eager to return because he saw his thought so inextricably bound up with the German language, and he believed he could have a greater impact in Germany. Horkheimer was hesitant. For example, he got the U.S. government to preserve his U.S. citizenship even after he returned to Germany. During his first visits to Frankfurt after the war, Horkheimer stayed in a hotel close to the train station, so he could leave very quickly if need be. Horkheimer was finally convinced only by the students who were eager to learn from him. His time in Germany after the war was often unpleasant, and he retired early in Switzerland after being subjected to anti-Semitic attacks from other professors in Frankfurt.
28. Adorno acknowledges this, even in his otherwise hostile report on Kracauer's "Totalitarian Propaganda" study of 1938, and notes, "We are not overly blessed with contributions of such writerly quality" (see paragraph 5 of the *Gutachten*). Adorno's appreciation of Kracauer's power of expression were strictly limited to his German-language publications. He lamented the shift to English and tried without success to persuade Kracauer to write in German again. Writing in English was to rob oneself of one's most precious insights, observations, and expressions, Adorno insisted, but to no avail. To his credit, Kracauer was unimpressed by such linguistic chauvinism.
29. See von Moltke and Rawson, eds., *Siegfried Kracauer's American Writings*, 2.
30. In 1952 he succeeded in becoming a staff member and then research director of the Bureau of Applied Social Research at Columbia University. See Ingrid Belke and Irina Renz, *Siegfried Kracauer, 1889–1966* (Marbach: Marbacher Magazin, 1988), 111.
31. He received funding from and became an adviser to both the Bollingen and Old Dominion Foundations, for example. He also received monies from the Chapelbrook Foundation.
32. Here, as published in *Public Opinion Quarterly* in 1949. Subsequently, a version under the amended title "How U.S. Films Portray Foreign Types: A Psychological View of British and Russians on Our Screens" appeared in *Films in Review* in March 1950.

REFERENCES

Adorno, Theodor W., Else Frenkel-Brunswick, Daniel J. Levinson, and R. Nevitt Sanford. *The Authoritarian Personality*. London: Verso, [1950] 2019.
———. "The Curious Realist" [*Der wunderliche Realist*]. *New German Critique*, no. 54 (1991): 159–77.

———. *The Psychological Technique of Martin Luther Thomas' Radio Addresses*. Stanford, CA: Stanford University Press, 2000.

Adorno, Theodor W., and Siegfried Kracauer. *Correspondence, 1923–1966*. Cambridge: Polity, 2020.

Belke, Ingrid, and Irina Renz. *Siegfried Kracauer, 1889–1966*. Marbach: Marbacher Magazin, 1988.

Carver, Harry. *Reluctant Skeptic: Siegfried Kracauer and the Crises of Weimar Culture*. New York: Berghahn, 2017.

Gemünden, Gerd, and Johannes von Moltke, eds. *Culture in the Anteroom: The Legacies of Siegfried Kracauer*. Ann Arbor: University of Michigan Press, 2012.

Giannakopoulou, Georgia, and Graeme Gilloch, eds. *The Detective of Modernity*. London: Routledge, 2020.

Gilloch, Graeme. *Siegfried Kracauer: Our Companion in Misfortune*. Cambridge: Polity, 2015.

Hansen, Miriam. *Cinema and Experience: Siegfried Kracauer, Walter Benjamin, and Theodor W. Adorno*. Berkeley: University of California Press, 2017.

Jay, Martin. *Permanent Exiles: Essays on the Intellectual Migration from Germany to America*. New York: Columbia University Press, 1986.

Jenemann, David. *Adorno in America*. Minneapolis: University of Minnesota Press, 2007.

Kracauer, Siegfried. *From Caligari to Hitler: A Psychological History of the German Film*. Princeton, NJ: Princeton University Press, [1947] 2004.

———. *Georg*. Frankfurt: Suhrkamp Verlag, 2016.

———. *Jacques Offenbach and the Paris of His Time*. New York: Zone, [1937] 2002.

———. *The Mass Ornament: Weimar Essays*. Cambridge, MA: Harvard University Press, 1995.

———. *The Salaried Masses: Duty and Distraction in Weimar Germany*. London: Verso, 1998.

———. *Theory of Film: The Redemption of Physical Reality*. Princeton, NJ: Princeton University Press, [1960] 1997.

Kracauer, Siegfried, and Paul L. Berkman. *Satellite Mentality: Political Attitudes and Propaganda Susceptibilities of Non-Communists in Hungary, Poland, and Czechoslovakia*. New York: F. A. Praeger, 1956.

Löwenthal, Leo, and Norbert Guterman. *Prophets of Deceit: A Study of the Techniques of the American Agitator*. Palo Alto, CA: Pacific [1949] 1970.

Später, Jörg. *Kracauer: A Biography*. Cambridge: Polity, 2020.

von Moltke, Johannes. *The Curious Humanist: Siegfried Kracauer in America*. Berkeley: University of California Press, 2016.

von Moltke, Johannes, and Kirsty Rawson, eds. *Siegfried Kracauer's American Writings*. Berkeley: University of California Press, 2012.

PART I

Studies of Totalitarianism, Propaganda, and the Masses (1936–1940)

INTRODUCTION

Notwithstanding his deep and longstanding attachment to Theodor W. Adorno and his enduring friendship with Leo Löwenthal, Siegfried Kracauer's personal, intellectual, and professional relations with the Institute for Social Research were, even at the best of times, complicated and tense. The period 1936–1938 was not the best of times. The fact that Kracauer was keen to write an article for inclusion in the Institute's house journal, the *Zeitschrift für Sozialforschung*—given his earlier insistence that he would have nothing to do with the Institute—is indicative less of a mellowing of attitudes or some growing rapprochement than of the acute predicament he found himself in at the time.[1] Having fled Germany in 1933 on the advice of his superiors at the *Frankfurter Zeitung* who were then only too quick to sever any contractual obligations with him, the life of an exile in Paris was a precarious one, eking out an existence by his writing, all the while reliant on publishers and publications abroad. The offer of an honorarium to produce a critical examination of contemporary totalitarian propaganda was an invitation Kracauer could scarcely refuse, despite whatever misgivings he might still have had about collaborating with the Institute. However much he claimed that such a subject corresponded felicitously with his existing plans and interests, he also needed the money (6000 French francs).

For his part, Max Horkheimer was far from enthusiastic about approaching Kracauer. He was, nevertheless, on this particular occasion, prepared to put aside his own strong personal antipathy toward Kracauer, appreciating that he did possess, after all, at least in matters of mass culture and communication, some expertise and insight. Kracauer would do what was asked of him so long as Adorno was to make clear their overall expectations of the main themes and approaches that were to inform the study. Kracauer was not to be left too much to his own designs and devices. In short: Horkheimer grudgingly offered the work; Kracauer grudgingly accepted. Hardly an auspicious beginning! But the work of a few months expanded into a text that took him nearly two years to complete. By the time Kracauer met with Friedrich Pollock on April 12, 1938, and handed over the final installment of his study, the whole thing comprised well in excess of 150 pages of typescript. It was no longer just a journal article at all; rather, it had become a small book. Perhaps Horkheimer anticipated something of the sort. In any case, he had already been careful to point out to Kracauer from the start that publication in the *Zeitschrift* was, of course, not a given, and that there were other equally valid and valuable alternative arrangements for texts that did not quite fit the bill: a place in the archive, with the possibility of publication later in one of the Institute's anthologies.[2]

Adorno had his own alternative. Deeming the first 106 pages sent by Kracauer as being "neither of real theoretical value nor sufficiently grounded in the empirical material" and without even waiting for the final installment to arrive, Adorno took it upon himself to edit the text, stripping away what he saw as repetition and verbosity, cutting redundant quotation, and honing, as he saw it, the actual argument.[3] Adorno thought he knew best. He pared down the script to between one-quarter and one-fifth of its original length and duly sent it for approval to Kracauer on June 28, 1938. But Kracauer, notwithstanding the difficulties that beset him, was having none of it. His text may have been cut short, but he himself was not to be so easily belittled. In his response of August 20, 1938, he refused point-blank to allow publication of Adorno's abbreviated version, proposing instead a compromise that would see two key sections of his original text printed in the journal—"'the chapter on the masses, and if possible also the concluding chapter'" (2013, 325). But the damage had been done. Kracauer's study was never to appear in the *Zeitschrift*, and his subsequent attempts to find a suitable location for publication elsewhere proved to be in vain. Somehow, somewhere, the typescript versions of the text were mislaid or went astray. Only a barely legible handwritten copy with numerous corrections and amendments survived to become part of the Kracauer Nachlass in Marbach am Neckar. Indeed, it was not until 2012 that a painstakingly transcribed version of this manuscript was finally published by Suhrkamp Verlag as part of volume 2 of Kracauer's *Werke*.

So far, so bad. The remarks above draw upon the Suhrkamp editors' contextualization in their afterword to the "Totalitarian Propaganda" study. True, the fate of this study is indeed a testament to the poor relations between Kracauer and the Institute. But the situation was actually *worse* than this, because what the editors *do not mention* is that right in the middle of this fiasco, in spring 1937, Kracauer's societal biography, *Jacques Offenbach and the Paris of His Time*, was published—a book derided by Adorno as "idiotic and shameless." Walter Benjamin readily agreed with him.[4] Leo Löwenthal argued that just reviewing the book in the *Zeitschrift*—which he helped to edit—would be to bestow undeserved honor upon it.[5] Nonetheless, Adorno's biting review did make it into the *Zeitschrift*, albeit in an ameliorated form, and the incident sparked a heated exchange of letters containing various accusations and counterarguments: Kracauer had no technical appreciation of music and could only critique the libretti; Adorno had no sense of the critical sensibility of Offenbach as a "mockingbird" of his times.[6] Adorno thought he knew best here, too. But a more sympathetic reader of the Offenbach study might have appreciated how prescient and pertinent its themes were in regard to the "Totalitarian Propaganda" text: the populist machinations and manipulations through which authoritarianism triumphs; the myth of overcoming class and class conflicts; the creation of an illusory "operetta-world," a *Scheinwelt* or pseudoreality; the "joy and glamour" of the Second Empire as a foretaste of "strength through joy" (*Kraft durch Freude*) of the Third Reich; imperial pomp and spectacle including grandiose architectural projects celebrating state power and cementing control (the Hausmannization of Paris as "strategic beautification"; Albert Speer's plans for the new capital of the Reich, Germania).[7] But while these thematic continuities are certainly of significance, it is principally Kracauer's earlier writings, especially those of the late 1920s, that influence and inform the "Totalitarian Propaganda" study. It is to these that we now turn.

Although the prevailing conditions and practices of Italian Fascism do feature in Kracauer's text, and the analyses of Ignazio Silone are frequently cited, it is nevertheless National Socialism in Germany that is Kracauer's main focus. His writings in the varied roles of journalist, cultural critic, and sociologist, which aimed to capture the "newest Germany" of the turbulent Weimar years, provide much of the contextual material, and theoretical and conceptual armature, of the later propaganda study. For example, in section A of his text under the rubric

"Genesis of Totalitarian Propaganda," Kracauer begins by noting the general importance of the traumatic experiences of the Great War and its aftermath for the creation of both a martial sensibility and an intense disaffection from civilian government. In terms that echo his own wartime reflections from 1917 to 1918 on the theme of friendship,[8] he recognizes the formation of a profound and powerful sense of solidarity among the soldiers on the front line, a deep and lasting "camaraderie of the trenches" (*Schutzenkamaradschaft*) that went far beyond both individual concerns and class interests.[9] He also observes that one has to acknowledge the keen sense of betrayal that was felt by demobilized soldiers, especially but not exclusively among the officer class, when Germany finally capitulated in 1918.[10] Protofascist psychological predispositions—such as an absolute trust in one's fellow soldiers; a contemptuous distrust of all things civilian and liberal; and an acute desensitization to the use of violence—could be easily activated by propagandistic calls for mobilization, first as Freikorps in the city streets and then as SA and SS at the mass rallies. A certain readiness and receptivity are essential if propaganda is not simply to fall on deaf ears.[11]

It should be no surprise to learn that Kracauer's "Mass Ornament" essay (1927) and *The Salaried Masses* (*Die Angestellten*) book (1930) are the two most important works underpinning the "Totalitarian Propaganda" study. Both are referred to explicitly in the text on a number of occasions. They capture something of both the preconditions for the success of National Socialist propaganda and aspects of its actual practice. There are at least three deeply interwoven aspects here: the masses, the leader, and the orchestration of power.

Firstly, there is the purposeful constitution of the mass itself. The fundamental point of departure for totalitarian propaganda is the production and propagation of the mass as an entity, as the decisive social and political phenomenon of the time. This involves a number of processes: the dissolution of the distinct individual as an autonomous and idiosyncratic subject (i.e., the erasure of difference); the fragmentation and disintegration of all other social and civic bonds, forms of solidarity, and common belonging, above all, the (illusory) overcoming of class membership and class antagonism; and the reconfiguration of these now isolated, atomistic selves into a new totality bearing such grandiose names as "the nation," "the people," or the *Volksgemeinschaft*.[12] The generation of the mass *as mass* is the primary, and always inevitably ongoing, task of such propaganda, for it is the very precondition for the success of all that follows. The mass is that which is formed by, and that which then allows itself to be reformed according to, totalitarian propaganda. In the case of German National Socialism, the vital role of white-collar employees—the most rapidly expanding social group in Weimar Germany—cannot be overstated. Lacking the *Bildung* and accomplishments of the professional classes, elites, and haute bourgeoisie, but at the same time utterly disdainful of the working class and of proletarian collectivism, the ranks of lower-middle-class office workers (clerks, secretaries, minor state functionaries, administrators, pen-pushers of all kinds) were for Kracauer an in-between, neither-nor socioeconomic strata. As the bearers of bureaucratic and Tayloristic discipline, they were the subject-objects of modern instrumental reason—the "Ratio," as he terms it. On the basis of his 1929–1930 Berlin-based ethnographic exploration of the terra incognita of this seemingly invisible, because actually ubiquitous, class in *Die Angestellten*, Kracauer concludes that they are "spiritually homeless" (1998, 88), a claim he reiterates in "Totalitarian Propaganda."[13] This pathological condition of insecurity and meaninglessness predisposes them to duplicitous notions of belonging and the appeal of an authentic life especially at moments of economic crisis and uncertainty. The white-collar workers were indeed the salaried *masses* and constituted something both quantitatively and qualitatively new.[14]

Moreover, as Kracauer is at pains to point out, there are masses, and then there are other masses. Communism, he claims, also produces the masses, calls into being the proletariat as mass, the mass as proletariat, for the express purpose of the revolutionary overthrow of capitalism and the abolition of class society. But here, crucially, the mass is only ever a temporary phenomenon, a necessary and short-lived means to an end. The alienated worker becomes part of the collective, the mass, in order thereby to overthrow the circumstances of his/her alienation. The revolution is (only) complete when the *mass abolishes itself* for the full realization of the liberated individual human subject.[15]

Kracauer counterpoises the revolutionary mass with the mass in Fascism and National Socialism: here, the mass is not a transient stage on the way to genuine liberation but, rather, a permanent condition. The mass is no longer the means but the end point itself, the destination, the longed-for "homeland" (*Heimat*).[16] The mass comes into being *to remain* as a mass. The fundamental task of propaganda here is to convince the mass that class divisions and conflict have been overcome as capitalist relations actually go unchanged. Fascist propaganda fosters the *illusion of classlessness*. This has two important consequences for Kracauer. Totalitarian propaganda is not just about winning power, after which it has served its purpose and may then be dispensed with; it is necessary to *sustain* power because Fascism is unable—in fact, never intends—to deliver on its various promises of abolishing class inequalities and creating an egalitarian Volksgemeinschaft. The people are, after all, *never* to be emancipated.[17] Propaganda then is always and inevitably *ongoing*; indeed, it must intensify as the contradictions produced by the unchanged capitalist system themselves continue and increase. And where propaganda fails to convince, there is always coercion, violence as threat or as actual punishment. Propaganda and terror go hand in hand.

Totalitarianism targets both the mind and body of its population as mass: propaganda and terror co-configure the "psycho-physical structure" of the mass human, the *Massenmensch*, as "regression" (a toxic mix of fear, sadism, cynicism, frustration, and resentment).

Sustaining the illusion of class reconciliation is significant for Kracauer in another way: it is part and parcel of a much wider set of deceptions and misrecognitions that totalitarianism presents as the real, as enlightenment. Under Fascism, reality is a pseudoreality in which what appears to be becomes taken for what actually is, and what is is merely what seems to be. Appearance (*Schein*) displaces and becomes being (*Sein*). The masses live in a world of spurious appearances (*Scheinwelt*). Misleading and misinforming, maintaining this confusion of truth and lies, blending and blurring one with the other, insisting on the fiction that these fictions are not in the least fictitious—all this again falls to the work of the tireless propagandists.

This continual generation and regeneration of the masses finds it corollary, its necessary counterpart, in the creation of the leader, the Führer, the unique charismatic figure who remains distinctive and apart.[18] He, the "agent of power" (*Machttyp*), is the one true personality in a mass society in which all other personalities have been relinquished or eradicated. Kracauer emphasizes this symbiotic relationship between the mass and the leader which is, at the same time, highly asymmetrical. While essential, *they*, the masses, are only ever the interchangeable backdrop, so much stage scenery so to speak, before and above which *he*, the dictator, stands out. *They* undoubtedly and unquestioningly revere *him*; that is their role. But *he*, in return, regards *them* with nothing but contempt and loathing. *He* is everything, *they* are nothing, though, paradoxically, *he is nothing without them*. The aim of fascist propaganda is to transform individuals into masses—that is, to reduce them to naïve, credulous, gullible targets of propaganda. The leader plays with their prejudices and panders to their resentments, makes easy promises, lies and deceives, stirs the emotions, points out their enemies both within and without, and directs their fervor and fury. Kracauer describes the Fascist dictator as a "charlatan," as a cheap trickster and second-rate magician under whose spell the masses are docile and compliant. Indeed, he repeatedly compares the Führer to a kind of hypnotist with the masses as his entranced and obedient instrument. Although he goes unmentioned here, precisely this combination of tyrannical personality, huckster, and hypnotist is to be found in the fictional figure of Dr. Caligari, the eponymous sideshow sorcerer who dispatches the sinister somnambulist Cesare to do his murderous bidding in Robert Wiene's 1919 film—the very film, of course, that Kracauer came to see as indicative of incipient authoritarian predispositions among postwar German cinema audiences. The Führer as despotic deceiver is the very embodiment of the Caligari complex. In this sense, the "Totalitarian Propaganda" study is the first star in the later Caligari constellation.

The hypnotic power of the dictator, Kracauer continues, derives from the use of the voice (as opposed to written texts). The form and temporality of writing appeals more to reason and opens itself up to reflection: one can reread the text, mull it over, return to it, question it, take exception to it, tear it up. But the human voice has an immediate impact allowing no time for scrutiny, no opportunity for interrogation. There is no possibility of—or intention to enable—dialogue, conversation, cross-examination. In this context, Kracauer notes the key role played by radio broadcasting in mass propaganda.[19] Not only does the radio provide for the comprehensive one-to-many one-way communication so suited to the dictator-mass relationship, but its reach and invasiveness ensure that there is no escape from the words of the Führer. It is not a coincidence that, shortly after coming to power, the Nazis began to mass produce an inexpensive radio, the Volksempfänger, and that radio ownership in Germany increased rapidly during the first few years of their rule, especially in small towns and more rural areas.[20] Kracauer states, "German radio has indeed been systematically developed as a vehicle for producing and vastly expanding the mass."[21] Furthermore, Kracauer stresses the significance of two long familiar but nevertheless still highly effective rhetorical devices: *repetition* and *rhythm*. Key to the success of totalitarian propaganda is the old adage that a lie repeated often enough eventually comes to be taken for the truth. This is how the *Scheinwelt* is produced and reproduced. And repetition also plays a role in the creation of a compelling rhythm: words insistently intoned and incessantly repeated become incantations. The leader is adept in such techniques of speech-making: sentences build slowly but surely one upon the other, the voice rising to a crescendo and then a momentary silence—that fleeting but decisive holding back for a few precious seconds of what is to come, to create tension and suspense, to ensure that what follows will not just be appreciated but ecstatically embraced—before at last the answer, the solution, the resolution, the appeal, the promise, the vision. The listener is drawn in, the breath is drawn in, and then held, and then released in a surge of euphoria.[22] Rhythm, too, Kracauer astutely notes, has its disciplinary aspect: hands clap in unison, voices chant slogans, drums beat together, martial bodies march and drill in time. The masses participate in, fall in line and in time to, the almost irresistible rhythm of the Ratio. As with the Tiller Girls, there are no soloists here. The mass is everything: moving together, working together, acting together, empowered together. All bar one. Of course, there is one and only one exception who stands alone, above and beyond.

Finally, this brings bring us to the notion of spectacle and ornament. Here, Kracauer not surprisingly refers to his own essay from 1927. The choreographed routines of the Tiller Girls anticipate the key principles of the mass rally: deindividualization, fragmentation, and homogenization; geometrical formations, abstraction, and machine-like function; synchronization and rhythmic repetition. Feathers were to be replaced by flags, costumes by uniforms, sequins by swastikas. Machine rhythms become martial ones. This is the very *orchestration of power* (via Latin from the Greek, *orkhēstra*, from *orkheisthai* "to dance"). The mass admires not only the parade passing before its eyes like a film strip, but also itself, its own image, its own sense of itself as mass, as the physical embodied expression of the "we." The mass becomes its own spectacle and all under the benign gaze of the choreographer in chief, the leader. The mass is the subject-object of ornamentation. Its decoration of power as "art of mass images" (*Massenbildkunst*) is not trivial or secondary; rather, like the propaganda of which it is an element, it is as necessary to the winning of power and the maintenance of hegemony as violence and terror.[23] Tellingly, at this point Kracauer refers to a study that had only recently been published in the *Zeitschrift*: Walter Benjamin's 1936 "The Work of Art in the Age of Its Technological Reproducibility." At the end of Benjamin's now-famous essay ones reads that Fascism involves the "aestheticization of politics" to which Communism responds with the "politicization of the aesthetic." The mass ornament *is* or *is at least fundamental* to this aestheticization of politics.[24] Indeed, totalitarian propaganda and aestheticized politics may be, in the final analysis, if not one and the same thing, then certainly two sides of the same coin.

NOTES

As editors of this current volume we were, ironically, faced by not the same but certainly a similar dilemma to that which confronted the editors of the *Zeitschrift* more than eighty years ago: What is one to do with Kracauer's text? It is far too long to include in its entirety here, and yet to leave it out completely would be wholly inappropriate and run counter to Kracauer's own express wishes. The full 150 pages plus of the "Totalitarian Propaganda" text can be neither fully included nor excluded. And so today, we, *unlike* Horkheimer et al., have taken up Kracauer's own suggestion. We present here translations of the two sections he himself saw as most important and proposed for publication back in 1938: chapter E, which foregrounds the concept of the masses, and the final chapter, G. We also include, as an appendix, John Abromeit's essay "Siegfried Kracauer and the Early Frankfurt School's Analysis of Fascism as Right-Wing Populism," which provides an overview and analysis of Kracauer's entire text. In his essay, Abromeit places Kracauer's study within the context of the Institute's writings on fascism during the 1930s and 1940s, and he also highlights the ongoing relevance of Kracauer's (and the early Frankfurt School's) analysis of fascism as a form of right-wing, authoritarian populism. We hope that this is an acceptable compromise and look forward to the future publication of an English translation of the full text of Kracauer's "Totalitarian Propaganda."

In the translations of the various "Totalitarian Propaganda" texts presented here we have, as far as possible, and despite inconsistencies in both the originals and in the published Suhrkamp editions, sought to use brackets in the following manner throughout:

(...) Kracauer's own brackets;
[...] brackets used by the Suhrkamp editors to indicate their own additions;
{...} brackets we use to indicate our additions.

We have tried to use {*sic*} as little as possible and have either corrected or noted certain errors (e.g., Kracauer's misuse of dates; the Suhrkamp editors' occasional lapses in page references). For ease of comparison, we have retained the footnote numbering as given in the 2013 Suhrkamp taschenbuch edition. We have only added endnotes where necessary and, in particular, for the presentation of abbreviated versions of the Suhrkamp editors' extensive and detailed comments and explanations (*Anmerkungen*) clarifying historical figures, events, and organizations.

1. In his letter to Gertrud and Richard Krautheimer of May 16, 1936, Kracauer states unequivocally: "The Institute is the only place in the world which we can have and want nothing to do with." *Totalitäre Propaganda* (TP), ed. Bernd Stiegler (Berlin: Suhrkamp Verlag, 2013), 313. Hereafter cited parenthetically.
2. Horkheimer writes: "Should it turn out at the end of the four months that the article, which will definitely be valuable to us, is not suitable for the purposes of the journal, we will then add it our archive, like some other important work. We hope to occasionally publish some of the pieces from this archive in an anthology" (TP, 320).
3. T. W. Adorno, "Report on the Work 'Totalitarian Propaganda in Germany and Italy' by Siegfried Kracauer, 1–106" (see appendix 1).
4. Adorno made this remark in a letter to Walter Benjamin on May 4, 1937. In his response to Adorno on May 9, Benjamin wrote, "I cannot believe our judgments about the book diverge in any way." See Theodor W. Adorno and Walter Benjamin, *The Complete Correspondence, 1928–1940*, ed. Henri Lonitz, trans. Nicholas Walker (Cambridge: Polity, 1999), 183, 186.
5. Writing to Adorno on September 21, 1937, Löwenthal observes that "the review does the book much credit simply by virtue of its being reviewed by us at all." Mappe A7: 205, Leo Löwenthal Archive, Frankfurt, Germany.
6. Siegfried Kracauer, *Jacques Offenbach and the Paris of His Time*, trans. G. David and E. Mosbacher (New York: Zone, [1937] 2002), 25. See also *Theodor W. Adorno and Siegfried Kracauer: Correspondence, 1923–1966*, ed. Wolfgang Schopf, trans. Susan Reynolds and Michael Winkler (Cambridge: Polity, 2020), 240–50; and Adorno's review of Kracauer's book on Offenbach in *Zeitschrift für Sozialforschung* 6, no. 3 (1936): 697–98.

7. Adorno, by contrast, was keen to emphasize the *discontinuity* between the Offenbach book and the "Totalitarian Propaganda" study, noting in his report the "huge effort" Kracauer had made to "work his way out of the sphere of commercial writing [*Warenschriftstellerei*]" (see appendix 1).
8. See Kracauer's essays "On Friendship" [*Über die Freundschaft*] (1917–1918) and "Thoughts on Friendship" [*Gedanken über Freundschaft*] (1921) in *Gedanken über die Freundschaft* (Frankfurt: Suhrkamp Verlag, 1971).
9. For one influential study of this camaraderie and its subsequent influence on the development of National Socialism in Germany, see Klaus Theweleit, *Male Fantasies*, vol. 1, *Women, Floods, Bodies, History*, and vol. 2, *Male Bodies: Psychoanalyzing the White Terror*, trans. Stephen Conway (Minneapolis: University of Minnesota Press, 1987).
10. In the "Disposition" from July 1937 (under section A.II), Kracauer terms these groupings "the excrescences of war" and notes the overall "sympathy of the army for the Fascist type."
11. Despite Kracauer and Horkheimer's chilly personal relations, one can see here an interesting theoretical affinity in their mutual interest in exploring the ways in which shared life experiences among specific social groups create psychological predispositions that can be mobilized by the leaders of both progressive and reactionary social movements. Horkheimer outlines such a project of "differentiated group psychology" in his 1932 essay "History and Psychology." He developed this project historically in his 1936 essay "Egoism and Freedom Movements: On the Anthropology of the Bourgeois Epoch." Through an analysis of the progressive and reactionary elements of early modern European social movements, Horkheimer sought to gain insight into the triumph of fascism in his own time. Thus, despite Horkheimer's refusal to publish Kracauer's essay—influenced no doubt by Adorno's negative assessment—in retrospect one can read it as complementing and supplementing Horkheimer's own theoretical project in the 1930s. In his study of fascist propaganda, Kracauer also approvingly cites Erich Fromm's introductory essay to the Institute's large-scale empirical project on authority and family, *Studien über Autorität und Familie* (Paris: Félix Alcan, 1936), which was also designed to apply and test Horkheimer's theory of differentiated group psychology. Fromm had already directed an earlier empirical study of the social psychology of blue- and white-collar workers in the Weimar Republic, *The Working Class in Weimar Germany: A Psychological and Sociological Study*, trans. Barbara Weininger (Cambridge, MA: Harvard University Press, 1984). Whereas Horkheimer had focused more on the sociohistorical roots of authoritarianism, in his substantial theoretical introduction to the *Studies on Authority and Family*, which has only recently been published in English translation, Fromm analyzes the social-psychological mechanisms in such movements. : Erich Fromm, "Studies on Authority and Family: Sociopsychological Dimensions," trans. Susan Kassouf, in *Fromm Forum: Journal of the International Erich Fromm Society* 24 (2020): 8–58. Kracauer draws on Fromm's essay to explain the ideological function of sadism in fascist propaganda. In short, despite the acrimonious personal relations between Kracauer and the Institute at this time, Kracauer's essay on fascist propaganda demonstrates important affinities with the early Critical

12. In his initial "Exposé. Mass and Propaganda," dated December 1936, Kracauer notes, "The concepts of the 'nation,' the 'people,' the 'honour' are placed in the centre and their function are magnified in propagandistic manner in order to paralyze the class struggle" (V.3c).
13. See, for example, the 1936 exposé, which foregrounds "the spiritual homelessness of the masses" as part of his wider discussion of "The Crisis After the War and Its Consequences" (II.2).
14. Kracauer draws most heavily on *The Salaried Masses* in section F of his essay "Totalitarian Propaganda," which we have not translated for this volume. But anyone capable of reading the original German, who is interested in seeing how Kracauer develops and fleshes out his analysis of the sociology and social psychology of the salaried masses in light of subsequent terrifying historical developments in Germany, should consult section F. See also the discussion of section F in John Abromeit's essay in appendix 2.
15. Here one sees clearly Kracauer engaging with arguments Horkheimer put forth in "Egoism and Freedom Movements" about how the function of the mass and the role of the leader is different in emancipatory movements than in reactionary social movements. Whereas Kracauer agrees with Horkheimer that that aim of emancipatory movements is to abolish the existence of the mass as such, Kracauer is more willing to accept the formation of the mass as a strategic means to accomplish the desired end of abolishing capitalism. For his part, Horkheimer writes, "The mass meeting is suitable for the purpose of exerting irrational influence; small groups of individuals with common interests are appropriate for discussions of theory, the analysis of a given historical situation, and the resulting considerations on the policy that should be followed. Movements striving to transcend the bourgeois order can therefore not use the mass meeting with the same exclusiveness and the same success." Max Horkheimer, *Between Philosophy and Social Science: Selected Early Writings* (Cambridge, MA: MIT Press, 1993), 78.
16. See, for example, "Disposition," C.II, in our volume, where a note in the left-hand margin reads "mass as homeland [*Heimat*]."
17. In contrast to antidemocratic traditional European conservatives, who rejected popular sovereignty, and protofascist theorists like Carl Schmitt, who purposefully conflate the concepts of "the mass" and "the people," in order to defend an authoritarian "concept of the political," Kracauer carefully distinguishes the concept of "the people" from the concept of "the masses" throughout his essay. In so doing Kracauer holds out the hope for a true democracy, in which the people are no longer a homogenous mass manipulated from above, but are instead concrete individuals able to articulate, pursue and satisfy their diverse needs. In other words, rather than rejecting the very notion of "the people," Kracauer argues that its emancipation can come only through the abolition of "the mass." Despite his sharp criticisms of Kracauer at this time, Adorno seems to have agreed with most of his arguments in regard to this concept. See Adorno's discussion of the concept of "the mass" in Institute für Sozialforschung, *Soziologische Exkurse: Nach Vorträgen und*

Diskussionen (Frankfurt: Europäische Verlagsanstalt, 1956), 70–82. In the "Totalitarian Propaganda" essay, Kracauer also argues that fascist propaganda relies heavily on the "principle of the personality [*Persönlichkeitsprinzip*]" and "never misses an opportunity to celebrate the "personality" at the expense of the mass." See beginning of section III in section E in our volume. This critique of the concept of personality represented a break with Kracauer's work from the 1920s, but one with which Adorno fully agreed, and which he often reiterated in his postwar writings. On these points, see Detlev Claussen, *One Last Genius*, trans. Rodney Livingstone (Cambridge, MA: Harvard University Press, 2008), 60–61; and Theodor Adorno, "Gloss on Personality," in *Critical Models: Interventions and Catchwords*, trans. Henry Pickford (New York: Columbia University Press, 1998), 161–66. As we saw in the case of Horkheimer, here again we can see with the case of Adorno that, despite the personal and theoretical differences that certainly existed between him and Kracauer, many important and perhaps unconscious affinities also existed, which make it possible and profitable to reread Kracauer's "Totalitarian Propaganda" essay as part of a larger project carried out by the Institute and thinkers with whom they were in dialogue, to understand the success, staying power and—in the postwar period—ongoing threat of fascism. On this history of Adorno and Kracauer's relationship, see Martin Jay, "Adorno and Kracauer: Notes on a Troubled Friendship," in *Permanent Exiles: Essays on the Intellectual Migration from Germany to America* (New York: Columbia University Press, 1986), 217–36.

18. Kracauer notes, "Postulating the ideal of the personality in no way refutes mass as ideal" ("Disposition," C.II.4).
19. Kracauer anticipates here Adorno's verdict on the radio as the "mouthpiece of the Führer" and sets up part of the rationale and agenda for the Institute's radio research on Fascist agitators undertaken by Adorno and Lazarsfeld and other "prophets of deceit" explored by Löwenthal and Norbert Gutermann in the 1940s. Theodor Adorno, *The Psychological Technique of Martin Luther Thomas' Radio Addresses* (Stanford, CA: Stanford University Press, 2000); Leo Löwenthal and Norbert Gutermann, *Prophets of Deceit: A Study of the Techniques of the American Agitator* (New York: Harper & Brothers, 1949).
20. Radio ownership in large German cities, such as Berlin, was already widespread before the Nazis came to power. On the role of the Nazis' attempts to expand radio ownership as part of their larger propaganda program, see *Zuhören und Gehörtwerden I. Radio im Nationalsozialismus: Zwischen Lenkung und Ablenkung*, ed. Inge Marßolek and Adelheid von Saldern (Tübingen: Editions Diskord, 1998).
21. See section III of section E.
22. Kracauer also notes "the long wait (to see Hitler)" ("Disposition," C.II.3a) of the masses at rallies for the arrival of the Führer and hence the creation of tension and sense of expectation.
23. See "Disposition" (C.II.4).
24. In his summary of Kracauer's essay, and in line with Kracauer's comments on the hypnotic powers of the Führer, Adorno paraphrases the following formulation by Kracauer: "The aestheticization of propaganda aims at the anaestheticization of the masses." Kracauer's formulation and Adorno's paraphrase can be found in TP, 64, 275.

I
Exposé. Mass and Propaganda. An Inquiry Into Fascist Propaganda

Dr. S. Kracauer
Paris (17ᵉ)
3, Avenue Mac-Mahon

PROBLEM

The methods of political propaganda developed in fascist countries represent an innovation. Never before has there been this connection between terror and mental manipulation—at least in the modern age—nor, until now, has propaganda been not only a means of realizing whatever political goals, but also politics itself to such an extent. To compare: the propaganda practiced in earlier dictatorships with that of today. An excursus on the role of propaganda in democratic countries would show that it is structurally different from fascist propaganda. Reference to advertising.

How did this propaganda emerge? What reality underlies it? What function is it given?

To simplify matters, I will extrapolate here primarily with reference to Germany, where fascist propaganda has been ingrained in a particularly systematic manner; I would like to note immediately, however, that in the planned project the most varied countries shall be considered. The continuous juxtaposition of the European dictatorships with the Soviet Union, on the one hand, and with the great democracies, on the other, appears essential to me. Crucially important above all is the inclusion of American efforts in the realm of advertising and propaganda.[1]

THE POSTWAR CRISIS AND ITS CONSEQUENCES

The economic crisis in the postwar period. In the countries susceptible to fascism, the economic crisis combines with the political one and assumes a total character.

The social consequences of the crisis: In Germany the crisis leads to the impoverishment of broad strata and to the emergence of new masses around the proletariat.

1. On the situation of the proletariat itself.
2. The proletarianized middle class. Drawing from the findings of my book on salaried employees, I demonstrate here how the German middle classes were partly dispossessed and partly proletarianized after the war.[2] The living conditions of salaried employees in the postwar economy come closer and closer to those of workers.
3. The unemployed.

The Ideological consequences of the crisis

1. Dissolution of the bourgeois value-hierarchy. Among other things, this means that the bourgeoisie loses its self-assurance, and that its lifestyle becomes problematic. The capitalist interests become nakedly apparent.
2. The spiritual homelessness of the masses. By and large, it can be said that, apart from those gripped by socialism, the masses that emerged on account of the crisis live in an ideological vacuum.

   a) The middle class: The precarious position of the middle class results from the fact that its members are proletarianized, on the one hand, and are completely entrenched in bourgeois traditions, on the other. Precisely because of these traditions, they virulently resist communism, but at the same time have to negate their place in the capitalist production process. They are no longer readily situated in the prevailing system. They therefore seek a change of this system, but are unable to support a dictatorship of the proletariat.

   b) The unemployed: They too are no longer able to be integrated as a result of the crisis and technological developments. Because of the length of the crisis, the army of millions of the unemployed is placed in a state of belief in miracles {*Wundergläubigkeit*}, which makes it susceptible to all extreme influences and promises. Typical for the mass of unemployed people: their constant wavering between National Socialism and communism.

Summary: Like the masses of workers, the newly emerging masses around them also reject the capitalist economy in its existing form. They view themselves as left to ruin economically and socially, and they feel even more lost on an ideological front when the bourgeoisie is hit with powerlessness and bears little appeal anymore.

THE DECISIVE STAGE OF THE CRISIS

Through the weight of the masses and the inability of the classes representing capitalism to win back the masses, the antagonism between the left-wing and right-wing parties, between communism and capitalism, intensifies in such a way that it is no longer bridgeable through democratic means.

Since one cannot count on a return of economic prosperity through which large parts of the masses could be absorbed after all, the situation is ripe for revolution. The task posed by this situation can also be formulated as follows:

How is it possible to reabsorb the masses?

The following is certain from the outset: the masses are no longer capable of ready reintegration into the existing economic system under the prevailing circumstances.

Communism offers itself as the only radical solution that would eliminate, with the capitalist economic system, the causes that led to the emergence of the masses characterized here. In a communist society, according to the theory, unemployment would be definitively abolished and the mass as mass would disappear.

The situation in Germany, however, is conditioned such that the communist solution comes up against incredibly strong resistance—even and especially among some of those who belong to the expatriated mass. The dispossessed middle class is a crucial supporter of the resistance.

The dilemma thus emerges: the masses should be reintegrated while maintaining the capitalist system, but are unable to be reintegrated. Only a pseudo-solution {*Scheinlösung*} is possible. Fascism is a pseudo-solution.

ADVENT OF THE FASCIST PSEUDOSOLUTION

Thesis: With the pseudo-solution, fascism not only fails to eliminate the mass (which would be impossible), but rather underlines its character as a mass all the more and furthermore tries, through appropriate measures, to create the impression that the mass is in fact reintegrated. To produce this pseudo-solution, fascism uses two interlocking methods:

    1. Terror, the necessity of which is explained by the facts

        a) that within the prevailing system class antagonisms exist that can only be violently stifled, and

b) that the acceptance of a pseudo-solution like the fascist one has to be continually forced;

2. Propaganda. Two general statements about fascist propaganda should be made straightaway:

a) Fascist propaganda is necessary if only because communist propaganda has to be counteracted. It develops in constant friction with the latter; in other words, it is fixated on communist propaganda.

b) Unlike its communist counterpart, fascist propaganda does not have the disappearance of the mass and therewith its own disappearance as its goal. It has—and this is its peculiar feature—no goal whatsoever after the realisation of which it can resign, but rather resists its objective in every such instance, since it would have to be guided to it ad absurdum. Its objective: *producing the illusion of the reintegration of the masses.* This illusion would dissipate immediately, however, if it were not maintained through constant propaganda. Fascist propaganda thus does not lead to its own demise like every other form of propaganda, but rather breeds itself anew time and again. Fascism can just as little do without propaganda as it can without terror. It subsists through propaganda.

V. THE ROLE OF PROPAGANDA IN FASCISM

1. To begin with, in order to avoid the dilemma identified above, fascist propaganda is forced to let the non-reintegratable mass persist as a mass, and indeed to exaggerate its mass character even more. Here would be the place for a critical excursus on the various theories of the masses.

How is the hypostatization of the mass achieved through propaganda?

a) One forces the mass to see itself everywhere (mass gatherings, mass marches, etc.). The mass is thus always present to itself, often in the aesthetically seductive form of an ornament or striking image.

b) With the aid of radio, the sitting room is transformed into a public space. (To the extent that men may still exist as individuals at all, their emotions are totally diverted from politics. Fascist propaganda confers to individuals only the sphere of "interiority" and otherwise seeks to transform them into a part of the mass.)

c) All mythical powers that the mass is capable of developing are exploited for the sake of underscoring the significance of the mass as a mass. To many it can thus seem that they are elevated above themselves in the mass.

The cult of the mass produces two desired side effects:

a) It enables a cult of personality, which is useful because it weakens the sense of reality.

b) It seems to legitimate terror.

2. By unleashing the cult of the mass, fascist propaganda succeeds in creating the necessary preconditions for its agenda. The mass as mass meets charlatanry halfway. Historical excursus on the charlatan. The relations between fascist propaganda and charlatanry are to be demonstrated here. (For example, the perpetual arousal of fantastic hopes, etc.)

3. The actual aim of fascist propaganda is the pseudo-reintegration of masses that it has primed in a workmanlike manner. It already achieves this aim by letting the masses march and generally occupying them nonstop, such that the masses gain the conviction that they already serve whatever functions as masses. More crucial, however, is the attempt of propaganda aimed at reintegration to disavow communist doctrine, which is considered to be the greatest danger. This attempt, which is undertaken with the help of middle-class ideologies—it is characteristic of the middle class that it lives on the periphery of the production process and can therefore preserve bourgeois traditions in the most uncontested manner—this attempt, I argue, culminates in the demonstrative refutation of the class struggle.

a) The masses are assembled such that they seem to belie the assumption of class struggle.

b) One appeals primarily to youth, who are still least subjected to the force of economic and social relations and are therefore seemingly classless.

c) One places the terms "nation," "Volk," and "honor" center stage and exaggerates their reality and function in a propagandistic manner in order to paralyze the class struggle. Excursus on the sociological function of the term "race" and of anti-Semitic propaganda. Further excursus on the propagandistic significance of fascist foreign policy.

d) Social laws are enacted that do not in fact change the relation of employer and employee—legal fronts {*Fassadengesetze*} that amount to the preservation of the capitalist economy, just like the establishment of the *Dopolavoro*.[3]

4. Since fascist propaganda represents a fictitious solution to the social problem that it faces, it quickly closes itself off. It displays its greatest strength *in statu nascendi*, during the conquest of power. After the seizure of power, it loses much of its original force. The actual relations shine through; the illusion emerges as illusion. Ideologues serve themselves in the realm of propaganda by aggressively working towards the realization of

propagandistic effects, in order to produce intense shocks. Otherwise, where fascism has prevailed, leadership maintains itself by withdrawing from sheer power—that is, from the army and authorities of terror—and by placing the palpable hunger for power and the military-political aspirations in place of the social ones, whereby the due solution of the social problem is deferred once again. Propaganda adapts itself to this.

The end of this main section would be followed by an analysis of communist propaganda, showing that hidden behind the formal similarity between communist and fascist propaganda, there are, nonetheless, differences in principle.

Postscript: This main section of the work is conceived as an inquiry that would work through copious material in a constructive manner. For this reason all the more, I had to restrict myself here to the briefest remarks.

SOME CONCLUSIONS

In this last section, I intend among other things to examine the extent to which social reality is affected by the fascist pseudo-solution; whereby I proceed from the assumption that the fascist pseudo-solution is a means of preserving the imperiled capitalist economy. Furthermore, I will consider here what importance is due to the traditions conserved by the middle class—traditions that render the fascist pseudo-solution preferable to a socialist solution.

Postscript: Let me emphasise once more that the project can only obtain its full worth when it is carried out on an *international* scale and also when it analyses the corresponding relations in the great democracies (above all in America).

S. Kracauer, December 1936.

NOTES

The preceding translation is by Nicholas Baer and originally appeared in *Film Studies* 16 (Spring 2017): 6–15. We are grateful for permission to republish the translation in this anthology.

1. Various letters were exchanged in November 1936 about whether Kracauer's study would focus on propaganda and/or advertising, with Adorno advancing the view that the distinction between the two terms was itself a product of the capitalist system and should be dissolved; see Christian Fleck and Bernd Stiegler, "Nachbemerkung und editorische Notiz," in Siegfried Kracauer, *Werke*, vol. 2.2 (Frankfurt: Suhrkamp Verlag, 2012), 838. Kracauer would also compose an unpublished

essay, "Popular Advertisement," in the late 1940s, which is included in this anthology.—Trans.
2. See Kracauer, *Salaried Masses: Duty and Distraction in Weimar Germany*, trans. Q. Hoare (New York: Verso, [1930] 1998).—Trans.
3. Founded in 1925, the Opera Nazionale Dopolavoro (OND) was an organization for leisure and recreational activity in fascist Italy. The OND attracted a large percentage of the nation's salaried workers.—Trans.

2

Totalitarian Propaganda

Section E. Propaganda as Instrument of Power

I.

If totalitarian propaganda must change the psycho-physical structure of people in order to lend some appeal to the facades it glorifies, in so doing it need not rely exclusively on terror. The psycho-physical structure can already be found in a changed form, which is suited to the needs of propaganda, wherever Germans appear not as individuals but as a mass. Thus, the second means that totalitarian propaganda uses to pursue its aims is the exploitation of the particular constitution of Germans who form a mass, and the ongoing production of masses for this aim.

As sure as it is that all masses demonstrate certain common characteristics—the concept of masses is used here to designate large gatherings of people—not all masses are constituted in the same way. In addition to masses of sundry persons fortuitously thrown together, there exist others that consist of individuals from one and the same population stratum. Speaking generally, the most politically important homogenous mass is the proletariat, which has recently been joined by the masses of salaried employees {*Angestellten*} and the proletarianized middle classes more broadly. The proletariat should also be called a mass even if its members do not form a mass. In conjunction with the industrial development of the previous century, and emerging as one of its consequences, the proletariat represents an enormous mass already in purely quantitative terms. Furthermore, workers are in fact employed en masse in the production process and, from the standpoint of those with more advanced training, are interchangeable like mass particles. In terms of his social function the individual worker is an element of the mass and he sees himself as such. It would not be a mistake to equate the revolutionary interest of the working class in a socialist transformation of existing relations with their interest in the elimination of conditions that reduced it to a mass. The emancipation of the proletariat is the negation {*Aufhebung*} of its existence in the form of a mass. Here it is once again confirmed that in principle communism originally had as its aim the consummation of democracy. It does not want to eternalize the mass, but instead to create a social order in which everyone—thus also and precisely the proletariat, which has been restrained at the level of the mass—attain the possibility to develop according to the measure of their individual abilities. But how can a proletariat that has become conscious realize its demands? Only by attempting to amass itself and to utilize its heft as a mass to exact recognition. The nature of the revolutionary interest conditions the specific character of the revolutionary mass, which is the means, not the end. The mass is not a goal, but instead a strategic necessity, of which the proletariat makes use on the basis of tactical reflections that emerge from a theoretical assessment of the current situation. One can see in the proletariat's relationship to theory that the goal is not their massification, but their liberation from the condition of mass particles. In revolutionary activity emphasis is placed not so much on the organization of mass meetings, as on uniting individuals in small groups and steeping them in theory. But this also means that the revolutionary mass escapes to a certain degree the psychic constitution that characterizes the masses in general. For one thing it contains, at least according to its guiding principles, an avant-garde of thematically schooled individuals. For another, it also lies in the revolutionary interest to activate the consciousness of this mass in such a way that they are able successfully to fight against massification. In an unpublished section of his essay, "The Work of Art in the Age of Mechanical Reproduction," Walter Benjamin makes a remark on the constitution of the proletarian mass that has far-reaching implications.[1] Horkheimer, as well, carefully distinguishes the revolutionary mass from other masses: "The speaker's goal then is for the masses to grasp the situation with their own consciousness; the action to be taken then follows from this as a logical consequence. What matters is that things are made clear [. . .] and the leader's personality can recede, since it is not itself supposed to act as an influencing factor."[2] He also underscores the circumstance that work in groups, in the service of expanding individual consciousness, is no less important for a flourishing revolutionary movement than mass gatherings. An episode related by Goebbels illustrates that he was striving exclusively for an expansion of the masses and that the group—if it could not be avoided altogether—was only valued as an opportunity to eliminate individual independence: "We could not yet put together any large militant rallies," he reports on the beginnings of the Berlin

movement (1926), "because the organization did not possess the inner strength for it. We had to limit ourselves to bringing together party members with supporters and fellow-travelers week after week in smaller rooms. In our speeches we focused less on discussing current issues, and much more on explaining the programmatic foundations of our worldview and hammering it into the heads of our party comrades so that they could recite it in their dreams, so to speak."[3]
(...)

Mussolini proclaims in the beginning of his ascent, "A period of history is now beginning that could be defined as a period of the politics of the masses."[4] And Goebbels regrets that "we are now living in an epoch, in which politics must win the support of the masses."[5] Both of these nearly identical explanations—as is clear from the very beginning—do not refer to the politically constituted revolutionary mass of the proletariat, upon which totalitarian propaganda has had relatively little effect. Hitler repeatedly gives vent to his disappointment about this: "The great mass of workers," he says to Otto Strasser, "do not want anything except for bread and circuses; they have no understanding for any ideals."[6] Another time—in the early days of the movement—he assures Oberst Hierl,* the first point is "to win the masses, even if only the petty bourgeois masses, then the workers will follow."[7] This second statement already demonstrates that his desire is less for homogenous masses than for masses as such. On the way to power he must undoubtedly strive to come into contact with masses—at the same time or one after another—which have originated on the basis of common afflictions and common interests; but the ideal is a mass whose composition is not uniform, one whose elements come from different social strata. "The street [...] is [...] the characteristic feature of modern politics," says Goebbels. "Whoever can conquer the street, can also conquer the masses."[8] One cannot express more clearly that the ideal mass is understood here as the one that has been taken from the street. Hitler's aforementioned claim, that the great mass of workers has no understanding for any ideals, goes a good way to explain totalitarian propaganda's pronounced inclination towards this type of street mass—which also and not coincidentally differs from the revolutionary mass in that one of its components is the mob. In reality, Hitler's criticism is directed against the strong attachment between the ideals and the

---

* {Konstantin Hierl (1875–1955) was a senior military figure who established one of the Freikorps units after the Great War and was involved in the suppression of the Spartacist uprising in 1919. He joined the National Socialists in 1927 and took a leading role from 1929. He was elected to the Reichstag in 1930 and from 1932 was involved in the organization and administration of the workforce and labor. He was convicted and imprisoned in 1948 for his participation in the Nazi regime and was released in 1953.}

interests of the revolutionary mass. Hitler can take power only when the evolving ideas have been established to the point where they can be manipulated independently of interests. So of course he must accuse the workers of a lack of understanding when they are unreceptive to his idea-montages {*Ideen-Montagen*}, because they do not see their own interests in them. In so doing he understandably confuses their indifference to such montages with a lack of appreciation for anything higher. Totalitarian propaganda targets a mass that is precisely not governed and guided by one interest. "Take away from the masses their leaders or seducers," as Goebbels says again, "then they are masterless and can easily be overcome."[9] But leaders and seducers of masses are not only persons but also interests. That is precisely the reason why National Socialism and Fascism prefer masses that can be called 'broad' conglomerates, in which many divergent interests clash and weaken one another. The other advantage of "masterless" masses is that they alone satisfy the will to power of the cliques; for as a mish-mash of population groups they seem to represent the people.

If a mass is a mass as such, then it is a "masterless" one; it must therefore embody in particular purity the character that more or less all masses possess. It represents a regression of character traits developed through civilization. As soon as people become an element of the mass, their consciousness deteriorates; the individual in the mass is no longer an individual. Hitler's detailed comments on this topic demonstrate remarkable insight and shed some light on the—to him—welcome fact that the 'broad masses' react primarily with their feelings. "The meager [abstract] knowledge they possess directs their sensibilities more towards the world of feelings."[10] Accordingly, propaganda claims that it must direct its efforts "at the emotions and only to a very limited degree at the so-called intellect."[11] Evidence of the destruction of consciousness, which is suffered by the individual reduced to a mass particle, is also found in the observations that the mass does not desire objectivity and that it feels more attracted to a doctrine "that tolerates no other besides itself than to one that grants liberal freedoms."[12] Hitler dwells particularly frequently upon the inchoate nature of their sentiments, which is so important for propaganda. "And this sentiment [...] is not complicated, but very simple and all of a piece. It does not have multiple shadings; it has a positive and a negative; love or hate, right or wrong, truth or lie, never half this way and half that way, never partially, etc."[13] And, "the psyche of the broad masses is not receptive to anything that is half-hearted or weak."[14] Through its submersion in the mass the individual is thus automatically forced into the same regression that totalitarian propaganda carries out consciously, a transformation that in one stroke transports the individual back to developmental stages that were overcome long ago. Ortega y Gasset says of the "mass-man" {German: *Massenmensch*; Spanish: *el hombre-masa*}, not only that he has the psyche of a "spoilt child,"[15] but also refers to him as a primitive. "The actual mass-man is, in fact, a primitive, who has slipped through the wings on to the age-old stage of civilization."[16] If archaic humanity arises in the mass, then it, the mass, must love its "great festive joy," cruelty. "When the mass acts independently," as the Spanish philosopher then also claims in a logically consistent and one-sided way, "it does so only in one way, for it knows no other: it lynches."[17] From this he (explains)* effortlessly that today since "the masses triumph, {...} violence should triumph and be made the one *Ratio*, the one doctrine."[18] Hitler's clarifications extend deeper than those just mentioned: "the broad masses are only a piece [of] nature."[19] As a piece of nature it is passive and active, wax and raging torrent. Hitler grasps its hermaphroditic composition; he knows about the "overwhelming power of the mass" that springs from its share in the masculine principle, but he focuses primarily on its feminine receptivity, in which he has a stronger interest.[20] "The people in their overwhelming majority are [...] feminine by nature and attitude."[21] Further, "Like the woman, whose psychic state is determined less by grounds of abstract reason than by an indefinable emotional longing for a force which will complement her nature, [...] likewise the masses love a commander more than a petitioner."[22]

II.

Hitler woos the mass like a woman. "Anyone who wants to win the broad masses must know the key that opens the door to their heart. Its name is [...] will and power."[23] Actually, it is called suggestion, and is not any regular key, but rather a skeleton key that can open or shut many different doors according to need.

An attenuation of consciousness certainly also occurs in the revolutionary mass. But this loss has a positive function insofar as it supports to a certain degree the revolutionary interest against the excesses of individualism, and the theoretical education of individuals is also an attempt to counteract this tendency. In any case the revolutionary side does not in principle profit from the psycho-physical structure of the mass particle, whereas the propaganda of the totalitarian movements ruthlessly exploits the willingness of the broad mass to be influenced. As a consequence of the attenuation of consciousness, the

---

* {"Explains" is in parentheses in the original text.}

"mass-man" finds himself in a condition that borders on hypnosis or at least greatly facilitates hypnosis. Totalitarian propaganda not only does not wake him, but lulls him into an even deeper sleep to impart suggestions to him. Totalitarian propaganda is exceptionally able in this task because its power-obsessed directors claim a right to unconditional authority. Erich Fromm writes, "Among relations between men that resemble hypnosis, the most socially significant is the relationship to authority. Like a hypnotist, it impresses those under its sway."[24] Those who hold power make no effort to conceal the methods they use to profit from the psychic {seelischen} disposition of the mass. Hitler banks on the assumption that everyone who participates in a mass rally feels the "overwhelming power of suggestive intoxication."[25] Goebbels emphasizes the "suggestion of an effective speech" and praises with the justified pride of an artist the day of the awakening nation—which he organized on March 4, 1933—as a perfect example of mass hypnosis.[26] "No one can doubt that this day was the greatest propagandistic achievement accomplished in Germany in human memory. But this achievement was only possible because we refrained from all other work for an entire week and kept the eyes of the people focused in a hypnotic trance solely on this one event. Then, of course, we were also able to record a major success."[27] For a skillful hypnotist it is in fact not impossible to distract good subjects from their interests and to excite their passions in regard to some goal or another. Hitler states, "the impetus to the mightiest upheavals on this earth has at all times consisted less in a scientific knowledge dominating the masses than in a fanaticism which inspired them and sometimes in a hysteria which drove them forward."[28] Does not a hysterical person behave capriciously? The mood of the inconstant mass can easily be changed by a Mark Antony.* Accordingly, Hitler pays most attention to their endurance. "Their emotional attitude at the same time conditions their extraordinary stability. Faith is harder to shake than knowledge, love succumbs less to change than respect, hate is more enduring than aversion."[29] This observation is meant formally; it refers to the unwavering obedience of the masses to the directives given to them. In fact, the hypnotists do everything possible and use their power both to fanaticize the masses and to extirpate their memory.

The entire style of the National Socialist and Fascist mass rally can be explained in terms of their aim to place the mass, which is already predisposed to it, completely into a hypnotic sleep. For this reason their rallies unfold—differently than

---

* {The German original has "Antonius." The editors of the Suhrkamp edition presume that the reference here is to Mark Antony (ca. 82–30 BCE) and his famous oratory in Shakespeare's *Tragedy of Julius Caesar* (1599).}

revolutionary mass gatherings, which are unmasking, not mystification, and whose basic features demonstrate a sober, unceremonial character—in a magical atmosphere, whose function is the further attenuation of consciousness. With the conscientiousness of a magician, who makes all the preparations necessary to increase the credulity of the audience, Hitler attempts to create such an atmosphere. As indicated by the previously cited statement,[30] he chooses the evening hours for his gatherings, because people put up less resistance to being violated by the will of another in the evening. He pays attention to space just as carefully as he does to time. "There are spaces that leave one cold for reasons that are difficult to discern."[31] And when he compels the mass gathering to wait for him for hours, his aim here as well is to tire them and thus put them in a condition that will permit him "to uproot emotional prejudices, attitudes, sensibilities, etc. and to replace them with others."[32] To support this undertaking the hypnotic powers of authority are brought to bear. "Any meeting that is protected exclusively by the police," says Hitler in a passage dedicated to the SA, "discredits its organizers in the eyes of the broad masses."[33] That means that the organizers do not appear in possession of the authority necessary to direct the mass. Hitler himself alludes to why he desires the display of power. "From the very beginning it was important to introduce blind discipline in our meetings and absolutely to guarantee the authority of the committee in charge. For what we said [...] in content and form was always suited to provoke a reply from our opponents. And opponents there were in our meetings!"[34] Put differently, the assertion of authority should stifle any independent impulses in the consciousness of the mass, so that the latter becomes even more lacking in will and alertness. It has the desired effect: "soon no more hecklers, no more dissenters dared to come forward," reports Heiden from the early days of National Socialism in Munich. "With what seemed like the wave of a magic wand, the mood in Hitler's gatherings became simpler, more unified and more faithful."[35] On a daily basis this wave of the wand helps those who are the Führer's fist to create miracles of belief that get people to entertain even the most absurd propositions. Hypnotists normally proceed by letting their patient stare at a shiny object. The shiny object used by totalitarian propaganda is the symbol that plays a decisive role in all the mass rallies it organizes. It is not as if the revolutionary mass does without, or even could do without symbols, but since the function of symbols always depends on the intention behind their use, in the case of the revolutionary mass they contribute principally to keeping progressive consciousness alert and protecting it from the integrating power of the status quo. The symbols enthroned by totalitarian propaganda, in contrast, refer to nothing at all that exists outside of the propaganda itself; instead, their meaning is exhausted in the role they play as an instrument of propaganda. "In *red*," so interprets Hitler the National Socialist flag, "we see the social idea of the movement, in *white* the nationalistic idea, in the swastika the mission of the struggle for the victory of the Aryan man, and, by the same token, the victory of the idea of creative work, which as such always has been and always will be anti-Semitic."³⁶ Graphic signs of inflammatory recruitment ideas, these symbols are intended to facilitate the manipulation of the mass, and to reinforce the docility with which the mass obeys the suggestions of the will to power. Horkheimer remarks aptly, "the great importance placed on symbols, ceremonies, uniforms, and phrases, which attain the same sanctity as flags and coats-of-arms, follows from the necessity of an irrational bond tying the masses to a policy which is not their own."³⁷ And, on a similar note, a sentence of {Ernst} Krieck's reveals just how much National Socialist symbols are intended to agitate people's drives and emotions {*Triebleben*}. Krieck praises the National Socialists' masterful practice of the "art of domination, of the excitement and manipulation of mass gatherings." He continues, "Based on the same instinct, National Socialism prefers to work with symbols, with their captivating visibility, rather than with rational concepts. The swastika, greeting rituals, and the Third Reich have the direct mobilizing power—akin to the subterranean—of all that is symbolic."* Totalitarian propaganda knows very well the reason why it amasses so many symbols. The denser the primeval forest of flags into which it lures the mass, the more submissively it follows the voice that rings out in the dark.

"The power which has always started the greatest religious and political avalanches in history rolling," says Hitler, "has from time immemorial been the magic power of the spoken word."³⁸ An insight followed directly by another: "particularly the broad masses of the people can be moved only by the power of speech."³⁹ But there is more. In order to underscore the defining political significance of mass speeches, Hitler and company usually play them off against political literature, which is denigrated as much as possible. In a passage that has already been cited, Hitler speaks—misrecognizing the connection between theory and praxis—with disdain of the "mode of writing of Marxist church fathers," who have allegedly contributed far less to conquering the working masses than the tens of thousands of propagandists and agitators.⁴⁰ And if Goebbels wants to express how much National Socialism owes to its public speakers,

---

* {No reference is given by Kracauer here. Ernst Krieck (1882–1947) was a leading and influential figure in the development and implementation of a National Socialist (NS) pedagogy. Trained as a teacher, he first agitated for an NS mode of education during the 1920s. He joined the Nazi Party (NSDAP) and published his *Nationalpolitische Erziehung* in 1932. He subsequently held various prominent positions in academia, including professor of philosophy and pedagogy and rector in Frankfurt-am-Main, professor in Heidelberg, and rector in Baden. He was, at the same time, a leading figure within the Nazi movement itself and the Sicherheitsdienst (SD). He was the editor of numerous pedagogic journals. Arrested after the war, he died in custody.}

he clothes this conclusion in the following form: "the National Socialist movement has grown through its speakers, not its journalists."[41] In short, totalitarian propaganda dedicates itself with conspicuous zeal to subordinating the written word to the spoken word. Undoubtedly this zeal comes from the fact that they view the former as an instrument of Enlightenment—the correct use of which could alienate them from the masses—and the latter as the principal means of influencing the masses. Goebbels weighs one against the other: "Even when a speaker can usually [...] reach only a few thousand people with his words—in contrast to a writer, who sometimes finds tens or hundreds of thousands of readers—the spoken word, in fact, influences not only those listening directly; they pass it along and carry it forward in hundreds and thousands of ways."[42] So, would the resonance of these two forms of communication be approximately the same from a quantitative point of view? But since the aim is, after all, not to awaken individual consciousness, but rather to direct an unconscious mass, Goebbels must of course opt for speech and come to the conclusion that "the suggestive power of an effective speech [...] still towers above the bookish suggestion of a leading article."[43] Indeed, based on this desire to use the power of suggestion, he demands of writers that they utilize the illusion of speech: "For us the leading political article (for example, in *Der Angriff*) was a written poster or, even more accurately, a speech in the street put onto paper. [...]* It intentionally presupposed as common knowledge that of which the reader should actually be convinced, and drew from this the inexorable consequences. The reader should get the impression that the author of the leading article is actually a speaker who is standing next to him and who wants to convert him to his opinion with simple and compelling thought processes."[44]

"Magical power of the spoken word."[45] The mass speech developed by totalitarian propaganda proves its magical power in that it escalates hypnotic sleep into deep sleep and then seizes control of the unconscious. Hitler describes (graphically) the rapport that the speaker should maintain with those souls who are manipulated in both senses of the term. "He will always let himself be borne by the great masses in such a way that instinctively the very words come to his lips that he needs to speak to the hearts of his audience. And if he errs, even in the slightest, he has the living correction before him."[46] In conjunction with

---

* Goebbels founded the weekly newspaper *Der Angriff* (The attack) in 1927. By 1932, there were two daily editions. Although Goebbels himself lost interest in the paper, its readership grew to over three hundred thousand copies by 1944. Its main contents were Nazi ideology, anti-Semitic and racist propaganda, and various attacks on the Weimar Republic in general and particular individual figures. It was temporarily prohibited in 1931.}

this, Hitler does not neglect to highlight and explain the function of the mass speech. "Here again it is not seldom a question of overcoming prejudices which are not based on reason, but, for the most part unconsciously, are supported only by sentiment. [...] False concepts and poor knowledge can be eliminated by instruction, the resistance of the emotions never. Here only an appeal to these mysterious powers themselves can be effective; and the writer can hardly ever accomplish this, but almost exclusively the orator."[47]

How is the speaker successful with such an appeal? In regard to the formal structure of the speech, he relies on two rhetorical devices: repetition and apodictic claims. "The mass," explains Hitler, "will commit to memory only a thousandfold repetition of the simplest concepts."[48] He incessantly repeats this conviction, which he once formulated succinctly as follows: "But the most brilliant propagandist technique will yield no success unless one fundamental principle is borne in mind constantly and with unflagging attention. It must confine itself to a few points and repeat them over and over. Here, as so often in this world, persistence is the first and most important requirement for success."[49] Reinforcing Hitler's experience, Goebbels concludes a speech in the Berlin Sports Palace with the dithyrambic quatrain:

Whoever wants the same and always only the same
He unlocks the vault of heaven
Before him even the Gods must bow
And say: come and take. You seize what is yours.[50]

When a mother reads fairy tales to children, they long for repetition, and not only of the meaning of the story; they always wish to hear the same exact words repeated. The child, lying gently within the wooden bars of the crib, is lulled to sleep by these familiar sounds, which in sleep become the building materials of dreams. By using the principle of repetition, the speaker pushes the mass down to the level of children and into a condition in which they no longer take in anything except what he constantly repeats. Stereotypical formulas attain enchanting power; passing through them, the mass identifies with them. The mass is what the words say that monotonously trickle down, presupposing of course that the material, out of which it should be composed—according to the will of totalitarian propaganda—is conveyed to them in a tone of absolute certainty. Since every doubt stirs slumbering consciousness, even the possibility of a doubt threatens to destroy the magic. "The level of speeches at National Socialist rallies," as Wilhelm Stapel spells out in his study, *Christianity and National Socialism*, "is characterized by very skillful methods of operating with the idea of mass individuals and avoiding factual arguments whenever possible."[51] Similarly, Krieck: "Based on a revolutionary instinct, National Socialist agitation works primarily not with intellectual proofs and arguments, but instead with the primordial power of rhythm."[52] Refraining from arguments is thus also motivated by the interest in deepening the hypnotic effects.

For totalitarian propaganda everything depends on whether or not the concrete suggestions of mass speeches—inflammatory arrangements of ideas, directions for behavior, posthypnotic tasks, etc.—can truly capture the "mysterious powers" that hold sway in the unconscious. This requires two things. First, the speaker must "speak the language that the mass understands," as explained by Goebbels, who provides additional, more detailed information about the foundations of this language.[53] According to him, the art consists in "the elimination of all arabesques and anything superfluous, in order to make these primitive thoughts clear to the people, but also to carry them into the public sphere with momentum and force."[54] This recipe demonstrates the intention of the mass speech to strengthen the tendency of the "broad" mass to regress to a primitive stage and cynically to take full advantage of it. Second, the speaker must set in motion the primitive instincts and feelings, to which he appeals, in such a way that his audience abandons all previous engagements and yields unconditionally to his suggestions. According to a statement taken by Münzenberg from Goebbels's book *Moderne Politische Propaganda*,[55] the "Reich propaganda division of the NSDAP"* set forth in its guidelines for rally themes that "sensational current events, scandals involving Jews or Marxists"[56] should be chosen in order to stimulate "curiosity, rage, or the hope of experiencing a sensation."[57] The totalitarian mass speech is indeed similar to sensational literature in that it produces images of horror and happiness. One minute the speaker invokes in the darkest of tones the diabolical machinations of real or imagined enemies, the next minute he indulges in messianic prophecies, in the vision of the "ultimate goal" {*Endziel*} that Hitler promises the mass again and again. He preaches the inevitable cataclysm and promises in the same breath the certainty of salvation—just like the medieval charlatans who appear at the annual fair in luxurious costumes and accompanied by music in order to peddle their elixirs. "Come and see! This

---

* {As of 1923, the NSDAP engaged a head of propaganda. Once reestablished in 1926 after the party's temporary prohibition, the propaganda division was led by Gregor Strasser, by Hitler himself and then, as of 1930, by Goebbels. It was responsible for the control and coordination of NSDAP propaganda, and, though there was much interconnection and sharing of personnel, it remained formally independent of the Ministry for Popular Enlightenment and Propaganda itself. In its early years, its focus was on the use of radio as a mass medium.}

cures all pains, bruises, tooth aches, rabies and scabies."[58] To be sure, the apotheosis forms the conclusion, but the dark chasm is exposed not only to make it appear more fascinating; rather the opposite is truer, namely, that enthusiasm also serves to intensify horror. Enthusiasm dissipates and the mass speech would soon cease to resonate if it appealed solely to easily generated hopes. Its intention is precisely to mobilize not only hope, but also curiosity or rage and, like other totalitarian propaganda events, to cause an oscillation of the elementary movements of the psyche {Seelenbewegungen}. For only if it produces such movement in the depths, is it able to take hold of the entire system of "mysterious powers" and put it in the service of their suggestions. But the mass soul will submit itself to these different suggestions even more blindly, if the speech also has the effect of replacing the repressed individual consciousness of the mass particles with a pseudo-consciousness that is in its control. "The Jew," declares Goebbels, "is the same thing for the people as a tuberculosis bacillus is for a lung. The tuberculosis bacillus is not dangerous until it comes into contact with a weak lung. The Jew becomes dangerous when he comes into contact with a weak people."[59] In National Socialist speeches one finds thousands of formulations like this, whose razor-sharp and primitive logic is reminiscent of children's drawings. They behave precisely as if they had the intellect of the mass in mind. In truth, however, the intellect to which they lay claim has its foundations in a psyche that has already been manipulated. This intellect is imposed through suggestion upon the mass in order to make them forget that their own intellect has been forfeited. Power prevents individual consciousness from sinking deeper roots in this psychic foundation, because it too has been artificially grafted onto mass-man.

With the aid of other hypnotic techniques, which are usually supplemented with the elementary rhythms of military marches, the mass speech successfully carries out a totalitarian manipulation of opinion. The mechanism of totalitarian propaganda functions so wonderfully that, once it has been set in motion, it hardly needs to function any longer. Neither is it necessary to implement all the propaganda devices, nor is it important that speeches are understood. A fleeting hint from the stage-production is all it takes, and the mass is already hypnotizing itself.

III

Although totalitarian propaganda does in fact attempt to win over the broad masses, it still cannot proclaim often enough—as has been demonstrated—that it holds them in contempt. As if it wanted to emphasize this contempt even more, it never misses an opportunity to celebrate the "personality" {*Persönlichkeit*} at the expense of the mass. Hitler commands the party to "promote respect for personality by all means,"[60] and comments upon this wish with the following words: "the organization must not only not prevent the emergence of thinking individuals from the mass; on the contrary, it must in the highest degree make this possible and easy by the nature of its own being. In this it must proceed from the principle that the salvation of mankind has never lain in the masses, but in its creative minds."[61] All efforts seem directed toward putting the person, instead of the mass, on center stage. "The greatest revolutionary changes and achievements of this earth, [...] the immortal deeds in the field of statesmanship, etc., are forever inseparably bound up with a name and are represented by it."[62] It is self-evident that these efforts to inflate the prestige of the person must culminate in the cultic idolization of Hitler and Mussolini. Their lives become myths and their names are spun into legends.

Thus, on the one hand, totalitarian propaganda imposes itself violently upon the mass; on the other hand, it strives to dismiss and devalue this same mass. Is this a contradiction? One should first recall the aforementioned observation that the concept of personality targeted at the masses by the National Socialists receives its particular stamp from the will to power that drives the movement forward. The Führer, as the embodiment of this will to power, commands the apparatus he founded through a hierarchy of demagogues {*Verführer*}, whose authority flows from his own absolute authority and also represents it within a more or less limited region of power. So when Hitler insists that "the state must have the personality principle anchored in its organization from the smallest community to the highest leadership of the entire Reich," he makes evident that for him personality means the representative of power.[63] The personality that he means can have no other character than the nihilistic one of National Socialism itself. Consequently, it manifests itself in the pursuit of power as such and rises above the mass through its ability to perform ruling functions. One sees once again, and more clearly than before, that for propaganda personality means that species of superior human {*Herrenmensch*} that is indispensable for the totalitarian regime in its pursuit of power. But one also sees that the National Socialist and the historically inherited concepts of personality cannot be reduced to a common denominator. Horkheimer returns repeatedly to the fact that the leaders of bourgeois revolutions in the past were not apotheosized any less than the modern dictators—which for him can be explained by the necessity of captivating the masses to distract them from certain social demands that the revolution, as precisely a bourgeois revolution, was not able to fulfill.* Deification of the irrational personality in the past as today. The image that one has of the person has changed fundamentally, and this transformation reveals changes in economic and social relations. As a fruit of the bourgeois revolutions, nineteenth-century democracy—with its parliamentarism and liberal capitalism—constructed itself on the belief in reason, which of course was limited to the extent that it did not come into conflict with the concerns of the bourgeoisie. Since individual consciousness is the point where reason enters into the world, that era celebrates the conviction that politics and the economy are regulated by the free competition of enlightened individuals. Democracy is put to use by the individual; so it must see in personality the perfected individual. It is not for nothing that personality in Goethe's sense is the individual who has developed his capacities in a harmonious and multifaceted way.† This ideal of personality associated with democracy is distinguished by the fact that it is directed against the formation of masses. In the context of a bourgeois-democratic regime, the leader is not celebrated as a ruler of the masses, but instead as a role model whom everyone should emulate. And, from this democratic perspective, the more that the masses dissolve into individuals, and the individuals mature into personalities, the more successful are economy, progress and civilization {Gesittung}. Whereas socialism affirms this valuation of the individual so unreservedly that it wants to achieve its universal recognition, the National Socialist movement uses the concept of personality in order to liquidate the individual. But they use it in such a way that differs from its original use just as monopoly capitalism differs from liberal capitalism, which illustrates once again their alliance with the capitalist powers. The interest of big capital, which has been pushed into a defensive position and become increasingly dependent on violence, is not the struggle of opinion—that it would lose—but instead the death of opinion; not the disappearance of the mass, but its domination; not the development of the individual into a personality, but the "personality" that knows how to subdue a mass. Whether the totalitarian dictatorships have been summoned to rescue capitalism in danger, or they are simply using it to enhance their own power—they are, in any case, breeding a type, without which capitalism would have to surrender: the type of the man of power, the mass hypnotist. Instead of working against the development of

---

* {The reference here is once again to Horkheimer's essay "Egoism and Freedom Movements: On the Anthropology of the Bourgeois Epoch."}
† {This theme is most evident in Goethe's second novel, *Wilhelm Meister's Apprenticeship* (1795–1796), a work that became the model of the bildungsroman.}

masses, this kind of personality compels their rise. It is one pole of the totalitarian regime; the mass is the other. They mutually condition each other. The personality demanded by National Socialist propaganda posits the mass and is posited by the mass. "A leader," says Goebbels, "does not emerge randomly [...]. He grows with the mass and the larger it gets, the more the genuine leader grows beyond the mass."[64]

And nonetheless totalitarian propaganda holds the masses in contempt? Without doubt, contempt is really the feeling that grips a ruler in relation to one who is dependent upon him. But whether this contempt is genuine or feigned, in all cases it is conspicuously displayed for propagandistic reasons. One time, this display—sublimely pursued—is likely the product of the cynicism mentioned earlier. It is intended to test the depth of the hypnotic sleep of the mass and also to inject them with the belief that they are insignificant in comparison to the personality {of the leader}. The next time, the mass is condemned in order to carry out an effective polemic against the workers' parties which, like the totalitarian movements, have to win with mass rallies. National Socialist propaganda tries again and again to protect itself from this troublesome competition by claiming that the revolutionary left is engaging in shameful idolatry with the mass, and the National Socialists are the first to treat them in the way they deserve. "The National Socialist movement," assures Goebbels, "does not blindly worship the mass and sheer numbers, as do the democratic-Marxist parties."[65] At the congress of the labor front, which met in Berlin on May 10, 1933, Hitler justifies the liquidation of Marxism and the union organizations with the following words: "For we know very well the final aim of this entire development, no, this struggle between fist and forehead {*Faust und Stirn*}, between mass, i.e. number, and quality: annihilation of the quality of the forehead.* But this means not only a blessing for the number, or simply the elevation of the worker; on the contrary, it means poverty, misery and privation."[66] Such typical mirror reflections demonstrate that the totalitarian, not the proletarian, movement targets the mass. Needlessly, Hitler even goes so far as to invoke the archetype {*Urbild*} of the truth, instead of its reflection {*Spiegelbild*}: "The mass rally is also necessary," according to *Mein Kampf*, "for the reason that in it the individual, who at first, while becoming a supporter of a young movement, feels lonely and easily succumbs to the fear of being alone, for the first time gets the picture of a larger community, which in most people has a

---

* {"Workers of the fist and the forehead" (Arbeiter der Faust und Stirn) was an expression used by the Nazis to refer to blue- and white-collar workers. Hitler used it—for example—on campaign posters during his run for president in 1932.}

strengthening, encouraging effect. [. . .] In the crowd he always feels somewhat sheltered [. . .], when the visible success and agreement of thousands confirm to him the rightness of the new doctrine and for the first time arouse doubt in the truth of his previous conviction—then he himself has succumbed to the magic influence of what we designate as 'mass suggestion.' "⁶⁷ According to this, the mass which is "massified" {*massierte*}* in both senses of the term by totalitarian propaganda, is supposed to function as a form of *Heimat*.† The revolutionary mass, in contrast, is always just a passageway to *Heimat*.‡ It turns out that contempt for the mass is not at all opposed to the need for it. By openly spurning the mass in the name of personality, National Socialism is merely expressing its own proclivity for the mass. For the personality, with which it is concerned, comes into its own only in the presence of large masses.

When totalitarian propaganda appropriates aspects of the revolutionary mass demonstration, such as parades, speaking in unison, etc., it does so not only to make its own mass event appear revolutionary, but also above all because the methods developed to activate the revolutionary mass can be utilized to consolidate masses in general. Such a consolidation is no doubt a side effect of the various actions of the revolutionary mass, but its decisive task remains to manifest the will that animates the homogenous proletarian mass before it has formed itself into a mass. As soon as totalitarian propaganda exploits the procedures used in the revolutionary camp, their function changes and the side effect becomes the main effect. The same actions and long-term developments, which the one side directs toward revolutionary goals, lose on the other side any purpose of transcending the mass, and now serve only to transform the mass into a tough, rigidly structured formation. These actions are limited to provisions to lend structure to the mass. Because the mass constantly appears here, there and everywhere {*an-, auf- und oben erscheint*} at the command of Fascist and

---

* {In German, *massieren* means to bring people together in one place, usually for military purposes. But Kracauer is also using the term here in the sense of transforming people into a mass in social-psychological terms.}

† {In German, *Heimat* means literally "homeland," but it also implies a tight-knit, organic community, often inextricable from a particular locale with long-standing traditions. The term usually has conservative implications and was popular among both the traditional and fascist right in the 1920s and 1930s.}

‡ {Here, Kracauer seems to be appropriating the conservative concept of "Heimat" (see footnote 11) and attempting to give it a revolutionary reinterpretation. Kracauer's appropriation here reminds one of similar moves by other Weimar leftist thinkers—such as Walter Benjamin and Ernst Bloch—who attempted to uncover the utopian and potentially emancipatory content of certain key conservative ideas. Bloch ends his three-volume magnum opus, *The Principle of Hope*, with a discussion of *Heimat*. Ernst Bloch, *The Principle of Hope*, vol. 3, trans. N. Plaice, S. Plaice, and P. Knight (Cambridge, MA: MIT Press, 1995), 1370.}

National Socialist propaganda, it gets caught up in a steady movement that takes hold of all its elements and the movement becomes an end in itself.* The mass as such {*das Massenhafte*} consolidates itself through the uninterrupted activity of the mass particles. The type of this activity makes it clear that it truly aims for nothing other than the thoroughgoing formation of the mass. In the actions of the revolutionary mass spontaneity appears, which demonstrates that these actions do not so much rigidify the mass, as instead express a common interest. The actions of the National Socialist and Fascist masses, in contrast, are directed from above and arranged as rituals. But they assume the character of ritual in order to create the illusion that the masses are performing cultic practices that increase their invincibility. As with symbols, totalitarian propaganda also accumulates many rites, because the more the masses must perform, the more firmly they are yoked, and the better (consequently) their cohesion is secured. Furthermore, the ceremonial duties with which the mass is burdened are so created that its usefulness increases along with its stability. This observation proves once again that the meaning of these duties does not extend beyond the mass. What is essential is not the content of the mass actions, but instead the rhythm of their execution. Krieck remarks in conjunction with a passage already cited,[68] National Socialist agitation works "with everything that is related to rhythm and that emanates its stimulating power, such as speaking in unison."[69] In other words, speaking in unison and other activities demanded of the masses aim to facilitate the handicraft of the propagandist. Some of these activities—as the description of Silone mentioned earlier illustrates—unfailingly induce self-hypnosis.

Being dependent upon the broad mass, totalitarian propaganda incessantly strives to artificially produce the broad mass. The prophecy of Mussolini, that a new period of history is dawning, which one could define as a period of the politics of the masses, was less a prophecy than a program: in fact, Fascists and National Socialists produce the masses for the sake of their own power politics.[70] One year after the seizure of power, Hitler assures the "Old Guard" in Munich: "Just as we used to address the people in ten thousand, in one hundred thousand single rallies, so in the future we must also continue this struggle with ten thousand and one hundred thousand rallies and mass meetings, in order at least once a year to make an appeal to the entire nation. If the appeal is not well received, no-one should say that the people are to blame; instead he should say that the movement has become lazy. The movement is no longer fighting properly, the movement has lost touch with the people. And from this

---

* {The editors of the German edition remark that "an-, auf- und oben erscheint" is conjectural, since the original text is unclear here. TP, 200.}

one will be able to learn once again how to immerse oneself in the people. This is where our strength lies."[71] The ideological vocabulary of these sentences hardly conceals Hitler's actual opinion, according to which the National Socialist movement fails at its task when it does not succeed in conveying the suggestion appropriate at any given time so effectively—through the constantly renewed formation of the mass—that one can rely upon such appeals to the nation being carried out. For this reason, mass gatherings have become the rule; so far, attendance at mass rallies has been obligatory. The totalitarian dictatorships do not assemble the masses when there is genuine reason to do so; instead, they create artificial reasons, which serve as a pretext to organize mass gatherings. Only the outsider will misunderstand these innumerable rallies, which interrupt the labor process again and again, and damage the entire land, as a superfluous and unproductive affair. In truth, they are, like terror, a prerequisite of the system. So much so, that even when the formation of the mass takes places on the occasion of a politically important event, the question remains open whether or not this event, notwithstanding its significance, has been conjured up in order to further the formation of the mass. Within the sphere of power of the totalitarian regime, propaganda is not merely an instrument of politics; politics is also an instrument of propaganda. The aforementioned explanation from Goebbels, who requires the radio to broadcast all possible events of national relevance, demonstrates not least that the imaginative powers of National Socialist and Fascist propaganda know no limits when it comes to conjuring up the mass out of nothing. German radio has indeed been systematically developed as a medium for producing and vastly expanding the mass.* Fritz Morstein Marx† emphasizes in his superb study "State Propaganda in Germany," the propagandistic value of the *Volksempfänger*, whose production was a National Socialist initiative.[72] This particular use of radio demonstrates that National Socialist propaganda is not actually trying to realize its

---

* {The National Socialists were quick to see and exploit the potential of the new radio medium for propaganda purposes. Goebbels himself recognized the need to leaven political news, speeches, and other propaganda broadcasts with popular entertainment to maximize the appeal and reach of the medium. The production of inexpensive radio sets (the Volksempfänger, or "People's Receiver," was introduced in 1933; the Deutscher Kleinempfänger, or "German Small Receiver," followed in 1938) resulted in a massive increase in radio ownership and audiences such that, by 1941, more than 60 percent of German households had a radio set. Public broadcasts were also used to reach those for whom the radio nevertheless remained unaffordable.}

† {Friedrich Wilhelm Julius Morstein Marx (1900–1969) was a German legal scholar who "emigrated" to the United States in 1933. He held various academic positions at U.S. institutions before returning to Germany after World War II. He was chair of comparative administration and public law at the Hochschule in Speyer where he became an emeritus professor in 1968.}

frequently proclaimed intention of transforming the mass into a people {*Volk*}; on the contrary, in the interest of the total manipulation of opinion it seeks to transform the entire people into a single mass susceptible to suggestion. The ideal is attained when the entire people permanently constitute themselves as a mass rally, or at least when all individuals find themselves constantly in the state of mass particles. This aim no doubt runs contrary to the tendency of the regime to celebrate the family, but one will yet see how their propaganda—precisely because of its totalizing ambitions—becomes caught up in antimonies over time and as a result is increasingly forced to shed all content and to reveal ever more nakedly the will to power that is its source. With its largely successful reduction of individuals to mass particles, it additionally bound together members of the people {*Volksangehörige*}, also in a progressive sense. It creates the illusion {*Schein*} of a unity of the different social groups or classes which, regardless of their divergent interests, belong together under the rule of monopoly capitalism, and not only in a spurious way.* For, in so far as monopoly capitalism also places previously privileged population groups into a state of dependency, it does reduce the violence of existing differences. The artificial production of the mass, which is supposed to make it possible for totalitarian propaganda to influence people against their own interests, reflects at the same time—of course, in a distorted way—a common interest, which may reveal itself sooner or later. Undertaken in order to maintain appearances {*Schein*}, it indirectly undermines social reality.

IV

Like terror, the mass addressed by the totalitarian movements is not only a means of propaganda, but is itself propaganda. It seduces in the first place because—in this regard also like terror—it represents power." [In his book] *Propaganda and National Power*, Hadamovsky recognizes that, "The most effective power of the mass rally is every palpable form of the expression of power, that is, in the first place the number of participants, the size of the rally, and beyond that, everything that appears as power, people with arms and in uniforms, weapons of all kinds."[73] The inherently appealing character of the mass already insures that it has an effect; add to this, that the power speculating on this type

---

* {In the text, Kracauer uses the abbreviation "MK" for "Monopolkapitalismus."}

of mass is not satisfied with its inherent power of attraction. Incapable of rational justification due to its nihilistic character, it tries twice as hard to dazzle. The totalitarian dictatorships know exactly why they constantly engage in grandiose actions and why they infuse the concepts of the imperium and the Reich—these projects and projectiles of their will to power—with such beguiling brilliance. The brilliance embellishes the tatters of those who bask in it, so that they become convinced they are wearing elegant apparel, not tatters. But the mass itself provides an excellent opportunity to dazzle, provided one makes use of the match-making services of an art that can be best designated as the art of mass images {*Massenbildkunst*}. This art, which has been systematically introduced by Fascist and National Socialist propaganda, consists in orchestrating the ensemble of the mass in such a way that it exerts an aesthetic attraction. By transferring the mass demonstration from the political or social realm into the aesthetic sphere of the monumental spectacle, which captivates the senses like the nihilistic parade, totalitarian propaganda not only increases the cohesion of the mass, it also nips in the bud—as has already been pointed out—any question of the purpose of forming masses.

A French observer describes how the works of the National Socialist art of mass images are produced and which sensations they evoke in the spectators: "And [...] in the same way that the leader has made himself into the organizer of the obedient masses," writes Erich Wernert in his study *L'art dans le Troisième Reich*, "he has also made himself the organizer of those mobilized masses, those human masses [...] or actually those masses that no longer have anything human about them and that form and reform themselves in an overwhelming rhythm."[74] The masses no longer have anything human about them; however, in their intention to annul the human as a standard, the totalitarian dictatorships realize the aesthetic grandiose in inhuman material. This is the overwhelming appearance of power; its function is to tear people out of the sphere of interests into a sphere in which they imagine they have been elevated above themselves and they are partaking in the magnificence that is presented to them, or that they themselves represent.

Totalitarian propaganda celebrates the people as the quintessence of power and its magnificence. Thus, in order to make the spell that emanates from the composition of the mass completely irresistible, National Socialism seeks by all means to create the illusion that it forms the mass into the people. It is not a coincidence that for the majority of its marches propaganda drums together only so-called deputations from the most diverse areas of the country; the more it churns up the population, the more it strengthens the impression of an identity of the people and the mass. It merely reflects this tendency when

Dressler-Andress,* the President of the Reich Chamber of Radio, goes so far as to claim that "the radio [...] is [...] the mouthpiece of the entire people," even though the National Socialist radio is in fact the mouthpiece that those in power use to belabor the broad masses.[75] To his previous assertion, Dressler-Andress adds another: "the radio has become the pioneer of a true culture and art of the people."[76] The claim of National Socialist propaganda, that demonstrations have conjured up the people, would be convincingly proven if the people's alleged resurrection manifested itself through cultural and artistic achievements. The National Socialist propagandists speak again and again about the necessity or even the existence of art that has its roots in the people, and in so doing take aim at contemporary art, which they view as degenerate and accuse of individualization, intellectualism and internationalism. "The deeper art springs from popular culture {dem Volkstum}, the higher will be its international standing," says Goebbels, although he simply conflates art that really does emerge from popular culture with the "people's art" that he propagates.[77] But what National Socialism considers art does not have the people as its origin, but instead as its target; more importantly, it is an art intended to cloud the impression that the broad mass is the people. However, by commanding art to march along this path, totalitarian propaganda stifles art. For art worthy of the name, it is precisely this criterion of judgment that cannot be used, namely, whether or not it—following Goebbels's formulation—springs from the depths of popular culture. Whether it presents itself as popular or esoteric, glorifies the people or not, has nothing to do with its origins. It depends much more on the respective artistic intentions and social relations. Without doubt, an artist like Picasso is more closely connected to the people than a random painter, who paints the people by order. And also art that takes the people as its subject is not by any means—as long as it is genuine—identical with National Socialist conceptions. Instead of enslaving itself to this or that doctrine, it shows the reality of the people that goes beyond such doctrines, particularly ones that are so unequivocally instrumental such as those of the totalitarian regime. In his wonderful book about Dickens, Chesterton† says the following about him: "in this matter

---

* {A veteran of World War I, Horst Dressler-Andress (1899–1979) became active in cabaret and theater in the 1920s and devised a political framework for radio and cultural organization within the NSDAP. He held various cultural positions within the party and the Ministry for Popular Enlightenment and Propaganda, including leadership of the KdF. He worked in various positions, including propaganda, in Poland during the war. After internment during 1945 and 1948, he became active again as a theater director and actor in the DDR.}

† {G. K. Chesterton (1874–1936) was an English journalist and writer. He is perhaps best known today for his creation of the Father Brown detective stories, several of which Kracauer himself reviewed at the time.}

he was the people. He alone in our literature is the voice not merely of the social substratum, but even of the subconsciousness of the substratum. He utters the secret anger of the humble."[78] Goebbels knows, of course, that art is not able to flourish under a diktat, and thus makes it seem as if the totalitarian regime granted complete artistic freedom, with the exception of absolutely necessary limitations. In his public remarks to filmmakers,* he emphasizes "that the national government does not intend to promote films with standardized clichés. This is not possible because art is free and should remain free. But certainly with one reservation. It must feel bound to certain political, moral and ideological {weltanschauliche} norms, that do indeed exist and without which a common national existence appears impossible."[79] But this argumentation is mere shadow-boxing, because the reservations in question are not simply an essential condition of common national existence; on the contrary, as a product of totalitarian propaganda, which eliminates the right to question and to individual freedom of opinion, they in fact rob art of the air it needs to breathe. "The aesthetic doctrine of the Third Reich," remarks Wernert, "insists on the existence of the constantly renewed cycle of the people, the artist, the people, etc. It views this cycle as the very essence of the artistic process. If the people is the purpose of all things, and also of art, then the artist bears a heavy responsibility [...]. This responsibility encompasses three domains of duty. Above all, the artist must give expression to the race, the nation and the ideal of Germanic beauty; furthermore, he must carefully ban from his art all elements that could corrupt the soul of the people {Volksseele}; finally, he must instruct the soul of the people and make it conscious of its unity and strength."[80] Wernert also sees that the inherent nature of these demands favors certain forms of art, which—like the art of mass images—are also well suited to influence masses of people in the desired way. "In order to glorify this totalitarian and unifying spirit, the regime has succeeded in strengthening and giving expression to certain forms of art that are better suited than any other to this collective action: for example, music, theater,

---

* {Goebbels recognized in film a key medium for mass propaganda. The Reichsfilmkammer (Chamber of Film) was a subcommittee of the Reichskulturkammer (Chamber of Culture), established in 1933, and was integrated into the Ministry for Popular Enlightenment and Propaganda. Since membership of the Reichsfilmkammer was a prerequisite for employment in the industry, some 1500 filmmakers, actors, technicians, and other workers, finding themselves either expelled or excluded because they were Jewish or on account of their political views, left Germany, some of them making their way to work in the expanding film studios in Hollywood. From 1934, the Lichtspielgesetz (Film Law) heightened the pre- and postcensorship regimes and intensified control of filmmaking and distribution. By 1941, the entire German film industry was under state control through the directorship of the Ufa-Film company.}

architecture, ceremony. Through the people's choir, the *Thingspiel** and the gigantic structures it erected, through the large national gatherings which were conducted masterfully, the regime has succeeded in drawing in the masses."[81] As a witness of artistic events, Wernert concludes that the arts favored by National Socialist doctrine have successfully fulfilled their duties. In a *Thingspiel* the choirs sang a march and all of Germany marched along: "One becomes aware of a tumultuous German mass, but one that is expanding everywhere: in the galleries, on the stage and also beyond the set. One is reassured, made happy, by the observation that all of Germany marches and that Germany is one's own self and all of the others. The old and romantic rumbling of the Germanic tribe runs through everyone present in the mass. The miracle occurs: for a few seconds the *Volksgemeinschaft* is a living reality."[82] Admittedly, National Socialist art aims for such psychological effects; so does this mean that it should be equated with the "genuine culture and art of the people" envisioned by Dressler-Andress?[83] If it were, the content of its creations would have to confirm the existence of the people: "In short, what can one say about contemporary German art? Only this: it is nothing more than a form of political propaganda, run like the economy, and mobilized like most other national activities."[84] Popular art? Utility art {*Volkskunst, Gebrauchskunst*}. First, National Socialists and Fascists deform the people into a manipulable mass, then they avail themselves of the arrangements, posters and decorations, in which utility art exhausts itself, in order to deceive the mass into thinking that they guarantee these values. Thus, the totalitarian regime commands the mass to remain in existence; but its domination is based on the reproduction of the mass.

V.

The analysis of the principles guiding totalitarian propaganda cannot be concluded any better than with the following words of Goebbels: "The National

---

* {As a particular form of open-air theater involving audiences in the dramatic action, the Thingspiel was developed primarily by Wilhelm Carl Gerst from 1929. Its usefulness was increasingly recognized by the Nazi authorities in the early 1930s, and it came under the auspices of the Ministry of Popular Enlightenment and Propaganda in 1933. By 1934, some sixty open-air theaters had been built, and, in the following years, between two hundred and four hundred more were planned or begun. A performance of a Thingspiel by Eberhardt Wolfgang Möller marked the Berlin Olympic Games in 1936. However, Gerst had by this time already lost his position and influence and the Thingspiel itself was renamed Freilichttheater (open-air theater). The cultic elements dramatized by the Thingspiel increasingly ceded importance to the new mass media of radio and film and their promulgation of the Führerkult.}

Socialist movement created its most active propaganda troops in the form of the SA. [...]* A modern political struggle is fought with modern political means, and the most modern of all political means is propaganda. Propaganda is basically the most dangerous weapon that a political movement can deploy. Against all other means there is a counter-measure; only propaganda is unstoppable in its effects. If, for example, a Marxist society is shaken in its belief [...] then it is already overcome because it immediately surrenders its power to resist."† Even if the last sentence turns out to be a propagandistic exaggeration—the nihilistic will to power that animates the Fascist and National Socialist cliques and leads them to monopoly capitalism, has created for itself in this propaganda—which functions with the combined methods of terror and the formation of masses—an instrument of incomparable force.

Translated by John Abromeit

NOTES

1. [Walter Benjamin, "The Work of Art in the Age of Mechanical Reproduction," trans. Harry Zohn, in *Illuminations: Essays and Reflections*, ed. Hannah Arendt (New York: Schocken, 1969), 217–52. See also "The Work of Art in the Age of Its Technological Reproducibility" (second version), trans. Edmund Jephcott and Harry Zohn, in *Walter Benjamin: Selected Writings, Vol. 3: 1935–1938*, ed. Howard Eiland and Michael Jennings (Cambridge, MA: Harvard University Press, 2002), 101–33. See also "The Work of Art in the Age of Its Technological Reproducibility" (third version), trans. Harry Zohn and Edmund Jephcott, in *Walter Benjamin: Selected Writings, Vol. 4: 1938–1940*, ed. Howard Eiland and Michael Jennings (Cambridge, MA: Harvard University Press, 2003), 251–83.]
2. [Max Horkheimer, "Egoism and Freedom Movements: On the Anthropology of the Bourgeois Epoch," in *Max Horkheimer: Between Philosophy and Social Science* (Cambridge, MA: MIT Press, 1995), 78.]

---

* {Founded in 1921 as the paramilitary wing of the Nazi movement, the SA (Sturmabteilung, or "Storm Detachment") were also known as the "Brownshirts" on account of their uniforms. They played a key role in the rise of the movement—intimidating opponents, carrying out acts of violence, providing "security" at rallies and speeches—and by 1933 numbered some three million men. Hitler, however, grew increasingly fearful of its power and influence under the leadership of Ernst Röhm. On June 30, 1934, the "Night of the Long Knives," up to two hundred leading figures of the SA were arrested and executed. Formerly just a subdivision of the SA, the SS (Schutzstaffel, or "Security Force") under Heinrich Himmler came to the fore as its replacement. Though overshadowed by the SS, the SA was not formally disbanded until 1945.}

† {Goebbels, *Kampf um Berlin*, 91. This quotation from Goebbels is actually missing in Kracauer's text. As the Suhrkamp editors point out, his reference system allows for the identification of the absent quote but not its precise extent.}

3. [Joseph Goebbels, *Kampf um Berlin Der Anfang*, vol. 1 (Munich: Franz Eher Nachfolger, 1934), 32.]
4. [Mussolini quoted in *Il Popolo d'Italia*, March 18, 1919; Kracauer citing Silone, *Der Fascismus, seine Entstehung und seine Entwicklung* (Zurich: Europa Verlag, 1934) 33.]
5. [Joseph Goebbels, speech given before the press on the construction of the Reich propaganda ministry on March 15, 1933, in Berlin, in Helmut Heiber, ed., *Goebbels-Reden, Vol. 1: 1932–1939* (Düsseldorf: Droste, 1971), 217–21, 220.]
6. [Adolf Hitler's conversation with Otto Strasser on May 21, 1930, is recounted in Otto Strasser, *Hitler und Ich* (Leipzig: Johannes Asmus Verlag, 1948), 137. Kracauer's citation is from Konrad Heiden, *Adolf Hitler: Eine Biographie*, vol. 1 (Zürich: Europa Verlag, 1936) 273.]
7. [This quotation preserved from Hitler can only be found in a relevant collection of National Socialist writings, which purports the existence of a correspondence between Hierl and Hitler: *Deutsche Sozialisten am Werk*, ed. Friedrich Christian zu Schaumburg-Lippe (Berlin: Deutsche Verlag für Politik und Wirtschaft, 1936), 17. Kracauer's citation is from Willi Münzenberg, *Propaganda als Waffe* (Paris: Editions du Carrefour, 1937), 146.]
8. [Goebbels, *Kampf um Berlin*, vol. 1, 86.]
9. [Goebbels, 68.]
10. [Adolf Hitler, *Mein Kampf*, vol. 1, *Eine Abrechnung* (Munich: F. Eher, 1934), 227.] {Our translation. Kracauer cites the wrong page here.}
11. [*Mein Kampf*, 197.] {English: Adolf Hitler, *Mein Kampf*, trans. Ralph Manheim (Boston: Houghton Mifflin: [1943] 1971), 180.}
12. [*Mein Kampf*, vol. 1, 44.] {42 (translation amended).}
13. [Hitler, vol. 1, 201.] {183 (translation amended).}
14. [Hitler, vol. 1, 44.] {42 (translation amended).}
15. [José Ortega y Gasset, *Der Aufstand der Massen* (1931), 41.] {English translation: *The Revolt of the Masses* (New York: W. W. Norton, [1932], 1957), 58.}
16. [Ortega y Gasset, *Der Aufstand*, 59.] {*Revolt of the Masses*, 82.}
17. [Ortega y Gasset, *Der Aufstand*, 86.] {*Revolt of the Masses*, 116.}
18. [Ortega y Gasset, *Der Aufstand*, 86.] {*Revolt of the Masses*, 116.}
19. [Hitler, *Mein Kampf*, vol. 1, 371.] {338. Brackets in Kracauer's original.}
20. [Hitler, vol. 1, 201.] {183.}
21. [Hitler, vol. 1, 201.] {183.}
22. [Hitler, vol. 1, 44.] {42.}
23. [Hitler, vol. 1, 371.] {338.}
24. [Erich Fromm, "Theoretische Entwürfe über Autorität und Familie: Sozialpsychologische Teil," in *Studien über Autorität und Familie: Forschungsberichte aus dem Institut für Sozialforschung* (Paris: Librairie F. Alcan, 1936), 107.]
25. [Hitler, *Mein Kampf*, vol. 1, 535.] {Our translation. The page Kracauer cites here is incorrect.}
26. [Goebbels, *Kampf um Berlin*, vol. 1, 19.]
27. [Joseph Goebbels, *Revolution der Deutschen* (Oldenburg: Stalling, 1933), 147f.]
28. [Hitler, *Mein Kampf*, vol. 1, 371.] {337–38.}
29. [Hitler, *Mein Kampf*, vol. 1, 371.] {337.}

30. [Kracauer, *Werke*, vol. 2.2 (Frankfurt: Suhrkamp Verlag, 2012), 73.] {*Totalitäre Propaganda* (hereafter TP), ed. Bernd Stiegler (Berlin: Suhrkamp Verlag, 2013), 62–63.}
31. [Hitler, *Mein Kampf*, vol. 2, 541.] {Our translation. Kracauer cites the wrong page here.}
32. [Hitler, vol. 2, 280.] {Our translation.}
33. [Hitler, vol. 2, 546.] {487.}
34. [Hitler, vol. 2, 541]. {483.}
35. [Konrad Heiden, *Adolf Hitler: das Zeitalter der Verantwortlosigkeit. Eine Biographie*, vol. 1 (Zurich: Europa Verlag, 1936), 113.]
36. [Hitler, *Mein Kampf*, vol. 2, 557.] {496–97. Kracauer incorrectly cites p. 554. He (or those who transcribed his manuscript) also writes "rationalistic" instead of "nationalistic."}
37. [Horkheimer, "Egoismus und Freiheitsbewegung," 177.] {English: "Egoism and Freedom Movements," 63.}
38. [Hitler, *Mein Kampf*, vol. 1, 116.] {106–7.}
39. [Hitler, vol. 1, 116]. {107.}
40. {Kracauer refers here to a passage in section B of this essay, which can be found in *Werke*, vol. 2.2, 73.}
41. [Goebbels, *Kampf um Berlin*, vol. 1, 19.]
42. [Goebbels, 19.]
43. [Goebbels, 19.]
44. [Goebbels, 200.]
45. [Kracauer, *Werke*, vol. 2.2, 100] {TP, 88.}
46. [Hitler, *Mein Kampf*, vol. 2, 527.] {470.}
47. [Hitler, vol. 2, 527–28]. {471.}
48. [Hitler, *Mein Kampf*, vol. 1, 203.] {Our translation.}
49. [Hitler, vol. 1, 202.] {184.}
50. [Joseph Goebbels, speech on February 10, 1933, at the Berlin Sports Palace, in Wilfried Bade, *Joseph Goebbels: Deutsches Volk und deutsche Männer*, vol. 5 (Lübeck: Charles Coleman, 1933), 70.]
51. [Wilhelm Reich, *Die Massenpsychologie des Faschismus* (Cologne: Kiepenhauer & Witsch, 1986), 54.] {Our translation.}
52. [Ernst Krieck, *Nationalpolitische Erziehung* (Leipzig: Armanen-Verlag, 1932), 38.]
53. [Goebbels, *Kampf um Berlin*, vol. 1, 46.]
54. [Goebbels, *Revolution der Deutschen*, 147.]
55. [Joseph Goebbels, ed., *Moderne Politische Propaganda* (Munich: F. Eher, 1930).]
56. [Also in: Reichspropaganda-Leitung der NSDAP, ed., *Kampfschrift*, vol. 1: *Arbeiterverrat* (Munich: F. Eher, 1932), 19.]
57. [*Kampfschrift*, 19.]
58. [According to the manuscript, Kracauer is quoting Roger Mauduit here. The quote could not be located.]
59. [Joseph Goebbels, "Um die deutsche Scholle," speech on May 11, 1930 in Munich, in *Revolution der Deutschen*, 27–34, 31.]
60. [Hitler, *Mein Kampf*, vol. 1, 387.] {352.}
61. [Hitler, *Mein Kampf*, vol. 2, 497]. {446.}

62. [Hitler, *Mein Kampf*, vol. 1, 387.] {352.}
63. [Hitler, *Mein Kampf*, vol. 2, 501.] {449.}
64. [Joseph Goebbels, "Hitler über Deutschland," radio program from the Siemens plants in Berlin during the celebration of the nation on October 11, 1933, in Goebbels, *Signale der neuen Zeit: 25 ausgewählte Reden* (Munich: F. Eher, 1934), 317–23, 318.]
65. [Goebbels, *Kampf um Berlin*, vol. 1, 40.]
66. [Adolf Hitler, *Die Reden Hitlers als Kanzler: das junge Deutschland will Arbeit und Frieden* (Munich, F. Eher, 1934), 46.]
67. [Hitler, *Mein Kampf*, vol. 2, 535–36.] {478–79. Translation amended.}
68. [Kracauer, *Werke*, 2.2, 103.] {TP, 91.}
69. [Krieck, *Nationalpolitische Erziehung*, 38.]
70. [Kracauer, *Werke*, 2.2, 93.] {TP, 81.}
71. [Adolf Hitler, speech to the "Old Guard" of the Party in Munich on March 19, 1934, in *Hitler: Reden und Proklamationen, 1932–1945*, vol. 1, ed. Max Domarus (Vienna: Löwit, 1973), 367.]
72. [Fritz Morstein Marx, "State Propaganda in Germany," in *Propaganda and Dictatorship: A Collection of Papers*, ed. Harwood Lawrence Childs (Princeton, NJ: Princeton University Press, 1936), 11–35.]
73. [Eugen Hadamovsky, *Propaganda und nationale Macht* (Oldenburg: Stalling, 1935), 52. Kracauer here citing Münzenberg, *Propaganda als Waffe*, 179.]
74. [Erich Wernert, *L'art dans le IIIe Reich: Une tentative d'esthétique dirigée* (Paris: Paul Hartmann, 1936), 7ff.]
75. [Horst Dressler-Andress, "Volkstum und Heimat," in *Der nationalsozialistische Staat: Grundlagen und Gestaltung. Urkunden des Aufbaus. Reden und Vorträge (bis zum November 1933)*, ed. Walther Gehl (Breslau: Hirt, 1933), 221–26, 221.]
76. [Dressler-Andress, "Volkstum und Heimat," 221–26.]
77. [Goebbels, *Revolution der Deutschen*, 191.]
78. {G. K. Chesterton, *Charles Dickens* (London: Methuen, 1913), 133.}
79. [Willi Krause, *Reichminister Dr. Goebbels* (Berlin: Verlag Deutsche Kultur-Wacht, 1933), 55.]
80. [Wernert, "L'art dan le IIIe Reich," 28.]
81. [Wernert, 120.]
82. [Wernert, 100.]
83. [Kracauer, *Werke*, 2.2, 116.] {TP, 102.}
84. [Kracauer, 116.]

2
Totalitarian Propaganda

Section G

I.

Propaganda orchestrated to win power cannot cease after the seizure of power. This follows necessarily from the principle according to which Fascism and National Socialism emerged. Were both movements to identify with a real societal interest, then their victory must effect not so much the continuance of propaganda as its dismantling, for the satisfaction of such an interest would speak for itself, and would not require total influence over opinion to earn them recognition. Should Moscow's propaganda have assumed totalitarian forms in the Soviet Union, that would be a sign of the regime's withdrawal from its original conception. Doubtless the totalitarian movements, invariably misrecognized, can and will satisfy one or another societal interest they encounter along the way, but their actions are not determined by such interests. Rather, they are predeterminately grounded in a nihilistic will to power {*Machtwille*} stemming from war, and this requires no lasting ties with any social interest. Thus, since the rulers see themselves as obliged to manipulate and disavow existing interests, and since they are also predisposed to take into account their experience in war that power is not won and upheld by force alone (Goebbels confirms in 1933 that "The national government has no intention of sitting on bayonets"), all their acts are necessarily accompanied by propaganda indeed are at the same time propaganda themselves.[1] Propaganda is not merely a means used only occasionally by modern dictatorships; it is anchored in the fundament of these dictatorships.

And, instead of carrying less weight after the seizure of power, propaganda becomes from this moment on effectively totalitarian. In his speech to the press, 16 {*sic*} March 1933, Goebbels states: "In setting up the new Ministry for Public

Enlightenment and Propaganda, I see a revolutionary act of government in as much as the new government no longer intends to leave the people to their own devices."[2] But he also says: "If this government is determined, never to yield . . . then it cannot be satisfied in the long run to know that 52 per cent are behind it, in order to terrorize the remaining 48 per cent with that figure, but will see its next task as winning over the 48 per cent."[3]

Obeying the impulse implanted in them, the dictatorships set to work after the seizure of power and prepare an adroit national apparatus of power, with the help of which they intend to realize their dream of the imperium or the Reich. These goals determine the course of National Socialist and Fascist foreign policy. In order to overcome difficulties arising in the domain of foreign policy, propaganda will have to proceed according to the same methods—appropriately modified, of course—used to seize power at home. Certain idea-montages are not without effect abroad, provided terror lends them sufficient force. But the purpose of this investigation is not to pursue the use within foreign policy of propaganda methods which have already been analyzed, but to indicate how propaganda develops once it has become a monopoly. The task is to reconstruct the development of effective totalitarian propaganda within its own dominion. In the course of this process, world propaganda of course assumes an ever more decisive role, and this will be taken into consideration at given points.

Despite all their differences, Fascist propaganda proceeds in the same direction as National Socialist propaganda. If the following representation refers more to conditions in Germany, then this is primarily because National Socialism—in this it was truly German—attached great importance to the constant "ideological" {*weltanschaulich*} legitimation of its procedures, and so is particularly revealing.

II.

The installation of total propaganda is tied to that of terror. "This statutory, almost absolute rule over life and death," declares Heiden of conditions after 1933, "was expanded and refined piece by piece."[4] And Silone: "Fascism has never eschewed the use of terror to dominate the country."[5] Totalitarian dictatorships eschew its use so little that they sweep aside the few bulwarks that protect against it and introduce a law that corresponds with the National Socialist rule "Whatever benefits the people is right"[6] {*"Recht ist, was dem deutschen Volke nützt"*}.* Since, as has been shown, the concept of the people {*das Volk*} is purely a cover term in National Socialist parlance for nothing more than the will of the ruling clique, then this statement must be understood along the lines of: what is right is—according to the definition of the National Socialist Huber—whatever heightens the "force of political power."[7] According to Huber, "Civil liberties, institution and institutional guarantees cease to exist in the people's constitution. The underlying reason for this is that the principle of 'guarantee' has itself been surmounted in a people's constitution. The liberal constitution was essentially a 'guarantee;' it is a system of safeguards and assurances vis-à-vis state power. The people's constitution does not have this guarantee function; on the contrary, it is meant to heighten the efficacy and force of political power. It is not supposed to protect individuals and groups from the whole, but instead serves the unity and entirety of the will against all individualistic and group-based disintegrations."[8] "There are workers' rights," writes Silone with reference to Alfredo Rocco,† who formulated the juristic doctrine of Fascism, "only as allowances of the state. They exist only as reflected rights. The authority of Fascist trade unions is a reflected authority, granted by the authority of the State.... This State authority is the only original, non-reflected authority, the source of all law. So, there is no Fascist legality, no written body of laws, out of which an opposition movement could derive a justification of its existence. The only law is that of the bourgeois {*bürgerlich*} state. All concessions it can make are nothing more than that: concessions, temporary allowances."[9] Allowances can be revoked, and the totalitarian regime really does not shy away from disavowing its own laws just as soon as their implementation might hinder its claim to totality. Elections to German works councils do not take place, the statutory provision of symmetry between the unions of employers and employees in Italy exists, according to Silone, only on paper.[10] The law that, in a democracy, regardless of its class character, still limits power {*Macht*}, is transformed into an instrument of pure power. The illegal power {*Gewalt*} exercised by the Gestapo and the Fascist militias, as explained above, must appear as doubly arbitrary if it is constantly accompanied by legal power; the terror effect

---

* {The Surhkamp editors include the correct citation from Hans Frank: "Alles, was dem Volk nützt, ist Recht; alles was ihm schadet, ist Unrecht": "All that is beneficial to the people is right and lawful, all that harms them is unlawful." The term "Recht" can be translated as "right," as "just," and as "law"/"lawful."}

† Alfredo Rocco (1875–1935) was a professor of commercial and economic law at a number of Italian universities prior to becoming justice minister (1925–1932). At one time a Marxist thinker, he later joined the Fascist movement, which adapted his notion of corporatism, according to which the state should intervene to mediate and harmonize otherwise conflictual class relations.}

produced by this association is further increased by the fact that the legal power itself only maintains the semblance of legality.[11] The installation of terror goes hand in hand with the artificial production of the masses, and once all measures have come into force which compel the desired shift in the psycho-physical structure, then totalitarian propaganda can become effective. It functions all the better when the dictatorship is in a position to corrupt wide strata via the allocation of positions, offices and sinecures.

The seizure of power imposes an obligation on totalitarian movements to make good their propagandist promises, or at least to attempt to fulfill them. The NS State accomplishes—no matter how—tasks which de facto fulfill promises: it promotes the political centralization of Germany, which wasn't even tackled by social democracy; it eliminates the problem of unemployment. Inasmuch as these accomplishments further real societal interests, they do so for reasons that are independent of these interests. The standardization of the state apparatus is meant to strengthen the power position of the regime, and the elimination of unemployment is for the sake of the prestige it will bring. Of course, the regime never fails to exploit for propaganda purposes the fact that some of its achievements meet societal needs. Indeed, we may venture to assert that one or another of these achievements arises not least from propagandist necessity. Motorways and drained Pontine Marshes are the Potemkin villages of totalitarian dictatorships.*

The real problem after the seizure of power is not, however, fulfilling what can be fulfilled, but dealing with those propagandist promises which the totalitarian movements cannot satisfy at all, in consequence of their approach. What is meant here is the creation of class equality {*Klassenausgleich*}, which in National Socialist Germany includes the creation of the *Volksgemeinschaft*. Mindful of Fascism's misuse of the concept of the trade union, Angelica Balabanoff elaborates:† "Here, too, we find the hallmark of Fascism: promises are not

---

* {Between 1933 and the outbreak of war in 1939, and starting with completion of a stretch between Frankfurt and Darmstadt, 3300 km of the German Autobahn system were constructed, a program continued as of 1940, using forced labor. In Italy, work to drain the Pontine Marshes southeast of Rome was abandoned in 1914 and then resumed under Mussolini's regime in 1930. Serving as a work creation scheme and photo opportunity, the project led to the drainage of 775 square km in a ten-year period though subsequent attempts to settle and utilize the land proved largely unsuccessful. The notion of a "Potemkin village" is a reference to the creation of fake or simulated scenery and villages in the newly conquered Crimea by its governor, Grigory Potemkin (1739–1791), during the reign of Catherine II.}

† {Born in Chernihiv in the Russian Empire, Angelica Balabanoff (1878–1965) was a Jewish Russian communist activist in Rome who, after spending time in Russia and breaking with the Bolshevik movement in 1922, returned to Italy and worked as a journalist. With the rise of Fascism, she went into exile firstly in

kept, cannot be kept, nevertheless the semblance {*Schein*} of fulfilment is created."¹² The compulsion to create this semblance requires the dictators to seize upon a series of measures which, from the outset, are acts of propaganda. Their function is to evoke the impression that class antagonism is liquidated and an internally unified people is a reality.

Among these acts of propaganda, the first to be highlighted are those groups which may be called direct since they behave as if they substantially changed the relationship between employees and employers; whether, like National Socialist employment law and the German Labor Front,* by treating both classes as symmetrical formations, or as organizations such as Strength through Joy (*Kraft durch Freude*, KdF)† or the Fascist *Dopolavoro*, by granting employees special privileges.‡ But the symmetry is exhausted in formalities, and the benefits leave the position of the employee in the production process untouched. Such procedures, that treat only the symptoms, do not in fact help the bourgeoisie in general, but do indeed benefit big business and, above all, the ruling clique. That they are undertaken in the interests of power and aim solely to lend weight to the illusion of class equality is revealed in the arguments put forward by Dr. Ley on 27 November 1933 before the German Labor Front as he establishes the "KdF" organization.§

"The words coined by the Führer stand above everything: 'How do we best sustain the nerves of the people, knowing that to pursue politics one needs a people with strong nerves?'"¹³ Thus, this organization is set up, neither for the sake of the workforce, nor for the people, but as a prerequisite for the power politics of the totalitarian dictatorship. The KdF serves to build up the National Socialist apparatus of power.

"Unfulfilled longing," Dr. Ley explains further, "generates envy. But when the German is allowed his share in life's bounty, he will no longer be filled with

---

Switzerland and then in the United States. After the war, she resumed working for the cause of socialism in Italy until her death in Rome at the age of eighty-seven.}

* {This served to cement a hierarchical relationship between employer and employee rather than an equal reciprocal contractual arrangement.}

† {The KdF was established in November 1933 under the auspices of the German Labor Front (Deutsche Arbeitsfront, DAF) and encompassed not only a wide range of recreational, sporting, and cultural activities, including mass tourism, but also various workplace improvements (e.g., the construction of modern canteens and washrooms). Its mission was essentially twofold: to boost industrial production, and to facilitate the integration of the workforce into the *Volksgemeinschaft*.}

‡ {The *Dopolavoro* (OND) was the Fascist Italian equivalent of the KdF.}

§ {A member of the Nazi Party since 1925, Robert Ley (1890–1945) was leader of the DAF in the period 1933–1945. He committed suicide while awaiting trial for war crimes at Nuremburg. Kracauer provides no details of the source of these quotations.}

envy and hatred, but with happiness and gratitude. This results in the second contribution of the movement.... It is to kill the inferiority complexes in the working people."[14] In other words: The institutional purpose of *Kraft durch Freude* is to render social resentments harmless by bestowing a few vicarious gratifications on proletarian and proletarianized strata within the framework of what already exists. Unable to remove the causes of inferiority complexes, it does not in truth eliminate them but sedates the "working people" so that they forget them.

"Thirdly, the organization should ward off boredom in the people. Boredom gives rise to stupid, rabble-rousing and, indeed, ultimately criminal ideas and thoughts. Dull tedium makes men brood, gives them a sense of homelessness {*Heimatlosigkeit*}, in a word: a feeling of absolute superfluity. Nothing is more dangerous for a state than that. And so we are going to build camps on heath and mountain, and all across the uplands of the Rhine, where Germans will spend their holidays in discipline and camaraderie."[15] Recreation is therefore structured to deprive its coerced consumers of joy of any free time in which they might come up with "criminal ideas and thoughts" i.e., pursue their class interest. Obviously, the way to prevent such trouble is by systematically filling the tiniest gaps in leisure time. In camps and on ships, it is easy to keep holidaymakers under the lasting influence of propaganda, and the more magnificent the natural setting, the more it too becomes a vehicle of propaganda.

"The Office for Teaching and Training {Amt für Unterricht und Ausbildung] will enable everyone to acquire knowledge and skills free of charge. We will, however, only promote this hunger for training in those who are truly suitable and capable."[16] These sentences declare that Dr. Ley's organization, in as much as it monopolizes education, prevents individual freedom of expression—the play of which must immediately destroy the illusion of class equality. It is not enough that the organization confiscates leisure, it promotes only the people of its choice. Anyone who doesn't pay homage to National Socialism will have difficulty accessing knowledge, and the knowledge that is on offer will from the outset be of a National Socialist persuasion. So it is that any thirst for knowledge that jeopardizes the totalitarian regime is manipulated.

Among the measures striving to deal directly with the unattainable, there are those related to the Volksgemeinschaft. Wishing to substantiate its existence, the party leaders collect on the streets for the winter relief programme {*Winterhilfswerk*}; in a similar vein, mass visual art and other aesthetic productions must have the same effect as these symbolic acts. Describing National Socialist architecture, Wernert writes: "Architectural monstrosities intended for gatherings of the people convey to those who gaze upon them no sense of balance, of scale and rhythm; they express only that relentless physical force, the force of the avalanche, the irresistible oppressive force; they evoke the masses who populate them, the German *Volk*."[17] Images of, and for, the masses, the purpose of which is to simulate the existence of the *Volk*, transform themselves thanks to their magic and all possible propagandistic ingredients into the very proofs of existence.

Direct acts of propaganda are supplemented by indirect. Passions are unleashed against some adversary outside the sphere of the class struggle—whose presence or absence incidentally makes no difference—and immediately any differences existing within the sphere lose their importance. Antisemitism indirectly deepens the impression of the unity of the people—and the economic beneficiaries of anti-Jewish legislation are those least likely to welcome any diminution of that impression. The same indirect effect is achieved by the cult of power and the leader; as power, through its glorification, appears to be elevated above the classes, so the psychological significance of class interest is automatically subdued. It is for this reason that the Nurnberg Congress Hall has to be the biggest.* Gigantic proportions call to mind the power that is becoming absolute, and precisely this glaring emphasis of its absolute nature means the conception of the real *Volk* can be surmounted by the fiction of the *Volksgemeinschaft*. Finally, there are those propaganda acts which serve only to reinforce. Fascism is concerned to ensure the punctuality of the trains; National Socialism promotes hygiene and values the publicity potential of beautifully arranged factory yards and workplaces. In their efforts to keep up appearances, every means of seduction is right.

"With us, seeming {*Schein*} has become being {*Sein*}"—with these words, spoken in 1932, Goebbels certainly also wishes to express the conviction that the National Socialist regime hopes to transfer the idea of class conciliation {*Klassenversöhnung*} and of the *Volksgemeinschaft* into reality.[18] The propaganda acts undertaken after the seizure of power do indeed conjure up a new reality in that they create numerous institutions and organizations and generally steer the whole conduct of the people. But this reality is to be bracketed since it only comes about under the pressure exerted by the terror and the production of the masses {*Massenerzeugung*}. The extent of its reliance on the unremitting assistance of totalitarian propaganda is made clear by the exhortation of the SA Gruppenführer Schöne

---

* {Designed by Albert Speer and Walter Brugmann, the foundation stone for this edifice was laid in 1935 but the building itself was never completed. It was part of a complex of sites in Nuremberg where the Nazi Party staged its rallies and events from 1933 to 1938.}

at a conference in East Prussia:* "We still haven't learned to see everything from the point of view of propaganda. Propaganda must therefore be used more."[19] Knowledge of the general rule covering the dictatorships' reality is also apparent in Silone's comments about Mussolini: "He is doomed to play carnival Caesar to the end of his days, to keep his facial expression in check at all times."[20] Reality in the totalitarian state is a pseudo-reality. For, if Fascism and National Socialism are unable to achieve the unity of the people, then they are obliged, of course, to create a synthetic reality in which unity seems to be an actuality. Thus, Goebbels's statement would more correctly read: "With us, seeming has become the semblance of being {*Schein des Seins*}." This pseudo-reality differs from the actual reality it has largely eliminated in that it is a product of the will to power as the latter becomes absolute, its actions disregarding societal requirements whenever necessary. "In a way, as of a certain point," Heiden says, "power is always right, as it no longer needs to adapt its assertions to circumstances but can change circumstances according to its assertions."[21] This helps to explain the consistency with which the world of pseudo-reality develops: what doesn't add up is made to add up. Another feature of this world is that it extends deep into the regions of the absurd; if the unattainable must be considered attained, then absurdity does become a necessity. As a result of its consistent and at the same time absurd character, the pseudo-reality has something of a drawing by the insane come to life.

For totalitarian dictatorships, everything depends on the maintenance of the psycho-physical constitution in which this pseudo-reality works as reality. "Once a Marxist following is shaken in its ability to believe . . ., then it is already overcome; for it instantly relinquishes its power to resist."[22] This remark from Goebbels illuminates, as a mirror reflection, the structure of National Socialist and Fascist rule. If Goebbels's theory is followed to the letter, then it seems that the totalitarian regime would fall apart if at any point, even for only a second, the total influence over opinion were interrupted. Hence the humorlessness of the modern dictatorships—humor might damage the fine weave of propaganda; hence their efforts to underpin the acts of propaganda with precautions, the sole purpose of which is to prevent any slippage from the sphere of pseudo-reality. And the more constantly people are kept in a state of eager anticipation of directives issued from above, the less fear there is of such slippage. Totalitarian propaganda incorporates its own agents of suspense. By privileging a heroic life over a happy one, and the *Volksgemeinschaft* over the individuals who comprise it,

---

* {Heinrich Schöne (1889–1945) joined the National Socialist movement in 1924 and the SA in 1925. Leader of the Hitler Youth movement (1926–1927) he rose to hold senior positions in the SA and became a leading Nazi politician and official. He was killed on the Russian front.}

propaganda encourages psychological forces of attraction to develop that thwart any individual's relapse into her/his special existence; with its time-limited plans, it constantly seeks new ways to keep all those subjected to it on tenterhooks. In his 1936 book, *Das deutsche Wirtschaftswunder*, Hans Erich Priester* remarks of the second German four-year plan[23]: "A prime concern remains the need to ensure that the first so-called four-year plan does not simply run without further ado, but to put something new in its place.... People want to be compensated for shortcomings in the present with change in the future."† This means that the four-year plans, like all projects tied to a deadline, serve to reinforce that state of mind in which the reader of sensational novels {*Kolportageromane*}, caught up in the suspense, will not stop reading at any price. The threat of armed conflict also creates tension, an effect not to be underestimated—it is a threat which produces the same oscillation between conflicting emotions and convictions that is so indispensable to propaganda. The presence of crisis has a similar effect as the calculated threat of war. A thoroughly dialectical relationship prevails between the totalitarian regime and crisis. On the one hand, Fascists and National Socialists wish to fulfil their promises of better times by overcoming the crisis; on the other hand, they need the crisis in order to justify the dictatorship to the masses. If there were no crisis, then it would have to be invented by the totalitarian movements. "Is there a way out of... the difficult situation?" writes Priester. "What Germany needs is the transition of the pseudo-economic growth into a real economy growth. This is not unattainable. However, one precondition must be met: The Third Reich must reach a political understanding with the world."[24] But this way conflicts not only with the will to power of National Socialism, but equally with its need for a continuation of the crisis, the value of which can hardly be overestimated. The pressure of the crisis strengthens the pressure of the terror and the tensions and vibrations emanating from the crisis reinforce the pseudo-reality. Incidentally, totalitarian propaganda likes to make use of the possibility of transforming some measures which originally had no propagandist significance into agents of suspense, simply by the way they are employed. It is not unusual for them to be used for acts of

---

* {Han Erich Priester (life dates unknown) was a journalist and commentator on economic affairs. He wrote critically on the German banking crisis of 1931 and in 1936 described what he saw as the success of National Socialist policies in eliminating unemployment.}

† {Announced at the party conference in 1936, this centered on the swift rearmament of Germany and preparations for what was seen as an inevitable war with Russia. Hermann Göring was commissioned to lead this program, which involved the reorientation of German businesses and industries away from consumer goods and toward military equipment.}

foreign policy, in order to relieve weariness with domestic policy. Fundamentally, then, any act can achieve the significance of an act of propaganda.

Plebiscites represent spot checks of the psycho-physical constitution associated with the pseudo-reality; to say nothing of the fact that their proliferation is intended to produce tension and their success to increase the prestige of the leadership at home and abroad. The positive outcome of these plebiscites is guaranteed, not only by terror, but also by the questions, which wisely refer to national existence. The plebiscites are not meant to establish the opinion of the masses, but on the contrary to show quite starkly the extent to which the masses have been deprived of their freedom of opinion. A proclamation of the will of the people turns into a proclamation of the power of the regime over the will of the people. What Silone said of the union elections is true also of the plebiscites: they are the "means by which the masses can confirm their connection {*Anschluß*} to the government."[25] In a turn of phrase already cited elsewhere, Hitler himself declares that the purpose of such voting manoeuvres is to demonstrate and control the steadfastness of this "connection." "If the appeal is not well received, no-one should say that the people are to blame; instead he should say that the movement has become lazy. The movement is no longer fighting properly.... And from this one will be able to learn once again how to immerse oneself in the people."[26] Like the plebiscite, the National Socialist Reichstag is a farce. Its eerie antics reveal at a stroke those of the entire pseudo-reality.

III.

The expansion of the apparatus of power keeps pace with the build-up of the propaganda machine. The ruling caste installs itself; it implements military armament and seeks to transform the army into its instrument; bending to the force of circumstances and the logic of the will to power, it develops the organized capitalism of the postwar period into a kind of steered economy—the so-called military economy, which takes its impetus from the regime's aims of imperialist expansion and in reality satisfies monopoly capitalist interests, though of course without wholly identifying with them....

But the question here is not the construction of the National Socialist and Fascist apparatus of power, but the course of totalitarian propaganda. Holding the monopoly, propaganda lines up act after act and assertion after assertion {*Setzung*} with absolute authority: are these acts and assertions such that they fit into a unified whole without special modifications? On the contrary: the more established the regime becomes, the more propaganda finds itself in the predicament of disavowing some of its own claims and striving to reconcile contradictions. Apart from very few contents, there is in fact nothing to which it would be able to commit definitively. As was said above of the pseudo-reality, what doesn't add up will be made to add up. The inconsistency consists precisely in the divergences that form in the field of propaganda.

They can be explained in the first instance by the fact that totalitarian dictatorships must take into account an intrinsically contradictory societal reality. Leaving aside the medley of interests with which foreign policy must deal, class differences at home are by no means a thing of the past, and nor are groupings of peasants, the middle classes, the churches, etc. Thus: "In the first flush of enthusiasm," writes Heiden, "the social problem is benumbed, but not resolved.... The social circumstances remain, and the class differences remain; these are the societal facts of the National Socialist dictatorship of 1937."[27] What is more, this reality is constantly being recast by the actions of the regime; new potential conflicts arise, new needs make themselves heard. A mix of criss-crossing interests and tendencies brings about necessarily heterogeneous situations—situations which could be addressed within the democracy through the struggle between parties. Since, according to its guiding principles, the totalitarian regime aspires to power per se and, in order to win this power, displays a nihilistic indifference toward all contents, it will not hesitate to modify its realization-convictions {*Realisierungs-Überzeugungen*} according to the current situation. As a consequence of the rupturing of the social fabric, it must go on and on annulling commitments made by the propaganda.

The glaring conflict between the acts of the dictatorships and their propagandist promises conjures up crises both in Italy and in Germany which threaten the collapse of the pseudo-reality. According to Silone, the Matteotti Crisis* is "the result of the blatant contradiction between the government policy of Fascism and the interests and wishes of the majority of the population, including

---

* {Giacomo Matteotti (1885–1924) was a socialist politician who warned of the threat of Fascism and, in a speech on May 30, 1924, denounced Fascist violence and fraud in the recent elections. He was abducted eleven days later and murdered. Among those arrested and convicted of this killing was Amerigo Dumini, a member of the Fascist secret police. This murder led to a temporary decline in support for the Fascists. Mussolini's involvement is still much debated. He accepted some responsibility for the killing in a speech in early 1925 but did not admit any direct link with the events. The crisis was a turning point in Mussolini's politics: from then on, his apparent efforts to work with parliamentary institutions gave way to a much more dictatorial approach. The threat that provincial Fascists might trigger civil war strengthened Mussolini's position in his dealings with the Italian monarchy, setting himself up as a guarantor of national stability.}

the Fascists."²⁸ And the National Socialist crisis of 1934 stems from the disappointment of the left wing of the party that the government is clearly moving with big business instead of fulfilling its pledge to find a socialist solution.* At that time, as the "second revolution" festers in Germany, the very propaganda that once demanded the communalization of the department stores and the nationalization of already socialized businesses heaps argument upon argument to make the discontented masses understand the contrary behaviour of the regime. At a rally on 14 May 1934, Goebbels rounds on the "moaners {*Miesmacher*}":† "No-one is going to take an economy which everyone knows has been mismanaged and replace false methods with wholly new ones in an instant. When an economy is fighting for its life, it first needs to be given a modicum of good health."²⁹ And, at a regional party congress in Essen on 25 June 1934, he declares: "A single blunder could destroy our economic life."³⁰ But such sophisms fail to make any real impression on the SA with its left-leaning old Freikorps leaders, and so they are replaced five days later by the execution squads, whose powers of persuasion are, of course, incontestable. The middle classes are more easily manipulated. Although they, too, despite their early solidarity with the National Socialist and Fascist movement, must likewise learn to think little of propaganda promises, they will—because the regime draws functionaries from their circles and breathes some life into middle-class illusions—always obscure the monopoly-capitalist character of the totalitarian dictatorships. In his study of the problem for small businesses in the Third Reich, *Das Mittelstandsproblem im Dritten Reich*, published in 1934, Benedict Schmittmann finds "that National Socialism has not lived up to the group-centred {*gruppenegoistisch*} hopes of the small business community {*gewerblicher Mittelstand*}."‡ This is no longer necessary, he continues, "since the

---

* {Material shortages and high unemployment in Germany compounded internal strife in the National Socialist party itself, with the leader of the SA, Ernst Röhm seeking to seeking to increase his own power and that of the SA vis-à-vis the Gestapo and SS. In what became known as the "Röhm Putsch," Hitler had Röhm and other leading figures in the SA, some two hundred in total, arrested and summarily executed. Around one hundred other opponents met a similar fate. Hitler sought to persuade the populace that this was necessary action against corruption. Retrospectively, these extrajudicial actions were legalized by the ruling cabinet and legitimized by Carl Schmitt.}

† {The rally actually took place on May 11, 1934. The "moaners" dismissed by Goebbels, according to an article of May 13–14, 1934, in the *Völkischer Beobachter*, were, typically, critics of the regime, Jews, and the foreign press.}

‡ {Benedict Schmittmann (1872–1939) was a Catholic social scientist, academic, and political figure calling for federalist reforms of the German Reich. He was arrested in 1933 and prohibited from teaching. Declining to emigrate, he was arrested again in 1939 and died of the effects of ill treatment in the Sachsenhausen concentration camp.}

Volksgemeinschaft puts an end to class division and, instead of class stratification, the movement itself, embodying the people, acts as an all-defining stratum and, through its leadership, reconciles interests."[31]

One by one, the contents of propaganda fall victim to the acts of the regime. The concept of autarky is removed from usage when the momentary requirements of National Socialist economic policy demand its abandonment, only to be back in the limelight to publicize the second Four-Year Plan. The concept of the entrepreneurial personality, played off against Marxism, evaporates before our eyes thanks to the economic measures of the regime. Writing in the *Völkische Beobachter* in early January 1934, Gottfried Feder assures the reader that "The danger of Marxist economic policy was precisely that it dragged the State down into the sphere of production and would have preferred to make the State itself into some gigantic economic machinery, with the result that every creative personality and every self-sufficiency in the economy would have been destroyed."[32] In the interim, National Socialism has in fact proven to stifle the very private initiative it extols. Its propaganda vows to sanctify the family and protect it from destruction at the hands of Marxism; its actions are dictated by the desire for total power and must therefore undermine any entity like the family. The eradication of the individual and the requisitioning of youth through the Party and the state run directly contrary to the cult of the family which has brought the petit-bourgeois masses to National Socialism. Moreover, the regime does not hesitate for a moment to intervene in the intimacy of the home. A recent decision of the chancery court in Frankfurt-Höchst, which was applauded by the magazine *Deutsches Recht*, denied a divorced mother custody of her two children "because she had registered the son in a boarding school and wanted the daughter to have a convent education."[33] Another recent verdict of a German court states that "derogatory remarks about Party leaders made in the family circle are to be considered public insults."[34] It is telling that, in the same edition of *Kulturkampf*, mention is made of an attempt by the SS magazine *Das Schwarze Korps* to justify male infidelity on biological grounds.* Marriage ceases to be an arcanum, and time spent inside four walls is like sitting on the street.

The independent existence of societal reality not only destines the dictatorships to incessant changes of direction in their actions but also frequently compels them to decide upon ever differing ways to propagandize one and the same action. Contents mean nothing, and if propaganda makes no impression with

---

* {This weekly newspaper was first published in March 1936 and was required reading for members of the SS. The print run increased from an initial 70,000 to approximately 750,000 by 1944, making it the second largest political weekly of the Third Reich.}

one motif, it will deliver a second and third in its place. "Obviously there is no discussion," Goebbels explains in an interview published by the *Berliner Börsen-Zeitung* on 5 December 1937, "about whether our politics is right or wrong; but we often think long and hard about whether the arguments we put forward are right and compelling enough for our political purposes. Once we have set a political course, we never depart from that line. But if we see that a policy we deem right has not sufficiently taken root in the people, then we make sure we improve the arguments that speak in its favour."[35] A method applied on a large and small scale. Initially, in order to underpin its anti-church political propaganda, the National Socialist regime maintained that the churches were sowing the seeds of confessional discord; now that the churches have united to form a defensive front, the sole aim of propaganda in the interests of anti-church policy is once again to incite the confessions against each other. In an article in the *Nationalsozialistischen Monatshefte* of July 1937 dedicated to the Oxford Conference of World Churches, the Protestant churches are urged, finally to recognize the danger posed by the Catholic church.[36] Each phase of the struggle calls for a change of position. Josef Grohé,* Gauleiter and state councillor in Cologne, writing in the *Westdeutschen Beobachter*,[37] has no scruples in restoring to Charlemagne—whom the propaganda has liked to dub "Saxon butcher"—the epithet of Greatness because it is useful at this moment to denounce the Aachen Pilgrimage of 1937 as a political demonstration and let Emperor Charles the Great appear as the true head of Christendom.[38] Indeed, not content with constantly changing its fixations, propaganda takes each fixation and extracts from it further contrasting meanings. Depending upon whether security needs are used to justify French or German armament, they are one minute decried as the contemptible product of bourgeois fear, the next hailed as the expression of a peaceful nation's will for self-preservation.

But even assuming the impossible, namely, that societal reality is inherently without contradiction and that the totalitarian regime need not therefore abandon a single item of propaganda content in the course of its own unfolding, even then propaganda (inasmuch as it sets the contents) would still not have won the game. For, since the will to power, which the dictatorships repress, stems from a nihilistic sensibility {*Gesinnung*}, it must in its realization become embroiled in antinomies. The will to power strives for total rule and represents nothingness

---

* {Josef Grohé (1902–1987) joined the National Socialist Party in 1922 and held various offices and positions in and around his native Cologne. In 1928 he was imprisoned for hate speech in an article for the *Westdeutscher Beobachter*. He served as a functionary within the party up until 1945. After the war, and a four-and-a-half-year prison sentence, he worked in the toy industry.}

{*das Nichts*}: the consequence of this is that it comes into conflict with its own totalizing claims. In the interest of power per se, Fascism and National Socialism have to suppress the spontaneity of the mind {*geistig*} which, if given free rein, exposes the illusion that sustains them both; and yet, without lifting the controls on this spontaneity, they cannot achieve power per se. An intractable dilemma: the dictatorships lay claim to absolute power, the very pursuance of which would call precisely their power into question. Thus, nihilism, if it enters the world, is taken to the point of absurdity; like the devil of Grimms' fairy tale swindled by the crafty farmer.*

In all areas of spontaneity of the mind {*geistig*}, the totalitarian dictatorship is thwarted by its own imperialism. In the interests of power, National Socialism endeavours to throttle religious freedoms completely; but for these very same interests, it must recognize them. If the churches are not tolerated, National Socialism calls into play spiritual {*geistig*} resistance, which cannot be overcome—at least not through propaganda. If, on the other hand, the churches are left unhindered, then National Socialism might gain their support, but be obliged to endure the withdrawal from its influence of a spiritual-intellectual {*geistig*} sphere capable of shattering the pseudo-reality at any time. This conflict is all the more intractable since its only possible removal would consist in the regime as it were absorbing the churches—a solution ruled out by its own irrationality. Hence the ambivalence of National Socialist church policy, its fluctuations clearly carrying over into propaganda. All that remains is for the regime to resort to compromise, though this compromises the absoluteness of power. In the domain of art, as in culture in general, the same antinomy has a disruptive effect. On the basis of the principle of totality, the dictatorships must prescribe the direction of artistic and cultural works; if, however, these become a variable of pure power, then the preconditions for their emergence no longer apply and they can at best be considered achievements within the pseudo-reality. Controlled art is wooden iron {*Gesteuerte Kunst ist hölzernes Eisen*}. "This general mobilization of art and the artistic powers of the nation for the benefit of the Volk," remarks Wernert, "has a weakness. This is not lost on the men of the hour. They have seen that there was an antinomy between the duties imposed on the artist and the freedom essential to any creative work of art worthy of the name. They have tried to find a solution, mainly simply by contesting that such an antinomy existed."[39] Goebbels himself recognises the antinomy in order to repudiate it. "If liberalism started out from the individual and positioned the

---

* {The reference here is to the tale "The Peasant and the Devil" ("Der Bauer und der Teufel") in which a cunning farmer twice outwits the Devil.}

single human being at the centre of all things," he declares, "then we have replaced individual with *Volk* and single human beings with *Gemeinschaft*." Goebbels is speaking to filmmakers at the opening of the Chamber of Culture {Reichskulturkammer} on November 15, 1933, and his words chime with his other explanations cited above: "And, of course, the freedom of the individual had to be limited inasmuch as it conflicted with or contradicted the freedom of the nation. This is not a restriction of the concept of freedom per se. Exaggerating the freedom of the individual means jeopardizing or even seriously endangering the freedom of the *Volk*. Thus, the limits of the concept of individual freedom abut upon those of the freedom of the *Volk*."[40] Since, in the meantime, the regime is not so much limiting individual freedom as abolishing it altogether—not in the interests of the freedom of the Volk, but for the sake of the National Socialist power apparatus, this argumentation merely glosses over the conflict rather than eliminating it. The antithesis coined by Goebbels in 1932 follows the same line: "Culture is there to serve the soul of the *Volk*, not poison it."[41] But culture is one with the life process of the Volk, and by contemplating the possibility that the soul could be poisoned by culture, Goebbels announces unequivocally that he understands culture as various pseudo-cultural events serving to uphold the National Socialist fiction of the Volk. What is more, belittling artistic and cultural life, as is the wont of the dictatorships, strikingly confirms the sense that the conflict between the claims of the mind {*Geist*} and those of power per se cannot be resolved. More ominously for power itself, this conflict comes to a head in the sphere of knowledge. Imbued with the significant conviction that freedom of scientific inquiry and totalitarian propaganda are mutually exclusive, the dictatorships do everything to bring schools and universities into line. Speaking at the assembly of the National Socialist Teachers' Federation [Nationalsozialistischer Lehrerbund, NSLB] in Frankfurt on 5 August 1934,* Reichsamtsleiter and State Minister Schemm† assures his audience that "in Germany's educational life today, there is no schoolwork and no science, no English, French or Greek, no mathematics, geography and no history that is not focused on a single goal, and that is Germany and its future."[42] The more divergences appear in the content of propaganda, the more the regime has to fear from spontaneous acts of knowledge; the pressure on science must

---

* {This association of National Socialist teachers grew enormously following the 1933 seizure of power (from approximately 12,000 to 250,000 members). However, its influence on educational policy remained limited.}

† {Hans Schemm (1891–1935) was a teacher in Bayreuth and joined the party in 1923. In 1928 he was elected to the Bavarian Assembly (Landtag) and founded the NSLB in 1929. Involved in numerous publications, including setting up a newspaper, he joined the SA and became Bavarian minister of culture in 1933. He was killed in a plane crash.}

therefore increase steadily over time. Only at a relatively late stage of the development is an agreement reached between Reichsminister Rust* of the Ministry for Science, Education, and Teaching {Reichsminister für Wissenschaft, Erziehung, und Unterricht} and Reichsleiter Bouhler, chair of the Official Party Inspection Commission for the Protection of National Socialist Literature {Parteiamtliche Prüfungskommission zum Schutze des nationalsozialistischen Schrifttums} to ensure the supervision of science in such a way that amounts to its total prescription.† The official rationale is that experience has shown the necessity of bringing scientific literature—as far as it deals with, or touches upon, questions of political worldview—broadly into line with National Socialist literature policy.[43] However, by gaining power over science, the totalitarian regime loses power itself, since scientific enquiry is bound to waste away if it cannot move freely and its decline will in turn limit the perfecting of the power apparatus desired by the regime. Already today, the military is openly critical of the training of new recruits; the latter leave much to be desired—not only in the humanities, but also in technical subjects. And so it even comes about that an official voice sometimes speaks out in favour of science; this means that propaganda begins to waver between the implementation and the suppression of its own totalitarian claims. As in its dealings with the churches, so too with science: the regime is reliant on compromise.

The continuing development of the totalitarian system therefore brings with it the dynamization of the contents of propaganda. Everywhere there are divergences demanding to be suppressed, vulnerable positions crying out to be covered, so that the task of propaganda visibly becomes nothing more than ordering ad hoc mobilizations of motifs and montages of ideas hither and thither like squadrons. During the mass trials of Catholic priests, it is noted that the charges of immorality are not firing up the public enough and immediately the emphasis

---

* {Bernhard Rust (1883–1945) joined the National Socialist Party in 1925 and, after losing his teaching position in 1930, entered politics. He oversaw the dismissal of thousands of teachers and academics on account of their political views and backgrounds. He sought to integrate Nazi ideology into the curriculum. His influence waned after 1936. He committed suicide on the day of the German capitulation.}

† {Philipp Bouhler (1899–1945) worked on the *Völkischer Beobachter* from 1921 and joined the National Socialist Party in 1922. He became a leading Nazi functionary and in 1933 achieved the position of Reichsleiter, the second highest rank in the party. A key figure in Hitler's central office, he was given oversight of cultural affairs and became chair of the Official Party Inspection Commission for the Protection of National Socialist Literature. From 1939, with Karl Brandt, he planned and coordinated the Aktion T4 program involving the mass killing of disabled people and psychiatric patients and the "special treatment" (*Sonderbehandlung*) program of mass murder in the concentration camps. He committed suicide after his arrest in 1945.}

is shifted to the accusation of treason.* Women in the workforce were once frowned upon, but a shortage of labor to keep pace with armament makes it necessary to resort to them again and promptly assert that homage has never been paid to any "Gretchen ideal" of German women. A shifting of convictions which gathers pace inexorably. For one thing, the formation of the pseudo-reality does not master the actual societal reality, but instead transforms it into a confused mishmash of conflicting interests and needs; for another, the antinomies in which the nihilistic will to power embroils itself become ever more apparent. The image presented by propaganda moves closer and closer to the fencer in the fairy tale who brandishes his sword with lightning speed to fend off raindrops.† The reproach levelled at science by National Socialism—that it professes unbridled relativism—can therefore more rightly be aimed at fully-fledged totalitarian propaganda itself. The result is that propaganda, inasmuch as it sets certain contents, must wear out. The totalitarian mobilization of convictions leads to the total liquidation of them all. The degree to which these are devalued emerges in the section Silone appends to his description detailed above of the radio transmission of a Mussolini speech: "Discussion is impossible for Fascism."[44]

IV.

The wearing out of the contents of propaganda by no means spells the end for totalitarian propaganda overall. Due to the increasing frequency of contradictions between the acts of the regime, between its acts and the assertions {Setzungen} of its propaganda, and between these assertions themselves, the convictions promulgated by propaganda have worn so thin that they no longer serve to uphold the pseudo-reality—and this despite the unbridled implementation of terror and the artificial creation of the masses. In response, the propaganda changes direction, plotting a course which will allow it to hold on to the masses after all. Unable to sustain an effect by means of particular contents, propaganda withdraws from those contents. Material propaganda turns into formal propaganda; the onus is not on the content, but on the manner of its presentation. The

---

* {The persecution of (mainly Catholic) clergy, accusing them of homosexuality, began in earnest in 1935 and reached its high point in 1938, when several thousand priests and other religious figures were condemned in show trials.}
† {A reference to Grimms' fairy tale "The Three Brothers."}

movement itself must become the substance—this goes for National Socialism as well as for Fascism. According to a statement by Krieck, cited above,[45] National Socialist agitators do not entice with intellectual proofs and arguments, but rather seduce with the "primordial energy of rhythm."[46] In fact, rhythmic formations gain the upper hand as, and to the extent that, the swarm of previous promises loses its value. Shocks are orchestrated in random material to prevent any respite from the tension; waves of propaganda are sent out and, as required, either build steadily or swiftly ebb away; and, in all cases, care is taken to coordinate tempi to good effect. These occurrences are lent propagandist significance by the rhythmic quality of the course they take: the skillful sequencing of quiet and action, of push and pull. If the proclamation of content, of substantive and attractive goals, was once decisive, now the appeal to the psycho-physical state associated with the pseudo-reality is predominantly through form—the form in which the propaganda accomplishes the requisite acts and resolutions. The further this process advances, the more the nihilism with which the propaganda handles all convictions reveals itself, of course, and the more undisguised is the eruption of the will to power, whose product is propaganda. Still, the "primordial energy of rhythm" could hardly provide lasting compensation for the destruction of the contents of propaganda if the propaganda didn't also succeed in making people forget about its own vacuity by stamping the now transparent will to power as the content itself. Whilst, at the beginning of their careers and in the interests of propaganda, National Socialism and Fascism must conceal that they seek nothing but power, they are now, inversely, likewise in the interests of propaganda, obliged to make power per se appear as the epitome of all that is desirable. The impulse to power, which engenders the totalitarian movements and drives them to monopoly capitalism, not only becomes manifest in this phase of development, but also and of necessity assumes the function of its devalued masquerades. The idea of class equality has vanished; what remains is the notion of the abundance of power as the central propagandist motif. In accordance with this theoretical conclusion, Heiden remarks: "If the strength of the dictatorship essentially consisted from its inception in the agreement of wide strata of the *Volk* and in the resignation of equally wide strata, then by the beginning of 1937 its strength consists in sheer power and in the absence of actual political opinion."[47] "Domination for its own sake," he also writes, "is the content of the dictatorship. Where the latter appears to engage in argumentation, persuasion, even logic, it is only ever an attempt to bolster domination by ostensibly intellectual means. [...] The power of persuasion at their rallies flows, not from the conclusiveness of what is said, but from the display of their power in having the last word."[48] Doubtless, the totalitarian regime uses every opportunity to display its power and, through the suggestive effect of such events, to replace any of its ideational montages which have expired. Just as propaganda uses the aesthetic magic of the well-organized power apparatus, so it also benefits from the sheen of military pomp. It is no coincidence that the army is summoned to all major political events; aircraft and tank parades, as means of publicity, help the lamest argument back onto its feet and still weave a seductive shimmer around nothingness. Such displays may again and again disguise the nihilist nature of the totalitarian claim to power, but they do not present to their masses the creditworthiness which alone would enable that claim to replace the worn-out contents of propaganda. The masses directly subjected to propaganda will at most give credit to the National Socialist and Fascist claim to power if it gains outward recognition. Indeed, nations in the economic situation of Germany and Italy—nations, moreover, whose unification has taken place comparatively recently—will function particularly willingly if such a claim appears to be identical with that of safeguarding and augmenting national standing. Since propaganda is shrinking while National Socialist and Fascist domination is consolidating, and since the shrinking process threatens to cancel out organizational consolidation, striving for imperialist goals is by no means at the discretion of the dictatorships; rather, they would perish along with their propaganda if they did not live out their will to power in the form of expansionism. In the interests of its own continued existence, upon which the existence of the entire regime depends, totalitarian propaganda must give ever greater emphasis to foreign policy.

This is not to say that propaganda hasn't been working on foreign policy material already from the days of the seizure of power, nor that it would refrain from inflammatory slogans to campaign for the National Socialist and Fascist politics of conquest. Corresponding in propaganda terms to Mussolini's proletarian nations, Hitler's words attacking the Bolshevization of Europe do so in the name of race and blood, laying claim to the incorporation of ethnic German minorities. Such assertions {*Setzungen*} seek to arouse sympathetic masses in the most varied countries and to create a mood of civil war; they indisputably owe a part of their effect to the terror which the dictatorships bring to bear on international public opinion through the extreme escalation of the potential for war. German armament and the second four-year plan are not least acts of world propaganda. "Ultimately," writes Priester, "the autarkic programme is meant to ease the situation in foreign policy and to move future negotiating partners towards the greatest possible concessions in colonial and trade questions."[49] Added to this comes the use of all remaining means of propaganda in the interests of foreign policy: vibrations are sent rippling through the international public, fixating it on promulgated slogans; relentless excitement is created so that the tragic effect of these slogans doesn't abate. In time, world propaganda undergoes the same process as domestic propaganda. Gradually, in the interests of the dictatorships' expansionist drive, propaganda must overturn the very watchwords it proclaimed itself because otherwise it would be unable to withstand the heterogenous situations evoked by the independent existence of foreign policy reality. Divergences and contradictions are the consequence. Tactical adaptation? But when the strategic goal is no less than world domination, everything that otherwise counts as substance falls within the sphere of the tactical. The course of Italian foreign policy is reminiscent of a temperature curve. And if National Socialist colonial propaganda believes that momentarily it can achieve nothing with the thesis "people without space" {*Volk ohne Raum*}, then it foists in its place the argument that what's needed is more space *and* more people.* The propaganda montages are constantly in flux, unless constancy in international relations necessitates their provisional retention. And through both their wearing out and the acts in which they culminate, what reveals itself—ever more unmistakeably—is the imperialism from which they stem. Subsequent to the declaration in the autumn of 1936 that Germany and Italy will not tolerate the establishment of a Bolshevist stronghold in Spain, events take place which conclusively show that the anti-Bolshevism of the dictatorships is not so much the expression of a Platonic ethos but rather represents the propagandist justification of armed intervention. Hitler's solemn renunciation of all claims to South Tyrol proves unequivocally that the dogma of all Germans belonging to the people as a whole {*Volksganze*} is only intended to camouflage the National Socialist will to conquer. Dogma is toppled, imperialism remains. Gradually world propaganda assumes a formal character; in any case it increasingly burdens the necessity or the fact of the increase in power per se. Hitler's Königsberg address, calling the people to the first greater German plebiscite on 10 April 1938, ends with: "On this day I will be the *Führer* of the greatest army in world history because when, on this 10th day of April, I place my ballot in the ballot box, I know: Behind me come 50 million, all of whom know only my rallying cry: One people and one Reich, Germany!"[50]

Although these words invariably exploit associations with the conquest of former German territories, the emphasis is quite clearly more on winning power.

---

* {Originally the title of a 1926 Hans Grimm novel, this became a key slogan of National Socialist propaganda and part of their manifesto.}

Portraying the electorate as the greatest army of world history is a singularly striking admission that National Socialism consists entirely in striving for the greatest possible power apparatus. But the use of such an image at these outstanding moments also betrays that undisguised imperialism is in fact becoming the decisive propaganda content. Totalitarian propaganda has no other choice: it must live on conquests, but it is dying. Its art consists now more in supplying renewed energy with the injection of imperialist motifs. War has been described as the recourse of dictatorships which fail internally. But war is an extreme case and, in the event of difficulties at home, at least the totalitarian regime has many propagandist tools of a foreign policy nature at its disposal; though it may push on towards war all the same and war may be its ultima ratio. Through the rhythmic gradations of its acts and resolutions, world propaganda can offset the loss of tension due to the decline hitherto of domestic propaganda, and, if psychophysical upheaval is called for, is never at a loss for ways to trigger shocks; not to mention that the slightest increase in external prestige contributes to strengthening the pseudo-reality, in which nothing appears quite as real as prestige itself. To be sure, the National Socialist colonial program provides for a string of functions which initially don't even concern the colonies. By shifting imperialism into the centre, the dictatorships not only find a replacement in the shape of world propaganda for home propaganda as it expires, but also directly fan the flames of the latter; for, as has been seen, an expansionist politics needs extensive propagandist preparations within the sphere of influence {*Machtbereich*} of the dictatorships themselves. In the end, world and domestic propaganda interlock so tightly that every foreign policy action at the same time satisfies inner propaganda needs and every domestic action seeks to serve the purposes of outward-looking propaganda. Fully corresponding totalitarian propaganda is of necessity propaganda on a world scale.

Looking at the play of this propaganda: blindly it whirls and swirls everything that appears fixed, since only by distorting and confusing the contents which it unleashed is it able to achieve total influence over opinion, the realization of which is a condition of its total claim to power. In the first phase, totalitarian propaganda becomes a technique for exciting the masses, no matter what methods are used. Up is down and down is up. Instead of ideologically transfiguring its colonial demands according to familiar patterns, National Socialist propaganda is in the habit of accounting for these demands with overt reference to economic interests. It says calico and means God*—the God who inspires

---

* {In section A of the manuscript, Kracauer approximates Theodor Fontane's comment: "When they, the English say Christ, and mean cotton."}

Mussolini's vision of the Mediterranean and Hitler's campaign to the southeast. Behind the tumult of totalitarian propaganda, a death's-head appears.[51]

Translated by Bernadette Boyle and Graeme Gilloch

NOTES

1. [Joseph Goebbels, *Revolution der Deutschen* (Oldenburg: Stalling, 1933), 140.]
2. [Joseph Goebbels, statement to the press on the establishment of the Reich Ministry for Public Enlightenment and Propaganda in Berlin, March 3, 1933, quoted in *Deutsche Geschichte 1933–1945: Dokumente zur Innen- und Außenpolitik*, ed. Wolfgang Michalka (Frankfurt: Fischer, 1992), 78f.]
3. [Goebbels, *Revolution der Deutschen*, 136.]
4. [Konrad Heiden, *Adolf Hitler*, vol. 2 (Zürich: Europa Verlag, 1937), 133.]
5. [Ignazio Silone, *Der Fascismus: Seine Entstehung und seine Entwicklung* (Zürich: Europa Verlag, 1934), 179.]
6. [Hans Frank, *Nationalsozialistisches Handbuch für Recht und Gesetzgebung*, 2nd ed. (Munich: F. Eher, 1935), 13.]
7. [Ernst Rudolf Huber, *Verfassungsrecht des Grossdeutschen Reiches* (Hamburg: Hanseatische Verlagsanstalt, 1939), 360.]
8. [Huber, *Verfassungsrecht*, 360.]
9. [Silone, *Der Fascismus*, 271.]
10. [Silone, 271.]
11. {Kracauer refers here to a passage in section E of this essay, which can be found here: Siegfried Kracauer, *Werke in neun Bänden*, vol. 2.2, *Studien zu Massenmedien und Propaganda*, ed. Christian Fleck and Bernd Stiegler (Frankfurt: Suhrkamp Verlag, 2012), 81.}
12. [Angelica Balabanoff, *Wesen und Werdegang des italienischen Faschismus* (Vienna: Hess/Verlag, 1931), 62.]
13. [Robert Ley at the German Labor Front rally in Berlin to mark the founding of the culture and leisure organization Kraft durch Freude (KdF) on November 27, 1933, quoted in *Der nationalsozialistische Staat*, ed. Walther Gehl (Breslau: Hirt, 1933/34), 90.]
14. [Robert Ley, *Durchbruch der sozialen Ehre* (Berlin: Mehden-Verlag, 1937), 34.]
15. [Ley, *Durchbruch*, 34.]
16. [Ley, 43.]
17. [Erich Wernert, *L'art dans le IIIe Reich* (Paris: Paul Hartmann, 1936), 112.]
18. [Goebbels, *Revolution der Deutschen*, 119.]
19. [This statement from Heinrich Schöne is found only in Willi Münzenberg, *Propaganda als Waffe* (Paris: Éditions du Carrefour, 1937), 273.]
20. [Silone, *Der Fascismus*, 266.]
21. [Heiden, *Adolf Hitler*, vol. 2, 212.]
22. [Joseph Goebbels, *Kampf um Berlin*, vol. 1 (Munich: F. Eher, 1935), 91.]

23. [Hans Erich Priester, *Das deutsche Wirtschaftswunder* (Amsterdam: Querido, 1936), 269.]
24. [Priester, *Das deutsche Wirtschaftswunder*, 323.]
25. [Silone, *Der Fascismus*, 204.]
26. [Max Domarus, ed., *Hitler: Reden und Proklamationen, Vol. 1: 1932–1945* (Vienna: Löwit, 1973), 367.]
27. [Heiden, *Adolf Hitler*, vol. 2, 150.]
28. [Silone, *Der Fascismus*, 175.]
29. [Joseph Goebbels, rally in Berlin Sports Palace, May 11, 1934, quoted in *Deutsches Reich 1933–1937, Vol. 1: Die Verfolgung und Ermordung der europäischen Juden durch das nationalsozialistische Deutschland, 1933–1945* (Munich: Oldenbourg, 2008), 337.]
30. [Joseph Goebbels, speech at party rally, Essen, June 25, 1934, quoted in Gehl, ed., *Der nationalsozialistische Staat*, 73.]
31. [Benedict Schmittmann, "Das Mittelstandsproblem im Dritten Reich," in Rosi Karfiol, *Mittelstandsprobleme*, vol. 4, *Kölner Sozialpolitische Studien*, ed. Benedict Schmittmann (Cologne: Reich und Heimat Verlag, 1934), 123.]
32. [Gottfried Feder, writing in the *Völkische Beobachter*, January 4, 1934, quoted in Gehl, ed., *Der nationalsozialistische Staat*, 74–76, 75.]
33. *Kulturkampf: Berichte aus dem Dritten Reich*, no. 75, November 29, 1937.
34. *Kulturkampf*, no. 74, November 18, 1937.
35. *Kulturkampf*, no. 76, December 8, 1937. [Goebbels in an interview for the *Berliner Börsenzeitung*, December 5, 1937.]
36. *Kulturkampf*, no. 62, July 19, 1937.
37. [Josef Grohé, "Zur Aachner Heiligtumsfahrt," *Westdeutscher Beobachter*, July 24, 1937.]
38. *Kulturkampf*, no. 63, July 28, 1937.
39. [Wernert, *L'art dans le IIIe Reich*, 31f.]
40. [Joseph Goebbels, speech on the opening of the Reich Chamber of Culture in Berlin, November 15, 1933, quoted in Helmut Heiber, ed., *Goebbels-Reden, Vol.1: 1932–1939* (Düsseldorf: Droste, 1971), 133–141, 134.]
41. [Goebbels, *Revolution der Deutschen*, 120.]
42. [NSDAP/Nationalsozialistischer Lehrerbund, ed., *Hans Schemm spricht: Seine Reden und sein Werk* (Gauverlag Bayerische Ostmark, 1941), 223.]
43. Cf. *Kulturkampf*, no. 62, July 19, 1937.
44. [Reference cannot be determined with certainty.]
45. [Kracauer, *Werke*, 2.2, 103.] {TP, 91.}
46. [Ernst Krieck, *Nationalpolitische Erziehung* (Leipzig: Armanen-Verlag, 1937), 38.]
47. [Heiden, *Adolf Hitler*, vol. 2, 148.]
48. [Heiden, 62.]
49. [Priester, *Das deutsche Wirtschaftswunder*, 269.]
50. [Adolf Hitler, speech in Königsberg, March 25, 1938, proclaiming Reichstag election on April 10, 1938, quoted in Domarus, ed., *Hitler*, 837. Kracauer also cites *Berliner Tageblatt* of March 27, 1938, nos. 145–46.]
51. [Kracauer, *Werke* 2.2, 17.] {TP, 11.}

3
Abridged Restricted Schema

8th July {1937}

1. <u>The role of the superstructure</u>
2. <u>Postwar situation in Germany and Italy</u>:
    a) Democracy not self-evident: therefore relationship between democracy and Bolshevism sensed
    b) Self-elaboration possible within democratic frame
3. <u>The Fascist Führer type</u>
    a) Monstrosities of War
    b) Social Contingency
    c) Mentality [preceded by:] Dependence on the army
    d) Power of the Nation, for this it must be unified.
        (Interests of the imperialistic monopoly capitalism of the dominant class,)
        (Interests of the people (and/or the state) people's front (enemy of the state)
4. How does the clique judge the political superstructure?
    It sees the slogans of the ideologies of the parties as fixed and frozen
    Strongest concept: socialism, this as in the possession of the SPD and KPD
5. Possibility for the clique: to seize at the point of a bayonet: this contradicted by the experience of the war (H[itler]'s war propaganda) and the experience of the SPD
    Thus propaganda: its content, mass-stimulating concepts torn from their underground realm

6. What the task of propaganda reveals about its essence
   a) Regression
   b) Totality
   c) Criterium: success alone
      α Movement and actualism
      ß Lie = Cynicism
7. Pre-given susceptibility to Fascist propaganda
   a) Crisis in general
   b) Middle class
   c) The unemployed
   d) Youth
      But not overly decisive: it concerns precisely the dissolution of strata, whose existence rigidity increases.[1]
      Goal: total influence of opinion as such
8. Terror
9. The production of the masses*
10. <u>Functioning</u> of propaganda. This is inherent in the regime. It cannot stop. Conquest of contradictions.
    What is propaganda, what action.

Translated by Bernadette Boyle, Graeme Gilloch, and Jaeho Kang

NOTE

1. [8 and 9 are connected by a preceding curved bracket.]

---

* {The meaning of the original is unclear here. This is a literal translation of "deren Bestand Verfestigung steigt."}

4
Schemata

5, 6, 7 July 37

I. The role of the superstructure.
    You learn nothing if you only listen to the ideology of the leaders. But you also learn nothing if do not pay attention to it at all and turn your back on things altogether. (Petit bourgeois paradise (...) see Horkheimer)*
    In the long run it is about what happens in the sphere of the superstructure.
II. Core leadership of National Socialism and Fascism only seen sociologically. On the concept of the adventurer. His mentality. (Power:)[1]
III. The situation, seen sociologically: (democratic character has not been able to establish itself).
    Post war:
    Class struggle: the semblance of democracy, capitalism stronger than denatured socialism. Most important situational factor: the rigidity {*Fixiertheit*}, the mass-mobilizing idea in heterogeneous parties.† Nothing

---

* {Kracauer's reference to Horkheimer here demonstrates that his interest in Horkheimer's analysis of the sociohistorical roots and social psychological mechanisms of authoritarianism in modern capitalist societies was genuine, not merely perfunctory.}

† {Kracauer is describing a shift in party affiliation in the latter half of the Weimar Republic, which has been documented by more recent historians of the period. In the early and especially the middle phase of the Weimar Republic, the party system became very fragmented and based on narrow self-interest. The Nazis succeeded in getting many people to abandon these parties and to join a populist "Volkspartei" that overcome this fragmentation and rigidity. See, for example, Peter Fritzsche, *Germans Into Nazis* (Cambridge, MA: Harvard University Press, 1998), 172–214.}

in-between. Socialism as the mass-mobilizing idea *kat exochen* {par excellence} in the possession of the SPD and KPD.

IV. Objectives of Fascism and National Socialism:

Not socialism, not capitalism, but class peace, i.e. taking the status quo in hand as it is. (Trustees!) For the purpose of national power (= imperialist monopoly capitalism). Therefore: not classlessness but the appearance of classlessness.

Hitler says: Only when the nation is in power can the worker thrive. The following overarching motif {*Motivik*} is true: Only when the working people are satisfied, will National Socialist power succeed.

V. The necessity to mobilize, to convince the masses, does not yet follow from this. One could. In Italy force sits first on the bayonet. But, on the other hand, war experience and experience with people shows the objectives of socialist propaganda. Therefore, one must already use the mass-mobilizing ideas.

Task: Go to the masses! i.e. prise the mass-mobilizing ideas away from their foundation: "Nation," "Socialism." These ideas accepted like images {*Bilder*}, not analyzed. Thus: entrenched mass-mobilizing ideas are set in motion and become more fluid: this is propaganda in the sense of counter-reformation. Task of Fascist propaganda, which corresponds to a particular historical situation.

VI. Given the image-like manner {*Bildhaftigkeit*} with which "Socialism" is understood, and given the necessity of propaganda, it follows for the character of the latter that:

1) it means the same as its *regressus*, i.e., anti-liberal, anti-Marxist (Roman Orion for *regressus* of course dialectical)[2]

2) it must lay claim to totality (in every sense: uniformity, not a single impulse left to itself)

3) its criterion is not coherence, but only success, for this reason it seeks to adapt successfully to every situation. (Controlling the basis: people or state) Therefore Fascism defined as a "movement." Actualism {*Aktualismus*} (...) with ambivalence fixed or resolutions: ruling class, property (...) therefore, in addition: deceit and cynicism (removes also the *regressus*).* Propaganda as art (National Socialist propaganda = the influence of opinion as such)

---

* {The meaning of some of these fragments is unclear in the original German. In such cases we provide a literal translation.}

VII. How can Fascist propaganda be implemented? Begin here by studying (in the period of the conquest of power) the pre-existing susceptibility for it in the social body. Schema of propaganda: nation—socialism—promise of happiness. Crisis creates work in many places.

Distinguish especially <u>middle classes</u> / <u>unemployed</u> / <u>youth</u>.

Conclusion: of this section: the inclusion of individual social strata {*Schichten*} is not decisive—what we are dealing with here is also a petit-bourgeois movement. But the most essential task of this propaganda is precisely the dissolution of social strata, the total influence of opinion itself. So, again: How can Fascist propaganda be implemented?

VIII. The use of force {*Gewalt*}, more precisely: of <u>terror</u>. For Mussolini's Arditi, very characteristic that Hitler views the SPD as terror.[3]

1) Force as regression
2) Force strengthens the semblance, makes it real;

Here: Terror is always exercised by the superior power: not out of cowardice, but because otherwise there would be no successful ignition.

Terror is denied, because taboo.

Terror <u>integrates</u> into the regime: its function: to create <u>fear</u>. The constant pressure of fear—decisive condition of the liquidation of all concepts and their largely arbitrary implementation. [Preceded by:] Fear = hysteria.

IX. The means of changing human beings to increase their receptivity. The artificial production of the mass, in which individuals find themselves in a hypnotic state.

Hitler on this: a classic of mass technique

The art of mass images {*Massenbildkunst*}

[Preceded by:] Stupefication {*Betäubung*}! The speech! Radio

(The lack of culture proves that it is not about the people. Nothing blossoms here)

[Preceded by:] Here also: aesthetic effect.

"Mass" in the socialist sense.

Concluding formulation: In the space staked out by terror, concepts are set in motion on the debris of concepts. In order to be injected into the masses in the appropriate manner . . .

X. <u>The functioning of propaganda</u>: propaganda is not an incidental aspect of the regime but intrinsic to it.[4] After the seizure of power, it really takes hold, since the antagonistic play of social forces is by no means eliminated; {this antagonism} must therefore be continuously concealed lest it run riot and explode "classlessness."

Fact: that the Fascism of the ruling class is different.

That it—pro gress*—realizes the neutral economy.
Contradictions:
Autocracy—export necessity
Family—state youth
Church—Volk/leader
Worker—Entrepreneur

[Like] a motorized troop, the propaganda wave is sent everywhere, where cracks are to be plastered over. Main motif of propaganda: never leave the people alone!

Important! Contradictions in the propaganda itself, but these generate shocks and fear—are therefore useful.

Chaos ensues, since no one knows what is propaganda and what action. Who serves whom? [Line added here to refer to:] Meyrowitz[†]

a) National Socialism used to oppose the relativism of science. Today science opposes the relativization of National Socialism. (But a bourgeois consciousness is forming)

b) Class is released from caste

c) Capital must make sacrifices in order to preserve itself [preceded by:] 9th July.

d) Against everything that the world contains: thus, against churches, against monisms.

e) Crimes against morality {*Sittlichkeitsverbrechen*}. Discontinued after a series of trials, since eroticism was not effective, and continued with new series of criminal trials for treason.

Translated by Bernadette Boyle, Graeme Gilloch, and Jaeho Kang

NOTES

1. [There follow after "Power" {*Macht*} a number of symbols that cannot be deciphered with certainty.]
2. [*Römischer Orion für Regressus natürlich dialektisch*: uncertain reading.]
3. [*ansieht*: uncertain reading.]
4. [*abgewandtes* {incidental}: uncertain reading.]

---

* {Space in "pro gress" here is present in the original text.}

† {Kracauer is probably referring here to Henri Meyrowitz, who was born in Darmstadt in 1909, studied law at the University of Frankfurt, and moved to Paris in 1933. He was the author of numerous books and articles on the law of armed conflicts.}

5
Disposition

[At the top of the page Kracauer records a "Titulary" of the planned essay/book:]
<u>Titulary</u>:
<u>Total Propaganda</u>

    A. The genesis of total propaganda
    B. The character of total propaganda
    C. The method of total propaganda
    D. Total propaganda on the way to power
    E. Total propaganda as instrument of power

DISPOSITION

10, 11, 12, 13 July 1937
    <u>Total Propaganda</u>

A.
Genesis of Totalitarian Propaganda

I. <u>The independent life of mental {*seelischen*} structures</u>, concepts, etc.* Their economic classification a new problem.

---

* {The underlining throughout this text appears in the original.}

II. The founders of total dictatorships. Identification of the core troops (demobilized officers, the déclassé, bohemians, adventurers). They are excrescences of war. About the direct postwar situation in Germany and Italy: national humiliation, ruination of the economic and social organism; defeat of the socialist upsurge. This situation and the war induced psychological {*seelischen*} structure of the core troops produce the mentality and objectives of the totalitarian type: nation and/or people as the ultimate entity. Enhancement of the national power apparatus. Dream of unlimited expansion of power of the nation (= people = people's front) and/or the state, the communities of the people {*Volksgruppen*} . . . In order to achieve this power once again, the people must be unified. (Interesting Strasser's dictum: first fight for power, then German socialism = national unity; de facto vice versa: first German unity, then win power. The extent to which this comes from the army demonstrates the sympathy of the army for the fascist type. Yoking the fascist type with the interests of imperialist big capital. Origins of Sorel and Nietzsche. *Völkisch*.

III. Interim considerations on the postwar situation. This consideration serves to assess the objective chances of the fascist type in Italy and Germany.
   1) Finding, that for the forceful subjugation of the socialist movement, fascism and/or National Socialism were not united. Socialism hoped that the bourgeois regimes would maintain the upper hand.* But:
   2) In both countries, democracy is a distorted picture. A democratic character has <u>not</u> been established in either country. Therefore, opposition to attacks by the agents of power {*Machttyps*} is lacking. What's more:
   3) Both in Italy and Germany, capital is pushing—to differing degrees and for different reasons—towards dictatorship.

IV. From the outset, one thing is certain for the agents of power: that the unity to be achieved cannot be maintained with bayonets, but only through the conviction of the masses. He must win the masses, put them in mental bondage {*geistig fesseln*}. Where does this fundamental desire come from? From the experience of propaganda during the war. From the

---

* {Kracauer is referring here to the more moderate Majority Social Democratic Party in Germany, which supported the Weimar Republic and cooperated with bourgeois parties that also supported the Republic.}

experience of socialism (*Mein Kampf*). As a result, for the agent of power propaganda becomes necessary.

V. How does the agent of power see the situation which is to be changed? His attitude defined by the will to re-establish and to perfect limitlessly the national power apparatus. Thus, he sees with hatred: the fragmentation into parties, into the right and the left, the class struggle. In the interest of resolving this fragmentation, he wishes to win the masses. Thus, he sees with hatred that the concepts that mobilize the masses are not only claimed as their own by various parties but also linked to modern pacific concepts. "Socialism," a great ideal, is linked with pacifism and internationalism: the <u>national idea</u>, to make use of this catchphrase, is commandeered by money powers and so devalued for the masses—by the money powers who are themselves engaged in class struggle. The agent of power cannot structurally consider that the parties and their conceptual linkages are anchored in real interests, are therefore only symptoms; he recognizes only the ready images, not their origins. It seems to him therefore worth fighting against: the class struggle, the rigid linking of useful concepts with those of the enemy, moreover their linkage with certain social strata and interests, i.e., rigidity per se. In the end the agent of power type views with hatred the blinded masses' inclination towards communism.[1]

[Preceded by:] New Montage of the Concepts

VI. The situation depicted gives rise to the task of organizing propaganda by the agent of power: the objectives that excite the masses must be freed from their rigid attachment to the parties and to certain combinations of ideas and used instead for one's own purposes. This means uprooting established conceptual formations, in order to set the superstructure in motion. This is tantamount to overcoming the class struggle in the interest of national unity, serving to perfect the national power apparatus. But this only in appearance [*Bild*], not reality. The intention is not to eliminate class struggle by abolishing exploitation, but to compel the warring classes to come together in a show of unity—a show of unity, because the cause of class struggle is not to be eliminated, merely the symptoms eradicated. Thus, much greater emphasis must be placed on transforming the superstructure. It is clear that these interests conform with those of the large landowners and of big capital. The task of propaganda is to liquidate the prevailing "system" of ideas, to uproot ideas that excite the masses and to manipulate them in the interests of power. This is "movement" in the strictest sense of the word. The Italian "<u>Actualism</u>."

B.
The Character of Total Propaganda

I. Total propaganda must have the character of <u>regression</u>. Its fundamental trait: to go back beyond the French Revolution. (Anti-liberalism, anti-Marxism—borne by the important insight that democracy and Marxism belong together; the latter supersedes the former; accordingly anti-intellectualism). Appeal to the lower classes (as in war!!). But this regression itself dialectical: the democratic fiction seen through: socialist internationalism too early. As <u>Russia</u> professes <u>socialism in one country</u>, and in so doing regresses itself, there remains in fact as a possible next stage: the realization of national imperialism for the benefit of the ruling class. Sign of the dialectical character of regression: the Roman salute—its interpretation.

II. Total propaganda must lay claim to <u>exclusivity</u>. Its claim to totality is determined by the character of the regression. If democracy and Marxism are to be eliminated, there has to be absolute control over the formation of opinion; all the more so since—as a result of the efforts not to overcome class differences, but only to force them together—all emphasis is placed on organizing the superstructure. The demand is for total power over opinion formation. This is why totalitarian propaganda strives for autocracy. Here for the first time about the <u>relationship to authority</u> with its command and obedience up to the power over and sacrifice of life and death.

III. Total propaganda must see its criterion only <u>in success</u>. It does not serve to win over the masses for a doctrine or a program; in fact, it has absolutely no doctrine and the program serves only to win over the masses, since the true objective of the agent of power—reconstruction of the national power apparatus for the use of capital—wouldn't exactly be a useful propaganda medium. Apart from a few items indicative of capitalism's ideological inventory, such as the retention of property rights, no further objective remains, so that success in winning over the masses becomes itself the ultimate criterion (see Hitler, Goebbels).[2]

Thus: Propaganda per se, <u>propaganda in "pure culture"</u> {*Reinkultur*} ... Here also: the mystifying concepts of "Volk" (in National Socialism) and "State" (in Fascism). Furthermore, the position of the "<u>program</u>" (Muss[olini] and Hitler). Almost complete <u>ambivalence</u> regarding promises.[3]

[Preceding addendum in margin:
Volk: leader and a vicious circle

Volk: romantic, Savigny

State: Roman empire

Romans]

Due to the fact that propaganda measures itself only in terms of success—a fact which betrays that the executors of this propaganda only value power per se, but in general are nihilistic in their conduct towards all values—it follows that:

1) The irrelevance of the lie.—This is a propaganda medium. Meyrow[itz].*
Fin-de-siècle attitude. Here the openness to forms advertising, that Hitler and Goebbels develop in their propaganda.[4]

2) The aesthetic-<u>cynical</u> attitude of the executors of the propaganda. This attitude legitimated from the standpoint of nihilistic power. Here already the guiding formula for this propaganda clearly emerges: it is the <u>technique [*Technik*] of totally influencing opinion as</u> such. No wonder that the best formulations about propaganda stem from Hitler.

[Addition in the left margin:] Here: total propaganda always suspects the opponent of what it is and wants itself. See Heilbut: essential objectives: recognized as phenomenon and called "mirror reflection." How is this to be interpreted? It is a forced confession! The urge to reveal the truth emerges as a mirror reflection.

C.
The Method of Total Propaganda

In order to set the superstructure in motion in the aforementioned sense, propaganda must change the psycho-physical structure of the people, indeed the psyche itself. This is dependent on two decisive conditions:

The systematic use of terror. Terror = the creation of fear by means of violence.

Demonstrated by fascist punishment expeditions and Feme murders.

1) Terror is not an end in itself, for the agent of power proceeds from the assumption that it is a question of winning over the opinion of the masses.

---

* {Kracauer is probably referring here to Henri Meyrowitz, who was born in Darmstadt in 1909, studied law at the University of Frankfurt, and moved to Paris in 1933. He was the author of numerous books and articles on the law of armed conflicts.}

But terror also corresponds intrinsically to the regressive character of the "movement." Open terror reveals the dismantling of layers of civilization and the affirmation of elementary, conspiring role of nature in exploitation as a "principle of nature." Terror as a sign of monopoly capitalism, of monopoly as such. Of course, regression is dialectical and so terror also contains a revelatory moment. Direct terror uncovers the terror basis of class society (Hitler on the "terror" of the SPD, Nazis in general on the "terror" of the system). Remark: terror always implemented by the dominant power, not out of cowardice, but in order to peel back layers of civilization; in order to create a passageway for raw nature.

2) Terror therefore not an end in itself, but a means to the end of carrying out the task of propaganda. It facilitates this task in a twofold way. Terror

   a) produces fear in the people to be won over, the fear takes the fear from the concepts, under its pressure mass-mobilizing concepts can be separated from their interests, put in motion and redirected.[5] (Terror, comparable with drumfire, the function of which is to wear down the enemy to prepare an assault on their position.) Examples of this fear (Paris World Exhibition?). Chronic fear creates hysteria, leads to a blurring of the lines between reality and semblance. The spell takes effect, the ground slips from under one's feet. Lies and inversion of images in this state are matter of course. [Preceded here by:] Corruption.

   Remark: terror is denied not out of a sense of shame, but because it must remain taboo in the interests of the propaganda and because its denial heightens fear further and, making the lie true tests the effect of the terror (just as with the lie of the grotesque = Aryanism).

   b) reaffirms the illusion—the illusion that class divisions have been overcome and a community of the people has been established. Blood appears to give truth to the illusion, to make it real.

3) terror not only the condition of total propaganda, but propaganda itself. It has appeal because

   a) it excites the (economically and socially determined) sadomasochistic structure of its executors and victims and

   b) it appears to be the product of limitless power. Power attracts. Why? (Reflect!) [How to include Horkheimer's interpretation of terror: terror as the revenge of those who have fared badly against the happiness of the fortunate.]*

---

* {The square brackets here are Kracauer's own. Here, also, we see another example of Kracauer's genuine interest in Horkheimer's analysis of authoritarianism.}

II. The Systematic Production of the Masses

1) The <u>structure of the mass</u>. Individual consciousness diminished in the mass. In addition, the mass as a source of energy.
2) But not every mass is a mass in the sense of the Moehl type.[6] Here, an analysis of the <u>revolutionary</u> mass: it consists in principle of members of the exploited class and subscribes to a doctrine. It is not the end, but the means. Its revolutionary energies are to be used. It is not a homeland [Heimat] either, (as the mass of the dictator), but by (all means) a passage or passageway to a homeland. The diminution of the individual consciousness has here a progressive aspect to it.

    [Noted in left-hand margin:] mass as homeland
3) The mass in the sense of the agent of power is instead a prerequisite of the effectiveness of total propaganda. What is it? The recipient of suggestions. Interject here that ideal mass is one which unites people with the most varied real interests = symbol of the community of the people [Volksgemeinschaft]. Mass from the street! In order to be that, the mass is sedated, hypnotized and prepared in every way. Means employed to this end:
    a) the long wait (see Hitler)
    b) the symbols
    c) the <u>speech</u> itself with its repetitions. <u>Speech</u> not <u>writing</u> (opposing the <u>Enlightenment</u>!) Written language enlightens.

    No matter what the subject of the speech, it always moves from horror to happiness. Like sensationalism, it exploits concepts that have been mobilized and that excite the masses. Horror and the promise of happiness both equally present. Ultimately, the content of the speech is not what really matters; instead, the mass hypnotizes itself (citation from Silone "Bread and Wine").

    [Preceding the paragraph:] Charlatan!
4) Since total propaganda depends on maximizing its influence, the preexisting "natural masses" do not suffice; instead, it systematically produces new masses.

    The innumerable gatherings, festivals, celebrations, radio masses.
    For the purpose of consolidating the mass:
    Marshalling the masses with rituals (marching = war and "movement") and the art of mass images [*Massenbildkunst*].

    [Preceded by:] The mass as "homeland" for Hitler

    The goal would be that each individual constantly finds themselves in that state in which they are a member of the mass (this is contradicted, however, by esteem for the family; but that belongs in the chapter on antinomies).

[Preceded by:] Speaking choir

Postulating the <u>ideal of the personality</u> in no way refutes mass as ideal. There have to be people there to manipulate the masses and what does personality mean here anyway—the superior man? Ley quotation about the superior caste (see Heiden I)

[Preceded by:] Myth

5) The crowd not only means of propaganda, but propaganda itself.
   a) It seems to represent national unity, the community of the people and its effect is therefore propagandistic (Hitler says: the individual finds his homeland in the mass). That the mass is not the people is proven by the lack of culture. National Socialism produces no culture.
   b) It represents power, which attracts
   c) Its effect (therefore becomes mass ornament) is aesthetically appealing. An effect in the material present. Embellishing existing conditions with aesthetic, decorative features, disables the forces aiming to change them.

Concluding remark: In the space demarcated by terror the superstructure is set in motion and, after the mass-mobilizing concepts are set free, they are injected at the most effective time and place into the masses. [as the most dangerous weapon, see Goebbels]*

D.
Total Propaganda on the Way to Power

1) Starting thesis: the propaganda of the power squad would not prevail if there were no existing receptivity for it. (Proof: the decline of National Socialism in the Dollar Years 1924–29, initially of bourgeois democracy): but such a link between propaganda and situation has to exist since, after all, propaganda develops in close contact with the situation.

   <u>The social basis of propaganda, its natural foundation:</u>

2) What matters to the propaganda of the agent of power: liquefying the superstructure = destruction of rigid parties, as already partially occurred during the postwar crises (= poor blanket term, must be discarded) . . . and

---

* {Kracauer's own square brackets here.}

the societal developments caused by them. The crises, etc. have the effect of objective terror, they generated in the different strata fear, which took the fear out of the concepts. In all circumstances, it is the "movement" which profits. A number of strata are particularly susceptible to its propaganda.
[Added here with an arrow:] Workers!
3) Outstanding role played by the middle class, that stratum stretching from the petit bourgeoisie to the liberal professions.
   a) Their abridged sociological analysis; they are partly regressive—partly progressive (white-collar employees)
   b) Proletarianized by the hyperinflation. As white-collar employees and academics, they become acquainted with unemployment during the crisis of 1929/30.
   c) What should the proletarianized, déclassé middle classes do? They originate in the bourgeoisie but find no representation of their interests in the bourgeois parties. <u>Economically</u> proletarianized, their <u>middle-class</u> interests are equally poorly <u>represented</u> in the proletarian parties. Should they, therefore, pledge allegiance to the proletariat? They are hindered by the glaring weaknesses and one-sidedness of the SPD and KPD (the latter international and unable to see the whole picture). Furthermore, the <u>risk of parting with a traditional psychological structure is too great</u> (see Horkheimer).*

The entire superstructure retreats from the middle classes, for as little as Marxism appears an alternative, they see though capitalist ideologies just as much. The spiritual wasteland which plagues them, the cult of distraction / dissipation (see work on "white-collar employees").†
   d) Important to add: the untenable position of the proletarianized middle classes between the parties, and their distance from the production process create a natural affinity between the mentalities of the middle-class mentality and the agent power. (the middle classes must also wish for a false reconciliation of class antagonisms, not their elimination {*Aufhebung*} in a sociological sense). Furthermore: the agent of power is, in fact, usually of middle-class origin.

---

* {Kracauer is referring here to Horkheimer's concept of "cultural lag," which he introduces in his introduction to the Institute's 1936 *Studies on Authority and Family*. For the English translation, see "Authority and the Family," trans. Matthew J. O'Connell, in Max Horkheimer, *Critical Theory: Selected Essays* (New York: Continuum, 1992), 47–68.}

† {Kracauer is referring here to his own study, *Die Angestellten*, which was first published in 1929. In English: Siegfried Kracauer, *The Salaried Masses: Duty and Distraction in Weimar Germany*, trans. Quintin Hoare (London: Verso, 1998).}

[But that does not mean that the "movement" is petit bourgeois!]
4) <u>The role of the unemployed</u>—lumpen proletariat—inadequately grasped by class concepts.
5) <u>The role of the youth</u>—also distant from class and inadequately grasped [by class concepts]
6) <u>Peasants</u>, etc.
7) The social process thus leads to the formation of masses particularly receptive to the propaganda of the agent of power. How is propaganda carried out in relation to the different strata of the population? It deals with each in its own way, promises each heaven on earth. (Program: "political advertising") (see, for example, Strasser's speeches intended for workers)—compare with Hitler's speeches in industrialist circles. Total propaganda has been reproached with this (it takes money)—very unjustly. In fact, it only uses given propensities, without identifying with a particular stratum. Its goal is precisely the dissolution of the strata which embody various interests, total influence over opinion formation per se, for the sake of power. It functions according to horror and happiness—sacrifice and bliss. That appeals to the sadomasochistic type.

[Preceded here by:] Heroism

E.
Propaganda as Instrument of Power

1) <u>After</u> the seizure of power—i.e., after the establishment of a totalitarian dictatorship—can propaganda cease? No! For two reasons:
   a) The construction of the national power apparatus is just one stage on the way to the imperialist goal. Thus, propaganda must be continued—as foreign policy—on an international scale. Installation of propaganda a./b. explicit propaganda acts.*
   b) Propaganda cannot stop domestically either since its content—community of the people, elimination of class struggle, etc.—is in reality not achievable. This means propaganda becomes an essential component of the dictatorship (Ministry of Propaganda and Public

---

* {It's unclear what "a./b." signifies in the original text.}

Enlightenment). Terror is incorporated into the system (jurisdiction), the mass eternalized.

2) No need to consider world propaganda here since it proceeds in the same way as domestic propaganda striving for power. [The implementation of terror is facilitated by perfecting the *potential de guerre*;* the incitements are, for example, the global threat of Bolshevism—Volk without living space—but all suggestions are of course interchangeable].† Investigate solely the—ideal typical—development of propaganda directed inwards; since it alone is an ongoing process.

[Added in margin, left:] Do not forget:
a) continuation of crisis
b) enforced censorship

3) After the seizure of power follow necessarily attempts to realize propagandistic promises. But these measures and institutions do not remove social antagonisms; at best they paper over them. Propaganda has to give the impression that semblance is not semblance, but reality. This takes place by:
a) creating, with these measures and institutions, sinecurists and beneficiaries of the regime who are happy to accept these attempts at face value; [Added in margin:] Corruption
b) pressing on with the relevant measure and institutions to the point of grotesque absurdity. The absurdity of the Aryan paragraph, for example, heightens terror and serves as a doctrine of faith.

Summary: All the fulfillments of propaganda are at the same time themselves propaganda; since they undeniably represent realizations, without however attacking the reality of class itself, they incline toward an attempt to uproot—at least psychologically—the concept of reality.

Comment: The more that total dictatorships develop, the more dominant the sphere of psychological pseudo-reality becomes in them, related to insanity. Pseudo-reality could only become reality if dictatorships succeeded in achieving their ideal of total autarchy, but that would mean attaining absolute world domination. But not even then, since pseudo-reality reveals itself as just that in the immanent contradictions in the superstructure of the regime (family, freedom of art, church, etc.).

4) Concurrent with this development of propaganda, there occurs in fact an enhancement of the national power apparatus. Its characteristics: fulfillment of the aspirations of the masses. Controlled national (military) economy

---

* {"Potential of war."}
† {Kracauer's own square brackets here.}

[progressive tendency]. All this under the pressure of the crisis (Mussolini's speech in Silone). Who profits from this? Large-scale industry, high finance. [Closely tied to capitalism, but the axis is the party. Does it call the shots? Can it shift over to the "second revolution," to Bolshevism?]*

5) At a certain stage propaganda becomes worn out insofar as it relies on specific convictions and the nihilistic character of the regime becomes ever more apparent.
   a) Propaganda must wear out because
      α) social antagonisms gradually break through again, which were only covered up and were not—even with the enhancement of the national power apparatus—done away with. Such antagonisms are:
         those of the classes
         those of autarchy and the world economy
         economic and social (...)
         as a result of this, various particular real interests and interest groups are created, which tend toward different ideologies.
      β) the <u>contents of the propaganda are in themselves contradictory</u>
         Family affirmed and denied
         Art free and bound
         Religion registered as a positive force and opposed as worldly
         Youth disciplined and anarchic
         Culture should be made and should not be made, etc.
   b) The nihilistic nature of power is revealed precisely in the regime's increasingly open reliance upon the armed forces, from which it originates, and in its imperialist objectives. Devaluation of the party.
6) To avoid economic decline, which would mean the end of the regime, the <u>propaganda must change</u>. Its change in function consists in the closer alignment of certain <u>contents and convictions</u>. The nihilism of the agent of power breaks through—as had the nihilism of the exercise of power—and increasingly reveals itself as what it was intended to be from the beginning: the technique of totally controlling opinion as such (—as trivialization). In view of the antagonisms and contradictions surfacing everywhere, it becomes complete power. Keeping the masses in line, regardless of how it's done. That is their function. The image of the fencer.

---

* {Kracauer's own square brackets in this paragraph.}

[But world propaganda also becomes the domestic agitator of the masses. Thus, the increasing importance of foreign policy. Foreign policy actions increasingly become means of propaganda.]*

Further: Wherever a weakness is exposed, similar to motorized troops, any old concepts and/or the ruins of concepts are hastily deployed. It is not about their content. Propaganda formalizes itself. More decisive than its content is the rhythm of the waves of propaganda, its artful acceleration or delay. The shock. The contradiction between word and deed can become propaganda, the change of the measures in itself. Interesting: NS Propaganda, which opposed/set itself up against relativism in art and objectivity in science, is driven to the complete relativization of all content. Mass mobilization for its own sake is its end and its nihilism becomes manifest. Born of war, it tends towards its own destruction in war.

Translated by Bernadette Boyle and Graeme Gilloch

NOTES

1. ["moreover" and "blinded" uncertain in Kracauer's original text.]
2. ["indicative" uncertain in Kracauer's original text.]
3. ["promises" uncertain in Kracauer's original text.]
4. ["advertising" uncertain in Kracauer's original text.]
5. ["takes the fear" uncertain in Kracauer's original text.]
6. [Kracauer is likely referring here to Ernst Moehl, *Hermann Goering. Ein deutscher Führer* (Paderborn und Würzburg, 1934).]

* {Kracauer's own square brackets here.}

PART 2

The Caligari Complex (1943–1947)

INTRODUCTION

In this section, we consider Kracauer's writings dating from his arrival in American exile in April 1941 to the publication of his retrospective social-psychological study of German film during the years of Weimar Republic, *From Caligari to Hitler* (1947), the major work that was so central in enabling Kracauer to obtain the requisite visas for leaving occupied France. All of these writings in some way orbit around the Caligari book, in which so many of his ideas come to fruition, and especially the attempt to interweave the study of particular images and their resonance with the inner workings of (certain) minds. Nevertheless, we can divide these texts into two main categories. First, there are those that examine specific propaganda techniques and motifs, as well as audience psychologies in relation to Nazi newsreels. These studies were seen as a direct contribution to the American war effort and to work combatting the spread of National Socialist ideas. Second, there are those that are concerned with studying American audiences for the important purposes of identifying, understanding and countering fascist mentalities and anti-Semitism in the United States itself—"the enemy within," so to speak. Most significantly, there are various drafts, sketches, and fragments pertaining to Kracauer's proposed test film project, a social-psychological investigation using film as an experimental device to expose latent anti-Semitism and other racist tendencies using selected American students as subjects. Although Kracauer himself drafted several versions of the screenplay of the film, it was never made, and the project came to naught. These various documents have never been published before in the original English.

Kracauer's research projects at this time on propaganda in general, and on the medium of newsreels in particular, were conceived against the background of his ongoing research on the Caligari project. Some of these studies first materialized in the United States with help from members of the faculty of the New School for Social Research, such as Alvin Johnson, Hans Speier, and Ernst Kris, as well as the director of the Museum of Modern Art Film Library, Iris Barry. Kracauer's first American publication, the review article "Hollywood, the Movie Colony—*The Movie Makers* by Leo C. Rosten," appeared in *Social Research* in 1942, a journal edited and published by the Graduate Faculty of the New School. The first tangible outcome in relation to German propaganda was a pamphlet, *Propaganda and the Nazi War Film*, issued in 1942 by the Museum of Modern Art Film Library, which explores two feature-length campaign films—*Feuertaufe* (*Baptism of Fire*, 1940) and *Sieg im Westen* (*Victory in the West*, 1941)—both of them largely composed of newsreel footage. The study emphasizes three key points regarding the efficacy of German war newsreels: they had to show the actual footage of events themselves and not simulations or reconstruction; these newsreels were extended in length (up to forty minutes); and they were subject to rapid distribution so that the scenes depicted were fresh from the frontline. Later this brochure was incorporated as a supplement into *From Caligari to Hitler* in 1947 (hence we omit it from our selection).

Working in the field of cultural sociology and communication studies in America in the 1940s, Kris and Speier, among other émigré scholars, were themselves extensively engaged with quantitative analyses of German media and political communications. Kris's work on German radio propaganda was highly influential in the early stages of media and propaganda research.[1] It is little wonder to find close theoretical affinities between Kracauer's and Speier's views on the impact of fascist propaganda on the transformation of white-collar workers. Since the mid-1930s, Speier had comprehensively researched the structural changes of salaried employees in modern society and, in particular, the role of German white-collar workers in the rise of Hitler. From the 1940s onward, Speier investigated how the radio communication of war news in Germany played a particular role in the transformation of the masses. Kracauer's second study of Nazi newsreels, "The Conquest of Europe on the Screen: The Nazi Newsreel, 1939–1940," was originally produced for the Experimental Division of the Study of Wartime Communication in 1943. It was published in an abbreviated version in a 1943 issue of *Social Research*, which included a major article by

Hans Herm, "Goebbels' Conception of Propaganda," and Speier's "Nazi Propaganda and its Decline."

Kracauer's short report contains some fascinating insights, including notions that figure prominently later in his theory of film. One reads, for example, that "film surpasses other arts in that it reflects the visible world, to an extent hitherto unknown. Everyday life, with its infinitesimal movements, its multitude of transitory actions, could be disclosed now there on the screen." Moreover, he notes how early German cinema presented pictures featuring "the city street as the place where the 'man of the crowd' perceives the kaleidoscopic configurations of everyday life; they are full of house facades, window dressings, strangely lit rooms and physiognomic details." The unique capacity of film for the redemption of physical reality is anticipated here—perhaps not surprisingly, since such ideas, as Miriam Hansen notes, had already been formulated in Kracauer's Marseilles notebooks as he was waiting to escape from occupied France.[2] As for the newsreels themselves, Kracauer emphasizes that their power derives from a number of key features. For one thing, they are able to construct the sense of a single unified narrative through the use of image sequences, which seem to merge into each other and stand in stark contrast, Kracauer suggests, to the plethora of heterogeneous episodes characteristic of contemporary American newsreels (a point later reiterated in his article "A Duck Crosses Main Street"; see part 3 in this volume). Additionally, Kracauer notes that the Nazi newsreels—grounded in the techniques, practices and skills perfected by German cinema during the Weimar years—give much greater emphasis to the images themselves rather than to the commentary and subtitles. Kracauer argues that images can speak for themselves to a much greater degree. This is important because they stimulate an emotional response from the audience. Propaganda does not rely on an appeal to reason and intellect; instead, it manipulates emotions and presents images in the form of an integrated totality. The spare commentary of German newsreels is far more effective than the verbosity of their American and British counterparts, which are distinguished by a deluge of words. Kracauer also notes the key role of music in the newsreels—not just Wagnerian symphonic music with its leitmotifs, but also popular songs and familiar melodies, prompting nostalgia, sympathy, and identification. The cinematic qualities of German newsreels are truly different from other forms of screen propaganda, especially that of the Allies. The clever use of intercutting, the presentation of dramatic landscapes and seascapes, and an overall emphasis on movement and dynamism all contribute to what Kracauer sees as an aestheticization of war—a clear echo of Benjamin's notion of the aestheticization of politics with which he concludes in his famous 1936 "Work of Art" essay.[3] Finally, Kracauer highlights how Nazi newsreels succeed in contrasting the figure of the Führer, as a solitary and distinct individual, to the mass into which the individual has been wholly dissolved. The mass itself becomes a motif in the form of an adoring crowd, victorious soldiers, flag-waving parades; the image of the mass itself becomes an ornament. This theme of the remote leader as an auratic figure—in Benjamin's sense, of maintaining a distance no matter how close it may be—is developed in Kracauer's article "The Hitler Image," which was published in 1944 in the *New Republic*. Here, Kracauer comments upon the way Nazi newsreels present the Führer as a quasi-mythical being, a kind of savior who heals the sick; as an artistic genius, who turns his marvel Olympia into a living being; as the "lord of hosts" directing his generals; and as a great leader, who is the object of adoring crowds. Kracauer suggests that, amid such sycophantic representation, attempts "to humanize the idol" by placing him among weeping children or next to a faithful warhorse, prove less than successful. Hitler is much more at home when pictured with dutiful soldiers—the cannon fodder of the Wehrmacht.

So far in this volume, we have been concerned with Kracauer's writings on totalitarianism, propaganda, and the masses. The materials pertaining to Kracauer's "Below the Surface" project are of a different kind. Kracauer's interest here is not so much in communication techniques, particular ideologies, or forms of persuasion, but rather in the development of a social-psychological experiment to test the susceptibility of America itself—that is, a liberal democratic capitalist society—to authoritarianism and anti-Semitism. Kracauer's beloved medium of film was not to be the object of the analysis; instead, it became a methodological tool used to investigate deep-seated and latent psychological predispositions, tendencies, and prejudices. The project came into being in the context of the Studies in Prejudice program—a collaboration that started in the late 1930s between the Scientific Research Department of the American Jewish Committee and the members of the Institute for Social Research, who, like Kracauer, found themselves in exile in New York. The possibility of using film as a tool of empirical social research, by depicting an incident and then using a series of questionnaires to tease out audiences' responses, seems to have originated with Horkheimer as early as 1941.[4] The involvement of Kracauer, newly arrived in America, remains unclear in this initial stage. The project was resumed in 1945 when Kracauer engaged in a flurry of communications with Horkheimer and Adorno in Los Angeles, and with Lowenthal and others in New York. The first version of the screenplay for the twenty-minute film was proposed under the title

"The Accident." The second version bore the title "Below the Surface," or "Below the Surface, Final Version," and was produced by Kracauer. There is also another version of the script in which some of characters involved are named for the first time. The project was dogged by competing suggestions and countersuggestions as to precisely which questions should be asked in the follow-up to the film screening. More seriously, the issue remained of who would make the film, and how exactly it would be funded; indeed, these were to prove fatal to the project as a whole. "Below the Surface" sank, but not without a trace. The documentation of the project was strewn between different archives, including those of Kracauer himself and Max Horkheimer, until it was eventually published in German translation.[5] We are publishing here a variety of documents relating to this failed enterprise for the first time in their original language.[6]

Although many of the details of "Below the Surface" remain unclear, the general intention is nonetheless evident. The film was to be shown to small groups of students drawn from American colleges, and then their responses to events on-screen were to form a data set in which levels and degrees of prejudice could be measured and established. In a manner that would probably fail our current ethical standards for research methodology, the student test subjects were supposed to remain ignorant of the purpose and design of the experiment itself. The film events themselves were intended to provide sufficient distraction and diversion to disguise its principle intention. In accordance with his long-standing emphasis upon methodological digression, Kracauer was at pains to emphasize that genuine attitudes could only be captured if the experimental subjects themselves were unaware of, or unable to second-guess, the experimental goals. The screenplay itself went through various changes, and, most importantly, it was decided that different variants of the film be shown in which the accused person would be Jewish or African American or white American white-collar workers—the latter as a kind of control variant. The action is as follows: on an overcrowded evening subway train taking commuters home from their workplaces in the city, a woman encumbered by a large vacuum cleaner falls through the rear door of the carriage but is saved by safety chains. Emergency brakes kick in, and the train stops in the tunnel. An argument breaks out among various passengers (an array of types) when the vicious accusation is made that the woman did not fall but was pushed, her assailant being Jewish, African American, or white. Passengers take a side, and the tensions rise. It is probably at this point that the film would have been paused, the questionnaires distributed, and the views of student subjects elicited. Would they share the prejudicial views—anti-Semitic, racist—of the lead accuser, the clubfoot peddler? Or would they see through such malicious allegations as the expression of bigotry and hatred? Once such data had been collected, the conclusion to the film could be shown. Now recovered from her ordeal, and unharmed by her near-death experience (the vacuum cleaner is completely destroyed!), the woman is able to refute the spurious allegations that have been made: she just tripped and fell. No one is to blame. Calm returns, and the train moves off. The End.

"Below the Surface" will probably not strike the reader today as a particularly subtle or sophisticated social-psychological experiment. Various characters involved in the events are certainly rather crude stereotypes, serving essentially as mouthpieces for different ideological positions. As we have made clear in our previous discussion of the screenplay, what one sees in this film is a veritable rogues gallery of figures embodying particular preoccupations of Critical Theory: the linkage of forms of ignorance and irrationalism; bourgeois prejudices that lie just below the surface in everyday life; working-class solidarity with the marginalized; and the spinelessness and supine attitude of (American) intellectuals. But if the plotting and characters are rather crude, nonetheless Kracauer's test film project remains of interest for us because its pioneering attempt to utilize the medium of film in social scientific research looks to get below the surface of public opinion and reveal the American unconscious. It is a fascinating example of Kracauer seeking, as Wiggershaus puts it, to "combine European ideas and American methods"—or, more precisely, to develop a new critical empirical research method as a key component of Critical Theory.[7]

NOTES

1. Ernst Kris and Hans Speier (and associates), *German Radio Propaganda: Report on Home Broadcasts During the War* (New York: Oxford University Press, 1944).
2. Kracauer was part of the larger émigré community in Marseilles at this time, which was memorably depicted in Anna Seghers's 1944 novel, *Transit*, and—more recently and more allegorically—in Christian Petzhold's 2018 film, *Transit*, which was based on Seghers's novel.
3. Kracauer attributes the camera's continual concern with figures in motion—especially columns of soldiers, military vehicles of all kinds, aircraft, and shipping—to pleasures of movement itself inculcated into German youth by such organizations such as the Wandervögel and other hiking groups. A more likely reason for the emphasis upon the speed and movement of troops, we suggest, would be as a contrast to the stasis and immobility that characterized trench war experiences of 1914–1918.
4. It is worth noting that the Institute would use a different version of this method in the Group Experiment (Gruppenexperiment): the first major empirical study it conducted after reestablishing itself in Frankfurt in 1949. This study analyzed West

Germans' attitudes about recent historical events and current political topics, such as World War II, the Holocaust, and American occupation. In this study, the subjects' responses were provoked not by a film, but by a fabricated "stimulus letter" that was supposedly written by an American military officer, who was skeptical about Germans' willingness to accept responsibility for the recent past. As with the film "The Accident," the stimulus letter was used to expose attitudes that lay below the surface and would not be revealed by standard questionnaire or interviews methods. See Friedrich Pollock and Theodor Adorno, *Group Experiment and Other Writings: The Frankfurt School on Public Opinion in Postwar Germany*, ed. and trans. Andrew J. Perrin and Jeffrey K. Olick (Cambridge, MA: Harvard University Press, 2011).

5. "Projekt eines Testfilmes," in Siegfried Kracauer, *Werke*, vol. 2.2 (Frankfurt: Suhrkamp Verlag, 2012), 470–99.

6. For a more detailed account of the history and themes of this ill-fated project, see Graeme Gilloch and Jaeho Kang, "'Below the Surface': Siegfried Kracauer's 'Test Film' Project," *New Formations*, no. 61 (2007): 149–60; and Graeme Gilloch, *Siegfried Kracauer: Our Companion in Misfortune* (Cambridge: Polity, 2015), 146–52.

7. Rolf Wiggershaus, *The Frankfurt School: Its History, Theories, and Political Significance*, trans. Michael Robertson (Cambridge: Polity, 1994), 410.

6

The Conquest of Europe on the Screen

The Nazi Newsreel, 1939–40

As far back as the early days of the Polish campaign the Nazis began a series of organizational steps to incorporate the newsreels in their system of war propaganda communications. They insisted upon authentic shots of warfare, extended the length of the newsreel, and speeded its release. In addition, every possible means was employed to force these pictorial records upon the naive population, and to spread them abroad in appropriate versions.[1] It is evident that such reorganization of the German newsreel could not be accomplished without changing its character. In terms of the standardized American film types, the Nazi war newsreel now keeps midway between the normal newsreels and the shorts.

The following comment is based on a set of eighteen Nazi newsreels issued during the years 1939 and 1940.[2] They cover the period from the Polish campaign to the Battle of Britain, and includes, besides the warfare proper, scenes of civilian life and activities in the occupied countries. As is well known, the newsreels of that period helped in undermining the moral resistance of neutral peoples and governments. It is true that their undeniable effectiveness may have been partly due to the profound impression then being made all over the world by the German conquests themselves; but the effectiveness of the Nazi newsreels is doubtless traceable to their own specific nature as well. The Nazis know how to arrange the propaganda content in a compelling way, and also they excel in persuasive cinematic devices. Because of space limitations only these devices can be presented here. The film devices used in the German newsreel command special attention, not only because they contrive to increase and supplement the effects of the topics, but also because they follow a line that deviates considerably from the ways of the American film of fact.

The normal newsreel consists of a more or less casual mixture of various bits of news. This applies both to the American newsreel of today and to the weekly record that was issued by the German U.F.A. before Hitler. It would be interesting to learn the full extent to which the Nazis have superseded that hodgepodge of episodes by a purposeful arrangement. Are there any rules governing the relations between episodes of military and civilian life, activities in the occupied countries and at the home front, political events and mass agglomerations? And how do the Nazis manage to canalize the spectator's mental processes through their planned succession?

Unfortunately, the material at hand is too limited to settle such problems. Only one compositional device can be determined with absolute certainty: the Nazi newsreel tends to unify the news instead of dividing it. Time and again several successive stories are connected to form a whole. Pictures of an unsuccessful English air raid over occupied Norway imperceptibly run into a lyric glorification of the German Spirit of attack against England; Hitler's visit to his soldiers is the middle part of a unit that opens with derisive shots of the English king and ends in the destroyed Maginot Line.

As a result of its use of these large units the Nazi war newsreel has not much in common with the American. It is a species combining traditionally fashioned episodes with sequences that vaguely recall the March of Time or World in Action series —-vaguely, for a closer approach reveals decisive differences between the American or British type of short and the "unit" within the Nazi newsreel. First, this unit is not necessarily concerned with one theme alone; second, the episodes of which it is composed are linked more frequently by pictorial than by verbal transitions. Such fusions of diversified contents have most often the character of picture units. But before their composition is dealt with, it is necessary to consider the share of the pictures, the commentary and the music in the organization of the whole newsreel.

I

The part these components play is easily recognized and defined: in the Nazi war newsreel, pictures prevail over the commentary. This preeminence of the visual element is an extremely important and consciously handled device. That it is peculiar to the Nazis can be proved by a quantitative comparison of their newsreels and analogous American films. The rough estimate that in the latter the words cover about 80 or 90 percent of the shots is certainly not exaggerated. In the Nazi newsreel the commentary inclines toward brevity and, for long intervals, lets the pictures explain themselves. Sixteen of the eighteen newsreels have been examined with regard to the quantitative relation between their verbal and visual parts; the result is the finding that, on an average, only 31 percent of the total number of shots are accompanied by words.[3] Thus the Nazi commentary does not even extend along one-third of the film's footage, while the American spreads over nearly its whole length.

To make the German newsreel in this way would scarcely be possible, of course, without the existence of numerous skilled cameramen capable of furnishing lavish material. The staffs of the High Command, the Propaganda Ministry and the film companies have neglected nothing in this respect. And it is solely due to their organizational preparations that the Nazi newsreel editors can shape a scene like that showing the welcome offered to troops returning from the front—a sequence brimful of pictorial details, such as two soldiers jumping together from a freight train, boys creeping into a tank turret, a raised hand holding a hat against dark foliage, and an old woman's head behind a gun barrel that slowly passes by. One recalls, too, the enormous stock of newsreel shots available for the full-length German campaign films; "Victory in the West" was drawn from film material of about one million feet.[4]

By subordinating the commentary to the visual element, the Nazis employ a truly cinematic procedure. The film surpasses other arts in that it reflects the visible world, to an extent hitherto unknown. Everyday life, with its infinitesimal movements, its multitude of transitory actions, could be disclosed nowhere but on the screen. That films cling to such little phenomena never consciously evaluated before, may be related to their descent: they originate in the sphere of popular art, and there is no doubt that the plain people are always intimate neighbors to the many objects surrounding them.[5] And this inclination toward the minute is furthered by technical possibilities inherent in the film. The ubiquitous camera can detail any subject or part of a subject, show it from various angles, and thereby approach its very nature. A work of art comes closest to perfection when it complies with the specific conditions under which it is achieved, and this is exactly what the Nazi newsreels set out to do. In so far as they play off the picture against the word, they expand within a dimension which belongs entirely to the film.

Their persistence in this line may be explained by the influence of powerful traditions. The German film grew up in a period of revolutionary crises and social insecurity. Chaos spread in Germany from 1918 to about 1923, and as its consequence the panic-stricken German mind was released from all the conventions that usually limit life. Under such conditions the unhappy, homeless soul not only drove straightaway toward the fantastic region of horrors, but also moved like a stranger through the world of normal reality, seeing its conventional forms in such a way as to change them into weird, abnormal structures. At that time Karl Grune, Lupu Pick, G. W. Pabst and other film directors portrayed apparently familiar objects and made them seem new. Their early pictures feature the city street as the place where the "man of the crowd" perceives the kaleidoscopic configurations of everyday life; they are full of house facades, window dressings, strangely lit rooms and physiognomic details.

Thus, the Germans introduced a cinematic realism deeply rooted in their particular experiences. And this was done with a perfect insight into the language of lights and shadows, and by means of a camera which, in "Variety" and "The Last Laugh," became as movable as the unfettered mind directing it. It is not astonishing that such a cinema felt strongly attracted by the realism in the Russian screen epics which, headed by "Potemkin," poured into Germany after 1926. In their desire to explore the human environment through pictures the Germans not only adopted many Russian camera and editing devices, but also took advantage of certain material contents stressed in those films. The same desire proved active in Ruttmann's "Berlin," a late silent composition which connected multifold shots of Berlin everyday life in a rhythmic way, so that this life seemed to exhibit itself on the screen. Ruttmann continued to work under Hitler until he was killed in Russia.

While the pre-Hitler Germans employed these techniques to conquer more and more provinces of the bible world, the Nazis are using them with quite another intent. In emphasizing the role of the visual they bolster those efforts that attempt to repress the intellect and directly affect the emotional life. The predominance of pictures in the Nazi newsreel is synonymous with a minimum of verbal explanations. In addition, the pictures themselves are so selected as to work in the desired direction. Taylor has said of the Nazi propaganda tracts that they supersede rational argumentation by "pictures and symbols." Nazi speeches, too, dwell upon metaphoric turns, for the spell of the image smothers the interest in motives and reasons. Totalitarian propaganda in general consciously attempts an approach to the unconscious language of primitive tribes. And this orientation directs also the visual element in film. Thus, many newsreel shots are not inserted simply to illustrate some event, but function, exactly like the images in Nazi speeches, as "pictures" within the pictures. Instead of enlarging the spectator's knowledge they aim at arresting his mind and shaping it through figurative meanings. Swastika flags hoisted on the roof of Versailles and the Eiffel Tower symbolize the significance of the French campaign, and, hence deepen its emotional resonance; clips of the reopened market in occupied

Brussels detail birds, girls, onlooking soldiers, cheese and other peaceful things for the obvious purpose of making a future German peace appear idyllic. All objects that function as current metaphors are widely exploited, particularly children and flowers; sufficiently piled up, they are indeed able to impart to the most sinister projects an air of radiant innocence. Thus, the succession of literal pictures is interrupted time and again by metaphoric pictures. Their frequency clearly indicates the reason such a conspicuous part is assigned to the visual element.

In the whole formed by the commentary, the visual element and the music, the last is an active partner. Although the score—a symphonic interweaving of themes of a Wagnerian character, popular melodies and songs—offers no interest in itself, it strikes any audience as a weighty contribution to the whole. One cannot look at Nazi newsreels without sensing that their music goes far beyond a mere accompaniment. Its expanded role is necessitated by the specific tasks it has to achieve. When in this kind of film the visual element lacks verbal elucidation, music proves indispensable in determining the effect of shots that imply several meanings. What could be intimated by a commentary can emerge also from an appropriate tune. The same stilted musical motif is synchronized with the market scene at Brussels and with an episode picturing occupied Copenhagen. This leitmotif of the little nations, as it might be called, is probably intended to give the impression that all conquered peoples are full of confidence in the Germans. But the faces on the screen lend themselves to other conclusions as well.

Besides its interpretative duty the music performs an even more vital function: that of shortening the way from the visual element to the senses. Nazi newsreel music makes the motor nerves vibrate; it works directly upon the bodily feelings. Like a fifth column these themes penetrate the spectator's subconscious and soften it up for an eventual invasion by pictorial suggestions. While Hitler visits the Strassburg cathedral the old German folksong is heard, "O Strassburg, O Strassburg, du wunderschöne Stadt..." Meeting both demands imposed upon the score, this song not only interprets Hitler's Strassburg excursion as a symbolic re-annexation of former German territory, but also drags the audience—at least any European one—into a sentimental mood. To many listeners the song has been familiar since childhood. And the emotions it arouses in them are likely to become identified with the accompanying pictures.

In their desire to utilize the whole stock of emotions the Nazis occasionally reverse the usual relation between the visual and musical elements. This is the case in the scene which, through juxtaposed shots of battleships, submarines and bombers, celebrates in a rather lyric way the offensive warfare against England. The synchronized song, a tune apparently popular in Nazi Germany, includes the words: "Give me your hand, your white hand, good-bye, my sweetheart, good-bye. For we are sailing, for we are sailing, against Eng-e-land— Eng-e-land, ahoy!" Words and melody alike attempt to express the feelings of soldiers determined to make the decisive attack. In this scene music goes beyond its mediating function and takes a leading role. It is complete; it shapes emotions itself, instead of merely opening the emotional sphere to pictorial assaults. Whereas normally music accompanies the pictures, here a visual accompaniment is synchronized with the music. Not by chance is the scene composed of a somewhat incoherent mixture of shots. They need not be connected, for they confine themselves to illustrating the meaning of the song.

II

The predominance of the visual element over the commentary results from two basic devices. The first of these concerns we might call the distribution of the contents. In the Nazi newsreel, as we have seen, the great majority of facts and propagandistically important topics are set forth through pictures. To be sure, there are a few episodes in which this rule is abrogated by shifting the burden to the commentary. One of them shows prominent enemy statesmen, such as Churchill, Eden, Duff Cooper, Reynaud and "the Jew" Mandel; since their faces cannot be transformed into odious caricatures, name-calling is resorted to, the shots becoming mere illustrations of exhaustive insults. Another sequence, concerning the German reconstruction efforts in conquered Norway, is intended to boast that more than sixty bridges were rebuilt and that the German Labor Service helped to finish a railway line planned by the Norwegians; here words are necessary to convey the information. The same holds true for an episode denying London's report that English bombers reduced Hamburg to ruins; the claim itself could have been denied with the aid of pictures alone, but the commentary takes the lead, the reason being that the Nazis wished in addition to advertise the death of twenty-two children whose corpses they did not like to picture, and also the presence of foreign newspapermen who are not recognizable as such on the screen. In all these sequences the propagandistic intention could be achieved only verbally. The words cover much footage, but they express nothing that might be expressed in the pictures.[6]

These, however, are exceptions. Throughout the newsreels a practice prevails that is closely connected with the Nazis' reluctance to give more than purely technical information, if any at all. But information is only one theme among others, and every normal newsreel episode reveals how rich in content a series of shots can be. The verbal statement, "Various armed formations push forward in Poland," refers to about eighteen clips which considerably enlarge the scope of that reserved sentence. They show columns of artillery and infantry on a highway; night conflagrations obviously caused by guns; heavy guns in action; a row of infantrymen taking cover along a slope; soldiers machine-gunning; soldiers running across a field; a cannonade; horse-drawn wagons moving.

It is interesting to compare this procedure, characteristic of the Nazi newsreel, with the American methods of narration. In one of the German reels the statement, "German Stukas start for an attack on military objectives in England," is accompanied by about twenty shots of the take-off and flight of the German squadron. A recent American newsreel uses about four shots to show a similar action: Army planes taking off from a carrier. But these few shots, amounting to only one-fifth of those in the Nazi film, are deluged by the following commentary: "Amy-Navy cooperation is graphically evident as an airplane carrier transports a fleet of Army fighting planes—though not taking them to any harbor. At sea, some distance off-shore, the speedy fighters take off and deliver themselves to their destination. One after another, they go. On to an undisclosed destination, and to the Army planes the Navy men say 'Happy landing'."

The point is that here and elsewhere the American commentator, not content with furnishing information, gets florid about the events on the screen. It is as though he were bent on outdistancing the pictures. Unlike the Nazi speaker, he formulates in words what doubtless would emerge from the pictures themselves if the many words allowed the audience to look at them. Precisely this is the trouble with the typical American and English procedure: it makes spectators uncertain whether they should follow the pictorial development or the verbal narration. And since they are not able to do both at the same time, their attention is divided, thus weakening the effect. Much could be gained by ending this competition.

The second basic device which makes the pictures predominate in Nazi newsreels concerns their structural relation to the commentary. As a result of purposeful arrangements, the pictorial part of the Nazi newsreel gives an impression of continuity. If we disregard those large units in which several successive stories are connected mainly by means of pictures, we can distinguish two methods that are employed to produce this impression. One of them is an appropriate timing of the verbal statements. When a newsreel episode ends and the subsequent one begins, it often happens that the commentary accompanying the new episode begins not with its fade-in but only after a certain lapse of time. In similar American films verbal explanation rarely fail to set in with the opening shot of a sequence, but in the Nazi newsreel, pictures generally precede the words. Five shots silently depict the construction of a suspension bridge, before the commentator tells that this bridge is part of the new German highway system. Preceding a verbal account of English troops in Egypt are two airplane shots of a mosque and the pyramids, indicating where the story will be located. And the statement about German Stukas starting for an attack on military objectives in England joins the pictures at a moment when they have already begun to develop the action. As a result of this method of timing, the pictorial parts of successive episodes seem to run into one another, despite their different content. Thus, the feeling grows in the spectator that he is carried along by a flow of pictures. In addition, the shots that come before the commentary refrain from revealing their meanings while they pass by, thus resulting not so much in straining the intellect as in loosening the emotions. Under the influence of these shots the whole pictorial flood tends to work in the same direction.

The other structural method for creating the impression of such a current consists in shaping verbal statements as incidental remarks to some shot. In the episode that pictures the welcome offered to returning troops two shots of soldiers enjoying the people's cordiality are accompanied by the words, "No one will ever forget this day." Similarly, the commentator extemporizes, "A bunker at the outskirts of the town," during a series of clips of Hitler's drive through Strassburg. Statements of this kind are frequent and seem to be inspired by the pictures. It is as though the speaker, confining himself to the role of a spectator, silently followed the course of the pictures and only here and there, struck by a detail or a sudden idea, felt the desire to comment. Particularly he likes shots that lend themselves to a propagandistic interpretation. One sequence shows the Bastille Square crowded with people listening to a loudspeaker announcing the Armistice conditions in French.[7] The camera, voluptuously dwelling on the people's dejection, turns after a while to a man who is haranguing a group, and the commentary speedily assumes: "Here one discusses Messrs. Reynaud and Mandel. The opinion about them is rather obvious." The subsequent shot is also exploited. It represents a conclave of four women, one of whom illustrates her chatter with a gesture simulating the secret pocketing of money. This provokes the bold conjecture that "Here one talks over the warmongers' flight abroad." By eliciting such propagandistic subtleties from the pictures, the speaker encourages the audience to plunge like him into their flood.[8]

While the Nazi commentary thus consciously submits to the hegemony of the pictures, the commentary in Anglo-Saxon films is always tempted to go even beyond their content. In the World in Action short, "Our Russian Ally," several shots of Russian troops and tanks moving across the snow are bound up with the elaborate narration: "From the trenches of Leningrad to the gates of Rostov they stood to arms all through the bitter winter of 1941. All winter long they wrote across the bloodstained snow a chapter of heroism of which the greatest armies of history might be proud. And come what may, on this two-thousand-mile battlefront, where the titanic forces of the swastika and the red badge of courage struggle for dominion over one-sixth of the earth's surface, Russia knows that her true war power lies not alone in arms and equipment but in the inner spirit of a people." As long as there is such a tendency to bury the pictures under a snow of words, there is a danger that the film will degenerate into an illustrated editorial.

So much for the structural relation between the visual element and the commentary, though it should be added that these two components have a certain inclination to run contrapuntally. Thus, the statement, "At noon military bands play in the towns of the occupied zone," belongs to a number of shots intended to show that German soldiers and French girls are mutually attracted. Another fascinating instance is provided by several shots of a big swastika flag hoisted on the Eiffel Tower—symbolizing the statement that "Paris is in the hands of the Germans"—which are followed without any marked interruption by pictures reveling in accumulated swastika banners and cheering crowds. Where does this spectacle take place? Instead of locating it the somewhat delayed commentary declares, "Marshall Pétain, deputy minister of the newly organized French government, asks the German government for the conditions of a possible armistice." In other words, the speaker, indifferent to what is shown on the screen, continues reporting on the events 'that sealed the French defeat. After two more shots he joins in again with the remark, "At a meeting in Munich between the Fuhrer and Mussolini terms of an armistice were agreed upon." Through this contrapuntal procedure the Nazis succeed in affecting the psychological system by at least two simultaneous suggestions.[9]

III

Since the visual element prevails in the Nazi newsreel, the camera and pictorial editing devices are of special interest. Some of them are not peculiar to the Nazis. Of these, one may be cited because it is used rather frequently: the falsification of reality by means of tricks. The sequence in which French girls and German soldiers seem to take to each other is decidedly not so much a true image of life as the illusory outcome of clever cutting. The mirage is accomplished through a series of clips that alternately picture smiling girls and gaily chattering soldiers. Then, to deepen the impression that the groups are really in touch with each other, the girls look toward the right, while, in the subsequent shot, the soldiers turn toward the left-whereupon the girls appear once again, seemingly pleased at having been noticed by the males. For a cutter with many newsreel clips at his disposal it was rather easy to palm this romance off as the finding of some cameraman. Sometimes it happens that the changes worked upon reality by studio specialists are admitted openly as such. British film material showing English recruits drilling on a barracks square has been re-edited with the aid of optical tricks to shape a comic strip for the purpose of making the audience laugh at England's amateurish soldiers. But the Nazis have no monopoly on cinematic jokes of this kind. In fact, the dance steps that Hitler's columns perform in Cavalcanti's "Schicklgruber Dancing the Lambeth Walk" are even funnier than the goose-steps of those caricatured English recruits.

One of the devices that seems to be confined to the Nazi film is an important, though simple, use of the camera to feature moving troops. It is not by chance that marching columns are the property of the Nazi regime. In calling them into existence, Hitler took advantage of traditions emanating from the old German Youth Movement—a revolt of middle-class youth against the obsolete conventions of the parental world. The rebels wanted to free and renew themselves. But since they failed to recognize the social and political reasons for their unrest, they were unable to visualize any real goal, and thus confounded true freedom with freedom as an end in itself. They opposed the adults by rambling in loose groups with guitars with no definite destination. This kind of wanderlust was animated by their belief in the then popular idealistic conception that the world is in eternal movement toward eternal ideals; these being inaccessible, the young idealists revered movement as a goal in itself, and as they wandered aimlessly they all had the gratifying feeling of expressing a metaphysical creed. After the last war this attitude persisted in the youth of middle-class Germany, which was then becoming increasingly affected by the worsening economic situation.

Hitler knew how to exploit these traditions. He persuaded the young people that he was sent to realize their ideals, and thus influenced them to join the S.A. The rambler movement was lost in the Nazi movement, the loose groups in uniformed, marching columns. And yet some of the young people may still have believed that nothing essential had changed, for Hitler was on his guard not to destroy the spell of the movement by a premature disclosure of his aims. Significantly, such official Nazi films as "Hitlerjunge Quex" and "Triumph of the Will" end with enormous S.A. columns marching off against the sky. It is as if these processions were intended to convince the spectator that they are carrying on the unending movement of the past. Because of their ideological importance, marching columns are a leitmotif of the Nazi war newsreel, making the audience itself participate in a spectacle that symbolizes irresistible advance.

All this accounts for the effort of the newsreel cameramen to cover the columns' movement as completely as possible. Placed near some highway or city street—usually at the outside of a curve—the camera first captures the whole scenery, with a column advancing toward the foreground, say from the left. As the formation moves on, steadily growing in size, the camera pans to keep it within the field of vision. Presently the column passes immediately before the camera. But is it still the column? The former long shot picturing it as a unit has now changed into a close shot that singles out several individual soldiers or even mere fragments of them: their heads, their torsos, their marching legs. Thus, the whole gives way to the puzzling movements of its parts. This disintegration not only testifies to the Nazis' desire to depict the movement from all conceivable angles, but also serves in an impressive way to prepare spectators for the reconstruction of the unit. The constantly panning camera still follows the soldiers, who now reappear as a column as they march on to the right. In the final position a long shot shows the scenery, with the now recreated column marching off. Time and again the Nazi newsreel uses this kind of drawn-out pan shot, which gives the movement of a column in all its details and yet never neglects to represent it as continuous.

Another characteristically Nazi device is the occasional insertion of beautiful natural settings, which are not, as a rule, given much attention in newsreels. Picturesque seascapes open the episode that lyrically glorifies the Battle of Britain, and also preface the shots of German Stukas starting for an attack on English territory. In the latter the camera proceeds like a painter: a motionless soldier and a little shore gun are silhouetted against a sea that quietly mirrors the sinking sun. Both newsreel items attempt to evoke the spirit of attack-which is evidenced, too, by the cheerful songs synchronized with the bulk of the pictures. The seascapes have the function of facilitating this attempt. Before an attack is launched, soldiers often receive an abundant alcohol ration designed to weaken their instinctive fear of the coming battle. The supposition that these pictures play, for the audience, about the same role as the alcohol plays for the soldiers is the more justified as the pictures appear at the beginning of the two episodes. Their beauty is expected to put the mind into a state of aesthetic delight and thus repress the scruples of everyday life.

Thus, the Nazis profit by the power of aesthetic impressions in overcoming psychological resistance. In fact, these seapieces, which recall the magnificent posters of transmarine travel bureaus, work exactly like a stimulant. And there is no doubt that an audience intoxicated by their charm will unconsciously transfer that feeling to the subsequent praise of the attack on England. It should be noted that for certain reasons, fascists generally tend to visualize war from an aesthetic point of view. By extolling the "beauty" of war they obscure its real significance.

An important device is used in the composition of those large units that extend over several episodes: successive episodes are sometimes selected and linked in such a way that the transition between them conveys a propagandistic meaning. A transition of this kind is found in a unit that consists of the following four stories: King George attending Air Raid Protection exercises; King George visiting a Scout camp; Hitler among his soldiers; Hitler inspecting Alsace and Lorraine. It is obvious that the first two and the last two stories belong together, and the transition between them is shaped in such a way as to bring the contrast to the fore and exploit it in favor of the regime. Toward the end of the second the King appears amid the singing Scouts, imitating almost timidly the droll gestures that are part of their ritual. To prepare the ground for the contrasting effect, the commentary outdoes itself in ridiculing his behavior. Then comes the transition. Usually pictures do the job, but in this instance it is exceptionally performed by a verbal statement which, instead of being delayed, has already started during the last shot of the Scout camp. "While His Majesty, at a moment when England begins to fight for her very existence, does not know of any better way to use his time, the Fuhrer of the German Reich shares the company of his soldiers." As this pompous sentence progresses the two opening shots of the third story picture a multitude of soldiers informally saluting Hitler, who, after a further shot, will leave his car to approach the old war horse. Because of the contents of the stories which it connects, the transition implies that England is in a state of complete decay, whereas Germany is young and virile.

When the pictorial transitions, more prevalent, assume propagandistic functions, they are of the same demagogic nature. One of them links two parades: the parade of French and English soldiers in 1938; and that of German troops celebrating the seizure of Paris. Drawn from enemy film material, the flashback has evidently been inserted to heighten the impressiveness of the Nazi soldiers, whose goose-step shakes the famous Paris avenue. The contrast between the episodes manifests itself at their juncture. When the survey of past splendor is about to end, the Nazi cutter manages to turn one's attention from the cadets of St. Cyr and the mountaineer formations to the French colonial troops. In fact, the sequence concludes with two close shots of Negro faces. They are followed immediately by a shot which anticipates the whole Nazi show: the camera first points to the upper part of the Arc de Triomphe, then tilts down to a German infantry column moving past the monument, and finally pans to reveal endless columns participating in the parade. By confronting the colonials with the representatives of the master race, the transition not only deepens the contrast between the former Allies and the Germans, but also gives one to understand that the Nazi victory must be an outcome of moral superiority.

No less pretentious is a transitional passage within the visual part of a unit that includes three sequences: a detailed depiction of the Maginot Line, taken from a French documentary; the German attack on the Maginot Line, indistinctly illustrated by about four shots; Hitler's return from the destroyed Maginot Line to Berlin. Here the transition—it connects the last two episodes— underscores not so much a contrast as a consequence, that of the victory over France, and does so by an ingenious shot. After having shown a demobilized French fort the camera turns toward the left, captures the French bank of the Rhine and slowly continues panning and traveling in this direction, with the result that it covers not only the whole width of the river but also its German bank. The shot, its location fully explained by the succeeding picture of Hitler's car moving over a pontoon bridge, leads from the conquered Maginot Line to Germany in a sustained movement that symbolically annexes Alsace and characterizes the Rhine as a German river. Only a man who passes his possessions in review surveys in this way. A simultaneous statement merely confirms the shot's significance. Thus, a simple transition between two successive events goes far beyond its immediate duties, in the interest of propaganda.

IV

Many devices are employed to stress the suggestive power of those episodes that picture excited crowds and are thereby intended to make the audience participate in the regime. The Nazis excel in organizing masses on the screen as well as on the street. In the newsreels such crowds appear nowhere with more magnificence than in the combination of sequences illustrating Hitler's reception in Berlin. These sequences cover the following events: Berlin people preparing for the reception; Hider's arrival at the Berlin station (*Anhalter Bahnhof*); Hitler leaving the station and walking to his car; crowds cheering Hitler on his drive to the *Reichskanzlei*; Hitler and Göring on the balcony, cheered by immense crowds. Except for the second episode, showing Hitler's reception by high dignitaries of the Reich in the station building itself, all sequences are devoted to one and the same task, that of sustaining a unique mass demonstration from beginning to end. Ninety-eight shots reproduce this demonstration, with a thoroughness that depends, of course, upon the lavish use of well-equipped cameras. Significant in this respect are the various angles from which Hitler's entrance into the grounds of the *Reichskanzlei* has been shot.

Flags and flowers are the accessories of the grandiose show. Its description starts with five shots of swastika flags and standards which because of the manner of their representation, acquire a specific meaning. The camera approaches them closely, with the result that the screen is alternately covered by waving flags and a forest of standards, reminiscent of the enchanted woods which Lang in his "Nibelungen" film shaped after Boecklin's "Great Pan." The spell of that forest reinforces the lulling effect of the flags' undulations. These pictures are an opiate, making spectators submit more readily to the image of the mass.[10] Immediately after the flags a number of girls strew flowers on the street under the eyes of the. waiting crowd, while the commentator asserts, "The streets from the *Anhalter Bahnhof* to the *Reichskanzlei* will be turned into one carpet of flowers." The propagandistic value of flowers, resulting from their figurative significance, is supplemented by a few pictures showing this carpet from above. Flowers spread all over the screen, and it would be difficult to decide whether they are a botanical or a human mass. Thus, the camera forces spectators to associate the impressions of an exalted crowd with flowers. What strikes one first in the cinematic shape of the mass itself is the constant alternation between the whole and details of the whole. Distance shots of the crowds and close shots of some face appear in turn. But this alternation is not in itself so important as the cutter's endeavor to shift the attention from the individual to the mass. A closer scrutiny of the sequences reveals that the depiction of the mass demonstration is divided into a succession of scenes which almost imperceptibly run into one another. They are composed in such a way as to determine the course the spectator's mind has to follow. One of them, forming the finish of the first sequence, that of preparation for the reception, begins and ends with a long shot of the mass before the Berlin station building; between these is a series of four close shots, interrupted by a further long shot, detailing the efforts of the S.A. and the police to stem the mass. Another scene, contained in the sequence of Hitler's drive to the *Reichskanzlei*, proceeds in the same way: clips of the huge crowd frame pictures that pick out raised arms and heads. This cycle, characteristic of all scenes, introduces a movement leading from the mass to the individual and back to the mass dimension. The movement's meaning is obvious: it isolates individuals for the sole purpose of drowning them in the crowd, thus implying that they are nothing more than its elements.

Other devices, too, aim at depriving the individual of any autonomous value, and, conversely, attempt to make the mass attractive. The close shots prefer the faces of women and children to those of men. Many an innocent boy emerges for a moment from the mass. This predilection is explained by the fact that women and children are particularly susceptible to the influences of mass excitement; Hitler himself has called the crowd feminine. One of the furies has a baby on her shoulder. The camera dwells upon their hysterical faces and never tires of presenting screaming youngsters and girls in transports. Are they still private beings? They are part of a delirious crowd. How little concerned the camera is with maintaining the individual can be seen by the frequency of pictures that offer diverse parts of human bodies. The head of a woman appears between a hand and a sharp chin; the legs of a girl try to push away the jackboots of two S.S. men. These pictures intimate that the individual is not all of a piece—an assumption buttressed by several close shots of confused mass elements. One of them shows an inextricable muddle of arms, little swastika flags and heads spreading over the screen. To complete the impression of the individual's nullity the camera always pans and travels while giving details. Its constant movement denies the independent existence of the man in the crowd. How different from the classic Russian films! Even though these also indulge in crowds, they manage to show that they are a rally of individuals. What remains of the advancing mass of revolutionary workers in Pudovkin's "Mother" is the self-possessed face of the woman heading the procession.

Whereas these close shots blend anarchy and ecstasy, the long shots reveal a crowd which, in contrast to its elements, affects the audience as an entity. The bird's eye view works particularly to this effect. Cameras set far above show the compactness of the mass and disclose the strange beauty of this enormous and eternally surging body which suggests comparison with an ocean or an endless wheat field. Now it becomes dear why the carpet of flowers has been shot to make it resemble a crowd. Through this pictorial analogy the attractiveness of the crowd is strongly amplified. It must be added that the cameras pan over the whole mass as well as over the fragments composing it. Its immensity could not otherwise be grasped.

But the mass is not entirely autonomous. It depends upon Hitler. That Hitler masters the crowd is implied by the organization of the last sequence. It consists of two scenes, the first of which opens with four long shots of the cheering mass before the *Reichskanzlei* and ends with a shot of Hitler surveying the spectacle below from his balcony. The space between is filled in with detailed shots of the mass. This arrangement, in leading from the mass to Hitler, clearly shifts the balance in his favor. The subsequent and concluding scene, which is the climax of the whole, settles Hitler's relation to the mass by means of a very clever editing device. While the first shots of the scene picture first Hitler and Göring on the balcony, and then the ocean-like mass, the last ones show exactly the same objects in reverse order, so that the scene ends with Hitler. His images encircle those of the crowd, definitely subordinating it to him. The unique sovereignty he thus acquires is sustained by two further shots which, mingling with the closeups of mass elements in the interval, likewise show him enjoying his triumph. These closeups record almost exclusively the faces of youngsters. The preference given to them doubtless originates in the desire to stress the relation between German youth and its Führer.

Of hundreds of thousands absorbed by a crowd, which itself lacks complete independence, Hitler alone appears as an individual. He is composed; he seems an end in himself. "Chattering on his balcony with Göring while crowds cheered him on his return from France, he smiled, but there was no timidity about his crooked mouth"—this is the impression he made on Howard K. Smith (*Last Train From Berlin*) during that mass demonstration. Cinematic expedients help in idealizing his personality. He is always contrasted with a particularly distorted face or fragment, if not with the mass as a whole. And no sooner do the incessantly moving cameras light upon Hitler than they come to a standstill. By stopping momentarily their ceaseless motion they feature him as the true source and goal of the mass below (New York City).

NOTES

1. These measures have been dealt with in the author's study on "Propaganda and the Nazi War Film," Museum of Modern Art Film Library (New York, 1949).
2. These newsreels were made accessible to me through the courtesy of the Museum of Modern Art Film Library. They are undated. Some of them are in German, while others have an English commentary and are obviously versions for Anglo-Saxon countries.
    As for the later German newsreels, those from the winter of 1940 on, they continued as long as possible to advertise bloodless victories and steady advances.

Flight Sergeant Bill Orndorff of the RAF who spent seven weeks in Nazi-occupied Europe, in 1942, tells the *New York Post*, on November 13, 1942, of a newsreel he had seen there: "It was a Nazi film about the capture of Rostov—which would have you believe that the Nazis never lose a plane." But the more peace faded and the German death toll rose, the stronger became the criticism in Germany itself of that kind of film propaganda. According to Ernst Kris ("The Imagery of War," *Dayton Art Institute Bulletin*, October 1942), the Nazi authorities were forced to take these reactions into account. Since they do not dare to present grave setbacks in place of easy conquests, or to substitute the now deadly serious soldiers for the former gay columns, they have reduced the frequency of newsreel showings. And in what is left they picture more the innocuous and irrelevant sides of life in occupied Europe than warfare proper or any real problems.

3. The most striking instance of the absence of words is the sequence picturing Hitler's reception at Berlin by means of about 85 shots. Since the commentator's two sentences cover not more than 3 of these shots, that is, 3.5 percent, almost the entire episode runs like a silent film—except for the synchronized music and cheering.
4. See "Propaganda and the Nazi War Film."
5. See Erwin Panofsky, "Style and Medium in Moving Pictures," *Transition*, no. 26 (1937): 121–33.
6. It is noteworthy, too, that the introductory parts of the two full-length Nazi campaign films, *Baptism of Fire* and *Victory in the West*, are on the whole, nothing more than verbal reports illustrated by suitable shots. This is a consequence of their purpose. They have to summarize, from a Nazi viewpoint, the historic events that led to the Polish and French campaigns. The intent is not so much to portray history as to sketch a background. The succeeding parts, dealing with the campaigns themselves, proceed like the newsreels in stressing the visual elements at the expense of commentary.
7. It is an amusing fact that the excerpt drawn from the Armistice treaty in this sequence deals with the future of the French fleet. The loudspeaker records the paragraph: "Le gouvernement allemand déclare en outre solennellement et expressement qu'il ne formulera aucune revendication vis à vis de la flotte francais lors de la conclusion de la paix."
8. Because of this pictorial continuity particular caution is necessary in including clips drawn from Nazi propaganda films in anti-Axis films.
9. For a fuller appraisal of such cinematic polyphony, see "Propaganda and the Nazi War Film." The question may be raised whether also the above quotation from "Our Russian Ally" is not connected with its pictorial accompaniment in a contrapuntal way. But even though the narration in that instance refers to many more things than the few shoots shown at the same time, the little scene is by no means a polyphonic composition. Instead of adding to the theme of the pictures a new theme, so that both can work together upon the audience, the narrator imposes such a multitude of ideas that under their weight the pictures lose their force. The contrapuntal method does not all weigh any one theme to push another aside, but weaves them into a unit in which they are sustained equally.
10. Here the flags have a function similar to that of the beautiful seascapes mentioned earlier.

7

The Hitler Image

Monday, January 3, 1944

In the Nazi war newsreels every possible means has been employed to create an image of Hitler that transforms impassive spectators into fanatic followers. Gros once painted Bonaparte's visit to plague-stricken soldiers in a Jaffa hospital in a manner suggesting that he, like the Christian saints in Italian paintings of the sixteenth and seventeenth centuries, was endowed with the magic power of healing touch. Taking up this tradition again, one recent Nazi newsreel episode assigns the traits of a savior to Hitler. He enters a room full of severely wounded soldiers, and as he strides from bed to bed, his raised arm seems to exorcise all infirmities, while cripples and invalids look at him with an excitement that implies their faith in his thaumaturgical faculties. "They live to see the proudest day of their lives," the commentary modestly adds.

Hitler's inspection of the Munich art exhibition in 1940 offered the Nazi cameraman a gratifying opportunity to reveal that the savior is also a genius. Having passed along a wall of paintings and admired such items as an old mill covered with snow or a Dolomite rock glowing in the sunset, the Führer approaches some sculptures, and here his genius manifests itself. The moment that he looks at a young marble or plaster woman, her naked body slowly becomes luminous and shines like the Dolomite rock. The solemnity of the process is augmented by an accompaniment of Wagnerian music. It is as if the illuminated body miraculously reflected the brightness of Hitler's inspirational powers—a phenomenon of transference that reminds one of spiritualistic seances. This episode seems to be proof of the great degree to which film propaganda can count on the credulity of the masses.

Frequently Hitler appears as the lord of hosts: followed by his generals, he reviews parades, surveys destroyed fortifications or makes his entrance into a conquered city. After Hitler's tremendous military success, it was not difficult to represent him as the "victorious field marshal," but it must also be noted that the German film makers are experts at finding effective pictorial formulas to magnify this role. Close-ups of Hitler's head and raised arm against a cloudy sky elevate him above all morals; another shot relates his head to the spire of a cathedral in such a way as to give the impression that Hitler, too, is a towering event in German history. Whenever themes of mythological significance are to be shaped, the Nazi film seldom fails to choose the right objects and angles.

Hitler triumphant is never seen without those crowds that have become a regular institution in Nazi Germany. The background of his relation to them is unveiled in the newsreel sequence of his train journey to a Berlin feverishly awaiting the *blitz* conqueror of France. This record, as well as the subsequent survey of his Berlin reception, was made at a moment when Germany thought a victorious peace imminent. Hope and happiness animated people's faces in that railway episode, and it was as though, thanks to the prospects opened by the overwhelming French defeat, the usually prearranged excitement seen in so many Nazi newsreels had for once given way to a true cordiality. Symptomatically, these pictures focus upon small groups or even single persons rather than upon huge crowds. Workmen and farmers wave to the passing train, village children form an improvised lane along the tracks, and as the car stops in provincial stations mobs gayly besiege the car. Hitler behaves exactly like a popular movie star where he smiles down at a blonde girl handing him a bouquet or autographs pictures of himself and hands them out through the car window. But the significant point is that he never leaves the train to mingle with those who, according to the commentary, offer him "tokens of love, loyalty and gratitude." The triumphant Fuhrer withholds any such gesture of genuine intimacy—an illuminating fact in a scene designed expressly to show the close contact between him and his people. Is his reluctance the outcome of fear? It rather reveals his concept of leadership. The Nazi regime depends upon its ability to manipulate people; in the interest of self-preservation it must suppress spontaneous feelings in favor of directed ones. Now the enthusiasm of the people in the railway sequence is no doubt sincere. But precisely for this reason Hitler cannot join them outdoors. For by doing so, he would implicitly recognize his crowd as individual people and thus deny the principles upon which his power is based.

To humanize the idol, an episode shows Hitler in informal contact with his troops. In this one sequence he walks across a field without any ceremony. "An old war horse is allowed to share in the breakfast," runs the commentary. Indeed,

Hitler approaches a horse and feeds it cautiously. But even though it is a harmless, worn-out animal of the kind that is used in theaters, he looks uncomfortable in staging this show. His uneasiness is that of a man who keeps all creatures at a distance and tries for a moment to overcome this habit. Instead of endowing Hitler with human traits, the scene only succeeds in confirming his unsocial character. It reminds one of a scene in the Nazi documentary "Für Uns," where Hitler comforts some weeping children of fallen partisans by patting them on their wet cheeks—a caress which fails to produce the intended effects because he absentmindedly looks in the other direction while doing so.

The intermezzo with the horse is followed by two shots picturing Hitler amid a multitude of soldiers who greatly enjoy his presence. Two soldiers in the background take snapshots of him as he smilingly returns to the waiting generals and cars on the highway. The little scene breathes confidence. "Hitler displays a familiarity during this visit, which the commentary celebrates with the lyric words: "The Führer and his soldiers—an insoluble community guaranteeing the victory of German arms." Yet the two shots neither suffice to illustrate such pretensions nor do they allow any inferences as to the nature of Hitler's relation to the people in general. For soldiers differ basically from people in that they form organized units subject to the laws of discipline. They are, like Hitler himself, men in uniform, and in judging them for a moment, the corporal of the last World War still remains within his peculiar sphere—a sphere strictly separated from the world over which he rules. This scene does not make him appear more human or humble, but rather exhibits how knowingly he handles the instrument "guaranteeing the victory of German arms." Thus, some light is thrown on the Hitler behind the scenes by his official image on the screen.

8

Below the Surface

Project of a Test Film

Our <u>hypothesis</u> is the following:

A person who tends to accuse a Jew or any member of another minority of an action which that group, on the basis of its professional and traditional background, cannot be expected to commit (at least not with greater probability than a member of any other group) must be biased in some way against this group.

The <u>basic hypothesis</u> is as follows:

A person determined by an antisemitic outlook will introduce a relation of cause and effect between two unrelated parts of a situation.

To explain: the occurrence of the accident, on the one hand, and the being Jewish of the accused person, on the other hand, are not related either in fact or perceptually (that there is no perceptual relation is established by the control experiment in which the accused person, playing the identical role, is Gentile).

The crucial question is whether the person introduces the causal relation where it does not exist. If he does, this can only be on the basis of an antisemitic orientation.

If this hypothesis is correct, then the reaction to the film indicates the presence or absence of an antisemitic orientation in the given situation. The validity of this inference can eventually be checked against the correspondence between the reactions to the film and the other data, such as interviews and attitude scales.

HYPOTHESES

1. The frequency with which the Jew is judged guilty will vary directly with the antisemitism of the groups; i.e., the frequency will be higher in antisemitic groups than in non-antisemitic groups.
2. There will be significant relationships between the reaction to the film and the scores on attitude scales.
3. The ambiguous events in the film will be structured in the direction of the final decision.
4. Upon a second showing of the film there will be a trend to maintain the verdict previously reached.
5. The minority of the people will be prone to mention the man who reads the newspaper, and those who do mention him will tend to endeavor to achieve a most objective appraisal of the situation.
6. The fur-coat lady would get unfavorable reactions from antisemites.
7. In a Jewish audience there will be significant differences of reaction according to socio-economic levels; those of lower socio-economic level tending to exonerate the Jew.
8. The difference between variation II and variation I will be greater in the antisemitic groups.
9. In the group which shows a higher degree of accusation of the Jew, there will be fewer refusals to judge and contrariwise. If the refusal is not due to lack of cooperation in general, the male antisemites will show a certain degree of lack of cooperation, not the females.
10. Antisemitism is connected with anti-intellectualism in the sense of "sophistication." Sophistication has a negative connotation with the antisemites.

Examples of questions which the audience
   Will be asked after the showing:

1. Give a short report on what you have just seen. Tell the events without any commentary.
2. Which were the leading characters? Describe each one of them.
3. List each of these characters according to whom you like best, next-best, a.s.o. {and so on}, until the one whom you disliked most, and give reason why.
4. Do you think the crowd designated as guilty the right man?
5. How did the man behave when he was accused by the crowd?
   Cowardly   Courageously   Correctly
6. How did the two nuns behave? Do you think their sympathies at the end were with the crowd or with the accused man?

NOTES

We might experiment with the fragment of the picture which ends immediately after the accident. Therefore, the production should be done in such a way that we can make a break after the accident and before the talk starts.

Once in a while we might show the picture twice to the same audience in order to see whether the second showing (without the slow-motion part) has an influence on the audience's opinion.

Perhaps it is a good idea to test the difference of reactions if the Jew is represented as rich or simply average. This could be done very easily. For example, at the end, when the crowd turns against the Jew, he would raise his hand and a member of the crowd would say: "Look at that big diamond ring!" This remark could be left out in other versions.

Another, and even better, way would be for the policeman to ask the man his business. Then, when he is questioned as to his employer, he answers: "I am the owner." The next question concerns the address of the business. When that is given the policeman inquires: "What floor are you on?" to which the man answers that the business occupies the entire floor. After hearing the name, the policeman could even say: "Oh, you are the Mr. . . . ."

It should be well understood that we do not expect that any cross-section of any group would react to the picture in the following way:

The part of the cross-section which will see the Gentile accused would be expected to say: "The Gentile is not guilty," and the part, or at least a fraction of the part, which would see the Jew accused would say: "The Jew is guilty."

What we expect is that some of the group which sees the Gentile accused will agree with the accusation. The percentage of the those who see the Jew accused and agree will be somewhat higher if the group of which the cross-section is typical is biased to some extent. This bias is not necessarily an expressed one. It might be that the whole cross-section, when asked, whether the Jews are as desirable as other groups, would answer, "Yes." It is just this latent prejudice which can be tested by such means as the picture.

NOTES RE{GARDING} PEOPLE TO BE IN THE CROWD

Either the one-legged man or another character must imitate the Jew.

There should be an old lady having {*sic*} a dog in a basket and crying: "My dog, My dog . . ." when the commotion starts.

There should be a child who cries in the panic.

There should be one intellectual with horn-rimmed glasses.

There should be one very elegant lady in a fur-coat.

There should be two shipyard workers, but they should be dirty enough as to enable the antisemite to say that they look suspicious.

PROJECT OF A TEST FILM

Audience reactions are significant only if they are expressed spontaneously, involuntarily. The purpose of this test film must therefore be veiled. The interest of the audience must be diverted from the test proper and concentrated upon something else; in this case, on the fact that the testimony of eye-witnesses is nearly always unreliable.

On the other hand, we cannot veil the purpose of the film so that the audience is completely sidetracked. It would be advisable to insert motifs which keep alive or even stimulate the more or less latent racial or religious prejudices.

The subject of this film is an accident in a subway car. The accident occurs at the beginning of the film. This theme has been selected:

(1) to shock the spectators from the outset into identifying themselves with the characters in the screen;
(2) to arouse the spectators' emotional reactions from the beginning;
(3) to create argument among the screen characters, a passionate dispute designed to evoke participation by the audience.

The film should be interesting as a movie. A dull film would weaken the interest of the audience in the problems involved, thereby reducing the value of the test.

OUTLINE OF THE PLOT

A subway car stops at a station. Pressing into the crowded car are people coming, perhaps, from a baseball game. Among them, a one-legged, elderly candyman, tries to get in.

He is pushed aside by an obviously Jewish man.[1]

The one-legged man finally gets in. A girl offers him her seat near the door leading to the next car. From this place he follows the events, and eventually becomes the mouthpiece of what seems the "public opinion" in the car after the accident.

The one-legged man is to arouse sympathetic feelings among the audience. He will express antisemitic sentiments.

This is to arouse a slight bias.

As the subway starts moving, a man in front of the one-legged man is seen reading a newspaper. It hides his face.

A woman with a big parcel containing a vacuum cleaner is squeezed against the door leading into the next car. When the train rounds a curve, she clasps the latch, trying to keep her balance, and the door swings open.

At this very moment, for unknown reasons, a violent commotion occurs, involving four men standing close to the door. One of them is the Jew. The three others are presumably Gentiles—among them a rather tough guy. Owing to this commotion or to some other cause, the woman is pushed out of the door; she seems to slip through the safety ropes between the cars. The woman screams. People leap from their seats. A flash: the lights go out, the subway stops. An isolated flashlight and occasionally lighted matches allow the camera to show that the short circuit has been cause by the vacuum cleaner which has fallen onto the rails. (An accident of this kind has recently been reported in the *New York Post*.) The woman herself, caught by the safety ropes, is dragged into the car and cared for by a doctor who happens to be among the passengers. She is more shocked than hurt.

The man with the newspaper, undisturbed, makes a futile attempt to continue reading with the aid of kitchen matches.

Mass hysteria and a general fight develop.

Suddenly the lights go on again.

A slight comic touch is needed to prepare the audience for the shock to come. This character represents indifference.

We can see immediately that the accident was not dangerous after all. This is done to mitigate the shock effect, so that the racial prejudices will not be overshadowed by other reactions.

Two cops, accompanied by a subway guard, enter the car by the door opposite the door of the accident and push through the crowd toward the four men. Each of the four men is accused by some member of the crowd.

The man with the newspaper is seen absorbed again in reading.

(From this point on the film has to be split into two variants)[2]

<u>Variant I</u>: implies that one of the Gentiles is guilty; claiming indemnity, the hurt woman expresses the definite opinion that she was pushed out of the door not by the Jew, but by one of the Gentiles—the tough guy. The crowd seems to adopt her opinion. Only the one-legged man is dissatisfied.

<u>Variant II</u>: implies that the Jew is guilty: The woman loudly claims indemnity, without being interested in the problem of guilt. The antisemitic atmosphere predominates. The one-legged man remains the accepted leader.

The film ends, in <u>both</u> variants, with the cops taking down the addresses of the four men and the eyewitnesses. While they are doing this, the camera pans over the crowd—an extended shot including a close-up of the one-legged man.

Slow fade-out.

Caption: You, too, have been eyewitnesses of the accident. What is your opinion?

Now the questionnaires are distributed among the audience. They include many questions regarding the cause of the accident and each character involved.

One question is:

"Is the suspected person really guilty, and why?"

<u>The purpose of the two variants</u>: Both variants are shown to a sample of the social group whose racial reactions are studied. But, variant I is shown to a sample composed of other individuals than the sample confronted with variant II.

The sample shown variant I may be called sample I.

The sample shown variant II may be called sample II.

The degree to which the answers of sample I tend to be fairer to the suspected man than the answers of sample II—if such a difference can be observed at all—would provide us with an index of the amount of prejudice.

BELOW THE SURFACE

A Test Film Prepared for the
American Jewish Committee for
selected showings in connection
with questionnaire.

An impressive view of lower Manhattan, looking down from an elevation. Camera pans across Broadway, which is relatively empty, and stops close on clock tower as the hands reach six o'clock. There follows a brief montage of New Yorkers quitting work for the day and starting home, including:

> Office workers getting up from desks—
> Looking at watches—
> Covering typewriters—
> Powdering noses in the washroom mirror—
> Slipping on hats and coats—
> A factory whistle blows and we see factory workers down tools—
> Pick up lunch pails and coats—
> Punch out through the time clock—

A close view of the tower clock reveals that it is now a couple of minutes after six, and as we pan from it to the original scene of Broadway, it is now crowded, with more people pouring out of offices, bound for a subway kiosk. Dissolve to—

Interior, car of a New York subway express, northbound from lower Manhattan, evening rush hour. The train is in motion. It is already fairly full of homegoing types, and the establishing shots will give the impression of average Americans at the end of the day's work, tired and slumping, swaying in hard-packed, involuntary contiguity, each isolated with his or her own reading matters, his or her own thoughts.

A pan of close-ups starts well up towards vestibule with (seated) an OLD GENTLEMAN WITH FINANCIAL PAGE, on which he has started to check stock reports. Ad lib, a young STENOGRAPHER chewing gum and deep in a "Confessions" magazine. In any case, neither of these will speak or take active part, their value throughout being only as figures of persistent disinterest.

Camera moves in close to A WOMAN WITH A VACUUM CLEANER. She is standing in vestibule, against end door, the handle of the half-wrapped bundle over her shoulder and leaning against the door's pane. She is a mousey, puritanical little woman, middle-aged, middle-class, clutching her too-big burden with an air of frustration. As camera moves so close that it excludes everyone else, we begin to hear her thoughts, as given by her own voice with special effect in re-recording.

As she unwraps little corner of bundle and peeks in:	VACUUM CLEANER WOMAN'S THOUGHTS
	All right, now it's repaired. Now I can get to work tonight cleaning up the house again. All that dust and dirt, infection, disease ... I won't have them in <u>my</u> house. Clara always laughs at me—calls it silly. But it isn't <u>what</u> you do that counts—it's <u>how</u> you <u>do</u> it! (indicating cleaner) Might start on the rugs tonight—

Pan to TWO SHIPYARD WORKERS, standing. They are in work clothes, grimed, weary. They share a newspaper, but neither really reads it as, with far-away expressions, their voices—via similar technique—give their thoughts.

Both pretend dumbly they are reading paper.	FIRST SHIPYARD WORKER'S THOUGHTS
	Oh, boy, corned-beef tonight—that's what she promised. And after that shipyard all day! But the old Gal won't let my stomach down. She knows what's what—knows a woman's place is in the home—not in the shipyard. She'll have it all ready to dish up, smoking hot: good, chunky, fatty red corned-beef!
First worker goes through elaborate dumb show of asking whether second is through with page. First nods yes. First turns page. Both continue gesture of reading.	SECOND SHIPYARD WORKER'S THOUGHTS
	Spaghetti tonight—out of a can! Don't expect anything else. Spaghetti last night—spaghetti the night before. And don't kid yourself, it'll be spaghetti again tomorrow. Don't know what she spends my money on—certainly ain't on my stomach. Rivettin' all and then—spaghetti!

Camera moves to a middled-aged WOMAN IN FUR COAT, seated. She is a stout creature, and the conspicuous mink makes her look even more so. She is looking around car, much enjoying her lack of enjoyment, her gaze ultimately settling on a NEGRO youth in a Harlem zoot suit who is standing near.

As she watches NEGRO:

FUR COAT WOMAN'S THOUGHTS
All that company to prepare for tonight—and I couldn't get a taxi home. Well, we all have to make sacrifices nowadays—and I'm no snob. I like people all—like this, mixed together. Even colored people! Though I must say, the way that maid walked out on me just because of tonight's party... After all I've done for her, the dresses I gave her. No gratitude, Negroes... no loyalty. The minute you treat them like equals—you just can't do it! But—she <u>did</u> make such <u>darling</u> canapes! Do hope I can manage...

Camera moves to a policeman.

POLICEMAN'S THOUGHTS
O.K., Sadie, I'm on my way home right now! Kin hardly wait to get there. I'll be

BELOW THE SURFACE 167

NEGRO VERSION

Pan to TWO SHIPYARD WORKERS, standing. They are in work clothes, grimed, weary. They share a newspaper, but neither really reads it as, with faraway expressions, their voices—via similar technique—give their thoughts.

Both pretend dumbly they are reading paper.

FIRST SHIPYARD WORKER'S THOUGHTS

Oh, boy, corned beef tonight—that's what she promised. And after that shipyard all day! But the old gal won't let my stomach down. She knows what's what—knows a woman's place is in the home—not in the shipyard. She'll have it all ready to dish up, smoking hot: good, chunky, fatty red corned beef!

First worker goes through elaborate dumb show of asking whether second is through with page. Second nods yes. First turns page. Both continue gesture of reading.

SECOND SHIPYARD WORKER'S THOUGHTS

Spaghetti tonight—out of a can! Don't expect anything else. Spaghetti last night—spaghetti the night before. And don't kid yourself, it'll be spaghetti again tomorrow. Don't know what she spends my money on—certainly ain't on my stomach. Rivettin' all day and then—spaghetti!

Camera moved to a middle-aged WOMAN IN FUR COAT, seated. She is a stout creature, and the conspicuous mink makes her look even more so. She whisks her coat away from contact with the JEW, and looks around the car, much enjoying her lack of enjoyment, her gaze ultimately settling on a NEGRO youth in Harlem zoot suit who is standing near.

making a beeline down the block, and up the stairs—to where Sadie'll be waiting—with a tub o' hot water that I'll put these poor old Staten Island feet into and just let 'em soak there all evenin! Good old Sadie! Kin hardly wait!

Camera moves to close-up of a man's fat paunch in tight vest, with a gold watch-chain strung from pocket to pocket. Then to figure of a PICKPOCKET, a slick ratty little chap, standing next to man with vest and eyeing the watch-chain intently.

> PICKPOCKET'S THOUGHTS
>
> Fat jewelry on a fat man ... it depresses me.

Camera returns to the vest of the bystander. The watch-chain has disappeared.

> PICKPOCKET'S THOUGHTS
>
> Wonder how many other chances I'll have this evening to rebuke society's bad taste.

Camera moves on to a dowdy OLD WOMAN, with satchel on her lap.

> OLD WOMAN'S THOUGHTS
>
> Wanna be home—safe. Something's gonna happen. The stars said so for today. Folks can make fun of it, but astrology explains a lot of things. I'll just set for the evening—safe.

Out of open lid of satchel pushes the snout and cocked eye of a PUPPY. A kid's hand comes into scene—stops before patting puppy. Camera now includes LITTLE GIRL, gazing at the puppy longingly.

She makes a move to pet dog, but is restrained by glare from owner.

> LITTLE GIRL'S THOUGHTS
>
> Oh, dear, wish I was going home to a dog—'stead of just a baby brother. I think I like dogs better than people. Look at that. Now, dogs, they wag their tails and you know they want to be friends with you. And you can't scratch people's stomachs, mostly, either!

Pan to TOUGH GUY. He is a huge, surly brute, Prussian type. He is thumbing through a collection receipt-book, grim satisfaction on his jaw:

Turning to next pages:	TOUGH GUY'S THOUGHTS
	Morrisey, two installments, paid—yeah, they paid all right, all right—sure tried to get out of it. Greenwald, one installment. Smith—they didn't get away with anything, either. That old gag about meeting hospital bills first—nuts! A good day's work.
Shuts book away. A grin of anticipatory bliss:	And now home to Mama. My ol' Mama. A guy who don't feel real love and respect for his parents is a heartless mut—an' no American, besides!

His elbow jogs WISE GUY, a small, wiry, grizzled type with ironical expression, slightly too good manners, and an evening tie and shirt-bosom visible under his turned-up light overcoat.

He shrugs—smiles whimsically.	WISE GUY'S THOUGHTS
	Everyone else going home except me. Upside-down me, I go to work.
	Still, nothing like work in a nightclub for getting to know human nature at a glance.
Eyeing WOMAN IN FUR COAT:	Now there's a sure dollar tip. Millionaires in subways . . . this is certainly a democracy.
Camera moves with his eyes to WOMAN WITH VACUUM CLEANER. He shakes his head.	Uh-uh. Strictly cafeteria!
His gaze moves on to INTELLECTUAL. Speculatively:	HM! Big shot? Or just wishes he was?

Close-up of INTELLECTUAL standing in vestibule corner: a large, impressive, health-radiating type in good tweeds and ribboned glasses. He glances at some notes and then looks up, delivering a speech in his imagination.

Then, in quieter vein,	INTELLECTUAL'S THOUGHTS
	"Gentlemen, it's a privilege to speak here tonight to your distinguished membership of—may I say 'Doers'!—businessmen and other red-blooded men of action.'"
	Good—they mustn't put me down as a freshwater college professor!

Resuming the speech, in his imagination:	"Admitted, gentlemen, that's what I am by vocation, yes, but not by instinct! I'm the first to protest against our colleges' emphasis on intellectual theory instead of the solid virtues—There are problems too important to be understood by the mind alone. Problems which call for fewer laws and for courageous leaders, instead of beaurocrats {sic}..."*
Seeing SOLDIER further down car:	...real leaders, who won't be afraid to keep the younger generation in training. After all, human nature being what it is, there'll always be war... And military training makes young folks think about the <u>important</u> things in life.
During above Camera has centered on SOLDIER, a tall, good-looking kid in uniform, pfc. {private first class}.	SOLDIER'S THOUGHTS (in slow Vermont twang) She sure has the trimmest ankle... and the rest of her fits the ankle!

In gangly position and melancholy Jimmy Stewart mood, he is looking wistfully across aisle through gap in standees at:

Close shot CADET NURSE. At first she appears to look away, as if annoyed by his gaze.

But, as the camera comes very close, we see that out of the corner of her eyes she is looking back at the SOLDIER with an interest that matches his.

	NURSE'S THOUGHTS Well, I made him look at me, anyway. Though, a lot of good it does to have him look! He won't try to pick me up... the nice ones never do.
Intercut between them during following:	SOLDIER'S THOUGHTS Look, soldier, don't be a Vermont jokel {sic}. How far do you think you could get with a slick society dame as pretty as—gee, she sure is, all right, she sure is pretty! Wish I could show her I think so!

---

* [This is spelled incorrectly in the original text. The editors are unsure if the misspelling is intentional.]

Giving SOLDIER a quiet once-over:	NURSE'S THOUGHTS
	Five foot eleven, I'd say. No extra fat. Nice straight nose. Won't go bald before he's fifty. But what would he want with just plain run-of-the-mill Bronx goods like me? Times Square, Chorus Girl Land, that's where he'll get off.
	SOLDIER'S THOUGHTS
	Okay, even supposing you did get to know her ...

A SUBWAY GUARD enters car at lower end, and comes forging through towards vestibule.

She has a Red Cross First Aid Manual in her lap.	NURSE'S THOUGHTS
	I—I wish he's {sic} pick it up. No, not me, just—it!

The little manual plops to floor. SOLDIER leans awkwardly forward to pick it up, but gets his finger caught under somebody's heel.

The SUBWAY GUARD swoops up the manual, returns it to the NURSE, and passes on. In vestibule, the WOMAN WITH VACUUM CLEANER has to make way for him to open end door and exit through. As she inches back against door, the handle of the cleaner over her shoulder catches in the crack and, unnoticed by anybody, prevents a complete closing of door. Camera back to NURSE and SOLDIER.

As she crams manual into pocket:	NURSE'S THOUGHTS
	Of all the cheap tricks—and I played it! Serves me right.
Sits nursing his finger:	SOLDIER'S THOUGHTS
	Serves y' right for thinkin' she did it a-purpose! Wonder how good she is at bindin' up ...?
	NURSE'S THOUGHTS
	Wonder if he'd let me bind it?
His eye on his wrist watch:	SOLDIER'S THOUGHTS
	Gosh, take y' two whole hours, probably, to get up nerve to ask her to have supper ... that'd be eight o'clock.

	NURSE'S THOUGHTS
	Doesn't anything ever happen to—to anybody, ever?
	SOLDIER'S THOUGHTS
	9:30 before she'd even think of asking you home—
	NURSE'S THOUGHTS
	I guess not. Not on a subway, ever.
	SOLDIER'S THOUGHTS
	—and by the time you really got under way it'd be midnight, and you'd have to beat it back to camp.
As she looks reluctantly away:	NURSE'S THOUGHTS
	Well, five foot eleven, I—I guess it's goodbye.
Ditto, in other direction:	SOLDIER'S THOUGHTS
	Well, so long, ankles.

The train clanks on. A resume-shot gives another general impression of the carful as the shadow mechanism behind window closest to vestibule slows down and indicates station stop. Through window or door-pane, as vestibule side-door slides open, group-shot of waiting passengers in cluster around pillar.

One passenger pushes out, the waiting crowd pushes on. Among these, most prominently, a JEW and a CLUB-FOOTED PEDDLER. The JEW is stocky, prosperous-looking, open-faced but slightly over-bearing. CLUB-FOOT is fairly elderly, tall, dominant in spite of his affliction, his face a mixture of piety, truculence, and dormant fanaticism. He is poorly clad, and is having trouble with his peddler's tray of shoelaces, pencils, etc. He tries to barge aboard ahead of JEW, who, with plausible indignation, elbows him off and gets there first. As they come onto train:

Jostled aside:	CLUBFOOT (aloud)
	Look out, where are you—?
Turning in vestibule, with that curt constrained politeness of the subway code:	JEW (aloud)
	All right, I'm sorry.

CLUBFOOT looks up toward INTEL-LECTUAL, against whom he has been pushed. He's about to apologize, but INTELLECTUAL has evidently seen part of incident and sides with CLUB-FOOT, for he volunteers

---

NEGRO VERSION

	SOLDIER'S THOUGHTS
	—and by the time you really got underway it'd be midnight, and you'd have to beat it back to camp.
As she looks reluctantly away:	NURSE'S THOUGHTS
	Well, five foot eleven, I—I guess it's goodbye.
Ditto, in other direction:	SOLDIER'S THOUGHTS
	Well, so long, ankles.

The train clanks on. A resume-shot gives another general impression of the carful as the shadow mechanism behind window closest to vestibule slows down and indicates station stop. Through window or door-pane, as vestibule side-door slides open, group-shot of waiting passengers in cluster around pillar.

One passenger rushes out, the waiting crowd pushes on. Among these, most prominently, a NEGRO and a CLUB-FOOTED PEDDLER. The NEGRO is a good-natured, carelessly mannered chap with too fresh a grin, and is dressed in a Harlem zoot suit, loud tie, etc. CLUB-FOOT is fairly elderly, tall, dominant in spite of his affliction, his face a mixture of piety, truculence, and dormant fanaticism. He is poorly clad, and is having trouble with his peddler's tray of shoelaces, pencils, etc. He tries to barge aboard ahead of NEGRO, who, with gleeful determination, elbows him and gets there first. As they come onto train:

Jostled aside:	CLUB-FOOT (aloud)
	Look out, where are you—?

WHITE COLLAR VERSION

	SOLDIER'S THOUGHTS
	—and by the time you really got under-way it'd be midnight, and you'd have to beat it back to camp.
As she looks reluctantly away:	NURSE'S THOUGHTS
	Well, five foot eleven, I—I guess it's goodbye.
Ditto, in other direction:	SOLDIER'S THOUGHTS
	Well, so long, ankles.

The train clanks on. A resume-shot gives another general impression of the carful as the shadow mechanism behind window closest to vestibule slows down and indicates station stop. Through window or door-pane, as vestibule side-door slides open, group-shot of waiting passengers in cluster around pillar.

One passenger rushes out, the waiting crowd pushes on. Among these, most prominently, a WHITE-COLLAR WORKER and a CLUB-FOOTED PEDDLER. The WHITE-COLLAR WORKER is a sallow, somewhat cranky, worried man, bookkeeper type, distinctly Protestant. CLUB-FOOT is fairly elderly, tall, dominant in spite of his affliction, his face a mixture of piety, truculence, and dormant fanaticism. He is poorly clad, and is having trouble with his peddler's tray of shoelaces, pencils, etc. He tries to barge aboard ahead of WHITE-COLLAR MAN who elbows him petulantly and gets there first. As they come onto train:

Jostled aside:	CLUB-FOOT (aloud)
	Look out, where are you—?
Turning in vestibule, with an ineffectual show of spite:	WHITE COLLAR (aloud)
	Very well, I'm sorry.
CLUBFOOT looks towards INTELLECTUAL, against whom he has been pushed. He's about to apologize, but INTELLECTUAL has evidently seen part of incident, and sides with CLUBFOOT, volunteering the ironic comment.	INTELLECTUAL (aloud)
	"Sorry"—but <u>after</u> he pushed you, of course!
	CLUBFOOT
	Sure, sneakin' right in—ahead o' me—not mindin' anything—a gentleman!

WHITE COLLAR has not heard this bitter but quiet comment. However, glancing down, he notices CLUBFOOT'S affliction and murmurs to himself, as if in understanding of the man's bitterness:

The ironic comment:

  INTELLECTUAL (aloud)

  "Sorry"—but <u>after</u> he pushed you, of course!

  CLUBFOOT

  Sure, always pushing in first, always grabbing the profits!

JEW has not heard this bitter but quiet comment. However, glancing down, he notices CLUB-FOOT'S affliction, and murmurs to himself, as if in understanding of the man's bitterness:

  JEW

  Oh!...

Looking up, he senses their hostility, but shrugs it off and is soon absorbed in searching for something in his pocket. Camera returns to CLUB-FOOT. He has evidently been encouraged by a sympathetic audience.

  CLUB-FOOT (quiet but ominous)

  It's time folks woke up to lots of things going on in this country!

CLUB-FOOT stomps on further into car, using his tray to cleave a passage. In doing so he grazes against POLICEMAN, who winces and nurses his sore feet. Interlude shots of SOLDIER and NURSE sneaking looks at each other, of TOUGH GUY lurching against WISE GUY as, indicated by swing of upheld newspapers, etc., the train begins to take a curve.

In vestibule, shot of WOMAN WITH VC as the door behind her slides back under leverage of the cleaner handle. Next to her the JEW has his wallet out and is searching for something therein, when the lurch of the train causes him partially to lose his balance. Now we see a longer shot of lurch and melee, with the movement of people in foreground partially obscuring the action in vestibule at background. However, we are able to discern that the JEW has lost his wallet as he exclaims:

  JEW

  My pocket-book! Gone!

We see him elbowing about. Then there is a woman's scream, and we barely glimpse the VC WOMAN falling—then disappearing through the door's empty blackness. There is a small electric flash—then total darkness, as all the train lights go out, and the train slows down to a quick stop. During this there is a second's silence. Then:

NEGRO VERSION

Turning in vestibule, with flip, rather offensive cheerfulness:

    NEGRO (aloud)
    Okay, boss, sorry.

CLUBFOOT looks toward INTELLECTUAL, against whom he has been pushed. He is about to apologize, but INTELLECTUAL has evidently seen part of incident, and sides with CLUBFOOT, for he volunteers the ironic comment:

    INTELLECTUAL (aloud)
    "Sorry"—but <u>after he</u> pushed you, of course!

    CLUBFOOT
    Sure, pushing in first—nowadays—as if they owned the earth!

NEGRO has not heard this bitter but quiet comment. However, glancing down, he notices CLUBFOOT's affliction, and murmurs to himself, as if in understanding of the man's bitterness:

    NEGRO
    Oh . . .

Looking up, he senses their hostility, but shrugs it off and is soon absorbed in searching for something in his pocket. Camera returns to CLUBFOOT. He has evidently been encouraged by a sympathetic audience.

    CLUBFOOT (quiet but ominous)
    It's time folks woke up to lots of things going on in this country!

CLUBFOOT stomps on further into car, using his tray to cleave a passage. In doing so he grazes against POLICEMAN, who winces and nurses his sore feet. Interlude shots of SOLDIER and NURSE sneaking looks at each other, of TOUGH GUY lurching against WISE GUY as, indicated by swing of upheld newspapers, etc., the train begins to take a curve.

In vestibule, shot of WOMAN WITH VC as the door behind her slides back under leverage of the cleaner handle. Next to her the NEGRO has his wallet out and is searching for something therein, when the lurch of the train causes him partially to lose his balance. Now we see a longer shot of lurch and melee, with the movement of people in foreground partially obscuring the action in vestibule at background. However, we are able to discern that the NEGRO has lost his wallet as he exclaims:

    NEGRO
    My dough—pocket book! Gone!

WHITE COLLAR VERSION

       WHITE COLLAR
       Oh...

Looking up, he senses their hostility, but shrugs it off and is soon absorbed in searching for something in his pocket. Camera returns to CLUBFOOT. He has evidently been encouraged by a sympathetic audience.

       CLUBFOOT (quiet but ominous)
       It's time folks woke up to lots of things going on in this country!

CLUBFOOT stomps on further into car, using his tray to cleave a passage. In doing so he grazes against POLICEMAN, who winces and nurses his sore feet. Interlude shots of SOLDIER and NURSE sneaking looks at each other, of TOUGH GUY lurching against WISE GUY as, indicated by swing of upheld newspapers, etc., the train begins to take a curve.

In vestibule, shot of WOMAN WITH VC as the door behind her slides back under leverage of the cleaner handle. Next to her the WHITE-COLLAR MAN has his wallet out and is searching for something therein, when the lurch of the train causes him partially to lose his balance. Now we see a longer shot of lurch and melee, with the movement of people in foreground partially obscuring the action in vestibule at background. However, we are able to discern that the WHITE-COLLAR MAN has lost his wallet as he exclaims:

       WHITE COLLAR
       My pocket book! Gone!

We see him elbowing about. Then there is a woman's scream, and we barely glimpse the VC WOMAN falling—then disappearing through the door's empty blackness. There is a small electric flash—then total darkness, as all the train lights go out, and the train slows down to a quick stop. During this there is a second's silence. Then:

       JEW
       My God!

Simultaneously:

       WISE GUY
       She'll be run over. Help!

Down the dark car, matches are being struck by indistinctly milling figures.

       VOICES FROM ALL AROUND CAR
       What's the matter? Lights! Get away from me! Here's a match! etc.

       WHITE COLLAR
       My wallet! It had money in it. It—

                              NEGRO

                              Lawdy, God!

                              WISE GUY (simultaneously)

                              She'll be run over. Help!

Down the dark car, matches are being   VOICES FROM ALL AROUND CAR
struck by indistinctly milling figures. What's the matter? Lights! Get away
                              from me! Here's a match! etc.

                              JEW'S VOICE

                              My wallet! It had money in it. It—

The POLICEMAN is tugging out flashlight. We get his silhouette fitfully against a series of weird short-circuit showers of sparks seen through open vestibule door.

                              POLICEMAN
As he pushes down through crowd, with   Now, now, keep calm, everybody—'n' off
lighted flash: my feet, besides! Whoa, there.
To INTELLECTUAL: You—what's the trouble?
To JEW: All right, then, you—what happened?

                              JEW

                              Somebody took my money!

Roughly, to JEW: TOUGH GUY

                              Never mind your damn money.

                              WISE GUY

                              A woman. A woman with—

                              TOUGH GUY

                              Out—like that—out there!

The CADET NURSE leaps from her seat, rushes down aisle into crowd. The SOLDIER is up and after her, gets his lank body ahead and pushes way through for her.

                              SOLDIER

                              Gangway!

                              NURSE

                              Thanks. Officer, I'm a nurse.

NEGRO VERSION

We see him elbowing about. Then there is a woman's scream, and we barely glimpse the VACUUM CLEANER WOMAN falling—then disappearing through the door's empty blackness. There is a small electric flash—then total darkness, as all the train lights go out, and the train slows down to a quick stop. During this there is a second's silence. Then:

        JEW
        My God!

Simultaneously: WISE GUY
        She'll be run over. Help!

Down the dark car, matches are being struck by indistinctly milling figures.
        VOICES FROM ALL AROUND CAR
        What's the matter: Lights! Get away from me! Here's a match! etc.

        NEGRO'S VOICE
        My wallet! It had dough in it. Ah want mah—

The POLICEMAN is tugging out flashlight. We get his silhouette fitfully against a series of weird short-circuit showers of sparks seen through open vestibule door.

        POLICEMAN

As he pushes down through crowd, with lighted flash:
        Now, now, keep calm, everybody—an' off my feet, besides! Whoa, there—
To INTELLECTUAL: You—what's the trouble?
To NEGRO: All right, then you—what happened?

        NEGRO
        Somebody took mah dough!

Roughly, to NEGRO: TOUGH GUY
        Never mind your damn dough!

        WISE GUY
        A woman. A woman with—

        TOUGH GUY
        Out—like that—out there!

WHITE COLLAR VERSION

The POLICEMAN is tugging out flashlight. We get his silhouette fitfully against a series of weird short-circuit showers of sparks seen through open vestibule door.

	POLICEMAN
As he pushes down through crowd, with lighted flash:	Now, now, keep calm, everybody—an' off my feet, besides! Whoa, there!
To INTELLECTUAL:	You—what's the trouble?
To WHITE COLLAR:	All right, then, <u>you</u>—what happened?
	WHITE COLLAR
	Somebody took my money!
Roughly, to WHITE COLLAR:	TOUGH GUY
	Never mind your damn money.
	WISE GUY
	A woman. A woman with—
	TOUGH GUY
	Out—like that—out there!

The CADET NURSE leaps from her seat, rushes down aisle, into crowd. The SOLDIER is up an after her, gets his lank body ahead and pushes way through for her.

SOLDIER

Gangway!

                    POLICEMAN
                    Yes 'm. Stand by.

SUBWAY GUARD reenters car, forges through to vestibule with emergency grappling apparatus. Ahead of him SOLDIER plunges into pitchy opening and then down out of sight.

                    POLICEMAN
                    Atta boy!

To INTELLECTUAL, as he shoves him aside: Look out, mister.

Off-scene, shouting: SOLDIER
                        Here she is.

Ditto: GUARD
          Careful. Lift her—

          POLICEMAN
          Back up, everybody. Here. Look out, soldier—look out for that third rail stuff.

Dark shot of SOLDIER and GUARD lifting muffled object back, former down on ground and unmindful of vacuum cleaner fallen to rails, sizzling and crackling there.

Anxious for SOLDIER: NURSE
As VC WOMAN's body is being hauled in: Oh please....
                                          Let me—

Leaping from seat and barging to vestibule: WOMAN IN FUR COAT
                                               Don't let her down on that dirty metal—here!

With impetuous motherliness, starts ripping off her mink coat.

                    NURSE
                    All right, officer. We'll take care of her.

Arms spread up over crowd: POLICEMAN
                              Yes'm. 'N' pipe down, everybody. If you really want to help, keep your shirts on ' n' tell me what happened.

In spite of his efforts, general hubbub. CLUB-FOOT starts pegging furiously back toward vestibule. As he passes LITTLE GIRL, who is crying with fright, and the yelping PUPPY:

CLUB-FOOT

Shut up, you!

Crowd in vestibule closes around POLICEMAN, masking the bent-down NURSE and the victim with head in lap of FUR COAT WOMAN. The SOLDIER is forcing the circle larger, POLICEMAN has his notebook out—is interrogating.

POLICEMAN

So what makes her fall out?

Knowingly, as he looks toward JEW: CLUB-FOOT

I've got a pretty good idea.

TOUGH GUY

Maybe she didn't. Maybe somebody—

CLUB-FOOT

Pushed her. That's it, pushed her!

POLICEMAN

To WISE GUY: Who?

You! What'd you see?

WISE GUY

Me? Why—nothing.

NEGRO

Me, neither, boss.

CLUBFOOT

Well, <u>somebody</u> did it!

During above the OLD LADY has lighted up with an air of triumphant prophecy. Abandoning her yelping pup, she leaps from seat, pushed out into vestibule crowd:

OLD LADY

And I know who!

NEGRO VERSION

	POLICEMAN
To WISE GUY:	Who?
	You! What'd you see?

WISE GUY

Me? Why—nothing.

JEW

Neither did I.

CLUBFOOT

Well, <u>somebody</u> did it!

During above the OLD LADY has lighted up with an air of triumphant prophecy. Abandoning her yelping pup, she leaps from seat, pushed out into vestibule crowd:

OLD LADY

And I know who!

POLICEMAN

Spill it.

OLD LADY

I knew it all along!

POLICEMAN

What? Who?

OLD LADY

In the stars for today. It just had to happen. Exactly like this.

POLICEMAN

Like what?

OLD LADY

The way it did. It had to. He did it just—

POLICEMAN

He? Who?

POLICEMAN
Spill it.

OLD LADY
I knew it all along!

POLICEMAN
What? Who?

OLD WOMAN
In the stars for today. It just had to happen. Exactly like this.

POLICEMAN
Like what?

OLD LADY
The way it did. It had to. He did it just—

POLICEMAN
He? Who?

Pointing wildly at JEW:

OLD WOMAN
Him, of course! He was standing right next to her, and —

Bewildered:

JEW
Me? I—I certainly did not.

CLUB-FOOT
You weren't next to her?

JEW
Yes, but—

CLUB-FOOT
So—you admit it!

JEW
Yes—I mean no! I mean—I was next to her—but I didn't push anybody!

NEGRO VERSION

Pointing wildly at NEGRO:

OLD LADY
Him, of course! He was standing right next to her, and—

NEGRO
Me? I—I sure didn't do no such—

CLUBFOOT
You weren't next to her?

NEGRO
Yeah, sure, but Ah—

CLUBFOOT
So—you admit it!

NEGRO
Sure—Ah mean no! Ah mean—I was next to her, yeah, but Ah didn' push nobody!

Imitating NEGRO's action during accident:

OLD LADY
Oh, yes, he did. I seen him, officer. Swingin' his hands—like so!

With growing alarm:

NEGRO
Shucks, Ah—was was jus' tryin' to find mah wallet, that's all. I felt it—all of a sudden—it was gone!

INTELLECTUAL shows a passing interest, but affects scientific objectivity:

INTELLECTUAL
Ah! So he did swing his hands. Point one—admitted.

NEGRO
No, only for mah wallet! Listen, you—all o' you—Lawdy God, Ah didn' have a thing to do with it!

Imitating NEGRO's dialect with coarse delight:

TOUGH GUY
Lawdy, Lawdy, oh, no—he didn't done a thing!

WHITE COLLAR VERSION

                                      OLD WOMAN
                                      The way it did. It had to. He did it just—

                                      POLICEMAN
                                      He? Who?

Pointing wildly at WHITE COLLAR: OLD WOMAN
                                      Him, of course! He was standing right next to her, and—

Bewildered: WHITE COLLAR
                                      Me? I—I certainly did not.

                                      CLUBFOOT
                                      You weren't next to her?

                                      WHITE COLLAR
                                      Why, yes, but—

                                      CLUBFOOT
                                      So—you admit it!

                                      WHITE COLLAR
                                      Yes—I mean, no! I mean—I was next to her, yes, but I didn't push anybody!

Imitating WHITE COLLAR's action   OLD WOMAN
during accident: Oh, yes, he did. I seen him, officer. Swingin' his hands—like so!

With growing alarm: WHITE COLLAR
                                      Sure, but I was trying to find my wallet. I felt it—suddenly it was gone!

INTELLECTUAL shows a passing interest, but affects scientific objectivity:

                                      INTELLECTUAL
                                      Ah! So he <u>did</u> swing his hands. Point one—admitted.

                                      WHITE COLLAR
                                      No, only for my wallet! Officer, I—absolutely did not have a thing to do with it.

	OLD WOMAN
Imitating JEW's action during accident:	Oh, yes, he did. I seen him, officer. Swingin' his hands—like so!
	JEW
With growing alarm:	Sure, but I was trying to find my wallet. I felt it—suddenly it was gone!

INTELLECTUAL shows a passing interest, but affects scientific objectivity:

INTELLECTUAL
Ah! So he <u>did</u> swing his hands. Point one—admitted.

JEW
No, only for my wallet! Officer! I—didn't haf a t'ing t' do vit it.

Imitating JEW's accent with coarse delight:	**TOUGH GUY** Oi- sure—he didn't haf a t'ing t'—
	OLD WOMAN He did, too! The stars don't lie!
Demanding around group:	**POLICEMAN** I'm askin' you, not the stars. Anybody else see him? You? or you?

WISE GUY
They couldn't. It went dark.

POLICEMAN
Oh—exactly.

INTELLECTUAL
Easy, don't make any statement that might be discredited.

CLUB-FOOT
We don't have to see what we know. We got proofs enough already to—

NEGRO VERSION

	OLD LADY He did, too! The stars don't lie!
Demanding around group:	POLICEMAN I'm askin' you, not the stars. Anybody else see him? You? or you?
	CLUBFOOT How could they? It went dark.
	POLICEMAN Uh-huh.
	CLUBFOOT But that don't matter. We don't have to see what we know. We got proofs enough to—
To NEGRO:	POLICEMAN Afterwards. Names first. Come on.
With defiant swagger he thrusts forward his wrist and shows a gold identification bracelet:	NEGRO Me? Yassur . . . That's me—middle name, address 'n' all.
	TOUGH GUY Yeah, solid gold. It would be.
As POLICEMAN writes:	NEGRO Ask anybody up in Harlem about me, boss.
To WISE GUY:	INTELLECTUAL Doesn't sound precisely humble, does he?
	NEGRO Mah jazz-band's famous—an' nobody pins nothin' on me, no, sir!

The SUBWAY GUARD climbs aboard again from below, with the blackened, half-melted remains of the vacuum cleaner in his grappler.

WHITE COLLAR VERSION

Imitating WHITE COLLAR with coarse delight:	**TOUGH GUY** Absolutely not a thing—oh, no!
	OLD WOMAN He did, too! The stars don't lie!
Demanding around group:	**POLICEMAN** I'm askin' you, not the stars. Anybody else see him? You? Or you?
	CLUBFOOT How could they? It went dark.
	POLICEMAN Uh-huh.
	CLUBFOOT But that don't matter. We don't have to see what we know. We got proofs enough to—
	POLICEMAN Afterwards. Names first.
Takes out gold fountain pen and, at POLICEMAN'S nod, proceeds to write it in notebook. With spiteful glance around:	**WHITE COLLAR** Me? Certainly. Here, I'll ... write it out for you. As head bookkeeper for a Wall Street firm, I happen to have an excellent handwriting— And <u>don't</u> care to shout my bosses' business address to the whole world.
Eyeing WHITE COLLAR'S pen:	**TOUGH GUY** Yeah, solid gold. It would be.
With smug complacency, as he writes:	**WHITE COLLAR** Exactly—and why not? For a twentieth Christmas bonus?
To WISE GUY:	**INTELLECTUAL** Doesn't sound precisely starving, does he?

	POLICEMAN Afterward. Names first.
Takes out gold fountain pen and, at POLICEMAN's nod, proceeds to write it in notebook.	**JEW** Me? Certainly. Here, I'll . . . write it out for you.
	TOUGH GUY Yeah, solid gold. It would be.
	INTELLECTUAL Doesn't sound precisely starving, does he?
Overhearing:	**JEW** No, I . . . even though I <u>have</u> been giving up three days a week to government work. See?
Ironically:	**INTELLECTUAL** Oh, yes . . . I believe there are a great many—of your people—in the Federal agencies nowadays.

The SUBWAY GUARD climbs aboard again from below, with the blackened, half-melted remains of the vacuum cleaner in his grappler.

Halting behind cluster around VC WOMAN:	**GUARD** Hurt bad? Conscious?
	NURSE Ssh! Not yet.
To POLICEMAN:	**GUARD** Here's all about her on this repair tag . . . what's left of it.
He hands damaged tag to POLICEMAN.	**POLICEMAN** Need any help to get started again?
	GUARD Could be.

NEGRO VERSION

Halting behind cluster around VACUUM CLEANER WOMAN:	GUARD Hurt bad? Conscious?
	NURSE Ssh! Not yet.
To POLICEMAN: He hands damaged tag to POLICEMAN.	GUARD Here's all about her on this repair tag... what's left of it.
	POLICEMAN Need any help to get started again?

GUARD shakes his head—starts through train. As he opens door to next car sounds of excitement well up. Turning back to POLICEMAN:

	GUARD But you might try to keep the tourist trade quiet.

POLICEMAN grins—follows GUARD—disappearing down train. People are crowding excitedly round group with VACUUM CLEANER WOMAN.

To CLUBFOOT:	SOLDIER Gosh—give 'em room, folks. You heard me—fall back!
Bitterly:	CLUBFOOT What? And let him get away with it?
	WISE GUY Who?
Staring vindictively at NEGRO. Then, appealing to TOUGH GUY:	CLUBFOOT Who? Him that did it. Pushed her out. That dinge there, him. Right?
	TOUGH GUY Right, I'll say—
	OLD WOMAN He did it, he did it!

WHITE COLLAR VERSION

Overhearing:	**WHITE COLLAR** No, I ... even though I have been giving up three evenings a week to draft board work, for instance!
	INTELLECTUAL Oh, yes ... Wall Street has undoubtedly done its part ... a great patriotic part, I'm sure.

The SUBWAY GUARD climbs aboard again from below, with the blackened, half-melted remains of the vacuum cleaner in his grappler.

Halting behind cluster around VACUUM CLEANER WOMAN:	**GUARD** Hurt bad? Conscious?
	NURSE Ssh! Not yet.
To POLICEMAN: He hands damaged tag to POLICEMAN.	**GUARD** Here's all about her on this repair tag ... what's left of it.
	POLICEMAN Need any help to get started again?

GUARD shakes his head—starts through train. As he opens door to next car sounds of excitement well up. Turning back to POLICEMAN:

	GUARD But you might try to keep the tourist trade quiet.

POLICEMAN grins—follows GUARD —disappearing down train. People are crowding excitedly around group with VACUUM CLEANER WOMAN.

To CLUBFOOT:	**SOLDIER** Gosh—give 'em room, folks. You heard me—fall back!
Bitterly:	**CLUBFOOT** What? And let him get away with it?

He starts through train. As he opens door to next car sounds of excitement well up. Turning back to POLICEMAN:

> GUARD
>
> AND you might try to keep the tourist trade quiet.

Before following GUARD, POLICEMAN bends over group round VC WOMAN— asks:

> POLICEMAN
>
> Managing all right?

NURSE'S head appears as she looks up for a moment from ministering to patient. She nods.

> NURSE
>
> If we could have a little more room
>
> POLICEMAN
>
> OK—back up everybody—don't crowd!

People ease back, and he exits toward next car from which we again hear irated {*sic*} clamour. As soon as he is gone, crowd closes in again.

To CLUBFOOT:

> SOLDIER
>
> Gosh—give 'em room, folks! Fall back!

Bitterly:

> CLUBFOOT
>
> What? And let him get away with it?
>
> WISE GUY
>
> Who?

Staring vindictively at JEW. Then, appealing to TOUGH GUY:

> CLUBFOOT
>
> Who! Him that did it. Pushed her out. Right?
>
> TOUGH GUY
>
> Right! I'll say—
>
> OLD WOMAN
>
> He did it, he did it!

Crowd's mood grows distinctly threatening as it tightens around JEW. The PUPPY adds to the confusion by running wildly around in dimness, yelping at legs, howling for its mistress. Above the din it makes, people must scream to be heard. Even the WISE GUY, coming for a moment to half-hearted, ineffectual defense of the JEW, goes high-pitched and squeaky.

WISE GUY

Oh, but ... I say, after all, we haven't really proved it, have we?

TOUGH GUY

No?

WISE GUY

Why, no, not—

TOUGH GUY

An' that proves he didn't do it—yeah?

CLUB-FOOT

And you want to testify, is that it? Against <u>us</u>?

TOUGH GUY

Make liars outer us, yeah? You—

His one little spurt of bravery subsiding fast as he looks around:

WISE GUY

Why, er—I didn't mean—except I couldn't say one way or the other, that's—

OLD WOMAN

Well, I can!

JEW

But I didn't do it. I tell you I—

CLUBFOOT

Sure, you tell 'em! Tell 'em how you pushed me before!

The TWO SHIPYARD WORKERS have been drawn down into the crowd. One of them, with burly kindness, starts to interfere:

NEGRO VERSION

Crowd's mood grows distinctly threatening as it tightens around NEGRO. The PUPPY adds to the confusion by running wildly around in the dimness, yelping at legs, howling for its mistress. Above the din it makes, people must scream to be heard. Even the WISE GUY, coming for a moment to half-hearted, ineffectual defense of the NEGRO, goes high-pitched and squeaky.

WISE GUY

Oh, but . . . I say, after all, we haven't really proved it, have we?

TOUGH GUY

No?

WISE GUY

Why, no, not —

TOUGH GUY

An' that proves he didn't do it—yeah?

CLUBFOOT

And you want to testify, is that it? Against us?

TOUGH GUY

Make liars outer us, yeah? You—

His one little spurt of bravery subsiding fast as he looks around:

WISE GUY

Why, er—I didn't mean—except I couldn't say one way or the other, that's —

OLD WOMAN

Well, I can!

NEGRO

But Ah didn' do it. Listen, you-all, Ah'm tellin' you—

CLUBFOOT

Sure, you tell 'em! Tell 'em how you pushed me before!

WHITE COLLAR VERSION

                                                  WISE GUY
                                                  Who?

Staring vindictively at WHITE COLLAR.   CLUBFOOT
Then appealing to TOUGH GUY: Who? Him that did it. Pushed her out. Right?

                                                TOUGH GUY
                                                Right! I'll say—

                                                OLD WOMAN
                                                He did it, he did it!

Mood of one faction grows distinctly threatening as it tightens around WHITE COLLAR. The PUPPY adds to the confusion by running wildly around in the dimness, yelping at legs, howling for its mistress. Above the din it makes, people must scream to be heard. Even the WISE GUY, coming for a moment to half-hearted, ineffectual defense of the WHITE COLLAR, goes high-pitched and squeaky.

                                                WISE GUY
                                                Oh, but . . . I say, after all, we haven't really proved it, have we?

                                                TOUGH GUY
                                                No?

                                                WISE GUY
                                                Why, no, not—

                                                TOUGH GUY
                                                An' that proves he didn't do it—yeah?

                                                CLUBFOOT
                                                And you want to testify, is that it? Against us?

                                                TOUGH GUY
                                                Make liars outer us, yeah? You—

His one little spurt of bravery subsiding   WISE GUY
fast as he looks around: Why, er—I didn't mean—except I couldn't say one way or the other, that's—

SHIPYARD WORKER
Hey, look, brother—

At JEW's confusion:

CLUB-FOOT
He pushed me. He can't deny it. He <u>doesn't</u> deny it. See? Him and his kind, they glory in it—they're <u>always</u> pushing!

JEW
But, my God—

TOUGH GUY
You leave God out of it, you!

CLUBFOOT
Stickin' together to push all the rest of us out o' their way—up! To shove—and shyster and—get away with it, every time you can.

Several more passengers have pushed in close behind CLUB-FOOT, murmuring agreement.

SECOND SHIPYARD WORKER
Hold it there, Mister. You better go sit down!

Other passengers murmur assent to this, aligning themselves against CLUBFOOT's faction.

CLUB-FOOT
Sit down? While his kind get away with it? Oh, no, I don't! If that poor woman's been killed—

JEW
Killed?

TOUGH GUY
You heard us!

FIRST SHIPYARD WORKER (to TOUGH GUY)
Sit down, yu' too, yu' scab—
Or do you want me to knock your block off!

NEGRO VERSION

The TWO SHIPYARD WORKERS have been drawn down into the crowd. One of them, with burly kindness, starts to interfere.

> SHIPYARD WORKER
> Hey, look, brother —

At NEGRO's confusion:

> CLUBFOOT
> He pushed me. He can't deny it. He <u>doesn't</u> deny it. See? Him and his kind, they can get away with anything these days, sassing back, rioting, mugging—

> NEGRO
> Lawdy, God—

> TOUGH GUY
> You leave God out of it, you!

> CLUBFOOT
> Defying all the rest of us to keep 'em in their place—to preserve ourselves from their impudence, an' filth an' crazy ways . . . To take our streets an' houses, snatch our jobs . . .

Several more passengers have pushed in close behind CLUBFOOT, murmuring agreement.

> SECOND SHIPYARD WORKER
> Hold it there, Mister, you better go sit down!

Other passengers murmur assent to this, aligning themselves against CLUBFOOT's faction.

> CLUBFOOT
> Sit down? While dinges like him get away with it? Oh, no, I don't. If that poor woman's been killed—

> NEGRO
> Killed?

> TOUGH GUY
> You heard us!

WHITE COLLAR VERSION

OLD WOMAN

Well, I can!

WHITE COLLAR

Ridiculous! I didn't do it. I tell you I—

CLUBFOOT

Sure, you tell 'em! Tell 'em how you pushed me before.

The TWO SHIPYARD WORKERS have been drawn down into the crowd. One of them, with burly kindness, starts to interfere.

SHIPYARD WORKER

Hey, look, brother—

At WHITE COLLAR'S confusion:

CLUBFOOT

He pushed me. He can't deny it. He <u>doesn't</u> deny it. See? Him and his smart kind, they glory in it—they're <u>always</u> pushing!

WHITE COLLAR

But, my God—

TOUGH GUY

You leave God out of it, you!

CLUBFOOT

Thinkin' themselves so much better than us with their bookkeepin' 'n' bankin'—'n' jugglin' their figures to keep us broke 'n' get away with it, every time they can!

Several more passengers have pushed in close behind CLUBFOOT, murmuring agreement.

SECOND SHIPYARD WORKER

Hold it there, Mister, you better go sit down.

Other passengers murmur assent to this, aligning themselves against CLUBFOOT'S faction.

	CLUB-FOOT
	Scab?
	SECOND SHIPYARD WORKER
	Sure, stooge for the bosses—wait till we're on top!
Brandishing fist:	CLUB-FOOT
	You don't have to wait that long!

Murmurs from both factions, as crowd takes sides.

	JEW
	Honest—all I was doing was—
	CLUBFOOT
	Reaching for your money, sure! For your dirty money, and not givin' a damn what else so long you get it. Shove, hurt, kill—
	SECOND SHIPYARD WORKER
	Aw, shut your dirty mouth!
	FIRST SHIPYARD WORKER
	I'll give you ten seconds to sit down.
	CLUB-FOOT
	Sit down, sure—and turn it all over to Reds like you? To Jews and Niggers and the like of them, the hell we will. There's times when us plain, decent, God-lovin' Christians—us white Americans—has got to take the law in our own hands and clean things up. Come on!

During above speech FIRST SHIPYARD WORKER has begun counting ominously, while tension and hostility mount within the crowd, emphasized by rising excitement in camera treatment and cutting. Thus, breaking in after first view {sic, few?} words above comes:

CLOSE SHOT—of group round CLUBFOOT pressing in closer.	FIRST SHIPYARD WORKER'S VOICE (grimly)
	One—
CLOSE SHOT GROUP aligned with FIRST SHIPYARD WORKER also presses in towards potential opponents.	Two—

NEGRO VERSION

To TOUGH GUY:

FIRST SHIPYARD WORKER

You sit down, too—before I knock your block off!

Murmurs from both factions, as crowd takes sides.

NEGRO

Honest, boss, all I was doing was—

CLUBFOOT

Reaching for your money, sure! For your Harlem jazz band money, and not giving a damn what else . . . shove, mug, razor, kill—

WISE GUY

Why not let the law handle it?

FIRST SHIPYARD WORKER

I'll give you ten seconds to sit down.

CLUBFOOT

Sit down and wait? What for? To turn it all over the Reds like you? To Niggers and Jews and the likes of them, the hell we will. There's times when us plain, decent, God-lovin' Christians—

WHITE COLLAR VERSION

CLUBFOOT

Sit down? While smarties like him get away with it? Oh, no, I don't. If that poor woman's been killed—

WHITE COLLAR

Killed?

TOUGH GUY

You heard us!

To TOUGH GUY: FIRST SHIPYARD WORKER

You sit down, too—before I knock your block off!

WHITE COLLAR

See here, all I was doing was—

CLUBFOOT

Reaching for your money, sure! For your dirty money, and not givin' a damn what else so long as you get it. Sneak, shove, outsmart, hurt, kill—

WISE GUY

Why not let the law handle it?

FIRST SHIPYARD WORKER

I'll give you ten seconds to sit down.

CLUBFOOT

Sit down—for what? What for? To turn it all over the Reds like you? To the Wall Street bankers and Jews and Niggers and the likes of them? The hell we will. There's times when us plain, decent, God-lovin' Christians—

BIG HEAD CLOSE-UP for CLUB-FOOT, continuing his speech defiantly, with mounting emotion.	Three—
BIG HEAD CLOSE-UP of FIRST WORKER, delivering his fourth count of warning with quiet grimness.	Four—
CLOSE-UP—a hand clenching into a menacing fist.	Five—
CLOSE-UP—corresponding fist action of opponent.	Six—
CLOSE-UP—a hand grasps a dinner pail, preparing to wield it as a weapon.	Seven—
CLOSE-UP—an opposing hand draws a knife slowly from pocket.	Eight—
CLOSE-UP—a hand smashes bottle against opened dinner pail and holds jagged glass menacingly.	Nine—

Suddenly the car lights flare on again.

Long-shot of the mob frozen into an ugly, sustained tableau. The antagonists still stand immobile, hate-bound. Pan to group in protective ring around JEW, who is nursing a bruised forehead.

The train starts again. Its motion relieves the tension of the rooted crowd. Behind the SOLDIER, a small stir as the NURSE rises, chuckling:

	NURSE
She leans down again, helps VC WOMAN to her feet, with FUR COAT WOMAN'S aid:	A crime, was it?
	Well, here's your victim—without one broken bone—or more than a six-inch bruise. Come on dear. Dazed? Sure, but—
To SOLDIER:	You helped save her.
	SOLDIER
	Me? Gosh, no, the guard-chains got there first.
	VACUUM CLEANER WOMAN
	I'm all right, really.
	SOLDIER
	They kept her from slipping through as neat as—

Bewildered but regathering wits:

VACUUM CLEANER WOMAN
Thank you, everybody, but I'm fine again ... It was God's decision I should be spared.

Desperately:

CLUB-FOOT
But who pushed you?

VACUUM CLEANER WOMAN
Pushed me? Did somebody—?

Pointing to JEW:

CLUB-FOOT
Of course they did. Him? Who? You mean to tell us you don't—?

SOLDIER
Leave her alone.

The WOMAN looks around for her vacuum cleaner. They show her the sad remains. She gives a long, dry sigh—stares wearily down the car.

NURSE
Don't worry, darling, the subway people will give you a new one.

OLD WOMAN WITH PUPPY has recovered her animal and pauses to assure VC WOMAN.

OLD WOMAN WITH PUPPY

She trundles on, to resume her seat. Unlucky day, that's what. There's those that scoffs at astrology, oh, yes, but—

JEW and CLUB-FOOT exchange a look and move off toward opposite ends of train. POLICEMAN re-enters car.

We hold for brief punctuation on a few people getting on and off. Then Camera comes close to SOLDIER and NURSE.

NURSE
Well ... that's that.

NEGRO VERSION

She trundles on, to resume her seat. those that scoffs at astrology, oh, yes, but—

NEGRO and CLUBFOOT exchange a look, move off toward opposite ends of train. POLICEMAN re-enters car.

We hold for brief punctuation on a few people getting on and off. Then Camera comes close to SOLDIER and NURSE.

                                NURSE
                                Well . . . that's that.

                                SOLDIER
                                Yes, I reckon it is.

Looking around: NURSE
                                Funny, a minute ago everybody was all excited and—now—

                                SOLDIER
                                Now they're right back where they started from. Us too. Where we started.

Nodding glumly; neither can think of anything to say. After an awkward pause: NURSE
                                Er—<u>did</u> we? Well, goodbye.

                                SOLDIER
                                Goodbye. Yeah.

She moves off toward seat. He turns in opposite direction.

The train settles down to a steady clanking, the passengers back in the same moods and occupations they had when first seen. Camera travels slowly among their faces, past the still absorbed MAN WITH THE FINANCIAL PAGE and STENOGRAPHER with "Confessions," picking up their thoughts as before.

                                TOUGH GUY'S THOUGHTS
                                  Well, anyway, Niggers are Niggers—pretty much alike. Me, I'm glad to be getting' home to Mama. . . .

Camera moves successively to following:

He smiles whimsically.   WISE GUY'S THOUGHTS
                                  Home—all going home—while I start to work!

WHITE COLLAR VERSION

She trundles on, to resume her seat. those that scoffs at astrology, oh, yes, but—

WHITE COLLAR MAN and CLUBFOOT exchange a look and move off toward opposite ends of train. POLICEMAN re-enters car.

We hold for brief punctuation on a few people getting on and off. Then Camera comes close to SOLDIER and NURSE.

                                    NURSE
                                    Well . . . that's that.

                                    SOLDIER
                                    Yes, I reckon it is.

Looking around: NURSE
                                    Funny, a minute ago everybody was all excited, and—now—

                                    SOLDIER
                                    Now they're right back where they started from. Us too. Where we started.

Nodding glumly; neither can think of   NURSE
anything to say. After an awkward   Er—<u>did</u> we? Well, goodbye.
pause:

                                    SOLDIER
                                    Goodbye. Yeah.

She moves off toward seat. He turns in opposite direction.

The train settles down to a steady clanking, the passengers back in the same moods and occupations they had when first seen. Camera travels slowly among their faces, past the still absorbed MAN WITH THE FINANCIAL PAGE and STENOGRAPHER with "Confessions," picking up their thoughts as before.

                                    TOUGH GUY'S THOUGHTS
                                    Well, anyway, the smart-allicks {sic}—the Wall Street hanger-ons—are pretty much all alike. Me, I'm glad to be gett'n home to Mama—

Camera moves successively to following:

                                SOLDIER
                                Yes, I reckon it is.

Looking around:
                                NURSE
                                Funny, a minute ago everybody was all excited and—now—

                                SOLDIER
                                Now they're right back where they started from. Us too. Where we started.

Nodding glumly; neither can think of anything to say. After an awkward pause:
                                NURSE
                                Er—_did_ we?
                                Well, goodbye.

                                SOLDIER
                                Goodbye. Yeah.

She moves off toward seat. He turns in opposite direction.

The train settles down to a steady clanking, the passengers back in the same moods and occupations they had when first seen. Camera travels slowly among their faces, past the still absorbed MAN WITH THE FINANCIAL PAGE and STENOGRAPHER with "Confessions," picking up their thoughts as before.

                                TOUGH GUY'S THOUGHTS
                                Well, anyway, Jews are Jews—pretty much all alike. Me, I'm glad to be gettin' home to Mamma—

Camera moves successively to following:

He smiles whimsically.
                                WISE GUY'S THOUGHTS
                                Home—all going home—while I start to work!

                                INTELLECTUAL'S THOUGHTS
                                This everlasting racial problem!... "Face it, gentlemen, we need strong leaders—doers, like Henry Ford..."

                                VC WOMAN'S THOUGHTS
                                That old dust and dirt still won't get the better of me! Just take some extra elbow-grease. That's not much, to show thanks for my deliverance. Might start on the rugs tonight—

> FIRST SHIPYARD WORKER'S THOUGHTS
>
> Corned beef—juicy, red corned beef!
>
> SECOND SHIPYARD WORKER'S THOUGHTS
>
> Spaghetti. I can't escape it—spaghetti!
>
> FUR COAT WOMAN'S THOUGHTS
>
> Now I won't even have time to dress, let alone fix the flowers ... that ungrateful girl!
>
> POLICEMAN'S THOUGHTS
>
> Home to Sadie—an' that big steamin' tub o' hot water!

Camera moves to LITTLE GIRL. She looks gravely around at all the rest of the people in the car—then down towards puppy next to her.

> LITTLE GIRL'S THOUGHTS
>
> You see, puppy ... people are such <u>children</u>, sometimes!

The train slows to a stop for the next station. Nothing seems to have been changed by the accident, not even the status between SOLDIER and NURSE, for she is still seated and apparently looking elsewhere as he moves towards exit. The door slides open—a few people start out ... SOLDIER among them. But suddenly she rises—moves toward him. And almost simultaneously he turns—pushes back against the stream of other people.

Simultaneously:

> SOLDIER
>
> Look, there's no <u>law</u> against talking!
>
> NURSE
>
> You know, if you'd rather <u>not</u> get off at Times Square—
>
> SOLDIER
>
> Not if you're free tonight.
>
> NURSE
>
> Free—and hungry.
>
> SOLDIER
>
> Well, of course! Supper comes with the invitation!

A lurch of the train brings them closer together.

       NURSE
       You know—if you don't mind eating in the kitchen—

       SOLDIER
       Mind? Say!

In the midst of his enthusiasm he looks suddenly at his wrist-watch.

       NURSE
       Worrying about the time?

He grins happily, shakes his head in response to her quizzical smile.

       SOLDIER
       We're three hours ahead of schedule already!

Camera pulls back to FULL SHOT of train as we:

FADE OUT

NOTES

1. To increase the usefulness of this film as an instrument of detecting (and measuring) emotional reactions, we suggest producing several versions in which the Jew may be replaced by (a) a Negro, (b) a German, (c) an Englishman.
2. Of course, similar variants have to be provided in the versions suggested in the footnote, p. 2.

PART 3

Postwar Publics (1948–1950)

INTRODUCTION

Under this heading, we collect together here a rather diverse range of texts penned by Kracauer toward the end of the 1940s, including a couple of essays intended as magazine articles, a report produced under the auspices of a wider UNESCO project, and a number of book reviews published in some leading newspapers and journals. These texts constitute a series of reflections upon the condition and tendencies of mass media and their audiences in postwar America. The heterogeneity of the materials themselves, and of the publication outlets in particular, is highly suggestive of Kracauer's precarious financial and intellectual position in postwar New York, as he sought to establish himself as a regular freelance writer for particular journals and newspapers and secure long-term positions as a researcher attached to different organizations and institutions in the wake of the publication of *From Caligari to Hitler* in 1947. Together these writings show a sustained concern with critically identifying and exploring the relationships between different forms of popular media, emerging consumer culture, and their reception and perception by American audiences in the context of what Adorno and Horkheimer would term "the culture industry" in their famous study *Dialectic of Enlightenment* (1947).

We begin with two reviews from 1948 published in the *New York Times Book Review*, exploring recent contributions to understanding propaganda and prospects of denazification measures then being undertaken by the Allied authorities as part of ongoing German postwar reconstruction. Kracauer provides a brief account of Marshall Knappen's own advocacy of a "soft program" of German reeducation undertaken by churches and community groups on the ground and the difficulties that hampered such work in the light of the proposed Morgenthau Plan. For Knappen, deindustrialization and the dismantling of a modern national economy would run counter to the fundamental and necessary processes for denazification and the creation of new liberal democratic Germany. While praising the book as "an honest piece of American self-criticism," Kracauer remained unconvinced by Knappen's optimism that economic growth enabled by the Marshall Plan—the option eventually chosen—would necessarily guarantee new political attitudes in Germany. It is noteworthy in this context of reconstruction of postwar Germany that the Kracauers themselves never returned to live in Germany despite the acute problems, economic and otherwise, that confronted them in America, whereas Adorno and Horkheimer were back in Frankfurt as early as 1949 to reestablish the Institute for Social Research in Frankfurt as part of the reeducation, reconstitution, and rehabilitation of Germany after the trauma of the Third Reich. Kracauer was not a part of this reeducation program; he and Elizabeth became American citizens instead.

Six months later, Kracauer reviewed the book *Public Opinion and Propaganda*, a study by the notable Yale psychologist Leonard W. Doob (1909–2000), who would publish his famous article "Goebbels' Principles of Propaganda" in 1950. While Doob's book is written, not surprisingly, from a psychological perspective, Kracauer is nonetheless enthusiastic about the book's scope and its attention not only to the makeup of individual personality but also to the formation of public opinion and the specifics of different types of media, such as press, radio, and film. While providing an "anatomy of propaganda" in terms of its techniques, Doob engages with a set of questions that are also close to Kracauer's own long-standing interest—for example, "How are people made to perceive propaganda, to respond to it, and eventually to follow its suggestions?" As we have already seen, the complex relationship between propaganda messages, forms of media, and the receptivity of audiences as a mass is central to Kracauer's thesis regarding the impact and efficacy of totalitarian propaganda. Kracauer's description of Doob as a "skeptical humanist" is perhaps also a self-characterization.

"Popular Advertisement" is rather a puzzling text. Originally intended for publication in the leading journal *Commentary*, in which Kracauer's work had previously appeared, this essay was never published in his lifetime. Moreover, while the date given for the text is January 15, 1949, the actual advertisement for "waterproof coffins" (!) with which Kracauer begins his reflection is dated as first appearing in 1957.[1] What is most striking, however, is that it seems to be his only direct engagement with American advertising in the course of his American writings. There are earlier examples and references to commercial adverts in his newspaper writings for the *FZ* during the Weimar era. Indeed, this blurring of news and publicity opens his 1927 photography essay, when one particular member of the Tiller Girls dance troupe smilingly welcomes the attention of what today we would describe as the paparazzi. Kracauer's reflection on advertising clearly resonates with the notion of the culture industry and anticipates Marcuse's vision of a "one-dimensional" America published some fifteen years later. Kracauer highlights three key themes: "conformity," "youthfulness," and "the happy consciousness." Just as totalitarian propaganda both produces and relies upon some notion of a homogeneous mass, the disappearance of the autonomous subject and the uniqueness and idiosyncrasy of genuine individual personality, so the advertising industry in postwar American advertising produces images and narratives marked by "insistence on conformity": "They aim at eliminating social diverseness and unconventional characters; and they ruthlessly regiment taste and manner down to the smallest detail." The use of "popular" is key here: whereas Horkheimer and Adorno wish to retain a critical moment in the term, as a reference to genuine critical impulses in folk and other cultural manifestations of and for the people, in contradistinction to the concept of "mass culture," Kracauer seems to use the term "popular" here with respect to a normative and normalizing set of expectations and social and psychological compulsions. We all crave to be popular, and to be popular is to be the same. To be the same is to share the taste and values of the multitude of others. To be popular is to be no different. Otherness is stigmatized and eradicated. And this popularity is about being young. Advertising is geared toward a fantasy of youthfulness (especially for those who are no longer youthful!) and identifies the young themselves (that new emerging category of teenager) as a particular target consumer group. Popular also means to be happy. The products and services that are promoted through advertising provide compensation for a life of boredom, repetition, and meaninglessness. The vacuity of our dispirited and disenchanted times is to be filled by the "joy and glamour" of fashion and consumption. Kracauer's essay on advertising is an early critique of consumer capitalism in the American context. Massification, youthful bodies, imaginary compensations for lives bereft of meaning—the principles of the contemporary advertisement are not so far from those undergirding techniques of propaganda. Kracauer's conclusions though are less pessimistic: the very dreamlike quality of the advertisements' images and delusions may yet come to have a critical edge when confronted with real-world, everyday experiences that fail to match up to these visions of harmony and happiness. Dreams can be also made to question that which is. Psychoanalytically speaking, dreams are, after all, the manifestations of what the world does not yet permit. Walter Benjamin and the Surrealists were, of course, among the first to see modern commodity culture as bound up with dreamlike experiences and anticipations. Kracauer suggests that those who are looking to sell us dreams, even the American dream, might be playing with fire: the consequences of peddling dreams may not be the ones that the advertising industry and capitalist culture have in mind.

Coauthored with the journalist Joseph Lyford, Kracauer's essay "A Duck Crosses Main Street" reflects upon the fragmented style of contemporary American newsreels and the disparate incidents they deem newsworthy, such as the eponymous foolhardy fowl. In a manner which recalls the start of Kracauer's "Below the Surface" screenplay, the text opens with an American citizen heading home from work, but instead of boarding the subway train and encountering the various characters created for the test film project, he misses his connection and instead seeks comfort at a movie theater to kill time waiting for the next train home. Kracauer proceeds to give an impression of the montage of disconnected news items with which he is confronted in the darkness of auditorium. Kracauer thereby reinforces the key point made in his earlier study of Nazi newsreels: how totalitarian propaganda seeks to bind otherwise disconnected and diverse images and episodes into a totality through the use of music and narration in order to tell a single story. The quick-fire montage of random incidents, in which the serious, catastrophic, sordid, sensational, comic, and quirky are all treated with the same indifference, is designed for those seeking mild distraction while they wait. The American newsreels place few demands on its audience, not even the need to concentrate on what is shown. When "A Duck Crosses Main Street" is news, the newsreel itself has lost any pretense at informing and educating its viewers about the contemporary social, economic, and political situation. News has become mere novelty, banal entertainment for the masses. For Kracauer, newsreels seem able to offer only a miniature "total work of art" (*Gesamtkunstwerk*) of fascist propaganda or the consumerist spectacle of fashion and frivolity.

The proliferation of popular advertising and the eclectic assemblage of moving images in the newsreels contribute to and constitute part of the current "deluge of pictures"—the title Kracauer adopts for his 1950 review of Lancelot Hogben's extensive overview of the history of visual representation, *From Cave Painting to Comic Strip*. In a passage highly reminiscent of his 1927 photography essay, Kracauer critically contrasts the meaningfulness of memory images to the meaninglessness of photographic images, and he laments the blinding consequences of the veritable blaze of images:

> Now pictures surround and besiege us. Through television, they silence our thoughts in that last and now insecure refuge of introspection, the bar; we

cannot pick up a printed piece of paper without being faced with an image. We are flooded with sights and spectacles—not with the originals, not with the sights and spectacles of nature, but with an intemperate outpouring of reproductions. Nature provides man with one spectacle at a time to which both intelligence and heart can respond; but man now provides himself with a mechanical, kaleidoscopic flurry of endlessly succeeding images. Instead of seeing clearly, he is almost blinded.[2]

Hogben's book, nevertheless, sees positive potential in this multiplicity of visual material in the modern world. Pictures encapsulate the possibility of language that transcends national differences, a kind of optical Esperanto for communication and mutual understanding between different linguistic communities. Kracauer himself will be drawn to the ideas and possibilities of what we would now term intercultural dialogue or transcultural communication in work he was to undertake at the behest of Department of Social Sciences at UNESCO. But he was unconvinced by Hogben's wide-eyed enthusiasm for the potential of images. Kracauer saw little prospect of popular cartoons, for example, being anything more than relatively trivial phenomena. Indiscriminate and uncritical, "The Deluge of Pictures" is more likely to overwhelm us with crass and crude stereotypes than to create and circulate genuine and nuanced portraits of others.

Developed from his 1949 "International Tensions" report for UNESCO, Kracauer's study "How U.S. Films Portray Foreign Types: A Psychological View of British and Russians on Our Screen," is a clear example of his penchant for the cinematic medium and his advocacy of its critical potential in reconceptualizing and reframing attitudes and perceptions with respect to individuals and collectives of other nations. While the films he refers to in this study are themselves (with one or two exceptions) now obscure, if not wholly forgotten, there are some interesting points, we suggest, that emerge from Kracauer's discussion. For instance, his study emphasizes the importance of audience perceptions, predispositions, and prejudices—what we might gather under the term "susceptibility." Echoing his earlier work on Weimar film in his recently published Caligari book, Kracauer focuses on our need to understand particular forms and patterns of audience receptivity to images and messages. For communications to be effective, Kracauer proposes, they must attune themselves and at least partially coincide with existing and well-established notions. In other words, radically new or discrepant messages, or film images radically at odds with preconceived ideas, are apt to fall flat and fail to engage audiences. To have the desired impact, film images always need to meet their spectators halfway. Propaganda does not work in a vacuum, and it cannot ignore the vagaries and contingences of context, history, and what Kracauer later refers to as the "total situation."

In the case of English and Russian characters and characterization—the twin foci of Kracauer's studies—prevailing ground reception are characterized by notions of an in- and an out-group, respectively. Relative familiarity with the English (e.g., in terms of long-standing common cultural traits, heritage, sympathy, and languages) ensure and enable American films to present a wide range of national and social types including but also extending well beyond the typical figure of the eccentric aristocratic snob. To be sure, the English are stereotyped in Hollywood films, but there is a multiplicity of guises and classes on display. Kracauer argues that this plethora of types enables a more diverse and hence representative set of "portraits" to emerge, which have some degree of verisimilitude. By contrast, Kracauer notes, Russian characters are far less common and diverse with only the mad Russian appearing as a recurrent figure. As an outgroup, Kracauer contends, the images of Russians are cruder caricatures. Members of out-groups appear as unsophisticated stereotypes, as the audience's level of familiarity and its expectations are much lower. Kracauer concludes that the less familiar a group is to typical audiences, the more important prevailing political interests are in their depiction: Russian stereotypes changed in accordance with fluctuating U.S.-Soviet relations. Hostility in the 1930s gave way to more positive images in the 1940s, which then returned to negative and antagonistic images in the postwar period. Two points emerge from this analysis. First, the more familiar populations are to their audience, the more difficult to stigmatize them in terms of, for example, class, ethnicity, and nationality; propaganda works best against out-groups. Second, film images—in this case in Hollywood productions, but in principle in any national cinema—may be seen as a kind of index or barometer of political relations between different countries. Films and film characters serve as a means of critically reading fluctuating international political relations and tensions.

NOTES

1. See the editorial notes in Siegfrid Kracauer, *Werke*, vol. 2.2 (Frankfurt: Suhrkamp Verlag, 2012), 725.
2. See p. 264.

9

Re-education Program for the Reich

January 4, 1948

Review of:
AND CALL IT PEACE
by Marshall Knappen
313 pp.
Chicago, IL, The University of Chicago Press. $3.

This book is a detailed account of German re-education as planned and implemented by the American Military Government. An insider has written it: Marshall Knappen, in civilian life a historian and political scientist at Michigan State College, was not only on the staff of the original planning unit, but after Germany's defeat continued to serve in a leading position. He tells a story of blunders, frustrated hopes and crippled achievements. And he tells it for a purpose.

When in March, 1944 a small British-American team assembled in southern England to draw up an education program for Germany, the three American members, among them Knappen started from two basic assumptions. First, they argued, Fascism in Germany and elsewhere must be traced to economic hardship rather than militarist leanings or ultra-nationalism. Secondly, if a group of people have been handicapped in the past by a poor inheritance, an improvement of environmental conditions will in time change these people themselves. In the light of such assumptions the hope seemed justified that economic reconstruction as promised by the Atlantic Charter to the vanquished might bring about a peaceable and democratic Germany. This optimistic outlook determined the program. It was a "soft program, based upon the supposition, reasonable in itself that the work of re-education would have to be undertaken by the Germans themselves. Provisions were made to re-establish schools and theological seminaries as quickly as possible, to counteract the consequences of denazification by energetic teacher training, to encourage the formation of church and community youth groups on a voluntary basis, etc. The whole breathed a spirit of indulgence toward German sensibilities.

But even before this well-intentioned program could take effect, it met two obstacles. One resulted from the inscrutable ways of the Army. Mr. Knappen exhaustively criticizes the meager understanding of military authorities, except perhaps on the top level, for educational problems—an acrimonious comment not only on occasional mistakes but on inherent narrowness. It deals with senior officers unable to grasp the importance of experts; with the infiltration of the Military Government by officers not desired elsewhere; with the belief, common among the brass, that reorientation was a matter of flogging the Germans or speedily metamorphosing them by ways of magic.

The second and more serious obstacle was the Morgenthau plan, with its demand for Germany's deindustrialization, which upset the very foundations of the education program. No sooner did this plan emerge than Washington reconsidered its occupation policy, insisting on tougher measures.

The subsequent survey of operations in Germany shows that despite these aggravating circumstances part of the original program could be carried out in a relatively short time. Schools were functioning by the spring of 1946; youth activities were initiated; adult education was revived in the major cities. The best points of this report on actual achievements are the interviews which Mr. Knappen as head of the Religious Affairs Section had with Cardinal Faulhaber and several dignitaries of the evangelical church. It is fresh material.

He gives a good account of Pastor Martin Niemoeller's intricate personality; and with some disappointment he admits that the pillars of German Protestantism not only advanced nationalistic viewpoints but showed themselves lenient toward the Nazis. Since, according to plan, outside interference with religious traditions was to be avoided, the churches were temporarily allowed to do their own housecleaning. Upon insistence of the Catholics the occupation authorities also conceded the re-establishment of denominational schools—a compromise which aroused much animosity among the anti-Nazi population.

However, the potential yield of these efforts was nipped in the bud by policy decisions from higher up, creating a climate even more unfavorable to reorientation than the Morgenthau intermezzo. Mr. Knappen takes great pains to attack the stern handling of denazification, which, in his opinion, thwarted any palpable solution in the educational field. He also elaborates upon the influence exerted by deteriorating living conditions in the wake of the Potsdam Agreement. And, of course, he again brings the Army on the carpet, dwelling at length upon the corruptive example set by its undiscriminating billeting procedures, its toleration of black market practices and its immature replacements.

Mr. Knappen's avowed purpose is to awaken the American people from their indifference. Prospects are gloomy in Germany, he asserts, and if we really wish to change the German mind we ourselves will have to change our policy. Or else history may once more repeat itself.

This book is useful as an honest piece of American self-criticism. Unfortunately, it is crowded with technicalities which sometimes obscure its underlying views. It also fails to take into account certain recent developments which point in the direction of the author's aims. Denazification measures have been modified. And should the Marshall plan come true, German economy, at least in the Western zones, would be reconstructed as a matter of course. In any case, since Mr. Byrnes' Stuttgart speech "environmental" changes are actually under way, and they conform exactly to what Mr. Knappen considers a necessary preliminary to German re-education. The one thing needed, as he remarks at one point, is "to give the German a job at steady wages which would take his mind off parading and putsching." Would it really? For a historian, Mr. Knappen seems rather oblivious of Germany's past. We can only hope that a future Germany will not give lie to his rosy basic assumptions.

10

How and Why the Public Responds to the Propagandist

July 4, 1948

Review of: *Public Opinion and Propaganda*
By Leonard W. Doob.
600 pp. New York: Henry Holt & Co. $5

This book should become a standard work in more than one respect. In it Professor Doob of Yale University organizes a vast, amorphous, and fluctuating body of material so masterfully that it becomes finite, articulate, and firm. What knowledge we have acquired in these fields is not only surveyed but also analyzed with a circumspection which owes much to the author's wealth of experience. Wartime observations which he made as Chief of the Bureau of Overseas Intelligence in the O.W.I. lend to many of his statements a color that makes his book very readable. And since it combines scholarship with a pronounced sense of human values, it is enlightening beyond its fundamental purpose.

Besides affecting each other in various ways, public opinion and propaganda have a common denominator: both are modes of human behavior. For this reason, the author approaches his double theme from a psychological angle. He calls his book an attempt "to extend some of the principles underlying individual behavior into the sphere of the inter-individual behavior, which is public opinion and propaganda."

His psychological outlook determines the route he chooses. The opening chapters deal with typical behavior patterns. He breaks down the over-all concept of personality into drives, attitudes, habits, etc., qualifying the influence of these properties on our responses to given stimuli. Here as elsewhere the specific flavor of Doob's definitions flows from his acute awareness of their provisional character. His is a kind of precision which never allows you to forget that every term is wrested from the raw material of life.

In the first major part the author examines, one by one, the factors that make up public opinion. Its emergence from a variety of social groups, its different modes of existence, its dependence on our cultural heritage, and its peculiar reactions to environmental changes and topical issues—all this is considered systematically. Yet the system is open; it is terra firma reclaimed from an ocean of possibilities which are permanently in view. The whole culminates in an exhaustive appraisal of current methods of measuring and evaluating public opinion. This section appears to me particularly important, because it treats popular polling techniques with sober caution.

The second major part is an anatomy of propaganda. Unaffected by the bad reputation of propaganda in Anglo-Saxon countries, Doob, always proceeding psychologically, stresses its resemblance to education—a resemblance of underlying attitudes—and then determines its particular nature as a social force. Intentional propaganda, whether revealed or concealed, is spread by such specialists as advertising men and journalists; and Doob, in a mood of relaxation, draws up profiles of them which are as judicious as they are amusing. After an inquiry into the existing methods of seizing upon propaganda content, he develops his main theme: the numerous devices used in driving home propaganda messages.

How are people made to perceive propaganda, to respond to it, and eventually to follow its suggestions? Doob methodically details the spells brought to bear on prospective believers. Often subpropaganda campaigns must be launched to induce novices to "learn" what it is all about. Unfavorable facts must be retouched, adverse attitudes counteracted. Simultaneously with these preparatory or defensive measures, the skilled propagandist strengthens positive reactions by evoking "related" responses, drawing on the prestige of the past, slightly varying ever-repeated appeals, etc. So, it goes on through the whole gamut of more or less tricky techniques. Doob insists that not all of them are so devilish as they seem to the naive; for instance, the propaganda device of simplification is common practice.

The third and last part surveys the media of communication—in particular the press, radio, and film. These three mass media not only reflect, and help to mold, public opinion, but are gigantic instruments of propaganda, whether intended or not. The role each medium plays as such an instrument is traced to its given characteristics, which, as Doob emphasizes, include a marked tendency toward concentration of power. Except, perhaps, for the chapter about radio, this part is not on the level he himself has set. His remarks on magazines, books and plays seem to be made merely for the sake of completeness. And the section on motion pictures is a loose assemblage of observations. Yet these minor shortcomings are really inevitable in a work of so wide a scope.

His sense of depth shows magnificently in the concluding chapter; in which he examines the value of his analytical enterprise. It proves itself to be rooted in a prudent, well-balanced conception of human affairs. "Without analysis," he says, "the feeling is likely to emerge that men are fatalistically tossed about by an irrational, unintelligible destiny. With analysis there is the beginning of self-control and social control, but neither can be guaranteed." The analyst, as it turns out, is a skeptical humanist.

11
Popular Advertisements

A coffin manufacturing company specializing in watertight caskets advertises its macabre merchandise by contending: "There's deep consolation ... for those who know the casket of a dear one is protected against water in the ground ..." This unfathomable statement is borne out by two pictures: a technical drawing demonstrating the casket's impermeability and the photo of a girl serene in the knowledge that her loved one will not suffer from the rain to which she is actually exposing herself. The whole is on a level with Evelyn Waugh's satire of American funeral rites.

And this nightmarish ad appeared in a weekly that reaches many millions of readers. Strange things are going on in our immediate surroundings. Let us, for once, take a look at them.

All popular advertisements try to engage us totally. Not content with interesting us in this or that product and for the rest leaving us in peace, they insatiably encroach on our thought processes and behavior patterns in general. To this end they more often than not cook up stories entirely unconnected with the articles they promote. It is as if the advertising agencies were guided by the conviction that the average individual will buy coffee or sanitary napkins only if he has such and such a personality structure. Hence their overwhelming desire for psychological domination. American ads sneak, octopus-like, into the remotest recesses of our minds, in a continuous effort to expand their hold on us.

Ours is a competitive society. It would therefore seem natural that the general views which, for instance, a soap manufacturer attempts to put over to us differ to some extent from those of a car manufacturer. Yet actually the contrary holds true: economic rivalry goes hand in hand with a complete consensus in the ideological field. The dream of the soap and the car manufacturer are strictly identical. However different their products, all advertisers propagandize one and the same *Weltanschauung,* one and the same outlook on life.

And in spreading this uniform message. (which will be discussed shortly), all of them urge us to accept it unreservedly. Perhaps the most conspicuous feature of ads is their insistence on conformity. They aim at eliminating social diverseness and unconventional characters; and they ruthlessly regiment taste and manner down to the smallest detail. A popular hair tonic ad has it that a boy with disheveled hair may well estrange his girl from him." How can a man as clever as he," the girl asks gloomily, "be so blind about his appearance?" Fortunately, the worst is averted. Upon her advice he uses the tonic and thus turns from a maladjusted individual into a regular fellow who reconquers the sympathies he was on the point of losing. In this way numerous ads threaten any freakish dissenter with the loss of love or social status.

Evidently this persistent plea for conformity is bound up with the requirements of mass production. Highly standardized goods cannot find sufficient outlets unless they satisfy highly standardized needs. The souls must come from the assembly line also, or else they may not absorb what really comes from it. As the world is shrinking and supply is apt to surpass demand, this tendency to condition—or, rather, precondition—the buying public psychologically is likely to increase. We are living in an era in which psychological imperialism supersedes political imperialism for the sake of a more intensive market policy.

And what kind of life do the ads hold out to us? It is a life of, by, and for the young. Most ad characters, I should guess, are below 30, if not plain 'teen-agers, including many married couples whom no one would credit with being married at so adolescent a stage was it not for the lovely children bestowed upon them by the commercial designers. The sight of these boys and girls is somewhat confusing because all of them look alike—pictorial testimonies to the urge for conformity behind ads. That they are glad to conform can be inferred from the boy in the above-mentioned hair tonic ad who begins to smile immediately after having normalized his disheveled hair. He is heretic returned to the fold. Like him everybody smiles—it is as if the Cheshire Cat had left behind its smile for general distribution. And the present owners of the smile, all these beautiful and healthy young people, radiate a confidence which reveals their ignorance of its weird origins.

They smile for good reasons.

First, life, as it were, offers them plenty of gratifications. Even the drudging housewives and gas station attendants manifest a cheerfulness which marks their seeming chores as veritable Pleasures. And most people are never seen drudging. If they are not kept busy by such outdoor activities as sports and travels, they usually indulge in the more intimate charms of nature. The scene is crowded with loving couples in closeup, after the manner of Hollywood films. A radio-television unit sets them dancing, and a dental cream stimulates them to a tête-à-tête as tender as it is hygienic. But perhaps the greatest enjoyment is family life, what with snapshots being taken of baby, homely fireplaces, folksy Main Street views, and nationally reputed beverages in the garden. Between porch and airliner, motionless well-being and utter speed, nothing is omitted in this itinerary of pastimes and diversions.

Secondly, wealth, prestige and power seem just around the corner. Here is where the middle-aged and old come in, who naturally keep on smiling. A few less privileged among them, it is true, have grown old only to tell us that a particular car tire lasts ten years and longer, or that the traditional ice cream Dixies are still the best. But the rest of them figure in the social register and the high income brackets—a choice tribe of presidents, vice-presidents and other business leaders. They thrive in the rarefied air of country clubs and Pullman suites, put in a shining appearance on social occasions, and surround themselves with de luxe secretaries, lords, prominent stars and expensive paintings. This display of glamor is obviously intended to suggest that it lies in the order of things for the young to become, in due time, big executives also. Everybody is predestined, to success. It may sound paradoxical, but even those, who, by an unexplainable whim of fate, do not precisely get to the top, are in a certain sense as successful as are the chosen ones. This is demonstrated by the many ads which show vice-presidents and genuine aristocrats reveling in some commonplace article, thus giving Tom, Dick and Harry the pleasant feeling that they are actually on a par with the upper crust. Any bottle of beer does the trick.

Thirdly, all these characters smile, it appears, because they are confident that nothing will ever interfere with their enjoyments and achievements. They live in an atmosphere of complete security, inaccessible to rumors of unemployment and failure. One may object here that, for instance, life insurance ads are bound to spread this atmosphere in the interest of their sponsors; that it is indeed their very business to exercise the nightmare of lean years to come by glowing pictures of middle-aged policy holders who, in a state of perfect contentment, are whiling their time away on the inevitable porch. But other ads with no such obligations follow exactly the same pattern. Whenever they conjure up the old frontier spirit—a giant truck meeting a ghost caravan of covered wagons, a mail coach stopping at a Wells-Fargo station—they usually do so with definite pride in present-day safety. And they invariably convey the impression that is the business enterprises they portray resemble our Constitution in their aloofness from the ugly vicissitudes of cycles and crises. Occasionally, this impression is deepened by a glorying in successful laboratory research which implies that such trials never entail errors. Ad characters need not even fear.

And finally, they are justified in believing that their blissful lives are going to continue forever. The ads create this illusion of a heaven on earth by omitting death and all that leads up to it. To be sure, undertakers and casket manufacturers want to have their say also. But they interfere only in isolated cases; and the ad for impermeable caskets, mentioned at the outset of my article, proves conclusively that their discretion is as waterproof as are their caskets. For even though this ad does not conceal the fact that our dear ones sometimes disappear, it so insistently dwells upon the technical perfection of their future abodes that we are led to think of their disappearance as a removal to just another and more comfortable place. It is merely a change of domicile after all. Like the characters in old epics, those in ads live eternally.

Much as they are privileged, however, they should not be mistaken for Fortuna's favorites who reap a harvest they never sowed. Rather, they get what they get by deliberately reaching out for it. From the moment at which the first snapshots of them are taken until such time as they depart for an unmentioned destination, they leave nothing to chance in their pursuit of happiness.

Ad characters are born planners. Here again I do not refer to their conduct in insurance ads which of course urge them to be prudent and farsighted, but to the way they scheme and act under less exacting circumstances. An ad for Pullman lounge cars lays bare the taut aspirations behind their effortless smile. In that car a gentleman of distinction and a college boy engage in a conversation which sets the latter raving soberly: "You meet regular people—*your* kind—in the lounge car. Me, I'm on good terms already with this Big Executive who's suggested I see him about a job next June: " These characters never relish an enjoyable situation without speculating on how to improve further their chances. Not even the ecstasy of love makes them forget the future in the present. It would seem natural for a boy to fall into incoherent stammer while embracing his girl before moonlit birch trees; instead, he voices in well-set words his dream of the home they will have and the chests or silver spoons they will buy.

Yet in being so preoccupied with their own future, these charming go-getters fulfil a mission transcending them.

They are not satisfied unless they get better refrigerators, milder cigarettes, smoother cars. Since for obvious reasons ads never mention the less recommendable refrigerators, cigarettes and cars to which they compare the praised ones, the words "better," "milder" and "smoother" are left hanging in midair—comparative which, for being grammatically impossible, all the more connote the idea of technological progress. In many ads explanatory statements reveling in improvements achieved, corroborate this implication of the fragmentary comparatives. All ad characters are progressive-minded. And they seem convinced that anything milder or smoother adds something invaluable to life in general; that technical progress infallibly results in human progress. Their conviction of a pre-established harmony between better machinery and better humanity gives their smile an ideal quality.

This then is, in one summary sentence, the American dream, as told by the ads in our popular magazines: the happily conforming young aspire to success and manage to attain it, thereby serving the ideal of progress. The dream sounds familiar. In fact, the magazine contents themselves resemble so closely the ads with which they alternate, that we sometimes find it difficult to differentiate between commercial inserts and pictorial or literary contributions. No Life reader will be immune to this delusion. It is a legitimate one, for in effect ads supplement rather than interrupt what popular magazines see fit to print. Commercials and editorials are often interchangeable. Many a Saturday Evening Post story advertises the very ideas which the interspersed ads narrate in true story fashion.

To be sure, the dream is a dream; and we do not depend on wild guesses to reveal it as such. A glance at the nonfiction bestseller list suffices. For a long time, the two books "Peace of Mind" and "How to Stop Worrying and Start Living" have succeeded in topping that list. The inevitable conclusion is that the counterparts in real life of the happy housewives and gas station attendants in the ads suffer from a lack of peace and do a great deal of worrying. They must be psychologically dissatisfied, or else they would not be spellbound by the magic of those book titles. That many of them are living under a mental strain is further confirmed by the ever-increasing vogue for psychoanalysis and the widespread concern with psychosomatic medicine—sciences which would hardly have become so popular were it not for a general want of emotional stability. All of this gives the lie to the pretended happiness of ad characters.

What are people worrying about? At first glance it seems hopeless to try to get an answer from the ads themselves, for they naturally deny the existence of any such worries. And yet it pays to question them. The reason is that effective mass propaganda must respond to real mass needs. Even Goebbels at his most fanciful could not manipulate away the vestiges of independent public opinion, but had to cope with them somehow and somewhere, thus enabling us to draw reasonable conclusions as to their nature. The same applies to ads: they cannot afford to pass over reality, however hostile, with a slight of hand, because its complete neglect might interfere with our acceptance of their propaganda messages. Of course, they attempt to camouflage real life by oblique innuendos and powerful suggestions; yet even so it is still present, and its smoldering presence is bound to affect the dream fabric they are weaving. Beneath this manifest dream story there runs another, less glamorous story which can be inferred from two problematic features of the dream itself: the ads' strange preoccupation with security and their wholesale absorption in the planning of success.

What is strange in their insistence on security is its one-sidedness. Ads are true products of a system rooted in competition with its inherent risks. One should therefore expect them to draw on the thrill of high stakes, on that adventurous spirit which underlies so many of our achievements. Instead, they feature a life in which safety prevails over adventure and the motif of contest emerges only in the field of sports—when some advertiser finds it opportune to refer to a horse race or a baseball champion. But this reluctance to acknowledge the fact of competition is inexplicable unless it is traced to a concern with actually existing mass dispositions. Through their singular bias in favor of security the advertising agencies betray their awareness that people are harassed by the lack of it. And their soothing language seems calculated to allay apprehensions.

In the light of this knowledge a new meaning accrues to a special tyro of ads—the foot ads, with their screaming colors and their giant displays of cuts of meat, tomato slices, and luscious pies. They are suggestive of an infatuation with food which often grows out of a state of anxiety or depression. A Canadian-made documentary film, *The Feeling of Hostility*, illustrates this familiar experience through the case history of a woman who, at a certain moment of her life, gobbles enormous quantities of sweets to compensate for her frustrations.

To be sure, this shrill and oversized victual cannot sufficiently be explained by culinary excesses in the wake of emotional troubles; but what may once have been a naive expression of bouncing vitality is now, I guess, being upheld by the feeling of insecurity that sweeps the masses.

The way ads emphasize the planning of success points to another source of general disquiet. Ad characters organize their lives with such an incomparable smoothness that we feel they have no psychological difficulties to overcome in getting along nicely. Nothing within them resists their upward flight; they seem devoid of unruly instincts and impracticable fancies. And what originality they possess is being used up in the process of climbing. Take the Whiskey ads: most of them appeal merely to the social ambitions of prospective buyers, implying that they are animated not so much by a genuine passion for Whiskey as the burning desire to "belong." Smiling eagerness for careers consumes the purposeless; love ceases to be an end in itself, as is evidenced by the ad with the two would-be lovers before moonlit birch trees. This indifference to self-sufficient human relations reaches its peak in an amazing ad for a new station wagon model: standing before the shining vehicle, a young man, possibly its owner, chats with a radiant young woman, and the caption, underlined in red, affirms: "The Beginning of a Beautiful Friendship:" The delighted reader is led to believe that he has finally come across a commercial which extols tender leanings for their own sake: yet no sooner does he continue reading than he learns that the beautiful friendship is meant to develop between the car owner and his car. Alas, the car's attractiveness outshines the sex appeal of the young woman.

Ad characters impress us as empty creatures. This impression is intensified by a few exceptional ads which, for whatever reasons, picture the opposite state of mind—emotional fullness. One of them, an ad for watches, shows an elderly couple taking leave of each other at an airport; untouched by the stirring bustle about them, both are visibly under the spell of emotions that evade measurement. They inhabit a universe in which slow growth and inner experience count more than space-devouring speed and surface glamor. It is the universe in which music evolves. This probably accounts for the presence of similarly mellow and cultured people in an isolated radio ad—people who, as they listen to the music from an expensive radio set, seem to defy the hollowness of chronological time. Stray visitors in the world of the ads, they and the elderly couple make us acutely aware of the shortcomings of its permanent residents—their two-dimensional flatness, their futile predilection for time-saving gadgets. What will the industrious housewives do with the time thus saved? The same problem is posed by the declared favorites of life insurance ads, those prematurely retired policy holders on their porches who represent nothing but infinite boredom.

In emphasizing their characters' unflinching purposefulness, ads reflect a widespread, economically desirable attitude. American mass production is, itself, a matter of methodical planning and calculating; and it naturally works at full steam only if it is supported by people susceptible to its demands. These people exist not only in ads; nor are they emotionally more articulate than ad characters. We know what they are like. Sinclair Lewis has exposed their inner workings, and John Marquand in his novels never tires of elaborating upon the atmosphere of emptiness that pervades our society.

Ads cannot help revealing this emptiness. At the same time, they try hard to minimize it, thus inadvertently admitting that many people currently suffer from the void within and about them. The dream must be cloudless. Hence the advertising agencies' desperate attempt to pass off technological advance as progress in general, human or otherwise—an equation difficult to maintain in the era of the atomic bomb. That they nevertheless perpetuate such an obvious illusion betrays their (presumably unconscious) desire to make up for the mass frustration from emptiness. The device is simple: people who believe themselves to be the standard-bearers of "progress" will be less aware of their lack of really substantial ideals. The idea of progress serves to ennoble the streamlined efficiency with which they rush ahead of the moment, even the most precious, in which they are actually living.

At this point the omnipresence of the young, in particular the "teen-agers" becomes understandable. The gratifications lavished on them in ads make them appear superficial, if not callous, in comparison with the elderly couple in the watch ad mentioned above. But youth is justified in behaving this way because it is still remote from death and because it can acquire experience only by playing around. A certain emptiness is natural for it. This may strengthen the publicity agents' determination to concentrate on youth. In doing so, they not only conform to a general trend which is what they want to do anyway, but achieve, probably without intending it, something more specific—they challenge the public to identify itself with an age group which need not feel frustrated for temporarily drifting along in a vacuum. The very emptiness which causes many to look out for books like "How to Stop Worrying and Start Living" is thus impressed upon us as a normal, by no means unpleasant state of mind. The whole amounts to an attempt to wheedle adults out of their frustrations by making them adolescents once more.

Here arises the problem of accounting for the tremendous impact of ads. Their flaws show glaringly; and many of their appeals and insinuations are too silly to deceive anyone in his senses. Yet all this does not prevent publicity agents from clinging doggedly to such doubtful patterns. And they certainly have the know-how.

Ads lure the masses for three reasons, the first of which is precisely their dream quality. But why does this particular dream with its boundless optimism, its undiscriminating promise of success and its naive outlook on human affairs prove so attractive? The answer is that it is a left-over from those days which Coolidge epitomized in declaring that the business of America is business. It is an obsolete dream, long since discredited by history. This, however, makes it all the more irresistible, for it caters to popular longings for that time of expansion and prosperity when, it appears, life was less involved and private initiative of more consequence. A clever mixture of Main Street mentality and managerial slickness, current ads look very much up-to-date; yet actually they are the last stragglers from the era that preceded the Great Depression. And nothing compares in splendor with the nostalgic memory of things irretrievably gone.

Secondly, ads are so effective because they are more than a dream. Their dream quality is every now and then suspended; their escapism is not consistent enough to conceal unescapable reality. Ads hint of the truth, if only by implication. And most people will grasp the truth instinctively. They will realize, however dimly, that the relation established in ads between planning and emptiness has a bearing on their own lives, and that the stereotyped smile of ad characters is in effect a smile under the stress of insecurity. As they look at ads, people may be haunted by the vision of the Cheshire Cat taking shape again and reclaiming the smile from its present owners, those insouciant housewives, gas station attendants and college students. But instead of disrupting the spell of ads, the reappearance of this weird animal increases their attractiveness. It causes the public constantly to waver between the two opposite poles of ads—the dream of happiness they spread and the pressure of the reality they admit. The psychological result is that the dream mitigates that pressure, which in turn makes the dream seem more palpable. This intermingling of life as it is and life as it might be having the intoxicating power of a drug.

And thirdly, ads are animated by an almost religious passion for producing and selling goods. Much as they affect us through their mixture of dream and reality, the very secret of their impact is this passion, which imbues any hair tonic or coffee manufacturer with the certitude that he has a gospel to impart, a mission to fulfil. His is so absorbing a belief in the immense signification of his particular product that he feels urged to propagandize, along with it, his whole outlook on Life—a life centering round shampoos or coffee beans. I have said at the beginning that all ads tend to engage us totally; this tendency must, at least in part, be traced to the advertisers' missionary zeal which often stirs them or their publicity agents to turn into veritable bards. "You'll be walking on air," a piece of authentic poetry reads, "... you'll be dancing with joy... you'll be feeling smug as silk ... once you have the body under the slimming, trimming, smoothing, soothing influence of this...... girdle or panty-girdle." It is the girdle, not the girl wearing it, that kindles this emotional conflagration. The passion enlivening commercials bears exclusively on merchandise, as the above-mentioned station wagon ad reveals once and for all through its express advocacy of responses to goods instead of responses to persons: its caption, "The Beginning of a Beautiful Friendship!" creates the illusion of the car owner's concern with his female companion for the sole purpose of driving home his amorous feelings for the ear.

Yet for all its indifference to human values this impassioned interest in business is something promising—a symptom of unbroken vitality, an expression of the creative energies instrumental in American life. Ads are so impressive because the vigor of the passion pervading them endows their otherwise problematic dream of youth and progress with a certain meaning. Besides serving as a means of escape, this dream manifests a belief in the future which is sustained by the existence of those creative energies. Why should they benefit only business? And the same belief in the future makes the glimpses of reality which ads afford appear less frightening. We somehow feel confident that our vitality will enable us to overcome both insecurity and emptiness.

Strong stimulants produce strong effects. Through their perpetual emphasis on conformity ads, along with the other media of mass communication, promote a state of mind which, should it further gain ground, would give the lie to that belief in the future. There are, to be sure, times when nonconformist behavior assumes threatening proportions; but at present the graver danger is what I have called "psychological imperialism"—a tendency, powerful in this country, to prefabricate souls as if they were houses. Ads belong among its most common carriers. The kind of conformity they propagandize not only undermines our creative faculties but helps increase the emptiness about us, thus favoring dispositions for such substitutes as race bias and authoritarian rule.

Fortunately, propaganda has its limits. Speaking of our press, film and radio, Harold J. Laski in his book, *The American Democracy* (New York, 1948, pp. 622–23), remarks that "the power of those who own and operate these major instruments of propaganda is always being challenged and is never as effective as, superficially, it might seem that it ought to be. There is something in the psychological climate of America which resists any ultimate regimentation of behavior or opinion. Something always escapes the net which is thrown about the people. Nonconformity is an element in American life which is always called into being by the spectacle of conformity." This statement has been clinched by the results of the November election.[1]

Our belief in the future is fairly warranted if we continue to disregard the gratuitous intimations of polls—or of ads, for that matter. Should this happen, then I foresee a time in which ad characters will drop their out-to-pattern smile; for ads not only influence people but are, on their part, influenced by what people do and think. Much can be done of which publicity agents are currently unaware. It seems possible, for instance, to feature a shampoo without contending that a boy with disheveled hair cannot be loved. It also seems possible to advertise watertight caskets and yet have death retain its dignity. Someday such possibilities may materialize. This would be a good sign indeed.

NOTE

1. Harry S. Truman, candidate of the Democratic Party, won the U.S. presidential election in 1948.—Eds.

12
A Duck Crosses Main Street

December 13, 1948

—That's news for American newsreel cameras, which focus mainly on wars, monkeys, volcanoes and pretty girls.

It happens at least once to every commuter. Cyrus Fairweather misses the 5:31 and walks into the newsreel theater in New York's Grand Central Station to while away an hour before the next train. He also has a vague idea that he might catch up on what is happening around the world, but as he settles back in his seat, what does he see and hear for his forty cents?

Kettledrums; a Voice of Doom; grinning, bearded Greeks firing a cannon at what looks like a mountain. According to the commentator, aggression is being stopped as Time Marches On in Greece.

There follows the up-to-the-minute news.

The battleship *New Jersey* is deactivated as granite-faced admirals salute and a boatswain's mate dramatically turns off the ship's ventilation systems;

Somewhere in the USA, a duck crosses Main Street;

A French wrestler, weight 276, grapples with a Belgian with a long, black beard; Secretary of the Treasury Snyder signs a check for $7.5 billion;

Girls in bathing suits dive from towers; girls in bathing suits parade before solemn judges; French girls in French bathing suits coyly assume sidewise poses for the prudish American cameras, while American girls in American bathing suits put on skis and fall down in the snow.

"The ski's the limit," cries the commentator, and Fairweather looks at his watch. His time is up, and he starts off for his train, his ears still buzzing from assorted squawks and explosions and his eyes watering from the quick shifting of the scenes.

As he emerges from the theater, Fairweather is little impressed by what he has seen that he immediately wonders what Mrs. F. is having for dinner.

Like thousands of other Americans Fairweather thinks of newsreel theaters as convenient places to wait for trains, get out of the rain, or cool off in air-conditioned comfort. The customer who really expects to see the news is a naive character.

The average moviegoer is so accustomed to bathing beauties, monkeys, baseball games, politicians, etc., that he would probably be mystified by a newsreel which attempted to give him fifty minutes of significant current events. Since he raises no effective objection to the status-quo, the newsreel producers are content to let things ride.

The result of this apathy has been to perpetuate a newsreel format that hasn't changed appreciably in the past twenty years. The same old subjects are given the same old treatment. In covering horse races, animals at the zoo, speeches, etc., the photographic techniques used by five major newsreel companies (20th Century-Fox Movietone, Warner-Pathé, Paramount, Universal, Hearst-M-G-M News of the Day) are as predictable as the days of the week.

As for authenticity, some newsreels are almost as phony as the old staged photographs of the sinking of the *Maine* in 1898, which were shown in the nickelodeons.

However, to attack the newsreel on artistic grounds, or as an agency for disseminating important news, is like hitting a man when he's down. Even the men who make them are far from proud of what they turn out. Their attitude is deprecating and, instead of plugging their product, they go into long explanations of why it is no better.

Problem number one is money. None of the newsreel companies makes more than a moderate return on its investments; at times they show a loss, which must be absorbed by the parent company in Hollywood. Unlike newspapers, they have no advertising revenue, and the cost of taking pictures, developing the negatives, making prints, etc., is high.

A second big problem is the difficulty of getting hold of enough spectacular or important news week after week. One harassed producer complains: "The *Daily News* can't always be bright with a good sex murder; the *Times* can't always be bright with an international situation; and so how in hell can you expect us to be bright every time some chump sits down in front of a camera and opens his mouth?"

Even if important news stories broke every day, limited budgets would make adequate coverage impossible. Most of the companies operate on a "stringer"-correspondent basis. Although they pay a few men a regular salary to obtain material, most of the work is done by stringers, who are paid small fees. This reliance on half-time correspondents gets half-time results.

In faraway places like China and Japan, the newsreels use a "pool" arrangement under which one cameraman works for several companies. This a cheap way of getting film, but it discourages imaginative reporting. Another example of pooling is the non-competitive way in which representatives of the major newsreel companies often cover a single big assignment such as a national convention. The cameramen travel in a tightly knit group, shoot the same stuff, and look with a fishy grin at colleagues who attempt to get exclusive stories.

A talk with a newsreel editor is roughly analogous to picking up an empty vase which you expected to be full; it throws you slightly off balance. The editors, conscious of the shortcomings of their output, add criticism of their own to the general uproar. For example, Newton Meltzer of Telenews admits that the commentary is much too verbose, and hopes that American newsreels will learn to emulate the European films' terse, reserved treatment.

For Movietone's Dan Daugherty, a red-headed newsreel veteran, faces criticism with equanimity. "We have made billions of mistakes," he agrees, "but when we do a good job nobody notices. For instance, we told the public about Hitler, Mussolini and the rest of their gang—filmed thousands of feet of speeches, parades, planes, and guns—but almost nobody believed us. What the hell? You show some people the truth, and they close their eyes. But if you miss something, that's different."

Two outstanding critics of newsreels are Bosley Crowther of the New York *Times* and the New York *Herald Tribune*'s John Crosby. M. D. Clofine, editor of Heast-M-G-M's News of the Day, blames the term "newsreel" for many of their adverse comments.

"What the critics don't see is that the newsreel has got to be more than just a documentary. As part of a theatre program it has two functions—to inform and to amuse. Since the entertainment factor has to enter our calculations, we often use light subjects in preference to a 'significant' piece of news that is pictorially dull."

Clofine also points out that the scope of the newsreel is limited by the requirements of the individual theater exhibitor, who, after all, is in the business to make money. Since the main features are the most important revenue-producers on his program, he allots most of his budget to them; the result is that when the exhibitor gets around to the newsreel he has very little left to spend. This simple economic fact explains why the newsreels are not as elaborate or as exhaustive as they might be. The producers cannot afford it.

Economic and technical difficulties may explain many of the newsreels' weaknesses, but not their editorial shortcomings. Newsreel material about world affairs, for instance, follows a singularly conventional course and, in most cases, industriously beats the drum for US foreign policy (Palestine is a possible exception).

The films are saturated with anti-Communist and pro-military propaganda. When Cardinal Spellman and President Truman spoke on St. Patrick's Day, it was the anti-Communist portions of their addresses that were singled out for screening. Extensive shots of army maneuvers, diving planes, smoking rockets and General MacArthur reviewing his troops in Japan are screened while sound tracks blare do-or-die college marching songs.

On the home front, the newsreels frequently make no bones about being partisan. Labor conflicts are usually treated with ill-concealed bias. During the soft-coal strike last year, elaborate shots of abandoned mines and joking, idle miners invited moviegoers to ponder the destructive effects of the shutdown. The cameras did not go into the miners' side of the story. The newsreels' way of treating the packinghouse workers' strike was to give prominence to signs in butcher shops proclaiming the rising cost of meat. Occasionally, however, impartiality is shown. Telenews' coverage of the Wall Street strike was fair to both sides, and also told the story in an interesting way.

There is little doubt that US newsreels distort current political events. Yet these distortions would do so little harm if it were not for the newsreels' tendency to blunt audience's critical faculties.

First, there is too much chatter. Newsreel audiences are spoon-fed a constant stream of words, wisecracks and loaded phrases. These are spoken in overemphasized tones of seriousness, despair, triumph or happiness that only the worst ham actor would dare to employ on stage. Not only is it corny; it is much too long. The comment in American newsreels takes up 80 percent of the screening time, while many of the European reels restrict commentary to a third as much footage.

Again, American newsreel sequences almost always alternate between disaster (floods, fires) and fun (gorilla eats birthday cake). The emotions of the newsreel fan are made to bob up and down like a yo-yo, and the effect of this jerky, kaleidoscopic attack on his eyes and ears is to induce a state of near paralysis. When he finally emerges from the theater, his memory is a hodgepodge of noises, faces, catastrophes and shifting backgrounds.

At least one major newsreel company, Telenews, is showing that new techniques can be evolved. In its short existence, Telenews has emphasized the "trend" approach to significant news stories, featuring intelligent interpretation of the scenes it records.

An excellent example of Telenews' reporting was its treatment of the Supreme Court decision invalidating restrictive covenants.[1] The sequence opened with shots of men picketing the White House in protest against the Negro segregation in the Army. Then came footage contrasting white and Negro housing in such cities as New York and Washington D.C. The narrator interviewed the Negro family which brought the case to the Supreme Court. The disputed portion of the covenant itself was enlarged on the screen, while a background voice slowly quoted that section of the Fourteenth Amendment which played a crucial part in the court decision. This was superb reporting—thorough, convincing, and original.

Sloppiness, distortion, and bias are probably unintentional. They may play up or omit certain topics for political reasons, but it would be preposterous to assume that they select and manipulate their material with a view to stupefying their audience. They seem to be indolent rather than totalitarian minded.

There is no valid reason why US newsreel companies should not try to develop patterns that challenge the intellect instead of blunting it. The newsreel need not be as bad as it is. The eternal mixture of disasters and silly jokes is not unavoidable, and even sports events can be depicted in a less stereotyped way.

But the most urgently needed reform is in structure. Commentary should be limited to essential supplementary information, while the pictures tell the actual story. The audience would then be in a position to digest material that now scarcely reaches its senses.

NOTE

1. Kracauer is referring here to the landmark United States Supreme Court case *Shelley v. Kraemer* (334 U.S. 1, 1948), that struck down racially restrictive housing covenants. On *Shelley v. Kraemer* and the history of racially restrictive housing covenants in the United States, see Richard Rothstein, *The Color of Law: A Forgotten History of How Our Government Segregated America* (New York: Liveright, 2017), 77–91.—Eds.

13
National Types as Hollywood Presents Them

Hollywood, and any national film industry for that matter, is both a leader and follower of public opinion. In portraying foreign characters it reflects what it believes to be the popular attitudes of the time, but it also turns these often vague attitudes into concrete images. This process is dramatically highlighted by the treatment which American films have given British and Russian characters from about 1933 to the present. Our images of foreign peoples result from a ratio between objective and subjective factors, and Hollywood can make a considerable contribution to international understanding by increasing the objective factor in its treatment of foreign characters to the extent that current public opinion will allow.

This study is one of a number of pilot studies undertaken in connection with the UNESCO project for studying international tensions.

The author is well known, both here and abroad, as a social psychologist specializing in analysis of the social and cultural implications of films. His analytical account of the German film, From Caligari to Hitler, *was published by the Princeton University Press in 1947.*

UNESCO has begun to inquire into the nature of tensions inimical to mutual understanding between the peoples of the world. Part of this "Tensions Project" is an analysis of "the conceptions which the people of one nation entertain of their own and of other nations."

It seems likely indeed that international understanding depends to some extent on the character of such conceptions- particularly if they assert themselves within the media of mass communication. Among these media the film is perhaps the most impressive.

If we are to study national images as presented in films, two broad areas for research immediately confront us. How do the films of any nation represent their own nation? And how do they represent others? The first of these two problems, increasingly dealt with in current writings, can be dismissed here in favor of the second which seems to me more important for UNESCO'S quest. It is a new problem, not yet posed in a general way. Along with a whole family of similar problems, it has come into focus only now that world government is a possibility and world domination a threat. Only now, in fact, has the goal of mutual understanding through knowledge changed from an intellectual pleasure to a vital concern of the democracies.

The following study is by no means intended to provide a comprehensive analysis of the various screen images which the peoples of the world have formed, and continue to form, of each other. It is a pilot study, and merely attempts to prepare the ground for such an investigation by examining a small sector of the total subject: the appearance of English and Russian characters in American fiction films since about 1933.[1]

In the universe of fiction films two types are of lesser importance—films about the past of the English and Russians, and screen adaptations of literary masterworks from the two countries. This is not to say that such films are rare. On the contrary, Hollywood finds Victorian England endearing and Catherine the Great amusing. Also, it often feels compelled to exchange entertainment for what it believes to be culture, and thus it eagerly exploits Shakespeare's plays and Tolstoy's novels, trying to make of them entertainment.[2] No doubt both these historical and literary films are well-established genres. And of course, I do not deny that they help build up the screen images of the foreign peoples to which they refer. Yet since they deal with remote events, they are decidedly less relevant to this study than films that have a direct bearing on present-day reality.

It is these latter films on which I am concentrating here—films, that is, which involve contemporary Russian and British characters in real-life situations. There has been no lack of them since 1933. I am thinking, for instance, of *Ninotchka* (1939), with its pleasantries at the expense of Soviet mentality, and of *Cavalcade* (1933), which follows the destinies of a well-to-do English family through two generations. What concepts the American screen entertains of the English and Russians can best be elicited from such more or less realistically handled comedies and dramas.

OBJECTIVE AND SUBJECTIVE FACTORS IN NATIONAL IMAGES

In the cases of individuals and peoples alike, knowledge of each other may progress from a state of ignorance to fair understanding. It is, for instance, a far cry from what the average American knows about the Japanese to Ruth Benedict's recent disclosure of the set of motives that determine Japanese attitudes and actions. Her study, The *Chrysanthemum and the Sword*, marks progress in objectivity; it challenges us to dispose of the familiar notions and common prejudices which help fashion our standard images of that people. Generally speaking, any such increase of knowledge is identical with a closer approach to the object we seek to penetrate.

This approach, however, is bound to remain asymptotic for two reasons, one of which lies in the object itself. An individual or a people is not so much a fixed entity as a living organism that develops along unforeseeable lines. Hence the difficulty of self-identification. It is true that the successive images a people create of its own character are as a rule more reliable than those it forms of a foreign people's; but they are not complete and definite either.

The other obstacle to perfect knowledge, alone important in this context, lies in ourselves. We perceive all objects in a perspective imposed upon us by our environment as well as by certain inalienable traditions. Our concepts of a foreigner necessarily reflect native habits of thought. Much as we try to curtail this subjective factor, as we are indeed forced to do in the interest of increased objectivity, we still view the other individual from a position which is once and for all ours. It is just as impossible for us to settle down in a vacuum as it would be to fuse with him.

Any image we draw up of an individual or a people is the resultant of an objective and a subjective factor. The former cannot grow indefinitely; nor can the latter be completely eliminated. What counts is the ratio between these two factors. Whether our image of a foreign people comes close to true likeness or merely serves as a vehicle of self-expression—that is, whether it is more of a portrait or more of a projection—depends upon the degree to which our urge for objectivity gets the better of naive subjectivity.

MEDIA INFLUENCES ON OBJECTIVITY-SUBJECTIVITY RATIO

The ratio between the objective and the subjective factor varies with the medium of communication. It is evident that within the medium of the printed word objectivity may go the limit. In the radio, also, objective information plays a considerable role, even though it is hampered by various restrictions, most of them inherent in the nature of this mass medium. Yet for all its limitations the radio registers any signal increase of knowledge. I do not doubt, for instance, that the evolution of modern anthropology—resulting from the necessities of psychological warfare and this country's engagements in international affairs—has been instrumental in bringing about recent radio programs which surveyed living conditions in other countries, and in particular focused on "the character and ideals of the Russian people."[3]

And what about the film? Hollywood's fiction films are commercial products designed for mass consumption at home and, if possible, abroad. The implications of this over-all principle are obvious: Hollywood must try to captivate the masses without endangering its affiliations with vested interests. In view of high production costs, it must try to avoid controversial issues lest box office receipts fall off. What the latter "must" means for the representation of foreigners is classically illustrated by the setback which the Remarque film, *All Quiet on the Western Front* (1930), suffered in Germany after a few Berlin performances, in December 1930. This film; with its emphasis on the anti-war mood of German soldiers in the years of trench warfare, stirred the Nazis to violent demonstrations which in turn caused the German government to suspend its further screening.[4] Similar experiences, made with vaguely anti-Fascist films in neutral countries shortly before World War II, have corroborated the sad truth that foreign peoples are as touchy as domestic groups, professional or otherwise. The film industry therefore "remains afraid of portraying characters or situations in a way which will offend its existing foreign market: why jeopardize a source of revenues?"[5]

Hollywood, then, is faced with the task of producing films that draw the masses, in particular the American masses. The problem of how it measures up to this task has long since been a subject of discussion. Many holds that Hollywood, with the support of its affiliated chains of movie houses, manages to sell films which do not give the masses what they really want. From this viewpoint it would seem that Hollywood films more often than not stultify and misdirect a public persuaded into accepting them by its own indolence and by overwhelming publicity. I do not believe that such a viewpoint is tenable. Experience has taught us that even totalitarian regimes cannot manipulate public opinion forever; and what holds true for them applies all the more to an industry which despite its monopolistic tendencies still functions within the framework of a competitive society. The film industry is forced by its profit interest to divine the nature of actually existing mass trends and to adjust its products to them. That this necessity leaves a margin for cultural initiative on the part of the industry does not alter the situation. To be sure, American audiences receive what Hollywood wants them to want; but in the long run audience desires, acute or dormant, determine the character of Hollywood films.[6]

The audiences also determine the way these films picture foreigners. The subjective factor in any such image is more or less identical with the notions

American public opinion entertains of the people portrayed. It is therefore highly improbable that a nation popular with the average American will be presented unfavorably; nor should we expect currently unpopular nations to be treated with condoning benevolence. Similarly, screen campaigns for or against a nation are not likely to be launched unless they can feed on strong environmental moods in their favor.

Yet its surrender to such moods need not prevent Hollywood from volunteering information about foreign peoples. It is true that we usually want to understand other nations because of our concern with mutual understanding; but fear and distrust of a people may no less urgently compel us to inquire into the motives behind its aspirations. The desire for knowledge, an essentially independent inner drive, thrives on both antipathy and sympathy. To what extent do Hollywood films satisfy this desire? Or, more specifically: what is the ratio between the subjective and the objective factor in American screen images of foreigners? And has this ratio been stable so far, or are we justified in assuming, for instance, that the images of 1948 surpass those of 1933 in objectivity?

HOLLYWOOD'S ESTIMATE OF ITS AUDIENCE

Without anticipating answers, I wish to formulate a principle derived from the all-powerful profit motive. Hollywood's attitude toward the presentation of any given piece of information ultimately depends on its estimate of how the masses of moviegoers respond to the spread of that information through fiction films. It seems to me important in this connection that the film industry calls itself an entertainment industry a term which, whatever it connotes, does not precisely make one think of films as carriers of knowledge (nor as works of art, for that matter). There has indeed been a widespread tendency not only to equate screen entertainment and relaxation, but to consider anything informative an undesirable admixture. This entertainment formula, championed as late as 1941 in the sophisticated Preston Sturges film *Sullivan's Travels*, rests upon the conviction that people want to relax when they go to the movies; and it further implies that the need for relaxation and the quest for knowledge oppose rather than attract each other. Of course, as always with such formulas, they characterize the mental climate without being strictly binding. Many a prewar film has defied the usual Hollywood pattern and has deepened our understanding of the world.

Only since the end of the war have ideological conventions undergone a change; and again this change must be traced to mass moods. Obviously inspired by the general desire for enlightenment in the wake of the war, spokesmen of the industry now advocate films that combine entertainment with information. "Motion pictures," says Jack L. Warner, "are entertainment—but they go far beyond that." And he coins the term "honest entertainment" to convey the impression of a Hollywood fighting for truth, democracy, international understanding, etc.[7] Eric Johnston, President of the Motion Picture Association, lends his authority to this view. In his statement, *The Right To Know*—which is none the less pertinent for referring to fiction films and factual films alike—he contends that "the motion picture, as an instrument for the promotion of knowledge and understanding among peoples, stands on the threshold of a tremendous era of expansion."[8]

Whether the American motion picture has already trespassed this threshold remains to be seen. On the purely domestic scene it has done so—at least up to a point and temporarily. Attacking social abuses, such films as *The Best Years of our Lives* (1946), *Boomerang* (1947), and *Gentleman's Agreement* (1947) reveal a progressive attitude which undoubtedly owes much to wartime experiences.[9] They still play to full houses, even though political pressures have meanwhile caused the industry to discontinue this trend. Will Hollywood revert to its old entertainment formula? For the time being, we must remain in suspense.

THE TIME ELEMENT

Such foreign peoples as one does see on the American screen do not appear consecutively in films about present-day life. The English were featured in a number of prewar films succeeding each other closely—among them were the above-mentioned *Cavalcade* (1933), *Of Human Bondage* (1934), *Ruggles of Red Gap* (1935), *The Lives of a Bengal Lancer* (1935), *Angel* (1937), *Lost Horizon* (1937), *A Yank at Oxford* (1938), *The Citadel* (1938), *The Sun Never Sets* (1939), *We Are Not Alone* (1939), *Rebecca* (1940), *Foreign Correspondent* (1940), and *How Green Was My Valley* (1941). No sooner did the United States enter the war than the frequency of topical films about Great Britain and her people increased, as is instanced by *Mrs. Miniver* (1942), *The Pied Piper* (1942), *Journey for Margaret* (1942), *The White Cliffs of Dover* (1944), etc.

This vogue broke off immediately after the war. To the best of my knowledge, the British postwar generation would be nonexistent in the cinematic medium, were it not for *The Paradine Case* (1948), a murder story without any bearing on current issues, and the international-minded melodrama Berlin

Express, released as late as May 1948. Between 1945 and 1948, there was a gap spanned only by a few films that focused exclusively on the past—Lubitsch's *Cluny Brown* (1946) which satirized prewar attitudes, fashionable or otherwise; *So Well Remembered* (1947), a social-minded chronicle of small-town life between the two wars; *Ivy* (1947); *Moss Rose* (1947); and *So Evil My Love* (1948). The last three were mystery thrillers playing in turn-of-the-century Britain, if not earlier. Though three years may not be a long period, this sustained unconcern for the present still seems a bit strange.

During the 'thirties, contemporary Russians were less in view than the English, without, however, being wholly neglected. I have already mentioned *Ninotchka* (1939). Other films of the period were *Tovarich* (1937), and *Comrade X* (December, 1940). In the war, when Stalin joined the Allies, Hollywood permitted no one to outdo it in glowing accounts of Russian heroism. *Mission to Moscow, Miss V. from Moscow, The North Star, Three Russian Girls, Song of Russia*—a veritable springtide of pro-Russian films—flooded the movie houses in 1943 and 1944. Then, exactly as in the case of the English, the Russians disappeared for three years. They disappeared even more completely than the English, for I do not know of a single, halfway important film since Lubitsch's resurrection of Catherine the Great (*A Royal Scandal*, 1945) which has dealt with their literature or past. Of course, I discount the "mad Russian," who reemerged in *The Specter of the Rose* (1946); this stereotyped favorite of American audiences—usually a Russian-born artist having sought shelter in the West—is on the whole too estranged from the country of his origin to be identified as a Soviet citizen. It is true that Russians were also rare on the prewar screen, but in those days they were not featured in other media either. What makes one wonder at the absence of Soviet Russia on the postwar screen is just the fact of her omnipresence in speech and print at this time. Between 1945 and 1948, the film alone seemed unaware of a mass obsession. That Hollywood behaved true to pattern in thus ignoring the Russians is proven by its equally conspicuous silence about the Nazis in the years preceding 1939. It is not as if Germany had played any noticeable role in American films prior to 1933. Yet precisely in the critical years 1930–1934 two grade-A films turned the spotlight on her—*All Quiet on the Western Front* and *Little Man, What Now?* (1934), a screen adaptation of Hans Fallada's pre-Hitler novel about unemployment in Germany. Hollywood, it appears, had become mildly interested in things German. And what came out of it? During the subsequent years Hitler was a topic everywhere but on the screen. If I am not mistaken, only two films with Germans in them appeared in this interval: *The Road Back* (1937) and *Three Comrades* (1938). Both were adapted from novels by Remarque, whose name meant business, and both were laid in the early Weimar Republic, which was dead and buried at the time of their release.

TIMES WHEN SILENCE SEEMS WISE

This temporary withdrawal from certain peoples at certain times can be explained only by factors affecting commercial film production. Significantly, prewar Germany as well as postwar Russia provoked impassioned controversy in the United States. Before the war the country was divided into isolationists and interventionists; immediately after the war it heatedly debated the problem of whether the U.S. should be tough or soft in her dealings with the Kremlin. I believe it is this split of public opinion which accounts for Hollywood's evasiveness in both cases. Hollywood, as I have pointed out earlier, is so sensitive to economic risks that it all but automatically shrinks from touching on anything controversial. Germany and Russia were tabooed as "hot stuff;" and they were hot stuff as long as everybody argued about them and a decisive settlement of this nation-wide strife was not yet in sight. They disappeared, that is, not in spite of their hold on the American mind, but because of it.

There has been no such controversy with regard to Anglo-American relations. Why, then, the scarcity of postwar Britons in Hollywood films? Considering the impact of mass attitudes on film content, this scarcity may well result from the uneasiness with which Americans react to Labor rule in Britain. Their disquiet is understandable, for what is now going on in Britain means a challenge to American belief in free enterprise and its particular virtues. In the United States any discussion of British affairs is therefore likely to touch off an argument about the advantages and disadvantages of the American way of life. But once this kind of argument gets started you never know where it will lead. The whole matter is extremely delicate and involved, and it is for such reasons, I submit, that Hollywood producers currently neglect, perhaps without consciously intending it, the living English in favor of their less problematic ancestors.[10]

...AND TIMES TO SPEAK OUT

These periods of silence may suddenly come to a close, with mimosa-like shyness yielding to uninhibited outspokenness. In the prewar era, the years 1938/39 marked a turning of the tide. At the very moment when the European crisis reached its height, the American screen first took notice of the Axis powers and their creeds. *Blockade* (1938), a Walter Wanger production, initiated this trend. It denounced the ruthless bombing of cities during the Spanish civil war, clearly sympathizing with the Loyalist cause which, however, was left unmentioned, as was Franco, the villain in the piece. Hollywood soon overcame these hesitations. *The Confessions of a Nazi Spy* (1939), a realistic rendering of Nazi activities in the U.S., overtly stigmatized Hitler Germany and all that it stood for. Then came the war, and anti-Nazi films, less realistic than well-intentioned, grew rampant.

During those fateful years 1938/39, other national film industries began to speak up also. The French released *Grand Illusion* (1938), which resurrected World War I in a pacifistic spirit, and *Double Crime in the Maginot Line* (1939) whose German characters were indistinct. Even though both these films shirked any direct mention of Nazi Germany, they effectively conjured up her giant shadow. A similar device was used by Eisenstein in his *Alexander Nevsky*, shown in the U.S. in 1939. In picturing the defeat which 13th century Russia inflicted upon the Teutonic Knights, Eisenstein—and through him Stalin—warned Hitler not to try the old game again.

Shortly after the release of *Blockade*, John C. Flinn, a *Variety* correspondent, emphasized Hollywood's vital interest in its career: "Upon its success financially revolve the plans of several of the major studios heretofore hesitant about tackling stories which treat with subjects of international economic and political controversy."[11] This expert statement sheds light on the motives that prompted the film industry into action. Despite the protests of certain Catholic groups, *Blockade* was a success financially; and though Hollywood might have felt tempted to produce anti-Nazi films even before *Blockade*, it did so only after having made fairly sure that they would be accepted on a nation-wide scale. The appearance of Nazis on the screen was connected with the evolution of public opinion in the United States. They appeared when, after the debacle in Spain and Austria's fall, the time of wavering controversy was practically over. Isolationism, to be sure, persisted; but the whole country bristled with indignation against the Nazis, and there was no longer any doubt that someday the world would have to stop Hitler and his associates. Since this conviction also prevailed in Britain, France, and elsewhere, Hollywood did not risk much in expressing sentiments so universally popular.

What happened in 1939, repeats itself in 1948: after a lull of three to four years, Russians now begin to reappear on the American screen as abruptly as did the Germans. The parallels between *The Iron Curtain* of May 1948 and *The Confession of a Nazi Spy* are striking. Like the latter film, this new one is a spy thriller—a pictorial account of the events that led to the discovery, in 1946, of a Russian-controlled spy ring in Canada. Both films are based on scripts by the same author; and both are narrated in documentary fashion. Should these similarities be symptomatic of analogous situations, as I believe they are, then *The*

Iron Curtain, with its avowed hostility toward the Soviet regime, would indicate that American public opinion has come out of the controversial stage in favor of a tough stand on Russia.

TREATMENT OF ENGLISH CHARACTERS

For a long time, Great Britain and the United States have been entertaining an alliance founded upon the community of race, language, historical experience, and political outlook. Interchange has been frequent; processes of symbiosis have been going on. To Americans the English are an "in-group" people; they belong, so to speak, to the family, while other peoples—"out-group" peoples—do not. Where such intimate bonds exist, knowledge of each other seems a matter of course. American screen images of Britons might therefore be expected to be true likenesses.

Hollywood has tried hard to justify such expectations. Many American films about the English are drawn from their own novels or stage plays; and the bulk of these films are shot on location, involving genuine mansions, lawns, 'and London streets. In addition, there is rarely an important English part in an American film that is not assigned to a native Britisher.

This insistence on authenticity and local color benefits films which cover a diversity of subjects: middle-class patriotism (*Cavalcade, Mrs. Miniver*); Empire glorification (*The Lives of a Bengal Lancer, The Sun Never Sets*, etc.); Anglo-American relations (*Ruggles of Red Gap*); upper-class ideology (again *Ruggles of Red Gap*, then *Angel, The White Cliffs of Dover*, etc.); sports (*A Yank at Oxford*); social issues, such as the status of physicians (*The Citadel*) and of coal miners (*How Green Was My Valley*), and so on. Strictly personal conflicts prevail in *Of Human Bondage* and *Rebecca*; public school life is featured in *Goodbye, Mr. Chips* (1939), a retrospective film. The wealth of themes engenders a wide range of types. I dare say that, taken together, American films offer a more complete cross-section of the English than they do of any other people. From night club musicians to Kiplingese colonels and from workers to diplomats nearly all strata of the population are presented on some occasion and somehow. Frequent among these types are well-to-do gentlemen and their manservants—a couple of figures forever illustrating the Lord-Butler relationship, which has been so delightfully patterned in *Ruggles of Red Gap*. Incidentally, in any film about foreigners the minor characters tend to be more true to type than the protagonists, because they are less deliberately constructed.

In short, the English are rendered substantially as befits the prominent place they hold in American traditions. The result is a fairly inclusive image of their national traits, an image which for all its emphasis on snobbish caste spirit permits the audience to catch glimpses of British imperturbability, doggedness, and sportsmanship. The *Lives of a Bengal Lancer*, which initiated a trend of cloak-and-dagger melodramas—films playing in an India or Africa faintly reminiscent of the Wild West—points up the frontier bravura of English Empire builders and their soldiery.[12] *The Pied Piper* in a highly amusing sequence shows members of a London club indulging in the native penchant for understatement, while German bombers noisily drop their loads.

This many-sided approach further testifies to Hollywood's concern with the British way of life. Small wonder that several prewar films succeeded in reflecting it faithfully. A model case of objectivity is *Cavalcade*, the well-known screen version of Noel Coward's play. Before this film with its English cast went into production, its original director filmed the whole London stage performance of the play so as not to miss any of those minutiae upon which the impression of genuineness depends. Such efforts paid: *Cavalcade*, according to a report from London, "convinced the most skeptical Englishmen that the American film capital can on occasion produce a much better British picture than any English studio has yet managed to achieve."[13]

At this point the problem of the ratio between the objective and the subjective factor arises. Can the latter be neglected in the case of the English? Or, rather, does experience show that in the long run subjective influences—influences exerted by American mass attitudes—win out over that urge for objectivity of which *Cavalcade* is so impressive an instance? I wish to make it clear from the outset that all the measures Hollywood has taken in the interest of authenticity do not suffice to eliminate distortions. A script may be one hundred per cent British and yet materialize in a film imbued with Hollywood spirit. Nor do views of the Tower or a Tudor castle warrant accuracy; documentary shots, as is proven by many propaganda films and newsreels, can be juxtaposed in such a way that they falsify the very reality which they candidly capture. But are not English actors a guarantee for the truthful representation of English life? They are not, for two reasons. First, the screen appearance of any actor results not only from his own acting, but from the various cinematic devices used in building up his image on the screen, and because of their share in its establishment this image may well express other meanings than those conveyed by the actor himself. Secondly, even though an English actor is under all circumstances an Englishman, he may have to appear in a film so little suggestive of typically English behavior and thought patterns that he finds no opportunity of substantiating them. He will be neutralized within such contexts. In other words, whether or not screen portrayals of a foreign people are convincing does not solely depend upon their being enacted by native actors. What counts most is the whole film's susceptibility to the characteristics of that people.

THE SNOB

The influence of American preconceptions shows in the selection of English character traits. Hollywood films establish a hierarchy among these traits in which snobbishness, as I have indicated, figures foremost. Inseparable from class-mindedness, snobbishness pervades the servant's quarters in numerous films, confers upon screen aristocrats an air of inimitable superiority, surrounds as a palpable halo all those Englishmen who by provision of the plots defend advanced colonial outposts or mingle with Americans and Frenchmen, and makes itself felt everywhere not only in the manner of speaking but at decisive turning-points of dialogue. It is the one British characteristic which American movies never tire of acknowledging, ridiculing, condoning or repudiating, according to the views expressed in them.

No doubt this trait actually exists. The English writer Margaret Cole, who is all against snobbishness, nevertheless admits that much in her recent *Harper's* article: "The British have a pretty lively sense of birth and upbringing: they like titles and honors, and they like to know people who have titles and honors . . . they are, most of them, pretty good snobs."[14] Yet this does not mean that the English are primarily snobs. Like any other people, they have a complex character structure; snobbishness therefore need not appear as their main trait. As a matter of fact, it could easily be shown that the films of different nations have conceived of Englishmen in quite different ways.[15] Take the German cinema: for all their surface similarities, the German and the American screen Britons are by no means counterparts. Such German peacetime films as dealt with the English at all paid tribute grudgingly to their way of life. Among the traits featured, however, correctness and decency (e.g. of British navy officers) were more conspicuous than snobbishness—a trait whose social implications eluded a people which had never had a society in the Western sense. And when war came the Germans expressed their pent-up resentments against the British Empire in films which made no bones about the ruthlessness of the English and about their alleged hypocrisy. The latter characteristic, passed off as an English cardinal vice by the Germans, is practically nonexistent in American films.

Any nation, it appears, sees other peoples in a perspective determined by its experience of them; and, of course, its cinema features those character traits of theirs which are an integral part of this experience. Hence the emphasis on English caste spirit in Hollywood films. To Americans this trait stands out among others because it affected them deeply under British rule. And since nations, like individuals, tend to build on their early impressions, the mass of Americans, among them swarms of Irish immigrants, took it for granted that the typical Briton is essentially a caste-proud snob. They reacted to him in two opposite ways—a further symptom of the imprint which his conduct, or, rather, their conception of it, had left on them. On the one side, they condemned British snobbishness for offending their sense of equality; on the other, they admired and imitated it. American snobbery contributes much to stabilizing the English snob on the screen; his recurrent image is both a reflection of and a protest against native cravings for nobility, Oxford, and authentic manners. This is confirmed by *Ruggles of Red Gap*, which mingles gentle gibes at the foreign idol with a solid satire of its Middle-West worshipers. Another case in point is Preston Sturges' brilliant comedy *Lady Eve* (1941). Even though this film does not include any Britishers, it does show a cute American girl who reconquers her lover by posing as Lady Eve, the daughter of an English aristocrat.

The American screen image of the English is more or less standardized. True as this image is to reality, as a stereotype it has also a life of its own, a life independent of that reality. The English snob, as he appears in Hollywood films, is a figure which has in some degree drifted away from its original to join those mythological figures that people the world of American imagination. Whether angry at him or fond of him, Americans consider this kind of Briton one of theirs. He "belongs"; like Huckleberry Finn or Mickey Mouse, he is part of their universe.

This permanent preoccupation with British snobbishness is not the only subjective element in Hollywood's portrayal of the English. Other influences, equally instrumental in its composition, arise from changes on the domestic scene. In prewar days, when relations between the United States and Great Britain developed along traditional lines, there was no reason why these changes should interfere with an objective rendering of Britons. Domestic mass desires asserted themselves merely in the preference given to such film subjects as were likely to draw American audiences at a specific moment. *Cavalcade* was particularly well-timed. This film, with its unflinching belief in Britain's greatness, appeared at the depths of the Depression, a comfort to all those Americans who despaired of the predicament they were in. Many wept when seeing the film, and more than one reviewer declared it to be a tribute to what is best in all national spirits. Two years later, *Ruggles of Red Gap*, a comedy about the molding of a class-conscious English butler into a free American, struck that tone of self-confidence which by then filled the air. And so it goes. It would, by the way, be tempting to inquire into the causes of the enormous popularity which films about British imperialism enjoyed for a stretch of years. That they had a definite bearing on domestic issues is evident even in their casting: the elder colonels in *The Lives of a Bengal Lancer* and *Gunga Din* fell to the charge of English actors, while the young protagonists, heroes or cowards, were played by stars genuinely American.

BRITISH CHARACTERS IN WARTIME

Once the war was on, national exigencies encroached on the tendency toward objectivity. American public opinion endorsed the war effort, and Britain was now an Ally. For these reasons Hollywood could no longer afford to approach the English in that spirit of impartiality which is indispensable for an understanding of others. Rather, it was faced with the task of endearing everything British to the American masses. The task was not simply to represent the English, but to make them seem acceptable even to those sections of the population whose pro-British feelings were doubtful.

Significantly, most Hollywood films about Britain at war attempt to weaken the existing antipathies against English snobbishness, thus reaffirming American obsession with this trait. *Mrs. Miniver*, representative of the whole trend, shows wartime Britain undergo processes of democratization tending to transform her national character. In this film, as a reviewer judiciously points out, "even Lady Beldon, the aged, local autocrat, finally realizes that her class-conscious, if gracious, civilization has been forged into the practical democracy of an entire country united against the enemy."[16] *The Pied Piper* features an old English gentleman whose noble impulses increasingly get the better of his outward standoffishness; *The White Cliffs of Dover*, a sentimental retrospect which tries to enlist audience sympathies for British upper-class people, ends with hints of their readiness to conform to more democratic standards. It is not that such motifs had been entirely omitted in prewar films; but during the war they grew into leitmotifs, coloring all films of the period and serving as their very justification.

Produced in response to powerful domestic urges, these films, I assume, would have misrepresented English reality even if they had been shot on location. To what extent they actually distorted it can be inferred from the criticism with which they were received in Britain itself. *Mrs. Miniver*, though recognized as a laudable American tribute to English war heroism, was nevertheless blamed for "its faults and frequent air of English unreality."[17] Of *The White Cliffs of Dover* the London *Times* said that it "misses the tones and accents of the country in which the action passes."[18] And with regard to *Random Harvest*, another Hollywood wartime production, a polite reviewer remarked that "Greer Garson and Ronald Colman act away the frequent obtrusion of error in English detail and behavior."[19]

ABSENCE OF THE POSTWAR BRITAIN

The war over, one might have expected Hollywood to resume its relatively objective approach to contemporary Britons. Yet it preferred, and still prefers, to ignore their existence. Nothing proves more conclusively the overpowering effect of domestic influences in the field of screen entertainment. Now that the English in some respects really live up to the image drawn up of them in all American war films class mindedness is on the decline and snobbery less domineering—it would seem natural for Hollywood to acknowledge what it praised only yesterday. Instead, it resolutely turns its back on Britain, for reasons at which I have made a guess in earlier contexts. During the war, folks at home took delight in a Lady Beldon who proved herself a convinced democrat; at present, the peculiar flavor of English democracy so little pleases many Americans that the Lady Beldons are being held incommunicado until further notice.

The meaning of this temporary blackout—all the more striking in view of the influx into America of English films about postwar life in Britain—is enhanced by those Hollywood productions which introduce British characters of the past. They not only reestablish the stereotype of the English snob (Cluny Brown), but draw on other familiar prewar patterns as well. All of them could have been made before 1941. In thus combining disregard of the present with uninhibited rendering of the past, Hollywood follows a rule of conduct which it has already practiced before. Nor is this treatment of foreign peoples unknown to other national film industries: at a time when the German pre-Hitler cinema was completely oblivious of Soviet Russia, it elaborated profusely on the blessings of the Czarist regime. I have reason to believe that in all such cases the emergence of films about the past of a people betrays discontent with its present state of affairs. What makes these films into vehicles of indirect criticism is the fact of their appearance at a moment when any direct mention of that people is strictly avoided. They manifest apprehensions not so much through their content as their sheer existence. Only occasionally do they come into the open, picturing past events for the thinly veiled purpose of dealing with present ones. In Alexander Nevsky the eyes that gleam through the visors of the Teutonic Knights are unmistakably the eyes of contemporary Nazis.

In sum, the objective factor in American screen images of the English is extremely vulnerable. Much as the age-old intimacy of Anglo-American relations favors its growth, the impact of subjective influences invariably tends to stunt it. Domestic needs and mass desires have on more than one occasion caused Hollywood to portray the English inadequately or not to portray them at all, which amounts to the same thing. There is no progress of knowledge noticeable as these portrayals succeed each other-in fact, *Cavalcade*, released as early as 1933, has probably never been surpassed in objectivity. Everything, it appears, hinges on market necessities which may or may not permit Hollywood to reflect the English closely.

RUSSIAN CHARACTERS

In their *America in Midpassage* the Beards mention the success of the first Russian Five-Year Plan among those foreign events which augmented American anxieties in the spring of 1933. "Still Russia was far off," they remark before turning to the more stirring repercussions of Hitler's rise to power, "and could be discounted as a bit oriental in its ways and values."[20]

To Americans the Russians are an "out-group" people indeed. There is a pronounced lack of traditions common to both countries, and there has never been an intermingling of their nationals as in the case of the English. The chasm separating the two countries is deepened by the antagonism between their regimes—an antagonism so laden with dynamite that it predetermines all popular notions Americans and Russians hold of each other. Unsustained by experience and inevitably biased, these notions are outright clichés. The average American has incorporated the figure of the "mad Russian" into the collection of his pet stereotypes; he knows that Russians are fond of music, ballet, and vodka. And, of course, innumerable editorials and the like have impressed upon him fixed concepts of Bolshevism as something with collective farms, secret police, and purges. Most of it is sheer hearsay, however true.

Hollywood, always inclined to capitalize on existing clichés, is not in the best of positions to breathe life into them. For obvious reasons American films about Russia are studio-made; and because of the scarcity of Russian actors in this country their native characters are as a rule assigned to Hollywood stars or to German actors who seem to have a knack for portraying Russians. In *The Last Command* (1928) Emil Jannings was a very convincing Czarist general. I have pointed out that even films with English actors in the cast may misrepresent the English; conversely, actors in the roles of foreigners need not under all circumstances miss the essentials. Nevertheless, it remains true that the reliance on outside portrayals in imitation settings thwarts rather than facilitates an objective rendering of other peoples.

Such scattered Hollywood films about contemporary Russia as did appear between 1927 and 1934 frowned upon the Soviet Union with an air of grave concern. Most of them were laid in, or referred to, the early days of the Russian Revolution when everything was still fluid. Even though they did not pass over the disastrous abuses of Czarist rule—how could they?—yet they managed to make you feel gloomy about the victory of a cause so obviously barbarian. I am thinking of *Mockery* (1927), *The Tempest* (1928), *The Last Command*, and *British Agent* (1934). Except for Sternberg's *Last Command*, each of these films culminated in a romance between a Russian Red and his, or her, class enemy, which drove home the humanly destructive effects of Bolshevist class hatred. *Forgotten Commandment* (1932), "a sermon on the evils of Soviet Land,"[21] accused Russia of having forsaken Christianity. Of these productions only the Sternberg film and perhaps *British Agent* had some merits. The Beards are right: "Russia was far off..."

She did not come nearer after her recognition by President Roosevelt late in 1933. Yet American attitudes changed. After a period of silence filled in by several films which involved Catherine the Great, Tolstoy's *Anna Karenina*, and Dostoievsky's *Crime and Punishment* (like the current films about the English past these may have conveyed polite discontent with the stubborn survival of Russian Communism), this change showed in Hollywood's transition from serious criticism to critical comedy. *Tovarich*, I believe, was the first film to endorse the fact of political recognition by substituting light skirmishes for heavy attacks. Hostilities continued, but they adjusted themselves to the improved relations with the Soviet Union which after all was here to stay. Lubitsch's *Ninotchka*, with Garbo in the title role, also marked a precarious rapprochement. This amusing piece of raillery which showed Marxist-trained Russians succumbing to the frivolous attractions of the West, viewed Soviet life with the condescension of an adult who watches fledgelings romp. It was a sort of shoulder-patting; why not finally grow up, the film seemed to ask. Its success bred other films in this vein: *He Stayed for Breakfast*, "a gay spoof of the

Communistic camaraderie that flourished in Paris before the war,"[22] and *Comrade X* which, laid in Moscow, equally jeered at the conversion of a rabid Communist. Released in 1940, both films not only lacked Lubitsch's finesse, but struck a tone of poignant aggressiveness absent in his *Ninotchka*. Of *Comrade X*, Bosley Crowther says: "... seldom has a film ... satirized a nation and its political system with such grim and malicious delight as does this ... comedy."[23]

THE WARTIME RUSSIAN

The English characters in American war films about Britain still resembled their predecessors of a few years before, but no such resemblances connected the intrepid Russian woman fighter glorified by Hollywood between 1942 and 1944 with the yielding Ninotchka so popular shortly before. This was not simply a shift of emphasis as in the case of the English, but a radical change of scene, with Stalin becoming Uncle Joe and collective farming a source of happiness. I scarcely need elaborate on characters and situations in *Mission to Moscow, The North Star*, and so on. All these films sprang from the overwhelming desire, on the part of the home front, to keep Russia in the war. The surprising thing is their unconcern for continuity: they idolized what had been condemned in times of peace, or winked at it unashamedly. It was a complete turnabout.

In thus wooing Russia for reasons of domestic self-interest, Hollywood ignored its otherwise guiding rule of leaving controversial issues untouched. Opposition against the Soviet regime was too stable a factor of American public opinion to be eliminated by the necessities of the war. Subdued as it was, it continued to smolder. This accounts for the criticism which in particular *Mission to Moscow* with its indulgent references to the Moscow trials met from diverse quarters. And about *The North Star*, which in its opening scenes extolled the insouciant life of Russian villagers before 1941, the Daily News wrote that this film is more Communistic "than the Russians themselves who have never pretended that prewar Russia was a musical-comedy paradise."[24]

... AND THE RUSSIAN OF TODAY

Now that the spell of amnesia from which Hollywood suffered in the postwar years is over, we are witnessing another turnabout. Gone are the brave Russian women fighters, the happy villagers, and the democratic allures of the rulers. In their places, somber bureaucrats, counterparts of the Nazis, spread an atmosphere of oppression. This at least is the way *The Iron Curtain* pictures Soviet officials—they appear as ruthless totalitarians obeyed by devout slaves. And the only "good" Russian is a man who so firmly believes in the superior value of Western civilization that he deserts Communism and betrays his country. Similar types were also advertised in American prewar comedies; but unlike *Ninotchka*, *The Iron Curtain* avoids any satirical overtones that might weaken the impact of its accusations. Other current films draw no less determinedly on the anti-Communist sentiments of American audiences. In *The Fugitive* (late 1947)—a deliberately fantastic film with exotic settings—humble priests are wantonly persecuted by all-powerful authorities which everybody is free to identify as Communists. The Russian black-market racketeer in *To the Victor* (April 1948) is no endearing figure either. And we may soon see some more anti-Soviet films; two or three have already been scheduled for production. This general insistence on toughness, however, seems to be slightly mitigated by the fearful prospect of another war: *Berlin Express* and *A Foreign Affair* (June 1948) both laid in Germany, indulge in a relatively amiable approach to their Russian characters, thus intimating that we should not give up hope for an understanding after all.

DOMINANCE OF THE SUBJECTIVE FACTOR

All this illustrates Hollywood's unconcern for Russian reality. Unlike the English characters in Hollywood films which at least give one a taste, however faint, of genuine life, American screen portrayals of Russians conform to what Americans imagine far-away Russians to be like. Even Russian-born actors are strangely colorless in plots based upon such subjective concepts; and, of course, Garbo in *Ninotchka* always remains Garbo in the guise of *Ninotchka*. The objective factor in these portrayals is negligible—they are not experienced, but constructed. Hence their remoteness from the originals they pretend to portray. Commenting on *The North Star*, Archer Winsten, one of the most observant New York film critics, states that its characters are "single-plane cutouts rather than those deeply modelled characterizations of the best Russian films..."[25] He might have added that the many Russian films shown in the United States have not in the slightest degree stimulated Hollywood to relinquish its home-bred notions of Russia.

These notions are of a political nature. All Hollywood films about Russia raise topical issues, and many of them, I presume, would have never been produced were it not for the purpose of externalizing American attitudes toward the Soviet regime. This explains why the characters in them are so poorly instrumented. As compared with English screen figures, Hollywood-made Russians are sheer abstractions. Instead of being introduced for their own sake as are the English in many cases, they merely serve to personify pros and cons in the ever-fluctuating debate on Russian Communism. It is as if they were drawn from editorials. They resemble marionettes, and you cannot help seeing the strings by which they are pulled.

And finally, these marionettes lack the relative stability of English characters. The English snob has survived the war, while Ninotchka was popular only for a transient moment. Her ephemeral vogue is symptomatic of the frequent, occasionally hectic changes which Russian characters undergo in American films. They succeed each other with a disregard for psychological consistency which again testifies to their function of conveying domestic views of Russia. In 1941, when these views changed so abruptly that films in keeping with the latest developments were not yet available, Hollywood tried to adjust an existing film to the new situation. Under the, heading: "Whitewashing Reds," *Variety*, of October 22, 1941, published the following notice: "Reflecting the changed public opinion in this country towards Russia, Metro has added an explanatory foreword on the film *Comrade X* to make clear that any spoofing of Russians in the picture was entirely intended as good clean fun." Metro simply was loath to shelve *Comrade X*, a film released only a few months before Hitler's invasion of Russia; yet this grim satire of Soviet life could not be kept in circulation unless it was made to appear as a meek banter among friends.

Russian characters in American films are projections rather than portraits. Chimerical figures, they unhesitatingly change with the political exigencies of the moment. Russia is far off.

CONCLUSIONS

The film industries of other democracies, I assume, behave in much the same way as Hollywood. Fiction films are mass entertainment everywhere, and what information they include is more or less a by-product. Any national cinema yields to the impact of subjective influences in portraying foreigners; these portrayals, that is, are strongly determined by such audience desires and political exigencies as currently prevail on the domestic scene. There are different degrees of subjectivity, though: peoples intimately connected by common experiences can be expected to form more objective screen images of each other than they do of peoples with whom they have little or nothing in common.

In other words, images of "in-group" peoples surpass those of "out-group" peoples in reliability. But even they are halfway reliable only as long as public opinion in the country of their origin does not interfere with their relatively unbiased approach. And under the pressure of alienating developments this may happen at any moment, as is instanced by Hollywood's conspicuous neglect of postwar Britons. On the whole, screen portrayals of foreigners are rarely true likenesses; more often than not they grow out of the urge for self-assertion rather than the thirst for knowledge, so that the resultant images reflect not so much the mentality of the other people as the state of mind of their own. International understanding is in its infancy.

Or, rather, does it begin to show signs of growing up? I have not yet mentioned a new international film trend which seems to justify Mr. Johnston's contention quoted above that the motion picture is on the point of becoming "an instrument for the promotion of knowledge and understanding among peoples." This trend, a spontaneous reaction to the effects of the war, originates in Europe. Representative of it are the somewhat sentimental Swiss pictures *Marie Louise* and *The Last Chance*, and the two Rossellini films, *Open City* and *Paisan*—wartime and postwar semi-documentaries much acclaimed by American audiences. In a similar vein is *The Search* (1948), a Metro-sponsored film about European war orphans which has been made by the producer of *The Last Chance* and his associates in collaboration with a Hollywood director. Hollywood seems to be interested in this genre.

It is by no means a new genre. D. W. Griffith, great innovator as he was, developed some of its inherent potentialities, and his ideas were followed up by Eisenstein and Pudovkin in their classic screen epics—masterful blends of reportage and fiction, matter-of-fact statements and emotional appeals. What is new in the most recent semi-documentaries is their content: a changed outlook on the world which, of course, entails changes of cinematic approach. All these films denounce Fascist lust for power and race hatred; and whatever they picture—Nazis torturing their enemies, scenes of heroic resistance, abandoned children, indescribable misery in bombed-out cities—is rendered with profound compassion for the tortured, the killed, the despondent. They are films with a message. They not only record the frightful encounters of persecutors and victims, masters and slaves, but glorify the bonds of love and sympathy that even now amidst lies, ruins, and horrors connect people of different nations. Their goal is mutual understanding between the peoples of the world.

I do not know a single prewar film which is so deliberately international as is any of these semi-documentaries. All of them reflect, in loosely knit episodes, the vicissitudes of the war, featuring chance meetings between soldiers and civilians of diverse countries. German refugees join company with a British officer; an American G.I. makes love to an Italian girl; undernourished French children regain health in Switzerland. And most of these figures are fashioned with a minimum of subjectivity on the part of the film makers. Instead of serving as outlets for domestic needs, they seem to be elicited from reality for no purpose other than that of mirroring it. They tend to increase our knowledge of other nations out of an overwhelming nostalgia for international cooperation.

CAN HOLLYWOOD AFFORD THE INTERNATIONAL TREND?

The whole trend, provided it is one, proves that screen portrayals of foreigners need not under all circumstances degenerate into stereotypes and projections. At this point the problem arises of what can be done to improve these images. It is a vital problem in view of the influence which entertainment films exert on the masses. There is no doubt that the screen images of other people help weaken or strengthen popular interest in mutual understanding.

This does not contradict the fact, emphasized throughout my study, that entertainment films on their part are strongly influenced by actually prevailing mass desires, latent tendencies of public opinion. Such desires and tendencies are more or less inarticulate, and do not materialize unless they are forced out of their pupa state; they must be identified and formulated to come into their own. Film industries everywhere, as I have mentioned earlier, are therefore faced with the task of divining audience expectations at any particular moment. Sometimes they miss their opportunities. The response which the Swiss and Italian semi-documentaries have found in the United States, for thematic rather than for aesthetic reasons, reveals a disposition in their favor on the part of American audiences which Hollywood has hitherto failed to recognize. On the other hand, Hollywood films occasionally react to well-nigh intangible emotional and social constellations with such a promptness that they seem to create desires out of nothing, especially in the dimension of taste. Characteristically, the trade has coined the term "sleeper" for films which are believed to be flops and, once released, prove themselves as hits. Film making involves constant experimenting—and many surprises.

What matters most in this context, then, is the essential ambiguity of mass dispositions. Because of their vagueness they usually admit of diverse interpretations. People are quick to reject things that they do not agree with, while they feel much less sure about the true objects of their leanings and longings. There is, accordingly, a margin left for film producers who aim at satisfying existing mass desires. Pent-up escapist needs, for instance, may be relieved in many different ways. Hence the permanent interaction between mass dispositions and film content. Each popular film conforms to certain popular wants; yet in conforming to them it inevitably does away with their inherent ambiguity. Any such film evolves these wants in a specific direction, confronts them with one among several possible meanings. Through their very definiteness films thus determine the nature of the inarticulate from which they emerge.

Once again, how can screen images of other peoples be improved? Since film producers, for all their dependence on current main trends of opinion and sentiment, retain some freedom of action, it may well be that they will find a more objective approach to foreign characters to be in their own interest. Hollywood is presently undergoing a crisis which challenges producers to probe into the minds of weary moviegoers, and documentary techniques, much-favored in Hollywood since *Boomerang*, lend themselves perfectly to objective portrayals. And has not *The Search* been a success? There is no reason why Hollywood should not explore this success and try its hand at films, semi-documentaries or not, which in however indirect a manner serve the cause of one world. U.S. audiences may even welcome a comprehensive rendering of Russian problems, or of life in Labor-governed Britain.

Or, of course, they may not. And Hollywood (any national film industry, for that matter) has some reason to believe that in the long run it knows best what spectators look out for in the movie houses. I doubt whether it will follow suggestions inconsistent with its estimate of audience reactions. Therefore, a campaign for better screen portrayals of foreigners—portrayals which are portraits rather than projections carries weight only if the motion picture industry is made to realize that the broad masses care about such portrayals. This accounts for the primary importance of mass education. Unless organizations such as UNESCO can stir up a mass desire for international understanding, prospects for the cooperation of film producers are slim. *The Last Chance* and *Paisan* come from countries where this desire was overwhelmingly strong. Can it be spread and sustained? Films help change mass attitudes on condition that these attitudes have already begun to change.

NOTES

1. Films of fact—documentaries and newsreels—will not be considered here, even though they frequently picture foreigners and events abroad. To exclude them is

not to belittle their significance as a means of conveying information, but is simply an acknowledgment of the fact that all but disappear in the mass of fiction films. Except perhaps for transitory wartime vogue, films of fact still belong among sideshows, at least in the U.S.

2. Professor Robert H. Ball, of Queens College, is presently preparing a survey of innumerable American and European screen versions of Shakespearean plays. In it he plans to comment on national differences between these versions as well as on changes have undergone in each country with the passing of time.

3. *You and the Russians: A Series of Five Programs Presented on the Columbia Broadcasting System*, a pamphlet issued by CBS. The programs were broadcast in November 1947.

4. Siegfried Kracauer, *From Caligari to Hitler: A Psychological History of the German Film* (Princeton, NJ: Princeton University Press, 1947), 206.

5. Leonard W. Doob, *Public Opinion and Propaganda* (New York: Henry Holt, 1948), 507.

6. For the whole argument, see Kracauer, *From Caligari to Hitler*, 5–6.

7. Jack L. Warner, "What Hollywood Isn't," publicity sheet issued by *Hollywood Citizen News and Advertiser*, 1946.

8. *Motion Picture Letter* (issued by the Public Information Committee of the Motion Picture Industry) 5, no. 6 (June 1946).

9. See Kracauer, "Those Movies with a Message," *Harper's Magazine*, June 1948, 567–72.

10. More immediate reasons for Hollywood's conduct may be found in the "cold war" between the American and British film industries and also in the gloomy aspect of life in Britain, hardly attractive to a screen infatuated with glamor. But what weight these reasons carry accrues to them from the atmospheric pressures on the political scene.

11. John C. Flinn, "Film Industry Watching 'Blockade' as B.O. Cue on Provocative Themes," *Variety*, June 22, 1938.

12. Other films in this vein: *The Charge of the Light Brigade* (1936), *Gunga Din* (1939), *The Sun Never Sets*, etc.

13. Ernest Marshall, "Featured Players and Costly Set . . .," *New York Times*, April 9, 1933 (quoted from a clipping which does not include the rest of the title).

14. Margaret Cole, "How Democratic Is Britain?," *Harper's Magazine*, July 1948, 106.

15. It even seems that the images which one and the same nation forms of a foreign people in different media of mass communication are far from concurring with each other. In American radio comedies, as Mr. Oscar Katz of Columbia Broadcasting System has informed me, the English are typecast as dull-witted fellows unable to understand a joke.

16. "Mrs. Miniver's War," *Newsweek*, June 15, 1942.

17. Evelyn Russel, "The Quarter's Films," *Sight and Sound* 2, no. 43 (Winter 1942): 69.

18. Lewis Gannett, "British Critics' Storm Lashes *White Cliffs*," *New York Herald Tribune*, August 20, 1944.

19. Evelyn Russel, "The Quarter's Films," *Sight and Sound* 12, no. 45 (Summer 1943): 17.

20. Charles A. Beard and Mary R. Beard, *America in Midpassage, Vol. 3: The Rise of American Civilization* (New York: Macmillan, 1941), 201.
21. "It Isn't the Screen; It's the Story," *New York World Telegram*, June 4, 1932.
22. Quoted from Kate Cameron's review of this film in the *New York Daily News*, August 3, 1940.
23. Quoted from Bosley Crowther's review of this film in the *New York Times*, December 26, 1940.
24. Quoted from Kate Cameron's review of this film in the *New York Daily News*, November 5, 1943.
25. Quoted from Archer Winsten's review of this film in the *New York Post*, November 5, 1943.

14
Deluge of Pictures

January 31, 1950

From Cave Painting to Comic Strip, by Lancelot Hogben (Chanticleer Press, New York, $5), is a peculiar book in this respect: Its 230 absorbing illustrations and their captions present a pleasant and temporary barrier between the reader and Mr. Hogben's text. Man is the only animal that makes pictures, says Mr. Hogben; his thought and progress would be impossible without pictures: numerals—pictures which permit mathematics; and the alphabet—pictures which permit writing. Man communicates through the visual. The author would be the first to understand our turning first to the pictures in his own book.

In deep caves in France and Spain, images of the bison and the reindeer are still visible on the walls; twenty thousand years ago, man painted them as an incantation to secure the real presence of these animals when he set forth to hunt. Later, man sought to give himself an identity through association with the stars in the heavens, and, here, in pictures of Mesopotamian seals, are the first Signs of the Zodiac. Man worried about the seasons, felt a need to measure time. The Pyramids of Gizeh in their east-west alignments permitted the Egyptians to observe the equinoxes; the stone avenue at Down Tor, Devon enabled the observer to note the interval (a solar year) between two occasions when the sun rises at exactly the same point on the horizon; in Peru a sun-tower was hewn from a single rock. All these are pictured in Mr. Hogben's pages.

The illustrations show the growth of mathematics—first the abacus, then the notation of numerals; the growth of the written word—first signs, then the alphabet. The images came first, then the means of reproducing them, and finally the great presses turning in our cities. Here, too, are the painters discovering perspective in response to the scientific unrest of Europe's fifteenth century. Finally come comic strips. Mr. Hogben takes them too seriously.

The story Mr. Hogben tells, when we leave the pictures for his text, is one of tragic setbacks, uneventful intervals, and gigantic conquests rendered possible by the contributions of peoples long since forgotten or sunk into apathy. He follows closely the developments which led from prehistoric cave paintings, primitive seals, and calendars, to the invention of the printing press and photography.

Now pictures surround and besiege us. Through television, they silence our thoughts in that last and now insecure refugee of introspection, the bar; we cannot pick up a printed piece of paper without being faced with an image. We are flooded with sights and spectacles—not with the originals, not with the sights and spectacles of nature, but with an intemperate outpouring of reproductions. Nature provides man with one spectacle at a time to which both intelligence and heart can respond; but man now provides himself with a mechanical, kaleidoscopic flurry of endlessly succeeding images. Instead of seeing clearly, he is almost blinded.

Mr. Hogben wants us to inaugurate some system of control. What advertising men call "mass media" are available for the first time in history; Mr. Hogben thinks that they might possibly be used with some intelligence, and that if they are not so used our civilization will follow others that have vanished.

Mr. Hogben is not an impassive historian. He is a fervent champion of federal world government, and very combative about it; he urges us to use the techniques of mass communications to bring such a government into being. Pictures, historically, came before words; in our present plight, Mr. Hogben thinks we must depend primarily on the use of pictures. Unless we succeed in establishing such a pictorial Esperanto, he gloomily contends, western civilization will fall back into barbarism. That is the fate that befalls people who fail to put the means of their communication to good use.

It is here that American mass culture comes into focus. Is it to be used to "coca-colonize" the world? Is it to induce everywhere a gibbering pleasure at the sight of ever-repeated photographs of dancing legs? Mr. Hogben indicts it for wasting invaluable energies on sheer entertainment. "If it is a platitude that America has given the world an object lesson in the popularity of the pictorial medium, it is also a truism to say that America has not as yet contributed to our common civilization any outstanding vindication of its potential value." His attacks against the American output in general culminate in a criticism of our comic strips. This excrescence on the body of American civilization delights millions of children and adults. Yet Americans have not waited for Mr. Hogben to worry about it and argue whether or not it leads to crime or simply illiteracy, and whether it can be used to teach the Bible and world literature. Mr. Hogben wants to capitalize on the entertainment value of comic strips (to this reviewer highly overrated) in order to promote educational ends.

This emphasis on the comics results from the book's thesis, which, rather arbitrarily, links all of man's progress to the history of the means, the action and interaction, through which he communicates his thought. Overemphasizing the role played by the comics, Mr. Hogben stops too soon. Of this trough in which we flounder there is more to be said. Contrary to what Mr. Hogben and others want us to believe, comic strips are at best, or at worst, a minor evil easily recognizable as such. The real danger lies in the uninterrupted use made of pictures for their own sake. Pictorialization has become a wanton habit. We show pictures to fill space. Many of them are not even particularly entertaining; all of them seem essentially stopgaps; they either remain unnoticed, like passers-by in a crowd, or the reactions they arouse are highly confused.

If looked at intently almost any picture will yield valuable information. But it is as if our picture-makers did not wish us to look at any picture long enough or with a concentration sufficient for us to pierce its meaning. They present their material in a manner which effectively forestalls our attempts to grasp its significance. When they put captions to their pictures, they tell us what to see in the pictures; they do not permit, far less encourage, us to look for ourselves. "This girl is smiling because she has a new automobile or a washing machine, or because she is brace and life must march on," the caption says but the girl is smiling because she has been paid to smile or because the mask of pain is very close to the mask of laughter. But when we look at her, we obey the editorial injunctions.

Our newsreels, documentaries, and feature films are overcrowded with verbal statements. The spectator is in a dilemma. If he wants to watch the picture, there are voices that intrude; if he listens to the voices, then it is the story *told*, rather than the story *seen* that dominates his imagination. Generally, the spectator succumbs to the insistence of the voice.

As a result, we are submerged by pictures and at the same time prevented from really perceiving them. The pictures become a veil between us and the visible world, dulling the edge of our intellect, stifling our imagination. We are so exposed to them that they blind us to the phenomena they render. Paradoxically, the more pictures we see, the less we are able or willing to practice the art of seeing. We no longer respond; our perceptive faculties threaten to decline. The incessant flow of visual material from the assembly belt has the soporific effect of a drug, adding to the drowsiness which our kind mass culture tends to spread.

Mr. Hogben loves pictures, believes in pictures, wants us to have even more pictures than there now are. But he wants them to be the right kind of pictures—world-federation pictures. He seems to maintain, in the final chapter of this otherwise stimulating and fascinating book, that world-wide visual education will not only promote international understanding, but also largely reduce the present waste of pictures and thus benefit the pictorial medium itself. This is improbable, for the simple reason that pictures serve many other purposes than those considered by Mr. Hogben. How can we assume that by using them deliberately as elements of a pictorial Esperanto we may succeed in channeling their overpowering flow? Whatever one feels about the desirability of either world federation or such an Esperanto, Mr. Hogben's plan cannot possibly be expected to become the organizing principle of pictorialization. Mr. Hogben's program resembles a publicity man's dream; he is so completely possessed by it that he overestimates its beneficent effect on picture-making in general, as well as its educational possibilities.

Mr. Hogben is a plain rationalist. It is significant that he believes we dissipate our strength by learning foreign languages and remaining faithful to the irrational spelling we have inherited. His dream of a uniform world culture omits the best that culture has to offer: depth.

PART 4

Cold War Tensions (1952–1958)

INTRODUCTION

In this section we bring together some key writings stemming principally from Kracauer's ongoing work with American governmental agencies and other organizations in the 1950s, in particular the Bureau of Applied Research at Columbia University, where Kracauer became a part-time research advisor in 1951. These diverse texts exemplify Kracauer's approach to the analysis of international political communication with respect to three particular and pressing issues: 1), the critical analysis and evaluation of Communist propaganda in terms of its proliferation and efficacy both within the Soviet bloc itself and along its margins; 2), a consideration of the prospects and possibilities of the "democratic" propaganda promulgated by America and the West in response; and 3), the search for appropriate and optimal methods for the empirical investigation and qualitative analysis of mass media images and texts.

Kracauer's own attitude to these studies in political communications is certainly complex and equivocal. On the one hand, they clearly exhibit a degree of continuity with the earlier writings from the 1940s addressed in the previous section and thus may be considered as an extension of his genuine and abiding preoccupation with the critique of authoritarian regimes. On the other hand, as Kracauer himself makes clear on a number of occasions in his correspondence, he considered these studies a mere *Brotarbeit*—that is to say, as driven by monetary rather than intellectual interests, and, accordingly, experienced as irritations and distractions impeding progress on his real critical focus, the book of film aesthetics that would appear in 1960 under the title *Theory of Film*. However much Kracauer perceived them as compromised, in our view these texts nonetheless provided him with an opportunity to develop certain critical ideas in English. For us, there is a great deal going on between the lines of these texts, and the critical reader should resist simple, superficial understandings of their contents. There is much of theoretical interest below the surface.

From 1950 onward, Leo Löwenthal and Paul Lazarsfeld played a decisive role in the development of Kracauer's communication research. In 1950, Löwenthal, then-director of the Evaluation Staff of the International Broadcasting Service (Voice of America) at the U.S. Department of State, offered Kracauer a post as research analyst. On November 2, 1951, Lazarsfeld wrote to Löwenthal, asking him "to form and chair a sub-committee on communications research in the international field." As a guest editor and chairman of the Committee on International Communications Research of the American Association for Public Opinion Research (AAPOR), Löwenthal invited Kracauer to contribute to the special issue of International Communication Research for *Public Opinion Quarterly*, the issue that included the seminal essays of Lazarsfeld and Harold Lasswell in the field of political communication. In 1951, Kracauer was appointed as a part-time research advisor of the Bureau of Applied Social Research (BASR) at Columbia University (founded by Paul Lazarsfeld in 1944). Throughout the 1950s, Kracauer tried to develop empirical studies of international communications and propaganda and to organize related research programs, characterizing his role with a certain degree of irony, if not cynicism, as a "roving consultant."

At this point, it is worth recalling how Lazarsfeld earlier ended his collegial relationship with Adorno, to help us understand the direction of Kracauer's study of communication research in an attempt to develop a critical theory of political communication. In a response to an article by Horkheimer, "Traditional and Critical Theory" (1937), Lazarsfeld wrote "Remarks on Administrative and Critical Communication Research" in the journal of the Institute for Social Research in Frankfurt, *Studies in Philosophy and Social Science* in 1941. Here, Lazarsfeld strongly recommended that Critical Theory be included in American communication studies along with his own style of research, which he termed "administrative communication research." The term refers to the way he envisaged the relationship between empirical research in the service of government and mass media institutions and his effort to "build a pluralist bridge to critical scholarship." In a move to inject critical thinking into empirical research, Lazarsfeld invited Adorno to join the Princeton Radio Research Project, but, as widely known, their collaboration ended in failure.[1] In 1951, Lazarsfeld invited Kracauer to the bureau, based on a similar motivation but with tempered enthusiasm, which is understandable given his bitter experience with the members of the Institute.

In this section, we include two exemplary instances of Kracauer's work for the BASR, in each case summarizing more extensive research programs. The first of these is a document from May 1952 marked "restricted" for the International Information Administration's (IIA) program in the Near and Middle East, entitled "Appeals to the Near and Middle East: Implications of the Communications Studies Along the Soviet Periphery." This text summarizes a series of earlier documents and reports that collectively explored various dimensions and specific national and regional case studies of then-contemporary propaganda practices and possibilities with particular reference to Voice of America radio. The second, "Attitudes Toward Various Communist Types in Hungary, Poland, and Czechoslovakia," is an overview written in 1955 of a substantial empirical study entitled *Satellite Mentality*, coauthored by Kracauer with the psychologist Paul L. Berkman, which explores the perceptions of recent refugees from Eastern Europe, as contained in transcripts documenting some three hundred interviews conducted in 1951–1952 with exiles from Hungary, Poland, and Czechoslovakia. In investigating the attitudes of non-Communists to their country's political regimes and social and economic systems, Kracauer and Berkman draw attention to the way Communist propaganda quickly dissipated once the promises of the party failed to materialize and the quality of the daily life became ever more impoverished. Importantly, the authors highlight the nuanced and highly differentiated set of categorization and attitudes held by refugees toward Communist Party members, depending upon reasons for affiliation, ideological enthusiasm, and life situations. Far from decrying party members as mere fanatics or functionaries, the interviewees demonstrate a sympathetic appreciation of varied motives and exigencies at work in these Soviet-dominated societies. Kracauer and Berkman also explore how the broadcasts of Radio Free Europe helped shape the perspectives of non-Communists toward their compatriots, and toward the Soviet Union, Western Europe, and the United States. Because these perspectives were frequently unrealistic and even utopian in character, they could become a potential source for future disenchantment; for example, when in due course these refugees came to discover that Western capitalism was not a workers' paradise of economic bounty, unrestrained liberty, and unalloyed justice for all.

At first sight, these two reports suggest that Kracauer was now extending his wartime work to interrogating forms of totalitarianism and the possibilities of individual and collective resistance, and gearing his labors explicitly to the U.S. Cold War effort. It is legitimate to ask whether in doing so Kracauer, as a recently inducted U.S. citizen, rather uncritically embraces its ideologies and values. And so one reads, for example, in the 1952 summary, sentences such as following: "Contrary to what they [Arab populations] believe, America does not sustain the status quo but is actually the driving power behind an effort to improve conditions and illiteracy"; and "Israel stands a fair chance of developing into a ferment for social and economic progress in the Middle East." One is left to wonder if these comments genuinely express Kracauer's own views. There are other possibilities, of course. He may well be writing with a degree of a bad faith for the purposes of appeasing the bureaucrats and functionaries in the state department for whose attention they were intended. Restricted documents do not have to be, indeed should not be considered as, the proper vehicle for the presentation of personal, idiosyncratic views and values. Kracauer would certainly not welcome their circulation among his Critical Theory colleagues at the Institute. There is another possibility: that Kracauer is being ironic, or that in eulogizing the United States he is in some way contrasting its lofty self-perceptions with the far less rosy reality of 1950s American political and economic life. Utopian categories and conceptions become a form of critique of existing conditions. Kracauer himself suggests the manifold meanings of words and phrases in the course of his methodological writings, so the reader of Kracauer's texts would be well advised not to assume that Kracauer is merely endorsing American values and ways of life in any simplistic manner.

It is clear from these two reports that Kracauer did have some insights into incipient political issues that have remained with us in an intensified and exacerbated form right up to today. These include the problem of Palestine as *the* determining factor of contemporary American and Arab relations, as well as acute anxieties over American expansionism and imperialism. They also include critiques not only of American political, economic, and social hegemony, but also of American culture. Its superficiality, sexualization, triviality, banality, and vulgarity as a way of life appeared as anathema to those who sought to preserve other forms of culture conceived as authenticity, historical tradition, and profound faith. Kracauer is not unaware of the ironies and contradictions here. While America is frequently lauded as a land of equality and opportunity, and an enviable standard of material comfort, as the very epitome of progressive, tolerant, and liberal modern society, it is also castigated for its shallowness and vacuity. Then as now, it seems that the world loves and loathes American cultural products in equal measure, something many Americans themselves still struggle to understand.

The use of what today would be deemed Orientalist language, in terms of both particular tropes and overall tone, should on no account go unmentioned. It deserves particular comment, not to excuse it by some complacent appeal to historical context but rather because Kracauer himself, always so attentive to the use of language, was perhaps not wholly unaware of it. In the lengthy 1954 paper "The Social Research Center on the Campus: Its Significance for the Social Sciences and Its Relations to the University and Society at Large," one finds the following reflection in relation to work on the "Satellite Mentality" study: "It is well-nigh inevitable that scientists and researchers should be affected from within and without by the powerful stereotypes that shape public opinion in the area of politics" (see page 375, this volume). Academic works themselves, even critical studies, are not so privileged as to be exempt from the danger of recycling the very clichés they purport to unmask and challenge. Our attention is drawn here to the inescapably ideological character of language itself and, importantly, to the figure of the intellectual who stands not outside or above the conditions of everyday life and concerns of wider communities, but is rather immersed in and imbued by them just like everyone else. Without wishing to overstate the case, one might suggest that for Kracauer the Critical Theorist imagined here is not the trailblazer leading the way for others to follow, but, rather, always and only with us, one of us, our loyal companion in misfortune.[2]

It is also worth noting that, although Kracauer's focus is primarily on radio broadcasts (in particular, the Voice of America), his discussion does include other forms of media and interpersonal communication as well. Film is not ignored in Kracauer's writing on the IIA paper on the Near and Middle East. Once again, he emphasizes the importance of receptivity to communications with respect to existing predispositions of audiences and spectators. Moreover, this emphasis reflects his "Below the Surface" project more than his *Caligari* book. Kracauer is at pains to emphasize that the messages are most effective when they are veiled or partially concealed. Three interesting observations result from this. Firstly, the more explicit propaganda is, the less effective it will be (propaganda conceived as such is not just useless but actively counterproductive). Secondly, feature films with a strong narrative enabling emotional attachment between audiences and characters are far more powerful than documentary films with their didacticism and direct advocacy. Finally, Kracauer underscores the importance of indirectness as a technique and method; digression is the surest way to achieve intended goals. In contemporary parlance, soft power needs to be soft if it wants to be powerful.

As outlined above, it should be clear that Kracauer's work on communications in the early 1950s was not lacking reflexivity; it explicitly analyzed different methods of communication, including the role of language, and how best to understand the functioning of the realm of ideas, opinions, and discourses. In short, epistemological and methodological issues were at the forefront of his thinking in undertaking these empirical social-scientific analyses and evaluations. This should come as no surprise, since Kracauer had long been concerned with such questions; for example, in his early writings on sociology as a "science," his "ethnography" of Berlin's white-collar workers, his study of "mass ornament," the societal biography of Jacques Offenbach, and also in the interpretive scheme underpinning *From Caligari to Hitler*.

In the early 1950s, Kracauer's ongoing concern with method is evident in his critical response to the BASR's one-sided focus on quantitative methods, which leads him to defend the virtues of qualitative techniques such as participant observation and in-depth interviews. Three essays particularly relevant to this issue are reproduced here: "Proposal for a Research Project Designed to Promote the Use of Qualitative Methods in the Social Sciences" (unpublished manuscript, 1950); "The Challenge of Qualitative Content Analysis" (*Public Opinion Quarterly*, 1953); and "On the Relation of Analysis to the Situational Factors in Case Studies" (unpublished manuscript, ca. 1958). In his "Proposal for a Research Project," Kracauer points to the limitations of content analysis as a method for the critical analysis of textual materials, questioning the usefulness of, for instance, simply coding and then counting the frequency of a particular word or phrase in a political speech or radio broadcast. Insisting upon the importance of contextual and situated hermeneutical readings to capture the actual sense and full significance of language use, he suggests the value of a study identifying and exploring the mutual benefits that would accrue such qualitative and quantitative approaches when used in tandem. For Kracauer, overreliance or overemphasis on quantitative content analysis leads to a neglect of qualitative research in communication research. According to Kracauer, quantitative analysis can, at best, disclose issues in a "roundabout way," but it often leads to "over-fine" categorizations and oversimplifications. Highlighting the complementary relation of the two methods, Kracauer identified some exemplary instances of the fruitful combination of quantitative and qualitative methods in communication research: Leo Löwenthal's "Biographies in Popular Magazines," Rudolf Arnheim's "World of the Daytime Serial," and the essays in Paul Lazarsfeld and Frank Stanton's edited book *Radio Research, 1942–1943*.

In 1958, he completed a twenty-six-page memorandum, "On the Relation of Analysis to the Situational Factors in Case Studies." In October 1960, Kracauer sent it to Adorno under his private pseudonym, Friedel. While thoroughly reviewing the diverse research perspectives on case studies, Kracauer criticized the overemphasis on "psychology" and dismissed the hope for generality in a case study as merely "an illusion." Kracauer also gave a critical assessment of the Institute's project *The Authoritarian Personality*. In his view, the project should have related their "personality syndrome" to "situational factors"—that is, the historical and national contexts in which it was conducted.[3] Defending his earlier empirical work as well as Löwenthal's study of biographies in popular magazines, he foregrounded the significance of the sociological dimension of the case studies to formulate the situational factors.[4] According to Jay, Adorno's response was to label Kracauer's research method as "anti-idealist and ultimately anti-philosophical" in an article he wrote in commemoration of Kracauer's seventy-fifth birthday.[5] Adorno was probably partly right when he attributed Kracauer's fundamental theoretical debt to Georg Simmel's sociological impressionism. Like Simmel, Kracauer was less an abstract philosopher than a critical sociologist of urban culture, who preferred experiencing the complexities of modern culture as concrete surface phenomena to theoretically generalizing it.

Our final text, the report "The Social Research Center on the Campus" (1954), examines "organized research" in social science research centers, or "social laboratories," taking the work of the BASR at Columbia as a paradigmatic case study. In distinguishing between three overlapping areas of activity—"autonomous research," "commissioned research," and research "training"—Kracauer provides a series of interesting and insightful reflections upon, among others, three key thematic foci of relevance for our anthology: communications and opinion formation, politics and political behavior, and methodology in the social sciences. While the various analyses of mass media discussed here concentrate on radio and radio audiences (including Kracauer's own Voice of America writings) there is also reference to studies of advertising and marketing, and the fundamental role of "opinion leaders" (akin to what Pierre Bourdieu would later term "cultural intermediaries"): "Interpersonal relations," Kracauer writes, "play a much larger role in decision making than mass communications proper." In a felicitous anticipation of the language of social media today, he speaks of the need to "locate relevant 'influentials' in four areas ... marketing, movie preferences, fashions and political affairs." Given his own intellectual marginal status and financial precarity, the institutional and professional ethical juggling of research led by genuine scholarly passions and that driven by commercial interests thematized under the rubric of "professional integrity" in this study was, of course, something that preoccupied Kracauer throughout his American exile and is acutely relevant for universities and academics today.

NOTES

1. On the Princeton Radio Research Project, and the Institute's relationship to Lazarsfeld and the Bureau of Applied Social Research more generally, see Thomas Wheatland, *The Frankfurt School in Exile* (Minneapolis: University of Minnesota Press, 2009), 86–94; and David Jenemann, *Adorno in America* (Minneapolis: University of Minnesota Press, 2007), 47–104.
2. Kracauer himself wryly observes: "Even atomic physicists have come to realize that they are not only scientists but also citizens and that in consequence they owe allegiance to two ethical codes which might easily conflict with each other" ("The Social Research Center on the Campus," 375).
3. In an unpublished commentary on *The Authoritarian Personality*, which Adorno penned in 1948, he essentially agreed with Kracauer's criticisms here, pointing out that the predominantly social-psychological methodology of the study would need to be supplemented by a more sociohistorical approach, in order to fully grasp the persistence of authoritarianism in modern capitalist societies. This text has recently been published: Theodor Adorno, "Remarks on *The Authoritarian Personality*," in T. W. Adorno, E. Frenkel-Brunswik, D. J. Levinson, and R. N. Sanford, *The Authoritarian Personality* (New York: Verso, 2019), xli–lxvi.
4. For more details about Löwenthal's work on popular biographies, see note 7 in the general introduction to this volume. In his memoir, Löwenthal reveals that "On the Relation of Analysis to the Situational Factors in Case Studies" was written at the suggestion of the research mangers at the BASR, but the essay "criticized their research enterprise as lacking a historical or truly political foundation." Despite his willingness to stay close to "sociological empirical research," Löwenthal adds, Kracauer's message in this essay explicitly shows that "you have to watch out that you don't do research in a vacuum but in a concrete political and cultural context." Leo Löwenthal, "As I Remember Friedel," no. 54 (Fall 1991): 13.
5. T. W. Adorno, "The Curious Realist: On Siegfried Kracauer," *New German Critique*, no. 54 (Fall 1991): 159–77; Martin Jay, "Adorno and Kracauer: Notes on a Troubled Friendship," in *Permanent Exiles* (New York: Columbia University Press, 1985), 232.

15
Appeals to the Near and Middle East

Implications of the Communications Studies Along the Soviet Periphery

Prepared for the Bureau of Applied Social Research
Columbia University

May, 1952

PREFACE

The Columbia University Bureau of Applied Social Research has recently completed an extensive research study on the general subject of communications behavior in the Near and Middle East. The results of this investigation have been presented to the Department of State in the following series of individual country reports, each giving attention to a particular aspect of the communications process:

"Greek Attitudes Toward the United States, Great Britain, U.S.S.R, and France"
"Radio Audiences in Greece"
"Mass Media in Greece"
"Information Monopolists in Rural Greece"
"Mass Communications Audiences in Turkey"
"The Radio Audiences of Lebanon"
"Communication and Public Opinion in Jordan"
"Climates of Opinion in Egypt"
"Syrian Attitudes Toward America and Russia"

"Partisanship and Communications Behavior in Iran"
"Political Extremism in Iran"

In addition, a special report comparing the communications behavior and political attitudes of different social groups of the four Arab countries studied (Jordan, Syria, Lebanon, and Egypt) has been prepared. It is called, "Communications Behavior and Political Attitudes in Four Arabic Countries." The present report, which is the last of the series, represents an attempt to bring together and codify those implications of the entire study which seem most directly relevant for the International Information Administration's program in the Near and Middle East. The recommendations which are made grow out of our experience in collecting, organizing, and analyzing the research data, they should be interpreted in the light of the manifold factors which must be considered in the formulation of policy.

RESTRICTED

CONTENTS

INTRODUCTION————277
I. MASS MEDIA AND POPULATIONS————279
A. THE COMMUNICATIONS SITUATION————279
B. THE IMPORTANCE OF THE LOWER STRATA OF POPULATION————281
C. SUGGESTIONS FOR THE HANDLING OF THE MEDIA————283
II. SIGNIFICANT APPEALS————288
A. SUGGESTIONS BEARING ON AUDIENCE DISPOSITIONS————288
1. Resentments and inferiority feelings————288
2. Distrust of U.S. political intentions————289
3. Oriental values————291
4. America as land of opportunity————294
B. SUGGESTIONS CONCERNING SEVERAL U. S. OBJECTIVES————295
1. Communism and Soviet Russia————295
2. Progress————298
3. UN and free-world solidarity————300

III. COMMUNICATING WITH THE ARABS―――――302
   A. ABOUT REGIONAL DIFFERENCES―――――302
   B. SPECIAL TREATMENT OF EGYPT―――――303
   C. POLITICAL ARGUMENTATION ―――――305

INTRODUCTION

PURPOSE

The studies of communications behavior along the Soviet periphery, conducted by the Bureau of Applied Social Research, Columbia University, carry many implications which might be of interest to the International Information Administration (IIA). Some of these implications are stated explicitly, while others still lie dormant in the material.

The report is intended

1. to assemble the former and bring out the latter;
2. to detail and supplement all of them in the interest of their usefulness for IIA.

This means that the report presents a body of proposals for the implementation of U.S. objectives: the fight against Communism and Soviet expansionism; collective security; the strengthening of the U.N. More likely than not many suggestions will only confirm what is already known and practiced.

METHODOLOGICAL QUESTIONS

1. The communications studies—called "studies" in the report—are based on interviews gathered at different periods: field work in Greece and Turkey was done during the last months of 1950; in Jordan, Syria, Lebanon and Egypt in the first half of 1951.

It is evident that the then existing local conditions bear on the content of the interviews as well as the inferences drawn from them. Should conditions meanwhile have changed, all those inferences palpably affected by the changes would have to be reconsidered in the light of the current situation.

For instance, the recent admission to NATO of Greece and Turkey disposes of Turkish discontent with the failure of the Western powers to recognize Turkey's strategic position (study of Turkey, p. 49). Also, rural Turkey is said now to receive many more radio sets than at the time of the interviews a new fact which calls for revision of what the interviews themselves suggest in this respect.

Wherever possible, changes of consequence are taken into account.

2. Different studies approach their common subject matter—communications behavior—from different angles; the consequence being that themes featured in one study are relegated to the background in others.

Attitudes toward Communism and Soviet Russia, one of the main topics of the Syria study play a negligible part in the studies of Turkey and Egypt. Nor are the various strata of population treated uniformly, light is shed now on the existing socio-economic groups (Egypt, Jordan), now on groupings defined by identical relations to the mass media (Greece Turkey the Lebanon) or identical political views (Syria); also, Greek, Turkish and Lebanese youth are in evidence, while little is said about young people in Egypt and Syria.

To be sure, this differential treatment has the great advantage of enabling the social scientist to tackle, one by one, the new problems he encounters in the field of' international communications research. But its undeniable disadvantage is that it renders unifications and comparisons difficult. Fortunately, these difficulties are surmountable in some oases vital to the report. Due to a plethora of data, the variegated groups of population singled out or constructed in different places can be reduced to a common denominator. It would also seem justified to infer from the actual statements on young people as to the potential role of youth throughout the Middle East. (The study of Lebanon, for instance, speaks of the emancipatory aspirations "of women and young people, particularly young women, in a society where East meets West," thus implying that these aspirations may not be confined to Lebanon alone. Page 53.)

PROCEDURE

The report is divided into three parts.

Part I centers around the basic proposition, implied in practically all studies, that special efforts should be made to reach the lower strata of population and the youth groups. Based on an appraisal of the whole communications situation, this proposition is broken down into a series of suggestions for the handling of the media along the Soviet periphery.

Part II deals with the content and the presentation of IIA communications, featuring such appeals as might best be suited to get these communications across in the Near and Middle East. Some of the suggestions offered bear on audience dispositions while others concern several U.S. objectives.

Part III develops the thesis that the Arabs should be approached in a different manner from the way in which the Greeks and the Turks are approached; then it concentrates on the problem of how to communicate with the better educated Arabs. Suggestions for a special treatment of the Egyptian elite are followed by an attempt to construct an appropriate line of political reasoning.

I. MASS MEDIA AND POPULATIONS

Recommendations for a purposeful handling of the mass media along the Soviet periphery must be based on an appraisal of the communications situation in that part of the world.

A. THE COMMUNICATIONS SITUATION

The studies reveal that in the whole territory the actual exposure to the mass media depends upon the educational level of the recipients which in turn correlates highly with their socio-economic status, otherwise expressed, different socio-economic groups of population can be expected to react to the mass media in different ways. Since demographic subtleties would only blur the picture, it may suffice to discriminate between the following three major groups which are more or less characteristic of all countries under consideration:

1. At the top there is the small group of the _elite_. It comprises government officials, the nobility, if any, big land owners and prosperous merchants, army officers, religious dignitaries, the cream of the professionals, and students. On an average, these people are well-educated and well-off, if not wealthy; they aggregate in the towns; and many of them show strong affinities for the West. The type of westernized intellectual is found exclusively in the elite. He commands one or two foreign languages, has traveled widely, end cannot help

admiring the West. Turkish state officials are recruited from young men who have studied abroad; well-to-do Egyptians are at home in the European capitals and spas. In the Arabic countries proper these "westerners" feel uneasy about the backwardness of their own peoples (Jordan study, p. 60) and the frequent conflict between their affinities for the West and their political convictions. Everywhere the elite are devotees of the mass media which they of all groups of population, are best in a position to patronize. Many listen regularly to foreign broadcasts, read newspapers as a matter of course, and make a habit of frequenting the movie houses. The intelligentsia manifests its cosmopolitan preferences by turning ·its back on the domestic radio stations and reveling in the riches of American magazines. In sum, the elite are familiar with the mass media and highly susceptible to the flow of international communications.

2. The broad masses at the bottom consist predominantly of peasants—either tenants of absentee landowners or small farmers subsisting on their own produce. There are, in addition, the nomads and semi-nomads, particularly frequent in Jordan, the service workers, the watchmen, and the groups of plain laborers and factory workers. Industrialization is only beginning; even in countries where unions are legalized the workers can hardly be said to form a strong and class-conscious vanguard, All the more it would seem justified to define these strata of population as submerged masses. They are illiterate, or at best near illiterate; their living standards range from poor to destitute. This in part accounts for their insufficient exposure to the mass media.

Print is inaccessible to them and how could they afford to buy radio sets? Things are rendered more difficult by an ingrained aversion, strongest in rural areas, to let the doubtful blessings of civilization interfere with age-old traditions. The Bedouins reject wholesale the infidels and their devilish inventions. And except perhaps for the Egyptian farmers, the peasants everywhere accept radio, if at all, only to the extent to which it confirms their outlook on life. As illustrated by the studies of Turkey and Greece, they are indifferent to the movies or even condemn them for being a source of sinful temptations. All in all, the communications habits of these submerged strata are still underdeveloped. Messages from the world at large pass above their heads.

However, this applies primarily to the older farmers, laborers or workers. Their progeny feels a natural urge for evading the strictures of tradition and custom. Many young people actually yield to the attractions of modern life. The movies cast a spell over them which stirs their elders to impassioned or elegiac complaints about the destructive forces of the Western world. In rural Greece, for instance, the difference in film attendance between the generations is very striking indeed. It is inevitable that parental authority should often clash with youthful determination to enjoy the forbidden fruits; the study of Turkey goes so far as to speak of a "conflict between generations engendered by movies in Turkey, as in other Middle Eastern countries" (p. 96). Yet there is some evidence that the traditional inhibitions and scruples of the old are slowly losing ground. Ever more young people of the depressed classes learn to read and write, thus gaining an unassailable prestige in districts marked by illiteracy. A typical case is the Greek farmer whose 12-year-old son plods through the newspaper for him (study of Greece, no. 4, p. 13). The discharged Turkish conscripts return to their villages as pillars of grammar-school wisdom. In Lebanon the poor farm villagers rely on their trained offspring for worldly information. The young educated peasant there is a mobile type who, during his stays in town, goes to the movies or lingers in a coffee house listening to the radio. His influence as a news carrier cannot be overestimated (study of Lebanon, pp. 131–46).

3. The contrast between the urban elite and the rural masses would even be more outspoken were it not for a variety of groups which somehow fill the vacuum in between. These middle strata, as they may be called, include such different occupations as taxi drivers, smaller shopkeepers and merchants, coffee house owners, government clerks, white-collar workers, technicians, teachers in primary schools, etc., It is a sort of middle class, with a considerable amount of petty bourgeoisie close to the submerged populations; but of course, transitions to the elite are fluid. Also, except for near illiteracy within the low reaches, the educational standards range from elementary school to high school level; living conditions vary between modest and better off. More urban than rural, these strata occupy a middle position with regard to their communications habits. Even though they go beyond the peasantry in availing themselves regularly of the mass media, yet they do not explore them in the manner of the elite because their whole outlook is localized and tradition-bound. Whether in coffee houses or at home, they prefer domestic radio stations to foreign stations and are mainly interested in news which bears on their immediate concerns or strictly national issues. The middle groups tend to keep aloof from international communications.

B. THE IMPORTANCE OF THE LOWER STRATA OF POPULATION

Practically all studies point to the possibility of improving the communications habits of those still unfamiliar with the mass media or not yet fully attuned to them. Greek villagers would like to learn about events abroad; the radio owners among Lebanese middle-class people can be defined as potential foreign listeners (study of Lebanon, p. 66); and even the Bedouins are not entirely allergic to news from the outside world with its "effeminate" cities. Such facts and symptoms give rise to the proposition, advanced or implied in several studies, that long-range attempts should be made to reach not only the better educated but the lower strata of population as well—strata which, roughly speaking, extend from the petty bourgeoisie down to the bottom. This basic proposition involves all media of communication. Diverse International Information Administration activities seem actually designed to substantiate it: special press features oater to the needs of worker groups; documentary films are shown in rural areas, etc. Yet it might be desirable to broaden and intensify these activities for the following reasons, all of which corroborate the basic proposition:

1. The poverty-stricken masses along the Soviet periphery seem to gain in political consciousness. Rural Turkey is on the move since the 1950 elections; the Lebanese villagers, it appears, are at a stage of transition; the discontented Egyptian farmers are undoubtedly aware of' the need for economic and social reforms. It is as if inertia were slowly receding. In the Arabic world this desire for change at the bottom, which inevitably affects the urban middle strata, is fostered by unsettled refugees from Palestine, to be sure nationalist passions may prolong the dozing, but their drugging effect is bound to wear off. In short, broad Middle East populations are about to enter into the political arena. And since an opinion vacuum is as dangerous as a power vacuum, their appearance on the scene alone would account for the necessity of establishing contacts with them.

2. Such early contacts are especially needed to immunize the masses against the potential impact of Communist propaganda. One might object here that in both rural and urban Greece precisely the less educated nurture the strongest anti-Russian sentiments and that among the submerged classes in Syria protestations of indifference to Communist (and American) influences are fairly frequent. It is also true that Arabic religiosity puts a strain on those inclined to favor Moscow's foreign policy. Yet all this does not preclude the possibility that in times of crisis the very populations which now are anti-Communist or just apathetic will succumb to Communist insinuations from without and within. And it is always advisable to try to mold a mind as long as it is still malleable.

3. Free-world solidarity requires good will on grass-roots level. This more than anything else makes for a sustained effort to reach the depressed and less educated. To leave them to themselves would mean not only to increase the threat of Communism but to abandon the ideas that have shaped the U.N.

A ferment of change, the youth of the lower strata represents one of the most important links between these strata and the West. Appeals to young people are therefore indispensable for an implementation of the basic proposition. Without such appeals communications for the bottom layers of' Middle East societies might easily fall flat.

And what does the basic proposition imply for the handling of the mass media?

C. SUGGESTIONS FOR THE HANDLING OF THE MEDIA

ALL MEDIA

The studies show that people of the lower strata, both rural and urban, are particularly eager for communications which bear on local topics and, for the rest, conform to their traditional style of life. The scope of their interests and experiences is limited, this also means that they are not conditioned to grasp information about remote or abstract subjects, such as international meetings and the like, conveyed to them in highly technical terms. Embedded in their environment, they are averse to breaking away from it mentally and linguistically. The farmer in Jordan, lucky enough to possess a radio, elicits from it only things familiar (study of Jordan, p. 33); the traditional Turk would find it difficult to generalize the circumstances responsible for his personal situation (study of Turkey, p. 18).

Suggestions

Messages to these people should be selected and phrased accordingly. Whenever international issues or themes of a more abstract nature are discussed, it is helpful to focus on what they may mean to a Greek farmer or Syrian taxi driver. The language must be concrete and in keeping with local custom. All this is a matter of course, mentioned only in a systematic interest. It is understood that the adjustments to audience mentality are supposed to work two ways, they should penetrate the peasant mind and at the same time free it from its narrow confines. The whole is a dialectic process requiring much discernment on the part of the communicator. Insufficiently adjusted messages will hardly affect the farmers or laborers, while overadjusted messages will leave them unchanged.

Since less educated people are suspicious of anything foreign, they can be expected to assimilate communications of a domestic origin more readily than appeals from plainly outlandish sources. In the Arabic world news from Egypt has a homely ring. A good way of approaching these people therefore is the use of local channels authorized to pass off foreign communications as domestic products. The material need not even be "planted," but may be prepared by a local agency with American backing. Such "gray" propaganda techniques greatly facilitate the task of getting in touch with the lower strata.

RADIO

PRELIMINARY REMARK: One of the reasons, if a minor one, why interviewees in Jordan and Lebanon prefer the BBC to the Voice of America is the greater signal strength of the British broadcasts. This argument points up the need for better VOICE transmissions to the Middle East.

1. The studies of Greece, Turkey, and Lebanon refer explicitly to the scarcity of radio receivers in rural areas.

Suggestions would be misplaced, for efforts are being made to fill the gap. For instance, in Turkey things have reportedly taken a turn for the better since the time at which the Turkey data have been gathered (see Introduction, Methodological Questions, no. 1, pp. 1–2).

2. The VOA is not yet popular in the Middle East, especially in the Arabic countries it ranges, along with the Moscow Radio, among the least known foreign senders, lagging far behind the BBC or I say, the Cairo station in this respect (see studies of Turkey, Lebanon, Jordan). The reasons must be traced to its poor transmission and the fact that it is a newcomer there.

Suggestions

Pictorial newspaper ads, leaflets, and announcements on local radio stations currently serve to increase the awareness of VOICE broadcasts. In the interest of broader publicity, it would seem advisable to produce a documentary film about the VOA, vividly illustrating its effects on ordinary people everywhere, such a film might tell rural audiences the story of the VOICE in terms familiar to them and tell it with an intensity unattainable in other media.

3. For obvious reasons public listening is widespread among the lower strata. Greek and Turkish) villagers assemble around a community receiver or frequent the home of some isolated radio owner, usually a person of standing

who may or may not admit everyone. And, of course, there is throughout the Middle East the institution of the coffee houses where those with time on their hands cannot help lending an ear to the radio. Most studies emphasize the importance of both rural and urban coffee houses as places of listening for the populations at large.

Yet these opportunities are far from being all inclusive. The coffee house is a male affair; many laborers or poor farmers may have to work when the radio is playing or people are just too tired to listen in. All this makes for the spread of information through word of mouth. Listeners relate the news to their families, friends, and neighbors, who in turn pass it on, until it lands somewhere in a shepherd's hut or a desert tent. In the whole area word of mouth is a vital means of communication.

This situation breeds dangers. Public listening compares unfavorably with private listening in that it lessens the attention (study of Greece, no. 2, pp. 10–19). Coffee houses are noisy; the obtrusive presence of crowds interferes with mental concentration. But even assuming that the news is fully digested, it will nevertheless be increasingly distorted in the course of its wanderings from mouth to mouth. Grapevine rumors color the news that has launched them with the fears and hopes of their carriers.

Suggestions

Indistinct or diffuse communications are bound to increase these dangers. Accordingly, VOICE messages to the lower strata should aspire to extreme plasticity so that their salient points can be absorbed and rendered without essential changes, a striking image condensing an otherwise abstract text will stand out long in the memory and thus help preserve the substance of that text. Perhaps it is also for mnemotechnic reasons that the Oriental mind likes to give and receive information in the form of tales, episodes, and anecdotes. Much may be learned in this respect from the Arabic story teller who knows how to drive home the gist of what he is telling in the markets.

PRINT

Among the Arabic lower strata word-of-mouth communications traceable to radio listening seem to prevail slightly over those originating with newspaper consumption; in Greece and Turkey the reverse holds true—no matter, for the rest, whether people do read or are merely read to. Yet such differences are negligible within this context, Since the trend to fight illiteracy, particularly strong in the last two countries, is in the long run irresistible, printed material for the less educated will gain momentum everywhere.

Suggestions

Like radio messages, printed communications to these strata should possess a plastic quality. Photos, cartoons, and picture books are of course indispensable, but they will serve the purpose only if selected with an eye to the recipient's capacity of assimilating them. This refers to their content as well as their quantity; the pictorial deluge flooding certain western magazines will not do. It might prove worthwhile to gather some information about the average responses of Middle East farmers to visual aids. Considering the role young people of the lower strata are playing, special efforts to supply these shook troops of literacy with adequate visuals and reading fodder would certainly pay.

FILM

The lower strata are exposed to the movies less than to radio and newspaper material. Many are too poor to pay the admission fee; and there is, even more important, a woeful lack of opportunities. At the time of the interviews, Turkey had only 275 movie houses, with, in addition, a scanty total of 6 mobile film units to cover its rural areas; and three quarters of the rural Greek interviewees said they had never attended a screening.

Cultural and religious prejudices, mentioned in earlier contexts, seem to hamper any changes in this situation. The prejudices are sustained by feature films rather than documentaries. In fact, only 56% of the moviegoing Greek interviewees remember having seen a documentary film and only a quarter of the workers and farmers in Egypt are acquainted with foreign products in this vein. (But are not most documentaries of western origin?) In terms of distribution Hollywood pictures are everywhere in the lead. And as the studies of Greece illustrate, it is precisely they which arouse serious opposition, thus keeping alive the existing bias against the medium. Older Greeks of all walks of life worry greatly about the corrupting influence which they believe Hollywood films with their small regard for traditions, their many scenes of violence and their shallow lavishness exert on the young generation. Significantly, the less educated in Greece feel most attracted to them while the better educated prefer British movies because of their cultural appeals and, morally relevant plots.

It looks as if the situation were not yet ripe for a systematic use of cinematic communications. Or rather, things would look this way were it not for several circumstances which alter the picture. The fact that young people of lower education patronize the movie houses decidedly invites an approach to them by way of films. In addition, the resistance of the older generation to the medium might yield to mild acceptance, once this age group is made to realize that not all screen spectacles indulge in frivolous entertainment; Turkish villagers are said to appreciate documentary showings. The situation is actually in flux. And since processes of this kind are irreversible, it would hardly be justified to leave the immense propaganda value of films unexplored.

Suggestions

1. Whatever is done to increase opportunities in rural areas will help overcome ingrained prejudices. Mobile film units are mental tractors conquering virgin territory.

2. A study or the impact of Hollywood films on populations in critical areas is long since due. This study would have to analyze all factors responsible for the selection of the films, to appraise typical audience reactions to them, and to discuss the implications of its findings.

3. Experience shows that people not yet adjusted to the cinema are unable to follow the events on the screen. Cinematic language is still unfamiliar to them. They may neglect the narrative proper in an unimportant incident reminiscent of their everyday life; and they may be utterly confused by flashbacks, closeups and transitions which an ordinary moviegoer takes in his stride. The treatment of documentaries for novices in the medium poses problems which should be studied carefully. To mention only one of them, documentaries will not yield all the effects of which films are capable if those in charge of production rely mainly on verbal communications to make themselves understood. What counts in a film is its pictorial communications. It is they rather than the spoken words which affect the spectator's unconscious and thus subtly sensitize him to the championed cause. Grierson who considers documentary film a godsend for propaganda messages once said that "in documentary you do not shoot with your head but also with your stomach muscles." And when asked whether in his opinion the illiterate peasants in India might profit by films popularizing reforms, Pudovkin used surprisingly similar terms: because it teaches "The film is the greatest not only through the brain but through the whole body." To reach and teach the submerged populations in the Middle East the film maker must subordinate the commentator's voice to such camera revelations as they are ready to grasp.

4. Much as good documentaries challenge the spectator to participate in them emotionally, they involve his total personality to a lesser extent than humanly absorbing feature film. Perhaps the most effective Russian and Nazi propaganda films are dramas centering around an individual conflict—films imbuing the spectator's whole being with the messages entrusted to them. Feature films, then, might call forth responses of an intensity which films of fact are unlikely to generate. This is a weighty argument in favor of their utilization. There is fortunately no lack of suggestive Hollywood pictures apt to strike a sympathetic chord in traditional Turks or Lebanese farmers; a few random titles will be named later. It would seem highly desirable to incorporate such pictures into the film programs for the lower strata.

II. SIGNIFICANT APPEALS

PRELIMINARY REMARK: ILA communications serve to implement U.S. objectives. To carry out their task, they must be adjusted to the mentality of the peoples or the groups of peoples they try to reach. What kinds of appeals are best suited to get them across in the Near and Middle East? The studies yield a number of pertinent suggestions.

Some of them bear on audience dispositions in these areas, while others concern several U.S. objectives of interest.

A. SUGGESTIONS BEARING ON AUDIENCE DISPOSITIONS

1. RESENTMENTS AND INFERIORITY FEELINGS

In all countries under consideration the elite and the better educated middle strata resent anything which strikes them as Western overbearance. Greek professionals are displeased with American interference in Greek domestic affairs and the "patronizing" attitude of American advisers on the spot. Before Turkey's admission to NATO college-trained Turks who showed strong sympathies for America nevertheless reproached the U.S. with neglecting Turkey politically and economically. In their touchiness these people sometimes suspect insolence where there is actually none. A Greek law student blames the VOA for callously elaborating upon UNESCO's intellectual activities while so many Greeks are starving (study of Greece, no. 2, p. 36). Throughout the Arabic territory the elite suffer from feelings of humiliation. Egyptian interviewees of this group are firmly convinced that the British and the Americans look down on them—the former because of their all-pervasive snobbishness the latter because of their equally snobbish bias against those of dark skin. Since the Egyptian elite are fully aware of their cultural leadership in the Moslem world, they may be particularly sensitive to symptoms of Western arrogance, real or imagined.

Suggestions

Several interviewees reveal, without intending it, how the problem of dissolving this inferiority complex can best be tackled. Two less educated Turks are very proud of America's respect for Turkish bravery in Korea (study of Turkey, pp. 50–51). And an Egyptian respondent states that "British troops never respected us or considered our feelings during the war" (study of Egypt, p. 12). These answers dovetail to perfection for they manifest both overt pride in respect and unavowed yearning for respect. Accordingly, all communications in radio and print should be imbued with respect for those on the receiving end. Besides being desirable humanly, such an attitude is a major political requirement; were it lacking, free-world cooperation would hardly ever materialize. In the case of the better educated Middle East populations an effort to increase their self-confidence suggests itself. Greater self-confidence disposes of inflated resentment. Perhaps they will be more poised psychologically if they are made to feel that Americans do justice to their difficult in-between position.

2. DISTRUST OF U.S. POLITICAL INTENTIONS

Suspicions as to the motives behind U.S. communications, especially VOA broadcasts, are articulate among the elite and the better educated middle groups without being confined to them however. For instance, an unemployed Greek clerk holds that for all her friendliness America tries to convert Greece into a military base on the Balkans, and of course not solely in the interest of Greece (study of Greece, no. 1, p. 82). Similarly, literate Turks on all educational levels believe VOICE messages to be motivated by America's own personal advantage. "I don't think that they do it just to please us," says a manufacturer (study of Turkey, p. 63). In the Arabic countries there is a tendency among professionals to differentiate between the VOICE and the BBC; the former is often considered a propaganda instrument, while even in anti-British circles the latter is credited with being impartial and reliable. For the rest, the Arabic elite mistrust not only

Great Britain as a matter of course, but drop hints that in their opinion the U.S. is also plotting and scheming. The Egyptians go furthest in this respect, some of them being convinced that American advertising skills pervade all manifestations of American politics. Many an Egyptian professional accuses the U.S. of imperialism and accordingly identifies American aid as a means of bribing poor but honest nations so that they will be softened up for American business penetration. As a physician puts it: "The United States is trying to control the whole world by her dollars" (study of Egypt, p. 82).

Suggestions

Since these suspicions are particularly strong among the better educated, VOICE broadcasts to them and printed communications should avoid concealing legitimate American self-interest behind protestations of friendship and the like. To be sure, any communicator will be prone to elaborate exclusively on feelings of friendship in cases in which friendship itself is a declared political aim; yet the evidence shows that he would be ill-advised if he did not also point out that the friendship he is talking about is actually a fusion of altruistic and egoistic motives. One shade too much of altruism, and audience suspicions of its material advantages for the other party are bound to soar. Frankness is good policy in communicating with these easily vulnerable people. It implies respect for their intelligence and thus helps remove the psychological causes of their distrust.

Reliability is no less important than frankness—in fact, frankness is one of the aspects of reliability. People of all walks of life prefer the BBC to the VOA for a variety of reasons; when asked to indicate them they frequently refer to their impression, mentioned above, that the British news reports are least tainted by propaganda, A comparative study of the two broadcasting systems would be highly desirable; it might bring out those qualities of the BBC which sustain its unrivaled prestige in the Middle East.[1] Meanwhile one is safe in assuming that listeners there consider reliability a main virtue of foreign broadcasts. How does the BBC manage to convey the impression of it? The interviews reveal at least one of the procedures. A Turkish merchant says of the BBC "They are not trying to shape the facts so that news favors their side. They always give you both sides of the argument" (study of Turkey, p. XXIV). And several Egyptians agree that their trust in the BBC is based on the fact that it also broadcasts news unfavorable to Britain (study of Egypt, pp. 77–78). Middle-Eastern listeners, it appears, want to form their own opinion in full freedom and are therefore loath to have it predigested for them—an insistence on independent judgment which may well serve as a compensation for their dependence upon foreign powers in real life. The implication is that VOICE messages to these audiences should manifest the same detachment which seems to radiate from British broadcasts. An occasional bit of news which admits an American drawback or acknowledges a success on the other side of the fence will do a great deal of good. Perhaps the best propaganda in these areas is to seem to make none.

3. ORIENTAL VALUES

Practically all strata of population are imbued with a mentality which for lack of another expression may be called Oriental—a compound of traits and attitudes palpably at variance with Western values and preferences. Even the elite cannot completely rid themselves of it, in spite of their aversion to Koran readings and their affinity for a more modern style of life. Well-educated Greeks voice concern with their cultural heritage. Part of the Egyptian professionals feel strongly about their religion. Of special interest is the case of the Judge of Islamic Legislation in Jordan who is said to be representative of an important minority. He is aware of being at the crossroads; his sense of moral obligation determines him to be open-minded about the West, but his emotional and spiritual allegiances draw him irresistibly back to the fold of tradition (study of Jordan, pp. 85–86).

Within these contexts it will suffice to mention only two groups of typically Oriental notions, one relating to the meaning of human existence, the other to the feasibility of social change. Greek interviewees are very outspoken in what they believe to be humanly significant. Their ideas show in the opinions they form about the American way of life. Many Greeks who sympathize with the American people praise not only its generosity and kindness but declare themselves greatly impressed by its practical sense and enormous "drive"—qualities which inspire admiration rather than love and may be found also in less cultured peoples. There is in effect no indication that those favorable to America would acknowledge her as a wellspring of cultural achievements. Rather, a strong minority of Greek interviewees object to America's lack of culture. Especially the better educated feel this way although it is understood that their criticism does not interfere with their appreciation of American aid. The critics characterize Americans as money-seeking, callous, and indifferent creatures and are fairly convinced that the American "drive" is nothing but a meaningless bustle resulting in complete standardization and mechanization. Such frenetic activity, it seems to them, contradicts everything they themselves value highest—sentiment, spontaneity, leisure. And this leads to the Oriental concept of time. A student argues that he would not like to live in America because "there is too much rush and hurry. . . . for me." And a teacher says, "I like to waste time once in a while and I like to live on a slowed down Eastern European rhythm" (study of Greece, no. 1, p. 53). All Middle-Eastern peoples live in a time which cannot be counted by minutes and hours. Leisure is vital for them. Their meditations resemble the involved patterns of their carpet weavers.

The other group of Oriental notions centers around the belief that man is not primarily called upon to change his social environment; spiritual preoccupations may overshadow his concern with poverty and injustice. This belief which breeds fatalism in worldly affairs extends beyond the Moslem world, its native soil. Better educated Greek interviewees said to represent a strong minority, manifest their disgust at government corruption by simply shunning the radio news which they say overflows with empty promises; it does not seem to occur to them that they might do something about the corruption (study of Greece, no. 2, pp. 29–30). Turkey is in a state of transition accelerated by the 1950 elections; the Turkish elite embark on social and educational reforms with a zeal which on the surface is about the opposite of fatalism. On the surface—for their infatuation with progress and modern life is too pronounced to affect one as entirely genuine. A middle-aged tobacco executive is quoted as saying that he would not like to live in Britain or America because these countries are not modern enough" (study of Turkey, p. XX). Such excessive opinions point to the possibility that the radicalism of modern Turks grows out of their fear, conscious or not, of being again overpowered by the paralyzing influences in their blood. It is true that many Turks of the lower strata develop a certain restlessness, but their progressive ambitions are timid rather than exacting. And the rural masses still believe themselves to be irrelevant politically. The average Turkish villager questions the propriety of taking interest in public affairs and cannot even imagine that he himself should have to decide upon improvements or changes. The same reluctance to intervene in the social processes pervades the Arabic countries proper. If in Lebanon the farmers are slightly more eager for reforms than elsewhere this may be laid to the strong Christian element which functions as a tonic. The study of Egypt dwells on the impotence of Egyptian nationalism, deriving it from both political and psychological factors; among the latter, fatalistic dispositions may well play an important role.

Suggestions

What many Greeks, but not Greeks alone, imagine to be American reality—frenetic commotion for no purpose other than money-grabbing—bears actually little resemblance to it. And of course, radio talks to all strata of population should try, as they presumably do, to revise this picture by emphasizing, say,

America's modified capitalism and various slow-pace areas in American life. Yet Oriental criticism goes further and deeper; it culminates in the conviction that Americans lack culture. Arabic professionals speak of the alleged mistakes of U.S. foreign policy with a condescension which implies that not too much should be expected of people who have no sense of spiritual values and intricate contexts. The problem of how to refute such opinions is well-nigh insoluble. Any attempt on the part of the communicator to inform Oriental audiences of America's cultural possessions and endeavors will make them think he is talking or writing about commercialized culture, this counterfeit of the genuine thing. For if they know anything they know that culture is a mode of existence not a commodity which can be advertised. Sales talks about cultural accomplishments are a sure means of convincing the critics that their verdict is justified. The same Greeks who complained about the uncultured conduct of Americans ware favorably impressed by this country's decision to take up arms against the Korean aggressor. America's readiness to fulfill her promises is an invaluable in their eyes. It is also an asset which does not lose significance for being communicated. All of which tends to suggest that it might be wisest to feature in messages to the Middle East such merits as are demonstrable and let culture speak for itself. True culture has a way of radiating silently. In view of the little radio time and the fact that criticism mainly originates with the better educated, printed statements on values are preferable to verbal messages, they also permit the communicator to meander, unhurried through the world of meanings.

The dire necessity of social changes in the Middle East calls for a long-range campaign against the existing fatalistic tendencies. These are rooted in psychological depths inaccessible to direct appeals. Nevertheless, to penetrate them such a campaign would have to work by indirection. Examples of active self-help are most likely to touch off mimetic processes in the audience—provided of course they do not seem to impart a moral. Also, they should present success through action on so modest a scale that they cannot possibly be mistaken for, and rejected as, illustrations of American drive. Anecdotes and biographical sketches in this vein which captivate the reader's or radio listener's imagination may stimulate him to ward off spells of inertia. Because of their impact on the unconscious films are particularly fit to affect established behavior patterns. Take Buster Keaton's *The Navigator* or one of the better Harold Lloyd comedies: it is quite possible that the hilarious resourcefulness of their heroes acts as an antidote against Oriental passivity. These films are understood by everyone and they have the additional advantage of illustrating American awareness of the dangers inherent in mechanization. The better educated in the Middle East are prone to voice suspicions of government corruption, politics and politicians, but their distrust, certainly well-founded in many cases, remains just a grumbling of no consequence. It might prove worthwhile to acquaint these more sophisticated audiences with films like *Mr. Smith Goes to Washington* and *Born Yesterday* which feature American initiative in fighting political abuses. There is at least a slim chance that such films. along with similar communications in radio and print, will canalize energies which otherwise disintegrate without leaving a trace.

4. AMERICA AS LAND OF OPPORTUNITY

It is true that people of all classes admire and love America as a country where the dream of human freedom seems to have materialized; and it is equally true that the Egyptian elite feels attracted to the West for cultural reasons. But the studies make it unmistakably clear that the lower strata are fascinated mainly by the glittering material advantages which they believe America offers people like them; the America they care about is a land of wealth and opportunity where jobs and riches can be had for the asking. A poor Greek maid servant says, "Living conditions are better there. They have refrigerators, washing machines...." A Greek customs agent who spent a short time in the States holds that "there are limitless opportunities for everybody in all fields" (study of Greece, no. 1, p. 50). A Turkish manufacturer chimes in "I would like to live in the United States.... anybody who works enough can make a decent life for himself" (study of Turkey, p. 51). Even the proud nomads are not entirely immune against dreams of what money can buy in countries tainted by Jews; a rich Bedouin in Jordan concedes that he might be willing to settle down in America "Because they are rich. If I go there I can open a ranch and keep thousands of sheep and horses" (study of Jordan, p. 16). Lebanese interviewees of the middle strata. express their crude materialism with disarming candor. "I can become rich in America," volunteers an officer in the government. And a chauffeur is pleasantly tickled by this very prospect "I hear people who go to America become rich.... I hope I can go there" (study of Lebanon, pp. 77–78). To Egyptian white-collar employees America is alluring because of its job opportunities. An Egyptian worker elaborating on the theme falls into outright daydreaming: "I heard that the workers are well paid there and they can lead a good life like big employees in Egypt" (study of Egypt, p. 197). It should be added that this picture of America which to all appearances is firmly established everywhere owes much of its glamor to letters from relatives and compatriots who either have been a success in America or do not want to admit their failure there.

Suggestions

The situation is somewhat embarrassing. Unequivocal support of these self-centered notions would not only reflect on U.S. ideology but run the risk of producing boomerang effects in the form of resentments against American opulence. Greek objections to the lavishness of Hollywood films reveal a sense of frustration. On the other hand it cannot be denied that emotional attachments to the U.S. profit greatly by the image of America as a terrestrial paradise where kin of the Lebanese chauffeur or the Egyptian worker pursue happiness in cars of their own. The communicator is faced with a dilemma: should he feature the material aspects of American life or had he better suppress them? A practicable method of overcoming this difficulty is applied in VOICE broadcasts; they mention opportunity, but do not mention it for its own sake, References to it are frequently interwoven with comparisons between America and Russia or hints of America's free-world activities, thus challenging the listener to forget his egocentric views in meditations of a more ideological nature. It should be possible to kill two birds with one stone by systematically combining the theme of opportunity with the motif of self-help. Even though most interviewees assume that work is prerequisite to wealth in America also, they nevertheless seem secretly convinced that wealth is one's share there, anyway—a miracle ingratiating itself with the Oriental mind. Emphasis on the fact that in America material success is the result of strenuous efforts and unrelenting initiative may make these people realize that self-help is indispensable for prosperity everywhere.

B. SUGGESTIONS CONCERNING SEVERAL U.S. OBJECTIVES

1. COMMUNISM AND SOVIET RUSSIA

The populations along the Soviet periphery have only the vaguest notions of Russia. There are no immigrants to Iron Curtain countries who would write letters home; nor is the flow of Soviet communications comparable to that of Western communications. In both Greece and Turkey numerous interviewees of all classes protest their ignorance of Russia or declare they have no opinions on the subject, whereby it is understood that some of these noncommittal answers may be inspired by the fear of revealing Communist affiliations. Much the same holds true in the Arabic countries. Many a professional there complains that he has to base his views of Russia on conflicting or distorted information. Among the less educated with their predominantly domestic concerns even such knowledge as comes from foreign broadcasts is absent. Lower-middle-class people in Jordan insist that Russia is a complete mystery to them and even those scattered Lebanese interviewees who admit sympathies for Russia are either unaware of Moscow's Arabic radio program or cannot afford the luxury of a radio. This lack of contact with what is going on behind the Iron Curtain produces the phenomenon of "psychological distance:" nearby Russia is felt to be far away while America beyond the seven seas seems to lie just around the corner (see study of Lebanon, p. III). In Syria, where living conditions continue to be primitive, information about Russia is spread by word of mouth; its source is obviously the domestic Communist Party which has a certain following among Armenians, Orthodox Christians and Kurds. If this "internal" propaganda does not succeed in luring the submerged classes out of their indifference, it nevertheless promotes pro-Russian sentiments in diverse other quarters. It is a rumor propaganda which has the undeniable advantage of being disseminated by friends or acquaintances and supplying wishful thinking with appropriate food. On the other hand, people can never be sure of its truth; and the doubts they presumably nurture will be increased by rumors from the opposite direction. Be this as it may, the fact that Russia now tries to reach the Arabic countries through the conventional radio channels may well indicate that it does not place too much trust in the effectiveness of sheer hearsay information.

Suggestions

Since so little is known about Stalinism and Soviet Russia, communications in all media and for all strata of population should discuss these central themes with great caution so as to avoid stirring up curiosity where there is perhaps none. It would seem best not to give more information than the current situation requires. And in passing the information on, the communicator should always be aware that the Arabic elite especially are inclined to interpret anything he says against Russia as a propaganda maneuver designed to manipulate their minds. An Egyptian student holds that news from the West about Russia is mostly biased (study of Egypt, p. 69). A lawyer in Jordan declares: "American and British propaganda.... have depicted Russia as an aggressive country seeking to drive the whole world into a ruthless and exterminating war to serve its own interests and welfare.... Who do you think in the Arab world believes American or English propaganda?" (study of Jordan, p. 96). This ingrained distrust, pointed up already in earlier contexts calls for sobriety in references to Russia. Anti-Communist intelligence will not get across in the Arabic world unless it is well-authenticated and restrained rather than exuberant; the surest way of thwarting its effect is to revel in black-and-white contrasts. (Remark for the VOICE: The Howard Mayer commentaries, likely to be explosives in Satellite countries may prove duds in the Middle East).

All this is to say that information about Russia should be strictly adjusted to the opinions held of it. For instance, the Greeks have a strong sense of freedom. Recalling the Civil War, a shepherd says: "We are free.... we are ready to fight anyone for this. Russia tried to enslave us through her bandits" (study of Greece, no. 1, p. 31). These sentiments, strongest among the less educated in both rural and urban areas, induce many Greeks to conceive of Russia as the land of fear and oppression. Anti-Russian messages which play upon such apprehensions stand a good chance of striking home. Incidentally, since the Greeks still have to put up with a Communist underground, they may endorse propositions on Communism which the Arabs would most certainly discount as Western propaganda. In the Arabic countries positive and negative images of Russia intermingle on all educational levels—a muddle increased by the Egyptian elite's readiness to view Russia with a friendly eye out of spite for Great Britain. (At the bottom of their hearts they presumably know that nothing could harm them more than an advance of Communism.) There is in various groups of population a tendency to praise Russian policy for its non-interference in Arabic domestic affairs; some middle-class interviewees in Jordan even toy with the idea of Russia as a possible ally. But these favorable comments also seem to be largely determined by the fact of Western interference in Palestine. More genuine is undoubtedly the belief, not infrequent among people of the lower strata, that Russia helps those in distress. As a credulous Lebanese village housewife puts it: "They give houses and money to the poor" (study of Lebanon, pp. 117–18).

For messages to the Arabs it is not enough to invalidate these opinions by pointing, for instance, to Russian expansionism (of which the elite in Jordan are quite aware) or to the rule of inequality in Iron Curtain countries rather, information about Russia will find response only if it succeeds in reinforcing the existing aversion to the Communist way of life. Hence the need for emphasizing such Russian characteristics as are incompatible with Oriental traditions and notions. The Arabs are individualists; this inspires information to the effect that Communism means a definite threat to their personal independence. Much more important, the Arabs are so deeply involved in religion that many of them dislike Russia for its anti-religious attitude. "They have no religion," objects a Lebanese farmer (study of Lebanon, p. 118). Even those who argue in favor of Russia do not know how to reconcile their political preferences with their religious loyalties. They are under a strain. News about Russia should exploit their ambivalence. But in keeping the Moslem world posted on oases of religious persecution in Russia and the Satellite countries care must be taken to present these cases as a matter of political expediency rather than the outcome of ideological consequence. The Arabs might prove sensitive to Communist intolerance if they get the impression that it is a variant of their own fanaticism. Tolerance is a virtue of civilization which they are hardly in a position to appreciate at least for the time being.

Because of the Arabs' gift for imagining propaganda traps, it is further advisable to proceed like the buyer in an antique shop who cunningly avoids manifesting a special interest in the object he covets. Statements which treat Russia in a casual way are likely to meet less resistance than the same statements made up as major revelations. In VOICE broadcasts such communications will immediately assume a more incidental character if they are tied up with, and subordinated to, positive incentives bearing on the West. For instance, information about agricultural collectives in Iron Curtain countries may emerge as an afterthought in a report on U.S. farmers. The VOICE actually takes advantage of this device.

Printed material should alert the Arabic elite to the game Moscow is playing and the risk they themselves are running in favoring the enemies of their "enemies." The odds are that they will be least suspicious of matter-of-fact literature which aspires to a fair exposure of the conflicting views.—A good way of sustaining or arousing anti-Communist moods through documentary films is to insert in them such footage from Soviet films as is apt to impress Middle-Eastern audiences unfavorably. It would be difficult for any spectator to deny the authenticity of these self-portrayals. The method has been successfully used in the Nazi war documentaries and the American army morale films.

2. PROGRESS

The study of Syria, which deals mainly with political attitudes, reaches the conclusion that Russian influence is strongest among the minority of those rank-and-file Syrians who are intense and active psychologically. They may be found at the extreme left as well as the extreme right; and this implies that they are impressed not so much by the Russian brand of Communism as by the radicalism of Russian practice. What makes them look to Russia is her enormous drive—one more reason, by the way, for not playing up Communist intransigence in messages to Arabic audiences (see pp. 30–31). Conversely, it is the moderate, emotionally lass intense Syrians who show sympathies for America. The bulk of them belongs to the middle strata; they outweigh the pro-Russians numerically. Unlike the latter, these people prefer slow reforms to abrupt social changes. Theirs is a middle-class spirit; if they are progress-minded they are so in a conservative way. All this amounts to saying that in the eyes of the Syrians America is more or less representative of the status quo while Russia appears to them as the symbol, if not carrier, of revolutionary events, welcome or not. It lies in the interest of the energetic radical minority to deepen the image of the U.S. as a stabilizing power so that palpable social changes will be laid to Russian rather than American influence. But social changes are needed and bound to come.

Suggestions

The example of Syria indicates that many people in the Middle East tend to misinterpret America's role in international affairs. Contrary to what they believe, America does not sustain the status quo but is actually the driving power behind efforts to improve conditions in all areas of economic distress and illiteracy, and that the U.S. refrains from interfering in Arabic politics certainly does not mean that it would side with absentee landowners against poor farmers. Since the existing tendencies to associate America with stagnation or reaction involve grave political dangers, it would be important indeed to try to check them. There is a real need for establishing in the minds an America which favors progress and initiates change.

Progress means different things to different strata of the population; among the better educated Greeks cases of apathy caused by disillusionment with politics are fairly frequent—a fact which makes one suspect that the political climate there does not precisely encourage progressive ardor (see study of Greece no. 2, pp. 29–30). In the Middle East proper the necessity for social reform is generally recognized but the upper strata feel ambivalent about it, except for Turkey where the leading circles seem genuinely progress-minded. The Arabic ruling class shies away from sacrifices, financial and otherwise; and the Arabic professionals have not yet developed a mature sense of social responsibility, this is illustrated by the Egyptian elite: they combine nationalist aspirations with a certain interest in economic questions, the result being that the concerns tend to weaken each other (study of Egypt, pp. 57–59). Communications for the upper strata should appeal to their instinct of self-preservation, that is, stress the argument that their chances of survival depend largely on their willingness to support and carry out measures in behalf of the submerged populations.

To the lower strata technical; economic and social progress is synonymous with higher standards of living. Their views of America reveal that they crave relief from their hardships but take it by and large for granted that any such relief is due to outside opportunities rather than efforts of their own. This is a further argument in favor of the earlier suggestion that messages to them should feature the theme of self-help (cf. pp. 23–24, 26). The established practice of referring in radio and print to labor union activities in America and elsewhere may help sensitize farmers, laborers or workers to the inexorable truth that nothing will change unless they join forces and put up a fight, yet something in them resists this truth. People of the lower strata are animated by the fear that the Western concept of progress entails a way of life which jeopardizes their most cherished traditions and beliefs, Religion and industry seem all but incompatible to them. Prodding is therefore not enough. Or rather, it will be more effective if it is supplemented by the proposition that progress need not destroy extant values, nothing is more important than to alleviate the fear of industrialization. The communicator may utilize examples from American everyday life which testify to a continued interpenetration of religious convictions and progressive endeavors. A pamphlet in simple language on this theme would seem desirable. The impact of modern technology on backward cultures is incomparably pictured in the late Flaherty's full-length documentary, *Louisiana Story*. Flaherty was in love with these cultures. He believed them to be the last remnants of unspoiled human nature and he was deeply concerned with what would happen to them after their inevitable exposure to Western capitalism. Since his *Louisiana Story* holds out the promise of a reconciliation between man and machine, primitive attitudes and technological requirements, it should be shown throughout the Middle East. The film is located in the Bayou region, and its hero is a native youth who by and by comes to terms with a freshly imported oil derrick.

3. U. N. AND FREE-WORLD SOLIDARITY

Knowledge about the mechanics of the U.N. and the diverse agencies implementing the American aid program is found exclusively among the elite who keep track of international news. In the middle strata information of this kind is rare and foggy. And the poorly educated rural masses have only the faintest idea of where the radios or tractors they get come from. This state of things, documented by all studies, must be laid to the existing communications habits as well as the actual character of the communications themselves. Judging by a small sample of fairly recent VOICE broadcasts to Greece, Turkey, and the Arabic countries, radio information about, say, the World Health Organization or the Point Four Program seems as a rule to be couched in terms which transmit just the bare facts on a highly abstract level. It is true that the small amount of radio time and the obligation of completeness call for short outs, but it is equally true that even a trained listener will sometimes find it difficult to realize the practical consequences of negotiations, decisions end measures imparted to him in such a way.

Suggestions

Since collective security depends to a large extent on the morale of ordinary people, systematic efforts should be made to bring the message of free-world solidarity and America's tremendous share in it down to the Greek shepherd and the Lebanese farmer. What counts is to explore the emotional appeal of this message so as to further the growth of allegiances which go beyond narrow nationalism. It is a task which demands that the communicator concretize international cooperation in all media. Nearly all studies insist that concreteness is a "must" for communications to the lower strata; and of course, the same applies to communications designed to involve the better educated emotionally. There is rarely a sample of VOICE programs that would not include colorless news items or an indifferent press survey, no doubt choice information is preferable to such mechanical completeness. Why not weed out the ballast and insert instead occasional talks which make the U. N. a living affair and the E.C.A. something people can really grasp? For instance, case histories which follow up a seemingly lofty decision of an international body from the council chambers to the beneficiaries of that decision in remote villages and suburbs will draw significant activities out of their anonymity and give the populations at large a sense of belonging. Incidentally, it would perhaps pay to test the appeal of Walt Whitman's passion for the whole world; the Arabic VOICE programs seem to indulge so exclusively in Arabic poems and songs that even the Arabs might welcome a sample of "Leaves of Grass" for a change—not to speak of the less biased Greeks or Turks. Pertinent biographical material in radio and print is another means of enlivening abstract concepts and contexts. To be sure, films are regularly used to these ends; yet it must also be mentioned that many U. N. and E. C. A. documentary suffers from ororverbalization, an unbearably extroverted commentator drowning all pictorial appeals that might get under the skin (cf. pp. 13–14). One of the best E. C. A. films is *Adventure in Sardinia* which pictures the fight against malaria.—To sum up, all communications in this line should imbue plain people but certainly not them alone, with the heart-warming feeling that free- world solidarity is a palpable reality affecting their everyday lives. Thus, pale notions of it may develop into deep-rooted beliefs which in turn may make that reality ever more real.

III. COMMUNICATING WITH THE ARABS

A. ABOUT REGIONAL DIFFERENCES

Indications that different countries require a different approach are already found in the preceding pages. Of enormous consequence in this respect is the following difference between the Arabs, on the one hand, and the Greeks and Turks, on the other. The latter two peoples are favorably disposed toward U.S. policy regarding their countries while the Arabic peoples, with the sole exception of Lebanon, are opposed to it.

In Greece the U. S. is very popular. Sympathies for America and the American people thrive in all strata of population, though not in all of them with the same intensity; the better educated criticize Americans for their lack of culture and their devotion to materialist values (cf. p. 20). Attitudes toward U.S. foreign policy are likewise positive, the sole difference between upper and lower strata being that the professionals endorse that policy with more reservations than, say, the farmers (cf. p. 15). Since U.S. firmness in Korea has influenced these attitudes in a favorable sense, the admission of Greece to N.A.T.O. is likely to work in the same direction. There is a definite correlation between the image the Greeks have formed of the American people and the attitude they entertain toward American policy. And this would justify the assumption that any change of the image provokes a similar change of attitude; that is, the communicator will all but automatically improve on the latter if he succeeds in deepening Greek attachments to the American people (study of Greece, no. 1, pp. 17–19).

A comparison between the studies of Greece and Turkey suggests that in Turkey pro-American attitudes are slightly more pronounced and slightly less qualified than in Greece. They are shared by a majority of interviewees on all educational levels. Only a small minority of Turks voices unfavorable opinions about America and the Americans, but even these critics are inclined to think of U.S. policy in positive terms —an attitude which, as in the case of the Greeks, has certainly been strengthened since Turkey's incorporation into N. A. T. O. The prevailing political pro-Americanism, then, goes hand in hand with widespread sympathies for America, and exactly as in the case of Greece, one feels tempted to assume that an increase of these human sympathies will affect the political preferences accordingly. In both countries the parallelism of political and human loyalties lends itself to being exploited by U.S. communications.

Unlike the Greeks and Turks, most Arabs are hostile to U.S. foreign policy. The difference is complicated by the fact that many better educated Arabs—the only group to be considered here—show a split in their allegiances. This applies, for instance, to the scattered VOICE listeners among the Lebanese elite; all of them identify themselves with the American character or feel like cultivating existing bonds between themselves and the U. S., yet their pro-American sentiments do not prevent them from criticizing America's behavior in world affairs (study of Lebanon, pp. 50–60). In Jordan the same conflict is experienced not only within the elite but by middle-class people as well (study of Jordan, pp. 68–71). Or take the few Egyptian professionals who are sufficiently well-balanced to acknowledge American generosity: in spite of this concession they indulge in the same political anti-Americanism which characterizes the rest of the Egyptian elite (study of Egypt, pp. 80–81). The facts available warrant the general statement that most of those better educated Arabs who manifest sympathies for Americans are nevertheless as opposed to U.S. foreign policy as Arabs lacking such sympathies—perhaps even more so because of their difficult psychological condition. Their inimical attitude toward America as a political power is at variance with their friendly image of America as a people. It is therefore doubtful whether attempts to increase Arabic affinity for the American way of life will by themselves alone suffice to reduce Arabic hostility to America's political conduct.

In sum, messages fanning good will toward Americans are likely to benefit political pro-Americanism much more in Greece and Turkey than in the Arabic countries—always provided, of course, that political conditions do not change. For instance, in Greece as well as in Syria and Lebanon existing attachments to America were strengthened by personal contacts with relatives and compatriots who have settled down in the States. Documentary films about the Greek and Arabic element in America would certainly vivify these contacts for the native populations, but the Arabic films should not be expected to improve the Arabs' political moods. The two country blocs must be treated differently. In communicating with the influential Arabic elite, adequate political reasoning is the thing that counts most.

B. SPECIAL TREATMENT OF EGYPT

To get political arguments across in the Moslem world, these arguments must strike home with the Egyptians because of Egypt's leading role in that part of the world (cf. p. 16). To many Arabs Egypt is something like the promised land. Two Syrian interviewees praise it for its glamorous civilization, and a Lebanese housewife is awed by the high development of its artistic culture (study of Egypt, pp. 14–15). Political adversaries will be affected only by arguments which play upon their particular fears and hopes. Hence the necessity of adjusting relevant reasoning to the outlook of the Egyptian elite—especially in communications for use in Egypt. These people admire the West and are quite aware that their country depends upon Western know-how for years to come; at the same time, however, they suffer from the obsession that the West reciprocates their admiration with unbearable loftiness. And this disregard, real or not, offends them all the more since they feel it cheapens their exalted standing in the Middle East, thus reflecting on the whole Arabic cause. Even though the Egyptian elite do not believe the Americans to be as snobbish as the hated British, they nevertheless reproach them with being prejudiced against colored people (cf. p. 16). "Would my dark color be a handicap to me there?" asks an interviewee whose misgivings in this respect dampen his desire to live in the US" (study of Egypt, p. 13). The tribute a woman doctor pays to America's economic and scientific standards adds to the bitterness of her criticism: "What I cannot understand about them is that they go on talking about human rights and they violate these rights by their marked attitude or hostility toward the colored in America—especially the Negroes" (ibid., p. 31). Under the impression of Western contempt many Egyptian professionals live in a state of frustration which accounts for their self-doubts and never-dying suspicions. This shows in their emotional instability. On the one hand, they are all aglow with Pan-Arabic aspirations on the other, they crave complete westernization— an urge which often inspires them to learn to speak English fluently, the unadulterated English the British are speaking, so as to convince the others and themselves that they actually match those who think they are superior to them (study of Egypt. pp. 21–23). It is inevitable that this wavering between extremes should lessen their will power. Their nationalism and their admiration of the West tend to neutralize each other (cf. pp. 22, 33).

SUGGESTIONS

As matters stand, the Egyptian elite will not be inclined to accept American reasoning unless the communicator succeeds in reducing their sense of frustration. What has been said in earlier contexts about the need for respectfulness (pp. 16, 18), applies in particular to this group. All messages reaching the better educated Egyptians should therefore imply that the U.S. acknowledges Egypt's cultural leadership in the Middle East. Since Egypt enjoys prestige all over the Arabic world, little harm would be done if hints of this kind occasionally emerged in the Arabic VOICE programs. A good place for them is of course the re-broadcasts to Egypt via Salonika. Favorable reviews, if possible, of Egyptian achievements in the fields of art and science might help relieve wounded pride. There is also a change that historical talks about medieval Arabic culture and its influence on the West will do something for Egyptian self-confidence. Any communication which thus confirms the Egyptians as Arabs is useful, it cautions them, by indirection, against the danger of alienation inherent in excessive westernization. Most messages in this line should be entrusted to print rather than radio for three reasons. First—the familiar argument— VOICE broadcasts are limited in time and crowded with obligations; second, Egyptian professionals are to all appearances assiduous readers; and finally, not everything told them need be spread about. What they know about American race bias hurts them deeply. It would seem advisable to place extensive literature on the American Negro problem into their hands. This might flatter the Egyptian elite as a symptom of trust in their understanding and also inform them of various efforts to fight prejudice in the U.S. Perhaps the recent Hollywood films against anti-Negro bias will lend force to the pamphlets and books, though it should be added that they lag behind *The Quiet One*, a full-length documentary about a Negro boy, in seriousness of intention. Speaking of films, another Hollywood picture; *Ruggles of Red Gap* (1935), seems pre-destined to be shown to advanced Egyptian audiences. It is a comedy which confronts British caste spirit with American freedom, ridiculing, along with that spirit, the awe it inspires in rich Middle-Western "socialites." Everything ends happily, for the English butler, this incarnation of snobbishness, turns out to be a jolly good fellow.

To say it once more, only in trying to remove the inferiority feelings of the Egyptian elite can the communicator hope to make these people who are so influential in the Arabic orbit more amenable to political argumentation.

C. POLITICAL ARGUMENTATION

Arabic hostility to American foreign policy is of recent date. Except for the pro-Russian extremists among the Syrian interviewees, most Arabs trace it to the odious fact that the U.S. championed the cause of the Jews in Palestine. (It should be noted in passing that Great Britain's anti-Jewish policy in those days seems to have left a much weaker imprint on the Arabs.) A better educated Egyptian interviewee says: "All the nations of the East loved the Americans, but after that case (Palestine) they became in doubt of it" (study of Egypt, p. 30).

And a clerk in Jordan declares that "the United States was very good before," the emphasis being on "before" (study of Jordan, p. 68). The hostility, then, has a temporary rather than enduring character.

Not satisfied with harping upon America's Palestine policy, many better educated Arabs condemn the U.S. for having developed into an imperialistic power, whereby it is not quite clear whether they also interpret that policy itself as an outcome of imperialism. Be this as it may, they invariably hold that America has taken a turn for the worse since Palestine. A Ministry of Education official in Jordan derives the growth of anti-American sentiments among the Arabs not so much from America's partiality for the Jews as from her imperialistic drive (but the two trends may well be identical in his eyes): "The U.S.A., is becoming and working to be an imperialistic state and thus are losing the love and respect they had in the hearts of men" (study of Jordan, p. 99). A lawyer, also in Jordan has it that America's behavior in world affairs is dictated exclusively by its own interests which, he feels, "are becoming more Imperialistic than those of Great Britain itself" (ibid.). And this leads straight to the suspicion, voiced by many an Egyptian intellectual, that the U.S. has evolved its whole aid program for the sole purpose of conquering the international markets (cf. p. 17).

In spite of such verdicts, good will toward America survives from pre-Palestine times as is illustrated by the numerous Arabs who show sympathies for Americans while opposing the U.S. politically. Previous remarks on this point (pp. 39-40) may be supplemented by the observation that the sympathies are mainly aroused by American kindliness—the qualities of the heart rather than the brain. As a college-trained interviewee in Jordan puts it: "Americans are very sincere and simple hearted and to be sincere is too bad because they follow their hearts and not their heads and as a result they do many foolish actions" (study of Jordan, p. 100). Some of his less educated compatriots advance similar views, stressing both their belief in American good heartedness and their disapproval of America's political course (ibid., pp. 68, 70). It is the generosity of the American people which attracts the Arabs even now that they are little disposed to admit such a weakness.

The continued ·existence of these smoldering sympathies accounts for the widespread opinion that Americans are not intrinsically bad like the British but act as they do because of their inexperience or immaturity. When for instance a bank accountant in Jordan says that "the United States are very fresh in world politics," he obviously says so out of a rational desire to explain the bad behavior of people whom he otherwise believes to be likeable (study of Jordan, p. 100). Explicit references to America's youthfulness are not infrequent. A Lebanese VOICE listener calls the U.S. a "young child" and adds that "it has not been taking the right steps" (study of Lebanon, p. 59). This notion appears to have gained foothold among middle-class people in Jordan; a clerk there declares that Americans 'are baby politicians so far," and a less optimistic goldsmith predicts that they "will always remain children as compared to the British or Russians" (study of Jordan, p. 69). The goldsmith's opinion falls into line with several statements to the effect that the Americans are the dupes of the British masterminds. In forming this image of America as a sort of adolescent who has been led astray by a wicked and more experienced friend, the Arabs evidently assign to themselves the role of old and wise people versed in the ways of the world. Yet their very condescension indicates that they do not completely dismiss the case. Except perhaps for the gloomy goldsmith, they seem to cherish the secret hope that the juvenile delinquent might reform after all.

SUGGESTIONS

In view of the fragile situation, political reasoning should conform closely to Arabic ways of thought. A few preliminary studies are likely to facilitate the necessary adjustments. It might prove useful, for instance, to inquire into the political opinions held by Arabic U.S, residents or citizens. Assuming their opinions on topical issues represent an amalgam of innate Arabic concepts and half-digested American concepts, much can be learned from them about such intricate matters as how to twist an argument to make it work and where exactly to put the emphasis. The study of Egypt advocates an analysis of current political writings in the Arabic countries; there is no doubt that this undertaking would pay dividends. The same holds true of the repeatedly submitted proposition that the Koran be scanned for fitting quotas and adequate methods of approach.

Political argumentation itself is primarily faced with the tasks of setting the Palestine issue in the right perspective and invalidating the Arabic saga of American imperialism. It has been shown previously that efforts in this direction would gain little by too heavy a reliance on Arabic sympathies for the American people (pp. 39–40); many Arabs, especially the better educated among them, concede that they entertain such sympathies and yet continue to chide U.S. policy. What counts is to proceed within the political dimension. Instead of humanizing politics, the communicator should try to convert the human factor into a political asset. This he might achieve by a line of reasoning which, for the sake of argument, accepts the Arabic viewpoint that politically Americans behave like adolescents. Adolescents may commit blunders, but at least they usually act from generous impulses. Again, it is the Arabs who speak of American generosity. Yet if they experience America this way they might as well follow up the, implications of their experience. One of them is that generosity is something genuine with Americans. In keeping with their own premises, the Arabs will have to admit that generosity is one of the essential motives behind U.S. policy—no matter, for the rest, whether this trait is thought of as interfering with American self-interest or forming an integral part of it. Once the Arabs admit that much, they are bound to go a step further and realize two things—that America's Palestine policy must also be laid to her generous compassion for a tormented people and that the talk about American imperialism does not make sense. Imperialism results from adult passion for power rather than youthful generosity. For Arabs to denounce American aid, including the help to Arabic refugees, as an imperialist maneuver is not only illogical but hardly compatible with their own generosity. Nor can the Arabs, versed in the ways of the world as they are, possibly mistake expanding business for political expansionism. There still remains the basic objection, however, that the U.S. has grossly blundered in supporting the Jews against the Arabs. Has it really? Granted that juvenile impetuosity is sometimes slow in grasping the views of other people and thus hurts their sensibilities, which is a blunder indeed, yet such rashness need not be without political vision. Contrary to what a wrathful Egyptian teacher says—that "Israel is a cancer in the body of the Middle East" (study of Egypt, p. 60)—Israel stands a fair chance of developing into a ferment of economic and social progress in the Middle East. This would meet a need recognized by the Arabs themselves, to be sure, under the present circumstances it is difficult for the Arabic elite to envisage a modus vivendi with the new state, but even now their old political wisdom will perhaps tell them that tiny Israel might become a valuable ally in their fight against Communist infiltration, and here is where their interest coincides with American interest. It is understood that this sketchy argumentation is only for background use. Its main purpose is to stimulate discussion.

NOTE

1. Something in this line is actually under way—a report on a small sample of VOA and BBC broadcasts to Greece, which is being prepared for the program Evaluations Branch of the Voice.

16
Attitudes Toward Various Communist Types in Hungary, Poland, and Czechoslovakia

Bureau of Applied Social Research, Columbia University.
*A paper read at the Annual Meeting of the American Sociological Society held of Urbana, Illinois, September 8–10 1954.

This paper represents one segment of a larger inquiry into the political attitudes and propaganda susceptibilities of non-Communists in countries behind the Iron Curtain. The segment was selected for presentation here because, among other things, its findings illuminate an opinion area of Soviet Satellite life which has generally been neglected in the literature on the subject. They are, moreover, considerably at variance with the kind of inferences that most Americans would probably draw from hitherto available facts about Satellite Communism. They indirectly demonstrate the danger of imputing to members of another political milieu the accepted norms of our own political climate.

Specifically, it is perhaps safe to wager that most people who know anything about the evils and sufferings associated with Satellite Communism would almost automatically assume that the non-Communist sufferers share inimical attitudes toward *all* adherents of their nation's Communist Party; for it is the Party, after all, that has been the immediate indigenous instrument of so-called Popular Democracy in Eastern Europe. But this assumption is proved fallacious by the data at hand, the data being three hundred intensive interviews with escapees from Hungary, Poland, and Czechoslovakia. The interviews were conducted abroad by International Research Associates, Inc. (INRA) in late 1951 and early 1952.

Before proceeding further with substance, a few words about method. Although systematic, it was qualitative in character, supplementing a basically quantitative study of the same material undertaken by INRA. (1) The qualitative portion focused primarily on those responses which were inadvertently and disparately evoked, which were not readily amenable to statistical manipulation, and which bore on five major issues of critical interest:

1. How do the captive non-Communists view both their Satellite regime and its Communist Party adherents?
2. What are their primary complaints about the regime in action, and conversely, are there any Communist accomplishments for which they concede a measure of admiration or respect?
3. Which are the Communist propaganda themes that appear to have been most successful, which have proved impotent or self-defeating, and how do captive peoples defend themselves against Communist propaganda influence?
4. What are the state and prospects of anti-Communist resistance?
5. How does their basic hope of liberation structure the non-Communists' perceptions of Western policy and of Western radio reportage of this policy?

Almost anyone with an interest in foreign affairs would be able to hazard relatively correct answers to some of these questions. Or, stated otherwise, the interviews confirm a number of fairly common notions about Satellite life–especially about the attitudes of non-Communists toward their regime as such. Whether materially or ideologically motivated, for example, they hate and fear it. They blame it for a host of economic deprivations. They recognize its systematic exploitations of human life. They identify it with an atmosphere of terror and total insecurity. And they tend to perceive their countries as colonies occupied by Moscow, with the indigenous Communist Party–that is, the regime—acting as a traitorous tool of the alien Soviet power.

Given the determination of these attitudes, it would superficially seem unreasonable to make an issue of attitudes held toward individual members of the Communist Party. Ordinarily, it is probably safe to assume that at least the direction of intensely held monolithic and disciplined group as the Communist Party will hold firm with reference to most people belonging to that group. And perhaps the issue would never have arisen were it not for the discovery that so many respondents un-wittingly alluded to personal friends who were Communist Party members or to similar friendships back home. This stimulated an intensive examination of all other interview evidence bearing on the subject. And the conclusion is that Satellite Non-Communists clearly discriminate among several types of Party members.

The first breakdown is between "real" or convinced" Communists on the one hand and *nominal* Communists who only pretend to Party conviction and loyalty on the other. Incidentally, there is substantial evidence that, numerically, the nominal types predominate in the Party, although to what extent it is impossible to estimate.

Attributes ascribed to the *real* Communist include a sincere belief in the Communist gospel as interpreted from Moscow, unconditional loyalty to the Party, ruthlessness in the performance of Party duties, and complete immersion in activities that serve the interests of the regime. This is the kind of Communist that centers in the "hard core" of the Party; and the respondents emphasize that the captive populations hate him, just as they do the regime itself. Toward the secret police this hatred is filled with overtones of impotence and dread. An intelligent Hungarian kulak speaks for many other escapees when he says: "Nobody knows when a police truck will stop outside his house and arrest the members of his family. At the beginning only the intelligentsia and the rich farmers feared this; now, however, this fear concerns all classes."

The *nominal* Communists do not constitute a single type, but rather, four subtypes. Toward each of them, characteristic attitudes are manifest.

The subtype most closely resembling the *real* Communist in outward behavior is the sheer *opportunist*, the calculating and unscrupulous careerist motivated exclusively by self-aggrandizement. Intent upon ingratiating himself with the powers that be, he is zealous, unprincipled, and persistent in the performance of the Party work—as long, that is, as there appears to be no real threat to the regime. But he is a potential turncoat and, according to several respondents, had already in 1951 begun to hedge against a future fraught with the possibility of war and Communist defeat. Along with the *real* Communist, he is both hated and feared; but he is treated with a kind of loathsome contempt for having "sold himself to the regime out of vile selfishness" and for his willingness to "denounce anybody simply to strengthen his position or to get ahead."

Now we come to those types of nominal Communists who evoke judgements so at variance with superficial and uncritical expectations. Adopting the language of the respondents, we have called them the *jobkeeper* Communist, the *forced* Communist, and the *disillusioned* Communist.

The *jobkeepers*, a fairly frequent topic in the interviews, are defined throughout by three distinct traits. First, as the name implies, they either want to keep the job they hold or to get one simply for the sake of survival above subsistence level. They are motivated by reasons of self-preservation and the well-being of their families. When referring to them, respondents generally agree that they joined the Party "only in order not to lose their job" or "only to provide daily bread for their families." Second jobkeepers are unanimously characterized as people who, like the great majority of non-Communists, detest the regime in whole or part and long for liberation. The testimony is filled with such statements as: "They have the same views as the rest of the nation . . . and wait for liberation." Third, while paying formal allegiance to Communism, the jobkeepers restrict their Party activity to a bare minimum: "They are very passive. Once a week they go to meetings. From time to time, they will shout 'Long live Stalin' and carry a Red banner. Then they have a week to rest and don't take interest in anything."

The *forced* Communist is identical in all respects to the jobkeeper type except that he joined the Party not to keep or get a job, but under such duress as the threat of arrest or the withdrawal of ration cards.

The *disillusioned* Communist is the idealist who originally joined because he accepted at face value the Party's professions of faith. Now, with his ideals betrayed and his expectations shattered, he shares most of the grievances animating the non-Communists.

The remarkable thing about non-Communist attitudes toward each of these three nominal Communist subtypes is the lack of animosity displayed. It would seem natural for escapees to castigate the jobkeeper and the forced Communist, especially the former, for having yielded to exactly the pressures they themselves resisted up to the very last. Yet what happens is practically the opposite: in spite of their intense animus toward the regime, almost all respondents who advance the subject accept as relatively valid and defensible the reasons that prompted the jobkeeper and the forced Communist to join the Party. Rather than accusing him of weakness or lack of character, they point to the dilemma he had to face and show sympathetic understanding of the way he resolved it.

As for the disillusioned Party member, respondents give the impression that they react to him not only with the tolerance shown the jobkeepers and forced Communists, but with a sort of camaraderie and respect as well. Jobkeepers, they seem to feel, should be excused for having made inevitable adjustments; whereas disillusioned Communists deserve a measure of indulgence for their original idealism, as well as for their personal integrity which makes them realize and admit what is so profoundly disturbing to any non-Communist—that is, the frightful discrepancy between promises and practices of the regime. As a Social Democratic Czech mechanic explains it. "Formerly they were perhaps convinced Communists. However, they did not become victims of Communist propaganda preserving for themselves an unbiased judgment and thus realizing that the Party has deceived them, not fulfilling its promises. They have remained with the Party only because they are forced to. But as far as their personal convictions are concerned, they already belong to the anti-Communist camp." In the words of another Czech, "now they are just like us."

Unfortunately, the interviews provide no completely satisfactory explanation for non-Communist tolerance of nominal party membership. But they do supply a few clues that would be worth pursuing in any future escapee studies.

First, there appears to be universal awareness that the regime, whenever in its interest, is determined to make individual economic survival hinge on Party membership. "If a non-Communist works in a better position, they importune him politically until he joins the Communist Party: or if he won't do it, the remove him from his position and send him ... to a worse one says a young Czech. Another recalls that "after February 1948 (when the Communists seized power in Czechoslovakia) a radical change took place in the average family: the father was forced to join the Communist Party in order to keep his former occupation." And a Hungarian small-town musician avers that "Party membership is decisive ... even in the field of entertainment ... Musicians who were Communist Party members got most of the bookings." That the respondents are constantly preoccupied with this theme can be inferred from other statements of this sort as well as from the image–or rather, counter-image–they have of America. Many define the United States as a country where "participation in politics is not a prerequisite for people's being able to succeed and to support their families," where "Party membership gives no advantages," where there is no need for the worker to join a party and to say things that the party makes him say." In short, the terrible lurking alternative of having to turn into a Communist or being condemned to virtual economic subsistence continues to haunt escapees. And perhaps their absorption in it moves them to sympathize with friends and acquaintances who, on the horns of this crucial dilemma, eventually preferred external adjustment to life in distress. They can afford the sympathy since their own virtue is intact.

Second, such understanding, feeding on friendships with nominal Communists, may be vitalized by another, very private experience: more likely than not various respondents themselves felt tempted to become jobkeepers on occasion. Actually, only one respondent refers directly to this experience, but since the interview circumstances did not favor the admission of questionable intentions his statement may be more representative than its isolated occurrence would seem to indicate. The respondent in question is an intelligent, twenty-nine-year-old Pole, who prior to his escape had been "in charge of the stores in a textile combine." He is forthright enough to tell about his one-time susceptibility to Communist allurements. "Ever since 1948," he recalls, "the members of the factory council strongly advised me to join the Party. They motivated their advice by saying that I was young, capable, and would achieve something. But somehow, I kept refusing—although I must admit I frequently wanted to join. Only my wife stopped me. I wanted to join in order to prove the living condition of my family. I'm married and have a five-year-old child." Several others mention situations in which they were encouraged to become party members, in some cases seeming to protest too much their immediate repulsion of the idea.

Third, it is clear that many of the current non-Communists were themselves, like the disillusioned idealists, at one time impressed with the lofty rhetoric and promises of Communism. Indeed, there is considerable stress in the interviews on the appreciable impact of Communist propaganda during the period immediately subsequent to the Party's seizure of power. More or less typical is the following statement by a Hungarian worker: "Until 1949 the people still believed the Communists sometimes. Life was relatively good then and some people could have thought that even the communists worked for a good-cause." Another goes even further when he says that "a great part of the people believed that Communism would bring good to them." But references to the initial success of Communist propaganda are inevitably followed by assurances that "it has no influence any more" or that "this belief doesn't exist anymore." In short, people are painfully aware that they have been let down and betrayed by the regime, just as the disillusioned Communists; so they are in a position to appreciate the latter group's original motivation as well as its current embitterment.

Fourth, there appears to be general recognition that once committed to the Party, its members are virtually trapped. A typical remark is: "Once you join the Party there is no way out."

Finally, there are two Hungarian-voiced suggestions that tolerance of the nominal Communists may owe something to the influence of Satellite-beamed Western radio broadcasts. A railway worker recalls that "plenty of workers joined the Party when Radio Free Europe advised them not to throw away their daily bread." And a knowledgeable businesswoman, herself an ex-member of the party, says: "From my own experience I know how important it would be if the Voice of America would sometimes address the well-intentioned Party members in the way Radio Free Europe already does. This would not only reassure them but would also encourage them secretly to give much more help to those who are persecuted." Even though no other respondent mentions a Western radio in this vein, it is not improbable that other Satellite radio listeners may have interpreted something said by Radio Free Europe in the same sense—thereby arriving at the conclusion that their nominality at least partially excuses some Party members from the stigma of their formal label.

Each of the above clues offers room for considerable speculation, but their relative importance can only be gauged by further studies designed to shed light on the problem of the nominal Communist.

A word in conclusion. Ordinarily, a qualitative study of the kind reported here is concluded with a deferential bow to precise methods of quantification. The fashionable thing to say is that of course qualitative studies are only valuable as a preliminary to rigorous quantitative conclusions. In this case, however, we feel that in all honesty only a slight and formal bow is necessary. In a sense, the present study is roughly quantitative; we can say, for example, that of the escapees in our sample who said anything spontaneously about the jobkeeper, the forced, or the disillusioned Communist, nearly all tolerated or condoned their behavior. And for any practical conclusions that may be drawn from this particular finding, that degree of quantification is probably enough.

REFERENCE

1. Richard C. Sheldon and John Duktowski discuss several phases of the project in "Are Soviet Satellite Refugee Interviews Projectable?," *Public Opinion Quarterly*, 16 (Winter 1952/53): 579–94.

17
Proposal for a Research Project Designed to Promote the Use of Qualitative Analysis in the Social Sciences

I. PREMISES

The ideal of exact science—to arrive at laws and predictions by way of experiment and measurement—has been adopted by many social scientists. Whether they investigate minority problems, group attitudes toward some topic, or communication contents, they invariably formulate hypotheses enabling them to break down their material into quantifiable elements. Applied social research is largely a matter of coding, scoring, counting and tabulating, with much thought given to statistical technicalities and the reliability of the procedures. Since social phenomena differ from the subject matter of exact science in that they are historical entities and as such carriers of unique values and qualities, we may also define the current major goal of our social sciences as follows: they aim at transforming quality into quantity, at revealing unchanging nature behind ever-changing history.

Much can be said in favor of this approach. The continuum of social phenomena ranges from cases of highly individual behavior to cases of uniform mass behavior, and whenever we concentrate on the latter we move through a region ruled by the law of averages, a region in which many problems of interest lend themselves readily to quantification and statistical elaboration. And there seems to be no reason why the same procedures should not be applied as well to the analysis of intensive interviews, propaganda communications and other more individual phenomena at the opposite end of the conditions. They too include characteristics that may profitably be measured and computed; it all depends on the questions we pose, on the answers we expect. Quantitative analysis is a legitimate attempt to establish a body of strictly objective knowledge in fields where theory has for a long time indulged in unverified speculations and apparently uncontrollable, if perhaps cogent, descriptions. It is inevitable that the exponents of a science aspiring to the status of exact science should reject wholesale what they vaguely call the "impressionist" approach. They indict it for relying on untouchable "intuition" rather than rational probing, on appropriate evaluations rather than estimates in clear-cut figures.

All this is justified in a way. However, there is sufficient evidence that the course our social sciences are taking, leads them ever farther away from basic problems and relevant questions. In their eagerness for statistical accuracy they lose sight of the driving powers behind our social life, leaving it to the historians or political scientists to survey expanses in which they themselves are seized with agoraphobia. Their preoccupation with ever-refined breakdowns makes them disregard or even overlook anything that cannot neatly be pigeonholed. Sheer technique threatens to become an end in itself. This shows distinctly in the treatment of social phenomena conspicuous for their individual features and approached with a view to bringing them out. It is the kind of job assigned to content analysis. Take a sample of VOICE OF AMERICA broadcasts to some foreign country: what matters much is their structure; for instance, do they capitalize on the effects that may be produced through an appropriate linkage of the successive bits of the news they convey? Such effects obviously deepen the impact of the news items themselves. But because of their involved nature these structural qualities of the material resist the mechanics of coding and, hence, cannot be processed in content-analysis fashion. Only qualitative analysis, however, decried for its alleged "impressionism," might be able to capture them. In other words, content analysis is even in this relatively simple case not in a position to isolate, and account for, vitally important content. Its seeming objectivity is bought at a price; its very goal prompts it to strip social entities of their individual fullness. It is certainly no coincidence that current social research deals largely with problems arising from managerial concerns. How are we to handle groups or masses for this or that purpose, in this or that situation? In tackling these problems on the level of collective behavior, quantitative analysis is in its element, for it need not inquire into the situation or the purpose itself, nor appraise any of the qualitative factors which emerge on more individual levels. Quantifying techniques conform perfectly to managerial techniques.

In short, our social sciences are in a critical condition. Their insistence on emulating exact science threatens them with starvation. Yet the only alternative left to them would seem to be their surrender to the very impressionism of which they are trying to rid themselves. Is there a way out of this dilemma? The time has come, it appears, to take a good look at the foundations of the social sciences.

We therefore propose a research project reconsidering the conceptions currently held of quantitative and qualitative analysis. This project should be based on the following two hypotheses.

II. HYPOTHESES

First Hypothesis: the breakdown of individual wholes into quantifiable elements involves a series of subjective considerations which inevitably color the ensuing measurements, qualifying their objectivity. To verify this hypothesis it seems advisable to examine the customary procedures of content analysis because of its special concern with highly individual material. We submit that, in processing much material, the content analyst is time and again bound to make assumptions and decisions which cannot deny their "impressionist" origins. He may happily count the number of times the word "America" occurs in an editorial, but in doing so he presumably neglects various indirect references to the concept "America"; evidently, his predilection for the computable must be traced to the "impressionist" assumption that it is more relevant to the meaning of the text than those uncomputable references. Or he may decide to score an attitude under the heading "very favorable" instead of "favorable," but he would be blind to qualities indeed were he not, in so deciding, haunted by some of the scruples inseparable from the "impressionist" approach. Even the tiniest element challenges the analyst to review the infinite contexts to which it belongs. Each waterdrop contains a universe.

This is rarely acknowledged, though. Content analysts are not accustomed to think in terms of qualities, and they follow rules and directives which farther prevent them from going astray. Yet despite these protective habits and conventions which, of course, make for high reliability, "impressionist" evaluations and preferences actually persist all down the line. The objectivity of applied social research and in particular content analysis imitates rather than equals that of exact science. It is always an exhilarating spectacle to watch rows of tidy figures, complete with decimals, floating like little islands in an ocean of doubts and pretending to unattainable exactness. This is said not so much to deprecate quantifying techniques as to point to their limits. They are extremely valuable when applied to social phenomena sufficiently primitive and widespread to admit of quantification without a noticeable loss of quality; they fail to yield results when applied to highly individual textures.

Second Hypothesis: Qualitative analysis—a convenient designation of hermeneutic techniques in these fields—is more reliable, more scientific, than the champions of content analysis are inclined to believe. But having made a bogey of the "impressionist" approach, they naturally throw the baby out with the bath and refuse to acknowledge the legitimacy of any breakdown that cannot be presented in tables and charts. It is unfortunate that under the impact of their preferences, increased by the aversion of most exegetes to concern themselves with quantifications, qualitative methods have rarely been applied and never systematically cultivated. There is a palpable lack of pertinent examples: they are found in scattered books, papers and reports, and till now little attention has been paid to their far-reaching implications. In the interest of our hypothesis we will have to study these few existing models. For the moment all that can be said in its support are the following considerations. Exactly like content analysis, qualitative analysis proceeds to break down a given whole into small elements or units; thus enabling us to disentangle the fabric of its qualities and compare them with those other, similar wholes. But unlike content analysis, it is not primarily interested in matters of quantification. Some of the elements at which it arrives may be quantifiable and therefore should by all means be coded, scored and computed; others, as has been exemplified above, obstruct any attempt at numerical formulation. What counts alone in qualitative analysis is the selection and rational organization of such small elements as are expressive of the essentials of the whole.

But how can we find out about these essentials without collapsing into plain subjectivism? The danger is not so great as it appears. For even though such subjective factors as the analyst's philosophical viewpoints, political convictions, etc. unavoidably influence his conception of the whole he is analyzing, they will to a large extent be naturalized in the process. Whether or not he states them overtly from the outset—he should indeed—they are bound to leak out anyway. And once the cards are on the table, these influences and their distorting effects can in a measure be controlled and discounted. For the rest, access to the essentials of social entities depends upon familiarity with anything that might have contributed to their emergence, a sense of history, a flair for ideological currents, and some experience of human behavior—not to forget the greatest virtue of all: circumspection in weighing and balancing against each other the various data assembled.

We submit that these abilities can be taught to the degree to which they are needed for the purpose at hand, and that it is equally possible to train students in the successive operations that lead from the first rough scheme of analysis to its satisfactory completion. The skills involved in carrying out mental experiments or imagining possible alternatives are as teachable as are the skills of a flyer. No "intuition" of the kind dreaded by content analysts is required to trace and make evident the structural characteristic of VOICE OF AMERICA broadcasts, despite their allergy to statistical procedures; nor is it likely that different qualitative analysts will account for them in different ways.

In fact, we contend that on many occasions the evaluations of qualitative analysis exceed the measurements of quantitative analysis in reliability and precision. The reason is that the latter, in its desire to reach the haven of statistics, often simplifies or obscures aspects of the material which are a genuine concern of the former. But how can we ascertain the validity of qualitative findings? Qualitative analysis insists on making evident any of its results; it aims at inclusive objectivity, the very objectivity which is aspired to in the humanities. To be sure, it does not, and can not, provide the evidences of exact science; yet this kind of evidence is unattainable to content analysis also.

III. SUGGESTIONS

At this early stage a detailed blueprint would seem premature. We prefer to offer, for further discussion, a few scant hints concerning the execution of the planned project and its specific aims.

The first step, we suggest, is to assemble and analyze existing examples of qualitative analysis, with a view to codifying the methods used in them. In a way it is a preparatory step.

We suggest that research itself be conducted in close connection with a large-scale project involving diverse quantifying techniques, especially content analysis—a project of the kind carried out by Columbia's Bureau of Applied Social Research and similar institutions.

From beginning to end an intimate working community should be established between the staffs of the two projects, thus affiliated, so that the researchers engaged in qualitative pursuits are in a position continually to compare notes with those in charge of quantifications.

Finally we suggest a staff which, if possible, does not exclusively consist of social science students. It might be a good idea to include a historian and perhaps a psychologist.

Provided research is organized in this way, we shall be able

1) to examine, step by step, quantifying procedures from the angle of qualitative analysis and, perhaps, to define their inevitable limitations;

> (Some pertinent problems: Is there a point beyond which the measurements of content analysis turn out to be meaningless? What portion of the material lends itself to statistical elaboration and what portion does not? Etc.)

2) to undertake a qualitative analysis of each parts of the material as demonstrably elude the grasp of the affiliated project;
3) to train the staff, prior to and during this undertaking, in qualitative techniques for the purpose of testing out contention that they are teachable;
4) to study, in collaboration with the staff of the affiliated project, the methodological and practical implication of this whole experiment—in particular the problem of how qualitative and quantitative analysis might complement each other in future social research.

18
The Challenge of Qualitative Content Analysis

Quantitative analysis has many limitations. In this paper, Siegfried Kracauer proposes that qualitative analysis may be a more fruitful procedure in some stages of international communications research.

Siegfried Kracauer, formerly a prominent journal editor in Germany, has published widely in the field of communications research. He is presently completing a book on the aesthetics of the film.

This paper submits three propositions regarding the significance of qualitative exegesis for communications research:

1. One-sided reliance on quantitative content analysis may lead to a neglect of qualitative explorations, thus reducing the accuracy of analysis.
2. The assumptions underlying quantitative analysis tend to preclude a judicious appraisal of the important role which qualitative considerations may play in communications research. Hence the need for theoretical reorientation.
3. The potentialities of communications research can be developed only if, as the result of such a reorientation, the emphasis is shifted from quantitative to qualitative procedures.

QUANTITATIVE ANALYSIS MAY REDUCE ACCURACY

Overemphasis on quantification tends to lessen the accuracy of analysis. Content analysis is frequently obliged to isolate and process the more intricate characteristics of a sample; and whenever this happens it runs the risk of treating them inadequately. Quantitative analyses for example, commonly attempt to determine the "direction" of a communication, i.e., the extent to which it is "for," "against," or "neutral" in regard to a given subject. In such instances coding is often performed on the basis of a graded scale which defines a continuum ranging from "very favorable" to "very unfavorable," from "very optimistic" to "very pessimistic," or the like. Some quantitative analysts admit, however, that despite such scales, direction "is not always easily analyzed in an objective fashion."[1] The actual rating of a given unit of the communication on one or another step of the continuum still involves qualitative considerations which may bear on the whole of the communication. Unless the communication is a peculiarly one-dimensional affair, these assessments require a great deal of circumspection and delicacy. In quest of reliability, the quantitative analyst may—and frequently does—therefore introduce elaborate directives, to permit selected coders to arrive at highly reliable decisions. Such a breakdown of a complex direction continuum into relatively elementary scales inevitably invites simplifications apt to blur the picture. They render arbitrary, for example, the real gap between "very favorable" and "favorable"; and they place under one uniform cover (e.g., "favorable"), a great variety of treatments whose differences are perhaps highly relevant to the purposes of the analysis.

At this point the objection may be raised that it is possible to attain any degree of precise distinction by introducing sufficiently subtle scales in sufficient number. Coders might be trained, for example, to distinguish between matter-of-fact neutralism and well-balanced neutralism. Yet even the most refined tools of measurement may not enable the analyst to reconstruct the direction of the original communications. His rigidly atomistic data are likely to preclude inferences as to the way in which the data are interrelated. Significantly, it is this very interrelationship which often contributes largely, and sometimes definitively, to determine the direction of the overall text. Gestalt psychologist or not, any literary critic knows that, due to their organization, communications often move in a "direction" at variance with what a computing of the directions of their elements would yield. In such cases precise quantification, used alone, will actually encourage inaccurate analysis.

Of course, it is theoretically conceivable that the content analyst might succeed in quantifying the interrelationships between the "plus" and "minus" units of the communication, and so be enabled to measure direction correctly. But such a procedure would necessarily involve categories in such number and of so refined a nature that the incidence of their use would often be minute. Since, with the decrease of sizable frequencies, qualitative appraisals play a larger role in interpretation anyway, there is no reason why such cumbersome quantitative techniques should be preferred to qualitative exegesis proper. At best they would lead, in a very roundabout way, to what the latter could disclose without unnecessary complications. Quantitative analysts in fact recognize the danger of "over-fine" categorization, and continually caution against it. And yet to avoid it is to run the risk of oversimplifying the more intricate characteristics of many communications.

Direction is by no means the only contextual characteristic which resists a breakdown into easily countable components or even the development of "indicators" that permit the unambiguous, let alone exhaustive, identification of such components. Suggested procedures are often inadequate. Berelson, for example, suggests that "sophistication" can be quantitatively analyzed by "the indicator of the amount of qualifications appearing in the content ('on the other hand,' 'however,' 'although')."[2] Even granted that the indicator "qualification" is an adequate index of the particular form of sophistication in the given text (and certainly this could not be true for all texts), the *number* of qualifications still need not indicate the *degree* of sophistication, which might rather depend, for example, on the intrinsic nature of the qualifications themselves. The analyst might, of course, break down their "nature" itself into quantifiable elements, but such a procedure would lead straight to the dangerous complications already discussed.

Since most communications include intricate characteristics, and since many of the hypotheses which prompt analysis cannot help drawing on them, it would appear that many quantitative investigations include frequency counts which rest on uncertain ground. Yet once the figures are secured from the material, they are as a rule taken for granted; in fact, the analysis often uses them as a base for statistical elaborations. Probabilities are calculated; correlations are established and interpreted. Since these operations evolve on a mathematical plane—that is, without further recourse to the content analyzed—it is possible that their results are more inaccurate and oblique and less truly representative of the communication than are the doubtful counts from which they take root.

THE ASSUMPTIONS OF QUALITATIVE ANALYSIS PRECLUDE QUALITATIVE CONSIDERATIONS

Among the assumptions underlying quantitative analysis two are of special interest in that they tend to preclude a judicious appraisal of the role which qualitative consideration might play.

There is first the basic assumption that, due to its quantifications and counts, quantitative analysis is the only possible objective systematic and reliable analysis of content. Many researchers consider this as axiomatic.[3]

The second assumption which is relevant restricts the meaningful application of quantitative techniques to communications whose manifest content does not lend itself to being interpreted in different ways. Berelson, for example, proposes:

"If one imagines a continuum along which various communications are placed depending upon the degree to which different members of the intended audience get the same understandings from them, one might place a simple news story on a train wreck at one end (since it is likely that every reader will get the same meanings from the content) and an obscure modern poem at the other (since it is likely that no two readers will get identical meanings from the content).... The analysis of manifest content is applicable to materials at the end of the continuum where understanding is simple and direct, and not at the other. Presumably, there is a point on the continuum beyond which the 'latency' of the content (i.e., the diversity of its understanding in the relevant audience) is too great for reliable analysis."[4]

These assumptions put communications research, particularly applied communications research, in an awkward position. While it may be able to avoid obscure poems, it is much concerned with texts in which latent meanings not only pervade the manifest content, but also are intricately related to the objectives for which the analysis is undertaken. Such latent elements may strongly resist quantification, and occasionally the quantification is actually foregone. For example, the Bureau of Applied Social Research at Columbia University bases its recent studies of communications habits along the Soviet periphery on interviews which involve the respondents' total life to such an extent that practically no word in the interview record is free of multiple connotations. Accordingly, the studies do not confine themselves to quantitative measurements but also analyze, in purely qualitative terms, the intrinsic essence of certain interviews, the possible significance of deviant attitudes, etc. That these qualitative explorations are often touched off by statistical accounts should not blind one to the cases in which they expose unique characteristics without regard for frequencies and the like. All in all, the nonquantitative part of the studies enjoys relative independence, in keeping with the character of both the interviews and the various hypotheses bearing on them. Analysts of international communications have likewise often found themselves in need of qualitative procedures. When an area specialist, for example, is asked to estimate the presumable effectiveness of certain themes and of the devices employed to get them across, he is forced to focus on characteristics and interrelations which it would be meaningless to count because of their highly individual nature.

It is inevitable that the champions of quantitative analysis should regard such nonquantitative explorations as precarious adventures in uncontrollable intuition rather than procedures of verifiable research. The common objection to these procedures is that they are "impressionistic," "unobjective," and lacking in "verifiable evidence." Such criticism follows logically from the basic assumptions of quantitative analysis. But what about the assumptions themselves?

THE ASSUMPTIONS EXAMINED

There is little doubt that quantitative analysis is meaningful if it keeps to communications at the extreme end of the continuum defined by descriptions of train wrecks and similar events. There intricate characteristics hardly enter the picture; should such a category as "direction" be needed at all, it would have to cover only the most elementary pros and cons. And their frequency counts are of major importance. Within this border region quantitative analysis is indeed the only objective, systematic, and reliable procedure of analysis. (It is not, however, necessarily exhaustive. If, for example, the content is set in historical perspective, its "latency" will immediately increase so that quantitative procedures no longer suffice to describe it adequately.)

Yet quantitative analysis does not confine itself to inquiring into these extreme cases. It is often applied to content somewhere along the continuum, content which, though not as obscure as the modern poem, is nevertheless more involved and allusive than the reports at the opposite pole. In addition, such investigations may seek to trace attitudes and interests of population groups, to determine the psychological states of persons and groups, to discover stylistic features—purposes which force the investigator to examine characteristics rarely found in the train-wreck region. But if quantitative analysis expands beyond the confines set up by one of its underlying assumptions—thus running all the risks discussed in the first section of this article—then the other basic assumption that it is the only objective and reliable analysis of content cannot be upheld either. As currently practiced, quantitative analysis is more "impressionistic" than its champions are inclined to admit. All of them, incidentally, readily grant the need for qualitative reasoning in the initial stages of category formation.[5] They more rarely admit, however, that the quantification processes themselves often require much conjecturing which is not in actuality tied to objective, impersonal definitions.

A recent "quantitative" analysis of Voice of America and BBC broadcasts classifies the "style" of contextual units as "matter-of-fact," "mildly emotional," and "highly emotional." Granted that this particular classification was labelled as experimental and the data as merely suggestive, it is nevertheless significant that the quantitative analysts made the classification "mainly with reference to value-laden terms,"[6] the emotional intensity of which they attempted to assess. Certainly no procedure could be more impressionistic. In addition, quantification by this particular indicator promotes a peculiarly fragmentary view of style. For certainly the very absence of value-laden terms in, for example, a sober announcement of the fall of a city, an army, or an individual may constitute a "matter-of-factness" which is in effect highly emotional.

The example is not unique. Numerous quantitative analyses are similarly threaded with impressionistic judgments. And these judgments may in fact be more unaccountable than those found in communications studies of a predominantly qualitative nature. For within the framework of quantitative analysis, qualitative exegesis is condemned to playing a black sheep role. Recognized mainly as a means to arrive at suitable quantifications, its use in analysis proper is regarded as shameful, and may in fact be pursued with guilty haste and lack of discipline. This explains why the qualitative considerations on which most content analysis studies must draw for classification so often fail to penetrate the given text. Being no end in themselves, they threaten to turn into opinion-laden short cuts. The reproach of impressionism which determined quantitative analysts direct against nonquantitative insight thus tends to boomerang. Quantitative analysis is in effect not as objective and reliable as they believe it to be.

POTENTIALITIES OF THE QUALITATIVE APPROACH

Since quantitative analysis proves to be inadequate to describe more involved communications, it would seem advisable to inquire into the prospects of an analytical approach which emphasizes qualitative rather than quantitative procedures. Can we assume that such an approach is more adequately descriptive? And, if so, what of its scientific relevance? Will its "impressionism," its "inevitable lack of objectivity," nullify the advantages it may otherwise offer?

Before considering these questions, it should be emphasized that the terms "qualitative analysis" and "quantitative analysis" do not refer to radically different approaches. Quantitative analysis includes qualitative aspects, for it both originates and culminates in qualitative considerations. On the other hand, qualitative analysis proper often requires quantification in the interest of exhaustive treatment. Far from being strict alternatives the two approaches actually overlap, and have in fact complemented and interpenetrated each other in several investigations.[7]

Qualitative analysis by definition differs from quantitative analysis in that it achieves its breakdowns without special regard for frequencies. What counts alone in qualitative analysis—if the verb is permissible in a context which defies counting—is the selection and rational organization of such categories as condense the substantive meanings of the given text, with a view to testing pertinent assumptions and hypotheses. These categories *may* or *may not* invite frequency counts. In order to demonstrate the greater adequacy of qualitative analysis to communications which exceed straight reporting, these two possibilities will be dealt with separately.

QUALITATIVE ANALYSIS AND FREQUENCY COUNTS

In the case of categories which do invite frequency counts, there is no real difference between the qualitative and quantitative approaches. In theory, both might produce identical classifications. And yet the odds are that the qualitative analyst will be the less inhibited of the two in discovering countable characteristics. As Berelson points out, qualitative studies usually focus not so much on the content of a communication as rather on its underlying intentions or its presumable effects on the audience; "quantitative analysis" on the other hand, "is more likely to focus first upon the straight description of the content itself, if for no other reason because of the amount of energy devoted to the counting procedure."[8] The more involved communications, however, reverberate with so many latent meanings that to isolate their manifest content and describe it in a "straight" manner is not only almost impossible, but can hardly be expected to yield significant results. Such a focus on manifest content everywhere implies a naive extension of the limits implicit in the assumption, per se legitimate, that quantitative techniques are meaningful at the train-wreck end of the continuum. This explains why the qualitative analyst is in a better position than the quantifier to trace relevant characteristics which admit of frequency counts. Free of any biasing prepossession with manifest content, the qualitative analyst explores the whole of the content in quest of important categories. And since he devotes all his energies to this quest, he stands a good chance of coming inadvertently across frequency categories which might have eluded his grasp had he been preoccupied with quantifications at the outset. People often find in passing the very things they have sought in vain.

Examples bearing out these observations are extremely rare because practically no texts have been subjected to independent analyses of both the quantitative and qualitative type. It is perhaps relevant, however, to note that although quantitative analyses have occasionally attempted to employ categories dealing, at least experimentally, with presumed effects, such categories have dealt almost exclusively with manifest aspects of atomistic units of the texts. The previously cited category of "style" in international communications is a case in point. Qualitative analyses of similar material have also framed *quantifiable* categories dealing with the "structure" of the text as a whole, i.e., the linkage, manifest or latent, which makes the atomistic units a Gestalt. Such freedom to seek and use *quantifiable* categories of latent content has, at least to date, been almost exclusively characteristic of qualitative exegesis.

Thus, qualitative analysis steals a march over quantitative analysis in fields common to both—i.e., in regard to categories which do invite frequency counts. But by virtue of its ability to use non-quantifiable frequencies, qualitative exegesis also penetrates textual dimensions which are completely inaccessible to quantitative techniques. An example of the limitations placed on quantitative analysis may be found in Berelson's statement that "Whenever one word or one phrase is as 'important' as the rest of the content taken together, quantitative analysis would not apply."[9] Qualitative exegesis would; and it would make its breakdowns hinge on this one word or one phrase. As a case in point, let us suppose that an international communicator wished to ascertain whether his texts evidenced respect for the audience. A good indicator of this characteristic, though certainly not the only one, is the way in which the communicator refers to his listeners. It is immediately evident, however, that neither the relative number of laudatory and critical references, nor distinctions between "moderate" and "excessive" praise or blame will give any valid picture of the degree of esteem in which the audience is actually held. Frequency counts will reveal the amount of different modes of praise or blame, but since any mode may spring from various psychological sources, the counts are unlikely to yield information about the characteristic "respect" itself. The absence or presence of respect could obviously be better inferred from the manner in which the positive and/or negative references to the audience are interwoven; recognizable patterns of reference would no doubt appear in the communication. Qualitative exegesis would attempt to bare these patterns and assess their presumable significance for the characteristic under consideration. This particular task would be facilitated by the common awareness that certain familiar patterns of interwoven praise and/or censure—"ideal types" in Max Weber's sense—are symptomatic of respectful or disrespectful conduct. For instance, a balanced mixture of friendly approval and frank censure, both being voiced on fitting occasions, would clearly indicate that the communicator is treating his audience as he would a friend or peer; conversely, a pattern of abrupt alternation between extreme praise and harsh criticisms or threats would indicate that the communicator was bluntly trying to manipulate the minds of his audience, which in turn would indicate his low opinion of their independence and dignity. It is particularly to be noted that one single instance of such a configuration of statements would suffice to color the entire communication. In reference to such characteristics, frequency counts are of little relevance. What is relevant are the patterns, the wholes, which can be made manifest by qualitative exegesis and which can throw light upon a textual characteristic which is allergic to quantitative breakdowns.

Unlike quantitative techniques, which draw guiltily upon hasty and incomplete impressionistic judgments, qualitative analysis is frankly and resolutely impressionistic. And it is precisely because of its resolute impressionism, that qualitative analysis may attain to an accuracy which quantitative techniques, with their undercurrent of impressionistic short cuts, cannot hope to achieve. Carrying its explorations beyond the point at which many content analysis investigations prematurely stop, as if fearful of drifting too far from the secure haven of statistics, qualitative exegesis is indeed capable of classifications and descriptions which conform far more closely to the texts than those commonly produced by quantitative analysis. The relative capabilities and limits of these two approaches are nowhere better manifested than in the frequent failure of full-blown quantitative studies to achieve the brilliant promise of their pilot or exploratory stages. The pioneering steps, performed on a small sample, invite attention to unique traits which are perhaps manifest in only one single configuration of statements. The insight into wholes which these unique patterns provide gives rise to observations and hypotheses of unusually rich relevance. The pilot study is, in fact, a model of qualitative exactitude and circumspection. But in the fuller study which follows, the development and testing of these rich hypotheses is entrusted to systematic quantification, in which both infrequencies are deemphasized, and the original overtly impressionistic and accurate insights are not developed for lack of the very spirit in which they were conceived.

DISCIPLINED SUBJECTIVITY

One might ask, of course, whether the superior precision attained by qualitative procedures is not bought at too high a price. For it is true that qualitative analysis, being inevitably subjective, cannot ascertain the accuracy and validity of its findings in the manner of an exact science. One and the same topic may invite different qualitative appraisals of almost equal plausibility; and no accumulation of evidence will determine, in an objective way, which is closer to truth. But though there is no objective truth in this field, the lack of it does not entail lawlessness; qualitative analysis is not a discipline that admits arbitrary speculations. The believers in exact science among the social scientists are inclined to exaggerate, along with the objectivity of quantitative analysis, the dangers which qualitative techniques incur because of their subjectivity. Any historical period produces only a limited number of major philosophical doctrines, moral trends and aesthetic preferences, and if qualitative analysis operates, as it should, below the level of sheer opinion, these influences can be discerned and controlled. Moreover, communications which are sufficiently outspoken to canalize the imagination usually prove a powerful factor in bringing about a convergence of viewpoints and approaches. It is therefore a reasonable guess that different analysts will arrive at similar conclusions with regard to many texts. An experiment to test the guess is now being designed.

Finally, one may legitimately ask whether communications research, as such, should really try to match exact science. Documents which are not simply agglomerations of facts participate in the process of living, and every word in them vibrates with the intentions in which they originate and simultaneously foreshadows the indefinite effects they may produce. Their content is no longer their content if it is detached from the texture of intimations and implications to which it belongs and taken literally; it exists only with and within this texture—a still fragmentary manifestation of life, which depends upon response to evolve its properties. Most communications are not so much fixed entities as ambivalent challenges. They challenge the reader or the analyst to absorb them and react to them. Only in approaching these wholes with his own whole being will the analyst be able both to discover and determine their meaning—or one of their meanings—and thus help them to fulfill themselves. Far from being an obstacle, subjectivity is in effect indispensable for the analysis of materials which vanish before our eyes when subjected to a treatment confounding them with dead matter. Quantitative analysis is not free of such nihilistic influence. Many quantitative investigations in effect mark the spot where a misplaced desire for objectivity has failed to reveal the inner dynamics of an atomized content.

One final suggestion: a codification of the main techniques used in qualitative analysis would be desirable.

NOTES

1. Bernard Berelson, *Content Analysis in Communications Research* (Glencoe, IL: Free Press, 1952), 151.
2. Berelson, *Content Analysis in Communications Research*, 163.
3. Berelson states: "By definition, content analysis must be objective" (171).
4. Berelson, 9–20.
5. Thus, Berelson and Lazarsfeld suggest that the analyst try to formalize into categories his "general subjective impressions" of the content, and that he then put the formulations aside and later come back to them afresh. Bernard Berelson and Paul F. Lazarsfeld, *The Analysis of Communication Content* (New York: Bureau of Applied Social Research, 1948), 115–17.
6. Marie Jahoda and Joseph T. Klapper, "From Social Bookkeeping to Social Research," in this issue of *Public Opinion Quarterly*, 623–30.
7. E.g., the previously cited studies of communications behavior along the Soviet periphery; also Löwenthal's study, "Biographies in Popular Magazines" and Arnheim's "World of the Daytime Serial," in Paul F. Lazarsfeld and Frank N. Stanton, eds., *Radio Research 1942–1943* (New York: Duell, Sloan & Pierce, 1944).
8. Berelson, *Content Analysis in Communications Research*, 122.
9. Berelson, 20.

19
On the Relation of Analysis to the Situational Factors in Case Studies

This memorandum should not be considered a full-fledged paper. It is the draft of an argument designed to serve as a basis for discussion.

The following observations—which, incidentally, are not the only ones I had an opportunity to make during my activities as a "roving" consultant to the Bureau since July 1957—center around two topics:

1. The degree of awareness of the generality level attained in case studies and multiple case studies.

    Instances of such studies are the drug study, several medical profession studies, etc. To simplify matters, the term "case study" will also be applied to research on multiple cases wherever a misunderstanding is likely.
2. The degree of consideration given in analysis to "situational" factors.[1]

    "Situational" factors or determinants are factors which account for the peculiar character of the case or the cases analyzed. This concept refers mainly, if not exclusively, to "sociological" factors—determinants, that is, which comprise structural or functional characteristics of the case on hand, economic and political conditions obtaining at the time of data collections, historical influences, etc. Often these determinants are not traceable to the properties, psychological or otherwise, of the individual respondents, in which case they seem to be identical with what Lazarsfeld-Mensel in their paper, "On the Relation Between Individual and Collective Properties," call "global collective properties."[2]

    The sum of situational factors relevant to a case may loosely be called the "total situation" at the time and place from which the material issues. (The total situation plays a role not only in case studies proper but in national surveys as well. This is illustrated by comparative studies on an international scale, such as Lipset-Bogoff's planned study of social mobility in the U. S. and Europe;[3] they tend to bring out, for each of the nations compared, situational determinants not considered in the analysis of the national samples themselves.)

My basic assumption is that, in order to fully define a case under investigation, attention must be paid to the situational factors bearing on it; altogether they determine its position in the social process.

II.

There are case studies which manifest a strange ambiguity regarding the level of generality reached in them. An interesting example is the drug study. Of course, Coleman-Mensel sharply define the range of their data[4]—four Illinois cities east of the Mississippi and north of the Mason and Dixon line, none under the shadow of a leading medical center and the largest not exceeding the 100,000 mark. Moreover, the investigators never forget to localize their material (and, I should like to add, they remain acutely aware of the practical purpose analysis is to serve). So far the study is clearly circumscribed and well in focus. All the more striking is the vague manner in which the issue of generality is treated. Coleman-Mensel declare that.

The major reasons for carrying out a study like this is to give knowledge about the way doctors generally come to incorporate a medical innovation in their practice. Yet the study was necessarily restricted to a single group of doctors and single medical innovation. Generalization to other doctors and to other medical innovations must be done with caution. From the present study it is impossible to know just how generally the results found here do hold true for other doctors and other innovations. (Intr.-15)

Then they say that, thanks to multi-variate analysis with its emphasis on relationships between variables, their findings "are quite likely to be valid for other generally similar populations and situations" (ibid.).[5]

What exactly does this mean? If I am not mistaken, it means that their findings do not apply generally or do apply only under very specific conditions—a certain geographical region, no leading medical center nearby, cities with 100,000 at most, etc. In other words, the hoped-for generality turns out to be an illusion; it covers only counterparts of the sample itself. Nevertheless,

Coleman-Mensel call generality the major reason for carrying out their study. On the one hand, they believe in generalizations if they are done with "caution"—a somewhat nebulous directive; on the other, they cut down generality to a minimum.

III.

Their wavering in this respect is symptomatic of many a case study. But before submitting further examples, I wish to advance the following proposition: in case studies the degree of awareness of the generality level is contingent on the degree of consideration given to the sociological factors. The less the latter are taken into account—what this means will be seen shortly—the more the issue of generality is likely to be blurred. (Of course, the reverse holds true also.) This proposition is almost self-evident; roughly speaking, a research analyzing the data of a case or a group of cases cannot ascertain the extent to which his findings are more generally valid unless he knows something, and does something about the determinants operative at the locus of his material. Lack of regard for them inevitably entails the kind of haziness instanced above. At this point a new terminological distinction suggests itself—that between "oriented" and "unoriented" case studies. The former tries to relate their variables to the total situation, whereas the latter do not sufficiently consider the impact of local influence and in consequence leave the degree of generality of their results in the open. Whenever the tendency toward unoriented research asserts itself, it is as if research evolved in a vacuum.

At first glance, the drug study does not seem to confirm my propositions. As I mentioned above, Coleman-Mensel refer throughout to the locus of their material (and, in addition, gear analysis to a practical purpose); and yet, contrary to what should be expected if the proposition were true, they make ambivalent statements about the range of validity of their findings. Now I believe it possible to show that, appearances notwithstanding, their wavering results exactly from the reason I indicated—a neglect of the situational determinants. To be sure, the investigators are constantly aware of their point of departure; their study is and remains a study of smaller cities remote from a leading medical school. But the fact that they keep the circumstances conditioning their sample in mind does not necessarily imply that they also consider, and explore for their research operations, relevant components of the total situation. There is more psychology than sociology in the study. Just to illustrate what I mean, the variable "social friendships between doctors" might have been related to an assumption about a "collective property" of cities which have only 100,000 inhabitants or less. Perhaps in such cities of limited size the professionals of this or that denomination is more in need of informal relations among each other than in the larger cities with their multiple social outlets. Considerations of this possibility would have established a connection between the size of the population and the importance of social friendships and thus helped localize the latter in sociological terms. So far as I remember, Colesman-Mensel in their descriptions of the sample do not attempt to account for the ration between the number of doctors in each of the four cities? More likely than not, the degree of saturation plays a role in the flow of information about a new drug; consequently, it might have paid to "operationalize" this sociological rather than psychological concept.

Other studies are even less "local-minded" than the technically superb drug study. Take Wagner Thielens' "Some Comparisons of Entrants to Medical and Law School,"[6] based on a sample from one Eastern medical and on Eastern law school:

The findings reported here, says Wagner Thielens, cannot, of course, be assumed to hold beyond the scope of the two schools, since without additional categories we do not know to what extent they must be interpreted only in terms of local situations within the two schools. But it is tentatively assumed that conditions obtaining more generally are reflected at least in part of these findings ("The Student-Physician," 131).

In contrast to the accuracy of his comparisons, Wagner Thielens's "tentative" assumption is surprisingly casual and vague. Add to this that he does not really care about the "local situations within the two schools." In the summary of his findings no mention is anymore made of their limited generality; as a matter of fact, they are represented in such a way that they almost look like results of general validity. To stay with "The Student-Physician," I would also count here, for instance, such case studies as Huntington's "The Development of a Professional Self-image," or Martin's "Preferences for Types of Patients." Kendall-Sevin's paper, "Tendencies Toward Specialization in Medical Training,"[7] on its part differs from the just-mentioned studies in that it not only shows an appreciable awareness of the source of the data and thus avoids inadvertently gliding into loose generalizations but traces one of its statistical findings to the presence of a non-psychological situational factor, namely, the possible influence of the staff of Cornell Medical College on the decisions of fourth-year students. However, such references from psychological variables back to sociological determinants are very rare indeed, I guess.

To sum up, numbers of case studies are in the nature of unoriented research. They treat the major issue of generality in a cursory and ambiguous manner which contrasts with the internal accuracy of the quantifications and therefore all the more suggests there is something wrong in the sub-structure. If my proposition holds, the vagueness about this issue is inextricably bound up with the reluctance to explore and utilize the situational factors which frame and condition the material analyzed. Unoriented research turns its back on the total situation. This explains why the studies I have in mind give a see-saw impression; they undecidedly waver between specifying and generalizing statements—whereby it should be noted that (unwarranted) preference for the latter is conspicuous in those case studies which are intended from the outset to illustrate something general, say, the drug behavior of doctors, processes of socialization, etc. They have a natural bent for hurrying away from the local of their sample and plunging into the unlocalizable limbo of psychological extrapolations from which, as may be anticipated, a return to sociological categories proves extremely difficult.

IV.

After having roughly outlined my position I had better pause a little and discuss at least one of the objections that may be raised against it.

This objection runs as follows: for analysis in case studies to start with a consideration of situational factors would mean to put the cart before the horse. The task of uncovering these factors can be carried out only in the analytical process itself. And the analytical process extends far beyond the single case study. Any such study calls for supplementation by a series of comparative studies which alone are able to shed light on the peculiarities of each of the cases under investigation, thereby permitting the researchers to sift out the more generally applicable findings. (I learned from Patty Kendall that, with this purpose in mind, questionnaires have been sent to all medical schools in the U.S., the intention being to achieve, in the medical profession studies, the high generality of a nation-wide survey.) To epitomize the argument, definition of the determinants of a case is contingent on a sequence of comparisons which can be expected successively to reveal all differential local influences. The total situation, that is, is not so much a starting point (in the form of hypotheses) as a result in the form of precise description). The indefinite generality of case studies is therefore nothing to worry about; it is just a sign that they are something like stepping-stones.

No doubt this argument carries weight. However, there is a methodological snag in it. (In speaking of a methodological snag, I immediately discount the fact that actually case studies are rarely followed up by systematic comparative research. For a variety of reasons, economic or otherwise, social research proceeds more haphazardly in this respect than research in the natural sciences.) Now what is methodologically wrong with too great a reliance on comparative studies is the following: if, as I assume, the situational factors have a bearing on the analysis of the situation to which they belong, then the variables selected for analytical treatment must refer, somehow, to these factors in order really to describe and interpret the situation under consideration. If they do not, analysis, in interrelating them, always runs the risk of reflecting obliquely the case investigated.

In the drug study Coleman-Mensel say that "scientifically-oriented doctors" were among the first to receive information on tetracycline and introduced it at an early stage, whereas graduates of competitive medical schools were relatively slow in introducing the drug. This statement, contradictory by implication, is commented upon as follows: "... the slower introduction of tetracycline by graduates of competitive schools is evidently not due to the greater scientific caution of these competitive school graduates but to some other variable. In the data which we have this variable is not evident; it may be some *spurious factor* (italics mine) existing in the particular sample of doctors examined. In any case, the relation, which is not a large one, remains unexplained" (18–19).

The summary characterization of the behavior of graduates form competitive medical schools as a "spurious factor" may be due to the obliqueness of the variables chosen. I have definitive misgivings about the consistency (and adequacy) of the concept "scientifically-oriented doctors." It is distilled from sundry data (Appendix D, 1–8) which is my opinion do not fully warrant its construction. Sometimes the desire for establishing, as fast as possible, statistically manipulable variables seems to get the better of the concern for their substantiality. Of course, frequently the variables are solid and virtually relevant to the local contexts. As mentioned previously, in the drug study the category "social friendships between doctors" might easily be related to a property of smaller cities. And in the previously mentioned Kendall-Selvin study analysis is so conducted that it directly brings a situational factor—faculty influence on fourth-year students—into focus. (Interestingly, the research design there such that the assumed existence of this factor comes almost as a surprise. This need not have been so. Perhaps it would have been possible to direct attention to the local determinants, including faculty influences, from the very outset and examine their bearing on the whole curve of student tendencies toward specialization, not only on the last phase of it.) Yet in case studies which are less sociologically oriented than Kendall-Selvin's the adequacy of the variables to the given situation is by no means certain. And whenever the variables are chosen and utilized with little regard for the pertinent sociological configuration so that analysis is apt partly to distort the reality it is supposed to describe. No comparative study or sequence of such studies should be expected to remove the ensuing opaqueness of the analytical description.

V.

I now propose to circumscribe the concept of situational factors in more detail. The first thing to do is; naturally, to point to existing studies which gravitate toward oriented research. Contextual analysis in studies of a family of cases ranks high as a systematic attempt to lay hold on, and operationalize, local determinants of each of the cases analyzed; in the Teachers Apprehension project, for instance, size, wealth, and political preferences of diverse colleges are brought into play. To mention a few other relevant studies, contextual or not, the ITU study establishes meaningful relationships between individual properties and such collective properties as the ideological climate in larger and smaller shops or even,[8] if my memory does not deceive me, the impact of tradition; the polio study takes structural features of national organizations into account; McPhee's program for research on television is crowded with assumptions on the total situation; and the study of the Religio-Psychiatric Clinic which is a single case study derives, with the aid of ideal-types and Parsonian dichotomic variable patterns, its psychological units from estimates of the total situation based on transcriptions of group discussions and participant observation.

Examination of these examples leads to two conclusions, one concerning the range of situational factors, the other the problem of their selection.

First, definition of the total situation involves various areas—not only sociology proper and social psychology (whereby, in view of the current bias in favor of "psychology" the emphasis should be put on the sociological rather than psychological component of this discipline) but also economics, politics, anthropology, history. The area of history belongs to the most neglected for the simple reason that, because of their understandable aspiration to generality, case studies tend to care little about the place which their case occupies in the historical process; they forget the longitudinal section in the cross section. But this oversight might endanger the precision of analytical description. The operational significance of the historical factor is prominent in research on institutions or groups with a live tradition and a history which palpably conditions their present shape and functioning. Take a study of church congregations: it requires the researcher to deal in images, concepts, and issues saturated with values and meanings which have accrued to them in the course of history. Accordingly, the contents of these motions are important in their own right; they figure as such and such contexts in the minds of the parishioners. Which in turn means that analysis is adequate only if it considers the possible implications of the contents themselves no less attentively than the attitudes toward them. A complete isolation, for analytical purposes, of attitudes from traditional notions whose content carries weight as this particular content may falsify the picture. At any rate, the authors of *The Authoritarian Personality* would have come closer to the truth if they had related their personality syndrome to the historical and national contexts in which it actually appears. It would also have been better psychology for being less of it.[9] A companion project to Benson's exemplifying the usefulness of the historical approach for social research under certain circumstances might prove extremely interesting.

Second, the selection of possibly relevant situational determinants depends upon the case investigated. Lowenthal in his study of biographies in popular magazines of a period of time orients research toward a historico-economic factor—the ongoing transition from a production economy to a consumption economy. When devising the report on Satellite mentality,[10] Berkman and I introduced, on the basis of a careful reading of the interviews, a number of politically important topics which then served us as a starting-point for analysis proper. Incidentally, a comparison between this report and the INRA report on the same interviews[11]—our qualitative analysis was to supplement, or complement, the quantitative analysis of the latter—makes it quite clear that the situational factors must be hypothesized at the outset in order to affect the analytical process. INRA's report was relatively unoriented; the researchers gave the material a routine workout without, at the beginning, culling from it clues to (significant) components of the given total situation and proceeding accordingly. But this precisely is what Berkman and I tried to do. So we felt justified in exploring the interviews for such topics as the "unreality" of the Satellite world, the distinctions made by Satellite non-Communists between several types of Communists, the different attitudes of non-Communists toward resistance in time of relative calm and time of acute crisis, etc.—topics referred to in the material but left unmentioned in the INRA report. The moral is that you cannot extricate from analysis what has not been tentatively put into it. To stress an important point, the decisive difference between the two reports is not that one prefers qualitative analysis (much of which might have easily been quantified) and the other indulges in quantifications; rather, the decisive difference must be sought in the research design: we made an attempt to utilize socio-political determinants, while the INRA did not.

As for the question of how to seize on relevant situational factors, I should like to suggest that it be taken up in the planned seminar; the best method is perhaps to discuss one or two unoriented case studies, with a view to reconstructing the total situation from which their samples stem.

VI.

It follows from what has been said till now that a case study is oriented only if its variables or units are related to the possibly relevant sociological determinants. Only then will research achieve "the precise description and analysis of social events" (quoted from Lazarsfeld-Barton's paper, "Social Research in the United States").[12] The task with which the researcher is thus confronted requires definition. Except for research on "global collective properties." practically all case studies analyse their sample for properties of the individuals and/or groups involved; it is the humans and the interrelationships that count after all. Altogether these properties—attitudes, behavior-patterns, preferences, status aspirations, etc.—belong to what may be called the "psychological dimension." Similarly, the situational factors on their port may be said to constitute the "sociological dimension." The necessity for case research to select the psychological properties which appear as variables of analysis in such a way that they have a distinct bearing on the pertinent total situation can now be formulated as follows: The sociological dimension takes precedence over the psychological dimension. Or conversely, in the interest of a "precise description and analysis of social events" any psychological unit must be traceable to the ensemble of sociological characteristics framing it. Within social research even a seemingly self-sufficient pattern of personality traits is not an entity in its own right.

Among the studies which acknowledge the primacy of the sociological dimension is Merton's recent paper, "Priorities in Scientific Discovery,"[13] is of special interest methodologically for two reasons. First, Merton shows that the recurrent priority disputes call for a sociological rather than psychological explanation; they persistently flare up because the code sanctioned by the fraternity of scientists requires that new findings be attributed to their discoverers. A phenomenon which on the surface appears to be motivated psychologically thus turns out to be a genuinely sociological phenomenon. (Had Merton been less aware of the dependence of psychological properties on sociological determinants, he might have "explained" the fact that in priority disputes scientists take up the cudgels from themselves as well as their confrères from some pattern of personality traits in which, at critical moments, the desire for recognition and prestige scores higher than self-denying modesty; patterns of this kind can be made to fit any event or situation; yet in insisting on the sociological nature of the phenomenon, he judiciously avoids the pitfalls of purely psychological constructs, which also permits him to leave the eternally fluctuating relation between modesty and prestige aspirations undefined.) Second, Merton arrives at his conclusions by way of a comparative survey of relevant causes which is oriented toward situational determinants from the beginning. The same applies to all the units of analysis as a matter of course. He does not rely, that is, on unoriented comparative research to define the sociological character of priority disputes; rather, he finds out about it in the course of comparisons which are permeated with sociological considerations. This highlights a point made in earlier contexts: that comparative studies whose units are impermeable to the sociological dimension stand little chance of detecting situational factors in the process.—As has already been indicated above, Klausner's study of the Religio-Psychiatric Clinic belongs here also.[14] True, it concentrates on the divergent attitudes toward psychotherapy of a number often cooperating minsters and psychiatrists, but attitudinal analysis is framed by a phenomenological description of the outlook of these people: They are identified as deviants; and their opinions about the functions of the church and the significance of therapy are confronted with the institutionalized views of the clergy and the medical profession. In other words, Klausner locates his variables in sociological space by relating them to the collective properties of two social systems.—In my own book *From Caligari to Hitler*,[15] I hypothesized, on the basis of my material, the existence of certain inner dispositions among the Germans of the Weimar Republic; instead of passing them off as independent entities, however, I tried to embed them in the sociological contexts of the period and to trace changes in collective psychological behavior to the changing economic, social and political conditions. It was psychology in the sociological dimension and sociology derived from psychological constants. (After my book appeared, a psychoanalyst told me: "Your psychological analysis is fairly correct so far as it goes. But it doesn't go far enough." This exactly was what I wanted to avoid.)

VII.

The current style of social research does not seem to encourage consideration of the situational factors. I infer that much from the fact that numbers of researchers shy away from the sociological dimension even in cases where it is fully exposed to view. They succumb to what may be called the "psychological fallacy."

Take Anderson's paper, "Some Contributions to the Study of Social Perception:"[16] based on data of the Teachers Apprehension study, it aims, among other things, at determining the impact of the college teachers' "caution," "worry," and "permissiveness" on their perception of "incidents" at the respective colleges. (The contextual part of analysis may be neglected here.) The underlying assumption is, of course, that the three variables "caution" and "worry"—by the way, how to differentiate between them?—does certainly not apply to the concept "permissiveness." It is no genuinely psychological concept. The six indices from which it is built amount to value statements about situations which would have in varying degrees involved political risks at the time of the data collection. Consequently, these indices bear not so much on the respondent's psychological make-up as on the range of his political judgement. Far from suggesting a psychological disposition like "caution," or "worry," or "tolerance," they at most denote a temporary attitude toward Communist infiltration, as it affects the campus and the traditional notions of academic freedom. Whether or not "permissiveness" is a substantial unit is at least controversial. But once it has been constructed, emphasis on its threadbare psychological dimension and the sociological dimension at the expense of the latter.

Professor Brunner and David Wilder told me that they have come across the same habit in their survey of existing research on adult education. In accordance with the declared preferences of the educators themselves, most studies investigate reasons for enrollment, student attitudes—do you like this course?—change in attitudes, the kind of gratifications derived from attendance, etc. The bulk of research—much of it consists or doctoral dissertations free from nonacademic obligations—centers around motivations, human interrelationships, group dynamics, and the like. Which is to say that, all in all, these studies give a wide berth to adult education as a movement which raises sociologically important issues. Adult education has the function of providing broad strata of the population with knowledge in the areas of concern. Well, does it fulfill this function? The run of the studies fails to breach the problem of communications content. And yet it would not be too difficult to ascertain and measure the gain in knowledge achieved by those who attend the courses. Another relevant issue pertains to the sociology of culture: what happens to high-level knowledge if it is passed on to relatively untrained students? The significance of this issue for adult education and its cultural objectives is obvious. An evaluation of transcripts of lectures by authorities on the subjects treated might yield yardsticks for the analysis of teaching performances and enable the researchers to score their adequacy.

And this leads to a consideration of the role which the educator's training plays in the communications process. Etc. The point I wish to make is simply that adult education poses problems which reach deep into the sociological dimension; that these problems stand out glaringly; and that nevertheless a great deal of autonomous research shows little regard for them. It is as if the "psychological fallacy" blinded many a researcher to their existence and at the same time compelled him to proceed along lines which virtually serve purely manipulative purposes.

VIII.

Let us look more closely into the structure of unoriented case studies. They share characteristics which result from the indifferences to the situational factors and the concomitant tendency to blur the level of generality. Analysis in such studies comprises a series of steps most of which do not directly bear on my argument and will therefore be omitted. Of interest here are only the two subsequent major operations.

1. Establishment of variables or units. According to premise, these variables are not identical with situational factors, they are "internal" variables. (Of course, the same applies to the hypothesis underlying them.) As a rule, the variables selected designate properties of individuals or groups—attitudes toward a minority, preferences for a political party or a musical genre, personality traits, prestige aspirations, and what not. These examples show that the units used in case studies mostly consist of a sociological and a psychological component; for instance, preference for a political party points to both the social entity preferred and an inclination of the individual preferring it. Even though the variables do not lie in the sociological dimension itself—amounting, say to a "global" property of smaller cities or the content of a tradition-laden notion—many of them might nevertheless permit the researcher to follow up the implications of their sociological component and this work his way toward the situational influences at the time and place of the data. In unoriented research, however, these communication lines are largely blocked. There the emphasis is on the self-sufficiency of the variables, their independence of the local determinants. Otherwise expressed, their psychological component is made to overshadow what they include in "system references." A major reason for their

isolation from the total situation is presumably the concern, at the outset of analysis, for exact measurements; attempts to account for the situational factors would introduce considerations apt to hamper, or even obstruct, the quantification processes. So, the attitudes toward a minority are essentially valued as a psychological property of individuals. Note that this preoccupation with the psychological component of the variables not only tends to obscure parts of social reality with which they potentially cover also, but may as well lead to problematic psychology. It is by no means certain whether all the attitudes, preferences, behavior-patterns, etc., elicited from the data for analytical treatment represent genuine properties of the individuals with whom they are associated. Individuals whom the evidence reveals to be biased against a minority may manifest such a bias only within the given social contexts. To be sure, one might argue that an unoriented case study dealing with antagonistic attitudes toward a minority does not assert any more than precisely this; but by disregarding the social concerns relevant to the case, the study creates the impression that the bias is, so to speak, a quality of the individuals showing it—an impression which may be deceptive.

To sum up, unoriented case studies tend to resort to variables which are not derived from hypotheses about situational factors. Although numbers of these variables are transparent to the sociological dimension, they are often used with manifest disregard for their references to that dimensions. Under the impact of the "psychological fallacy" all the light falls on their psychological component. Yet for this does not necessarily transform them into intrinsically psychological units either. It is as if those which do not belong here not there occupied a twilight region. Generally speaking, we are confronted with the problem of whether the variables of unoriented research really facilitate "the precise description and analysis of social events." (Incidentally, it is a problem which also concerns contextual analysis. In order to get hold of the total situation contextual analysis may either start from sociological assumptions and constructs its variables accordingly, or avail itself of the kind of variables characterized just above and reinsert them into sociological contexts. on principle, the second alternative should be expected eventually to yield as much information about relevant sociological determinants as the first. However, my guess is that the first alternative—selection of sociological variables at the outset—is more likely than the second to attain the goal of contextual analysis. For in operating with variables relatively remote from the sociological dimension, this type of analysis runs the risk of tapering off into an asymptotic approach to the situational factors or at least becoming increasingly cumbersome. Of course, this need not be so. But even supposing that the second alternative fully serves the purpose, I cannot help feeling that it relates to the first in about the same way as the Ptolemaic system to the Copernican.)

Statistical analysis. The statistical processing of case material establishes, as accurately as possible, the existing relationships between the occurrences which fell under the variables selected. It may be taken for granted that quantitative analysis results in a refined description of any case analyzed—a description which, I hasten to add, is naturally limited to such aspects of the case as the variables denote. The problem I want to raise here has nothing whatsoever to do with these mathematical operations themselves but bears on the following matter: does, in unoriented case research, the analytical treatment to which data are subjected affect the signifying poser of the variables covering them? My tentative preposition is that it does. To be more precise, it appears that in the studies under consideration the statistical elaborations tend further to divert attention from what the guiding units include in sociological references. The reason is this: As has been submitted above, many units or variables point to both the psychological and the sociological dimension. And even though the researcher indifferent to the latter actually concentrates on the psychological component of the variables, he is theoretically still at liberty to look about and follow up to the clues they offer to the situational factors. The variables themselves preserve their double character; they are not yet isolated from the sociological determinants, but continue to be in a measure suggestive of the total situation. Now notice what happens when the data defined by those variables are statistically analyzed for correlations, other kinds of relationships, deviations from observed relationships, etc. In unoriented research the operations which are then taking place involve the variables not as units belonging to the sociological as well as the psychological dimension but as elements independent of any allegiance that might impinge on the researcher's freedom to combine and interlink them at will. They must be considered self-sufficient or else they cannot be correlated freely. (It is understood that I do not think here of large-scale surveys in which statistical regularities are the point of departure for interpretation; nor do I speak of such statistical operations as may be called for within the framework of case research which incorporates the sociological dimension.) Due to an unrestrained emphasis on statistical analysis, the psychological component of each variable becomes automatically all-important and eventually stands for the whole of it. In consequence, the mathematical workout given the variables does not increase our awareness of their references to the sociological determinants but on the contrary leads even farther away from them. Instead of bringing the social influences at the locus of the material again into view, it renders their reconstruction more difficult.

IX.

And what about the findings of unoriented case studies? To begin with, they are ambiguous as to location. On the one hand, it is obvious that they relate to data assembled at a certain time and place; to this extent they are well-localized. On the other hand, they are not embedded in the social contexts from which the material issues so that their location remains indistinct; and this being so, they tend to evoke the illusion of a generality similar to that of the natural sciences. Hence the haziness about the generality level discussed above. Suffice it again to mention this ambiguity which is only in the nature of a symptom after all.

It is symptomatic of the way in which the findings describe the social events on which they bear. There is no doubt, of course, that all the relationships discovered and established in the course of analysis reflect actual relationships. The findings portray accurately existing occurrences and expose to view much of their otherwise inaccessible interplay. The question is only what part of the social events do they cover? Since analysis not initially framed by sociological considerations disregards the situational factors, its results will not take them into account either. So the findings are likely to neglect essential aspects of the case they are intended to describe. They amount to a fine-spun texture of correlations and relationships all of which, however, are left undefined in terms of the social circumstances generating them. Once again, the configurations revealed by unoriented analysis do exist; yet the render not so much the social events in their fullness as the sentiments which these events deposit in the psychological dimension or somewhere between it and the sociological dimension. Otherwise expressed, it is the shadows of the events rather than the events themselves which are summoned by analysis unaware of the sociological determinants. This corroborates an observation advanced above—that unoriented case studies are threatened with rendering their cases obliquely. To be sure, the relationships established in any such study are true to fact; but from the angle of hypotheses about the total situation it may well prove necessary (1) to assign to these relationships new weights, and (2) to introduce sociological variables. Both measures would completely alter the picture, without for that reason giving the lie to the factuality of the previously established findings. The accuracy of statistical analysis should not be confused with precision in the description of social events. (My FCQ article, "The Challenge of Qualitative Analysis,"[17] includes some remarks on this point.)

Unoriented research, then yields findings of indeterminate generality and doubtful relevance to the cases at issue. Because of their unrelatedness to social reality proper they lack a frame of reference. Its absence is of consequence. It accounts for the unhampered sprawling of analysis, the emergence, among the findings, of relationships which it is true, grow out of the analytical process but have no other merit than to occur at the place of the data. They are just transient happenings. This indiscriminate exhibition of all that can be brought out by mathematical operations may be traced to two reasons. First it almost is as if the accumulations of findings of problematic significance, and the preoccupation with utmost accuracy in securing them had the function of substituting for the omitted situational factors; as if the researcher felt there is a gap that must be filled and then filled it with everything that he is able to wrest from the material. Second, his insistence on doing so may also spring from the belief that procedures in social research are identical with those in the natural sciences and that therefore seemingly insignificant results of analysis stand as good a chance as significant ones of being recognized, someday, as indispensable contributions. Yet is there really an identity of method and goal? Let alone other integrant differences between the two approaches, the findings of social case studies cannot lay claim to the genuine generality inseparable from all findings in physics. So it happens that at least part of unoriented research appears to be in excess of what would be needed were research framed by considerations of the possibly relevant sociological determinants. Or to say the same in the reverse way: if there were more analysis guided by assumptions about the total situation, much of what now hangs loosely in mid-air would automatically disappear. Orientation would dispose of the sprawling: sociology would do away with the "psychological fallacy."

X.

At the end I wish to submit a guess for what it is worth—that one of the origins of unoriented research is market research. Most of the foregoing comment on the former does not apply to the latter. Being as a rule concerned with short-term causes and effects, market research need not inquire into the total situation; and it is oriented inasmuch as its analytical efforts are geared to, and this limited by, a practical purpose, however insignificant from a sociological point of view. But no sooner does case research lose sight of a practical purpose and inadvertently cease to confine itself to findings of short-term validity than it immediately assumes that character of unoriented research, provided it does not at the same time integrate into analysis the situational factors.

NOTES

1. When referring to "analysis" I assume throughout that all the procedures it involves are carried out competently.
2. {We were unable to locate a reference for this paper.}
3. {We were unable to locate a reference for this paper.}
4. {We were unable to locate a reference for this paper.}
5. {This is a quote in the original text, although the reference is unclear.}
6. {Wagner Thielens, "Some Comparisons of Entrants to Medical and Law School," *Journal of Legal Education* 11, no. 2 (1958): 153–70.}
7. {We were unable to locate a reference for any of these three papers.}
8. {It is unclear which study Kracauer is referring to here.}
9. {T. W. Adorno, E. Frenkel-Brunswik, D. J. Levinson, and R. N. Sanford, *The Authoritarian Personality* (New York: Harper & Brothers, 1950).}
10. {See Siegfried Kracauer and Paul L. Berkman, "Attitudes Toward Various Communist Types in Hungary, Poland and Czechoslovakia," which we have included in this volume.}
11. {It is unclear which study Kracauer is referring to here.}
12. {We were unable to locate a reference for this paper.}
13. {Robert K. Merton, "Priorities in Scientific Discovery: A Chapter in the Sociology of Science," *American Sociological Review* 22, no. 6 (1957): 635–59.}
14. {We were unable to locate a reference for this paper.}
15. {Siegfried Kracauer, *From Caligari to Hitler: A Psychological History of the German Film* (Princeton, NJ: Princeton University Press, 1947).}
16. {We were unable to locate a reference for this paper.}
17. {See Kracauer, "The Challenge of Qualitative Analysis," which we have included in this volume.}

20

The Social Research Center on the Campus

Its Significance for the Social Sciences and Its Relations to the University and Society at Large

CONTENTS
INTRODUCTION———350
I: AUTONOMOUS RESEARCH———353
II: COMMISSIONED RESEARCH———369
III: TRAINING———379

INTRODUCTION

The study outlined in the following pages is intended as an inclusive and systematic contribution to the running controversy about the significance of organized social research in the university.

It is noteworthy that such a study could not even have been conceived twenty years ago when social research groups, if any, were as a rule ephemeral organizations set up to implement a specific research goal and disbanded after having served the purpose. A kind of transition between past and future was the research organization which Professor Odum, a dedicated Southerner, founded in North Carolina as far back as 1925; characteristically, its destination was to evolve propositions that might help the South. This would corroborate an interesting observation of Professor Lazarsfeld's—that regional thinking belongs among the substantive roots of contemporary empirical research.

Only since 1935 or so have more and more universities in this country and abroad seen fit to incorporate or create permanent social research centers. This powerful movement toward institutionalized research may be traced to two reasons: the new scientific developments in the collection of primary data (e.g., sample survey) which call for exploration and application by groups with special skills, technical facilities and research traditions, and the seemingly increasing inclination of governmental departments, social agencies and business enterprises to have such groups tackle their particular problems. (The fact that various public and private organizations entertain research staffs of their own in order better to cope with difficulties and needs in the areas of propaganda effects, publicity appeals, labor-management relations, etc., confirms the high market value of applied social research.) Both science and society at large have favored the trend under consideration. {Be this} as it may, there is no doubt that the social research centers on the campus show a strong capacity for survival. And now that they have developed stable habits and characteristics, the time has come to examine them more closely.

For the purpose of a first orientation it may suffice to present the arguments which part of the academic world raises against organized research. Since they bring the major topics and contents of the debate into focus, they serve as an appropriate point of departure. Whether or not these arguments are relevant is of little interest at the moment; nor is there any use in reproducing the customary counterarguments, however weighty. The task of assessing the significance of group research will devolve upon the study itself; and it may well prove necessary in the process to re-define the pros and cons which are current now.

The controversy, rarely outspoken but forever smoldering, centers around three issues of vital concern to the scholar. The first issue involves the genuinely scientific pursuits of research organizations—that part of their program which may conveniently be called <u>autonomous research</u>. Especially scientists with a broad scholarly background argue that the inevitable absorption of permanent research groups with empirical data and the methods of processing them all but automatically stifles their susceptibility to basic social problems. Thus the interest in the size and composition of a given radio audience tends to win out over the preoccupation with the meaning of radio listening as such. The Hollerith machines must be fed; and they would be doomed to starvation were research organizations more concerned than they actually are with that kind of knowledge which grows out of wide experience, thoughtful circumspection and imaginative insight.

Another objection which overlaps this one and comes from about the same academic quarters is directed against the aspiration of organized research to attain to the objectivity of exact science. Indeed, it cannot be defined that all social research centers more or less try to live up to this aspiration which incidentally is in perfect harmony with their inherent desire for permanence. Hence their insistence on quantification and reliability, upheld by the underlying conviction that general laws and valid predictions are within reach. The critics of organized research hold that the conception of sociology and social psychology as a sort of human physics threatens unduly to narrow the potential scope of these sciences. More specifically, they are afraid lest the emulation of exact science might entail disregard for the qualitative components of the phenomena analyzed as well as indifference to propositions which do not favor numerical breakdowns.

The second and most obvious issue of the controversy concerns the dependence of all or nearly all social research centers on substantial support from sources outside the campus. Founded for the sake of autonomous research, these organizations feel nevertheless urged, out of their instinct of self-preservation, to take on a considerable amount of <u>commissioned research</u>. And the latter may even exceed and slow down the former—despite the availability of Foundation subsidies for purely scientific projects. This state of affairs is responsible for a particularly conspicuous argument against group research: many a champion of professional integrity contends that university institutes indulging in market research and the like compromise academic standards and goals. Speaking crudely, what he means is that social scientists prostitute themselves in submitting, somehow, to the claims and aims of their donors. There the matter will have to rest provisionally. It should be added, though, that the feeling of integrity at the bottom of this argument is no less intense among the exponents of organized research themselves and that it actually challenges them to give much thought to their precarious situation between science and business, the university and the outside world.

The third issue bears on the <u>training</u> which students receive in the social research centers. In keeping with their obligations as university institutes, practically all centers consider it one of their tasks to contribute to the formation of future social scientists. And there is a strong belief in the camp of group research that the kind of training these organizations are able to provide complements the theoretical courses in a most fortunate manner. The critic of research centers on his part attacks their educational activities with an argument which follows straight from his doubts about their autonomous research. In his opinion these "social laboratories," as they sometimes call themselves, stress technical efficiency at the expense of full comprehension and in consequence produce versatile specialists rather than authentic scientists.

So much for the main issues of the controversy. They delimit three areas of investigation—autonomous research, commissioned research and training. To explore these areas thoroughly one might think of a comparative study covering the operations and products of the most important research organizations since their inception. Yet such a study would be impractical because of its excessive scope. Nor is it absolutely needed. The objectives of this project can be attained by a semi-comparative study—a study, that is, which concentrates on a single research group and makes comparisons only in the form of excursions designed to round out the picture. The Bureau of Applied Social Research, Columbia University—called "Bureau" in the following—suggest itself as a fairly paradigmatic case. It is one of the oldest university institutes in the field; and it has done a great deal of pioneering work, influencing similar organizations in this country and abroad. In fact, some of them are patterned on it. A historico-systematic study of the Bureau—its activities in the areas indicated and its related organizational patterns—would therefore seem to constitute an adequate approach. Provided it lives up to its comparative duties, this relatively limited investigation is likely to afford insight into the inner workings of organized social research, clarify its significance for the social sciences, and shed light on both its academic and social functions.

I. AUTONOMOUS RESEARCH

The controversy about research organizations, then, resolves around activities in the three areas of autonomous research, commissioned research, and student training. The best way of putting the debate on solid ground is obviously to scrutinize the actual achievements of organized research within each of these areas. It would seem advisable to investigate the latter in the order in which they have just been mentioned. The first area to be considered, therefore, is autonomous research.

Yet before examining this area, the meaning and the range of the term "autonomous research" must be clarified. As has already been pointed out above, it refers to pursuits intended to enlarge the body of existing knowledge, evolve a new method, test some significant theory, etc. Which implies that, for instance, a routine study which confines itself to informing a business company about customer reactions to its product can hardly be said to fall under this title. A certain spontaneity of research design is inseparable from "autonomous" projects; that is, they are not just meant to tackle the problems of private or public social agencies but grow out of the scientist's desire to advance his science and will have to be structured accordingly. Understandably enough, projects in this vein are frequently carried out with the aid of foundations or other organizations devoted to sponsoring scholarly undertakings. However, in view of the intrinsic character of empirical social research as well as the research center's financial needs—which are not or perhaps cannot be met by the university and foundations alone —, it is inevitable that autonomous intentions should also try to assert themselves in assignments from outside the campus, as is strikingly illustrated by the "American Soldier." There is no clear dividing line between autonomous research and commissioned research; rather, the former may well materialize in, or at least capitalize on, projects sponsored by clients who are not primarily concerned with scientific aims and procedures. Nevertheless, it would seem indicated to treat the autonomous endeavors of the research institute separately. For even though they often come true in commissioned projects, they do not exhaust themselves in catering to the client's demands but can be expected to follow ways of their own likely to lead beyond the confines of the commissions occasioning them. Hence the legitimacy of exemplifying autonomous developments and aspirations by references to such commissioned studies; the references bear not so much on the practical purpose of these studies as on what they include, perhaps as a by-product, in scientific accomplishments.[1]

Analysis of the research institute's autonomous output will be oriented toward two objectives. First, it aims at defining the scientific significance of all projects in this vein. The underlying assumption is that the significance of a project grows in the measure in which it advances methodology and/or raises issues involving the structure and character of our society. To simplify matters in this outline, emphasis will be placed on studies of substantive issues rather than methodological contributions—which of course is not meant to belittle the signal importance of methodology. (As a matter of fact, both approaches interpenetrate each other). All other circumstances being equal, a study of the social implications of radio listening is certainly significant in this sense, while a study focusing on the size and composition of a given radio audience is much less so.[2] This is not said to minimize the relative value of the latter studies; they are often prerequisite to propositions of some significance. A case in point is the study "Social Stratification of the Radio Audience" which H. M. Beville Jr. prepared for the Princeton Office of Radio Research in 1939. In his preface to this statistical survey Prof. Lazarsfeld points out that its systematic exploration might increase our knowledge of widespread attitudes and behavior patterns and thus pose problems bearing on the whole of American society; for instance, Beville's data challenge one to inquire into the reasons for which low income groups respond more readily than the economically privileged to "psychological" programs and dramatizations.

This implies, incidentally, that any speculation on the significance of the subject matter analyzed is meaningless. Rather, everything depends on the manner in which a topic is approached. Audience responses may be studied mainly for bookkeeping purposes or with a view to finding out about their implications for society in general. The theme itself—audience responses—is so to speak neutral; what counts is the way it is treated. (Hence the possibility that a very specialized monograph affords insight far beyond its subject matter)

Yet even so it is advisable to retain the classification of projects according to their level of significance. Many less significant projects which perhaps carry weighty implications are left unexplored for lack of time, money or brains and, hence, must be evaluated as low-level projects for the time being, in spite of their potentialities. And after all, not all low-level studies show promise; a study, say, of the images which people form of competing brands of soap might be just that, i.e., defy attempts at further exploration.

Second, analysis is intended to define and appraise the institutional properties of a permanent research organization in their bearing on autonomous scientific endeavors. In what ways does the existence of such an organization benefit and/or obstruct independent and, so to speak, spontaneous research? But these problems will be discussed only after the analysis of autonomous research itself.

The Bureau's autonomous research activities comprise long-range programs in the following areas:

(1) Communications and opinion formation. Research in this area, the Bureau's initial concern, has resulted in series of projects studying the effects of the mass media. It might be added already now that the tremendous task of finding out about these effects has led the researchers to shift, temporarily or not, the emphasis from the mass media themselves to factors held to play a more important role than they in the processes of decision making. Within the framework of the communications program proper much attention is paid of late to the functions which modern mass communications assume on the international scene, particularly in pre-industrial societies.

(2) Political behavior. This program, intimately connected with the mass media studies, materializes in projects investigating the influences behind voting decisions as well as the organizational characteristics of political parties and "private governments." An interdisciplinary long-term project designed to codify our current knowledge of the political process in America, is under way.

(3) Population. Under this title the growth of urbanization is being studied in its relation to other trends symptomatic of our civilization, such as the tendencies toward industrialization and literacy. Two major studies are in

preparation—a "world urban resources index" and a publication on "patterns of world urbanization."

(4) Sociology of professions. The idea behind this program is to analyze processes of socialization. The current main project, based on data which were gathered in a medical school, centers around the transformation of medical novices into budding young doctors, trying to account for the extent to which the attitudinal changes involved are brought about by institutional influences and the value-laden atmosphere in which they occur.

(5) Special projects. This program division which includes studies outside the areas just delineated belongs here inasmuch as some of the projects administered under it are carried out in the hope that they will open up new fields of research. There is, for instance, the long-term study of the epidemiology of hypertension; along with related projects, it is likely to develop into an autonomous program covering the areas of public health and social medicine. Similarly, a special project sponsored by the National Council of the Protestant Episcopal Church for the purpose of learning about the effects, and responses to, its activities in certain secular fields may well prepare the ground for a large-scale program devoted to the sociology of religion.

(6) Methods. The "methods" program consists of projects which serve to innovate and refine new tools of research—perhaps especially those needed for the implementation of studies in progress. Thus the Lazarsfeld-Stanton Program Analyzer grew out of the researchers' preoccupation with audience reactions to mass media content. Other methods evolved or furthered by the Bureau and presumably connected with its substantive autonomous pursuits are the focused interview, the panel technique, the integration of qualitative and quantitative research, etc. New developments in the field of sample survey techniques owe much to Lazarsfeld's conceptual and mathematical ingenuity. As a matter of course, all research groups are requested to participate in this program.

In order to cover the material adequately, the planned study will have to meet two major obligations: it must review each program separately and then check on the possible interrelationships between all of them; and it must pay attention to the evolution of research designs. Such a double approach—systematic and historical—is indispensable in the case of material which clearly represents a sequence in time. It will be seen that with autonomous research the two approaches overlap.

The first task—analysis and evaluation of each program—requires a series of procedures which will be presented here schematically.

Assuming a specific program is under consideration, one might conveniently begin with ascertaining its scope. Since, by definition, the program covers long-range activities and therefore extends over an unlimited period, it should be expected to materialize in a large number of projects. The communications program, which dates as far back as 1937, certainly does. The professions program, initiated in 1950, is designed to investigate not only the development of physicians, which is being done now, but the socialization processes in other professions as well; and this may not be the end of it. The possibility that a research institute intent on continuing a promising program is forced to postpone or disrupt it for overriding organizational reasons will be considered in due time.

The next step consists in defining the degree of continuity attained by the program's consecutive projects. That continuity is of the essence within this context can be inferred from a simple theoretical reflection. One is safe in assuming that empirical research, as practiced in the research centers on the campus, is animated by a desire for the objectivity of exact science. In any case, when probing into the given social phenomena it tends to rid itself of preconceived ideas about the whole of society. However, phenomena which are not viewed from the angle of an idea encompassing them, immediately change from definable entities into indeterminate complexes pregnant with numerous possibilities and potentialities. Merton hints of this indeterminacy when comparing the different roles which two types of experts assume in advising, say, our policy makers—(1) the "unattached intellectual," a university teacher or so who may give advice unhampered by administrative consideration, and (2) the "bureaucratic intellectual" who, as an official, must keep his suggestions within the framework of directives binding for all office-holders. Unlike the latter, the "unattached" expert is free to submit to the policy makers an "indeterminate" number of alternatives and choices (which however, as Merton judiciously adds, are rarely needed because of their all but unavoidable remoteness from bureaucratic concerns and "practicable" solutions—indeterminacy thus marking a kind of freedom which to the expert means a "purgatory" rather than a blessing) Conversely, whether the "bureaucratic" expert resents the limitations imposed upon him or succeeds in rationalizing them, these very limitations predetermine the range of his propositions. He operates in a well-contoured area instead of having to ponder indeterminate possibilities. In the words of Merton, the bureaucratic intellectual often "finds himself in a position where he is called upon to provide information for alternative or specific policies which have already been formulated by policy makers.... His perspectives are fixed accordingly.... He may or may not be aware that he is ignoring possible alternatives in his research by focusing on the consequences or modes of implementing limited alternatives which have been presented to him. He may overlook the fact that view to alternatives A and B means ignoring alternatives C and D."[3]

In view of the inherent indeterminacy of scientific pursuits it is well-nigh inevitable that any particular undertaking of organized research should yield only fragmentary results—fragmentary in the sense that they leave unanswered many a question arising in the course of research. Supposing a program includes the projects A, B, C, etc.: then each project is likely to investigate at least one aspect of the problems bound up with the overall themes or issues of that program; but in doing so it will presumably open up new aspects not yet considered. Accordingly, the following alternatives suggest themselves (provided the program is not discontinued at a certain stage of its implementation for scientific or organizational reasons):

(1) The projects of a program represent scattered rather than mutually connected attempts to approach what may cursorily be called the objectives of that program. The Bureau material does not include fitting examples. Nevertheless, to illustrate this alternative, it is perhaps permissible to discount, for the sake of experiment, the unity of intentions actually underlying the political behavior program. Then "political behavior" appears as a conglomerate of projects which have not much in common, except for the fact that their subject matter lies in the area of politics. These projects, or rather groups of projects, are: (a) studies of voting decisions which to a large extent must be traced to the concern, inherent in communications research, with mass media effects; (b) a major study of the Printers' Union which, among other things, tries to explain why this union is the only one to retain the two-party system; (c) research in institutional patterns typical of parties and other organizations; (d) codification of our current knowledge of the political process in America. At least on the surface there is a definite lack of coherence between the pursuits under the title "political behavior." To say it once more, they are in effect interrelated and the impression that they are not has been created only to help the reader imagine a program whose variegated projects do not seem to converge toward a common goal or so. It is of course possible that such divergent approaches will be successfully combined or synthesized in a later stage of research. This has happened more than once in the natural sciences.

(2) The projects of a program form a sequence of substantially interlinked propositions, with B starting from where A ends and C being contingent on B. Development in the field of "communications and opinion formation" can be interpreted as following this pattern. Interest in the effects of mass

communications, especially short-term campaigns, originally led the investigators to concentrate on "audience research," mass media content, relevant differences between the media, and the respondents' psychological predispositions—factors supposed to influence, if not change, given opinions and attitudes. Yet studies of the political effects of radio and newspapers showed that, along with the social environment, interpersonal relations play a much larger role in decision making than mass communications proper. Hence a marked shift of emphasis to the respondent's group affiliations the functions which small everyday groups with their "opinion leaders," and gate-keepers, etc. assume in the mass persuasion process. The forthcoming Elmira study, says Mcphee, stresses "social processes as compared to the mass media by a ratio of perhaps five to one in page volume and at least double that ratio in intellectual concern."[4] This new orientation, which belongs among the more recent phases of the program, resulted in increasing awareness of the "two-step (or multiple-step) flow" of communications.[5] Also, once the primary group was recognized as a sort of shunting station, an intermediary center through which most media messages pass—and rarely pass without being refracted or changed—the real effects of latter could be defined more accurately than was possible before.

It is noteworthy that this very sequence of approaches, so characteristic of the whole program, recurs in one of its subgroups which, under the heading "international communications," comprises a series of studies of mass media effects in the Near and Middle East. The first report (on Greece) was essentially audience research with the emphasis on communications behavior, while the report on Egypt, carried out at a later date, featured the role of social stratifications and interpersonal relations in the communications process. In addition, as research advanced, typical attitudes toward the great issues of traditionalism and Westernization were brought into focus.

(3) A third alternative, presumably the most frequent one, would be a palpable continuity of research designs, punctuated with projects which somehow sidetrack the main line of evolution. They may be in the nature of excursions, as was the case with several studies under the population program—one tackling problems of fertility in the Caribbean islands, another dealing with long-term population predictions; sponsored by this program division, both studies were only loosely connected with its more permanent pursuits. There are also projects or groups of projects which deviate from the overall course of the program inasmuch as they mark a trend abandoned later on; they represent, or are believed to represent, a dead end rather than a link in the chain of approaches. The question is whether some of these seeming blind alleys were not actually valuable advances unrecognized as such at the time. It may be assumed in retrospect that the

content analysis studies of the early 'forties—studies motivated by an interest in the possible effects of mass media content—were given up prematurely. This would seem to follow from Arnheim's study, "The World of the Daytime Serial" (*Radio Research, 1942–1943*) in which he elaborates on the frequent occurrence and paramount significance of the "leader" figure in soap operas. He characterizes the leader as an "influential" in the current sense, describes him in reference to small groups and explicitly mentions that he is often of low social standing. But since subsequent investigations failed to build from those first exercises in qualitative content analysis, the clues which the latter offered to existing behavior patterns and communications habits were not followed up either. Were it not for this neglect, the variable of interpersonal relations might have been discovered at an earlier stage of research.

In case some sort of continuity is discernible, analysis is faced with the task of assessing its direction. Three types of direction stand out conspicuously.

First type: It may be assumed that the program under consideration opens with a project rich in findings. Nevertheless, this project can hardly be expected to fulfill the objectives envisaged; rather, the contributions it makes will raise new problems which demand to be tackled also. Yet instead of proceeding from problem to problem with the vigor of the initial project, the subsequent investigations just elaborate on its necessarily fragmentary solutions. In other words, the theoretical impetus behind the opening moves wears off; and for lack of it research threatens to lose itself in sheer technicalities and a jungle of empirical facts. From the viewpoint of the study this would be a downhill movement. There is no Bureau program that deteriorates in such a way. But what about this or that section of a program? If isolated artificially, the projects which made up radio audience research might serve as an example. All of them were based on the assumption that radio provides stimuli which more or less directly affect the listeners' opinion and attitudes. Hence the sustained concern with medium exposure, audience likes and dislikes, etc. The sequence of studies in this field, most of them commissions, moved in a direction marked by increasingly refined statistical measurements and analytical procedures (see, for instance, Herta Herzog's comparison between listeners and non-listeners in "What Do We Really Know About Daytime Serial Listeners?"); however, the basic assumptions which kept research on the move were taken for granted throughout. To be precise, they were actually questioned: as has been mentioned above, some of the pertinent studies brought out implications transcending the scope of audience research proper; and after all, the limitations of this particular approach are now fully recognized. And yet one gets the impression that the research trend under consideration tended to perpetuate itself even after its sources had dried out and that, for lack of new substantive problems, the technical refinements it produced became more and more an end in itself.

The second type manifests itself in a sequence of projects which actually do explore various aspects of the problems involved. Yet none of these projects poses more relevant questions than the others. Assuming the first of them is on a medium level of significance, then the sequence does not gravitate toward issues of greater or lesser consequence but unfolds from beginning to end on the level thus defined—the very level to which Merton's middle-ground argument refers. Evidently the sequence follows a course which is much in the nature of an indeterminate meandering through the maze of social reality. To the extent to which the population program organizes information about urbanization it might be representative of such an evolution. Or take again communications research: the consecutive projects of this program can be conceived as a continuity evolving on about the same medium level. In order to account for the causes of mass media effects, they have emphasized one possible influence after another in the process, from media content via psychological predispositions to interpersonal relations. These successive propositions presumably parallel each other with regard to their relative significance. Provided the series they form is not cut short by a new approach putting them so to speak into brackets—a possibility which seems to come true especially in the Elmira study—there is no earthly reason why exploration of the las-mentioned factor of interpersonal relations should not challenge the researchers to introduce a new factor, and so one. The series might be continued. To be sure, this movement from aspect to aspect, position to position, results in an accumulation of knowledge within the areas investigated, but it does not amount to progress in the sense that it would yield increasingly significant knowledge.

Here is where the third type of direction comes in: instead of evolving invariably on the same level of significance, the successive pursuits advance toward the frontiers of empirical research, regions in which basic problems and far-reaching issues begin to assert themselves. It is fairly obvious that Merton insists on middle-ground theories only because he considers them a prerequisite of the transition from empirical to basic research; that is, they would somehow resemble the artificial satellites indispensable for space travel. This advance toward the frontiers—or is it rather a return of empirical research to its origins?—may be illustrated by shat has just been called a new approach in the area where communications research and research in decision-making processes join forces. The following is a more or less hypothetical reconstruction of latest developments in this area. They lead, it may be assumed, from the recognition of the influence which interpersonal relations exert on the individual's opinions and attitudes to an awareness that the individual is also exposed to the impact of the larger groups to which he belongs, such as church communities, unions, political organizations, etc. Now any larger group is a historical unit; and its specific character owes much to the changes it has it has undergone in the course of time. Consequently, in order to interpret these groups as influences that play a role in decision making, the social scientist must study not only their current sociological structure but set them in a historical perspective as well. For instance, it is quite conceivable that successive generations differ in their stand on the goals which their respective groups promote and that they thus alter the nature of the goals themselves. And it is equally conceivable that the historical sequence of such differences and alternations follows a definable pattern. The authors of the Elmira study, it appears, assume precisely this; in any case they trace some changes in attitudes and opinions to the tendency, believed to be inherent in each new generation, to evolve a new set of preferences. Research, then extends its interpretative effort to include what may be termed the "historical factor." It is important to grasp the meaning of this step. In achieving it, the researchers do not simply add an explanatory factor on the same level of medium significance as those preceding it—an alternative exemplified above—but definitely go beyond that level. Indeed, the inclusion of history confronts them with such basic problems as how to integrate historical exegesis and sociological analysis or how to utilize historical entities within the framework of empirical procedures. Similar advances toward basic theory are noticeable elsewhere. In the Printers' Union study the customary empirical approach is supplemented by an exposition of relevant historical processes. And one is safe in conjecturing that the religious program in the making will have to come to grips with the history of the Churches and the institutional implications of various theological concepts. All of which implies that the involvement in basic theory and the concern with substantive issues of high significance are closely interrelated. Otherwise expressed, the incorporation of the "historical factor" challenges research to raise questions that bear on large provinces of social reality, if not on the character of our society as a whole.

The scheme presented, then, serves to analyze each program for its scope, its inner coherence and the course it is taking. It need hardly be mentioned that the scheme has no function other than to give a general idea of how any program should be approached. Actually the material may call for variations in treatment and/or additional queries. This would, for instance, apply to projects carried out with other university agencies. Take the long-term study of social factors relating to hypertension: a joint enterprise of the Bureau and Columbia's School of

Public Health, its evolution is certainly conditioned by the fact that it grows out of interdisciplinary research. The necessity for social scientists and medical experts to collaborate in this field is obvious. Nevertheless, one will also have to consider the possibility that such teamwork entails compromises lowering the intensity of design. This might happen, for example, when one expert group nurtures doubts about certain notions of the other but, for lack of competence, must somehow put up with them. The task of reconciling divergent approaches not only mechanically poses problems which involve the organizational setup. It would therefore seem desirable to examine the organizational aspects of the hypertension project with a view to finding out about their impact, if any, on its scientific significance.

After the autonomous programs have been checked individually, the question of whether or not they are interrelated arises. In the case of the Bureau most of them are. It has already been shown that a large section of the political behavior program—all the projects inquiring into the motivations behind voting decisions—is an outgrowth of the communications program with its emphasis on the role which the mass media play in decision making. As has equally been pointed out, research under these programs arrives at the conclusion that an individual's decisions are strongly influenced by the small everyday groups to which he belongs. Well, the factor of interpersonal relations is also taken into account in the professions program; the study of trainees at a medical school combs student diaries for indications about the kind of influence which the "opinion leaders" among the trainees exert on their fellow-students.[6] And this suggests that the interest in the socialization of professionals and the preoccupation with voting behavior have something in common. Both bear on changes in attitudes and opinions. The main difference between the study of medical trainees on the one hand and some study of an election campaign on the other is perhaps that the former investigates long-term transformation processes, while the latter concentrates on such changes as may be effected by short-term operations. That the absorption in social dynamics does not lead to a neglect of social issues is demonstrated by the Bureau's efforts to develop a major program covering the sociology of religion. There is little doubt that this program falls into line with the afore-mentioned autonomous pursuits. It is likely to parallel and complement the studies of the political process in America. It will definitely carry over institutional research to a new area. And it may well add to our knowledge of the substantive influences that condition widespread attitudes; interestingly enough, the data on which the current Polio study draws intimate that people's choices and decisions are in a measure determined by their religious affiliations. Threads thus lead from area to area, unit to unit. Only the population program is relatively unconnected with the rest of the autonomous output—a lack of coherence which has certainly facilitated its recent organizational separation from the Bureau.

Finally, some thought should be given to the interplay between substantive and methodological endeavors. It is evident that these two branches of research depend upon each other: substantive problems cannot be effectively tackled unless appropriate methods for getting at them have been devised; and conversely, any advance in methodology stands a fair chance of bringing hitherto unsuspected aspects of substantive problems into view. Substance calls for method, and method makes appear substance. The latter sequence—from research techniques to new aspects of social phenomena—is of particular interest. Take the panel method: application of this technique, which the Bureau developed as a means of studying the dynamics of attitudes and opinions, yielded insight, otherwise difficult to gain, into the "regressive" effects of campaigns launched during an election period or so to win over opponents and entice the indifferent; actually, instead of swaying the minds, such pressures often strengthen group resistance to the campaign goals and also prompt the individual to revert to the very ideas they combat. The differentiation between high-motivated and low-motivated decisions at which the researchers arrived when utilizing reason analysis is likewise of substantive interest. What latent structure analysis implies for the projective tests and for depth psychology in general remains to be seen.

It has been tacitly assumed till now that there is an equilibrium between substantive and methodological pursuits. But the possibility that one branch of research grows rampant at the expense of the other should not be overlooked. Any such lack of balance has dangerous consequences; to paraphrase a famous statement of Kant's, substantive concepts without appropriate methods are "blind," while methods without substantive concepts are "empty." Affinity for substance being rare, the second alternative is more likely to occur. And this leads back to the Bureau. The question is whether its absorption in methodology has ever exceeded its genuine preoccupation with social problems proper. In their recent paper, "Friendship As a Social Process: A Substantive and Methodological Analysis," which is based on the housing study, Lazarsfeld and Merton focus on this particular issue, trying to demonstrate that methodological explorations are prerequisite to substantive discoveries or at least facilitate them considerably. Since the paper can be assumed to be representative of the Bureau's research intentions, a thorough probing into it—a probing into its latent emphases rather than manifest arguments—might reveal something about the kind of relationship which the Bureau tends to establish between these two independent modes of research.

So far the material has been dealt with systematically. Now the history of the research institute's autonomous activities will have to be considered. Not all of it, though; for systematic analysis has already involved the dynamics of these activities, if in a fragmentary manner. Indeed, the preceding paragraphs about the continuity (or noncontinuity) of successive research propositions and the direction in which they follow each other take in a measure care of developments in this field. What counts in the present stage is to supplement the fragmentary data thus provided by information enabling us to see the various sequences of autonomous aspirations and realizations in their historical context. Speaking of the Bureau, one would for instance like to learn whether it has always patterned the relationship between methodological and substantive analysis on the model set in the Lazarsfeld-Merton paper mentioned above. Along with such conceptual changes, the historical survey would also have to cover the impact of several relatively external factors on the evolution of the Bureau's autonomous research. No doubt university influences play a role in this evolution; and so do, perhaps, atmospheric conditions—the ideas and moods that frame people's outlook in any given period. The emphasis which the Bureau has placed throughout on a psychological approach to social phenomena presumably reflects the still undiminished prestige of psychology in this country. Nor is it by sheer accident that during the war the Bureau manifested a certain preference for content analysis studies; general concern with the effectiveness of our propaganda message in those years decidedly favored research along these lines. By the same token, the Bureau's increasing interest in religion may have something to do with a change in intellectual climate; judging from the non-fiction column of the bestseller lists, there seems to be a growing desire for values and contents apt to imbue life with meaning.[7]

What holds true of the Bureau, may not, or not completely, apply to other organizations of similar status, it is therefore planned to review also the autonomous output of, say, the research centers at the Universities of Chicago, Michigan and Harvard. This investigation will not be exhaustive, for this sole purpose is to provide such additional information as is indispensable for an evaluation of autonomous research in general.

In order to evaluate the material analyzed, two questions—both formulated at the outset—will have to be answered: What is the significance of autonomous research, as cultivated by the institutes on the campus? And in what ways may the latter's organizational requirements affect the character of these pursuits?

Regarding the first question, it has been assumed in the preceding pages that the significance of empirical research grows with its increasing immersion in social theory and in substantive problems leading up to the whole of society or even bringing it into play. Hence the necessity of ascertaining the extent to which autonomous research actually acknowledges these central concerns of sociology. Here is the place where, in the case of the Bureau, all the previous appraisals of its activities in the areas of communications research, political behavior, etc. must be integrated into an evaluation of its total autonomous output.

Yet this is only part of the story, if perhaps its most important part. Viewed from another angle, autonomous research reveals itself to be significant for reasons which have nothing to do with its greater or lesser devotion to basic theory and major issues. An analogy may illustrate this kind of significance which should not be neglected at the final stage of evaluation. Supposing a culture-minded person who has been exposed to abstract art for years and years without, however, grasping its meaning, drops into an exhibition of recent portraits all of which indulge, unmoved, in the old realistic manner. What he experiences there is presumably this: even though he is reluctant to endorse abstract painting, he nevertheless feels deeply disturbed at the sight of pictures which pretend to ignore its existence. They strike him as unreal—as more unreal, in effect, than any of the abstract approaches. And this in turn will prompt him to realize the element of necessity in modern art. Similarly, now that the methods of collecting and processing empirical data have become a matter of course, even the most significant speculations about the nature of society take on a ghost-like character if no attempt is made to test them with all the available means. In an era of organized social research their magic wears thin—a change in atmosphere which perhaps the speculative minds themselves would be the las to deny. There seems to be something inevitable and compelling about the movement toward institutionalized research. But as the product of an irreversible evolution this type of research with its empiricism and its emulation of exact science is certainly significant in its own right. (The task of defining its peculiar meanings would involve an inquiry into the characteristics of contemporary thought).

The second question concerns the implications of organizational permanence for autonomous research. Among the advantages of a research center the following may be mentioned:

(1) It offers to scientists, lone scholars or not, facilities that could not be had otherwise. Projects which involve extensive sampling, tabulating, etc.,

largely depend on the existence of an institute geared to assembling and processing the material needed.

(2) Permanence insures large-scale autonomous research. There is every reason to assume that such autonomous projects as the Elmira study or the Decatur study—projects requiring a relatively long incubation period and the utilization of variegated research experiences—could be developed only within the framework of the Bureau. The same applies, of course, to any long-term program; he professions program, for instance, is bound to unfold in a series of interrelated projects and therefore presupposes institutional stability. Nor should it be forgotten that permanence affords the administrative advantage of staffing a project according to the requirements of the moment. The evolution of the population program is a case in point; it started, so to speak, with no staff at all and then gradually took on larger proportions, whereby the Bureau with its University affiliations was in a position to supply adequate personnel whenever needed.

Organizational continuity does not warrant the continuity of research propositions. Several co-existing autonomous programs may or may not be interrelated. In the case of their interdependence all of them appear to stem from unified and truly spontaneous research intentions. But is this unity, ideal as it may seem, under all circumstances preferable to a conglomerate of programs which show no affinity for each other? It is entirely conceivable that the organization in charge of the latter considers it its foremost task to follow up the mutually unconnected propositions of different scholars. And provided these propositions are on a high level of significance, the unity reached in the first case need not be superior to the incoherence in the second. As has been pointed out above (pp. 23–24), the Bureau has on the whole given preference to the first alternative—programs forming a unit of closely interlinked queries and approaches; in fact, only its population program is somewhat out of tune with the rest of its autonomous output. This tendency toward coherence testifies to the theoretical interests of the Bureau's leading scientists.

(3) Permanence breeds traditions, thereby assuming functions vitally important in fields where reading cannot substitute for training and a pooling of skills is of the essence. However, traditions might also render those conditioned by them less flexible in their dealings with new problems. Has the Bureau succeeded in evading these dangers? That its staff members are sensitive to the tradition which grows on them and consider it a positive influence rather than a burden, can be inferred from the fact that they value highly what one of them calls "Bureau culture" and another "communalized language and behavior." Should these favorable responses turn out to be justified, one might try to

establish a correlation between the particular "culture" of the Bureau and its aversion to organizational rigidity. Indeed, the Bureau has always been reluctant to enforce a strict division of labor, with technical experts specializing in the diverse research operations. Perhaps such a relative looseness of organization accounts to an extent for traditions which do not stifle intellectual enterprise; on the other hand, this very laxity, if laxity it is, is likely to interfere with streamlined efficiency.

(4) In the interest of its survival any academic research center is obliged to take on assignments from private or public social organizations. But contrary to what might be expected, this necessity sometimes proves to be an advantage. For certain assignments either raise problems in line with the center's existing autonomous endeavors or involve data stimulating it to turn the spotlight on areas not yet investigated. These possibilities will be discussed and exemplified in the subsequent chapter.

And so will the disadvantages bound up with organizational permanence. Suffice it here to epitomize them in a slogan-like manner: commissioned research tends to obstruct autonomous research. (The just-mentioned assignments benefiting it represent hardly ever more than a minority of cases after all). Otherwise expressed, in order to achieve permanence, this condition prerequisite to sustained autonomous activities, the institute on the campus cannot help endangering the latter—means threatening to defeat the ends. The paradoxical situation in which the institute thus finds itself because of its eternal need for support is amply illustrated by the history of the Bureau. In 1946, for instance, the Bureau planned to prepare a much-needed syllabus on research methods and their application. Since the Foundations showed little interest in this proposition, the funds required for its execution had to be derived from the profits of commercial projects. The Bureau, that is, was forced to accept a number of "bread and butter" assignments for the sole purpose of being able to finance the syllabus. However, these assignments were such a strain on the staff's time that work on the syllabus itself, which should have been completed in 1949, fell far behind schedule. In fact, the job is not yet finished.

Its inherent desire for permanence, then, puts the research center into a permanent dilemma. It must constantly try to reconcile, somehow, autonomous interests with economic needs. And it cannot do so without compromising the institute's standards and goals. Scientists associated with it may have to devote some time and effort to securing new funds. Projects unlikely to prove rewarding scientifically may have to be accepted. The Bureau's list of unpublished reports includes studies of the effects of toothpaste and Ex-Lax commercials and of the reasons for which razor blade consumers change their brands—investigations whose main value presumably consists in enabling the Bureau to get over a financial crisis. (It is understood, of course, that, given enough time and money, even an inquiry into the responses to Ex-Lax commercials might afford insight of consequence).

II. COMMISSIONED RESEARCH

The second area to be investigated is commissioned research. For lack of sufficient university support the social research center must accept or even covet commissions from outside the campus in order to be able to fulfill its academic obligations, let alone survive. That much has been anticipated in the last pages of the preceding chapter. Most organizations of this kind are largely self-sustaining.

Analysis is faced with the task of bringing out the characteristics of the center's commissioned research as well as the problems bound up with it. The subsequent two schemes, analogous to those for autonomous research, roughly illustrate how this objective might best be achieved. The first is devised to explore the common subject matter in a systematic manner, while the second—a series of questions rather than a scheme—serves to cover its evolution.

To begin with the systematic part of analysis, support may come from (philanthropic) foundations, social welfare of social action groups, government agencies and private business organizations. It would seem advisable to check at the very outset on the function which foundations assume as sponsors. To be sure, like most donors they can be expected to grant funds only for work in areas in which they themselves are particularly interested, but once this limitation is taken into account, one will in all fairness have to admit that at least part of them tend to support scholarly enterprises which otherwise might have be dropped. In any case, the Bureau requested, and received, foundation subsidies mainly for the sake of its autonomous pursuits. Assuming, this holds true in a general way, foundation-sponsored projects do not strictly fall under the title of commissioned research and may therefore be disregarded in the following.

There remain, then, all those projects which issue from the vortex of society itself. They put two grave problems before the research institute on the campus: To what extent do they conform to its scholarly aspirations? And are they compatible with its ethical code, professional or otherwise? The first question gives rise to a breakdown of commissioned research according to its scientific significance. It appears that two different kinds of commissions can be considered relevant scientifically—projects in keeping with the institute's existing autonomous programs and projects opening up new areas of research. (What the latter alternative means remains to be seen.) But since the institute may also have to take on assignments which offer little scientific interest, altogether three types of projects claim attention here. They will be discussed presently.

The first type comprises projects which somehow fall into line with the institute's actual autonomous activities, supplementing them or leading beyond them in this or that direction. Their most desirable emergence may be a luck coincidence, as in the case of the so-called "drug" study which the Bureau was recently asked to prepare. Since the client wants to learn why doctors prefer certain drugs to others which have likewise been brought to their attentions, this study, as it were, invites further analysis of the factors behind personal influences and the processes of decision making. Yet assignments of this type are less infrequent than the slim chance of a windfall would lead one to expect. The reason is that the research center does not just wait for them. There is always the possibility of personal relations between the exponents of research and those in need of it; and such relations, especially if grounded in "value-homophily," may well give rise to "fitting" projects—fitting in the sense that they satisfy both the client's demands and the autonomous requirements. Here belong the Bureau's commissioned Middle-East studies which look exactly as if they were a straight extension of its communications research. Also, the institute may manage to "plant" a project which it would like to carry out for reasons of its own. It is evident that projects in this vein must be tailored to the presumable wishes of potential clients. A good case in point is the Decatur study which covers a wide range of personal influences. The Bureau approached a publishing company which specializes in popular low-brow magazines with the idea of this study, arguing as follows: In order to increase your success with the audience, you should know more about the way in which it is actually affected. Now advanced research shows that most people are strongly determined in their choices by the judgements of other people—in particular those who enjoy some prestige as "opinion leaders." You will be all the more interested in the kind of influence these opinion leaders exert since they are also found among your readers and advertisers. Let us therefore locate relevant "influentials" in four areas of concern to you: marketing, movie preferences, fashions and political affairs. Etc., etc. The argumentation clicked with the publishing house, and the resultant study built from the Bureau's autonomous propositions.

However, even the most "fitting" project may have strings attached to it. This observation calls for an excursion into contractor-client relationships and their possible consequences for research. To start with the embryonic stage of a commission, the prospective client is not a blank but has certain problems on his mind which he wants to research institute to solve. For instance, a government agency may wish to learn about the implications of organizational measures whose affectiveness is open to doubt and to get suggestions for an improvement of its organizational setup (see the unpublished Bureau report: "Problems of Film Production in Underdeveloped Countries"). To decline research is not so much an end in itself as a means to an end. In the course of his preliminary discussions with the representative of the institute—the contractor—his problems and ideas, usually vague at the beginning, can be expected to develop into a manageable project which may or may not be promising scientifically. If the latter possibility is discounted for the moment, the project either fits into the institute's autonomous output or—to anticipate the second type of commissions—bears on scientifically important issues not yet covered by the research group. But even so the contractor may feel dissatisfied with this or that condition which the client would like to impose. It is quite conceivable, for example, that the client is interested in questions which could be fully answered only by way of research operations requiring larger expenses than he is prepared to defray. Presumably the contractor will try to obtain more adequate terms. There are several instances in which the Bureau successfully prevailed upon the client to expand the scope of the commission. In the case of the tea study—a project intended to explain why people might change over to tea—the client agreed to the inclusion of a reason analysis which was not originally planned. Similarly, the sponsors of the oil progress project let themselves be convinced that they should enable the Bureau to use the data assembled for an additional latent structure analysis apt to inform them about the character of permanent consumer attitudes toward the oil industry.

Assuming now the client does not remove the restrictions which tend to interface with a satisfactory performance as envisioned by the contractor, then the latter is of course free to reject the assignment. Yet he may as well accept it because of (1) its financial attractiveness, (2) the opportunity it offers for student training, and (3) its scientific potentialities. The first two reasons will be considered shortly. Regarding the last, the following case is fairly typical: A client, concerned with problems which are not particularly alluring from a scholarly angle, insists on financing research only for a period of time long enough to tackle these problems but not sufficiently long to do justice to the more interesting features of the project. In such a case the research institute may or may not be able to go beyond the commission proper and subject, on its own account, the material involved to a new analysis. The history of the Bureau provides examples of both alternatives, especially the first one. Thus the Middle-East studies were followed up in a number of papers, among them an article demonstrating the inherent possibilities of "secondary analysis";[8] moreover, a book on the Middle East is now being prepared which reverts to the interviews from which the original studies were drawn in an attempt to delineate a few conspicuous personality types in this area and their different relations to the forces of traditionalism and Westernization. The forthcoming Decatur study re-analyzes the date of commissioned report for a variety of novel approaches. The report on Satellite mentality—a qualitative analysis of interviews with escapes from behind the Iron Curtain—will have a sequel also. On the other hand, it happened repeatedly that the Bureau just delivered the goods and left it at that for lack of time and money. To be sure, the girl scout study answered the questions raised by this organization as the stand of its volunteer workers on religiously restricted troops and on the policy which national headquarters should follow in the denominational field; yet from the angle of autonomous research the study had to be abandoned prematurely, for there was no opportunity to bring out its scientifically rewarding implications. The same applies to the Quick study; the hundred depth interviews with Quick readers on which it is based still wait for further exploration. Nor was the Bureau able till now to meet the challenge of the report on the social factors concomitant with venereal diseases. Generally speaking, whether or not frustrations prevail over fulfillments may be inferred from the research center's total record. Whatever the Bureau's achievements and failures in this respect, one is safe in assuming that it shows throughout a propensity for carrying on promising investigations beyond their commissioned stage, even though external conditions prevent it from doing so in a number of cases. It would be interesting to check on the amount of Bureau material which lies dormant for the time being.

As has been summarily indicated above, the commissioned projects of the second type open up new areas of research; that is, they involve issues which the research institute has not yet considered but now finds worth-while because of their scientific relevance. Perhaps the projects hint of hitherto unsuspected changes in social structure or prove rewarding for methodological reasons. It is also conceivable that they impress upon the researchers an aspect of social life which calls for further treatment. The Bureau has carried out enough projects which might give rise to additional large-scale programs. For instance, the studies in the fields of hypertension and venereal diseases suggest the development of a program covering various problems of social medicine. By the same token, the polio projects, the girl scout project, and the Episcopal study—an inquiry into the responses of clergy and parishioners to the secular activities of the Episcopal

Church—make, independently of each other, inroads in the area of institutional research; hence the possibility that the Bureau will sometime find it desirable to gather the loose ends they contain and investigate this relatively unexplored area under a separate title. Incidentally, the Episcopal study may well be the nucleus of a future major program on religion. to add a last example, the Decatur study and, perhaps, also the so-called disk jockey study (which was commissioned by Broadway Music Inc. and concerned itself not only with the motives behind the disc jockey's choice of records but involved, up to a point, the organization and the functioning of the popular music business) would seem to encourage new approaches to the substantive issue of popular culture. The Decatur study does so explicitly by pointing to the need for a special research program devoted to the uses which people make of the mass media as well as the gratifications they derive from them.

It is true that any research center tends to develop certain preferences which in turn and likely to attract assignments of specific interest to it; but despite these preselective influences such commissions must be considered fortunate accidents. Originating with private or public social agencies they cannot possible be predicted. The moral is that applied social research is of the essence. A research center confining itself to purely spontaneous pursuits, would perhaps never chance upon the significant issues and themes which society at large continually brings to this attention. Otherwise expressed, autonomous research is not the only raison d'être of a university institute. Rather, its' very scientific interests challenge any such organization to rely in a measure on unforeseeable commissions. Even supposing the organization is financially not obliged to accept assignments from outside the campus, it nevertheless will have to lie in wait for them in order to live up to its academic duties; it must so to speak leave the campus to achieve full scholarly status within its confines. Only by taking advantage of the "accidental" questions which society raises—questions which form the viewpoint of society itself are of course anything but accidental—can the social scientist hope to keep tabs on the living matter he is called upon to study. That organized research exposes him to the hazards of empirical ventures is perhaps its most peculiar contribution to the social sciences. For true as it is that empirical research serves to verify theoretical speculation, it is no less true that social theory may be advanced by empirical research feeding on chance opportunities. " 'Applied' research," says Stouffer who also declares himself in favor of a constant shuttling back and forth between theory and empirical data, "can speed up thinking about the kind of basic theory that is needed. . . . Often the pressure to 'explain' or interpret a surprising empirical practical finding may lead to a reflection which organizes a good many such finding."[9] Merton holds the same opinion, trying to substantiate it throughout his writings. The above examples intimate that the Bureau is ready to seize upon providential "accidents" whenever possible. Sometimes it even takes the initiative in bringing them about. Thus the Bureau presently aims at establishing, with the cooperation of other Columbia units, a Research Center for greater New York designed to survey the problems and need of the New York community; this project which definitely belongs to applied research may set off many a contribution to social theory.

The third type of commissioned research includes projects of little, if any, scientific interest. It should be kept in mind, though, what has already been said in earlier contexts—that even a seemingly insignificant commission, such as a study to improve the sales of some toothpaste brand, may lead up to important substantive problems, provided the researchers have sufficient time on their hands to get at them (p. 32). To be sure, since applied social research is currently in demand, well-reputed research organizations are perhaps in a position to select from among the assignments offered them those which conform best to their essential goals. Yet whether or not this slight margin of choices yields the hoped-for results depends upon the character of the inflowing commissions. In addition, an organization's need for support may be so pressing that it defeats all selective efforts. Hence the possibility or even likelihood that many a university institute carries out projects which just amount to "hackwork." The above-mentioned studies, chosen at random from the list of the Bureau's unpublished reports (p. 32), are certainly true to type and they are by no means the only ones. But it should not be forgotten that at least some of these projects benefit the institute's training program and thus assume an academic function after all. In the Bureau such unavoidable chores may be entrusted to relative beginners who, in executing them under supervision, learn how to develop a code, train the coders, instruct the machine room, and build tables from the tabulated data.

Decisions about the acceptance or rejection of a commission hinge on moral considerations no less than on estimates of its scientific relevance. These considerations stem from two sources—the professional ethics of the university institute and the general ethical code to which it feels it should submit as a member of society. To deal first with matters of professional integrity, there is little need for dragging in instances in which the client's inquisitiveness goes hand in hand with a desire to influence, however subtly, the outcome of research. The institutes on the campus can be relied upon to resist attempts at manipulation.[10] Yet for familiar reasons they will not always be in a position to reject assignments which center around uninteresting goals—say, fund raising for a social action group—or insignificant social topics and under the given conditions involve mainly drudgery. Examples of Bureau reports in this vein have been cited above. Referring to several remarks equally made in earlier contexts, one might object that hack work is the work of hacks; that only hacks are likely to ignore the significant implications or connotations of otherwise insignificant subjects. But this objection is not really valid. for even a genius will hardly consider a report on the possible effects of some Ex-Lax commercial a fitting starting- point for excursions into the lofty regions of social theory—let alone that such commissions rarely permit him to take wings.

Academic organizations thus indulging in drudgery evidently lower their scholarly standard; and by the same token, one is inclined to argue, they sin against the rules of conduct obtaining in the university. From the viewpoint of professional ethics, however, their apparent weakness is controversial rather than just objectionable. Supposing an institute cannot survive unless it takes on scientifically insignificant commissions, then the (moral) problem arises whether it is not justified in doing no for the sake of its autonomous pursuits. Should it cease to exist, valuable projects and ideas might never see the light of day. On the other hand, the time consumed by hack work may excessively curtail the time left for the things that count, and in general bad means spoil good ends. Arguments and counterarguments are inexhaustible—which amounts to saying that each case will have to be judged according to its individual merits.

Professional integrity may also be severely tested during the execution of certain projects, scientifically interesting or not. Take the following hypothetical case patterned on the Bureau's above-mentioned study of Satellite mentality (p. 38): A government agency wants to get material analyzed and evaluated which has a direct bearing on cold-war issues—whereby it assumed that the agency does not try to restrict independent research. Yet since the assignment calls for a discussion of real-life conditions behind the Iron Curtain, the presumable effects of Communist propaganda and U.S. propaganda, etc., it is well-nigh inevitable that scientists and researchers should be affected from without and within by the powerful stereotypes that shape public opinion in the area of politics. And the problem is whether or not their moral energies and intense enough to neutralize these all-pervasive influences which tend to color their findings from the outset and even before.

Even atomic physicists have come to realize that they are not only scientists but also citizens and that in consequence they owe allegiance to two ethical codes which might easily conflict with each other. Social scientists are in the same boat; they too may find themselves in a dilemma of conflicting loyalties. Three alternatives present themselves to the mind.

(1) Ethico-political bias vs. a detached scientific approach. A case in point is the Bureau study: "The 'New Internationalism' Under Attack" which was financed by the United World Federalists, an organization interested in a content analysis of some of the publications opposing "World Government." Once the Bureau had accepted this assignment, the staff member in charge of it was faced, consciously or not, with a dilemma, involving the objectivity of research. As a scientist he was certainly eager to present the pros and cons of the movement attacked with complete equanimity; but as a member of the larger community he might have felt urged—out of sympathy for the cause of the client, the very sympathy which, perhaps, prompted the Bureau to take on the commission—to underrate the significance of the counterarguments found in these publications. Actually he seems unwittingly to have succumbed to the latter temptation; it is almost impossible to overlook the apologetic character of his report. In cases like these the research institute had better state explicitly its political preferences or convictions at the very outset so as to avoid being reproached with unscientific partiality. What makes the report under consideration look equivocal, is of course not its underlying concern with world government but its pretense to scientific detachment.

(2) Ethically desirable drudgery. It is entirely possible that a social agency requests some institute on the campus to engage in research which, for all its lack of scientific interest, promises information beneficial to broad strata of the population. For instance, the Health Council of a New Jersey community commissioned the Bureau to determine the extent to which people within the Council's sphere of influence are aware of, and utilize, the public health facilities available to them in their neighborhood. It is evident that such a project represents a service to the larger community. And if one assumes that in case of a conflict between the social and academic codes of ethics the former has precedence over the latter, the Bureau was certainly justified in accepting this professionally unattractive commission. The whole argument adds to the moral controversy about "hack work" by demonstrating that it may be defensible on certain well-defined occasions.

(3) Ethically undesirable projects which, however, might prove attractive scientifically. Here would belong assignments from one political party or factory studies unsupported by the unions. But as Lazarsfeld remarks in a recent memorandum, in many cases it is unfortunately impossible to foresee the category in which an investigation belongs. For instance, a study of employee morale can be used for exploitative as well as remedial purposes and therefore may be morally admissible or undesirable.

At this point an important question arises: to what extent does the professional and ethical behavior of a research center result from conscious reasoning about what academic and civic probity may require in delicate situations? Suffice it to pose the question, which can be answered only on the basis of complete familiarity with the center's unwritten rules and organizational habits. To add a general observation for what it is worth, the sensitivity of an academic organization to professionally and/or socially problematic assignments is likely to increase in direct ratio to its involvement in basis social theory. (Regarding the Bureau, one gets the impression that the soul-searching among its staff member in cases of controversial commissions is matched only by their depressive awareness of the existing financial necessities).

Systematic analysis will have to be supplemented by an inquiry into the dynamics of commissioned research. Among the pertinent variables three are of special interest: the degree of dependence of a research center on outside support; its attitudes toward assignment from such sources; and the character of the assignments themselves. To begin with the first variable, the center's need for support may or may not have remained stable throughout its evolution. Under this title one would like to learn whether, other circumstances being equal, the growth of the center entails an increasing demand for commissions so as to take care of the increase in overhead expenses and keep the larger staff busy. But be this as it may, the Bureau is now as desperately in want of funds as it was in the past. Economic crises continue to mark the normal state of affairs; and much time is still lost in merely soliciting studies (cf. p. 32).

If one keeps the factor of support constant for the sake of simplification, the second variable—attitudes toward commissions—can easily be isolated, provided changes in the nature of the commissions themselves are provisionally disregarded. One of the major questions is obviously whether the research center's policy with regard to scientifically irrelevant studies has undergone significant changes. And if so, in what direction? In order to exemplify procedures, it may be hypothesized that the Bureau originally manifested some laxity in matters of commercial projects and that the laxity of the beginnings has by and by yielded to greater selectivity—a hypothesis, incidentally, which does not seem to be far from the truth. Once this is taken for granted, one will have to speculate on the presumable reasons for such a development from indiscriminate acceptance of any assignment to a less compromising attitude. Both external and internal reasons may account for it: pressures exerted by part of the academic world and influences traceable to the immanent evolution of research itself. In fact, always assuming that the Bureau has actually moved in this direction, it is quite conceivable that is has done so also because its research activities have, by dint of their inner logic, brought into focus increasingly significant issues which in turn have conditioned it to become more critical in its choice. And what about changes in the area of social ethics? According to the general observation advanced above, such a more critical attitude in the professional field might correlate highly with refined notions of what is morally admissible.

So much for attitudes. Concerning commissions—the third variable—they too may have changed their character with the passing of time as a result of changes in social structure and/or a reorientation of the research center itself. The latter alternative can be illustrated by the history of the Bureau, as would seem to follow from an unpublished report on Bureau activities written in 1949 or so. Having stated that, for the first ten years of its existence, the bulk of the Bureau's support came from commercial clients, the author of the report continues: "In the last few years, the Bureau has sought to divorce itself more and more from such sources of support and has increasingly oriented its fund raising activities around philanthropic foundations, social welfare and social action groups, and government departments. This policy has proven relatively successful..." It might be added that under the present Administration assignments from government agencies are dwindling. Study of these changes is indispensable for the correct evaluation of attitudinal developments. Supposing during a given period commissions become more and more scientifically irrelevant, while the Bureau itself, in accordance with the above assumption, show a tendency, constantly gaining in strength, to turn down scientifically unrewarding projects. The Bureau's rejection of hack work during that period—even though this may endanger its financial situation—would surely be proof of its growing awareness of scholarly responsibilities. Conversely, should even those commissions which are not directly solicited by the Bureau more and more center around issues of consequence, the Bureau's increasing affinity for precisely such commissions may also be due to their increasing incidence.

In the interest of an inclusive and well-balanced picture comparative excursions are a "must." Accordingly, it would seem advisable to consult the Harvard, Chicago and Michigan institutes, suggested above for comparisons in the dimensions of autonomous research, on account of their commissioned output as well. On the basis of the whole survey, an attempt can be made to appraise the presumable effects of different interrelationships between these two large groups of research activities. Supposing an institute accepts so many commissions, scientifically attractive or not, that it is no longer in a position to follow up spontaneous research designs: is the preference it thus gives to practical tasks likely to lessen the quality of the solutions it offers? Technically streamlined solutions may be poor in depth and outlook. Perhaps it is possible to determine the ideal ration between autonomous and commissioned research—a ratio acknowledging the double necessity for a university institute to aspire to goals of its own and at the same time profit by such accidental commissions as enable it to feel the pulse of society. And finally, one might try to derive from this "ideal ration" the theoretically desirable proportion between university support and outside support.

There still remain enough queries, but they go beyond the scope of the present study. One of the most impressive themes looming at the horizon is the interplay between applied research and society. If approached from the angle of the former, this theme would call for an inquiry into the actual impact of commissioned research on our social environment. That is, one would have to try to find out about the extent to which public and private social agencies have heeded the suggestions of research institutes and to assess the changes effected. At least part of the ground thus defined might be covered by a project, now under way, of the Ford Foundation which Lazarsfeld mentions in his above-quoted memorandum (p. 46)—a study of the extent to which knowledge in the behavioral sciences has proved useful in practical affairs. The same theme of the interrelationships between applied research and society will also have to be treated with the emphasis on the changing needs and preferences of the latter. Then it would invite examination of the reasons why so many organs of society feel urged to request the services of organized research. And since this is a relatively new and powerful trend, one would eventually have to speculate on its origins. Is it symptomatic of certain changes in the deeper layers of society itself? Yet these questions belong to the future.

III. TRAINING

The third and last area to be investigated is training.

The university institute usually engages in two kinds of training activities—in-service and out-service training. To begin with the latter, it may comprise various educational measures not involving apprenticeship proper. The Bureau provides technical assistance to students on the graduate level, thus supplementing their formal education within the university curriculum. This technical assistance program accommodates students who are preparing term papers, master's theses or doctoral dissertations in two ways: (a) It affords them an opportunity to consult Bureau staff members and at the same time puts at their disposal all the resources in material, machinery, etc., which they may need for their projects. And (b) it acquaints them with specific research operations, such as questionnaire construction, sampling, coding and processing of survey data, etc., by arranging "tutorial" seminars organized on a workshop basis. These seminars are also for the benefit of the in-service trainees, challenging them to acquire skills in areas not yet familiar to them.[11] — In addition, the Bureau occasionally holds courses for groups outside the campus so as to initiate them into the advanced techniques of social research. Such courses were made available, for instance, to executives of a large manufacturing concern, Latin American census officials and German, Japanese and Korean radio broadcasters.

In-service training is to a large extent training on the job. The personnel policy of the Bureau is to provide for a turnover of the research staff every two or three years. Only a small core staff is granted permanent positions in the interest of the work to be done as well as the preservation of the steadily accumulating know-how. Indeed, apprenticeship at a research center would seem to be all the more valuable since certain major research operations—e.g. the "analysis phase" of the survey method—are largely uncodified. They can be learned only in practice. It may also be assumed that of all the contributions which the center makes to the formation of future social scientists intramural training is probably the one which molds them most effectively. In any case, a majority of Bureau trainees feels this way.[12] Analysis will therefore concentrate on in-service training.

The following scheme is divided into two sections, the first bearing on the character of this kind of training, the second on its presumable effect. Regarding its character, three factors can be said to determine it at any given period: (1) the general gals and emphases of the research center; (2) the ways and means of indoctrination; and (3) the "raw material" itself—that is, the criteria by which students are selected and the reasons for which they may wish to join the staff. From the viewpoint of training procedures it would seem more logical to study the last two factors in the reserve order; but since within these contexts special attention is paid to training in its relations to the other functions and obligations of the university institute, the sequence as established here is perhaps preferable.

1. What matters first, then, is the general outlook of the research organization—its prevailing research interests and its overall training objectives. With respect to the former (which show in the output of the center and, therefore, can be inferred from the analyses suggested in the preceding chapters), one is safe in assuming that they condition the scope and direction of training. In fact, because of its well-known preferences in program selection the Bureau

provides fairly intensive training in the areas of communications and political behavior, while somewhat neglecting skills like participation observation or small group dynamics analysis which play a less important role in these areas (cf. p. 40). (Yet a certain one-sidedness is perhaps unavoidable. And it need not harm training. For the task of training is not to teach the trainee all imaginable techniques but to give him a working knowledge of how to acquire, should the need arise, these he has not been taught.)

Carrying this line of investigation a bit further, one might also inquire into the impact on training of changes in research interests. The hypothesis that the style of training will be affected by a shift of emphasis, say, from substantive issues to essentially methodological problems does not seem farfetched. It is quite conceivable that similar emphases tend to prevail in both fields of activities.

By the same token, the views which a research center forms of the purpose of training account for certain characteristics of its educational approach. To say it more cautiously, these particular characteristics strike one as resulting from such views. Thus the institute may fulfill its training duties with an eye to the student's scientific competence rather than his fitness to meet future job requirements—training here being viewed from a predominantly academic angle. Or the institute may feel that, in addition to conforming to the university standards, it should also try to prepare the trainees for the positions available to them upon leaving the campus. Whether or not the line followed by the institute can be traced to its greater or lesser preoccupation with significant autonomous pursuits is an open question. In case of the second alternative—training taking into account the students' careers—one is perhaps entitled to assume that changes in job opportunities will influence educational emphases and procedures.— There is no evidence that the Bureau cares about career prospects beyond the academic confines; it is not "outward-directed" in this sense.

2. Analysis of the ways and means of practical indoctrination requires criteria for what ideal training should be like. A few assumptions may therefore be made at the outset. First, ideal training can be achieved only if the apprentice is confronted, in an ordered progression and under adequate supervision, with all the tasks which a sizeable research project involves from its inception to its last, interpretative stage. Second, ideal training is contingent on favorable environmental conditions—especially the existence of a qualified and dedicated team of staff members who make the novice realize the significance of integrated collective work for empirical research. Many apprentices at the Bureau are aware of what has been labelled its "culture" in earlier contexts (p. 31) and consider it definitely an asset for training.[13] Such culture may somewhat compensate for the

Bureau's one-sidedness in program selection. Third, ideal training should in a meaningful way complement the formal education which the student receives in the disciplines of his choice. To simplify matters, only the first assumption will serve as a frame of reference in the following. The reason is that it alone bears on the training procedure proper.

Before examining these procedures, however, it is advisable to deal separately with two inherent features of academic research organizations and their possible consequences for the training process.

(a) Much as projects advancing autonomous research are of the essence, they may turn out to be a disadvantage to training: centering around high-level prepositions, they require skills which elude the grasp of the beginner. They presuppose training instead of serving its ends. The history of the Bureau, says Pratt, suggest that, in terms of basic training, "routine" projects are preferable to new approaches. Generally speaking, like any complex organization, the research center assumes a variety of functions which it is often difficult to reconcile with each other. Its research goals tend to conflict with its training goals. Accordingly, the higher the status of research for its own sake, the less prestige enjoys training as an end in itself. This seems to hold true of the Bureau. In case of conflict, it has more than once sacrificed its educational aspirations to its scientific aims by giving priority to pioneering studies with a low training potential.

(b) The research center's economic dependence on assignments from social agencies may affect implementation of its training program in two ways.

To find out about these influences one will, first, have to inquire into the reasons for which the center accepts some commission. To be more precise, to what extent is it motivated by pedagogic constructions? In the Bureau the fitness of a commercial project for training purposes seem to be at best a supporting argument in its favor. Other criteria, such as its compatibility with the Bureau's research programs or its value for new developments, are likely to carry more weight. And as might be expected, the awareness that additional funds are needed to keep things going frequently enough tips the balance. This would mean that the training potential of most available projects is a matter of chance rather than planning.

Second, once a project is accepted, the research center assumes responsibilities toward the sponsor which inevitably take precedence of its training duties. And as can be inferred from the passages about the relations between contractor and client (pp. 35–38), the latter often imposes conditions which, though perhaps acceptable in other respects, render efficient training very difficult indeed. Here as everywhere insufficient funds obstruct ideal solutions. It has already been indicated above that, in the case of many a commission, limited support forced the Bureau to concern itself strictly with the practical problems raised by the sponsor even though it would have liked, of course, to carry research beyond them into areas of greater scientific interest. Since such assignments cannot be used to acquaint advanced trainees with the more sophisticated and least codified research operations, educational frustrations add to the scientific ones. They may to deepened by stipulations as to the time period within which the project must be finished. Indeed, the client usually expects the research center to base its time schedule on an estimate of how long it would take an experienced staff to conduct the research involved. Hence the probability that there is rarely enough time left for adequate training. In the Bureau the trainee is frequently put on a job tailored not so much to his specific needs as the needs of the commission under way. And the instruction he receives mainly serves to secure adequate execution of this commission. Many a Bureau trainee realizes that his position is that of a hired help or a technical assistant rather than a trainee. "If the Bureau," says one of them," is to keep on having to furnish work for money, it will be difficult to train people well since this work is more important and always comes first. It cannot be held up for training periods or for responsibilities in the hand of inexperienced people."[14] This appears to be all the more plausible since the necessity of meeting the deadline more often than not puts the project staff under heavy pressure, especially in the crucial final stages. Considering the frequent incidence of rush work in connection with commissions, some thought should be given to its implications. On the surface, it just seems to reduce further the time for training, in particular high-level training. On the other hand, it might have the advantage of conditioning the trainee to a common real-life situation.

At this point the training process itself comes into view. It can be conceived of as a resultant of the efforts made to attain the ideal training goal and the organizational aims and obligations interfering with them. Assuming a beginner holds a job as a coder. The task of training not only consists in teaching him, by way of practice and theory, everything that there is to teach in matters of coding, but also requires that he be prepared for more difficult research operations and then actually promoted according to his capacities. Inclusive training, then, comprises three interrelated steps or activities: (a) training on a specific job; (b) instruction beyond job training proper; and © promotion to successively higher positions. This cycle is likely to renew itself until the highest position is reached.

(a) Training on the job. Along with the above-mentioned constraints arising from the needs of commissioned projects, the research center's commitments may also cause it to keep, say, a coder much longer on his relatively simple job—if simple it is—than would be justified from the viewpoint of training. This possibility is illustrated by the fact that Bureau trainees, mostly beginners, are often retained in one and the same low-level position far beyond the period normally required to get the hang of it. External pressures may thus defeat the beat educational intentions.

(b) Instruction. Training on the job alone is not enough. In order to enable trainees to rise from the ranks, they will have to be initiated into the total aspects of the project in which they participate and also introduced to research procedures on higher levels. This indoctrination may be provided in the form of seminars, such as the Bureau's "tutorial" seminars mentioned at the beginning of the training chapter, or through staff meetings of varying range. Within the framework of its professions program, the Bureau has held regular meetings rallying the staff members of the medical project down to the rank and file. There are also committee sessions which offer interested trainees an opportunity to learn about Bureau activities with which they are not directly concerned. Altogether these measures represent an attempt to reduce the dangerous consequences—dangerous to training—of the Bureau's strong dependence on commercial assignments. As has been hinted above, it is true that Bureau staff members in charge of a commission have often too much work on their hands—what with client meetings, organization of the project, its representation, etc.—to expand training beyond the immediate job requirements. But it is equally true that the Bureau is aware of the strangling effects of its organizational set-up and tries hard to alleviate them. Of course, whether its countermeasures—those meetings and seminars which, incidentally, tax heavily the time of its staff—really serve the purpose, cannot be answered offhand.

Nor should be it be forgotten that trainees may also be indoctrinated in a casual way; private discussions are likely to ventilate harassing problems and yield lacking bits of information, thus effectively supplementing the more official occasions. According to Pratt, the advanced trainees in the Bureau are very positive about this informal extension of their training, while the trainees in lower positions feel that the personal contact they were able to develop did not prove very helpful. Obviously a certain training period is needed for apprentices to learn to participate in the peculiar life of the Bureau which owes so much to communications through informal channels.

(c) Promotion. Any research center will want to give its trainees a fair chance of moving on to higher positions in accordance with their abilities and interests. And evidently the purposes of this job rotation is served best if the supervisors keep a watchful eye on the performances of their charges and evaluate them thoroughly. In other words, meaningful upward mobility calls for constant "reselection" and sifting. These selective processes, along with disturbing interferences from organizational necessities, will be touched upon in the subsequent section.

3. So much for the training procedures. And what about the human "material" processed? Analysis will have to differentiate between (a) the initial selection of the trainees, and (b) their just-mentioned reselection in the course of training.

(a) Initial selection can be effected by way of two methods or a combination of them. There is, first, the active approach: the research center selects from among the graduate students those whom it believes to be most gifted or most fit for the jobs available—here is where organizational needs come in—or both. This approach requires competitions of various types, with the winners being hired. The same result may also be obtained in less formal ways. For instance, in selecting trainees, the Bureau sometimes consults members of the Sociology Department and/or follows their spontaneous suggestions; or it acts according to the judgment of those of its own members who are acquainted with eligible individuals.

And there is, secondly, the passive type of recruitment which leaves most of the initiative to the future trainee himself. This method raises several questions which, of course, can be satisfactorily answered only with the aid of interviews on the campus. To begin with, how do those who approach the research center upon their own initiative learn about it? No doubt the center's popularity among students correlates with its general prestige. In many cases the applicant's awareness of the Bureau was due to its publications, references to it by university instructors, student gossip, etc.

Another question concerns the image which the student forms of the research center on the basis of what he heard of it. Interestingly enough, the Bureau seems to be envisioned not as a training center but as a place where certain skills may be learned. Applicants, that is, do as a rule not except to be really trained there; rather, they anticipate jobs which incidentally provide training.

Finally, for what reasons may sociology students—or students from neighboring departments, for that matter—feel attracted to the institute on the campus? Some of them are perhaps all the more eager to complete their education in it since empirical research has visibly gained foothold in the university curriculum—a fact likely to increase the institute's reputation as a center of learning. Other may believe that they are predisposed for the kind of activities they attribute to organized research. Add to the ideological incentives motivations of a more practical nature—among the acute need for money and the hope, founded or not, of the aspirants that their association with the institute will help them in preparing a doctoral thesis and/or prove an asset later on. Actually, many trainees flocked to the Bureau because they had to make a living, wanted to learn practical skills, and planned a research career. Whether or not such differences in intention affect the character of training remains to be seen; but the hypothesis that they do influence its outcome sounds very plausible indeed.— It might be added that the Bureau relies largely on passive recruitment.

No matter how applicants are preselected, the final decision will more likely than not hinge on personal interviews with them, at least this holds true of the Bureau. It would seem indicated here to pose again the familiar question as to the implications of conflicts between the research centers' multiple aspirations: for instance, to what extent are appointments determined by considerations bearing on the training goals proper and to what extent by the center's obligations toward its clients? Various alternatives are possible. Assuming the conflicting tendencies usually result in a compromise, then analysis will, in each case, have to bring out its specific nature and trace the organizational factor responsible for it. Regarding the Bureau, inferences drawn by applicants from the interview questions they were asked confirm what has already been stated above—that the prospective trainee is often "hired" not so much for his own good as in the interest of running commissions.[15] And since there is as a rule not time and money for experimenting in the highest dimensions of research, leading Bureau positions—those requiring some experience in advanced analysis and organizational skills—may well be entrusted to already-tested young scientists rather than staff members having reached the training stage before the last. Pratt has it that otherwise capable apprentices have risen only to positions which did not involve full professional responsibilities. The policy, well-nigh inevitable for academic research centers in need of outside support, of hiring for specific jobs thus represents a danger to training; but it should not be forgotten either that in each academic generation relatively few students belong among the elected.

(b) Once the applicant has been accepted and put on a job. his fate as a trainee depends to a large extent on the "reselection" processes. In the ideal case his supervisors will watch his gropings, evaluate his performances and in the end promote his accordingly. They may wish to find out about the trainee's special abilities and inclinations and then give him tasks in keeping with them. Or they may attempt to overcome outspoken one-sidedness by entrusting, for instance, the predominantly theory-minded with assignments which force them to concentrate on the technical side of research. And of course, they will always see to it that the student learns as many skills on as many levels as desirable in his particular case. It need hardly be mentioned that here as elsewhere organizational constraints, well-know by now, call for makeshift solutions, thus interfering with systematic sifting and advancement. In the Bureau job mobility often seems to be a matter of sheer chance and of persistence on the part of the trainee.[16] Analysis is faced with the task of tracing and assessing the various influences that come to bear on reselection. For instance, its irrationality may be a variable of the research center's size. In fact, if an organization grows beyond a certain size, the result is frequently lack of coordination between its departments, and this in turn is likely to affect the promotion prospects. Take the Bureau with its currently variegated activities: the odds are that trainees with approximately the same record may nevertheless have unequal opportunities if attached to different administrative units.

A final remark on the whole training effort suggests itself. One might ask whether a more formal or a more informal approach to training yields better results. Should activities in this field be completely systematized? Or rather, is it preferable to handle things in a somewhat loose manner, placing only moderate trust, say, in unified measurements of student performances and the like? It is meaningful to speculate on the pros and cons of these two alternatives. Suffice it here to advance an assumption in favor of the second. Informality in matters of training carries at least the advantage of precluding mechanization of the procedures and ratings involved—that kind of mechanization which threatens to blunt sensitivity to the individual trainee's potentialities. Presumably this also applies to the research center's autonomous pursuits; they too may suffer from over-rigid control of their scope and direction. In scientific ventures as well as delicate human affairs something must be left to intuition and spontaneous action. It is perhaps to the credit of the Bureau that it has never aspired to streamlined organization.

The second section of the scheme of analysis is devoted to the effect of in-service training. What type of social scientists have actually been produced by the institute on the campus? One thing is sure: however purposeful its training efforts, the ultimate result does not depend upon them alone. As has been suggested above, the trainee's motives and expectations may well play a part in forming his intellectual physiognomy. And is not, in addition, each generation prompted by urges of its own, urges pregnant with changes in perspective and direction?

In order to uncover the effect of training, one will have to construct a typology which virtually encompasses all possible varieties of sociologists. A fairly convenient typology can be developed from a breakdown according to the different relations which scientists may entertain to social theory and empirical research—those two branches of knowledge whose interdependence has been stressed throughout the essay. If the idea of such a breakdown is adopted, two major groups present themselves to the mind: scientists sufficiently "integrated" to work in both the theoretical and empirical fields; and scientists who are not integrated in this sense.

This last group comprises two types—not to mention transitions and borderline cases. There is, first, the technician; he would have to be defined as a professional versed in the established techniques of research yet relatively unconcerned for the basic problems of sociology. As has been pointed out in the introductory chapter, the critics of organized research hold that this precisely is the type which the research center on the campus tends to produce. In the case of the Bureau the situation is not so simple. Due, perhaps, to its traditional interest in methodological issues, the Bureau discourages rather than challenges its staff members to specialize in any one technical operation.

The second type of interest in this group is the technicians opposite number—scientists with an outspoken penchant for theorizing but not inclined or equipped to verify their grouping empirically. The technician, as imagined here, lacks sensitivity to theoretical thought, while the theorizer fails to enter into the spirit of empirical research and therefore misses the kind of insight accessible to it.

The other major group includes, by definition, all those who have a good grasp of theoretical concerns as well as empirical procedures. It appears that the Bureau's training effort favors the emergence of such fairly integrated scientists; in Pratt's words, they represent the "middle class" of the Bureau. Another observer familiar with the inside story of the Bureau characterizes this type as follows: "He will be sell grounded in the empirical research which has been done in his field and will probably have the ability to integrate this knowledge in any new research he may undertake. He will be equipped if confronted with a research problem to express an intelligent judgment as to the methodology to be employed to best solve the problem and to ably design a study to this effect.... Where he is likely to fall down, however, is in not having a real sense of direction; of being a man with many tools without having a real sense of what to use them on; of being well acquainted with the means but of groping for the ends." True as this description may be, its emotional overtones are not entirely justified. A sense of direction is extremely rare, and trading cannot possibly aim at producing geniuses.

Yet even though they achieve a measure of integration, these "middle-class" scientists may nevertheless be specialists in on dimension or another. The actual types of integrated specialists are unforeseeable; hence the tentative character of the following alternatives. It is possible to distinguish between the more theory-minded and the more research-oriented—the latter coming close to the technician, the former having traits of the theorizer. (However, they should not be confused with either of these nonintegrated types). And it is equally possible to group the pertinent types according to their affinity for methodological questions or substantive issues. The last subgroup evidently calls for further differentiation since each important issue requires special treatment. There remains the type of the fully integrated social scientist who masters both theory and practice with an inclusiveness denied to specialists. His pursuits in various dimensions of research might lead him to evolve and follow up theories on the highest level of significance.

This typology serves to frame (and evaluate) interviews with scientists who have received their training in the Bureau. In view of the changes which the Bureau has presumably undergone in the course of its evolution one will have to approach ex-trainees of different years. To round out the picture selected scientists from other research institutes should be interviewed also. On the basis of the findings it is perhaps possible to trace the actual results of training to the different factors instrumental in the training effort itself and thus isolate the particular contribution of each of them. This in turn might induce the institute on the campus to reconsider its training program and try to improve it if needed.

NOTES

1. See Robert K. Merton and Alice S. Kitt, "Contributions to the Theory of Reference Group Behavior," in *Continuities in Social Research* (New York: Free Press, 1950), 40–105. There the authors remark: "As is not infrequently the case with applied research, the by-product may prove more significant for the discipline of sociology than the direct application of findings" (81).
2. For "significant" studies in the area of communications research, see, for instance, Suchman, "Invitation to Music" (*Radio Research 1942–1943*), Herzog, "What Do We Really Know About Daytime Serials Listeners?" (*Radio Research, 1942–1943*), Lazarsfeld, "The People Look at Radio" (1946), etc. What characterizes these authors is the imaginative circumspection with which they incorporate their data—data either purposefully assembled or drawn from available sources—into large and socially relevant contexts. In "The People Look at Radio," Lazarsfeld examines not only audience responses but also the "social structure and social implications of the radio industry" (4). And his follow-up study of 1948, "Radio Listening in America," adds to these two yardsticks for evaluation a third one: the query of whether radio lives up to a high standard.
3. Robert K. Merton, "Role of the Intellectual in Public Bureaucracy," in *Social Theory and Social Structure* (New York: Free Press, 1949), 169–70.
4. W. W. McPhee, "New Strategies for Research on the Mass Media."

5. Elihu Katz, "The Part Played by People: A New Focus for the Study of Mass Media Effects."
6. With interpersonal relations coming into focus, sociometric analyses gain momentum. The housing study is largely devoted to them.
7. To be sure, scope and continuity of a research center's autonomous activities also depend upon its organizational needs. But the organizational factor will be treated separately.
8. Benjamin B. Ringer and David L. Sills, "Political Extremists in Iran: A Secondary Analysis of Communications Data," *Public Opinion Quarterly* (Winter 1952–1953): 689–701.
9. Samuel A. Stouffer, "Some Afterthoughts of a Contributor to 'The American Soldier,'" in *Continuities in Social Research* (New York: Free Press, 1950), 199.
10. What they cannot prevent, however, is the distortion of their findings by the client. Take the following case: the Bureau undertook a study for a newspaper organization to measure the relative impact of newspaper and radio advertising. Even though the findings were inconclusive in that either medium was found to have certain positive qualities not present in the other, the sponsoring organization actively promoted only these figures that were in favor of newspaper advertising while suppressing the balance. This led to attacks against the study by the radio industry. To be sure, it was easy to prove that they were unwarranted, but one is safe in assuming that they nevertheless left a residue of ill-feeling and bias against the Bureau. Such unpreventable manipulations are apt to injure the reputation of the research center and strengthen the position of its academic opponents.
11. It might be mentioned here that the Bureau receives a $16,000 university subsidy per year for training purposes.
12. See the unpublished Bureau report "The In-Service Training Program of the Bureau of Applied Social Research," by Samuel Pratt. Its factual findings are used throughout this chapter.
13. See Pratt, "In-Service Training Program."
14. See Pratt.
15. "In most cases," says Pratt, "the specific selective factor was the ability to do the given job then available. The applicant was in competition with others only on this point. He was not considered as a whole. His student record and qualifications were not considered comparatively with other possible candidates. It was a hiring process. It was not a trainee selection process."
16. "According to the long-term trainees," says Pratt, "selection for an advancement is based on luck and other non-rational factors."

APPENDIX 1

Report on the Work "Totalitarian Propaganda in Germany and Italy," by Siegfried Kracauer, pp. 1–106

T. W. ADORNO

In evaluating Kracauer's text, which in terms of length will comprise approximately half the overall piece, it seems to me insufficient simply to confront him with our categories and to examine the extent to which he is in unison with them.[1] Instead, we should presume from the outset that Kracauer is neither committed to us in terms of his theoretical approach, nor does he rank as a scholarly {*wissenschaftlich*} writer in terms of his working methods. The question then is, having acknowledged these preconditions familiar to us, does his work have anything to offer us, and what can we best use—be it for publication or for developing our own theory.

I would like to formulate my impression as a preliminary thesis as follows: the work is neither of real theoretical value nor sufficiently grounded in the empirical material, but it does occasionally express in highly useful literary formulations particular experiences and observations whose validity transcends the outsider position of the author.

As regards the theoretical side, it should be noted that Kracauer is not a trained Marxist and as a result constructs the relationship of fascism and fascistic propaganda with the current phase of capitalism in more or less vague analogies and sometimes betrays an aversion to Marxist methodology itself, springing from individualistic reservations. Furthermore, his social-psychological reflections are not truly grounded, and psychoanalysis, in particular, plays the role of stopgap. This becomes clear, for example, in his remarks about sadomasochism, where the decisive difference between repressed and practised sadism is completely overlooked, so that Kracauer, who constantly refers to Horkheimer's theses, twists them to mean just the opposite. In the place of a sound theoretical foundation, Kracauer's text relies instead on a trove of convictions popular among present-day left-wing intellectuals, in which Marxist and psychoanalytic concepts quietly take their place alongside vulgar psychological and sociological notions and common-sense argumentation. Kracauer's inventory of categories is not so far removed from the leftist bourgeois writer of Stefan Zweig's ilk, as the pretension of the expression makes us think. The consequence of this is a certain non-binding informality and contingency of the theoretical underpinnings, which at times borders on the amateurish. This is particularly true of the derivation of fascism from the principle of the war, which is conceptualized in a socially neutral way. Thus, the entire introduction of the work, at least up to p. 30, probably even longer, is unusable—about which, incidentally, our group appears to be unanimous.

As for its empirical-scholarly {*empirisch-wissenschaftlich*} credentials, it should be stated that Kracauer—for reasons, I assume, connected with his precarious situation—has not studied the sources enough. His citations are mostly second hand, and the direct quotations from Hitler, some of which are extraordinarily interesting, are not evaluated sufficiently. The material about Italy is taken almost exclusively from Silone, who seems to me in no way above suspicion as a Marxist authority. I would therefore like to propose that all sections referring to Italy are dropped from any publication.

The strengths of the work lie for me in the quality of observation, of the literary experience of many formulations (we are not overly blessed with contributions of such writerly quality) and in a certain ability to arrange the factual material which at times compensates for what the work lacks in actual theoretical prowess. I would like to draw particular attention to pp. 53–57, which remain strictly within a purely phenomenological framework, but must, by these standards, be considered truly extraordinary. The thesis of the mobility of partial ideologies in fascism; much in the representation of Terror; the method and insights of drawing conclusions about fascism from the "mirror reflection"—that is, from the fascist representation of non-fascist facts; what's more, the theses about the constant reproduction of the mass through fascism and the critique of the opposition between the personality of the leader and the mass as a mere pseudo-opposition (a critique, incidentally, which could be made even sharper). I find all this so illuminating, and also new, that we should publish it.

Even though all these analyses lack economic rigor, one can say in Kracauer's defense that an economic theory of monopoly capitalism, which could support the analysis of fascism, does not yet exist; but also that precisely the detailed description of the fascist propaganda mechanism can call into question the kind of naively economistic approach which hinders Marxism at the current stage. One could, so to speak, make a Marxist virtue of Kracauer's theoretical necessity. Regarding this point, I would like to draw particular attention to the passage in Kracauer's text where he criticizes the argument that fascist mass events and the fascist construction of façades, more generally, are "unprofitable."

Since the positive elements of the work are beset throughout with theoretical improvisation and naiveties, and furthermore, since the work extends far beyond the space available in the journal—even if the first 30 or pages were omitted—I would like to suggest working through to find the usable sections, to note these down under headings and separate them out from Kracauer's context, inasmuch as this context appears arbitrary. On the other hand, Kracauer's useful classifications ought to be retained. This material would then be used to produce a new article no longer than two journal signatures {*Zeitschriftenbogen*}.[2] I am willing to commit to completing this task.

I would like us to bear in mind one thing: Kracauer has clearly made a herculean effort in this work to work his way out of the sphere of market-driven writing, to which the Offenbach book belongs. I commend his effort highly. Essentially, the quality of the work improves as it progresses. I therefore consider it entirely possible that the as yet uncompleted second part of the work will be better than the first. It therefore perhaps makes sense to wait for the arrival of the second part before we embark upon editing.

Finally, I don't think I'm guilty of any sentimentality if I say that, in the case of a victim of emigration like Kracauer who is, after all, making an honest effort to regain his intellectual standard, the morale boost that a publication has on an author should be taken seriously and not left out of our considerations as we reach a decision.

At the same time, in the course of the European propaganda campaign I have repeatedly encountered the wish for more contributions on political sociology, and the edited Kracauer essay could well meet this desideratum, without overly burdening us politically.

New York, 5 March 1938

Translated by John Abromeit

NOTES

1. {Adorno was reviewing the sections of the text that Kracauer had finished and sent to him and Horkheimer by the beginning of March, 1938. Adorno did not yet have the complete text at his disposal. See the editor Bernd Stiegler's "Nachwort," in

Siegfried Kracauer, *Totalitäre Propaganda*, ed. Bernd Stiegler (Berlin: Suhrkamp Verlag, 2013), 322–23.}

2. {In printing, a "signature" (the equivalent of a "Druckbogen") is four sheets cut and bound together to form sixteen pages. So, this means that the article was intended to be two signatures—that is, thirty-two pages long.}

APPENDIX 2

Siegfried Kracauer and the Early Frankfurt School's Analysis of Fascism as Right-Wing Populism

JOHN ABROMEIT

INTRODUCTION

Contrary to the traditional historicist approach to studying the past "wie es eigentlich gewesen ist," theoretically reflexive scholars have long recognized that our understanding of the past is always shaped by current social conditions and political tendencies.[1] The remarkable—and ominous—growth of right-wing populist movements and parties in Europe, the United States, and many other parts of the world in the past three decades has heightened public and scholarly interest in both the history of populism and the relationship of populism to fascism. As Theodor Adorno dramatically emphasized in his reformulation of Kant's categorical imperative "after Auschwitz," the subjective and objective conditions that made fascism possible did not disappear with its military defeat in 1945.[2] The recrudescence of authoritarian populist movements in Europe, the United States, and elsewhere since Adorno's death in 1969 underscores the truth content of his new categorical imperative. Part of the task of arranging our thoughts and actions so that something like Auschwitz will not happen again is certainly the effort to gain a better historical and theoretical understanding of how and why fascist movements so successfully appropriated populist political strategies and ideology. This essay aims to contribute to that effort.

In what follows, I will build upon my own research on the historical links between populism and fascism, in general, and the early Frankfurt School's analysis of those links, in particular. I will focus on a lengthy essay Kracauer wrote between 1936 and 1938, "Totalitarian Propaganda," which he submitted for publication in the *Zeitschrift für Sozialforschung*, the house journal of Max Horkheimer's Institute for Social Research. Due to its excessive length and alleged theoretical shortcomings—identified primarily by Adorno—Kracauer's essay did not appear in the *Zeitschrift*. The full, original German version of the essay was not published until 2012. In this volume we have translated into English and published for the first time two of the seven sections of the essay.[3] Kracauer's essay is noteworthy for several reasons. First, it offers unparalleled insights into Kracauer's understanding of fascism and the crucial role that authoritarian populist ideology played in its historical triumph. Second, Kracauer's essay has never been translated and remains virtually unknown outside of Germany. Third, Kracauer draws extensively upon Horkheimer's and Erich Fromm's writings from the 1930s—what I have called elsewhere the "early model of Critical Theory."[4] Kracauer is able to address some of the weaknesses in his own analysis of fascism by drawing upon Horkheimer and Fromm's work. But, as we shall see, Kracauer's analysis also complements and supplements Horkheimer's and Fromm's writings in important ways. After discussing the main arguments in Kracauer's essay, the way it sheds light on the authoritarian populist aspects of fascism, and its relationship to Horkheimer and Fromm's writings, I will briefly discuss Theodor Adorno's critique of the essay, which we are also publishing here for the first time in English translation. Adorno's predominately negative evaluation of it sheds light on some important differences between Kracauer's theoretical approach to fascism, and the approach of the Institute, which Adorno was in the process of assimilating during this time, the late 1930s. Here again, though, I will argue that not all of Adorno's criticisms are compelling, and that certain aspects of Kracauer's analysis can supplement the Institute's own important—and still very relevant—work on fascism and authoritarian populism. In other words, when taken together as a whole—along with other key Institute studies, such as Adorno's contributions to *The Authoritarian Personality* and Leo Löwenthal and Norbert Gutermann's *Prophets of Deceit*—Kracauer and the early Critical Theorists' writings can still provide us with an excellent theoretical foundation for grasping the persistence of right-wing populist movements into the present.[5] Throughout the essay I will also discuss the many ways in which Kracauer and the early Frankfurt School's analyses of fascism and authoritarian populism have anticipated more recent scholarly findings in these fields.

KRACAUER'S ESSAY ON TOTALITARIAN PROPAGANDA

Kracauer's essay "Totalitarian Propaganda" is divided into seven sections. In what follows I will first provide a brief overview of each section and then focus on his analysis of fascism as a form of right-wing populism. Section A of the essay addresses the recent historical origins of fascism—in Germany's defeat in World War I—and the central role of demobilized soldiers and officers, but also politicized workers who were disappointed with the reformist stance of the Social Democratic Party.[6] In the first section Kracauer also introduces key elements of his theoretical interpretation of fascism. He distinguishes his own approach from the traditional Marxist "base-superstructure" model, and from any version of sociological reductionism, which would explain fascism as a manifestation of the material interests of any distinct class or social group. Like Horkheimer, Kracauer moves beyond traditional Marxism in his defense of the relative autonomy of culture and psychological character structures, which allows him to place propaganda—as a complex and overdetermined form of ideology—at the very center of his analysis of fascism.[7] As we shall see, for Kracauer propaganda as ideology is not a mere reflex, but is *socially necessary*—indeed, even more necessary in a fascist than in a liberal capitalist society.

The specifically populist elements in the first section of Kracauer's essay are his emphasis on the broad appeal of fascist ideology and its strong emphasis on national unity, especially as expressed in the concept of "das Volk." Historians and political theorists have long recognized that what set the National Socialist German Workers Party (NSDAP) apart from others parties in the Weimar Republic, and what secured their electoral breakthroughs in 1930 and 1932, was their ability to attract voters from across the social and political spectrum.[8] Whereas the relatively stable, middle phase of the Weimar Republic (1924–1929) was characterized by a fragmentation of voters into diverse interest-group parties, in its final phase (1930–1933) many voters abandoned these small parties—but also the larger, more established parties as well—in order to cast their lot with the NSDAP.[9] Kracauer acknowledges this fact when he writes, "One cannot understand the constitution of totalitarian dictatorships, if one views them only as the product of bourgeois or also petty bourgeois movements."[10] Related to this point, Kracauer also emphasizes the important role not only of demobilized soldiers and officers in the early stages of the fascist movements in Germany and Italy, but also of radicalized workers who were disappointed with the socialist parties. Anticipating the important research done later on Italian fascism by Zeev Sternhell, Kracauer emphasizes the crucial role of "national-syndicalist workers" in the formation of Mussolini's movement.[11] Kracauer concludes that the social background of the fascist movement was "rather mixed."[12]

The ideological expression of such a movement that drew support from across the social and political spectrum was a strong emphasis on national unity, pushed to the point of "national fanaticism."[13] Kracauer cites Ignaz Silone's argument that an "enraged, revolutionary patriotism" was the defining feature of the early Italian fascist movement,[14] and Kracauer himself argues that "not so much the state, as the racially chosen people" is the central concept of Hitler's ideology.[15] Just as all the social differences of bourgeois society disappeared in the trenches of World War I, so the Nazis' concept of the Volksgemeinschaft (community of the people) appealed to the desires of many Germans to overcome the deep social divisions of the Weimar Republic. Of course, Kracauer was aware of the ideological content of such concepts. The leading question of his essay is "What is being concealed behind the 'enraged and revolutionary patriotism' of the core troops of fascism and National Socialism?"[16] The first and rather unsatisfying answer that Kracauer provides to this question is that Nazi ideology was driven by a "nihilistic will to power." This response begs the question of what lies behind such a "will to power" and, more important, how and why it was successful. In subsequent sections of his essay, Kracauer presents theoretical and sociological insights that point beyond this initial and inadequate answer.

In section B, Kracauer focuses on the role of fascist propaganda in establishing an emotional bond between the leader and his followers. Following Horkheimer, Kracauer emphasizes that the authority of the fascist leader cannot rest on violence alone.[17] Kracauer describes how Hitler, Gregor Strasser, Goebbels, and other Nazi leaders in the 1920s grasped intuitively the necessity of moving beyond a rational politics based on material interests and logical arguments to an irrational politics based on the creation of an imagined community of followers bound together emotionally through an identification with the leader and his "ideas." Kracauer describes as Hitler's main aim "to emotionally bind the masses as a whole to himself."[18] Kracauer also cites Goebbels's definition of the mission of propaganda—namely, "to win people over to any idea in such an integral and vital way, that they completely succumb to it and can no longer part with it."[19] Hitler and Goebbels both formulate here the necessity of mobilizing certain social-psychological mechanisms with propaganda in order to create an irrational bond between the leader and the mass. In this context Kracauer discusses Hitler's conviction that Germany lost World War I due to the superiority of the Entente Powers' propaganda, which led to Hitler's own successful efforts to systematically develop Nazi propaganda. In this section Kracauer also discusses the crucial role of Gregor Strasser, who was the Nazis' national leader for propaganda in 1926 and 1927, and who helped transform the NSDAP from a small, southern German splinter party into a national party with mass appeal. Kracauer stresses the central role of the concept of "German community" in Strasser's propaganda, but also Strasser's populist, even anticapitalist, rhetoric.

Kracauer argues that Strasser wanted to remove nationalism from capitalism, and socialism from internationalism, in order to create "national socialism." Strasser plays a similar role in Kracauer's analysis of Germany, as does national syndicalism in his analysis of Italy. Kracauer emphasizes the genuinely populist, antielitist, and (and least rhetorically) anticapitalist thrust of Strasser's propaganda, which appealed not only to German workers but also to large swaths of the middle- and lower-middle class. But, for Hitler's taste, Strasser's approach was too anticapitalist and thus ran the risk of scaring away potential supporters who would be alienated by such left-wing rhetoric. At a party gathering in Bamberg in 1926, Hitler cemented his own leadership of the NSDAP by criticizing Strasser's "National Bolshevism"; Hitler's rivalry with Strasser continued into the early 1930s and ended with Strasser's murder during the Night of the Long Knives in 1934. The displacement of Strasser's and the consolidation of Hitler's ideological position can be interpreted as the triumph of a right-wing, authoritarian form of populism over a left-wing, anticapitalist form.

In section B, Kracauer draws explicitly on Max Horkheimer's essay "Egoism and Freedom Movements" in order to explain some of the social-psychological mechanisms at work in such forms of right-wing, authoritarian populism.[20] Hitler and Goebbels argued that propaganda must seek to bind the masses to fascist leaders by winning them over to specific ideas, such as the national or racial community of the people. Ideas play such an important role, according to Kracauer, because they have the potential to separate individuals from their concrete *interests*. Horkheimer explained the irrational and authoritarian dynamics existing between the leaders and followers of early modern bourgeois freedom movements precisely in terms of such a conflict between ideology and interests. In the case of the NSDAP, they articulated a vehement critique of both the myriad interest parties that existed in Weimar Germany in the mid-1920s, and the entire party system as such. The right-wing populism of the Nazis consisted precisely in their attempt to replace the political fragmentation of interest conflicts with a unified "German community" or "people's community," in which only one political party would continue to exist. As Horkheimer also emphasized, in order to mobilize people to act in ways that are ultimately against their own interest—in order to prepare them, in other words, for self-sacrifice—they must become fixated upon an idea. Kracauer writes that Hitler is concerned not "with the defending interests, but with controlling the masses, independently of their interests.... Most important for him is that interests are transformed into ideas."[21] Unwittingly, Kracauer also highlights here an important continuity that existed between right-wing theorists of group psychology, such as Gustav Le Bon, and fascist theorists, such as Giovanni Gentile. Both Le Bon and

Gentile adamantly emphasize the idealist and antimaterialist character of authoritarian mass mobilization. Looking back on human history (in a superficial and dilettantish way), Le Bon concludes that all great social and political movements have been driven by "lofty" ideas, not petty material interests.[22] Gentile explicitly stresses the idealist nature of fascism and opposes it to the materialism of socialism and liberalism, which are grounded in collective or individual interests.[23] Hitler and Goebbels both believe that people are much more willing to die for a collective idea than for their own petty interests. The task of propaganda, and of the fascist leader, is to bind them emotionally to these ideas.

In section C of the essay, Kracauer discusses the relationship of fascism to democracy. He emphasizes the desire of fascism to completely erase the entire Enlightenment tradition in politics, which includes liberalism, democracy, and the French Revolution. As we just saw, fascists view socialism as the logical historical development of these traditions. Kracauer also mentions the "democratic deficit" in Italy and Germany. On the one hand, he does—like later defenders of the so-called Sonderweg thesis—view the comparatively late establishment and relatively weak institutional grounding of liberal democracy in Italy and Germany (in comparison to France, Britain, and the United States) as a factor in the success of fascism. On the other hand, and in contrast to the defenders of the Sonderweg thesis, Kracauer has no illusions about Germany lagging behind other Western democracies in terms of its economic development. For Kracauer the powerful antidemocratic forces pushing for the development of new forms of totalitarian monopoly capitalism[24] are more important for the success of fascism than a "democracy" or "modernization" deficit.[25] Like his colleagues at the Institute, Kracauer never equated capitalist modernization with automatic political and social progress. On the contrary, in the essay he clearly recognizes and emphasizes the common interests that brought advocates of monopoly capitalism and fascism together. The former opposed democracy because socialists and trade unions, backed by the constitution of the Weimar Republic, fought to safeguard the rights and secure a decent quality of living for workers and thereby tied the hands and diminished the profits of big industry.

In section C, Kracauer also continues his analysis of fascism as a form of right-wing populism through a lengthy discussion of the fascist concept of the Volk, and a briefer discussion of the fascist aestheticization of politics and the social-psychological dimensions of fascist mass spectacle. Regarding the former, Kracauer stresses the purely ideological character of the fascist concept of the Volk, which is grounded in the basic contradiction between fascism's rejection of democracy and its need to represent the will of the Führer as identical to the will of "the people." This positive (if also, of course, purely ideological) concept of "the people" is what separated fascism from traditional, nineteenth-century European conservative political traditions, which made no attempt to conceal their antidemocratic politics with ideological façades. Fascism represented a qualitatively new political phenomenon precisely because of its ability to mobilize the masses for an antidemocratic and antisocialist—that is, essentially conservative—political, social, economic, and moral agenda.[26] Kracauer's lengthy discussion of Gregor Strasser and his eventual defeat by Hitler illustrates well the fascist instrumentalization of democratic and even socialist themes, as well as the fact that such themes must remain in the rhetorical realm. Fascist populism must remain right-wing, authoritarian populism, because the fascist concept of "the people" is used primarily to conceal the contradictions and social domination that continue to exist (indeed, are heightened) within fascist monopoly-state capitalism. Kracauer cites Goebbels, who expresses the fascists' antiliberal, anti-Enlightenment concept of the people in the following way: "What is essential in this revolutionary development is that individualism is destroyed and that 'the people' takes the place of the individual and its deification."[27] In contrast to the liberal-democratic and socialist concept of "the people," which Kracauer emphatically defends, the fascist concept of "the people" is unitary and collectivist.

Kracauer argues that fascism sees its primary task as eliminating any possibility of popular self-determination, by transforming the people into a passive mass. The end of fascist propaganda is the creation of such a powerless mass, and the primary means is the ideology of "the people." Kracauer writes:

> Due to its totalitarian presumptions, National Socialist propaganda must disempower the real people and impose upon them its own directives; however, at the same time, it has to replace the idea of the real people with the illusion of a people that is worthy of divine worship. Only by pretending to serve the phantom of a racially superior people can National Socialism demand for itself the sovereign power that created it. This sovereign power deifies the will of an imaginary people so that the real people will not notice that they are deifying themselves. The National Socialist concept of the people is a capsule without content.[28]

Kracauer's formulation here echoes not only Marx's Feuerbachian theory of religion as the fetishization of one own's alienated powers—which, in his early writings, Marx also used to critique the ideological *political* forms of modern capitalist society.[29] Interestingly, Kracauer's description of the fascist concept of

"Volk" as a "capsule without content" also anticipates Ernesto Laclau's later argument that populism rests on a concept of "the people" as an "empty signifier."[30] In marked contrast to Laclau—or at least his later, "post-Marxist" work on populism—Kracauer's approach remains essentially Marxist, insofar as he grounds the "empty" nature of the fascists' right-wing populist concept of "the people" in the need to conceal underlying *social* contradictions. In his earlier, very suggestive work on populism and fascism, Laclau still worked within a Marxian framework, but in his later work he insisted upon the "primacy of the political" and disputed any attempt to explain popular will formation in terms of underlying social constellations.[31] Whereas for Kracauer the "empty" nature of the fascist concept of the people points unmistakably to its ideological character, Laclau views this emptiness as an opportunity to forge broad coalitions with the potential for a revolutionary transformation of power relations.

In section D of his essay, Kracauer describes how fascist regimes use terror, spectacle, and welfare to make propaganda "indispensable like a drug" for the masses they dominate.[32] As a tool of totalitarian propaganda, terror has two interrelated tasks. It must, first, create fear in order to, second, separate individuals from their concrete interests and subordinate them to the imagined national or racial "community of the people." Kracauer writes, "Fear [*Angst*] brings people under its power in such a way that they no longer listen to propaganda out of fear, but instead because everything becomes uncertain—precisely as a result of fear—which, in turn, makes them capable of belief."[33] As we have seen, however, Kracauer also recognizes that authority—even in a fascist society—does not rest on violence alone, which explains the crucial role of spectacle and welfare in creating a "mass addiction" to totalitarian propaganda. Terror also aims to have the indirect effect of convincing individuals to *willingly* abdicate their own ability to judge reality and to accept instead the fabricated "reality" of totalitarian propaganda. Kracauer underscores the theatrical nature of fascist spectacle, which encourages the masses to accept fiction for reality and teaches them that "the play is more than a play, and madness is the norm."[34] Kracauer's remarks here presciently anticipate the Nazis' use of film to create their own version of reality and impose it upon the German public. One could hardly find a better example of what Kracauer is saying here than the Nazi propaganda film *Kolberg*, which was made near the end of the war to encourage Germans to fight until the bitter end against the rapidly approaching Red Army. During the production of the film thousands of desperately need soldiers were called back from the Eastern Front to serve as extras in massive battle scenes, which illustrated clearly Goebbels's conviction that the maintenance of the illusory world created by propaganda was every bit as important as fighting the actual war.[35] Finally, the Nazi construction of a far-reaching system of welfare also aimed, as Kracauer notes, to win *willing* consent to their total program. Kracauer mentions the Nazis' Winterhilfswerk program, which ran from 1933 to 1945 and provided food, clothing, fuel, and other items during the winter months to Germans who needed them. Kracauer argues that the main aim of this and other Nazi welfare programs was to provide a "feeling of security" to counteract widespread feelings of impotence and anxiety, which were themselves consciously created by Nazi propaganda.[36]

Kracauer adds to his analysis of the right-wing populist dimensions of fascism in section D by discussing two ways in which totalitarian propaganda relied upon a friend-enemy dichotomy. One of the essential characteristics of populism—in both its left- and right-wing variants—is its stylized portrayal of society as being starkly divided between "the people" and "the enemies of the people."[37] This populist trope played a key role in the French Revolution and in subsequent democratic and socialist movements in the nineteenth century. Fascism adopts the "friend-enemy" form of the trope, while at the same transforming its ideological content from the Left to the Right, by redefining the basic contradiction in terms that obscure the actual social antagonisms in modern capitalist societies.[38] Kracauer provides a clear example of this dynamic, when he describes the Italian fascists' and German National Socialists' violent attacks upon workers' organizations and their leaders, which are intended to "liquidate proletarian organizations" and to force workers to identify with the ideological concept of the "Volk" rather than with each other. More than anything else, fascism must convince workers that the basic contradiction is not between capital and wage labor, but between the virtuous and productive "people" and the immoral and parasitic "enemies of the people"—which the Nazis referred to as the *schaffend* (productive) and the *raffend* (parasitic) elements of the population.[39] Fascist propaganda applies the "producer-parasite" dichotomy even to capital itself, with industrial capital portrayed as belonging the former—that is, on the same side as productive workers and peasants—and finance capital as belonging to the latter. In this way, workers are separated from the material interests that bind them together as workers, and are integrated ideologically into the false totality of the Volk.

If the primary *political* function of the right-wing populist "friend-enemy" dichotomy is to separate workers from their material interests, the dichotomy also performs a crucial *social-psychological* function. By portraying social conflict in the Manichean terms of a conflict between the Volk and its enemies, fascists—consciously or unconsciously—succeed in heightening, harnessing, and redirecting psychic energies created by the antagonistic relations of modern capitalism. Drawing on Erich Fromm's introductory essay to the Institute's *Studies on Authority and Family*, Kracauer highlights the role of masochism in maintaining social bonds and socially necessary ideology under fascism. The feeling of security created by identifying with the imagined community of the Volk not only counteracts what Fromm described as a "feeling of powerlessness" that is pervasive in modern societies; it also satisfies the masochistic need to identify with the powerful social forces that seem beyond individuals' control.[40] According to Kracauer, these individuals "obtain from the totalitarian dictatorship the pleasure of being subordinated to persons embodying an overwhelming fate. These persons control him and provide his masochistic desire to obey with delectable sensations."[41] Kracauer claims further that Fromm was right to argue that "the liberation from autonomous decision making and, with it, from doubt is one of the greatest satisfactions that the authoritarian state has to offer its followers."[42] Whereas Kracauer draws on Fromm's work from the 1930s to explain the masochistic components of fascist ideology, he draws again on Horkheimer's seminal essay "Egoism and Freedom Movements" to demonstrate why sadism fulfills such an important social-psychological function within it. As Horkheimer spells out in rich historical detail, when the masses are mobilized in the name of bourgeois political, social, and moral ideas, sadism provides a form of ersatz gratification for the demands made upon them to sacrifice their material interests and desires. The more sacrifices are demanded and the less the bourgeois leader is able to fulfill his promises to improve the material life conditions of the masses, the more sadistic compensation becomes necessary to reinforce the emotional bonds that unify the "people" against their "enemies." Official enemies become fair game for the ersatz sadistic gratification of libidinal drives that individuals must repress in order to become members of the new populist collective created by fascist propaganda.[43]

In section E of his essay (which we have translated and included in this volume), Kracauer first discusses the key difference between his concepts of "the masses" and "the people." Although Kracauer analyzes throughout the essay how the Nazis instrumentalize the concept of "the people" for their own ideological purposes, he does preserve a positive concept of "the people," which he views as an essential component of democratic and socialist politics, and which he distinguishes sharply from the concept of "the masses." Whereas, according to Kracauer, one of the primary aims of totalitarian propaganda is to transform the people into atomized, passive, and obedient "mass particles," truly democratic and socialist movements seek to abolish the conditions that give rise to such masses by empowering the people to actively determine their own fate.[44] Kracauer elaborates upon this crucial distinction by analyzing the difference between socialist and fascist mass rallies. Drawing once again on Horkheimer's essay, Kracauer points out that socialist rallies rely much more heavily upon appeals to reason than fascist rallies, insofar as the former aim to enlighten workers about the root causes of their exploitation and to encourage them to act collectively to pursue their own best interests. The latter, in contrast, rely much more heavily on appeals to emotion and on conscious attempts to manipulate the unconscious of the masses, whom the fascist leaders hold in contempt—as Hitler made abundantly clear in *Mein Kampf*. As examples of the antirational and manipulative character of fascist rallies, Kracauer mentions their privileging of the spoken over the written word, their mind-numbing repetition of slogans, their highly structured and ritualistic character, and their heavy reliance upon irrational gestures and symbols. As Gustav Le Bon, Sigmund Freud, and other theorists of crowd behavior and group psychology—whom Kracauer, strangely, does not discuss in his essay—had long emphasized, individuals in crowds have a tendency to *regress*. Kracauer writes, "By using the principle of repetition, the speaker pushes the mass down to the level of children and into a condition in which they no longer take in anything except what he constantly repeats."[45] It is precisely such regression that fascist propaganda seeks to reinforce with the "magical power of the spoken word."[46]

The two other key characteristics of fascist propaganda, which Kracauer discusses in section E, are its "cult of personality" and its "aestheticization of politics." He offers two different explanations of the former concept. The first links the authoritarian fetishization of the leader to what Kracauer himself describes earlier in the essay as the "nihilistic will to power" of fascism, its striving for power solely for its own sake. The second, and more convincing, explanation is based on Horkheimer's sociohistorical analysis of leader/follower dynamics in bourgeois social movements during the early modern period. Kracauer follows and elaborates upon Horkheimer's analysis of both the authoritarian "charisma" of bourgeois leaders, and the transformation of the (progressive) bourgeois celebration of individual autonomy and free development into its opposite. Kracauer agrees with Horkheimer that the primary cause of this apotheosis of leaders lies in "the necessity of captivating the masses to distract them from certain social demands."[47] In fascist propaganda, "all efforts seem directed toward putting the person, instead of the mass, on center stage."[48] Kracauer demonstrates how this fascist celebration of the "personality" represents an abstract, not a determinate, negation of the bourgeois concept of the free individual. Bourgeois society in its "heroic" period celebrated the autonomous individual as the cornerstone of a free society. In the nineteenth century, bourgeois philosophers and poets, such as John Stuart Mill and Goethe, sang the praises of the free and comprehensive development of the individual personality. Kracauer argues that the socialist movement, which also emerged in the nineteenth century, "affirms this valuation of the individual so unreservedly, that it wants to achieve its universal recognition."[49] But, as Horkheimer argued, the regressive economic development of bourgeois society in the late nineteenth and early twentieth century—that is, the transformation of liberal capitalism into monopoly and authoritarian state capitalism—also robbed the central philosophical concepts of the bourgeoisie of their content and transformed them into mere fig leaves for the new repressive social order.[50] Kracauer writes, "The interest of big capital, which has been pushed into a defensive position and become increasingly dependent on violence, is not the struggle of opinion . . . but instead the death of opinion;. . . not the development of the individual into a personality, but the 'personality' that knows how to subdue a mass."[51] For Kracauer, in other words, the fascist cult of personality is just the opposite of the progressive aspects of the bourgeois concept of personality. Rather than inhibiting, it reinforces the formation of regressive masses. In fascist propaganda, the "personality" and the mass "mutually condition each other."[52]

In section E, Kracauer also elaborates upon some comments he made earlier on the fascist aestheticization of politics.[53] In section C he had argued that "many techniques of totalitarian propaganda are calculated exclusively to be aesthetically fascinating," and "the aestheticization of propaganda is intended to anesthetize the masses."[54] Playing here, wittingly or unwittingly, on the ancient Greek etymological roots of "aesthetic," as having to do not only with art, but also with the senses, Kracauer goes on to spell out the links between artistically and sensually pleasing fascist spectacle and mass domination.[55] To grasp this phenomenon, Kracauer coins the term "Massenbildkunst," which means literally an "art of mass images." Kracauer points out that fascism views the constant reconstitution of the masses as not just as a means of delivering propaganda to the people, but itself as a form of propaganda. Seeing immaculately composed and efficiently functioning mass events such as rallies and marches provides aesthetic pleasure, in a manner not unlike watching a Tiller Girls performance. Fascist propaganda actively encouraged its audience to imagine themselves as an integral part—what Kracauer again calls a "mass particle"—of such a Volksgemeinschaft, in which different parts of Germany are combined into one large, efficiently functioning and formidable machine.[56] It is not a coincidence, Kracauer notes, that the Nazis actively recruited representatives from different parts of Germany to participate in their marches. This tactic is also on display in the famous scene from *Triumph of the Will*, in which twelve soldiers from different regions call out the names of their various "homelands." When cut and edited in rapid succession, the calls form an aesthetically gratifying montage of a unified national community. Kracauer takes seriously Hitler's claim that "the correct utilization of propaganda is a true art, of which the bourgeois parties were and are virtually unaware."[57] Whereas Hitler became a master of this art through long practice, Kracauer draws extensively upon Horkheimer and Fromm's social-psychological theoretical reflections to understand how and why the propagandist must be a "virtuoso of the instrument of the soul."[58] Drawing upon and reinforcing the authoritaritarian character structures that are the "natural" by-product of modern capitalist societies, the most important task of the fascist propagandist is to bind individuals to a social order that runs contrary to their own best interests. Kracauer writes, "the aesthetic grandiose... is the overwhelming appearance of power; its function is to tear people out of the sphere of interests into a sphere in which they imagine they have been elevated above themselves and are partaking in the magnificence that is presented to them, or that they themselves represent."[59] In other words, the fascist aestheticization of politics has the same function as its cult of personality: preparing individuals to sacrifice themselves for an imagined community that, in reality, remains dominated by particular interests.

Kracauer's discussion of the differences between fascist and socialist rallies, but also his analysis of the fascist cult of personality, are helpful in explaining why fascism is a form of right-wing populism, and how right-wing populism differs from left-wing populism and socialism. In addition to what was already written above, what is crucial to emphasize is fascism's appropriation and exploitation—as Kracauer himself puts it—of political forms and strategies, such as the mass rally, that were developed by democratic and socialist movements and parties in the nineteenth century.[60] One of the main reasons why fascism was so effective and why it represented an historically unprecedented political formation was precisely this transformation of left-wing populist political forms and their successful implementation for a right-wing populist political project. As Gustav Le Bon had already pointedly remarked in his introduction to *The Crowd* in 1895, if conservative elites hoped to maintain their positions of power in the new age of democracy, they would have to learn to play the game of mass politics and mass manipulation.[61] Fascism's successful *transformation* of left-wing into right-wing populist political forms, whose mass appeal eventually outstripped the appeal of socialism, can certainly be seen as fulfilling Le Bon's prognostication.[62] Like Horkheimer, Kracauer pays very close attention to the subtle and not so subtle shifts in the movement from left to right that occurs in the fascists' appropriation of populist forms. In addition to the crucial shift from a focus on rational interests to emotional compensation, Kracauer emphasizes the inversion of means and ends in the fascist transformation of populism. He writes, "As soon as totalitarian propaganda exploits the procedures used in the revolutionary camp, their function changes.... The same actions ... that the one side directs toward revolutionary goals, lose on the other side any purpose transcending the mass, and now serve only to transform the mass into a tough, rigidly structured formation.... The movement becomes an end in itself."[63] One of the consequences of the movement becoming an end in itself in this way is that a state of total mobilization must be permanently maintained in order to stifle any doubts about the authenticity of the illusory world created by propaganda. This need for permanent reaffirmation of the totalitarian Weltanschauung also explains the fact that leaders play a much more significant role in right-wing populist and fascist movements than in left-wing populist and socialist movements. In the latter, the leader's function is primarily to articulate the best means to achieve the material interests of the individuals in the movement. In the latter, the primary function of the leader is social-psychological: he must create and maintain the emotional ties that bind the imagined community together. Indeed, he must become the physical embodiment and symbol of that community. Neither Kracauer nor Horkheimer deny that such emotional bonds also exist in left-wing populism and socialism, but they insist that they are secondary to the primary, rational function of leaders in those movements.[64] If such emotional attachments to the leader begin to eclipse the rational pursuit of material interests, than the movement runs the risk of transforming itself into a right-wing populist movement—which is, historically, hardly a rare phenomenon.[65]

Section F of Kracauer's essay contains an important and distinctive contribution to a historically specific theory of the rise of fascism. With the possible exception of Franz Neumann's *Behemoth*, Kracauer's analysis here of the recent social and historical preconditions of fascism surpasses anything that the other Institute members wrote on the topic. As we have seen, Kracauer draws liberally upon Horkheimer's macrological analysis of the sociohistorical roots of fascism in modern bourgeois society as a whole, and Fromm's analysis of the social-psychological mechanisms at work in fascism, but neither Horkheimer nor Fromm provide a sustained analysis of the social and political situation in Germany in the 1920s, which set the stage for the triumph of National Socialism. As Kracauer vigorously emphasizes, fascist propaganda can succeed only under specific social conditions. He writes, "If the society, into which propaganda is introduced had not been receptive to it, it would have never been as successful as it was."[66] What, then, according to Kracauer, were the specific social conditions in Weimar Germany that made fascism possible? Above all, he stresses the political consequences of the hyperinflation of 1923, which hit the German middle class particularly hard and delegitimated the ruling parties in their eyes. The interlude of economic recovery brought by the Dawes Plan succeeded temporarily in holding the anger and distrust of the middle class in abeyance, but when the economy collapsed for a second time after the Great Crash of 1929, many came to the conclusion that Germany's experiment with liberal democracy had failed, and that a radical alternative was necessary. Kracauer argues that the experience of the hyperinflation had created anticapitalist attitudes among large section of the middle classes. He also discusses how these attitudes were reinforced by the strong tendencies toward the concentration of capital in the mid-1920s, with the "rationalization" of the production process and the formation of ever larger monopolies. Many members of the *alter Mittelstand* ("old" middle classes) were further damaged by these tendencies, while at the same time the ranks of the *neuer Mittelstand* ("new" middle classes) swelled, as the massive new companies hired white-collar workers to staff their bureaucracies.

Kracauer had, of course, already established himself as a leading authority on these *Angestellten*: the salaried white-collar workers who formed the most rapidly growing social group in Germany in the 1920s.[67] As in his earlier study, here too Kracauer stressed the social dislocation (*Obdachlosigkeit*) of the salaried masses, and their illusory belief that they somehow stood outside the social antagonisms of modern capitalist society. Kracauer points explicitly to Marx's remarks about the social position of the petty bourgeoisie, which leads them falsely to believe they were "extra-territorial in relation to class," and to yearn for a reconciliation of class antagonisms brought about by a powerful outside force—such as the state.[68] Kracauer argues that Marx's analysis "can also be applied to the new middle class masses."[69] Like Freder in the sickly sentimental ending of Fritz Lang's *Metropolis*,[70] who extends one hand to his father (the capitalist boss) and the other to the representative of the working class, in a naïve effort to mediate between the "head" and the "hands" of the industrial society of the future, the new middle classes dream of playing a "constructive mediating role" between wage labor and capital.[71] Despite their anticapitalist attitudes—which were, according to Kracauer, more pronounced among the German than the Italian middle class—they refused to join their logical ally, the workers, for two main reasons. The first reason was that the Socialist and Communist Parties had become too fixated on the industrial working class as the sole "subject" of revolution and failed to welcome the politically radicalized middle classes. The second reason (and here Kracauer draws on Horkheimer's concept of a "cultural lag" in his introduction to the Institute's *Studies on Authority and Family*) was that the consciousness of middle class remained firmly bourgeois even though the material life conditions of much of the old and new middle class differed little from that of the working class—especially after the hyperinflation.⁷²

Kracauer concludes section F with a discussion of how the Nazis adapted their own propaganda to fit perfectly with the confused belief system of the downwardly mobile, and politically mobilized, middle class. If fascist propaganda must adapt itself to the preexisting attitudes of its audience in order to strike a chord with them, "National Socialist propaganda plays every string correctly and resonates perfectly with the impoverished middle classes."⁷³ Rather than dismissing it as an obvious contradiction, the middle class recognizes its own inchoate feelings and beliefs in the Nazis' amalgamation of anticapitalist and anti-Marxist propaganda. Above all, however, they recognize the Nazis' determination to reestablish strong authority. As Kracauer puts it, "The middle classes know instinctively that a class reconciliation within the framework of the dominant economic system could only be imposed and maintained by unlimited authority."⁷⁴

Kracauer's analysis in this section of the dynamic social relations in Weimar Germany, as a necessary condition of the success of Nazi propaganda, contributes to our understanding of the essential right-wing populist dimensions of fascism in at least three ways. First, his critique of the Social Democratic (SPD) and German Communist (KPD) Parties anticipate a suggestive argument made nearly four decades later by Ernesto Laclau.⁷⁵ Like Laclau, Kracauer castigates both the SPD and the KPD for focusing too narrowly on the working class as the sole possible subject of the revolutionary transformation of society. In so doing, the SPD and KPD leave the door wide open for fascists to appeal to the déclassé middle classes, who had developed anticapitalist attitudes, but who were spurned by the Socialists and the Communists. Drawing on progressive populist (democratic and republican) and socialist ideas from the nineteenth century, fascism transforms these ideas into a right-wing populist direction, which culminates in their radical nationalist concept of "das Volk." Kracauer describes this failure to reach out to the disaffected middle classes in terms of the socialists' loss of a "total vision of society."⁷⁶ He argues that "during the crisis the workers' parties completely lost sight of their former vision of society as a whole, even though the surge of new masses should have drawn their attention to society as a whole."⁷⁷ Also, importantly, Kracauer criticizes the SPD for its reluctance to carry out a true revolution. Even though power fell right into its lap, the Social Democrats did not understand how to use it, and their pusillanimous revisionism made them "forgot to take control of the judicial and military apparatus," thereby leaving the conservative elites from the Kaiserreich firmly entrenched in their positions, where they would patiently wait for their opportunity to undermine the Republic. Kracauer concludes that "the absence of a real revolution heightens the appeal of a pseudo-revolution among the proletarianized middle classes."[78]

The second, closely related way in which Kracauer underscores the right-wing populist dimensions of fascism is his description of how the Nazis steal the very idea of socialism from the SPD and KPD. Here he develops further arguments from earlier in the essay relating to the aim of propaganda to separate people from their material interests, and how the delegitimation of the party system—which was based precisely on representing those interests—greatly facilitated this task. Kracauer writes:

> The dissolution of structures, which totalitarian propaganda was determined to destroy, had already been set in motion by the collapse of the party system. This collapse set the stage for this propaganda by creating a breach into which it could leap. The more the German workers' parties failed to meet expectations, the easier it was for National Socialist propaganda to attract the masses produced by the crisis with the idea of socialism, while at the same time suppressing the interests upon which socialism was based.[79]

Here Kracauer gives us not only an excellent example of the fascist appropriation of left-wing political ideas and their transformation into right-wing populist ideology; he also provides us with a compelling explanation of why such transformations are *socially necessary*—in precisely the sense Marx discussed in his theory of ideology. If liberal political and economic ideas were the socially necessary form of ideology in the liberal capitalist societies of the nineteenth century, the rapid concentration of capital in the monopoly and state capitalist societies of the twentieth century created the need for new forms of right-wing populist ideology, which assume their most extreme and virulent form in fascist and National Socialist propaganda. Kracauer buttresses his argument here with the following statement from Ignacio Silone: "In a country like Germany, in which almost three-quarters of all voters are employees, a bourgeois parliamentary majority is only possible if the capitalist parties present themselves as populists [volkstümlich auftreten] and make all kinds of promises to the poor masses.... The dictatorship in Germany was necessary."[80] In short, as society becomes dominated by an increasingly narrow group of particular interests, ideology must become increasingly intense and sophisticated in order to conceal blatant contradictions and to cajole the majority into sacrificing their clear interest in an emancipatory transformation of capitalist social relations.

As we have seen, social-psychological mechanisms come to play an increasingly important role in this transformation of capitalist ideology from liberalism to right-wing populism. According to Horkheimer, psychoanalysis has little to teach us about rational social movements, which are grounded in the pursuit of individuals' material interests, but it has much to teach us about the irrational mobilization of masses for aims that run contrary to their own interests.[81] The third and final lesson to be learned in this section about fascism and right-wing populism is related to the social psychology of totalitarian propaganda. Elaborating upon the remarks he made in section E, on the crucial role of sadism in fascist movements, Kracauer identifies the basic social-psychological mechanism of totalitarian propaganda as "arousing elementary passions and directing them against external objects."[82] The consciously pursued end of this tactic is mass deception: "The more intense the rage that is fixated on such objects, the less capable the bedazzled masses are of seeing the contradictions in the propaganda."[83] So, Kracauer clearly recognizes the central importance of such psychological mechanisms at work in the right-wing populists' need to constantly fabricate a clear and present danger posed to the people by their internal and external enemies. Yet, as Adorno points out in his critique of Kracauer's essay, his appropriation of psychoanalysis is not sophisticated enough to articulate theoretically how and why these mechanisms functioned. For this reason, Kracauer also relies heavily on the more theoretically sophisticated synthesis of Marx and Freud developed in the 1930s by Horkheimer and Fromm.

A brief discussion of the final section will suffice, since it mainly summarizes the rest the essay and since we have included a translation of it in this volume for the reader's own perusal. In section G, Kracauer reiterates the crucial point that propaganda is socially necessary for fascist regimes. He writes, "Propaganda is not just something used occasionally by modern dictators, it is anchored in the foundations of these dictatorships."[84] He discusses the fascist instrumentalization of law, and its reduction to "whatever is useful to the German people."[85] But for a much more penetrating theory of the fascist destruction of the rule of law, one should rely on Franz Neumann, not Kracauer.[86] Pointing to the organization of leisure time in fascist Germany by the Nazis' *Kraft durch Freude*, and in Italy by Mussolini's *Dopolavoro* programs, Kracauer gives further concrete examples of the important role of psychological compensation and the maintenance of the illusion of class equality in both regimes. Perhaps the most important point, however, in the conclusion of Kracauer's essay, is his strong emphasis on the social origins of fascism, and on the concomitant necessity to develop a critical *social* theory of fascism. In contrast to Carl Schmitt and later theorists such as Ernesto Laclau who were influenced by him, who move away from social theory, and who see in the pronounced populist dimensions of fascism evidence of the "primacy of the political," Kracauer remains—like Horkheimer, Fromm, and Adorno—a critical Marxist who rejects the autonomy of "the political" from social and socioeconomic relations. Kracauer states clearly his conviction that "the autonomous life [*Eigenleben*] of social reality determines the dictatorships."[87]

ADORNO'S CRITIQUE OF KRACAUER'S ESSAY

Next, I would like to briefly examine Theodor Adorno's evaluation of Kracauer's essay in order to reflect more generally upon the strengths and weaknesses of Kracauer's analysis of fascism, and also upon the ways in which his analysis was indebted to Horkheimer and Fromm. In March 1938, Adorno wrote an evaluation of Kracauer's essay for Horkheimer, to aid him in deciding whether or not Horkheimer should publish it in the *Zeitschrift für Sozialforschung*. Adorno argues first that Kracauer is not rigorous enough theoretically, especially in regard to his inadequate grasp of historical materialism and psychoanalysis. For Adorno, this alleged shortcoming also meant that Kracauer did not share the same theoretical premises as the Institute, and that he did not adequately grasp Horkheimer's writings, upon which he had relied so heavily in the essay. Adorno's second main criticism of Kracauer was that his essay was not sufficiently grounded empirically, that his conclusions were based on a spotty sampling of the scholarly literature on fascism up to that point. Although Adorno's overall evaluation of Kracauer's essay was negative, he did find some things to praise. Adorno states that Kracauer had succeeded in giving clear and nuanced expression in literary form to many important features of fascism, which he and others had experienced personally in the 1920s and early 1930s. Adorno praises the astuteness of Kracauer's observations and attributes their high quality to his "phenomenological" approach to the subject. Adorno also appreciates Kracauer's argument that fascism must constantly produce the masses, and that the fetishization of the personality of the leader cannot be separated from this ideological necessity.

Adorno's criticisms of Kracauer are most justified in relation to his inadequate grasp of psychoanalysis, and of social psychology and mass psychology more generally. Kracauer's theoretical weaknesses in these areas are precisely what led him to draw so heavily upon Horkheimer and Fromm's writings from the 1930s, which pioneered a qualitatively new approach to critical social theory that was grounded in a sophisticated synthesis of historical materialism and psychoanalysis. Although many of Kracauer's astute observations could be used as examples of the social-psychological mechanisms at work in fascism, one should not seek in his work a rigorous, conceptual explanation of how they function. In this regard, Horkheimer and Fromm's writings from the 1930s, as well as Adorno's writings on the social psychology of fascism in the 1940s, are without doubt superior to Kracauer's essay.[88] Also, as noted, Kracauer's failure to address the literature on mass psychology, from Gustav Le Bon and William McDougall (among others) to Freud's *Group Psychology and the Analysis of the Ego* (which was published in 1921), also underscores Kracauer's inadequate theoretical grasp of social psychology, group psychology, and psychoanalysis. With regard to Kracauer's allegedly insufficient understanding of Marx's theoretical categories, Adorno's argument is less convincing. We have seen here how Kracauer avoided the reductionism of traditional Marxist approaches, which failed to grasp the crucial right-wing populist dimensions of fascism. Kracauer's more supple interpretation of Marx, combined with his astute sociological observations, led him to focus precisely on this key aspect of fascism, particularly as it manifested itself in the realm of fascist propaganda. Although Lukacs's interpretation of Marx was certainly more sophisticated than Kracauer's—Adorno drew liberally upon Lukacs's pathbreaking reinterpretation of Marx in his own writings—Lukacs's fetishization of the proletariat as the "subject-object" of history prevented him from grasping the crucial populist dimensions of fascism in the way that Kracauer had.[89] At the same time, Kracauer remained enough of a Marxist to see through the spurious claim, made by theorists then (Schmitt) and later (Laclau), that fascism signified the replacement of socioeconomic relations by politics as the new foundation of society.

Adorno's second main criticism of Kracauer's essay, that it lacked solid empirical foundations and was not adequately grounded in the scholarly literature on fascism, is justified to a certain extent. As Adorno points out, in the sections of his essay on Italian fascism Kracauer relies almost exclusively on Ignazio Silone's writings. Kracauer stands on firmer ground in the sections on National Socialism, in which he draws not only upon studies by respected contemporary scholars—such as Arthur Rosenberg, Erwin von Beckerath, and Eric Wernert—but also extensively upon the writings and speeches of Nazi leaders, such as Adolf Hitler, Joseph Goebbels, Gregor Strasser, Hermann Göring, and Rudolf Hess. Kracauer also makes us of a number of studies of propaganda from both German and English-speaking scholars. Finally, Kracauer draws extensively on the writings of Fromm and, to an even greater extent, Horkheimer throughout the essay. Although Kracauer's theoretical premises were not the same as Horkheimer's, it is not the case, as Adorno claimed, that Kracauer failed to understand their writings. On the contrary, Kracauer seemed to have intuited his own theoretical weaknesses and to have used Horkheimer and Fromm's writings effectively to supplement his own analysis of fascism. The fact that Adorno was engaged at this time in an intense and ultimately successful attempt to win Horkheimer's loyalty, not to mention Adorno's troubled personal relations with Kracauer and his rivalry with Erich Fromm, probably contributed to Adorno's tendentiously negative evaluation of Kracauer's essay and of his appropriation of Horkheimer and Fromm's writings.[90] That said, Adorno did praise the power of Kracauer's "literary" and "phenomenological" observations, which could themselves be seen as a form of "empirical" evidence. In any case, Kracauer's analysis of fascism was grounded in earlier "empirical" studies he had carried out—most notably, of the burgeoning group of white-collar workers (*Die Angestellten*) in Weimar Germany. As I have argued here, some of Kracauer's most original and insightful analyses of fascism (especially in section F) are clearly indebted to these earlier analyses. Finally, I have also tried to point out throughout this essay the many remarkable ways in which Kracauer's analyses anticipated later scholarship on a variety of issues, including Zeev Sternhell's writings on the important role of national-syndicalist workers in the formation of Italian fascism, Ernesto Laclau's early writings on fascism and populism, to Peter Fritzsche's and Geoff Eley's emphasis on the centrality of populist ideology to the success of Nazism.[91] Even if Kracauer's essay may not have had sufficient empirical foundations, subsequent scholarship has demonstrated the truth content of many of his insights.

In addition to summarizing the main arguments in Kracauer's essay, I have attempted to demonstrate here what the essay can still teach us about the crucial links between right-wing, authoritarian populism and fascism. Kracauer's lengthy essay on fascism provides us with many important insights into the ways in which Italian fascism and German National Socialism relied upon right-wing populist ideology and political tactics to secure their catastrophic victory. These include the following: the Manichean—and ideologically motivated—division of society into the friends and enemies of the people, with the former portrayed as virtuous and productive, and the latter as immoral and parasitic; the stress on patriotism and national unity, and the suppression of individual and group interests in the name of the good of the imagined community as a whole; the mobilization of the masses, with the seemingly contrary aim of making people politically passive, individually isolated, and powerless; the central role of psychological compensation, in the form of both sadism (permission to hate and harm official enemies) and masochism (identification with the overwhelming power of the rulers); identification with powerful leaders;, the replacement of one's own ego ideal with the ego ideal of the leader; the crucial role of economic crises in greatly enhancing the appeal of populist movements and parties; the ideological appropriation of key concepts ("the people," "socialism") and strategies (mass rallies) from the left and their transformation into tools of social domination.

The resurgence of right-wing, authoritarian populist movements and parties in Europe, the United States, Latin America, and other parts of the globe in more recent times has generated new interest in both the history of populism and fascism, and the historical links between them.[92] Although it may be conceptually imprecise to label contemporary right-wing, authoritarian populist movements as "fascist," it is justified, conversely, to view fascism as a subspecies of the larger category of "right-wing populism." Fascism can be seen as an extreme, and National Socialism as perhaps the most extreme, form of right-wing, authoritarian populism. Hence, we can still learn important lessons about contemporary right-wing, authoritarian populist movements by studying the history of fascism, and the historical transformation of populism from left to right, that was so essential to the success of fascist movements in Europe in the 1920s and 1930s. The analysis of fascism by Kracauer and the other Frankfurt School Critical Theorists can also teach us important lessons about why right-wing populist ideology has *persisted*—in other words, why it has remained *socially necessary*—in advanced capitalist societies right up to the present day.[93]

NOTES

1. "As it actually was," here referring to Leopold von Ranke's famous dictum about the study of history. On the difference between Ranke's *traditional* historicism and the *critical* historicism of Marx, see John Abromeit, review of Gareth Stedman Jones, *Karl Marx: Greatness and Illusion, Journal of Modern History* 90, no. 4 (December 2018): 968–71. On the centrality of critical historicism to Horkheimer's early Critical Theory, see John Abromeit, "Reconsidering the Critical Historicism of Karl Korsch and the Early Max Horkheimer," in *Karl Korsch zwischen Rechts- und Sozialwissenschaft: ein Beitrag zur Thüringischen Rechts- und Justizgeschichte*, ed. A. Seifert, K. Vieweg, A. Ecker, and E. Eichenhofer (Stuttgart: Boorberg, 2018), 151–76.
2. Theodor Adorno, *Negative Dialektik* (Frankfurt: Suhrkamp Verlag, 1966), 358.
3. As mentioned in the introduction to the first section of our volume, sections E and G of "Totalitarian Propaganda" were the ones that Kracauer himself saw as most important and had proposed to Horkheimer for publication in 1938.

4. John Abromeit, *Max Horkheimer and the Foundations of the Frankfurt School* (Cambridge: Cambridge University Press, 2011), 1–5.
5. John Abromeit, "Critical Theory and the Persistence of Right-Wing Populism," *Logos: A Journal of Modern Society and Culture* 15, no. 2 (September 2016): http://logosjournal.com/2016/abromeit/ (accessed June 28, 2021).
6. Here we follow the designation of the different sections of the essay with successive capital letters (e.g., section A, section B) as it appears in Siegfried Kracauer, *Totalitäre Propaganda* (hereafter TP), ed. Bernd Stiegler (Frankfurt: Suhrkamp Verlag, 2013).
7. John Abromeit, "Max Horkheimer et le concept matérialiste de la culture," in *Les Normes et le possible: Héritage et perspectives de l'École de Francfort*, ed. P. F. Noppen, G. Raulet, and I. Macdonald (Paris: Éditions de la Maison des sciences de l'homme, 2012), 53–70.
8. Ernesto Laclau, *Politics and Ideology in Marxist Theory: Capitalism, Fascism, Populism* (London: New Left, 1977); Peter Fritzsche, *Rehearsals for Fascism: Populism and Political Mobilization in Weimar Germany* (New York: Oxford University Press, 1990); and Peter Fritzsche, *Germans Into Nazis* (Cambridge, MA: Harvard University Press, 1998).
9. Peter Fritzsche, "The Role of 'the People' and the Rise of the Nazis," in *Transformations of Populism in Europe and the Americas*, ed. J. Abromeit, B. Chesterton, G. Marotta, and Y. Norman (London: Bloomsbury, 2016), 5–14.
10. TP, 16.
11. Zeev Sternhell, with Mario Sznaider and Maia Asheri, *The Birth of Fascist Ideology: From Political Rebellion to Political Revolution*, trans. David Maisel (Princeton, NJ: Princeton University Press, 1994).
12. TP, 16.
13. TP, 20.
14. TP, 18.
15. TP, 26.
16. TP, 23.
17. TP, 29; Max Horkheimer, "Authority and the Family," trans. M. J. O'Connell, in *Critical Theory: Selected Essays* (New York: Continuum, 1992), 68ff.
18. TP, 29.
19. TP, 39.
20. Max Horkheimer, "Egoism and Freedom Movements: On the Anthropology of the Bourgeois Epoch," trans. G. F. Hunter, in *Between Philosophy and Social Science: Selected Early Writings* (Cambridge, MA: MIT Press, 1995), 49–110.
21. TP, 34–35.
22. Gustave Le Bon, *The Crowd: A Study of the Popular Mind* (New York: Penguin, 1977), 13–14.
23. Giovanni Gentile, "The Origins and Doctrine of Fascism," in *Origins and Doctrine of Fascism: With Selections from Other Works*, ed. and trans. A. James Gregor (New York: Routledge, 2017), 1–11.
24. To use Franz Neumann's term; Kracauer speaks mainly of "monopoly capitalism," but also emphasizes the desire of monopoly capitalism to establish a much stronger

state, in order to run the economy in a more authoritarian and autonomous manner. Franz Neumann, *Behemoth: Struktur und Praxis des Nationalsozialismus, 1933–1944* (Frankfurt: Fischer, 1984), 269–86.
25. For one astute critique of the Sonderweg thesis as applied to Germany, see Geoff Eley, "In Search of the Bourgeois Revolution: The Peculiarities of German History," *Political Power and Social Theory* 7 (1988): 105–33.
26. Symptomatic of the new right-wing populist strategy was the arch-conservative *Kreuz-Zeitung*, which changed its masthead after World War I from "Vorwärts mit Gott für König und Vaterland" (Forward with God for king and fatherland) to "Für das deutsche Volk" (For the German people). Peter Fritzsche, *Germans Into Nazis*, 111.
27. TP, 48.
28. TP, 57.
29. Karl Marx, "Contribution to the Critique of Hegel's *Philosophy of Right*," in *The Marx-Engels Reader*, 2nd ed., ed. R. Tucker (New York: Norton, 1978), 16–23.
30. Ernesto Laclau, *On Populist Reason* (New York: Verso, 2005), 67–128.
31. Laclau, *Politics and Ideology*.
32. TP, 78.
33. TP, 69.
34. TP, 72.
35. On Kolberg as Goebbels's last desperate attempt to maintain the illusory world of Nazi propaganda, see David Welch, "Nazi Film Policy: Control, Ideology, and Propaganda," in *National Socialist Cultural Policy*, ed. G. R. Cuomo (New York: St. Martin's, 1995), 115–18.
36. For a more recent study of Nazi Germany that emphasizes the importance of the Nazis' creation of a "welfare state," see Götz Aly, *Hitler's Beneficiaries: Plunder, Racial War, and the Nazi Welfare State*, trans. Jefferson Chase (New York: Henry Holt, 2008).
37. For an ideal typical analysis of the commonalities and differences between left and right-wing populism, see Abromeit et al., eds., *Transformations of Populism*, xvi.
38. See John Abromeit, "Transformations of Producerist Populism in Western Europe," in *Transformations of Populism*, 231–64.
39. See Horkheimer and Adorno's analysis of this important trope of Nazi ideology—in terms of what they call "bourgeois anti-Semitism"— in *Dialectic of Enlightenment*, ed. Gunzelin Schmid Noerr, trans. Edmund Jephcott (Stanford, CA: Stanford University Press, 2002), 141–44. Kracauer also mentions this same trope in his essay; he cites Hitler's statement that "schaffende Arbeit" (productive labor) is "ewig anti-Semitisch" (eternally anti-Semitic). TP, 87.
40. Erich Fromm, "Zum Gefühl der Ohnmacht," in *Zeitschrift für Sozialforschung* 6 (1937): 95–119.
41. TP, 76.
42. Erich Fromm, "Theoretische Entwürfe über Autorität und Familie," in *Studien über Autorität und Familie*, ed. Max Horkheimer (Paris: Felix Alcan, 1936), 127, cited here by Kracauer, TP, 76.
43. TP, 75–76. One of the most striking examples of the links between sadism and populism in Nazi propaganda can be found in the film *Jud Süß*, which was

commissioned by Goebbels and released in 1940 to prepare the German population for the so-called "final solution" to the Jewish question. In the film, which is set in eighteenth-century Württemberg, the virtuous and hard-working German people are portrayed as the victims of a sinister, lecherous, and parasitic Jew by the name of Joseph Süß Oppenheimer, who succeeds in bringing the guileless and profligate Duke of Württemberg under his control by granting him loans he is unable to pay back. Oppenheimer uses his influence over the Duke to repeal the laws against Jews living in Stuttgart, the capital city of Württemberg. Oppenheimer also aggressively pursues a married Christian woman, and, after she repeatedly refuses his advances, he rapes her. Soon thereafter the virtuous German people rise up to liberate Stuttgart and Württemberg from the sinister machinations of Oppenheimer, who is given a summary trial and executed (to great fanfare) at the end of the film.

44. Here a more detailed comparison of Kracauer's emphasis on the centrality of atomization in totalitarian regimes with Hannah Arendt's analysis of the same in *The Origins of Totalitarianism* would be interesting.
45. P. 65.
46. P. 64.
47. P. 68. Kracauer is paraphrasing Horkheimer here.
48. P. 68.
49. P. 69.
50. See, for example, Horkheimer's critical historicist analysis of the concept of "skepticism" in these terms, or Herbert Marcuse's analysis of the concept of "Kultur" along the same lines: Max Horkheimer, "Montaigne and the Function of Skepticism," in Hunter, ed., *Between Philosophy and Social Science*, 265–312; Herbert Marcuse, "On the Affirmative Character of Culture," in *Negations: Essays in Critical Theory*, trans. Jeremy J. Shapiro (Boston: Beacon, 1969), 88–133.
51. P. 69.
52. P. 70.
53. Kracauer does mention Walter Benjamin's famous essay "The Work of Art in the Age of Mechanical Reproduction," in which he develops the concepts of the "aestheticization of politics." But Kracauer mentions the essay in the context of a different discussion, and seems to develop his ideas on the aestheticization of politics independently of Benjamin. TP, 80.
54. TP, 64.
55. For a more detailed discussion of the evolution of the concept of the aesthetic from "pertaining to the senses" to the "philosophical study of art," see Herbert Marcuse, *Eros and Civilization: A Philosophical Inquiry into Freud* (Boston: Beacon, 1955), 172–96.
56. P. 72.
57. TP, 63.
58. TP, 64.
59. P. 75.
60. Pp. 60–67.
61. Le Bon, *Crowd*, 13–21.

62. For an elaboration and case study of this argument, see Abromeit, "Transformations of Producerist Populism in Western Europe."
63. P. 72.
64. Pp. 60–62. For Horkheimer's discussion of the crucial differences between genuinely progressive and authoritarian leaders, see "Egoism and Freedom Movements," 77–79. In the more recent literature on populism there is also a lively debate about the role of the leader in contemporary right-wing populist movements. See John Abromeit, "A Critical Review of the Recent Literature on Populism," *Politics and Governance* 5, no. 4 (2017): 177–86.
65. Abromeit et al., eds., *Transformations of Populism*, xvii–ix.
66. TP, 106.
67. Siegfried Kracauer, *The Salaried Masses: Duty and Distraction in Weimar Germany*, trans. Quintin Hoare (London: Verso, 1998).
68. As Kracauer puts it: "Beyond class." TP, 119.
69. TP, 119.
70. In his own analysis of *Metropolis* about ten years later, Kracauer states that "Maria's demand that the heart mediate between hand and brain could well have been formulated by Goebbels. He, too, appealed to the heart—in the interest of totalitarian propaganda." Siegfried Kracauer, *From Caligari to Hitler: A Psychological History of the German Film* (Princeton, NJ: Princeton University Press, 1947), 163–64.
71. TP, 120.
72. Max Horkheimer, "Authority and the Family," in *Critical Theory: Selected Essays* (New York: Continuum, 1965), 65.
73. TP, 126.
74. TP, 124.
75. Ernesto Laclau, *Politics and Ideology in Marxist Theory: Capitalism, Populism, Fascism* (London: New Left, 1977), 81–142.
76. TP, 112. He takes this idea from Ignacio Silone.
77. TP, 111–12.
78. TP, 115.
79. TP, 115.
80. TP, 115.
81. See Horkheimer, "Egoism and Freedom Movements," 95–110.
82. TP, 130.
83. TP, 130.
84. TP, 132.
85. TP, 132, 134.
86. Franz Neumann, *The Democratic and the Authoritarian State: Essays in Political and Legal Theory*, ed. Herbert Marcuse (New York: Free Press, 1957).
87. TP, 146.
88. See, for example, Theodor Adorno, "Anti-Semitism and Fascist Propaganda"; and "Freudian Theory and the Pattern of Fascist Propaganda," in *Soziologische Schriften*, vol. 1 (Frankfurt: Suhrkamp, 1979), 397–433.
89. Lukacs's notorious rejection of psychoanalysis certainly also played a role in his inability to move beyond a traditional Marxist interpretation of fascism.

90. On Adorno's efforts to win Horkheimer's loyalty in the mid- to late 1930s, and his rivalry with Erich Fromm, see John Abromeit, *Max Horkheimer and the Foundations of the Frankfurt School* (Cambridge: Cambridge University Press, 2011), 349–82; on Adorno's difficult relationship with Kracauer, see Martin Jay, "Adorno and Kracauer: Notes on a Trouble Friendship," in *Permanent Exiles: Essays on the Intellectual Migration from Germany to America* (New York: Columbia University Press, 1986), 217–36.
91. Sternhell, *Birth of Fascist Ideology*; Laclau, *Politics and Ideology in Marxist Theory*; Fritzsche, *Germans Into Nazis*; Geoff Eley, *Nazism as Fascism: Violence, Ideology, and the Ground of Consent in Germany, 1930–1945* (New York: Routledge, 2013).
92. For one suggestive attempt to conceptualize the historical relationship between fascism and right-wing populism, see Federico Finchelstein, *From Fascism to Populism in History* (Oakland: University of California Press, 2017).
93. Abromeit, "Critical Theory."

Bibliography

WORKS BY SIEGFRIED KRACAUER

Siegfried Kracauer Werke, 9 vols., edited by Inka Mülder-Bach and Ingrid Belke (Berlin: Suhrkamp Verlag, 2004–2012).

Vol. 1 *Soziologie als Wissenschaft. Der Detektiv-Roman. Die Angestellten*
Vol. 2.1 *Von Caligari zu Hitler*
Vol. 2.2 *Studien zu Massenmedien und Propaganda*
Vol. 3 *Theorie des Films: Die Errettung der äußeren Wirklichkeit*
Vol. 4 *Geschichte—Vor den letzten Dingen*
Vol. 5.1 *Essays, Feuilletons, Rezensionen, 1906–1923*
Vol. 5.2 *Essays, Feuilletons, Rezensionen, 1924–1927*
Vol. 5.3 *Essays, Feuilletons, Rezensionen, 1908–1931*
Vol. 5.4 *Essays, Feuilletons, Rezensionen, 1932–1965*
Vol. 6.1 *Kleine Schriften zum Film, 1921–1927*
Vol. 6.2 *Kleine Schriften zum Film, 1928–1931*
Vol. 6.3 *Kleine Schriften zum Film 1932–1961*
Vol. 7 *Romane und Erzählungen*
Vol. 8 *Jacques Offenbach und das Paris seiner Zeit*
Vol. 9 *Frühe Schriften aus dem Nachlaß*

Totalitäre Propaganda, edited by Bernd Stiegler (Berlin: Suhrkamp Verlag, 2013).

BOOKS IN ENGLISH

The Salaried Masses: Duty and Distraction in Weimar Germany. Translated by Quintin Hoare. New York: Verso, [1930] 1998.
Jacques Offenbach and the Paris of His Time. Translated by Gwenda David and Eric Mosbacher. New York: Zone, [1937] 2002.
From Caligari to Hitler: A Psychological History of the German Film. Princeton, NJ: Princeton University Press, [1947] 2019.
Theory of Film: The Redemption of Physical Reality. Princeton, NJ: Princeton University Press, [1960] 1997.
The Mass Ornament: Weimar Essays. Translated by Thomas Y. Levin. Cambridge, MA: Harvard University Press, [1963] 1995.
History: The Last Things Before the Last. Oxford: Oxford University Press, 1969.
Siegfried Kracauer's American Writings: Essays on Film and Popular Culture. Edited by Johannes von Moltke and Kristy Rawson. Berkeley: University of California Press, 2012.
The Past's Threshold: Essays on Photography. Edited by Philippe Despoix and Maria Zinfert. Translated by Conor Joyce. Berlin: Diaphanes, 2014.
Georg. Translated by Carl Skoggard. Troy, NY: Publication Studio Hudson, 2016.
Theodor W. Adorno and Siegfried Kracauer: Correspondence, 1923–1966. Edited by Wolfgang Schopf. Translated by Susan Reynolds and Michael Winkler. Cambridge: Polity, 2020.

SELECTED SECONDARY LITERATURE (ENGLISH, SINCE 1991)

Books

Barnouw, Dagmar. *Critical Realism: History, Photography, and the Work of Siegfried Kracauer.* Baltimore, MD: Johns Hopkins University Press, 1994.
Craver, Harry T. *Reluctant Skeptic: Siegfried Kracauer and the Crises of Weimar Culture.* New York: Berghahn, 2017.
Fisher, Peter S. *Weimar Controversies: Explorations in Popular Culture with Siegfried Kracauer.* Berlin: Transcript, 2020.
Forrest, Tara. *The Politics of Imagination: Benjamin, Kracauer, Kluge.* New York: Columbia University Press, 2007.
Gemünden, Gerd, and Johannes Von Moltke, eds. *Culture in the Anteroom: The Legacies of Siegfried Kracauer.* Ann Arbor: University of Michigan Press, 2012.
Gilloch, Graeme. *Siegfried Kracauer: Our Companion in Misfortune.* Cambridge: Polity, 2015.
Hansen, Miriam B. *Cinema and Experience: Siegfried Kracauer, Walter Benjamin and Theodor W. Adorno.* Berkeley: University of California Press, 2012.
Koch, Gertrud. *Siegfried Kracauer: An Introduction.* Translated by Jeremy Gaines. Princeton, NJ: Princeton University Press, 2000.
Martin, Adrian. *Last Day Every Day: Figural Thinking from Auerbach and Kracauer to Agamben and Brenez.* Santa Barbara, CA: Punctum, 2012.
Reeh, Henrik. *Ornaments of the Metropolis: Siegfried Kracauer and Modern Urban Culture.* Cambridge, MA: MIT Press, 2004.
Später, Jörg. *Kracauer: A Biography.* Translated by Daniel Steuer. Cambridge: Polity, 2020.
Vedda, Miguel. *Siegfried Kracauer, or, The Allegories of Improvisation.* Cham: Palgrave Macmillan, 2021.

von Moltke, Johannes. *The Curious Humanist: Siegfried Kracauer in America*. Berkeley: University of California Press, 2016.

Book Chapters

Elsaesser, Thomas. "Expressionist Film or Weimar Cinema? With Siegfried Kracauer and Lotte Eisner (Once More) to the Movies." In *Weimar Cinema and After: Germany's Historical Imaginary*, 18–60. New York: Routledge, 2000.
Gilloch, Graeme. " '*Hamlet wird Detekiv*': Reflections on Kracauer, Benjamin, and (Neo)-Noir." In *The Detective of Modernity: Essays on the Work of David Frisby*, edited by Georgia Giannakopoulou and Graeme Gilloch, 181–95. New York: Routledge, 2020.
——. "Impromptus of a Great City: Siegfried Kracauer's Strassen in Berlin und Anderswo." In *Tracing Modernity: Manifestations of the Modern in Architecture and the City*, edited by Mari Hvattum and Christian Hermansen, 291–306. New York: Routledge, 2004.
——. "Orpheus in Hollywood: Siegfried Kracauer's Offenbach Film." In *Tracing Modernity: Manifestations of the Modern in Architecture and the City*, edited by Mari Hvattum and Christian Hermansen, 307–23. New York: Routledge, 2004.
——. "Sunshine and Noir: Benjamin, Kracauer, and Roth Visit the White Cities." In *Walter Benjamin and the Aesthetics of Change*, edited by Anca M. Pusca, 82–94. New York: Palgrave Macmillan, 2010.
Hansen, Miriam B. "America, Paris, the Alps: Kracauer (and Benjamin) on Cinema and Modernity." In *Cinema and the Invention of Modern Life*, edited by Leo Charney and Vanessa R. Schwartz, 362–402. Berkeley: University of California Press, 1995.
Infante, Ignacio. "States of Exile: Kracauer's Extraterritoriality, and the Poetics of Memory in Cristina Peri Rossi's *Estado de exilio* (2003)." In *Liquid Borders: Migration as Resistance*, edited by Mabel Moraña, 131–42. London: Routledge, 2021.
Jarosinski, Eric. "Urban Mediations: The Theoretical Space of Siegfried Kracauer's Ginster." In *Spatial Turns: Space, Place, and Mobility in German Literary and Visual Culture*, edited by Jaimey Fisher and Barbara C. Mennel, 171–88. Amsterdam: Rodopi, 2010.
Jennings, Michael W. "Walter Benjamin, Siegfried Kracauer, and Weimar Criticism." In *Weimar Thought: A Contested Legacy*, edited by Peter E. Gordon and John P. McCormick, 203–19. Princeton, NJ: Princeton University Press, 2013.
Kaes, Anton. "Siegfried Kracauer: The Film Historian in Exile." In *"Escape to Life": German Intellectuals in New York—A Compendium on Exile After 1933*, edited by Eckart Goebel and Sigrid Weigel, 236–69. Vienna: De Gruyter, 2012.
Leslie, Esther. "Siegfried Kracauer and Walter Benjamin: Memory from Weimar to Hitler." In *Memory: Histories, Theories, Debates*, edited by Susannah Radstone and Bill Schwarz, 123–35. New York: Fordham University Press, 2010.
Linfield, Susan. "Kael and Kracauer: The (Very) Odd Couple." In *Talking About Pauline Kael: Critics, Filmmakers, and Scholars Remember an Icon*, edited by Wayne Stengel, 145–58. Washington, DC: Rowman & Littlefield, 2015.
Martins, Ansgar. "Siegfried Kracauer: Documentary Realist and Critic of Ideological 'Homelessness.' " Translated by Lars Fischer. In *The SAGE Handbook of Frankfurt School Critical Theory*, edited by Beverley Best, Werner Bonefeld, and Chris O'Kane, 234–51. Newbuy Park, CA: SAGE, 2018.
Miller, Sanda. "Siegfried Kracauer: Critical Observations on the Discreet Charm of the Metropolis." In *Revisiting the Frankfurt School: Essays on Culture, Media, and Theory*, edited by David Berry, 7–25. New York: Routledge, 2012.
Morelock, Jeremiah. "Siegfried Kracauer and the Interpretation of Films." In *How to Critique Authoritarian Populism: Methodologies of the Frankfurt School*, 391–411. Leiden: Brill, 2021.

Reeh, Henrik. "Fragmentation, Improvisation, and Urban Quality: A Heterotopian Motif in Siegfried Kracauer." In *Chora, Vol. 3: Intervals in the Philosophy of Architecture*, edited by Alberto Perez-Gomez and Stephen Parcell, 157–78. Toronto: McGill-Queen's University Press, 1999.

Richter, Gerhard. "Homeless Images: Kracauer's Extraterritoriality, Derrida's Monolingualism of the Other." In *Thought-Images: Frankfurt School Writers' Reflections from Damaged Life*, 107–46. Stanford, CA: Stanford University Press, 2007.

Robnik, Drehli. "Siegfried Kracauer." In *Film, Theory, and Philosophy: The Key Thinkers*, edited by Felicity Colman, 40–50. Stocksfield: Acumen, 2009.

Steiner, Henriette. "The Sea, the City, the Ruin, and the Whore: Siegfried Kracauer in Marseilles." In *New Essays on the Frankfurt School of Critical Theory*, edited by Alfred J. Drake, 285–305. Cambridge: Cambridge Scholars, 2009.

Tanca, Marcello. "Corpore praesenti: Walking in Urbanscape with Siegfried Kracauer and Georges Perec." In *Philosophy of Landscape: Think, Walk, Act*, edited by Adriana V. Serrão and Moirika Reker, 221–37. Lisbon: Centre for Philosophy at the University of Lisbon, 2019.

Taylor, Paul A., and Jan LI Harris. "Siegfried Kracauer's Mass Ornament." In *Critical Theories of Mass Media: Then and Now*, 39–61. London: Open University Press, 2008.

von Moltke, Johannes. "2 February, 1956: Siegfried Kracauer Advocates a Socio-Aesthetic Approach to Film in a Letter to Enno Patalas." In *A New History of German Cinema*, edited by Jennifer M. Kapczynski and Michael D. Richardson, 359–64. Rochester, NY: Camden House, 2012.

Wils, Tyson. "Phenomenology, Theology, and 'Physical Reality': The Film Theory Realism of Siegfried Kracauer." In *The Major Realist Film Theorists: A Critical Anthology*, edited by Ian Aitken, 67–80. Edinburgh: Edinburgh University Press, 2016.

Zakai, Avihu. "Siegfried Kracauer's *From Caligari to Hitler*: Weimar Cinema as Pandora's Box." In *Jewish Exiles' Psychological Interpretations of Nazism*, 71–116. New York: Palgrave Macmillan, 2020.

Zaslove, Jerry. " 'The Reparation of Dead Souls': Siegfried Kracauer's Archimedean Exile—The Prophetic Journey from Death to Bildung." In *Exile, Science, and Bildung: The Contested Legacies of German Émigré Intellectuals*, edited by David Kettler and Gerhard Lauer, 139–55. New York: Palgrave Macmillan, 2005.

Journal Articles

Abbate, Carolyn. "Offenbach, Kracauer, and Ethical Frivolity." *Opera Quarterly* 33, no. 1 (2017): 62–86.

Aitken, Ian. "Distraction and Redemption: Kracauer, Surrealism, and Phenomenology." *Screen* 39, no. 2 (1998): 124–40.

———. "Physical Reality: The Role of the Empirical in the Film Theory of Siegfried Kracauer, John Grierson, André Bazin, and Georg Lukács." *Studies in Documentary Film* 1, no. 2 (2007): 105–21.

Allen, John. "The Cultural Spaces of Siegfried Kracauer: The Many Surfaces of Berlin." *New Formations*, no. 61 (2007): 20–33.

Anderson, Mark M. "Siegfried Kracauer and Meyer Schapiro: A Friendship." *New German Critique*, no. 54 (1991): 19–29.

Baer, Nicholas. "Historical Turns: On Caligari, Kracauer, and New Film History." *Research in Film and History*, no. 1 (2018): 1–16.

Bardach-Yalov, Elina. "Analyzing Russian Propaganda: Application of Siegfried Kracauer's Qualitative Content Analysis Method." *Journal of Information Warfare* 11, no. 2 (2012): 24–36.

Benjamin, Andrew. "What, in Truth, Is Photography? Notes After Kracauer." *Oxford Literary Review* 32, no. 2 (2010): 189–201.

Blatterer, Harry. "Siegfried Kracauer's Differentiating Approach to Friendship." *Journal of Historical Sociology* 32, no. 2 (2019): 173–88.

Brett, Donna MF. "The Uncanny Return: Documenting Place in Post-war German Photography." *Photographies* 3, no. 1 (2010): 7–22.
Campbell, Jan. "Are Your Dreams Wishes or Desires? Hysteria as Distraction and Character in the Work of Siegfried Kracauer." *New Formations*, no. 61 (2007): 132–48.
Carroll, Noël. "The Cabinet of Dr. Kracauer." *Millennium Film Journal* 1, no. 2 (1998): 77–85.
Clucas, Stephen. "Cultural Phenomenology and the Everyday." *Critical Quarterly* 42, no. 1 (2000): 8–34.
Craver, Harry T. "Dismantling the Subject: Concepts of the Individual in the Weimar Writings of Siegfried Kracauer and Gottfried Benn." *New German Critique*, no. 127 (2016): 1–35.
Culbert, David. "The Rockefeller Foundation, the Museum of Modern Art Film Library, and Siegfried Kracauer, 1941." *Historical Journal of Film, Radio, and Television* 13, no. 4 (1993): 495–511.
Dimendberg, Edward. "Down These Seen Streets a Man Must Go: Siegfried Kracauer, 'Hollywood's Terror Films,' and the Spatiality of Film Noir." *New German Critique*, no. 89 (2003): 113–43.
Donald, James. "Kracauer and the Dancing Girls." *New Formations*, no. 61 (2007): 49–63.
Eksteins, Modris. "Rag-picker: Siegfried Kracauer and the Mass Ornament." *International Journal of Politics, Culture, and Society* 10, no. 4 (1997): 609–13.
Elsaesser, Thomas. "Siegfried Kracauer's Affinities." *NECSUS: European Journal of Media Studies* 3, no. 1 (2014): 5–20.
Ermarth, Michael. "Girls Gone Wild in Weimar Germany: Siegfried Kracauer on Girlkultur and the Unkultur of Americanism." *Modernism/Modernity* 19, no. 1 (2012): 1–18.
Ethis, Emmanuel. "From Siegfried Kracauer to Darth Vader: Shots on Cinema and Social Sciences." *Sociétés* 96, no. 2 (2007): 9–20.
Fay, Jennifer. "Antarctica and Siegfried Kracauer's Cold Love." *Discourse* 33, no. 3 (2011): 291–321.
Fleischer, Molly. "The Gaze of the Flaneur in Siegfried Kracauer's 'Das Ornament Der Masse.'" *German Life and Letters* 54, no. 1 (2001): 10–24.
Frey, Mattias. "Filmkritik, with and Without Italics: Kracauerism and Its Limits in Postwar German Film Criticism." *New German Critique*, no. 120 (2013): 85–110.
Frisby, David. "Between the Spheres: Siegfried Kracauer and the Detective Novel." *Theory, Culture & Society* 9, no. 2 (1992): 1–22.
Giles, Steve. "Making Visible, Making Strange: Photography and Representation in Kracauer, Brecht, and Benjamin." *New Formations*, no. 61 (2007): 64-75.
Gilloch, Graeme. "Fragments, Cityscapes, Modernity: Kracauer on the Cannebière." *Journal of Classical Sociology* 13, no. 1 (2012): 20–29.
———. "Urban Optics: Film, Phantasmagoria, and the City in Benjamin and Kracauer." *New Formations*, no. 61 (2007): 115–31.
Gilloch, Graeme, and Jaeho Kang. " 'Below the Surface': Siegfried Kracauer's 'Test-Film' Project." *New Formations*, no. 61 (2007): 149–60.
Hales, Barbara. "Taming the Technological Shrew: Woman as Machine in Weimar Culture." *Neophilologus* 94, no. 2 (2010): 301–16.
Handelman, Matthew. "The Dialectics of Otherness: Siegfried Kracauer's Figurations of the Jew, Judaism, and Jewishness." *Yearbook for European Jewish Literature Studies* 2, no. 1 (2015): 90–111.
———. "The Forgotten Conversation: Five Letters from Franz Rosenzweig to Siegfried Kracauer, 1921–1923." *Scientia Poetica* 15, no. 2011 (2011): 234–51.
Hansen, Miriam B. "Decentric Perspectives: Kracauer's Early Writings on Film and Mass Culture." *New German Critique*, no. 54 (1991): 47–76.
———. "Mass Culture as Hieroglyphic Writing: Adorno, Derrida, Kracauer." *New German Critique*, no. 56 (1992): 43–73.
Itkin, Alan. "Orpheus, Perseus, Ahasuerus: Reflection and Representation in Siegfried Kracauer's Underworlds of History." *Germanic Review: Literature, Culture, Theory* 87, no. 2 (2012): 175–202.

Jacobs, Steven, and Hilde D'haeyere. "Frankfurter Slapstick: Benjamin, Kracauer, and Adorno on American Screen Comedy." *October*, no. 160 (2017): 30–50.
Jay, Martin. "The Little Shopgirls Enter the Public Sphere." *New German Critique*, no. 122 (2014): 159–69.
Katz, Marc. "The Hotel Kracauer." *Differences: A Journal of Feminist Cultural Studies* 11, no. 2 (1999): 134–52.
Kent, James. "The Present's Historical Task: Kracauer as Reader of Collingwood." *Critical Horizons* 17, nos. 3–4 (2016): 338–57.
Koch, Gertrud. "A Curious Realism: Redeeming Kracauer's Film Theory Through Whitehead's Process Philosophy." *Screen* 61, no. 2 (2020): 280–87.
Koch, Gertrud, and Jeremy Gaines. " 'Not Yet Accepted Anywhere': Exile, Memory, and Image in Kracauer's Conception of History." *New German Critique*, no. 54 (1991): 95-109.
Kouvaros, George. "The Old Greeks." *Cultural Studies Review* 22, no. 2 (2016): 149–57.
Langfor, Barry. " 'The strangest of station names': Changing Trains with Kracauer and Benjamin." *New Formations*, no. 61 (2007): 104–14.
Lauterbach, Burkhart. " 'The New Majority' Scholarly Folklore Studies on German White-collar Culture." *Studies in Cultures, Organizations, and Societies* 3, no. 2 (1997): 211–28.
Lovett, Dustin. "The Politics of Translation in the Press: Siegfried Kracauer and Cultural Mediation in the Periodicals of the Weimar Republic." *Translation and Interpreting Studies* 14, no. 2 (2019): 265–82.
Luke, Megan R. "The Photographic Reproduction of Space: Wölfflin, Panofsky, Kracauer." *RES: Anthropology and Aesthetics* 57, no. 1 (2010): 339–43.
Mack, Michael. "Film as Memory: Siegfried Kracauer's Psychological History of German 'National Culture.'" *Journal of European Studies* 30, no. 118 (2000): 157–81.
———. "Literature and Theory: Siegfried Kracauer's Law, Walter Benjamin's Allegory, and G. K. Chesterton's *The Innocence of Father Brown*." *Orbis Litterarum* 54, no. 6 (1999): 399–423.
McCann, Andrew. "Melancholy and the Masses: Siegfried Kracauer and the Media Concept." *Discourse* 43, no. 1 (2021): 150–70.
Mehring, Christine. "Siegfried Kracauer's Theories of Photography: From Weimar to New York." *History of Photography* 21, no. 2 (1997): 129–36.
Mülder-Bach, Inka. "Cinematic Ethnology: Siegfried Kracauer's 'The White-collar Masses.' " *New Left Review*, no. 226 (1997): 41–56.
Ockman, Joan. "Between Ornament and Monument: Siegfried Kracauer and the Architectural Implications of the Mass Ornament." *Thesis: wissenschaftliche Zeitschrift der Bauhaus-Universität Weimar* 49, no. 3 (2003): 75–91.
Petro, Patrice. "Kracauer's Epistemological Shift." *New German Critique*, no. 54 (1991): 127–38.
Ponten, Frederic. "Tremor, Tick, and Trance: Siegfried Kracauer and Gregory Bateson in the Film Library of the Museum of Modern Art." *New German Critique*, no. 139 (2020): 141–72.
Rabot, Jean-Martin. "Siegfried Kracauer: From Critical Sociology to Aesthetic Sociology." *Sociétés* 110, no. 4 (2010): 47–56.
Rheindorf, Markus. "Film as Language: The Politics of Early Film Theory (1920–1960)." *Journal of Language and Politics* 4, no. 1 (2005): 143–59.
Richter, Gerhard. "Siegfried Kracauer and the Folds of Friendship." *German Quarterly* 70, no. 3 (1997): 233–46.
Rühse, Viola. "Luxurious Cinema Palaces in the Roaring Twenties and the Twenty-First Century: Critical Analyses of Movie Theatres by Siegfried Kracauer and Their Relevance Today." *Cultural Intertexts* 10, no. 10 (2020): 13–30.
Schlüpmann, Heide, and Drehli Robnik. "History: From 'the Other Frankfurt School" to 'Cinema and Experience.' " *New German Critique*, no. 122 (2014): 3–6.

Schlüpmann, Heide, and Ishbel Flett. "Re-reading Nietzsche through Kracauer: Towards a Feminist Perspective on Film History." *Film History* 6, no. 1 (1994): 80–93.

Schroeder, Tyler. "Siegfried Kracauer and Ernst Jünger: Writing Between History and the Beyond." *New German Critique*, no. 136 (2019): 167–96.

Sieg, Christian. "Beyond Realism: Siegfried Kracauer and the Ornaments of the Ordinary." *New German Critique*, no. 109 (2010): 99–118.

von Arburg, Hans-Georg. "The Last Dwelling Before the Last: Siegfried Kracauer's Critical Contribution to the Modernist Housing Debate in Weimar Germany." *New German Critique*, no. 141 (2020): 99–140.

von Moltke, Johannes. "The Anonymity of Siegfried Kracauer." *New German Critique*, no. 132 (2017): 83–103.

———. "Teddie and Friedel: Theodor W. Adorno, Siegfried Kracauer, and the Erotics of Friendship." *Criticism* 51, no. 4 (2009): 683–94.

Wigoder, Meir. "History Begins at Home: Photography and Memory in the Writings of Siegfried Kracauer and Roland Barthes." *History & Memory* 13, no. 1 (2001): 19–59.

Zinfert, Maria. "On the Photographic Practice of Lili and Siegfried Kracauer: Portrait Photographs from the Estate in the Deutsches Literaturarchiv (Marbach am Neckar)." *Germanic Review: Literature, Culture, Theory* 88, no. 4 (2013): 435–43.

Sources

1. STUDIES OF TOTALITARIANISM, PROPAGANDA, AND THE MASSES (1936–1940)

1. "Exposé. Mass and Propaganda. An Inquiry Into Fascist Propaganda [Exposé: Masse und Propaganda]," in *Siegfried Kracauer Werke Band 2.2. Studien zu Massenmedien und Propaganda*, ed. Christian Fleck and Bernd Stiegler (Berlin: Suhrkamp Verlag, 2012), 9–16.
2. "Totalitarian Propaganda [Totalitäre Propaganda]," in *Siegfried Kracauer Werke Band 2.2. Studien zu Massenmedien und Propaganda*, ed. Christian Fleck and Bernd Stiegler (Berlin: Suhrkamp Verlag, 2012), 90–119, 147–73.
3. "Abridged Restricted Schema [Abgekürztes gestrafftes Schema]," in *Totalitäre Propaganda*, ed. Bernd Stiegler (Berlin: Suhrkamp Verlag, 2013), 238–39.
4. "Schema [Schemata]," in *Totalitäre Propaganda*, ed. Bernd Stiegler (Berlin: Suhrkamp Verlag, 2013), 240–43.
5. "Disposition," in *Totalitäre Propaganda*, ed. Bernd Stiegler (Berlin: Suhrkamp Verlag, 2013), 244–58.

2. THE CALIGARI COMPLEX (1943–1947)

6. "The Conquest of Europe on the Screen: The Nazi Newsreel, 1939–1940," *Social Research* 10, no. 3 (September 1943): 337–57. Originally written as a report: Document No. 50, May 1, 1943, Experimental Division for the Study of War Time Communications, Library of Congress, Washington, DC.

7. "The Hitler Image," *New Republic* 110, no. 1 (1944): 22.
8. "Below the Surface: Project of a Test Film," typescript, 38 pages, Max Horkheimer and Leo Löwenthal Archives, Archivzentrum of the Stadt- und Universitätsbibliothek, Johann Wolfgang Goethe University, Frankfurt am Main, and Kracauer-Nachlaß, Deutsches Literaturarchiv, Marbach am Neckar.

3. POSTWAR PUBLICS (1948–1950)

9. "Reeducation Program for the Reich," review of *And Call It Peace* by Marshall Knappen, *New York Times Book Review*, January 4, 1948, 6, 18.
10. "How and Why the Public Responds to the Propagandist," review of *Public Opinion and Propaganda* by Leonard W. Doob, *New York Times Book Review*, July 4, 1948, 3.
11. "Popular Advertisements," typescript, 19 pages, January 15, 1949, Kracauer Nachlaß.
12. "A Duck Crosses Main Street" (with Joseph Lyford), *New Republic*, December 13, 1948, 13–15.
13. "National Types as Hollywood Presents Them," *Public Opinion Quarterly* 13, no. 1 (Spring 1949): 53–72.
14. "Deluge of Pictures" review of *From Cave Painting to Comic Strip* by Lancelot Hogben, *Reporter*, January 31, 1950, 39–40.

4. COLD WAR TENSIONS (1952–1958)

15. "Appeals to the Near and Middle East: Implications of the Communications Studies Along the Soviet Periphery," May 1952, prepared for the Bureau of Applied Social Research Columbia University, Max Horkheimer and Leo Löwenthal Archives, Archivzentrum of the Stadt- und Universitätsbibliothek, Johann Wolfgang Goethe University, Frankfurt am Main.
16. "Attitudes Toward Various Communist Types in Hungary, Poland, and Czechoslovakia" (with Paul L. Berkman), *Social Problems* 3, no. 2 (October 1955): 109–14.
17. Proposal for a Research Project Designed to Promote the Use of Qualitative Analysis in the Social Sciences, typescript, 9 pages, December 10, 1950, Kracauer Nachlaß, DLA Marbach, H: Kracauer, Siegfried.

18. "The Challenge of Qualitative Content Analysis," in "International Communications Research," special issue, *Public Opinion Quarterly* 16, no. 4. (Winter 1952/53): 631–42.
19. "On the Relation of Analysis to the Situational Factors in Case Studies," typescript. 26 pages, April 1958. Max Horkheimer and Leo Löwenthal Archives, Archivzentrum of the Stadt- und Universitätsbibliothek, Johann Wolfgang Goethe University, Frankfurt am Main.
20. "The Social Research Center on the Campus: Its Significance for the Social Sciences and Its Relations to the University and Society at Large," typescript. 67 pages, ca. 1954. Kracauer Nachlaß, DLA Marbach, A: Kracauer, Siegfried / Bureau of Applied Social Research.

APPENDICES

1. T. W. Adorno, "Report on the Work 'Totalitarian Propaganda in Germany and Italy' by Siegfried Kracauer, 1–106" in *Totalitäre Propaganda*, ed. Bernd Stiegler (Berlin: Suhrkamp Verlag, 2013), 262–65.
2. John Abromeit, "Siegfried Kracauer and the Early Frankfurt School's Analysis of Fascism as Right-Wing Populism," in *Théorie critique de la propaganda*, ed. Pierre-François Noppen and Gérard Raulet (Paris: Éditions de la Maison des sciences de l'homme, 2020), 251–77.

Index

Aachen Pilgrimage, 96
AAPOR. *See* American Association for Public Opinion Research
Abromeit, John, 32
Abstractness, 18
Academic organizations, 375
Academic research centers, 368
Administrative communication research, 268
Administrative units, 387
Adorno, Theodor W., 2, 3, 5, 8, 22, 273, 340; on advertising, 54n1; "Below the Surface" and, 130, 131; categorical imperative and, 395; critique of Kracauer, 31–32, 38, 413, 415; culture industry and, 211; on *Jacques Offenbach and the Paris of His Time* (Kracauer), 39; Lazarsfeld and, 269; on radio broadcasting, 48n19
Adult education, 343–44
Adventure in Sardinia (1950), 301
Advertising, 27, 54n1, 223; American dream and, 227; characters in, 224, 225, 226, 227, 229, 231; conformity and, 224, 232; dream quality of, 230; emptiness revealed by, 229; illusion of heaven on earth in, 226; impact of, 230; Kracauer on, 213; life as presented by, 224–25; security, preoccupation with, 228; for Whiskey, 228
Aestheticized politics, 44, 400, 405, 406
Alcohol, 146
Alexander Nevsky (Eisenstein), 246
Alienation, 19

All Quiet on the Western Front (1930), 241, 244
American Association for Public Opinion Research (AAPOR), 268
American civilization, 264
American Democracy, The (Laski), 232
American dream, 227
American Jewish Committee, 15, 130
American Military Government, 217
American newsreels, 28, 214
Analytical procedures, 360
And Call It Peace (Knappen), 26
Angel (1937), 243
Anglo-American relations, 253
Anglo-Saxon countries, 221
Anglo-Saxon films, 143
Anna Karenina (Tolstoy), 254
Anti-Americanism, 303
Anti-Bolshevism, 103
Anti-intellectualism, 156
Anti-Jewish legislation, 89
Anti-Semitism, 2, 3, 53; film and, 155–56; in U.S., 127, 130
"Appeals to the Near and Middle East" (Kracauer), 29, 269, 275–308
Appearance (*Schein*), 42
Applied communications research, 325
Applied research, 379
Applied social research, 318, 374
Apprenticeship, 380
Architecture, 88
Arnheim, Rudolf, 273, 360

Artistic freedom, 76
"Art of mass images" (*Massenbildkunst*), 44
Atlantic Charter, 217
Atomistic units of text, 329
Atomization, 21
Attenuation of consciousness, 60
"Attitudes Toward Various Communist Types in Hungary, Poland, and Czechoslovakia" (Kracauer), 269, 309–15
Audience research, 359
Auschwitz, 395
Authenticity, 248
Authoritarianism, 3; embrace of, 14; Frankfurt School on, 20
Authoritarian mass mobilization, 400
Authoritarian Personality, The (Adorno), 273, 340, 396
Authoritarian populism, 32, 395, 396, 399, 415, 416
Authoritarian propaganda, 2
Autonomous activities, 365
Autonomous interests, 368
Autonomous research, 351, 352, 355, 356; commissioned research and, 345, 368, 379; dimensions of, 378; evaluation of, 365; large-scale, 367; meaning and range of, 353; projects advancing, 382; significance of, 366
Axis powers, 245

Balabanoff, Angelica, 86
Baptism of Fire (1940), 128, 151n6
Barry, Iris, 128
Base-superstructure model, 397
BASR. *See* Bureau of Applied Social Research
Bastille Square, 142
Battle of Britain, 135, 145
Baudelaire, Charles, 10
BBC. *See* British Broadcasting Company
Beckerath, Erwin von, 414
Bedouins, 280, 282, 294
Behavior patterns, 360
Behemoth (Neumann), 408
Being (*Sein*), 42
"Below the Surface" project (Kracauer), 130, 131, 132, 155–209, 214, 271
Benedict, Ruth, 240
Benjamin, Walter, 2, 7, 13; dreams and, 214; on fascism, 22, 44, 129; financial existence of, 10; on *Jacques Offenbach and the Paris of His Time* (Kracauer), 39; on proletariat, 57
Berelson, Bernard, 324, 325, 328, 329
Berkman, Paul L., 30, 269, 340
Berlin, 7, 8, 41; Hitler in, 148, 151n3, 153; Kracauer move to, 9; white-collar workers in, 30
Berliner Börsen-Zeitung (newspaper), 96
Berlin Express (1948), 256
Berlin movement, 57–58
Best Years of our Lives, The (1946), 243
Beville, H. M. Jr., 354
Bildung (Education), 9
"Biographies in Popular Magazines" (Löwenthal), 273
"Biography as an Art Form of the New Bourgeoisie, The" (Kracauer), 5
blitz, 153
Blockade (1938), 245, 246
Bolshevism, 103, 107, 253
Bonaparte, Napoleon, 11, 152
Boomerang (1947), 243, 260
Born Yesterday (1950), 294
Bourgeois philosophers, 405
Bourgeois prejudices, 132
Bourgeois revolutions, 68–69
British Agent (1934), 254
British Broadcasting Company (BBC), 284, 289, 290, 327
Broad mass, 72
Brussels, 139
Bureaucratic intellectuals, 357
Bureau of Applied Social Research (BASR), 29, 30, 31, 268, 269, 272, 273, 275, 325, 353
Bureau of Overseas Intelligence, 220

Caligari complex, 43
"Camaraderie of the trenches" (*Schutzenkamaradschaft*), 40
Campaign films, 137, 151n6
Capitalism, 13, 19, 51, 109, 293; fascism and, 391; ideology of, 412; liberal, 69, 411; monopoly, 74, 79, 101, 392, 400; revolutionary overthrow of, 41; totalitarianism and, 22
Caribbean islands, 359
Carnegie, Dale, 227, 230
Case studies, 333, 344; numbers of, 337; rarely followed, 338; unoriented, 335, 347
Categorical imperative, 395

Catherine the Great, 239, 244
Catholic priests, 99
Cavalcade (1933), 239, 243, 248, 250, 253
Cave paintings, 264
Censorship, 123
Chesterton, G. K., 76
China, 235
Christianity and National Socialism (Stapel), 65
Chrysanthemum and the Sword (Benedict), 240
Church communities, 362
Churchill, Winston, 140
Church policy, 97
Cinematic approach, 17
Cinematic language, 287
Cinematic realism, 138
Citadel, The (1938), 243
Civic bonds, 40
Civic projects, 11
Civilian government, 40
Civil liberties, 85
Class antagonism, 87
Class division, 118
Class equality, 86
Class-mindedness, 249
Class reconciliation, 42
Class society, 41
Class struggle, 89, 109, 115, 122
Clofine, M. D., 235
Cluny Brown (1946), 244
Coffee houses, 285
Cold War, 4, 16, 29
Cole, Margaret, 249
Collective action, 77
Collective farms, 253
Collective security, 301
Columbia University, 267
Comic strips, 264, 265
Commentary (journal), 212
Commercial film production, 245
Commissioned research, 352, 369–70; acceptance or rejection of, 374; autonomous research and, 345, 368, 379; character of, 378; dynamics of, 377; scientifically insignificant commissions, 375
Commodity culture, 214
Communication research, 272–73
Communications content, 343
Communications habits, 360
Communications process, 344

Communications research, 322, 325, 331, 361, 366
Communications studies, 327
Communism, 41, 50, 256, 277, 278, 282; disillusioned Communists, 311–12, 315; forced Communists, 311–12; jobkeeper Communists, 311; nominal Communists, 311, 313, 315; Satellite Communism, 309
Communist Party, 269, 309–11
Communist propaganda, 30, 52, 54, 267, 269, 375
Comparative studies, 338, 339, 353
Comrade X (1940), 244, 255, 257
Concentration of power, 221
Confessions of a Nazi Spy, The (1939), 246
Conformity, 213, 224, 232
"Conquest of Europe on the Screen, The" (Kracauer), 24, 128
Consciousness, 59, 60
Consumer attitudes, 371
Content analysis, 317, 318, 319, 320, 322
Continuity, 360
Contractor-client relationships, 370–71
Coolidge, Calvin, 230
Cooper, Duff, 140
Copenhagen, 139
Correlations, 324
Countable characteristics, 328
Coward, Noel, 248
Creative energies, 231
Crime and Punishment (Dostoevsky), 254
Crimes against morality (*Sittlichkeitsverbrechen*), 112
Critical references, 329
Critical Theory, 3, 7, 20, 32, 132, 396; concrete application of, 24; Lazarsfeld and, 268
Crosby, John, 235
Crowd, The (Le Bon), 407
Crowds, 148, 149
Crowther, Bosley, 235, 255
Cult of personality, 405
Culture (*Kultur*), 9
Culture industry, 2, 5, 211
Czarist regime, 252
Czechoslovakia, 30, 269, 309, 313

Das Cabinet des Dr. Caligari (Wiene), 14
Das deutsche Wirtschaftswunder (Priester), 91
Das Mittelstandsproblem im Dritten Reich (Schmittmann), 94
Das Schwarze Korps (magazine), 95

Daugherty, Dan, 235
Dawes Plan, 409
Decatur study, 367, 370, 372, 373
Deindividualized mass existence, 4
Deindustrialization, 212, 218
Demobilized soldiers, 40
Democracy, 57, 107, 114; fascism and, 400; liberal, 2; movements for, 404
Denazification, 26, 211, 219
Department of State, U.S., 268, 275
Destruction of consciousness, 59
Detached scientific approach, 376
Deutsches Recht (magazine), 95
Deviant attitudes, 325
Dialectical critique, 6
Dialectic of Enlightenment (Horkheimer and Adorno), 5, 211
Dickens, Charles, 76
Dictators, 43
Dictatorships, 20, 84, 97, 122, 123
Didacticism, 271
Die Nibelungen (1924), 148
Differentiated group psychology, 46n11
Direction, sense of, 388
Direction of communication, 323, 324
Disillusioned Communists, 311–12, 315
Doctoral dissertations, 343
Documentary films, 271, 284, 287, 288
Domestic propaganda, 122–23
Doob, Leonard W., 212, 220, 221
Dopolavoro programs, 412
Dostoevsky, Fyodor, 254
Double Crime in the Maginot Line (1939), 246
Dreams, 213–14
Dressler-Andress, Horst, 76, 78
Drug study, 333, 334, 335, 336, 338, 370
"Duck Crosses Main Street, A" (Kracauer and Lyford), 28, 214, 233–37

Eastern Europe, 30
East Prussia, 90
Economic crises, 11, 50, 377
Economic decline, 124
Economic policy, 95
Economic progress, 299
Economic rivalry, 223
Economic theory, 392
Education (*Bildung*), 9
Educational approach, 381

"Egoism and Freedom Movements" (Horkheimer), 46n11, 399, 404
Egypt, 277, 278, 284, 289, 305, 307; elite in, 294, 299, 304; leading role in Middle East, 303; nationalism in, 292
Eisenstein, Sergei, 246
Eley, Geoff, 415
Elmira study, 359, 361, 362, 367
Emotional intensity, 327
Emotional stability, 227
Empirical data, 351
Empirical facts, 360
Empirical procedures, 388
Empirical research, 20, 350, 366
Empirical-scholarly (*empirisch-wissenschaftlich*), 392
Empirical social research, 354
Empirisch-wissenschaftlich (empirical-scholarly), 392
Employment law, 87
Emptiness, 229
England, 136, 140, 144, 247, 251
English characters in film, 238, 239, 243, 247; misrepresentation of, 252; snobbishness and, 249, 250, 257; traits of, 248; upper-class people, 251
Entertainment films, 259
Entertainment industry, 9, 242
Entrepreneurial personality, 95
Environmental changes, 221
Environmental conditions, 381
Escapism, 230
Ethically desirable drudgery, 376
Ethically undesirable projects, 376
Ethico-political bias, 376
Europe, right-wing populist movements in, 395, 416
European conservatives, 47n17
Exact science: believers in, 331; content analysis and, 318; emulation of, 352, 366; evidences of, 320; ideal of, 316; objectivity of, 351, 357; status of, 317
Exclusivity, 116

Fallada, Hans, 244
Fascism, 3, 411; aestheticized politics and, 44, 400, 405, 406; Benjamin on, 22, 44, 129; capitalism and, 391; democracy and, 400; foreign policy of, 84; formation of, 83;

Frankfurt School and, 20, 32, 416; idealist nature of, 400; impulse to power of, 101; Italian, 10, 39, 397–98, 414, 415; Kracauer on, 22, 396, 401, 408; Laclau on, 415; leaders and, 54; mass as political phenomenon and, 41; mass rallies for, 61, 405, 407; monopoly capitalism and, 392; objectives of, 109; politics of conquest of, 102; populism and, 395; protofascist psychological predispositions, 40; pseudo-reality of, 42, 90; pseudo-solution of, 51, 54; rise of, 408; social origins of, 412; social-psychological mechanisms of, 412, 414; sociohistorical roots of, 408
Fascist agitators, 20
Fascist mass events, 393
Fascist propaganda, 21, 22, 75, 405; aims of, 42; communist propaganda and, 52; cult of mass and, 53; as form of mass culture, 24; in Germany, 49; imaginative powers of, 73; implementation of, 110; leaders and, 398; National Socialist propaganda and, 84; personality and, 406; "producer-parasite" dichotomy and, 403; susceptibility to, 108; white-collar workers and, 128
Fatalism, 292
Faulhaber (Cardinal), 218
Feder, Gottfried, 95
Feeling of Hostility, The (1948), 228
Feme murders, 117
Fertility, 359
Fiction films, 239, 241, 242, 243, 257
Film, 1, 132, 241; aesthetics of, 268; analysis of, 13, 19; Anglo-Saxon films, 143; anti-Semitism and, 155–56; campaign films, 137, 151n6; commercial production of, 245; documentary, 271, 284, 287, 288; entertainment, 259; fiction, 239, 241, 242, 243, 257; German cinema, 23; Greece and, 286; industry, 242, 259; Kracauer and, 2, 12, 14, 24, 268; national images as presented in, 238, 248; Nazi films, 145; realistic tendency of, 16, 17; reviews of, 16; Turkey and, 286; Weimar cinema, 28, 215. *See also* English characters in film; German film; Hollywood; Russian characters in film
Financial attractiveness, 371
Financial crisis, 369
Financial speculation, 11
Flaherty, Robert J., 300

Flinn, John C., 246
Flowers, propagandistic value of, 148, 149
Forced Communists, 311–12
Ford Foundation, 379
Foreign Affair, A (1948), 256
Foreign Correspondent (1940), 243
Foreign policy, 84, 102, 103, 282; propagandist tools of, 104; of U.S., 236, 293, 302, 305, 308
Formal education, 379, 382
Formal propaganda, 100
Formative tendency, 17
France, 16, 127, 263
Franco, Francisco, 246
Frankfurter Zeitung (FZ), 7, 8, 12, 16, 37, 213
Frankfurt School, 2, 3; authoritarian populism and, 39, 396; fascism and, 20, 32, 416
Frankness, 290
Freedom of expression, 88
Free-world solidarity, 282
Freikorps, 94
French Revolution, 116, 400
Frequency counts, 328, 329, 330
Freud, Sigmund, 405, 412, 414
Freund, Karl, 17
"Friendship As a Social Process" (Lazarsfeld and Merton), 364
Fritzsche, Peter, 415
From Caligari to Hitler (Kracauer), 7, 12, 15, 127, 211; Cold War and, 16; German cinema and, 23; interpretive scheme underpinning, 272
From Cave Painting to Comic Strip (Hogben), 28, 214, 263
Fromm, Erich, 46n11, 61, 396, 403, 407, 412, 414–15
Fugitive, The (1947), 256
Führer, figure of, 42, 43, 68, 107, 153; Nazi newsreels and, 130; will of, 400
"Für Uns" (Nazi documentary), 154
Future, belief in, 231, 232
FZ. See Frankfurter Zeitung

Garbo, Greta, 254
Generality, 334, 337; aspiration to, 339; genuine, 348; indeterminate, 347; levels of, 333, 344; minimizing, 335; natural sciences and, 347
Genocide, 4
Gentile, Giovanni, 399–400
Gentiles, 158, 163
Gentleman's Agreement (1947), 243

Georg (Kracauer), 10
George (King), 146
German Communist Party (KPD), 410
German community, 398, 399
German film, 13, 23, 127, 137, 238; early, 129; Hollywood and, 249
German Labor Front, 87
German Labor Service, 140
German middle-class, 409
German Protestantism, 218
"German Radio Propaganda" (Kris), 24
German reeducation, 212, 217
German women, 100
German works councils, 85
Germany, 37, 93; chaos spreading in, 137; defeat of, 217; deindustrialization of, 218; economic situation of, 102; fascist propaganda in, 49; Hollywood and, 244; postwar situation in, 114
German Youth Movement, 144
Gestapo, 85
Global collective properties, 341
Goebbels, Joseph, 57–59, 61, 63–65, 83–84, 90, 227, 398, 418*n*43; artistic freedom and, 76; on *miesmacher*, 94; personality and, 70; popular culture and, 76; principles guiding totalitarian propaganda and, 78; radio broadcasting and, 73; totalitarian propaganda and, 66
"Goebbels' Conception of Propaganda" (Herm), 23, 24, 129
"Goebbels' Principles of Propaganda" (Kracauer), 212
Goethe, Johann Wolfgang, 69, 405
Goodbye, Mr. Chips (1939), 247
Goods, producing and selling, 231
Göring, Hermann, 150, 414
Government agencies, 371
Governmental departments, 351
Grand Illusion (1938), 246
Great Depression, 230
Great War, 40
Greece, 277, 289; admission to NATO of, 278; domestic affairs in, 288; film and, 286; rural, 280; Soviet Union and, 295; U.S. popularity in, 302; well-educated people in, 291; word-of-mouth communications in, 286
Griffith, D. W., 258

Gros, Antoine-Jean, 152
Group psychology, 405
Group Psychology and the Analysis of the Ego (Freud), 414
Grune, Karl, 138
Gunga Din (1939), 251
Gutermann, Norbert, 396

Hack work, 374, 375, 376, 378
Hadamovsky, Eugen, 74
Hamburg, 140
Hansen, Miriam, 129
Happy consciousness, 213
Harper's (magazine), 249
Harvard, 365, 378
Haute bourgeoisie, 40
Heiden, Konrad, 62, 84, 93
Heimat ("homeland"), 41, 71
Herm, Hans, 23, 24, 129
Hess, Rudolf, 414
He Stayed for Breakfast (1940), 254
Hierl, Oberst, 58
High finance, 124
Historical exegesis, 362
Historical factor, 340, 362
Historical materialist analysis, 12
"History and Psychology" (Horkheimer), 46*n*11
Hitler, Adolf, 24, 58–59, 62, 102, 105, 130, 398, 405, 407; in Berlin, 148, 151*n*3, 153; idolization of, 67; Königsberg address, 103; Kracauer quotations of, 392; at Maginot Line, 147; Marxism, liquidation of, 70; mass as political phenomenon and, 150; masses and, 60, 61; military success of, 153; in Nazi newsreels, 146, 152; Old Guard and, 72–73; *Reichskanzlei* and, 148–49; rise to power of, 26; spoken word and, 64–65; at Strassburg cathedral, 139; G. Strasser and, 399, 401; terror and, 111; uneasiness with horse, 154
"Hitler Image, The" (Kracauer), 130
"Hitlerjunge Quex" (Nazi film), 145
Hogben, Lancelot, 28, 214, 215, 263, 264, 266
Hollywood, 28, 238, 239, 242, 252, 258, 260, 286, 295; audiences of, 241; authenticity and, 248; clichés used by, 254; desires created by, 259; domestic self-interest of, 255; economic risks and, 245; English characters in, 247; entertainment formula of, 243; German film and, 249; Germany and, 244; impact

of, 287; public opinion and, 251; Russian heroism in, 244; Soviet Union and, 254
"Hollywood, the Movie Colony" (Kracauer), 128
Holocaust, 4, 25
"Homeland" (*Heimat*), 41, 71
Horkheimer, Max, 3, 5, 10, 12, 22, 395–96, 399, 404, 407, 414–15; "Below the Surface" and, 130, 131; on bourgeois revolutions, 68; culture industry and, 211; Kracauer and, 38, 46*n*11; on leader/follower dynamics, 405; Marxism and, 397; on revolutionary mass, 57; sadomasochism and, 391; on sociohistorical roots of fascism, 408; synthesis Marx and Freud by, 412; "Traditional and Critical Theory," 268
How Green Was My Valley (1941), 243
"How to Stop Worrying and Start Living" (Carnegie), 227, 230
"How U.S. Films Portray Foreign Types" (Kracauer), 215
Huber, Ernst Rudolf, 85
Huckleberry Finn (fictional character), 250
Human behavior, 319
Hungary, 30, 269, 309, 313, 314
Hyperinflation, 121, 409
Hypertension, 362, 363, 372
Hypnotic effects, 43, 61, 62, 66, 67, 69

Idealism, 400
Ideal-types, 330, 339
Idea-montages, 84
Ideology, 19
Ignorance, 132
IIA. *See* International Information Administration
Illegal power, 85
Illinois, 334
Illiteracy, 299
Imagination, 265
Imperialism, 103, 104, 224, 232, 251, 270, 307
Important categories of qualitative analysis, 329
Impressionism, 317, 318, 327, 330
Impulse to power, 101
Inclusive training, 383
Indeterminacy, 357, 358
India, 287
Individual consciousness, 119
Individualism, 4, 40, 297

Individualization, 76
Individual personality, 21, 213
Industrialization, 355
Infrastructural renewal, 11
Injustice, 292
INRA. *See* International Research Associates, Inc.
Insecurity, pathological condition of, 41
In-service training, 379, 380, 387
Institute for Social Research, 2, 7, 10, 15, 268; American Jewish Committee and, 130; empirical research agenda of, 20; Kracauer relationship with, 27, 37. *See also* Frankfurt School
Institutionalized research, 351
Institutional research, 363, 373
Institutional stability, 367
Instruction, 384
Intellectual climate, 365
Intellectualism, 76
Intelligentsia, 280
Internal accuracy, 337
Internal variables, 344
International Broadcasting Service, 268
International communications, 280, 281, 325
International Information Administration (IIA), 269, 271, 276, 277, 279, 282
Internationalism, 76
International Research Associates, Inc. (INRA), 309, 340, 341
"International Tensions" report (Kracauer), 215
International understanding, 238
Interpersonal relations, 273, 359, 360, 362
Iron Curtain, 295, 296, 297, 298, 309, 372, 375
Iron Curtain, The (1948), 246–47, 256
Irrationalism, 13, 32, 132
Israel, 308
Italian fascism, 10, 39, 397–98, 414, 415
Italy, 10, 85, 93; economic situation of, 102; postwar situation in, 114
Ivy (1947), 244

Jacques Offenbach and the Paris of His Time (Kracauer), 7, 21, 39
Jannings, Emil, 254
Japan, 235
Jewish people, 155–56, 158, 305–6
Jobkeeper Communists, 311
Johnson, Alvin, 23, 128

Johnston, Eric, 243
Jordan, 277, 280, 283, 284, 306; Bedouins in, 294; Judge of Islamic Legislation, 291; lower middle-class people in, 296; middle class in, 303, 307
Journey for Margaret (1942), 243
Judge of Islamic Legislation, 291
Jud Süß (1940), 418n43

Kant, Immanuel, 8, 364, 395
KdF. *See* Kraft durch Freude
Keaton, Buster, 293
Knappen, Marshall, 26, 212, 217–18, 219
Kolberg (Nazi propaganda), 402
Königsberg address (Hitler), 103
KPD. *See* German Communist Party
Kracauer, Siegfried, 1, 214, 215, 233–37, 309–15, 393; on abstractness, 18; Adorno critique of, 31–32, 38, 413, 415; on advertising, 213; American newsreels and, 28; "Appeals to the Near and Middle East," 29, 269, 275–308; "Below the Surface" project, 130, 131, 132, 155–209, 214, 271; on cinematic approach, 17; Cold War and, 16; on democracy, 400; dialectical critique and, 6; discontinuities in work of, 20; Eastern Europe and, 30; embrace of U.S. ideologies, 270; on fascism, 22, 396, 401, 408; film and, 2, 12, 14, 24, 268; financial existence of, 10; first U.S. publication of, 128; on formative tendency, 17; Frankfurt School and, 39; Fromm and, 415; German cinema and, 23; Horkheimer and, 38, 46n11; on hyperinflation, 409; on interpersonal relations, 273; journalistic career of, 8; Knappen and, 212; Lazarsfeld and, 268, 269; leaving occupied France, 127; Löwenthal friendship with, 37; main books by, 7; Marseilles notebooks of, 129; Marx and, 414; Marxism and, 397; on mass as political phenomenon, 41; move to Berlin, 9; on Nazi newsreels, 128, 130; New York Museum of Modern Art and, 13; Orientalism and, 271, 285; on party system, 411; in postwar New York, 211; on qualitative analysis, 322; quotations of Hitler, 392; on radio broadcasting, 43, 48n19; remaining in America, 25, 26; Simmel and, 4; "The Social Research Center on the Campus," 31, 271, 273, 350–90; on SPD and KPD, 410; G. Strasser and, 399; "test film" project, 3, 15; theoretical approach of, 391; on total situation, 216; trajectory of, 15; on traumatic experiences of Great War, 40; white-collar workers and, 272; work with U.S. governmental agencies, 267; World War I and, 3; Zweig and, 392.
See also specific writings
Kraft durch Freude (KdF), 87–88
Kremlin, 245
Krieck, Ernst, 63, 66, 72
Kris, Ernst, 23, 24, 128
Kultur (Culture), 9
Kulturkampf (magazine), 95

Laclau, Ernesto, 402, 410, 412, 415
Lady Eve (1941), 250
Lang, Fritz, 14, 148, 409
Large-scale industry, 124
L'art dans le Troisième Reich (Wernert), 75
Laski, Harold J., 232
Last Chance, The (1945), 258, 260
Last Command, The (1928), 254
Latent content, 329
Latent structure analysis, 371
Latin America, 416
Laudatory references, 329
Law school, 336
Lazarsfeld, Paul, 268, 269, 273, 333, 350, 356, 364, 365, 376
Leader/follower dynamics, 405
Leaders, 42; fascism and, 54; fascist propaganda and, 398; personality of, 413
Lean years, 225
Lebanon, 277, 278, 281, 284
Le Bon, Gustav, 399–400, 405, 407, 414
Left-wing intellectuals, 392
Left-wing populism, 407
Legal power, 85–86
Leisure, 292
Lewis, Sinclair, 229
Liberal capitalism, 69, 411
Liberal democracy, 2
Liberalism, 400
Libidinal drives, 404
Liebman, Joshua L., 227
Listener opinions, 360
Literacy, 355
Literature policy, 99
Little Man, What Now? (1934), 244

Lives of a Bengal Lancer, The (1935), 243, 248, 251
Lloyd, Harold, 293
Local influence, 335
London, 140
Lost Horizon (1937), 243
Louisiana Story (1948), 300
Löwenthal, Leo, 25, 27, 130, 268, 273, 396; on *Jacques Offenbach and the Paris of His Time* (Kracuaer), 39; Kracauer friendship with, 37; study of biographies in popular magazines, 340
Lower-middle-class office workers, 41
Lower-middle-class people, 296
Low-income groups, 354
Lubitsch, Ernst, 244, 254
Lukacs, György, 414
Lumpen proletariat, 122
Lyford, Joseph, 28, 214, 233–37

MacArthur, Douglas, 236
Maginot Line, 136, 147
Malaria, 301
Marcuse, Herbert, 25, 27, 213
Market research, 348
Marquand, John, 229
Marshall Plan, 26, 212, 219
Martial sensibility, 40
Marx, Karl, 401, 412, 414
Marxism, 12, 19, 79, 95, 121; base-superstructure model of, 397; Hitler liquidation of, 70; Horkheimer and, 397; Kracauer and, 397; left-wing intellectuals and, 392; methodology of, 391; post-Marxism, 402
Mason and Dixon line, 334
Mass as political phenomenon, 40, 47*n*17; cult of, 53; formation of, 72; Hitler and, 150; leaders and, 42; significance of, 52; structure of, 119; totalitarianism and, 42
Mass communication, 238, 261*n*15, 273, 355; effects of, 358–59; techniques of, 264
Mass culture, 213; Fascist propaganda as, 24; as ideology, 19
Mass desires, 253
Mass dispositions, 259, 260
Massenbildkunst ("Art of mass images"), 44
Mass entertainment, 257
Masses, 404; appealing character of, 74; artificial creation of, 100; common characteristics of, 56; credulity of, 152; expansion of, 57; formation of, 79, 122; Hitler and, 60, 61; masterless, 59; personality and, 69; production of, 108; proletarian, 71; reabsorption of, 51; reproduction of, 78; revolutionary mass and, 57; spiritual homelessness of, 50; totalitarian propaganda and, 70, 213
Mass-man, 60, 61
Mass media, 14, 211, 264, 267, 279, 280, 355; Middle East and, 359; rise of, 5
Mass mobilization, authoritarian, 400
"Mass Ornament, The" (Kracuaer), 6, 11, 13; *The Salaried Masses*, 40; "Totalitarian Propaganda" study and, 40
Mass particles, 74
Mass production, 229
Mass propaganda, 43
Mass rallies, 61, 62, 405, 407
Mass soul, 67
Mass speeches, 66, 67
Materialism, 400
Material issues, 333
Material propaganda, 100
Mathematics, 263
Matteotti Crisis, 93
Matter-of-factness, 327
Matter-of-fact neutralism, 323
Mayer, Carl, 17, 18
McDougall, William, 414
McPhee, W. W., 339, 359
Meaninglessness, pathological condition of, 41
Media and communications, 31
Medical schools, 336, 338, 363
Medium significance, 361, 362
Mein Kampf (Hitler), 70, 405
Meisel, Edmund, 17
Meltzer, Newton, 235
Menzel, Herbert, 333
Merton, Robert K., 341, 357, 361, 364, 365, 373–74
Methodological explorations, 364
Metropolis (1927), 14, 409
"Metropolis and Mental Life, The" (Simmel), 4
Metropolitan society, 11
Mickey Mouse (fictional character), 250
Middle class, 50, 56, 410; German, 409; in Jordan, 303, 307; Lebanese, 281; lower, 296; proletarianized, 121; youth, 144

Middle East, 278, 279, 282, 283, 287; BBC in, 290; coffee houses in, 285; educated populations in, 289; Egypt leading role in, 303; leisure in, 292; mass media and, 359; social changes in, 293, 308; Voice of America and, 284
Middle-ground theories, 361
Miesmacher (moaners), 94
Military marches, 67
Mill, John Stuart, 405
Mission to Moscow (1943), 255
Moaners (*miesmacher*), 94
Mockery (1927), 254
Moderne Politische Propaganda (Goebbels), 66
Modernity, 4, 7
Moehl, Ernst, 119
Monopoly capitalism, 74, 79, 101, 392, 400
Morgenthau Plan, 212, 218
Moss Rose (1947), 244
"Mother" (Pudovkin), 149
Motion Picture Association, 243
Moviegoers, 242
Movietone, 235
Mrs. Miniver (1942), 243, 251
Mr. Smith Goes to Washington (1939), 294
Museum of Modern Art Film Library, 23, 128
Music, 129, 139, 152
Mussolini, Benito, 58, 72, 90, 100, 105, 397, 412; idolization of, 67; terror and, 111
Mutually assured destruction, 4
Mutual understanding, 242

National Bolshevism, 399
National Council of the Protestant Episcopal Church, 356
National fanaticism, 397
National figures, 5
National humiliation, 114
National images as presented in film, 238, 248
Nationalism, 292, 304
National power apparatus, 122
National Socialism, 20, 39, 50, 59, 75, 408; architecture of, 88; church policy and, 97; colonial program of, 104; crisis of 1934, 94; employment law of, 87; foreign policy of, 84; formation of, 83; Heiden and, 62; impulse to power of, 101; literature policy of, 99; mass as political phenomenon and, 41; mass rallies and, 61; objectives of, 109; personality and, 68, 70; politics of conquest of, 102; pseudo-reality of, 90; science and, 112; symbols of, 63; white-collar workers and, 40; will to power of, 91
National Socialist German Workers Party (NSDAP), 397, 398, 399
National Socialist propaganda, 10, 40, 72, 75, 411; fascist propaganda and, 84; imaginative powers of, 73; relativism and, 125
National Socialist Reichstag, 92
Nationalsozialistischen Monatshefte (magazine), 96
Nationalsozialistischer Lehrerbund (NSLB), 98
National-syndicalist workers, 397
NATO. *See* North Atlantic Treaty Organization
Natural sciences, 347
Navigator, The (1924), 293
Nazi campaign films, 151n6
Nazi films, 145
Nazi Germany, 7, 11, 15, 140, 153
Nazi newsreels, 24, 127, 128, 136, 140; beautiful natural settings in, 145; commentary in, 137; crowds in, 148, 149; effectiveness of, 135; Führer and, 130; German film and, 129; Hitler in, 146, 152; information in, 141; music of, 139; panning shots in, 145; pictorial content of, 141–42, 144
Nazi propaganda, 28; *Kolberg*, 402; Winterhilfswerk program and, 403
"Nazi Propaganda and Its Decline" (Speier), 24, 129
Nazism, 3, 415
Nazi soldiers, 147
Neoliberalism, 3
Neumann, Franz, 408
Neutralism, 323
Nevsky, Alexander, 253
New media, 5
New School for Social Research, 23
Newspaper consumption, 285
Newsreel audiences, 236
Newsreel cameramen, 235
Newsreel companies, 234, 237
Newsreel editors, 235, 236
Newsreel theaters, 233, 234
New York Museum of Modern Art, 13
New York Times (newspaper), 26, 235
New York Times Book Review (magazine), 211

Niemoeller, Martin, 218
Night of the Long Knives, 399
Nihilism, 79, 83, 97, 100, 101, 102, 117, 124, 125, 398, 405
Ninotchka (1939), 239, 244, 254, 256
Nominal Communists, 311, 313, 315
Non-Communists, 309, 312, 314
Nonconformity, 232
Nonfiction bestseller lists, 227
Non-quantifiable frequencies, 329
North Atlantic Treaty Organization (NATO), 278, 288, 302
North Star, The (1943), 255, 256
NSDAP. *See* National Socialist German Workers Party
NSLB. *See* Nationalsozialistischer Lehrerbund

Obdachlosigkeit (Social dislocation), 409
Objective information, 240
Objectivity, 317, 318, 327; of exact science, 351, 357; organized research and, 351; of quantitative analysis, 331–32
Occupied France, 16, 127
Offenbach, Jacques, 10, 11, 39, 393
Office of War Information (OWI), 220
Of Human Bondage (1934), 243, 247
Old Guard, 72–73
"On the Relation Between Individual and Collective Properties" (Lazarsfeld and Menzel), 333
Open City (1945), 258
Open terror, 118
Operational significance, 339
Opinion formation, 355, 358
Opinion leaders, 359, 363, 370
Orchestration of power, 44
Organizational continuity, 367
Organizational measures, 371
Organizational rigidity, 368
Organizational separation, 364
Organized research, 379; critics of, 352; fragmentary results of, 358; objectivity and, 351
Organized social research, 366
Orientalism, 271, 285
Oriented case studies, 335
Ornament, 22, 44
Ortega y Gasset, José, 59
"Our Russian Ally" (World in Action short), 143

Out-service training, 379
Over-fine categorization, 324
OWI. *See* Office of War Information
Oxford Conference of World Churches, 96

Pabst, G. W., 138
Paisan (1946), 258, 260
Palestine, 282, 297, 305–6, 307
Paradine Case (1948), 243
Paris, 37, 147
Parliamentarism, 69
Parsonian dichotomic variable patterns, 339
Passive recruitment, 385, 386
Patriotism, 247
"Peace of Mind" (Liebman), 227
Peasants, 122, 280
"People without space" (*Volk ohne Raum*), 103
Permanence, 367, 368
Permanent research organizations, 355
Personality, 120, 413; cult of, 405; entrepreneurial, 95; fascist propaganda and, 406; individual, 21, 213; masses and, 69; National Socialism and, 68, 70
Personality traits, 344
Petty bourgeoisie, 281
Photography, 5
"Photography" (Kracauer), 28
Pick, Lupu, 138
Pictorialization, 265, 266
Pied Piper, The (1942), 243, 248, 251
Plebiscites, 92
Point Four Program, 300
Poland, 30, 141, 269, 309
Polio, 363
Political behavior, 358, 363, 366, 381
Political consciousness, 282
Political fanaticism, 6
Political organizations, 362
Political power, 85
Political propaganda, 49
Political struggle, 79
Political superstructure, 107
Politics of conquest, 102
Pollock, Friedrich, 38
Polls, 232
"Popular Advertisements" (Kracauer), 27, 212
Popular art, 78
Popular culture, 1, 4, 5, 12, 76
Popular sovereignty, 47n17

Population groups, 326
Populism: authoritarian, 32, 395, 396, 399, 415, 416; "friend-enemy" dichotomy of, 403; Laclau on, 415; left-wing, 407; right-wing, 395, 397, 399, 407, 411, 412, 415, 416
Post-Marxism, 402
Postwar period, 50
Postwar reconstruction, 211
Potsdam Agreement, 219
Poverty, 292
Practical indoctrination, 381
Practical skills, 386
Pratt, Samuel, 382, 384, 386, 388
Prejudice, 3, 6, 15
Priester, Hans Erich, 91, 102
Primary data, 351
Princeton Office of Radio Research, 354
Princeton Radio Research Project, 269
Printed material, 285–86, 298
Printers' Union study, 358, 362
Private discussions, 384
Private social agencies, 373
Probabilities, 324
"Producer-parasite" dichotomy, 403
Professional integrity, 274, 352, 374
Professionally problematic assignments, 377
Proletarian collectivism, 41
Proletarianized middle class, 121
Proletarian mass, 71
Proletariat, 50, 88, 414; collectivism, 41; emancipation of, 57; revolutionary mass of, 58
Propaganda and National Power (Hadamovsky), 74
Propaganda and the Nazi War Film (pamphlet), 23, 128
Property rights, 116
Prophets of Deceit (Löwenthal and Guterman), 396
Protestantism, 218
Protofascist psychological predispositions, 40
Pseudo-reality, 90, 92, 100, 123
Psychoanalytic concepts, 392, 412, 413
Psychological components, 345
Psychological constants, 342
Psychological dimension, 341
Psychological domination, 223
Psychological fallacy, 348

Psychological imperialism, 224, 232
Psychological resistance, 146
Psychological-sociological-historical thesis, 14
Psychological states of population groups, 326
Psychological warfare, 15, 241
Psycho-physical structure of people, 56
Psycho-physical upheaval, 104
Psychotherapy, 342
Public listening, 284–85
Public opinion, 221, 227, 245; Hollywood and, 251; manipulation of, 241; in U.S., 242
Public Opinion and Propaganda (Doob), 212
Public Opinion Quarterly (journal), 268
Public social agencies, 373
Pudovkin, Vsevolod, 149, 258, 287

Qualifications, 324
Qualitative analysis, 319, 320; communications studies and, 327; first exercises in, 360; important categories of, 329; impressionism of, 330; Kracauer on, 322; precision attained by, 331; quantitative analysis and, 328, 340
Qualitative exegesis, 329–30
Qualitative reasoning, 326
Quantifiable categories of latent content, 329
Quantification processes, 326
Quantitative analysis, 316, 317, 325, 346; of BBC, 327; direction of communication determined by, 323; nonquantitative explorations and, 326; objectivity of, 331–32; qualitative analysis and, 328, 340; of Voice of America, 327
Quantitative content analysis, 322
Quantitative investigations, 324
Quantitative techniques, 324
Quick study, 372
Quiet One, The (1948), 305

Radio broadcasting, 43, 48n19, 52, 272, 314; Goebbels and, 73; Kris on, 128; meaning of, 351; objective information and, 240; public listening to, 284–85
Radio Free Europe, 30, 269, 314
Radio Research, 1942–1943 (Stanton), 273
Railway line, 140
Random Harvest (1942), 252
Ratio, 7, 18, 41, 43, 60

Realisierungs-Überzeugungen (Realization-convictions), 93
Realistic tendency, 16, 17
Realization-convictions (*Realisierungs-Überzeugungen*), 93
Rebecca (1940), 243, 247
Refugees, 269
Reich Chamber of Radio, 76
Reichskanzlei, 148–49
Reichstag Fire, 7
Relativism, 100, 125
Relevant causes, 342
Reliability, 290, 323
Religious affiliation, 363
Religious mysticism, 6
Religious persecution, 298
"Remarks on Administrative and Critical Communication Research" (Lazarsfeld), 268
Remarque, Erich Maria, 241, 244
Repetition and rhythm of totalitarian propaganda, 43
Research designs, 359, 378
Research institutes, 389
Research intentions, 367
Research organizations, 353, 380
Research propositions, 365
Respect, 329
Revolutionary mass, 57, 119; gatherings of, 62; of proletariat, 58
Riefenstahl, Leni, 19
Right To Know, The (Johnston), 243
Right-wing populism, 32, 395, 397, 399, 407, 411, 412, 415, 416
Road Back, The (1937), 244
Rocco, Alfredo, 85
Rosenberg, Arthur, 414
Rossellini, Roberto, 258
Ruggles of Red Gap (1935), 243, 247, 250, 251, 305
Rural masses, 281, 300
Russian characters in film, 238, 239, 244; actors portraying, 254; clichés in, 253; as sheer abstractions, 257
Russian Five-Year Plan, 253
Russian stereotypes, 216
Ruttmann, Walter, 17, 18, 19, 138

Sadomasochism, 391
SA Gruppenführer Schöne, 89

Salaried Masses, The (Kracauer), 7, 9, 40
Satellite Communism, 309
Satellite mentality, 340, 375
"Satellite Mentality" (Kracauer and Berkman), 30, 269
Schein (Appearance), 42
Scheinwelt (World of spurious appearances), 39, 42, 43
Schmitt, Carl, 47n17, 412
Schmittmann, Benedict, 94
Scholarly standards, 375
Schutzenkamaradschaft ("Camaraderie of the trenches"), 40
Scientific accomplishments, 354
Scientifically insignificant commissions, 375
Scientifically oriented doctors, 338
Scientific potentialities, 371
Search, The (1948), 258, 260
Secondary analysis, 372
Second Empire, 10, 11, 30, 39
Security, 228
Sein (Being), 42
Self-determination, 401
Self-identification, 240
Sex appeal, 229
Shakespeare, William, 239
Silone, Ignazio, 39, 72, 84, 90, 92, 93, 397, 414
Simmel, Georg, 4, 8, 16, 273
Sittlichkeitsverbrechen (Crimes against morality), 112
Situational determinants: selection of, 340; survey of relevant causes oriented toward, 342
Situational factors, 333, 337, 338, 339; attempts to account for, 345; consideration of, 342; omitted, 348; relevant, 341
Smith, Howard K., 150
Snobbishness, 249, 250
Social agencies, 373, 382
Social antagonisms, 124
Social bonds, 40
Social contradictions, 402
Social Democratic Party (SPD), 107, 110, 111, 118, 119, 397, 410
Social dislocation (*Obdachlosigkeit*), 409
Social dynamics, 363
Social environment, 359
Social factors, 362

Socialism, 50, 69, 107, 109, 115, 400, 411; forceful subjugation of, 114; mass rallies for, 405, 407; movements for, 404; in one country, 116
Socialization, 337, 356, 357
Social laboratories, 352
Socially problematic assignments, 377
Social mobility, 334
Social phenomena, 316, 318
Social problems, 351
Social progress, 299
Social-psychological mechanisms, 412, 414
Social psychology, 339, 352
Social reality, 361, 362
Social Research (journal), 23, 128
"Social Research Center on the Campus, The" (Kracauer), 31, 271, 273, 350–90
Social research centers, 350, 351
Social sciences, 316–17
"Social Stratification of the Radio Audience" (Beville), 354
Social theory, 366
Societal interests, 83, 86
Socio-economic status, 279
Sociological analysis, 362
Sociological configurations, 339
Sociological determinants, 336, 341, 346, 347
Sociological dimension, 341
Sociological reductionism, 397
Sociology of culture, 343
Sociology of professions, 356
Sociology students, 385
So Evil My Love (1948), 244
Soft power, 272
Solidarity, 40
"Some Comparisons of Entrants to Medical and Law School" (Thielens), 336
Sonderweg thesis, 400
Sophistication, degree of, 156, 324
Soviet bloc, 30, 267
Soviet mentality, 239
Soviet periphery, 282, 295, 325
Soviet propaganda, 29
Soviet Union, 30, 49, 83, 252, 269, 278, 295–96; Hollywood and, 254; U.S. relations with, 216
So Well Remembered (1947), 244
Spain, 263
Spanish civil war, 245

SPD. *See* Social Democratic Party
Special research programs, 373
Spectacle, 7, 21, 22, 44
Spectators, 265
Specter of the Rose, The (1946), 244
Speier, Hans, 23, 24, 128, 129
Spellman, Francis, 236
Spiritual shelterlessness, 16, 21
Spoken word, 64–65
Spontaneous research designs, 378
Stalin, Joseph, 244, 255, 296
Stalinism, 3
Standardized goods, 224
Stanton, Frank, 273
Stapel, Wilhelm, 65
States of exception, 20
Statistical analysis, 346
Statistical measurements, 360
Sternhell, Zeev, 397
Strassburg cathedral, 139
Strasser, Gregor, 398, 399, 401
Strasser, Otto, 58
Studies in Philosophy and Social Science (journal), 268
Studies on Authority and Family (Fromm), 404
Study of War Time Communication, 128
Sturges, Preston, 242, 250
Subjectivity, 21, 240, 248, 257
Subpropaganda campaigns, 221
Substantive problems, 364
Success, planning of, 228
Sullivan's Travels (1941), 242
Sun Never Sets, The (1939), 243
Superstructure, 107, 109, 117; base-superstructure model, 397; terror and, 120
Supreme Court, 237
Susceptibility, 215
Swastika, 44, 63, 139, 143
Syria, 277, 278, 283, 296, 298–99
Systematic analysis, 377
Systematic quantification, 330
System references, 344

Tales of Hoffmann (Offenbach), 11
Taylor, Paul A., 138
Teachers Apprehension study, 343
Teaching performances, 344
Technical assistance, 379

Technocratic reason, 7
Technocratic systems, 6
Technological advances, 229
Teen-agers, 224, 230
Telenews, 235, 237
Tempest, The (1928), 254
"Tensions Project" (UNESCO), 238
Terror, 41, 51, 56, 74, 84, 108; formation of masses and, 79; implementation of, 100; Mussolini and, 111; open terror, 118; pressure of, 91; superstructure and, 120; systematic use of, 117; totalitarian propaganda and, 402
"Test film" project, 3, 15
Teutonic Knights, 253
Theory of Film (Kracauer), 5, 25; Cold War and, 16; film aesthetics and, 268; precepts of, 17, 18
Thielens, Wagner, 336
Thingspiel, 78
Third Reich, 39, 63, 77, 91, 212
Three Comrades (1938), 244
Tiller Girls, 6–7, 18, 43–44, 213, 406
Tolerance, 298
Tolstoy, Leo, 239, 254
Totalitarian dictatorships, 75, 90, 93, 397
Totalitarianism, 3, 270; capitalism and, 22; embrace of, 14; mass as political phenomenon and, 42
Totalitarian movements, 60, 83, 86, 101
Totalitarian propaganda, 2, 10, 58, 59, 90, 91, 138; aestheticized politics and, 44; aims of, 404; broad mass and, 72; effective, 84; examination of, 37; foreign policy and, 102; Goebbels and, 66; imposition of, 68; masses and, 70, 213; mass-man and, 61; mass rallies and, 62; mass speeches and, 66; mechanism of, 67; point of departure for, 40; power sustained by, 41; principles guiding, 78; psycho-physical structure of people and, 56; quintessence of power and, 75; repetition and rhythm of, 43; spoken word and, 64; terror and, 402
"Totalitarian Propaganda" study, 12, 15, 21, 24, 27, 32, 395; afterword to, 39; sections of, 396–97; theoretical shortcomings of, 396; works underpinning, 40

Totalitarian regimes, 73, 241
Total propaganda, 113, 117; character of, 116; influence of, 119; terror and, 118
Total situation, 216, 333, 335, 337, 339; isolation from, 345; reconstructing, 341; variables and, 346
Total war, 3
To the Victor (1948), 256
Tovarich (1937), 244, 254
Trade unions, 86
"Traditional and Critical Theory" (Horkheimer), 268
Traditionalism, 359, 372
Traditions, 367
Training, 352, 371, 387; activities, 379; formal education and, 382; inclusive, 383; initial selection for, 385; instruction and, 384; intensive, 381; procedures, 380; process of, 383; results of, 389
Triumph of the Will (1934), 19, 245, 406
Truman, Harry S., 236
Turkey, 277, 280, 302; admission to NATO of, 278; documentary films in, 287; film and, 286; rural, 282; Soviet Union and, 295; word-of-mouth communications in, 286

Ultra-nationalism, 217
U.N. *See* United Nations
Unattached intellectuals, 357
Unemployed people, 50, 122
Unemployment, 86, 225, 244
UNESCO. *See* United Nations Educational, Scientific and Cultural Organization
Union elections, 92
Unions, 362
United Nations (U.N.), 300, 301
United Nations Educational, Scientific and Cultural Organization (UNESCO), 211, 215, 238, 260, 288
United States (U.S.), 269; American civilization, 264; American dream, 227; American expansionism, 270; anti-Semitism in, 127, 130; audiences in, 241; creative energies instrumental in, 231; Department of State, 268, 275; distrust of, 289–90; England and, 247; foreign policy of, 236, 293, 302, 305, 308; government, 15;

United States (U.S.) (*continued*)
  imperialism of, 307; Kracauer embrace of ideologies of, 270; Kracauer first publication in, 128; Kracauer work with governmental agencies of, 267; mass production in, 229; newsreel companies in, 237; Palestine and, 305–6; political process in, 358, 363; popularity in Greece of, 302; propaganda, 375; public opinion in, 242; right-wing populist movements in, 395, 416; role in international affairs, 299; Soviet relations with, 216
United World Federalists, 376
Units of communication, 323
University curriculum, 379
University of Chicago, 365, 378
University of Michigan, 365, 378
Unoriented case studies, 335, 347
Unoriented research, 337
Upper-class ideology, 247
Upward mobility, 384
Urban culture, 273
Urban elite, 281
Urbanization, 355
Urban renewal, 11
U.S. *See* United States
Utility art, 78

Variables, 344, 345, 346
Variety (magazine), 246, 257
Verbal statements, 265
Verifiable research, 326
Verlag, Suhrkamp, 1, 23
Victorian England, 239
Victory in the West (1941), 128, 137, 151n6
Violence, 69, 74
Visual education, 266
Visual media, 5
Vitality, 231–32
Voice of America, 268, 269, 284, 288, 289, 290, 314, 317; quantitative analysis of, 327; structural characteristic of, 320
Volk, 85, 101, 197, 410; as "capsule without content," 402; conception of, 89; false totality of, 403; ideological character of, 400; individuals replaced with, 98; masses transformed into, 74; mystifying concept of, 116
Völkische Beobachter (newspaper), 95

Volk ohne Raum ("People without space"), 103
Volksgemeinschaft, 40, 41, 78, 88, 90, 398

Wagnerian music, 152
Wanger, Walter, 245
Warner, Jack L., 243
War propaganda, 135
Waugh, Evelyn, 223
We Are Not Alone (1939), 243
Weber, Max, 9, 330
Weimar cinema, 28, 215
Weimar culture, 12
Weimar Germany, 40
Weimar Republic, 8, 46n11, 127, 244, 397; inner dispositions among Germans of, 342; social divisions of, 398
Welfare, 403
Well-balanced neutralism, 323
Weltanschauung, 224, 408
Werke (Kracauer), 1, 23, 39
Wernert, Erich, 75, 77, 78, 88, 414
Westdeutschen Beobachter (newspaper), 96
Western civilization, 256
Western Europe, 269
Westernization, 304, 359, 372
Whiskey, 228
White Cliffs of Dover, The (1944), 243, 251, 252
White-collar workers, 12, 24, 30, 40, 46n11, 272, 294; fascist propaganda and, 128; hyperinflation and, 121; new category of, 41
Wiene, Robert, 14, 42
Wilder, David, 343
Will to power, 59, 74, 75, 96; eruption of, 101; expansionism and, 102; Führer as embodiment of, 68; logic of, 92; of National Socialism, 91; nihilistic, 79, 83, 100, 398, 405; products of, 90; suggestions of, 63
Winsten, Archer, 256
Winterhilfswerk program, 403
Women, 100
Word-of-mouth communications, 285
Working class, 41, 57
"Work of Art in the Age of Mechanical Reproduction, The" (Benjamin), 44, 57, 129

World Health Organization, 300
World in Action, 143
World of spurious appearances (*Scheinwelt*), 39, 42, 43
"World of the Daytime Serial" (Arnheim), 273, 360
World propaganda, 123
World War I, 3, 246
World War II, 23, 241

Xenophobia, 2

Yank at Oxford, A (1938), 243
Youth, 230
Youthfulness, 213

Zeitschrift für Sozialforschung (journal), 12, 25, 31–32, 37, 38, 44, 395–96, 413
Zweig, Stefan, 392

NEW DIRECTIONS IN CRITICAL THEORY

Amy Allen, General Editor

Narrating Evil: A Postmetaphysical Theory of Reflective Judgment, María Pía Lara

The Politics of Our Selves: Power, Autonomy, and Gender in Contemporary Critical Theory, Amy Allen

Democracy and the Political Unconscious, Noëlle McAfee

The Force of the Example: Explorations in the Paradigm of Judgment, Alessandro Ferrara

Horrorism: Naming Contemporary Violence, Adriana Cavarero

Scales of Justice: Reimagining Political Space in a Globalizing World, Nancy Fraser

Pathologies of Reason: On the Legacy of Critical Theory, Axel Honneth

States Without Nations: Citizenship for Mortals, Jacqueline Stevens

The Racial Discourses of Life Philosophy: Négritude, Vitalism, and Modernity, Donna V. Jones

Democracy in What State?, Giorgio Agamben, Alain Badiou, Daniel Bensaïd, Wendy Brown, Jean-Luc Nancy, Jacques Rancière, Kristin Ross, Slavoj Žižek

Politics of Culture and the Spirit of Critique: Dialogues, edited by Gabriel Rockhill and Alfredo Gomez-Muller

Mute Speech: Literature, Critical Theory, and Politics, Jacques Rancière

The Right to Justification: Elements of Constructivist Theory of Justice, Rainer Forst

The Scandal of Reason: A Critical Theory of Political Judgment, Albena Azmanova

The Wrath of Capital: Neoliberalism and Climate Change Politics, Adrian Parr

Media of Reason: A Theory of Rationality, Matthias Vogel

Social Acceleration: A New Theory of Modernity, Hartmut Rosa

The Disclosure of Politics: Struggles Over the Semantics of Secularization, María Pía Lara

Radical Cosmopolitics: The Ethics and Politics of Democratic Universalism, James Ingram

Freedom's Right: The Social Foundations of Democratic Life, Axel Honneth

Imaginal Politics: Images Beyond Imagination and the Imaginary, Chiara Bottici

Alienation, Rahel Jaeggi

The Power of Tolerance: A Debate, Wendy Brown and Rainer Forst, edited by Luca Di Blasi and Christoph F. E. Holzhey

Radical History and the Politics of Art, Gabriel Rockhill

Starve and Immolate: The Politics of Human Weapons, Banu Bargu

The Highway of Despair: Critical Theory After Hegel, Robyn Marasco

A Political Economy of the Senses: Neoliberalism, Reification, Critique, Anita Chari

The End of Progress: Decolonizing the Normative Foundations of Critical Theory, Amy Allen

Recognition or Disagreement: A Critical Encounter on the Politics of Freedom, Equality, and Identity, Axel Honneth and Jacques Rancière, edited by Katia Genel and Jean-Philippe Deranty

What Is a People?, Alain Badiou, Pierre Bourdieu, Judith Butler, Georges Didi-Huberman, Sadri Khiari, and Jacques Rancière

Death and Mastery: Psychoanalytic Drive Theory and the Subject of Late Capitalism, Benjamin Y. Fong

Left-Wing Melancholia: Marxism, History, and Memory, Enzo Traverso

Foucault/Derrida Fifty Years Later: The Futures of Genealogy, Deconstruction, and Politics, edited by Olivia Custer, Penelope Deutscher, and Samir Haddad

The Habermas Handbook, edited by Hauke Brunkhorst, Regina Kreide, and Cristina Lafont

Birth of a New Earth: The Radical Politics of Environmentalism, Adrian Parr

Genealogies of Terrorism: Revolution, State Violence, Empire, Verena Erlenbusch-Anderson

The Practice of Political Theory: Rorty and Continental Thought, Clayton Chin

Queer Terror: Life, Death, and Desire in the Settler Colony, C. Heike Schotten

Naming Violence: A Critical Theory of Genocide, Torture, and Terrorism, Mathias Thaler

Avicenna and the Aristotelian Left, Ernst Bloch

The Experience of Injustice: A Theory of Recognition, Emmanuel Renault

Fear of Breakdown: Politics and the Work of Psychoanalysis, Noëlle McAfee

Transitional Subjects: Critical Theory and Object Relations, edited by Amy Allen and Brian O'Connor

Capitalism on Edge: How Fighting Precarity Can Achieve Radical Change Without Crisis or Utopia, Albena Azmanova

Hermeneutics as Critique: Science, Politics, Race and Culture, Lorenzo C. Simpson

Critique on the Couch: Why Critical Theory Needs Psychoanalysis, Amy Allen

Recognition and Ambivalence, edited by Heikki Ikäheimo, Kristina Lepold, and Titus Stahl

Praxis and Revolution: A Theory of Social Transformation, Eva von Redecker

GPSR Authorized Representative: Easy Access System Europe, Mustamäe tee 50, 10621 Tallinn, Estonia, gpsr.requests@easproject.com